THE IMPERIAL ORDER

THE
IMPERIAL ORDER

ROBERT G. WESSON

UNIVERSITY OF CALIFORNIA PRESS
BERKELEY AND LOS ANGELES

1967

University of California Press
Berkeley and Los Angeles, California

Cambridge University Press
London, England

© by The Regents of the University of California
Library of Congress Catalog Card Number: 67-11938

Designed by Bud Mall
Printed in the United States of America

PREFACE

A sage observer of human nature, Aesop, related that the frog people of a marsh once prayed for a king to rule over them. Indulgent Zeus granted them a fine log. The frogs soon learned that they could climb over their King Log with impunity; disappointed that it was so unawesome, they pleaded for a more kingly ruler. Annoyed, the god sent King Stork, who proceeded to gobble his subjects.

Unhappily, governments often have inclinations, like the stork, to interfere with their subjects' lives and to consume their substance. Rulers, whatever their professions, seldom act solely and entirely in the interests of those whom they govern; and no system has been able to compel them to do so. Politicians everywhere strive, within the channels of the political culture, for the sweetness of command, honor, and position; and the urge to power is opposite to almost all hungerings in that it is not appeased but energized by the attainment of its desires. The everlasting fondness for managing and commanding others is essential for effective joint action and the useful organization of human efforts, but it all too often outgrows its rational purposes. Power asserts itself for the sake of power, and the more freely it is exercised the more inescapable and harmful its misuse.

It is a thesis of this book that the degree to which power or political motivation dominates society depends largely upon the degree to which it is checked by contrary power, that is, the degree to which power is divided. If various entities somehow offset one another, there can be no single firm order and omnipotent arbitrary rule; if there are no independent powers, an autocrat is politically unbounded, free to work his will as the stork upon the frogs.

Political power may be variously checked: national or religious cleavages often set parts of a nation against each other, fearful lest any secure absolute predominance; economic groups may be able to exert pressure in their own defense; an accepted constitutional structure may split powers functionally or, more effectively, territorially. But the most fundamental and in the long run the strongest of divisions is that into independent states which, so far as they are in contact, tend to check one another. In a system of independent states, no ruler can suppose himself king of the universe; competition compels some attention to the needs of the people; foreign ideas can never be entirely excluded; there are always potential sources of inspiration and support for dissidents. On the other hand, political power is freest and most readily made absolute and all-pervading in a great empire that encompasses its world, where there are no equal neighbors or where neighbors are so distant that men cannot look to them, as in imperial China or the Roman empire. Such great unified states, on whose horizons dwell only barbarians or minor states, have always been given over, for good and ill, to unlimited power.

Consequently, one might best see the effects of political power where it is purest, in the vast and noncompetitive empires that largely stand apart from or above the interaction of states. In them one should perceive the results of power unleashed, its means of fortifying itself, the abuses to which it is prone, and the course of its decay. If the divided system is conducive to individualism, inquiry, political freedom, and variety, the unified order favors a rigid and conformist social system, an unassailable ideology, autocratic government, and general uniformity. It is characteristic of the great empires that local and independent authorities are ground down or suppressed, that churches are made subservient to the political center, that rulers are deified or surrounded with great pomp and an aura of sanctity, that a large and usually swelling bureaucracy is set up to carry out the supreme will but serves itself, that the political struggle commonly retreats behind the scenes and to the palace corridors.

Many devices are evolved to protect and fortify the sacred power, the most important of which is perhaps the shaping of minds; obedience is incomplete unless voluntary, and an effective rule must be made philosophically acceptable. Impatient of dissent, the autocratic power discourages free inquiry; resting upon acceptance of the established order, it tends to formalism and conservatism. Where no law stands over the will, there is no measure of morality; and the higher the government stands over its subjects, the more difficult to restrain itself, to avoid capricious abuse of power, corruption, and internal rot.

It is the purpose of this book to consider the grandest creations of humanity and its most monumental failures, the great imperial systems, in which one sees the potency of human masses mobilized by a single will and yet much more the incapacity of men to govern themselves for the general welfare. Their common traits, from the Roman and the Mogul to the Inca empire, may be taken as the result of great and undivided power. That this is pertinent for a world forever beset by tendencies to concentration of power needs no stressing. Moreover, the study of the imperial order is a study of power itself. Wherever there is strong organization there is an element of command, giving some men opportunities of bending others to their purposes. Just as there is every shade and degree of despotism — from the Sapa Inca who decreed immediate death by raising his hand, down to the freedom and equality of a medieval Swiss commune, where no one could be bound without the consent of the whole community — so likewise there are exploitative and coercive elements in all complex societies; in all manner of hierarchies power is a prime motive and men seek to rise and better themselves by controlling their fellows. Most of the ailments of society are related to the inability to manage power. What may be seen in an extreme in the great power-oriented empires is a general sickness, the germs of which are never absent in civilization.

Not a little has been written about these matters, of empires and civilizations, growth, corruption and decay, and the uses of authority. If the present work seeks to go beyond others, it is mostly in stressing the primary role of the political configuration in the shaping of the rest. For example, it is taken herein that kings have been deified primarily because they were in a position to deify themselves and they liked it or it suited the purposes of rule. It may be contended, to the contrary, that deified kingship corresponds to needs for a powerful father symbol and the reassurance it brings, or to religious institutions identifying a symbolic person with the people and making him a necessary link with the supernatural. Imperial decay is here regarded as primarily a result of the misuse of power which follows inevitably from its concentration. Many have felt that an oppressive empire is less the cause than the result of a moral decay, because of which men cease to value independence and freedom; that then, as corruption progresses, economic and intellectual decline breeds tyranny, and despotism becomes less resisted and more necessary to hold together the fabric of society. Most treatments rather incline toward the second approach, so far as they venture explanation; that is, they see the political setup as the result of economic or cultural factors rather than the opposite, or view all as bound into a nexus from which cause can hardly be dissected.

It is, indeed, somewhat venturesome to speak of causes in matters so infinitely complicated as the rise and decay of great empires. It is justified only to the extent that emphasis on certain aspects may improve understanding and make more intelligible otherwise confusing developments. It is not a strictly verifiable statement of fact that the formation of a universal empire causes intellectual stagnation, but it is an observable regularity; and, when one considers reasons for the autocratic power to choke individual thinking and ways in which it can do so, this relation and allied ones become fairly understandable.

If something has remained to be explored in this direction, it is partly because only in the past few decades have studies of the great imperial societies of the past advanced sufficiently to permit much comparison. Whatever his perspicacity, Montesquieu lacked factual material for a morphology of the imperial system; he was practically limited to Roman history. In our day, historical studies have burgeoned at an ever-increasing rate, and the student, in connection with the better-known empires, is not starved but overfed. Moreover, there has been some disinclination to stress political power. Almost all of us have some covert admiration for power and a tendency to respect those who can make themselves powerful. At the same time, it has practically been taken for granted until recent years that political studies were concerned with the right uses and management of power, exceptionally, as in Machiavelli, with the means of its increase. The great absolutist or totalitarian states of the twentieth century have contributed much to our sophistication in this regard.

If the glorious universal empires are treated here with less respect than is ordinarily given them, this is not the result of initial prejudice but of convictions that grew during the study. The quest was undertaken, to be sure, with considerable skepticism about the claims of the empires and their apologists, but with no desire to blacken them. Empires have certainly accomplished great, or at least very impressive, things. But so far as they have been unrestrained one should not expect them to be good.

Preface

Thanks are due above all to my wife, Deborah, who has made innumerable suggestions of form and content and who, with care beyond price, has typed and retyped the entire work. I wish also to express gratitude to the University of California, which facilitated the completion of the manuscript through a Summer Faculty Fellowship.

R. G. W.

University of California
Santa Barbara

CONTENTS

Contents

Contents

Contents

1   VICTORIOUS EMPIRES

CONQUEST FROM THE FRINGES

Western culture has risen out of individualism, division, plurality, and contention. It has not known a universal hegemony since the Roman empire nor a general moral authority since the Reformation; its millennial history is of wars and diplomacy, the continual competition and intermittent strife of free and sovereign polities. Consciously or unconsciously, we take such a world for granted; children of the greatest of state systems, we find this international order or disorder the natural way of civilized existence.

This is only a perspective of good fortune. Systems of states in close contact and yet independent have been exceptional and usually transitory; ordinarily single states have ruled areas rather large in terms of their means of communication; and international contact, except for wars, has been of secondary importance. Most humans during the millennia of civilization have lived and died with hardly a glance beyond the horizons of a single state.

This follows because empires are much more easily made than state systems. The latter, indeed, are not made at all but can evolve only where conditions happen to be favorable, while empires can be formed whenever states or leaders can muster military power to carve them, and they can go as far as arms can carry them. Moreover, empires are dedicated to self-preservation, and usually rather effectively so; but a large part of the energies of contending states is directed toward pulling down opponents, which, if successful, means the destruction of the balanced system. This outcome is seemingly inevitable in the nature of sovereignty. As independent states are free to use force at their own discretion, to make war and get the better of their neighbors, and as inequalities of power are always arising, a system of closely interacting units can continue to exist for a long time only when special circumstances fortify the independence of the several units. The balance of power is helpful, but it is complex and delicate and can never give full security; independence is enduringly precarious so long as sovereignties

1

hope to increase power at the expense of their fellows. In a state system there is always danger, and fears increase the urge to conquest and so the dangers to all.

Hence the state systems of the past have all been engulfed, after a few centuries of vigorous life, by a conquering nation that has assumed the burden and glory of empire, ending quarrels and imposing a supreme rule, replacing plurality and disorder by unity and supreme government. The earliest recorded example is the downfall of the city-states of Sumeria, the chief originators of civilization. In the generations after 2500 B.C. tensions seem to have been increasing, as wars grew sharper and armies became better organized and professional. One or another of the city-states came to the fore until Lugalzagezzi of Umma about 2300 B.C. made himself hegemon of all Sumeria. He introduced the idea of world rule, proclaiming that he would water the earth with joy [132, I, 224] as all sovereigns lay before him like cows at pasture [135, p. 122]; but he was able to set up no firm empire. Holding to traditional ways and claiming authority not by prerogative but by election in the cities under his sway, he could really rule only the area adjacent to his seat. [100, pp. 172–182, 197–201] Lugalzagezzi enjoyed only brief glory; within a few years he was overthrown by a stronger imperialist, Sargon of Akkad. The latter, a Semite from north of the ancient center, built up a new disciplined mass army based on archers instead of the chariots and spearmen of the older style, and smashed to unexampled conquest. In his campaign against Lugalzagezzi he boasted of killing or capturing fifty chiefs. After conquering Sumeria, he marched far beyond, extending his power from the Persian Gulf to the Black Sea and the Mediterranean, perhaps as far as Cyprus [109, p. 24], to form a truly stupendous empire for the times. It is a token of the greatness of his work that Akkadian became and for a thousand years remained the diplomatic language of the Near East.

Although he may have owed much to the model of Egypt, a large state then close to a millennium old, Sargon is the first empire builder of whom we have much knowledge. Having begun his career as an administrator under the king of Kish, he applied his talents to ruling the Sumerian cities as they had never been ruled. It was his practice to destroy the city walls, take leading men as hostages, and install his own governors supported by a garrison. [136, p. 50] He must have built an imperial apparatus of rule; according to his boast, "5,400 men ate bread daily before him." Inaugurating a new era, he chose not to install himself in one of the ancient cities consecrated by tradition, but built a new, artificial capital, Akkad, said to have been the most resplendent city of its day. [*122*, p. 61]

Not yet, however, were the Sumerians prepared to bow their heads meekly. Each succession after Sargon saw a revolt of the still proud cities, although the apparatus of rule was successively improved. When the dynasty of Sargon was overthrown after about two centuries by new invaders from the relatively barbarian north, something of the old Sumeria reemerged. For approximately a century the cities again enjoyed a degree of independence. Then the ancient leading city of Ur established a new empire, more compact than the Akkadian but similarly administered by governors posted to each city. [*136*, p. 57] This strictly Sumerian empire lasted slightly more than a century, only to give way to a new group of small competing powers, with shifting leadership and instable alliances. In this Indian summer of more than two hundred years, Sumerian culture, although its highest creativity was long past, reached its apogee of splendor. Thereafter, the whole area was brought into the Babylonian empire by Hammurabi. Since then, the cradle of civilization has almost always paid tribute to alien rulers, of whom the Hittites, Assyrians, Persians, Macedonians, Romans, Arabs, and Turks are only the better known; and it has remained as relatively backward as it once was progressive.

Greek independence was not so long in dying as the Sumerian, perhaps because the Greeks were never out of sight of imperial rule, as perfected and exemplified by the magnificent Persian empire of Cyrus, Darius, and Xerxes. The Peloponnesian wars, coming when Hellenic culture was reaching its zenith, bled, drained, and partly demoralized Greece. The successive failure of the greatest cities, Athens, Sparta, and Thebes, to secure dominion seemed to show that only an outside force could unite the land. Philip of Macedon undertook this task. He developed his political ideas during three years spent as a hostage at Thebes; there also he learned strategy from Epaminondas, Greece's greatest general. Returning to Macedon, a kingdom large compared with a Greek polis, he introduced a much stronger and tighter phalanx supported by a fuller panoply of mobile weapons, light infantry, and archers.

It was an instrument impossible for the Greeks, who relied mostly on the valor, physical fitness, and discipline of their citizens.

Philip rather easily won ascendancy over the individualistic Greeks, unable as ever to unite against an invader; but he had too much respect for Greek culture to make them his subjects. The Macedonian yoke was never heavy; it never brought Greek intellectual and political life to a halt, and it was largely shaken off in a few generations. Then Greek political life partly revived, much as the Sumerian did after the Akkadian empire.

But hardly had Macedonian power receded when a far greater, the Roman, loomed on the edge of the Greek cultural sphere. The Roman empire was peculiarly, not the work of a single driving strategist, organizer, and conqueror, but the accomplishment of a people of imperial virtues, courage, and especially unflinching determination never to accept defeat. Rome had many leaders, good and bad, and many setbacks, but always returned to carry the attack to victory. Rome must, consequently, owe most to its institutions; and various writers, like Polybius, credited it with just the proper degree of oligarchy tempered by democracy. This meant the successful combination of strong leadership with the intense involvement of the citizens, the patriotic dedication of a partly democratic city-state guided by a purposeful Senate instead of a fickle assembly.

Rome did not swoop to empire as Macedon had, but built slowly and surely. The struggle for Italy was most arduous, and many times Rome suffered setbacks. Very early, however, it displayed an imperial bent by refusing to make peace except with a beaten enemy. Dogged determination often turned near defeat into victory; Rome was always victorious in war after 387 B.C., and the long series of triumphs gave confidence in divine favor and the Roman mission. Moreover, a certain forbearance, at least within Italy, added strength. Defeated Italian cities were not so much pillaged as brought into federation; they were made not mere subjects but allies. To be sure, alliance with Rome was permanent and involuntary, and attempts to break away were punished by war, while the Romans interpreted treaties to suit themselves. But Rome was much more successful than Athens or Sparta in gaining the allegiance of conquered neighbors. Roman citizenship, full or partial, was given to many Italians. [285, p. 62] And whereas Athens demanded money from subject towns, Rome required the Latins to furnish soldiers, a less resented form of tribute. Not only were men cheap; they were often quite willing to share the spoils of Roman victory. Adding to military strength by conquest, Rome thus built up in fertile and populous Italy a solid basis for power which no Greek state could hope to rival.

The empire came of age when Rome moved out of peninsular Italy to acquire Sicily, formerly mostly under Carthaginian control; and the crucial time of Roman expansion was the long struggle with Carthage, lasting with intermissions from 265 to 146 B.C. Carthage was the strongest rival in the Mediterranean world. The Greek city-states had faded to relative obscurity, while the major Hellenistic powers of Alexander's successors were preoccupied with one another and had little westward thrust after the defeat of Pyrrhus, against whom Rome and Carthage once briefly joined in alliance. Hence, although Rome was agricultural and Carthage commercial, expansion inevitably brought the two powers into collision. The First Punic War, fought mostly in and for Sicily, was a hard-earned victory for Rome. In the Second Punic War, Hannibal by sheer virtuosity gained spectacular success, but in the hour of darkness Rome refused to think of compromise and was saved by the faithfulness of the Latin allies. Carthage was unable or unwilling to dedicate the forces necessary for complete victory, and the Romans carried the war to Africa and beat the Carthaginians on their home ground.

Before the decisive battle of Zama, Scipio encouraged his legions by promising that the victor would rule the world [562, p. 57]; and he saw clearly. With Carthage disposed of, there was no great independent state to contest the western Mediterranean, and the gates to the East were open. There was still much hard fighting, and the Hellenistic states from time to time won victories, but the Roman tide was inexorable. When any two nations fought, Rome always sought to interpose its arbitration and usually came out the winner. To be known to be rich was to invite attack by Rome, and concessions made were followed by new demands. Western lands were generally made provinces; Eastern realms of older civilization were made allies — alliance with Rome being a condition of inferiority. Nominal alliance was converted insensibly, as Gibbon notes, into real servitude. [314, I, 31] As the lands that had learned obedience were made provinces under proconsuls, Rome by degrees became capital and ruler of the world, *orbis terrarum*, an empire that almost coincided with civilization as seen from Italy. Except for the Parthians, too distant for real concern, outside the Roman sphere were left only savage tribes, warlike, often nomadic peoples, from whom nothing could be extracted to repay the cost of conquest.

At nearly the same time that the classical Mediterranean world was being engulfed by the Roman empire, the classical China of many contending states was being forged into the Chinese empire. Again, the state that made itself master of a ripe civilization was one on the rim of the circle, accessible to Chinese culture but slightly alien to it, trained to military ways, as were Prussia and Rome, by contact with still less civilized peoples and by successful expansion against them.

Centuries earlier there had been a more or less united state in the Yellow River valley, and imperial unification might have seemed easier in China because men looked back to and idealized the golden age when sage kings had ruled all China. In fact, however, the continued existence of a shadowy imperial power long impeded a new master's rise, just as the Holy Roman Empire served not to unite Germany but to support its feudal division. In 722 B.C., when the old Chou dynasty became practically impotent, there were some 170 independent or nearly independent states. In centuries of wars, the weaker or less fortunate were gradually eliminated, until by 481 B.C. thirteen independent powers remained. Jealousies among these continued for a remarkably long time to maintain a balance of power, but one by one the feebler or less determined were swallowed up by the stronger and more aggressive, and the contest for position became more intense and wars fiercer. Chivalry and moderation were forgotten in the struggle; in the final stages of the Ch'in campaign for supremacy it is recorded (probably with horrified exaggeration) that 400,000 soldiers who surrendered on a promise of mercy were butchered, and this was only the worst of many atrocities.

The two principal contenders for supremacy were Chu, to the south, the first to annex a major state, and Ch'in, to the southwest of the Yellow River valley center of Chinese culture. Both were hardened by conflict with barbarians outside the polite code and less bound to the conventions of civilization. [5, p. 7] The Ch'in people themselves at one time were considered barbarians by the refined folk of the inner circle. Ch'in never produced a scholar of consequence but was fashioned into an efficient military state by political advisers from abroad, who imported and applied the stern philosophy of Legalism. A response to the increasing tensions of international relations, somewhat akin to fascism in spirit, Legalism exalted the state and its needs as the principle of right and justified coercion for the sake of power. It also excused harsh rule on the grounds that people had to be controlled because they had multiplied overmuch. [*11*, p. 123] In accordance with this doctrine, families were organized into groups directly under the central power instead of under the feudal nobility. Everyone was expected to watch his neighbors and denounce crimes or suffer the penalties imposed on the criminals; taxes were increased, rewards given for military service, weights and measures standardized, potential soldiers lured from neighboring states by the promise of free land, and the nobility largely supplanted by a bureaucratic administration. Measures were taken to penalize commerce (trade was less important for Ch'in than for more central states) and to favor agriculture and industry. [*21*, pp. 205–208] The police was made efficient and powerful, and movement was controlled by passports. The army was given mobility with mounted archers in nomad style while other states still relied on chariots. [*30*, p. 95]

By such authoritarian measures, Ch'in mobilized, under a Machiavellian foreign prime minister, the strength necessary to vanquish the last rival in 221 B.C. The king of Ch'in then proclaimed himself First Emperor. But the harsh tactics suitable for winning an empire were no way to rule it. After the death of the First Emperor, rebellion broke out, and the dynasty was overthrown. There was then an attempt to reestablish the old states. But it was too late; after a year or two, the Han dynasty restored universal empire and set the pattern of Chinese life for the next two thousand years.

On the other side of the world, the Inca conquerors of Andean civilization likewise came from a region somewhat apart from the old center of civilization. So far as the rapid course of Inca expansion was peculiar, it was in the importance of political organization and methods. The Incas seem to have introduced no important military innovations, but they were superlative organizers, as conquering peoples must be. They also strove perhaps more successfully than any other empire builders to impose their yoke smoothly.

They sent emissaries to mix blandishments and fair words with dire threats, explaining the advantages of the rule of the Son of the Sun. [*171*, p. 219] It seems that nations often preferred peaceful incorporation to a doubtful resistance, accepting their new masters as bringers of order out of chaos. [*172*, p. 13] The Incas made this choice easier by avoiding plunder and treating gently those who laid down their arms. [*179*, p. 88] Subsequently, for those who found themselves laboring mightily for alien lords, resistance was impossible.

Such gatherings of a group of independent states into a broad empire show a certain regularity in that the conquering state stands close enough to the center of civilization to learn the advanced arts of war and administration but far enough apart not to share fully its civilized values. Something like this has occurred often throughout history: the less civilized men of Upper Egypt marched across the delta to unite Egypt; the Hittites and various other conquerors of Mesopotamia (although not the Assyrians) came from the wilder north, as did the Persians; the state of Magadha, which united India in 325 B.C., although itself a cultural center of some importance [*204*, p. 18], lay to the east of the old center of Indian culture; the Mongols, history's most successful conquerors, were semibarbarian tribes on the edge of Chinese civilization before Genghis Khan forged them into a mighty force; the Turkic founders of the Mogul empire swooped down from Central Asia to feast on the civilized delights of India; the Aztecs came into central Mexico from the ruder north; the partly Slavic Prussians were slightly crude to the Rhinelanders who came under their aegis.

The superiority of such empire builders has never lain in a higher degree of general civilization nor usually in technical superiority of weaponry. But peripheral states have several advantages. Most obviously, they are likely to be bigger. Macedon had more substantial resources than any single Greek polis, and it was much easier for Rome than for Athens or Sparta to build up a broad base of land power. Ch'in could enlarge its domains and manpower at the expense of weaker and less cultured peoples, whereas the more civilized states of central China could expand only at the expense of one another and against the fiercest resistance. Similarly, the small free states of Italy, after having led European civilization for centuries, were helpless when France and Spain were forged into national powers. On a larger scale, while the states of Europe were battling for frontier fortresses and provinces, often passing them back and forth with shifting alliances, achieving little or nothing at the cost of much blood, Russia was able to spread over hundreds of thousands of square miles to the south and east against feeble resistance. Consequently, by the middle of the twentieth century Russia would have been in a position, but for the fortuitous rise of another huge extra-European power, to assert hegemony of the continent. Big states on the edge of civilization have a moral advantage, too; with the experience of incorporating and managing an imposing territory, they feel capable of governing the world and enjoy the idea that they may be called upon to do so.

Such states may also be more acceptable masters. Although the peoples of a culture-building area may regard the powers on the edges as crude and unpolished, they may resist the hegemony of an outsider less than that of one of their own number. Traditional quarrels run very deep; the new power stepping into the arena more convincingly proclaims its doctrines of peace and order and presents itself as deliverer as well as master; many are prepared to accept it as protector. For some Greeks it seemed less humiliating to bow to Macedonians or even the cruel Romans than to yield independence to Athens, Thebes, or Sparta. The Italian city-states of the Renaissance bitterly resisted moves toward supremacy by any of their system, but many towns carelessly if not joyously opened their gates to the French invaders, and masses of Italians hailed the French king as a savior. Likewise it would seem that, in the years following the Second World War, Europeans have been more prone to accept American or Russian hegemony than that of any European power. They have been much more easily persuaded of the unselfishness of America (or Russia) than of that of England, France, or Germany; the outside arbiter at least would not favor any one of the ancient rivals over the others. Radical parties could more easily accept dictation from Moscow than from Paris, London, or Rome. The commander of NATO forces in Europe for the defense of Europe could only be an American; and European statesmen have pleaded earnestly for the reduction of old-fashioned nationalism in deference to American leadership as they could not for the benefit of any of their own.

Even if the states of ripe civilization were acceptable as imperial unifiers, they seem to have been poorly qualified for the role. If Lugalzagezzi, becoming master of all Sumeria, had been able to organize his rule with stern imperial efficiency, he surely would not have been so quickly toppled. The strongest Greek cities were singularly incapable of organizing their domain. After the defeat of Persia, Athens was able to make a large number of cities its tributaries but had no notion of cementing them into a firm union. In the Peloponnesian wars, the Athenian vassals were of very little help to the metropolis; unlike the allies of Rome, they were more inclined to rebel than to aid in the hour of need. How far the Athenians were from an imperial mentality is exemplified by their overfrank statement to the Melians (according to Thucydides) that they would rule simply by right of strength; proper imperialists would have expounded their duties as protectors of civilization and bringers of order for the benefit of weak and strong alike, and would have done much to give this an appearance of truth. A sugar-coating of righteousness can cover much of the bitterness of subjugation. Sparta, after defeating Athens, had a much better opportunity to cement Greek unity under its sword and, as a land power accustomed to the rule of a surrounding territory, should have been better qualified. But it failed entirely. The Spartan harmosts, or proconsuls, had no concerted imperial policy or direction; and they and the supporting garrisons were soon withdrawn or expelled. Subsequently, Thebes became briefly the strongest power in Greece but made no serious effort to weld the cities together. The Italian city-states of the Middle Ages were likewise unadept in making conquered lands a source of new power.

So have been the nation-states of Europe, even while building, thanks to enormous technical superiority, huge colonial empires. It is particularly instructive how little vocation the British, once overlords of a quarter of the land and the people of the globe by virtue of sea power and economic leadership, have shown for the incorporation of alien peoples. Despite more than seven hundred years of rule they failed entirely to bend the Irish, and even on their own little island they have never entirely overcome the separateness of the Scots and Welsh. To this day, for example, the British struggle with the duality of the Scottish and English legal systems, while Scottish and Welsh nationalist parties are a recurrent nuisance. The British have been too respectful of rights simply to sweep away the obstacles to unity and uniformity. In their overseas colonies, they have taught not so much their own mission of rulership as lessons of law, freedom, and human rights. The West generally has educated dependent peoples not to bow humbly before the supreme power but to aspire to independence; almost all the leaders of nationalist and anticolonialist movements have been formed in Western schools. Free states, by their philosophy, laws, and institutions, give ideas of freedom even when they would not. Weaker but less enlightened and less scrupulous Portugal has known better how to keep its subjects submissive, while Russia, tsarist or communist, has been little troubled by independence movements in Central Asia.

The marginal states thus enjoy a manifold superiority: they have greater resources; they can place themselves above the long-time divisions and enmities of contending states; moreover, they are less inhibited in fighting and in imposing their rule. They are likely to be more warlike because of close contact with still less civilized peoples, while their mentality is less tempered by the experience of dealing with equals. Thus, Rome felt that war should be concluded only by victory; and it was the usage of many world conquerors, like the Mongols and the early Persian kings, never to settle with those who resisted until they were made prisoners. [317, p. 103] Such attitudes would be impossible within a functioning state system like the ancient Greek or modern European. More readily borrowing arts of war than values of civilization, enjoying military ascendancy while suffering cultural inferiority, peripheral states find compensation in the former and stress the values of power. Military and political domination is particularly satisfying to the uncultivated; if we are scorned as uncouth, our sword can speak for us. The will to dominion rises stronger in those who sense their own crudity but are confident of their strength. It may be also that the outer state, less advanced in ways of business and production, sees military power as the easiest way to riches; and success gives huge confidence in the rightness of strength.

Contact with a more advanced civilization seems frequently to bring about a strengthening of rulership among peoples who previously enjoyed more easygoing government. The king or the oligarchs are better situated than their people to learn from abroad, and the lessons that most interest them are those of power. Thus the state of Ch'in, aiming at hegemony in China, imported foreign scholars to teach not the people but the court; and the state was thereby successfully reorganized into a machine for conquest. Peter the Great tightened his control over his vast and unwieldy realm by bringing in Western techniques and advisers; only long afterward, as enlightenment filtered to broader circles, did Westernization become a liberalizing influence. Similarly, in the Hawaiian Islands at the end of the eighteenth century, foreign ideas and counselors helped King Kamehameha to build up a little despotic empire such as the islands had never known; not until decades later did the infiltration of modern ideas bring more freedom.

Inferiority in the more sophisticated aspects of civilization is thus an asset for empire builders. Among states, the most effective qualification for supreme power is the driving urge to clutch it — unqualified self-righteousness and determined will uneroded by civilized refinement.

DECADENCE OF THE FREE

The more successful of universal empires, such as the Roman or the Chinese, have taken over or inherited the civilization of a group of independent states. These, then, failed. Yet free competitive states have sometimes been exuberantly vigorous. Like western Europe from the late Middle Ages until our day, the Greek city-states for centuries were setting up colonies all around the Mediterranean and the Black Sea and ever more widely expanding their cultural sphere. In the creative period of classical Chinese culture, the time of Contending States, there was a strong political and cultural outward thrust against the surrounding barbarian peoples. Probably this has been true of every area of great cultural growth: by improvement of technology, by their morale and good organization, the creators of a new civilization find themselves immensely superior to peoples around and extend their influence or sway as naturally as water flows downhill. It is then a sharp reversal when the thrust comes from outside against the center, as though in delayed vengeance for a long history of cultural and political imperialism: Greece colonized Italy, and Italy conquered Greece; the Europe that gave its civilization to America and Russia finds itself pressed between the two.

This reversal suggests that civilizations have their time of vitality and vigor, as of youth, after which they age and decay to dull impotence; then it is almost an act of mercy to sweep them into an orderly empire. Thus it has been contended that Rome was practically fulfilling a duty in asserting dominion over Greek states whose day was done and whose life had essentially departed. But if aging is a tangible reality in an organism, it is difficult to define in a society, whose parts are continually renewed as new generations and fresh minds come forward. It is clear only if there are material causes for decline, as when a mining community comes to the end of its ore; some of the miners move away while others fall into poverty, and abandoned streets are the image of decay. The exhaustion of silver deposits at Laurium certainly added to the woes of Athens. Wearing out of the soil has been suggested as a possible cause of the mysterious abandonment of Mayan cities in Guatemala; pests or plagues may also be guessed to have played some role. Any sort of change of natural conditions may be postulated as a cause of decay; so far as a favorable environment contributes to the rise of a civilization, the random changes of centuries are likely to be detrimental. Possibly, too, there has been genetic deterioration; a great civilization creates artificial conditions of breeding, the effects of which may be supposed deleterious.

But the search for material causes for the decay of cultures has not been very fruitful. The creativity of the Sumerian city-states appears to have continued up to the time when they were conquered; at most one may suppose that they had lost martial virtues. The Chinese Contending States were in the full bloom of cultural growth up to the day they were cut down; the worst to be said of them was that they were unable adequately to mobilize, although they fought energetically against the militaristic state of Ch'in. In Greece, the Hellenistic period may be considered decadent by comparison with the classical period; but its cultural creation, if in some ways inferior, was in other ways superior and generally far more abundant. In particular, it was much the best season for natural science until modern days, and its high fertility endured until crushed by superior power. The Roman sword was sufficient cause of death for Greek civilization, as for its greatest mathematician, Archimedes, struck down by the plunderers of Syracuse. Nor does there seem to have been any marked failure of courage. The siege of Syracuse, defended by the genius of Archimedes, was long and hard-fought and was brought to an end only by treason. Likewise, in their last battles for freedom, the Greeks displayed a valor worthy of the men of Marathon.

There appears to be no general law of decay. The Phoenicians maintained a high vitality much longer than the Greeks. The trading towns on the Lebanese coast were in the vanguard of civilization by the twelfth century B.C. or earlier, masters, despite their puny size, of much of the Mediterranean. Although the life and ways of commerce are sometimes denigrated as especially debilitating, the Phoenicians were still youthfully vigorous after more than a thousand years of prosperity. Tyre resisted Alexander in 333–332 B.C. with more spirit than any other people he met on his epic march of conquest. And perhaps the best, certainly the noblest, time of Carthage came at the close of Phoenician independence, after defeat in the Second Punic War. Then the Carthaginians so energetically rebuilt that the Romans found their freedom dangerous, although they were stripped of outlying possessions and military power. In three years of nearly hopeless struggle against the Roman hordes, Carthage showed the most magnificent spirit and courage. No people, in the hour of despair, could have seemed less effete, less ready to be slaves.

The West has been developing with great energy for a thousand years; and, while the leadership has shifted from region to region and some areas have fallen behind, there has been no real interruption of the onward sweep. The great rise up to the Renaissance, to which the Italians contributed most, was much less the work of supposedly fresh and vital Germanic invaders, who comprised the nobility, than of the supposedly weary peoples of the decayed Roman empire, the artisans and merchants of the towns. In our time, it seemed to some that Europe, torn and bled by two terrible wars, had come near the end of its historic role. Yet since the Second World War, and perhaps benefiting by the cataclysmic shaking, Europe has shown exceptional economic vitality.

There may be reasons to suppose that a society of free states is especially resistant to decay. Division is an advantage in that a rot afflicting one area need not hurt the rest, as one or another section can take up the banner of progress. Competition should certainly help to keep states alive, as they are driven by fear and pride to keep up with their neighbors. The free community cannot be so stiff and tradition-bound as the great hierarchic empire. Institutions become irrational largely because of inability to adapt to changing circumstances; and the free states of a competitive community, forever driven to reexamination and change by their contacts and conflicts, are most adaptable of all. And if any grow staid and smug, they are likely one day to be aroused from lethargy, as Poland was stirred by partitions, or the complacent Netherlands of the eighteenth century shaken by the French Revolution. Moreover, the more open the political system and the freer the intellectual air, the more capable the society should be of absorbing change and taking measures necessary to combat any real sickness.

No society, however, has been capable of preventing lamentable changes, and debilitation may be inherent in high civilization. The idealization of rural life as purer and healthier than urban is not based entirely on myth. The inhabitant of the slum is usually a less inspiring specimen than his equally poor country cousin, and generals prefer recruits from the farms. Accumulation of wealth, important as it is in providing opportunities for cultural progress, has its dangers, as it may lead to inequality, social tensions, and loss of community spirit. A propertyless proletariat may well be indifferent to what befalls the state. Yet attempts to convert formal into real equality lead to social conflict and possibly to turmoil and dictatorship. At the same time, success and wealth often lead to overconfidence and smug complacency. In free societies, intellectual criticism may undermine all values and social discipline, leaving a sort of moral anarchy. Life in a high civilization comes to seem excessively and dishearteningly complex; the community will is weakened, and pessimism enters as material progress brings more confusion than happiness.

Thus free societies in their ripe maturity may suffer some atrophy of will and determination to be free. In the widening of mental horizons, men look more beyond their own state or nation and think more of the general and universal on the one hand and of the self on the other, thereby weakening attachment to the native land. So far as values are eroded, self-seeking is left alone, and individualism leads to withdrawal from concern for the community, to inwardness and indifference to civic concerns. In late-classical Athens, as in the modern West, people came to think less of their duties to the state and more of what the state owed them. The Theoric Fund, Athenian counterpart of the welfare state, rose to dominate politics as citizenship changed from wholehearted participation to a gainful status; and free distribution of grain was a regular demand and practice in the cities of Hellenistic Greece. Possibly, too, men become a little weary of the uncertainties and unsettlement of freedom, which promises no peace of mind.

Perhaps something like this has occurred in the maturity of each great state system. Certainly, the Chinese states that preceded the Ch'in empire, the Indian states that gave way to the Maurya, and the Hellenistic states that Rome swept away all showed an intellectual ferment and weakening of traditional loyalties which must have encouraged their respective conquerors. The Italian city-states of the Middle Ages in their heyday of leadership in civilization likewise lived in intellectual and moral turmoil. The contemporary world strikes many as decadent, in the loosening of the moral fabric and the relaxation of standards and values. As old and consecrated ways are abandoned, our society seems disordered, feverish, and at odds with itself. But it also boasts a productivity in most realms of human creativity which is phenomenal for quantity and variety, if not for depth. Never has human knowledge grown at any faintly comparable speed, and the explosive potency of modern technology is beyond the daydreams of centuries past. If this is decadence, it is quite opposite to the decay of stagnant old universal empires, such as the Roman of the fourth and fifth centuries or the Chinese in the downward half of each successive dynastic cycle, marked by material and intellectual poverty, institutional rigidity, and apathy. The aging empires suffer anemia, desiccation, and somnolence; the sickness of modernity is an indigestible excess of change.

It may be, then, that free societies wear themselves out and ease the way for the conqueror who would replace their disorderly diversity and frustrating conflicts with the simplicity of a great and orderly union. However, one can only guess how important such imponderable factors may have been. More obvious and substantial is the breakdown of the international order.

NEED FOR UNION

Only unity promises stability. The existence of a plurality of free states in close contact is always precarious. The anarchy is uncontrollable. By definition, sovereign states are free to injure and destroy one another so far as this is within their capacities. International relations are inherently more hostile than friendly. Between individuals the need to cooperate usually outweighs the impulses of greed or jealousy and the fear of one's neighbor; the existence of others around us is commonly advantageous to us. In international relations, on the contrary, the gains from cooperation are usually marginal and are submerged by political motives. Other states are most important not as partners in production of goods but as actual or potential antagonists or allies. The clashes of interests are compounded by clashes of ideals, as a large number of people closely joined together reinforce their own prejudices and give moral support to the collective egotism. The drive for power and position is insatiable, and all states are driven by a mixture of ambitions and fears. There are always bones of contention, and states invariably have a higher opinion of their rights and of their capacities for enforcing these rights than others are prepared to concede. There is no definite limit to the range of influence of any state; it might always expand in power or territory and can hope by this expansion to increase its precious security and glorious prestige. One man can enslave others only with the support of his society, but it is very difficult to form an international society able to prevent the subjection of one people by another; and the oppression of nations is more practical and profitable than that of individuals.

For such reasons, a community of states can be born and live only where conditions are somehow favorable to the maintenance of independence of a number of states in close contact and so tempted to aggression; when conditions change and favor amalgamation rather than sovereign independence, then the state system can be expected to die. But if the free states by their lively interaction bring about great material progress, precisely this outmodes them. Indeed, progress is greatest when the ease of communication, density of population, and administrative and military techniques are such as to invite more centralized authority than exists.

Progress inevitably pushes together. With more travel and broader horizons, men come to think more in universal terms; particularism and willingness to die for one's state decrease. Even in federal systems, progress invariably undermines the smaller units, as attention is drawn away from them toward larger spheres. Economic unification and increased dependence upon foreign trade reduce the apparent viability of small states, raise interest in controlling foreign markets, trade routes, and sources of supplies, and make the extension of frontiers seem more natural and inviting. The improvement of means of transportation, roads and ships, invites their increased use not only by merchants but by armies. Improvement of weapons (perhaps accompanied by decreased willingness of the citizenry to serve as soldiers) brings military professionalism; and the military profession, gaining political importance, thinks not in terms of political balance but of dominant power.

Perhaps most important, as communications and means of administration improve, size increasingly becomes an asset. When little states come to seem outmoded, rulers are more drawn to conquest as they feel capable of profitably managing more extensive lands. If victory promises only a little glory and perhaps a moderate indemnity, war is no serious problem; when it becomes evident that one state can and will engulf another entirely and gain greatly in power thereby, fears and ambitions rise together.

The troubles of the community of states are compounded when, as inevitably occurs, many of the smaller units are swallowed up while a few emerge preeminent as prospective masters. Decreased numbers and increased inequality make international equilibrium harder to maintain, reduce the flexibility and mutuality of the system, and make for the polarization of power; weaker states, despairing of defending themselves, often become clients of stronger ones in hopes of retaining some freedom by submission, while the leaders stand forth as potential champions. Thus the rise of commercial and imperial Athens evoked the fears and hostility of other cities, led by Sparta, and divided Greece into two bitterly opposed camps until Athenian power was broken. Similarly, the rise of Germany by virtue of Bismarck's unification and the country's subsequent industrial growth strained to the utmost the European balance of power. As a result, Europe was frozen into opposing alliances, and the resulting general war would have overthrown the state system entirely had not an outside power, America, come to its rescue.

As the system becomes instable, the stakes of conflict change from limited gains and improvement or loss of position to the supreme glory of universal rule or national extinction. The thirst for power and total control rises as princes and ministers drink. Their problems will be solved, as they see it, not by dealing with opposition but by sweeping it away. The nearer the goal of empire, the more alluring; and the assertion of expansive might brings confidence within and reputation for invincibility without. As the gap between supremacy and degradation narrows, the contest becomes one preeminently for power and only slightly for material interests. There was little economic reason for the antagonism of commercial Athens and agricultural Sparta, or for that between Rome and Carthage, similarly land and sea powers. Prior to the First World War, the Austro-German and Franco-Russian alliances were driven much more by fear than by hopes of gain. Today, America and Russia have no claims upon the possessions or vital economic interests of each other; but no two powers can share world leadership in comfort.

In these circumstances of tension, what little international order the community of states was able to build up in better days is lost. The more insecurity, the less room for morality. As the worst sin against the international order, assault, becomes a gainful and accepted practice, there is no longer any sense of community or consensus upon which to base international law, and only a sham remains. Reputation for honor ceases to be important beside reputation for strength; the imperialistic state wishes more to be feared than to be esteemed. Arbitration becomes impossible as issues become more critical and neutrality loses standing. The laws of war are forgotten as wars become desperate, and losers can no longer expect mercy. The era of empire building reverts to barbarism in international politics. Thus, in China, India, Greece, and Europe, the community of states has built up a code to moderate war, and in each case it has been trampled underfoot in the decline of the state system. [For India, see *188*, p. 298]

As the struggle grows more critical, the role of the state rises and its mission of power becomes overriding. Militaristic parties, seeking fulfillment in the drive for empire, may assume the direction of society. The state may be reshaped for the needs of military power, as rulers of Ch'in or Macedon and many others have purposefully made their nations into machines for conquest; and when energies are harnessed to the war chariot, it is hard to resist driving it forward.

As the open international system decays into a narrow power struggle, there is less room for freedom and criticism; the state can only strengthen its domination over minds and bodies. There is also likely to be developed an authoritarian doctrine, an ideology of empire and conquest to help strengthen internally and give moral justification for the high costs of power and the shattering of the old system. The imperialists want to feel right as well as strong, and conviction of rightness adds immensely to strength. Chinese

Legalists served up a sophisticated political amoralism well suited for ruthless leaders. In India, Kautilya helped his empire-building master of Magadha by sanctioning any means of statecraft, however ruthless and cynical, if it were only justified by probable success. In the decline of the Italian system, Machiavelli advised the prince who would unite Italy to break faith and murder as necessary. In recent times, Prussianism built up an impressive literature of power worship rationalizing the drive for unification of Germany. Most strongly after the First World War, as the obsolescence of the European state system became apparent, fascism arose as a frank espousal of power as the criterion of values and the goal of being.

As Napoleon said, perhaps with some wishful thinking, "One fine day, I am sure, we will see the Empire of the West reborn because the weary peoples will cast themselves under the yoke of the best-governed nation." [512, p. 312] The troubles and instability of contending states lead some to long for total dominion, but in others they cause weariness of strife. Must our civilization be split into fragments burdened with separate defense forces, cultivating mutual hatred of men who really belong together, spreading death and destruction in fruitless wars for the sport of kings, the profit of merchants, or causes no one really knows? Should we not have peace and unity, universal order for the strength and prosperity of mankind? Should not all be joined in the universal brotherhood, as dreamed the Stoics and Mo, the Chinese philosopher of love? Or might not a bygone imperial order be restored, as proposed by Mencius and Dante? The mind sighs for simplicity and order, the end of chaos and fratricidal strife. The drive of the competing states is narrow, petty, selfish, and repugnant to high ideals; nationalism elicited by conflict but discredited by violence is seen, not as a vivifying force, but as a nuisance and a danger; the empire builder writes the half-mythical passion of the peoples for peace and united harmony upon his banners in service of his ruthless cause. International relations are the most disorderly and irrational or uncontrollable aspect of human existence, the area of greatest wastage and futility; all attempts to order them by agreement or through international organization fail or are made to fail by the ambitions of the great. From the various Greek leagues through the Concert of Europe and the League of Nations, history has shown that only force can hammer quarreling sovereignties into unity. Despising alike the dreams of the internationalists and the supposed cynicism of balance of power politics, the maker of empire, standing at once for untempered violence and peaceful order, for perfection of society and scorn for humans, would make an end to all by conquest.

The free states may thus be viewed as victims of their success, as progressive civilization brings instability both internally and externally. Then, with increased strains and a weariness of contention and apparent injustice, ambitious men begin to look to overthrowing the system itself, both domestic and international; and domestic and international conflicts often merge. A struggle between oligarchs and populace has complicated many a drive for unification, as that of Rome against the Hellenistic city-states, or that of Muscovy against independent Novgorod. The coming of universal empire may thus meet real psychological and political needs, just as it answers the economic need for ending barriers to trade. But it hardly answers a demand; seldom has any people gladly bowed to foreign rule, however hypocritically varnished. The empire represents triumphant force. As a knowing imperialist, Adolf Hitler, once said, "The wild mustang does not take upon itself the yoke imposed by man voluntarily or joyfully; neither does one people welcome the violence of another." [Quoted by 536, p. 46]

Swept up by the universal empire, the peoples of once-free states find themselves in a new order, in which contention and competition have been overcome and simplicity and uniformity replace the complexity and disorder which are at once the richness, strength, and weakness of the open system. Tumult yields to order and stability. Yet the universal empires last no longer than the state systems they have smashed and usually not so long. If there have been many more great empires than state systems, it is simply that a monopoly of power comes easier to humanity than its stable partitioning.

UNIVERSAL EMPIRES

In all ways the antithesis of a group of small states sharing a sphere and contending for leadership within it, the universal empire is a political world to itself, a single and essentially self-contained entity. Hardly aware of states beyond, or, if perhaps troubled by them at times, scornful of them as unworthy inferiors, it is an unchallengeable power standing over its world, so vast as to appear to exalted masters and humble subjects alike as infinite in grandeur. Such an empire rests upon conquest and hence can be established wherever geography permits a great state to be built and held together. Most of the very large empires of history seem, however, to rest upon a foundation of an earlier state system. It is easier to forge into a single polity peoples of a common cultural background; moreover, extensive conquest usually implies a superiority of technology, if not of organization, and this the empire expropriates from the free culture builders. The chief seats of empire thus have been areas where a state system once built up a high civilization. But whereas the state system, once undone, seems to be lost forever, when a vast empire disintegrates a new one is usually, after a time of disorder, put into its place; the drive to union is more compelling than the urge to freedom.

Earliest of the empires that might be called universal was that of Egypt, which followed upon a dimly known but highly creative state of division. The Old Kingdom, established about 2850 B.C., was not enormously extensive by modern standards; but it must have struck the ancient Egyptians as equivalent to the world that mattered. Extending hundreds of miles along the valley and delta of the Nile, it held all the good land; beyond were endless deserts or the sea. After some six hundred years, the Old Kingdom broke down; there followed a long time of disorder, the looser Middle Kingdom, more disorder, and finally a reincarnation of the strong empire in the New Kingdom, beginning in 1550 B.C. Meanwhile, in the distant Indus Valley there had also grown up a civilization known from the sites of the presumed capitals, Harappa and Mohenjo-Daro. It seems to have formed an extensive empire, much larger than that of Egypt and even stabler. It had no successor, however, and left no record of its institutions.

Between the Nile and the Indus, the ample valley of Mesopotamia was more favorable for the dispersal of power, and there the Sumerian state system endured a long age. It was brought to an end by the truly magnificent conquests of Sargon. But his Akkadian empire was relatively brief, and for about two millennia this area, unlike Egypt, saw a series of passing empires, mostly lasting only a century or so, of varying scope, especially the Third Dynasty of

Ur; the Babylonian empire of Hammurabi, barely outlasting its creator; the Hittite empire; and the Assyrian, famed for its sternness. Much better known is the greater empire that succeeded them, the Achaemenid Persian, which stretched over unnumbered nations from India and Central Asia into northern Greece and to the Upper Nile, a true world state. Half a millennium after the fall of the last Darius, the Persian empire had under the Sassanids a second life, weaker but still glorious and worthy of some attention.

To the west of the ancient Near Eastern center there was built up, chiefly by the Greeks, a new and better civilization, which served as the basis for ephemeral Macedonian and subsequently the enduring Roman empire. The latter, closest to Western history and one of the best documented, was almost complete in its dominion. On its borders there remained no civilized and highly organized state except that of the Parthians in the distant east. The Roman empire was also outstanding in its longevity, about five centuries in the main part; its eastern limb, the Byzantine empire, managed to exist for another thousand years. The latter held a smaller territory, yet until the eleventh century it was extensive, stretching from the Danube into Armenia, to the Euphrates, and across southern Italy. Constantinople was long the largest city of Europe. Center of an efficient administration, it was hardly ever, even during the frequent struggles for the succession, troubled by revolt of any of the diverse subject peoples. [287, pp. 327–328] Its traditions and infinite pretensions qualify it for consideration along with effectively greater empires.

To the east of the most ancient cultural center and roughly contemporaneous with classic civilization, there grew up another creative state system, that of Hindu-Buddhist India. It likewise provided the foundation for a universal empire, that of the Mauryas, encompassing nearly all the Indian subcontinent. Walled off by impassable mountains, this area forms a natural geographic unit, and one might suppose that its subsequent history would be a tale of unity. However, Indian social structure, based on caste, seems inherently divisive and disunity has been the rule. The Maurya empire lasted less than a century and a half and was followed by much disorder. Centuries later there arose partial empires, as the Gupta and the Harsha, ending in the seventh century; but these were much less absolute than the Maurya, politically as well as territorially. [216, pp. 80–81] There followed more centuries of confusion and ephemeral empires until the arrival of the Turks or Mongols, as raiders or conquerors, in the thirteenth century. Only in the sixteenth century was the Mogul empire able to gather to itself as much of India as the Mauryans held nearly two thousand years earlier. Even then it had only loose control over many princes and tributaries. Nor did the invaders ever assimilate the subject peoples or the empire rise much above a system of crudest exploitation.

China, on the other hand, is the land par excellence of universal empire and of what is often called oriental despotism. Bounded by jungle and rugged uplands to the southwest, by high mountains and arid plateaus to the west, by steppe and desert to the northwest, by cold forests to the north, and for the rest by the forbiddingly broad Pacific, China is a natural unit and has had a cultural and political development as autonomous as any region of the Old World. After the period of Contending States (as it is appropriately called in Chinese histories), roughly contemporaneous with the state system of India and classical civilization in the West, unifying dynasties have followed one another with successively shorter intervals of division or disorder down to modern times. The dynasties, each carrying on the traditions of its predecessors, may be regarded either as phases of a single universal empire, subject to breakdown and restoration, or as repeated empires on the same ground and within the same cultural frame.

Some other large empires have had a rather different provenance. The Turks, magnificent warriors whose hatred of the infidel was fortified by love of plunder, put together much of their Asiatic background, the heritage of Byzantium, and their own inventions of military rule to hold firmly and lastingly a huge area without geographic, racial, national, or religious coherence, stretching from Persia and the Caucasus to Austria and Poland, across North Africa and Arabia, from the Atlantic to Ethiopia and the Indian Ocean. Aspiring to universal dominion by the beginning of the fifteenth century [438, p. 1] as they were flooding over the Balkans, the Turks made the Hapsburgs their tributaries in the sixteenth century and thought seriously of conquering the entire globe. Indifferent to the outside world, they maintained exceptional self-assurance until shaken by the disastrous defeats of the second half of the eighteenth century. [432, Part I, p. 19] Even then, notions of grandeur persisted; at the end of the eighteenth century, court officials shouted at the reception of ambassadors, "Praise be to the Eternal that infidels must come and give homage to our gloriously brilliant scepter." [*518*, p. 75]

Like the Turkish, the Russian empire fell short of true universality, but Muscovy rapidly took on imperial ways after casting off the Mongol yoke and gathering the Russian lands under its aegis. Ivan III, consolidator of the Muscovite state and tripler of its area, was the first to take an attitude of distant superiority to his underlings; a German visitor found his successor, Vassily III, to be the most absolute monarch in the world, master of the property and lives of all. [*365*, p. 135] Ivan IV (the Terrible), first to be crowned as tsar and consecrated by the patriarch, brought the autocracy to its fullness. According to the English ambassador, who considered a mission to his court extremely dangerous, he counted himself emperor of all nations and cared nothing for the law of nations. [*405*, p. cxxiii] Subsequent tremendous expansion, mostly into the weakly held or thinly populated lands to the east and southeast, maintained and affirmed the Russian sense of empire; by the end of the seventeenth century, Russia had stretched all the way across Siberia. But the Russians could never forget, despite their territorial immensity, that other powers were as strong or stronger, and, in military technology, much superior. Even in the sixteenth and seventeenth centuries the Russians had an uncomfortable sense of inferiority, like a country lad seeking recognition by polite society [*359*, p. 187], and Ivan the Terrible began the purposeful borrowing of Western technology. [*408*, p. 125] Peter the Great, a man as though designed by nature to be an autocrat, sought desperately to hammer his land into an instrument of his will; but his mission of wholesale introduction of foreign inventions and ways was woefully out of keeping with the pretenses of a universal monarch. Shortly after him, Western influence was strong enough to compel Anne to grant a constitution. [*412*, p. 47] Since then, Westernization has been perennially pressing, more powerfully in times of weakness and less so when the empire was victorious, against the political framework shaped by vast dominion. [*385*, p. 20]

Especially edifying is the great South American empire of the Incas. Unlike the loose Aztec empire of Mexico, the Inca empire was large and populous, a strip of western South America about 2,500 miles long containing some six million subjects in an extension the more remarkable in view of the lack of efficient animals, like the horse, to facilitate communications and travel. Virtually alone, facing important independent peoples only at its northern and southern extremities, it was a despotism of exemplary tight organization.

Over the range of history, numerous other states, by reasons of special power, traditions, or isolation, have shown something of the universal empire but are less appropriate for the present study. For example, Philip II of Spain, ruler of an enormous and rich American domain, felt himself virtual sovereign of the world; Louis XIV, whose France overshadowed Europe, did likewise to a somewhat lesser degree. But Spain and France were much involved in the complex interaction of European powers. On the other hand, the most extensive of all empires, that of the Mongols, unfortunately for our study, broke up after only two generations and before its forms could much evolve. One must also pass over, albeit with regrets, the large and thoroughly despotic kingdoms of Southeast Asia, as the great but very poorly known Javanese empire of Madjapahit.

These, then, are the great empires available for the study of the uses of power as unlimited as it can be in human affairs. They are not a little alike, presumably because they are all to some extent purposefully designed for a common task, the control of large numbers of people by a few. Since their similarities seem basic and their differences more accidental, it is suitable to consider them less individually, as one might discuss a number of quite diverse states, than topically, using examples to illustrate the common anatomy and ways of the imperial order.

PATTERN OF EMPIRE

Freedom means diversity. The Eskimo communities, the ancient Greek city-states, the city-republics of the Middle Ages, the Swiss cantons, and modern democracies have in common, as free societies, mostly the absence of strong rule. There is more sameness in vast empires than in small states because they are creations of unlimited government, and principles of domination are everywhere as alike as human psychology. Empires are born of conquest and are an imposition; they are more designed, shaped by a few wills, and less the outcome of organic growth and the interaction of different political forces. They represent dominion extended far beyond the bounds of elemental cohesion and easy administration; for them, problems of external enemies have receded while the internal problems of unity, order, and exploitation loom larger. This presupposes a strong political organization, a purposeful structure dedicated to government of the world. Having outgrown human community, the universal empire is a work of political engineering.

Great empires may also be alike because they have borrowed ideas and forms, one from another. Ever since the beginnings of culture, useful and even rather complicated ideas have traveled over long distances. The basic inventions of the Bronze Age were carried from the Near East to China, western Europe, and North Africa; as city life arose about the same time, within a few centuries, in Egypt, Mesopotamia, and the Indus Valley, the very idea of civilization must have spread. But the arts and techniques of domination are quite as easy to understand as the use of copper, and no less useful and interesting. Even rulers indifferent to new styles of building, not to speak of humbler crafts, take eagerly the lessons of political power, the forms and means appropriate for the mastery of peoples. Perhaps only the techniques of warfare are equally susceptible of imitation; and the more arbitrary the ruler, the freer to copy whatever is useful to his state.

The empire is indeed an artifact to be copied; the idea represents a tremendous invention for the powerful. Primitive groups ordinarily fight for lust, honor, or gain, not to impose their rule upon their neighbors. Even if they take slaves, it is easier to carry the prisoners home and set them to work like cattle; the small and intimate society, without a bureaucracy and regular taxation, with few distinctions of status or class, cannot imagine imposing a profitable rule upon subjects in a foreign territory. The chief and council may make war by common agreement; in victory they may impose respect or demand concessions. But repression at a distance does not fit into their ways.

Empire building requires war with incorporation of the defeated. The first step is an attempt to make victory permanent by imposing a regular tribute beyond the spoils taken or the indemnity demanded in the moment of triumph. But this system is unstable, for the victims will always seek to shake off the yoke. To keep fear in their hearts, they must be frequently punished. Nor can the conqueror rule from a distance peoples much more numerous than his own, for they are always likely to combine against their oppressor. A next stage is to quarter troops on the conquered to keep them disarmed and to ensure obedience. This permits a wider empire but deprives the master state of forces. True empire building requires that the subjected be made firmly to support their servitude, that conquered lands not drain off soldiers to garrison them but provide recruits for the army and taxes to sustain the government, that conquest be politically and economically profitable. For these purposes, there must be an elaborate apparatus to ensure compliance, voluntary or coerced.

The vast empire is thus a highly artificial form which men do not easily think of unless it is suggested to them, a political artifact to be reached only through successive steps of invention. A leader cannot govern, without organizational discipline, a troop of more than about thirty men. [494, pp. 18–19] It is prima facie ridiculous that a million men should prostrate themselves before another likewise of flesh and blood, that an autocrat should deem himself the proprietor of far-reaching lands he has perhaps never trod and peoples he has never seen. It is naïve to hold that men are born free and equal, only to be everywhere enchained; but it is absurd that they be divided into a very few with total powers and very many subject to arbitrary rule. The inborn powers of men differ as those of leader and followers in tribal society, not as despot and his slaves; and the chiefs of small bands, unlike the despots of huge empires, have to justify by their prowess the authority entrusted to them. A half-democratic government of consultation, or an aristocracy of respected elders, perhaps with a leader accepted for his qualities, is much more humanly sensible and easily evolved than a traditional empire, which defies logic by attributing all power to a few, probably to a single individual, and wherein the privileges of the rulers are utterly disproportionate to their merits.

By the same token, it may be considered a bit unnatural that the area of the state should be much larger than the ordinary range of human interaction. It is understandable that those who live and work together and know their common needs should manage their common affairs, defend the community, and give their resources and themselves for the general good. On the other hand, that men should obey and give a large part of the fruit of their labors to a distant authority that they know only by hearsay, that they should fight and risk their skins to defend far-off borders against peoples of whom they know nothing — all this represents great institutional development over the simpler state of mankind.

Perhaps there were extensive empires in neolithic times; the Incas and others, like the Zulus, have shown that a huge and very effective empire can be sustained on a technology in most respects very primitive. But so far as is known, the Egyptians invented the imperial state. The compact domain, a single huge oasis blessed with easy transportation on the Nile and bound together by irrigation canals, uniquely invited unification. Yet it seems to have required centuries of development before the centralized bureaucratic regime appeared full-blown about 2850 B.C.

Sumeria was very slow to follow the Egyptian example. Although there had been hegemonic cities for ages past, the Sumerian city-states enjoyed at least 1,000 years of freedom after attaining a fair cultural level; and one may guess that they were still attached to their old ways when Sargon of Akkad pressed them into his splendid empire about 2350 B.C. How much Sargon may have been influenced by the Egyptian model is conjectural, but such influence can hardly have been absent, as Egypt and Sumeria had been in contact for many centuries. Like a pharaoh, Sargon set up a great palace in a capital of his own, supported by a centralized taxing bureaucracy. [*129*, p. 154] It was indicative of the incompleteness of Sargon's work that his empire, like many initial efforts to unify a world, was soon troubled by revolts [*119*, p. 72]; but it was in turn an inspiring example. There was also trade and travel eastward from Mesopotamia, and it is not improbable that the great Indus Valley empire — if empire it was — drew upon the work of Sargon. [*218*, p. 102] This, least known of ancient empires, was much the largest until ages later and was seemingly the most stable.

Since Akkadian times the Near East, a region with little protection of geography, has never been long without imperial rule; and successive rulers, no matter what their cultural origins, took over much of the style of their predecessors. The Third Dynasty of Ur put together a state less extensive than that of Sargon but more thoroughly bureaucratic. The Babylonians were succeeded by the Kassites; after them the Hittites matured from limited kingship and loose authority to autocracy of Egyptian style in about 150 years. [*101*, pp. 157–159] The next memorable makers of empire were the Assyrians, who, thanks to better military organization, iron weapons, and specialized cavalry, were able to rule sternly and advance imperial techniques of tax gathering and control of conquered provinces. [*127*, pp. 81–83; *102*, p. 183]

The Persians spent some centuries absorbing Mesopotamian ways before their career of conquest; as a minor power, they modeled their court on that of Assyria. [*253*, I, 131–132] As masters of the Near East, they took over Assyrian governorships as satrapies and generally incorporated the old bureaucracy into their state. [*249*, pp. 74, 86] When Cambyses conquered Egypt, he became an Egyptian divinity like the pharaohs. [*246*, p. 60] Surrounded by the pomp of the universe, the Persian rulers dwelt like gods in palaces gleaming with gold and crowded with the fairest concubines. Beside them, ordinary men were slaves to be slain at the slightest whim. Thus, when a general dashed up to save Artaxerxes from a lion at a hunt, he was condemned to death for daring to come between the Great King and his quarry. [*253*, I, 217] Even nature was supposed to bow to the Persian monarch. Xerxes, Herodotus relates, had his slaves lash the Hellespont for its temerity in tearing away his bridge.

The ideals and forms of the semidivine Persian king long outlasted the empire of Darius and spread far beyond its bounds. In Persia itself successive strong states sought to emulate or improve upon the Achaemenids; the Sassanid monarchs (226–641 A.D.) in particular set themselves up as divine autocrats of unlimited pretensions, secluded from the people in incomparable magnificence. When the Arabs overran the region, they brought with them simpler and more modest political forms from the desert; but soon the old pattern was restored as the Abbasid Califate frankly looked back with pride to its Sassanid predecessors, infidel as they were. [B. Spuler, in *409*, p. 347] Like them, the califate cherished the forms and pomp of the despotic world state and godlike absolutism. [*486*, pp. 155–156]

The Mauryan empire (320–180 B.C.), which united nearly all of India, also took over Persian styles of court and administration, even borrowing the Persian word for satrap or governor. [*215*, pp. 124–145] The inscriptions of Asoka seem in various ways modeled after those of Darius. [*249*, p. 122] Mauryan ways, in turn, became part of the permanent Indian tradition of kingship, more or less absolutist and divine.

Persian kingship entered the Western tradition, too, through the Hellenistic monarchies, which inherited the ephemeral empire of Alexander and eventually much impressed the Romans. Julius Caesar, practical founder of the empire, spent his early years of military service in the East and later had pleasant experiences of divine kingship in the company of Cleopatra. Caesar's fondness for the trappings of despotism was his undoing, as many leading Romans were still fond of the republic, and Augustus was somewhat more modest. The deification of the autocrat progressed even under Augustus, however; if his proconsuls were worshiped by obsequious Eastern peoples trained by centuries of humility, the ruler of the civilized world could expect no less. And respect for the Senate did not prevent Augustus from forming an informal imperial council of "friends" after the Hellenistic-Persian mode. [299, p. 137] Later, as the empire became more frankly despotic, it borrowed more freely. Galerius (305–310 A.D.) openly called for the imitation of the Sassanids, and in the latter empire, or Dominate, many outward trappings if not much of the Persian spirit were copied. [299, p. 141]

The weary Roman empire gradually split into western and eastern halves, never rejoined after 395 when Theodosius bequeathed the parts to his two sons. The imperial glory was broken and faded in the West (to be dimly revived in the Holy Roman Empire); in the "New Rome" of the Byzantine empire it was long maintained. Caesars there for yet ten centuries called themselves "Lord and Governor of the Inhabited World," and even while speaking Greek, the people of the empire proudly called themselves Romans. [311, p. 185] For centuries, the Germanic kings of Western states sought the approval of the Byzantine emperor, put his image on coins, and probably believed him something like a god on earth. [353, p. 134] When the Turkish warrior bands smashed the enfeebled Byzantine state, they did not replace the old imperial institutions but revarnished them, much as the great church of St. Sophia was converted into a mosque. [438, p. 20] They freely adopted Byzantine royal styles, ornaments, and titles; the Turkish ruler of Constantinople called himself "Kaisar-i-Rum." [436, pp. 17, 179–180]

The institutions of empire in China may not have been entirely autochthonous, as many an idea was passed among the Near East,

India, and China from long before recorded history. But the evolution of the relatively isolated Middle Kingdom was independent, as a series of dynasties consciously tried to avoid the errors of their predecessors and step by step improved the arts of rule. The ways of despotism have in China been brought to their highest perfection, if one may make such comparisons; certainly in Neo-Confucianism the Chinese shaped the best rationalization and moral support for autocracy yet invented.

Whether or not they are indebted to anyone for lessons in imperial government, the Chinese have been effective teachers. The Japanese, for example, copied Chinese political forms, court ceremonial, and many matters of administration and taxation, as well as Chinese art and literature. In Japan, to be sure, centralized government after the Chinese image was never much more than a veneer. An essential feature of the Chinese system was excluded by Japan; civil service rank or position by service to the sovereign remained subordinate to nobility or position by birth. [E. Reischauer, in 466, p. 28] But the theory was powerful; the emperorship was as idealized as in China, and the Japanese were infected by fancies of world rule. In the sixteenth century a Japanese conqueror dreamed of ruling the universe through Peking; he began by attacking Korea. [53, pp. 75–76]

Various other peoples on the rim of China were enabled to conquer the Chinese partly by learning arts of rule from them. For example, the Manchus learned Chinese administrative techniques in their native Manchuria long before they took advantage of the calamities of the Ming dynasty to appropriate the realm. [20, p. 80] Even more spectacular was the success of the Mongols, who could never have come to hold the world's largest empire without Chinese help. When disunited, the Mongol tribes had a rather free and loosely organized society, and the chiefs' authority rested on little more than their personal qualities. But when Genghis Khan forged them into a prime instrument of conquest and overran vast subject lands, he rapidly and effectively, partly with the help of Chinese advisers, made himself into an emperor in Chinese style. He also acquired the outlook of universal empire, accepting the decree of heaven that he was to rule the world and establish peace everywhere. By Mongol law any nation that refused obedience was a rebel, just as the Chinese claimed: "In Heaven there is only one eternal God, and on earth there is only one lord, Genghis Khan, the Son of God." [*416*, p. 102]

Making themselves masters of China, the Mongols ruled as earlier great dynasties had done, while their armies spread the ways and ideas of empire from eastern Europe to the South Seas. It was when the Mongol-Chinese forces invading Indonesia were repelled in 1292 that a capable minister was inspired to undertake to subdue the entire archipelago. [*560*, pp. 5–13] Within some forty years he succeeded, mostly by naval action, in subjecting the whole watery sphere of Indonesia and parts of Malaya. This Madjapahit empire, so far as known, seems to have been typical of such creations. The vizier who made the empire for the glory of his sovereign codified laws and set up a regular administrative system. Villages, inhabitants, and fields were registered and taxed; everyone was made subject to labor service. The Hindu and Buddhist churches were part of the state, supervised by officials. To preserve the fullness of autocracy, the duties of the vizier were divided on the demise of the great founder. [*503*, pp. 141–142] The capital grew from a village to a city of several hundred thousand, crowded with those living by and from the king and palace. The king, who largely withdrew from active government to enjoy his pleasures and his harem, was held to be Shiva incarnate, so sacred that it was a blessing to be slain by him. [*560*, pp. 63–66] But in a century the great empire collapsed in chaos.

A branch of the Mongols went into India to establish the Mogul empire, which included that subcontinent plus Afghanistan. The Moguls brought with them not only leftovers of Mongol-Chinese political doctrine, but ideas picked up from the practice of Persia and the Abbasid Califate. [*213*, p. 4] Mongol ways were also blended by the Turks of Central Asia with those of the Byzantine empire, which they replaced.

Mongol and Byzantine elements also went into the shaping of the Russian empire. The Mongols were, in effect, the first unifiers of Russia; their invasion swept over a land split into many small states by the practice of dividing the realm among the sons of the prince. Two hundred and fifty years of subjection and paying tribute to the Mongols raised the demand for unity and strength to throw off the foreign yoke; and the state that led the struggle, Muscovy, naturally claimed hegemony. At the same time, the Mongols cooperated with the princes in the destruction of such popular government as remained. [*416*, p. 345] The occupation forces, with Russian conscripts, gave Russia the experience of a standing army. [*412*, p. 16] The Mongols also furnished the intellectual and administrative model of the universal empire, and centralization was forwarded by the census and the taxes they imposed. [*404*, p. 80] Indeed, the Tartar organization for gathering tribute was taken over and became part of the Russian state. [*360*, p. 25] The institution of landholding for official service may also have been taken from the khans. [K. Wittfogel in *409*, p. 327] Doubtless more important, Russian princes learned to grovel before the khan; it was not so difficult to continue groveling before the strongest of their own number. It was as tax gatherer for the Mongols that Ivan Kalita was able to raise his position over the other princes and meanwhile gradually reduce the tribute paid. With the enfeeblement of Mongol power, Ivan III was able in 1480 finally to renounce the sovereignty of the Golden Horde and become autocrat in his own right.

Freed from foreign control and steadily expanding their realm, the rulers of Muscovy came to regard themselves as true emperors. The fall of Constantinople (1453), attributed to the betrayal of Orthodoxy by compromise with Rome, came opportunely to support the view that the Roman-Byzantine mantle had passed to the holy Russian state. It also increased the xenophobia of Russia, which had long looked up to the Greeks in cultural and religious matters, gave feelings of great self-importance, and seemed to thrust Moscow forward as the defender of faith and civilization. [*404*, p. 113] Ivan III, who built up a very large state embracing nearly all the Russians, married Zoë, niece of the last Byzantine emperor, and so assumed something of the succession of the Caesars. He also borrowed the double eagle, which became symbol of the tsars, reconstructed the palace, prescribed formalities on the Byzantine model and affected court rituals with a new phraseology of exaltation, instituted the coronation as a solemn religious ceremony, and took for himself the Byzantine title of autocrat and Caesar, slavicized to czar or tsar. In short, he put himself forward as the political and ecclesiastical successor of the Roman emperor. [*404*, p. 117; *388*, II, 19]

The idea of the divine sovereign prospered under Ivan III's successors, Vassily III and Ivan IV, the Terrible. [*416*, p. 168] The latter, crowned in Byzantine style, claimed that autocracy was the essence of government and that rights of subjects were pure mischief; he also embraced the theory, then recently enunciated, that Moscow was the Third Rome, successor to Rome and Byzantium, the legitimate, last, and most glorious ruler of the world, temporal and spiritual. He also traced his ancestry to Augustus Caesar. [379, p. 47; 377, pp. 165, 186] His court patterned itself closely after the Byzantine in etiquette, dress, and entertainments [301, p. 269], while cherishing attitudes of self-righteousness and suspicion toward foreigners quite unlike the attitudes of earlier times. [404, p. 218] Ivan also looked eastward. Much interested in Asiatic customs, ceremonial, and government, he had many Eastern princes in Moscow; and a number of his chief administrators were Tartars. [408, p. 128] Having made himself khan of Kazan and Astrakhan, he used this as an argument for recognition of his title of tsar. Some said, with justice, that he was more orientalizer than reformer. [359, p. 175n]

As these examples indicate, ways of empire are borrowable, like metallurgical techniques. The very idea of commanding and exploiting distant alien peoples would hardly occur to anyone unless it had been done by others, and he who sets out to make himself master of an empire will almost inevitably follow the successful practitioners of the art. This is both easier and safer than trying to experiment and devise for oneself the suitable machinery, accouterments, and forms of the greatest of organizations. Indeed, no one has enough acumen to construct an imperial administration without also acquiring much political learning. Conquerors are the more inclined to ape their competitors or predecessors because they value power more than originality and, being stern men of action, often lack artistic imagination. If great and would-be great rulers do not spend more time in analyzing the experience of others, it may be because they are not very intellectually inclined and are too self-assured to feel much need to learn.

But the great empires not only suggest ways and forms for governing the world. As the very incarnation of political success, they recommend themselves to all proud rulers, great and less great. Rulers of midget states would fancy themselves like the monarch of the world, just as poor men dream of riches; and if they cannot have great states, they can try to run little domains in great style. Thus the German princelings of the eighteenth century all tried to keep imitation Versailles, even if they had only a few hundred subjects. After the huge Arabian empire broke up, numerous small successor states did their best to keep up the despotic style, with court eunuchs, harems, and liberal beheadings. When Solomon forged a strong little state among the Jews, he felt it necessary to ape the ostentation, court, and harem customary in the Near Eastern empires; also in the manner of the great, he instituted heavy taxes, took over profitable trade, and put religion under royal protection. [462, p. 40; 322, p. 83] Moreover, the people in the shadows of the empires come to accept the essential rightness of their forms. The way of the great should be the way of greatness. The elders of Israel said to Samuel, "We will have a king over us, that we may be like all the nations." [I Samuel 8:5] When slaves from the Near East revolted against their Roman masters about 140 B.C., they could devise nothing better than a little Hellenistic state, with an autocrat surrounded by his lords and an elaborate household down to the royal shampooer. [332, p. 7]

But however much may be copied from one empire by another, their essential alikeness in varied climates, cultures, and economic conditions probably owes more to the logic of single rule over tremendous areas and multitudes. The overgreat state resting primarily on force practically requires, as symbol of authority and final arbiter, a single and all-powerful ruler, whose person is elevated far above ordinary mortals. To govern, there must be a large corps of professional administrators in a pyramid beneath the throne. Checked only by its self-restraint or incapacity, the imperial state feels free to interfere with the economy, to take wealth to its own uses, and to tax mercilessly. Finding criticism inconvenient, it inevitably checks free expression; on the other hand, it finds it advantageous to propagate a suitable religion or ideology. And the autocrat will surely have a huge court, overflowing with ornaments, pleasures, toadies, and parasites.

These are some of the logical results of total power in a universal empire. It is instructive to find them all, even in an exaggerated degree, in the Inca empire, which must have built upon previous Peruvian imperial experiments, but which drew nothing from the empires of the Old World or even, so far as is known, from those of Central America. The Inca rulers, deified and trapped in the utmost splendor, had absolute and arbitrary authority over their subjects, from highest to lowest. A swollen bureaucracy drained off the larger part of the produce of the land. Political controls were everywhere, and obedience was inculcated by an apparatus of propaganda as well as by the cult of the sun-god. One may well imagine that a noble of the court of the Sapa Inca would have felt himself tolerably at home, except for the exteriors of life, in the entourage of Constantine, the Great Mogul, or the Son of Heaven.

2 UNIVERSALISM

REACHING FOR THE WORLD

The hunger for power is unlike that for food or fair women, and a conqueror can be happy only in ever more conquest. The imperial career is an accelerating one: by its great victories the on-marching state at once eliminates rivals and enemies and adds to its own forces and confidence. Past the point where a coalition can hope to check its rise, the way is open in all directions. Without, those who might oppose are overawed and demoralized so that they may see fit to yield peacefully and accept protection or can make only a halfhearted resistance; within, the exultant sense of world mission rises to the skies, and ever more victories are a wonderful tonic and solve political problems. Hence it is hard for the new master of civilization to desist from sending his armies on and on, nor has he any reason for self-restraint. His state is organized for war and has armies that are better kept occupied against the foreigners; the administrative machine likes ever more positions to fill and lands to rule; the treasury always needs more plunder or revenue. Rome found expansion a great antidote for social discontent, and Turkish sultans had to go to war whether they wished or not because the Janissaries expected a campaign at least every three years and became dangerously restive while unoccupied. [436, pp. 78–79]

Security combines with pride to require that the last independent powers be eliminated. For the omnipotent ruler it is an injury and an insult that men anywhere should defy his law. Patronizing the weak, hating and scorning the barbarians who arrogantly flout the will that is the law of the world, the would-be total authority can countenance only vassals. Independent states are at best a base for bandits and disturbers of tranquillity for the absolutism that can feel quite secure only when it is alone; at worst, they are a constant menace. They cannot be allowed to succeed lest others be encouraged to emulate their presumption. The monarch should be, as said the greatest of the Moguls, Akbar, "ever intent on conquest, otherwise his enemies rise in arms against him." [212, p. 304] The greater the realm, the less the inclination to respect the independence of others, the stronger the feeling that its way is universally valid and that all should have the benefit of it, and the more compelling the pleasant duty to secure the peace and order of the universe, while those who resist are, ipso facto, evil. Self-interest combines with inflated pretenses and responsibility for civilization to drive ever onward, and the conquering empire would swell itself infinitely.

Thus the empires that have come into the ownership of a culture-building area have not been satisfied but have been propelled far beyond. Even for Egypt, with its uninviting environs, strong unification meant foreign expansion. As soon as the Old Kingdom was quite firm, Snefru and his successor Khufu, of the pyramid-building Fourth Dynasty, went into Lybia and Nubia, whence came gold, ivory, and slaves, and made excursions up the Mediterranean coast, across Sinai to Phoenicia. Centuries later, when the New Kingdom had expelled the foreign Hyksos, it set out forthwith to appropriate distant lands, from the Upper Nile to Syria and the Euphrates. In Mesopotamia, Lugalzagezzi, having brought together a Sumerian empire of sorts, must have envisioned more, as he spoke of ruling "from the sunrise to the sunset." After him, Sargon appropriated a far larger area between the Black Sea, the Mediterranean, and the Persian Gulf, and called himself "King of the Whole Universe," as did countless later Near Eastern rulers. The earliest great Assyrian conqueror, although he held only a middling empire, called himself "King of All." For the Assyrians, all who did not submit were enemies, subject to the sanctions their monarchs boasted: "Their heads I cut off, by the sides of their cities like grain heaps I piled up. Their spoil, their property, their possessions to an unnumbered quantity I brought out." [*127*, pp. 52, 63, 66]

In this tradition of ambition, Cyrus, builder of the Persian empire, on taking Babylon proclaimed himself ruler of the four quarters of the earth. "I am Cyrus, King of the Universe, Mighty King, King of Babylon, King of Sumer and Akkad, King of the World Quarters" [*252*, p. 51]; he demanded to be accepted not as a foreign but as universal monarch. Darius wrote of himself, "I am Darius, the Great King, King of kings, King of countries containing all kinds of men, King in this great earth far and wide. . . ." When little more than Greece remained to flaunt independence, Xerxes said that, by conquering Greece, "We shall bring all mankind under our yoke, alike those who are guilty and those who are innocent of doing us wrong." [Herodotus, Bk. VII, chap. 8]

For centuries Rome grew slowly, until after it vanquished its greatest rival, Carthage. Then, in little more than a century, continually impelled by needs of defense against evil forces without or by the requirements of honor [542, p. 66], Rome transformed itself from an Italian power to master of the classical world. The only posture the Romans found acceptable in others was that of kneeling. As Virgil said, it was Rome's mission to humble the proud; that is, only Rome should indulge pride. Augustus' first boast, in the long inscription recounting his deeds, was that he "brought the whole world under the rule of the Roman people." So it must have seemed, and decrees of the Caesars were addressed not to Romans and their subjects but to all "throughout the world." So firmly set was the idea that the Roman emperor rightfully ruled the world that in 1393, when the power of the Byzantine Caesar had all but melted away, the patriarch wrote that there was but one lawful emperor in the universe, beside whom all others were imposters. [377, p. 140]

Somewhat differently, the Mauryan emperor Asoka, who in horror of bloodshed gave up military action after nearly completing the conquest of India, expected to prevail still more widely by word and example; the remaining independent states should give him heed. "I consider that I must promote the welfare of the whole world," he wrote in one of his edicts; and he sent missions of *Dhamma*, or virtue, to propagate his ideals far and wide, even to the Greeks and others. "Even where the envoys of the Beloved of God have not gone, people hear of his conduct according to *Dhamma*, his precepts and his instructions in *Dhamma*, and they follow *Dhamma* and will continue to follow it. What is obtained by this is victory everywhere, and everywhere victory is pleasant." [217, pp. 253, 256]

The king of Ch'in wanted to "lift up the whole world in his arms and tie the four seas in a sack" [16, p. 2], and as soon as he had gobbled up the competing states he went on to conquer far beyond the core area of China in the Yellow River valley, especially to the south, reaching as far as the Mekong delta and annexing this land, so different from the Chinese homeland. Shortly afterward the Han dynasty extended Chinese power in the second century B.C. approximately to its ultimate limits, as far west as Afghanistan.

This empire was much larger than the contemporary Roman empire and stretched farther from the capital, without the benefit of communications by inland sea. Later, strong dynasties have repeatedly, after times of weakness and retreat, pushed the borders far out. Chinese emperors, like Asoka, have held the pious principle that good example should prevail and the lesser nations should, in the Confucianist scheme, accept their inequality and welcome Chinese culture and tutelage; it was demanded, for example, that border states use the imperial calendar. [53, p. 16] If virtuous example were not enough, an army might be sent to purify hearts, as when the T'ang felt that, despite financial troubles, they must conquer Korea, simply because an independent state was inadmissible. Following Mencius' dictum that "In the sky there is only one sun and above the people there is only one emperor" [45, p. 43], the general objective of Chinese thought became, in the words of a Chinese scholar, "all under Heaven," or the whole of mankind. "Their political thinking has always been in terms of all mankind, with world peace as the final goal, and family and nation as transitional stages to the perfecting of the World Order." [46, pp. 7, 175] Chinese sovereigns maintained such all-embracing claims as long as the empire lasted. Upon his coronation the emperor, it was said, "received from Heaven and revolving nature the government of the world." [76, I, 311] In 1816 the British ambassador was expelled for refusal to kowtow to the "Ruler of all under Heaven." [45, p. 18] In 1840, two years before the Opium War, a high official wrote to Queen Victoria: "If you submit humbly to the Celestial Dynasty and tender your allegiance, it may give you a chance to purge yourself of your past sins. But if you persist in your path of obstinate delusion, your three islands will be laid waste and your people pounded into mincemeat as soon as the armies of his Divine Majesty set foot upon your shores." [4, p. 396]

Many others have intended no less. The Inca ruler informed those he would annex that he had come to make all men without distinction hear the voice of reason; that if strife and disorder occurred anywhere, it was his duty alone to sit in judgment, and it was their duty to recognize his law, while he looked only to his father, the Sun, for guidance. [181, p. 58] Resistance to this catholic beneficence merited enslavement or massacre [173, p. 119]; and the greater the empire became, the more readily did overawed peoples submit. More advanced peoples have with less reason

fondled such visions of universality. The monk who in 1510 proclaimed Moscow to be the Third Rome, wrote to his tsar: "Thou
art the only Christian sovereign in the whole world and, because
of this, sovereign of all Christians." In the sixteenth century Selim
the Grim, who doubled the area of the Turkish empire, aspired to
rule the entire world. [*434*, p. 261]

Such has been the ambition of the very great. Half a world is
not enough. But there is sense as well as vanity in the urge to rule
everywhere. Universality not only eliminates the irritant and threat
outside; it makes the yoke inside easier to bear or harder to shake
off. A man must be sorely driven to raise his hand against the lord
of all peoples. When so many once-proud nations are bowed alike,
their subjugation must be divine justice. Standing over the world,
probably calling itself simply the empire or the Middle Kingdom
or the four quarters, the universal empire seems to itself the natural
and inevitable order of mankind.

THE SWORD SHEATHED

Despite infinite ambition and pretensions, universal empires have
not succeeded in conquering the world. Perhaps none, in fact, has
incorporated all the powers with which it had fairly easy communications; always some lesser powers have remained around the
periphery. Thus Chinese dynasties have regularly, in their times
of early strength, expanded to roughly the limits of present-day
China; but they have never gone much beyond. After the great
expansions early in the Han, T'ang, Ming, and Ch'ing dynasties,
forward movement ceased and control over outlying areas was relaxed or relinquished. Usually the Chinese have been satisfied to
exercise a slight or nominal suzerainty over such areas as Indochina,
Tibet, and Korea. Their empire never approached in size that of
the Mongols, a far less numerous but more warlike people who
seem to have felt more strongly the urge to boundless aggrandizement. Unlike the Mongols, the Chinese never even tried to conquer
Japan, in spite of haughty condescension toward the Japanese
ruler. When the expansive thrust of a new and vigorous dynasty
had spent itself, the Chinese sought to deal politically rather than
militarily with the independent nations on their borders. Instead
of trying to subdue the nomads, it seemed cheaper and more politic

to buy them off or to conciliate them by sending Chinese princesses, who introduced Chinese culture and softened barbarian manners. [*24*, pp. 79–80] Titles were given to Tibetan, Turkic, or Mongol leaders who seemed threatening enough to merit them. The necessity of war was deemed a reflection on the character of the Son of Heaven, who should in the Confucian view sway the world by his example, keeping order at home and pacifying the barbarians by his virtue. Tributaries might have to be reminded of their obligations by punitive expeditions; but it was easier to encourage the bringing of tributes by giving in return gifts of similar or greater value, thus satisfying the requirements of imperial dignity with least trouble. [*56*, p. 236]

This story might be detailed of many empires, from the days when the Old Kingdom spread north and south hundreds of miles beyond the confines of Egypt, then halted and eventually withdrew, aggressive policies giving way to pacific, pursuit of the unsubmissive to their appeasement. The Roman example is illustrative. From the acquisition of Sicily (completed in 241 B.C.) to that of Gaul by Julius Caesar, the progress of Roman arms was like a swelling tide. Interrupted by the civil wars after Caesar's assassination, it was never really resumed. Augustus rounded out the empire to the Danube but, accepting defeat in a manner contrary to old Roman tradition, abandoned the conquest of Germany between the Rhine and the Elbe and desisted from seeking revenge for the humiliating defeat of a Roman army by the Parthians. His advice to his successors was that they content themselves with the borders he had established, and generally they did so. The chief subsequent acquisition was that of Britain, although some eastern territories were held for varying periods. From the end of the republic Rome began appeasing barbarians, and Roman citizenship was given to chiefs who would nominally submit to Roman authority. Domitian (81–96 A.D.) concluded that it was more practical to negotiate with the Dacians than to fight them, and granted them a subvention for keeping the peace. [*338*, p. 47] Although a few years later the more ambitious Trajan attacked and annexed Dacia, the conquests he made in Asia Minor were promptly surrendered by his successor, Hadrian. The latter preferred the easier way of checking barbarians by negotiation and presents, and instead of pursuing Teutonic intruders, tried to keep them out by a wall and palisade from the Rhine to the Danube.

[*314*, I, 287] Marcus Aurelius likewise failed to follow up victories and hold lands taken in Central Europe. By the time of Caracalla (211–217 A.D.) it was standard practice to buy off potential raiders. Far from trembling at the might of Rome, the barbarians came generally to expect subsidies — which the Romans represented as imperial largess — and were infuriated when these were not paid.

Such a reversal of roles is anomalous. The building of empire signifies above all the mobilization of resources, domestic and captured, for power and further advancement. Yet, having amassed resources immensely superior to those of all antagonists, the empire halts as though paralyzed. Yet the anomaly is not inexplicable. Empire building may be considered as primarily the work of overwhelming political will (aided, no doubt, by fortunate circumstances); but the will to power of nations is not insatiable. Paradoxically, expansion is not consonant with the mature imperial society.

After a certain point, the rewards of expansion become less. It is less attractive to try to incorporate more alien outlying peoples; this is supposedly the prime reason why Korea, although not difficult of access, was permitted by the Chinese to remain separate even though at times it was politically subject. The administration of an overlarge realm presents problems; doubtless many a time the emperor or his ministers must have felt that new provinces of which they knew little and with which communications were poor caused more headaches than they were worth. When moral decay had not yet progressed far, Augustus was hampered in his rule by lack of capable and patriotic administrators, especially for the less attractive and lucrative provinces. [*308*, p. 235] The later Roman empire won not a few victories over the barbarians, but territories were not annexed as they would have been in earlier centuries; it would have been too difficult to administer them. At the same time, the barbarians had little treasure to plunder; if the Germans had had rich cities and temples full of gold to despoil, the Romans would doubtless have felt it necessary to civilize them. Augustus at first did not impose taxes on the Germans. [*308*, p. 281] When he tried to, they rose and inflicted a frightful defeat on the legions, ending forever Roman power beyond the Rhine. The political drive to eliminate potential menaces also diminishes as the empire becomes very great and very self-satisfied. Unsubdued nations may be nuisances, but they can be ignored. Thus there is little to gain by pushing conquest beyond reasonable limits.

There is something to lose, perhaps an empire. Wars require active armies, and armies represent power not only against the enemy but against the civil government. If the emperor is a great war leader, this may cause no worry. A Genghis Khan is sure of the loyalty of troops and generals. But the rulership of a great empire is primarily a civilian occupation; and, to the ruler, the military force represents an unceasing danger, a competing force that can overthrow him at any time it musters the will to do so. For example, an Assyrian general rebelled and made himself Sargon II. In the empire that best knew how to control the armies, the Chinese, generals from time to time revolted, although they were rarely successful. Many Caesars, even outstanding military leaders, were undone by the armies; all of them had to give great attention to the demands, especially for pay, of the legions. Hence it is much preferable if, by a pacific policy, the army may be reduced. Safest is a demilitarized society in which the low status of the military, as in China, discourages both risings and coups. Very likely it seems more prudent to hire barbarian mercenaries as keepers of order, as the hirelings should be more controllable than armed citizens.

It is also expensive to keep up a large force capable of foreign wars. When prospects of plunder fade, money is more pleasantly spent on luxury and display at home. As the borders are pushed beyond the horizon, people and rulers alike lose interest in far-off wars. Self-sufficient and self-regarding, glorying in boundless superiority, the universal empire has more than enough to do at home without troubling itself with distant bandits. Perhaps the main business of the sovereign is the maintenance of his own position, and the dangerous enemies or rivals are not foreign but domestic. It becomes more important to control the people at home than to attack abroad, and it is easier and safer to plunder one's own subjects than to look for distant booty. The descendants of bold conquerors, raised in the palace hothouse, become lazy and luxury-loving; they fasten their attention not upon the frontiers but upon the palace. The interest of Roman aristocrats from the time of Julius Caesar increasingly turned from frontier battles to taxes and politics. For Commodus it was much better sport to fight wild beasts in the arena in Rome than Germans in the northern forests.

Even the relatively enterprising Louis XIV was less troubled by battles in Flanders than by disputes over precedence at dinner. [523, p. 225] If, as commonly happens, power gravitates to the inner court or household of the autocrat, to the harem and enuchs, mistresses, courtiers, and obscure intrigants, these have neither will nor spirit for foreign adventures. The whispers of palace passageways are of cunning schemes and plots for personal advancement, not of forceful imperial expansion. Those who wield power by flattering and tickling the senses of the master would either ignore distant troubles or solve them in more devious ways, like the Chinese who paid barbarians to fight each other or sent Buddhist missionaries to lure them into monasteries.

As often noted, one can conquer but not rule with bayonets, and the ideology that drives for conquest is inadequate for peaceful administration and stable government. The Legalism that was successful in the drive of Ch'in for empire failed once empire was achieved and was largely replaced by the more subtle and pacific doctrines of Confucianism. One might see something of the same change in the adoption, belated to be sure, of Christianity as the religion of Rome. In our day, if the Nazis had been able to retain mastery of Europe they certainly would have felt the need of a sounder teaching than the racism that helped to galvanize their armies. In the event, when Europe lay at their feet they had no idea what to do with it.

If the philosophy of the universal empire, representing peace and secure order over a huge expanse, must be different from that of the warrior state driving for hegemony, equally must the spirit of the people be different. In the noncompetitive world, the great union of nations, nationalism fades away. There may be patriotic talk but little deep feeling remains, as men are indifferent to a state too vast for love. Loyalty is more resignation and acceptance of the unavoidable than enthusiasm. The empire teaches men not to fight but to obey. It should not be surprised if they become passive and timorous.

Thus the very great empires in their maturity are rather pacific and, despite proud arrogance toward outsiders, may be slow to anger. Clumsy and lazy, having gained what is to be gained by violence, they would like to see violence abolished that peace and security may reign; and creeping conservatism and lethargy want only calm. Despite the wish to remove examples of independence and freedom from the borders, they may shrink, in a growing lassitude, from acquiring new territories and responsibilities, and may content themselves with the outward deference of the border peoples.

THE SELF-CENTERED STATE

If the universal empire abates its drive for total sovereignty, it does not retreat from its claims to superiority or acknowledge the rights of others. Upholding the ideal of cosmic order, the highei right derived from overwhelming greatness, it admits no legitimate dissent, but stands for a single law, which is its law. There is right, as Thucydides pointed out, only between equals; the universal empire acknowledges no international law as restricting its sovereignty; whatever it finds fitting for itself is just. Recognizing no peers, it retreats to a primitive idea of international relations, or has no international relations at all, as these are understood in a community of states. Those who are so backward as to refuse to recognize the supreme order are barbarians and evil rebels, to be brought to submission or tamed if possible, to be conciliated or bribed if necessary. The universal empire has no sense of international contest but views weakness as the only cause of conflict. Frequently the great empires have refused to recognize definite frontiers because an acknowledged boundary implies a limit to the claim of sovereignty. The imperial borders, perhaps marked by a desert strip, are thus apt to be vague and to shift with the power of the armies.

Self-engrossed, the empires turn away from foreign affairs or subordinate them to domestic concerns. In a sense, they automatically become more parochial as they grow larger, since dealings with foreigners become relatively less important. Moreover, they deliberately reduce contacts, building something of a Chinese Wall around themselves to avoid annoyances and contagion from without and to keep subjects at home. Foreign ideas are unnecessary and unwelcome. If men could depart freely they would feel less need to be obedient; they might plot abroad or give aid and instruction to the barbarians. Even nonpolitical trade is a potential source of infection to be strictly controlled. It is better that subjects be taught that there is nothing for them to learn or desire beyond the sacred sphere of the empire.

Before coming in sight of supremacy the Romans dealt with other states more or less as equals; after downing Carthage and Macedon, they turned from reciprocity to insistence always upon superiority, and became ever more overbearing as their power continued to rise. [*341*, I, 103] While going far in the systematization of domestic law, imperial Rome accepted no restrictions on the Roman right, that is, no international law; the *jus gentium*, of which much was made, was rather universal law, sanctioned by Rome for private relations among persons of different national legal systems in the Roman sphere. Treaties and dealings with outside powers were measured only by Roman law and forms. Roman treaties, unlike those of the Greeks, aimed not at restoration of peace but at the definition of vassalage, and they were not for a fixed period, as in the earlier style, but for perpetuity. [M. Rostovtzeff, in *563*, pp. 61–62] International usages were also left behind. Republican Rome had an established place and procedure for the reception of foreign envoys, but they fell into desuetude under the empire. [*320*, p. 11] There had been in early times some concern for the propriety of declarations of war. A foreign nation was accused and given a chance to make redress for wrongs; the College of Fetials then decided whether there was injury requiring action and so reported to the Senate. As the empire grew, these forms became the merest formality, as Roman wars were automatically held legal and just. [*320*, p. 9; *526*, p. 17]

When Rome gave up attempts to subdue the tribes beyond the Rhine and the Parthians to the east, there was never an admission that it lacked the right to march anywhere; it was not the practice to make peace but to hold a fortified line. Between Rome and the one major civilized state on its border, Parthia, there was little intercourse. It was attempted where feasible to wall or fence the empire around, as with Hadrian's Wall; in some places there was left a waste or desert zone. [*338*, pp. 224–225; *345*, p. 159] Roman law prohibited leaving the empire and trade was limited. Export of iron and bronze, later of wine and oil, and of arms in general, was forbidden. [*326*, p. 827] Even the reduced Byzantine continuation of the Roman empire had few and hostile relations with its neighbors and was not greatly interested in peaceful intercourse. Outsiders were still held to be barbarians, failing in the duty of submission, and their envoys were received by the "Bureau for Barbarians." [525, p. 304]

Other empires have similarly held themselves apart. The land and sea frontiers of Egypt were closed except for persons with special permits; travelers had to pay taxes and pass by designated stations. [117, pp. 173–176] The Mauryas had a board to watch over foreigners, prevent their spying, and conduct them back to the frontier when their business was accomplished. [537, p. 41] The Moguls hardly had diplomatic relations beyond the reception of gifts; early in the seventeenth century a British mission wasted many months trying to get a treaty of commerce. [199, p. 216] The Turkish disdain for infidels was traditional. The frontier belt of the empire tended to be depopulated by ceaseless marauding, and beyond it lay the "land of war," to be conquered whenever practicable. [435, p. 29] Not until the sixteenth century were foreign envoys admitted, and they were treated scurvily, usually being held practically as prisoners. [436, p. 110] Only in 1793 did the Turks deign to send an ambassador abroad. [526, p. 89; 488, p. 14]

Although the Russian empire always had to borrow foreign technology, it cherished a sense of special mission in the world, combined with distrust and dislike of foreigners. [380, II, 327] From the beginnings of Muscovite greatness, foreigners were forbidden to enter the land without special permission, and Russians could not travel abroad without official license. [379, p. 49] The frontier was closely watched in the days of Ivan the Terrible, and it was proposed to allow foreign merchants to come only to border towns. [G. Fletcher in 405, p. 63] In the disturbed times of the early seventeenth century, many foreigners came to Russia, but after midcentury they had to reside in a special sector of Moscow. A Dutch embassy in the latter part of the century were practically jailed and could not go around without a guard; to keep them from learning about the country they were not allowed to hire a Russian-language teacher. [457, p. 208] Conversely, Muscovites were forbidden to have teachers of foreign languages and were allowed to communicate with inhabitants of the foreign quarter on business only. [413, p. 19] Peter saw much more keenly the need to learn from the West and brought in more visitors. Many of them, however, were detained, as had been done in the past, for years or decades against their will. [379, p. 50; 403, p. 9] The government was also much embarrassed by the frequent desertion of those sent abroad to study. Peter's envoys were extremely boorish and careless of manners, perhaps less from lack of education than from indifference to Western opinion. [G. A. Craig in 393, pp. 354–355] Russian diplomats seldom showed respect for recognized procedure and had little idea of diplomatic bargaining until the nineteenth century. But even then, as Western influences were penetrating powerfully, Nicholas I tried to slam the doors shut, curtailing foreign travel and excluding foreign books and papers on principle. [404, p. 360] On the eve of the First World War, of the European powers, only Russia and Turkey required passports.

The land best situated to indulge in contempt and exclusiveness has been China. Geography dictated that there could be no major country adjacent to the Middle Kingdom, and India was far away. China was thus not only the political but cultural center of eastern Asia, and felt with some reason that peripheral peoples were respectable only in the measure that they accepted Chinese civilization and superiority. To be non-Chinese was to be despicable. An eleventh-century writer held that foreigners, that is, barbarians, "must be regarded as resembling birds and beasts." [53, p. 12] In the nineteenth century the Chinese believed, or were taught, that other peoples lived in holes and dressed in leaves for lack of the wisdom of the sage kings. [14, II, 421] Usually the Chinese court held no substantial sway over the borderlands, but much emphasis was placed on gestures of deference, formal submission, and sending of tribute by such states as Annam, Korea, Burma, Nepal, and parts of the Indies. The tribute bearers were treated with great disdain, perhaps kept for months waiting to kowtow in a manner designed for their maximum humiliation; then it mattered little that the Chinese commonly gave more than they received and made the tributary relation a form of foreign aid to secure the loyalty of the dependent state. Foreign princes were also expected to accept investiture from the emperor. [38, p. 22] Not only immediate neighbors but all foreign powers were held to be naturally subordinate. For example, in 607 A.D. the Sui emperor refused to accept a letter from the Japanese ruler addressed to him in terms of equality, but insisted that the Japanese, like everyone else, must be vassals. In 1596 the Ming emperor sent a patronizing letter graciously investing the Japanese emperor with the kingship of his islands. Only the Russian tsar was recognized in the seventeenth century as an approximately equal though still junior sovereign. As ruler of an expanse larger than China itself, the tsar might well be recognized as truly independent; but as Chinese strength recovered in the eighteenth century, the attitude toward Russia became loftier and there was an inclination to demote even this mammoth state to tributary status. All foreign affairs were handled by the Department of Rites, which received tribute. Only in 1861 was there established a regular organization for foreign affairs to fill imperative needs of dealing with Western powers, which for decades had been forcefully demonstrating their practical superiority. [56, p. 238] In defiance of constitutional theory, a foreign ministry was established in 1901.

A chief reason for carrying on foreign relations of any kind was to spread Chinese culture [53, p. 98]; otherwise there was little desire for intercourse with the outside world. It could not be admitted that China needed anything from the barbarians. The first attempt to solve the problem was made by the Ch'in unifiers of China, who sought by the Great Wall to divide the waste from the sown, the civilized from the savage. Some subsequent dynasties, like the Sui and the early T'ang, following four centuries of disunity, were more friendly to foreign intercourse; but by the late T'ang, China had turned inward again and Chinese were forbidden to leave the empire. [40, p. 205; 61, p. 185] Early Ming rulers sent out a great exploratory flotilla as far as Africa but afterward thought better of it, ended sorties, and closed the gates. From then on to modern times the tendency has been to regard foreign trade as superfluous or noxious. It was a reminder of a world beyond the pale of good society, beneficial only to the barbarians, while Chinese who went abroad were potential if not actual traitors. It was preferred to conduct trade, so far as any was permitted, as an adjunct of the tributary missions. Particularly remarkable was the virtual lack of intercourse with Korea, a nearby civilized and politically subordinate country whose culture and institutions had been largely borrowed from the Chinese. The border was closed and marked by a strip many miles wide, from which the population was removed. Trade by sea was not allowed; by land it took place only at supervised fairs held at the border three or four times yearly. The regular tribute parties were allowed to carry on a little business also, but the total quantity of goods exchanged was trivial. [53, pp. 84, 96]

While Europeans, conscious of some superiority of their own, were coming to China to trade or evangelize in the eighteenth and nineteenth centuries, the emperor continued to think that he ruled "all under Heaven's canopy," or at least all really worthwhile parts of the earth. [76, p. 309] An edict of 1832 proclaimed: "I, the minister of Heaven, am placed over mankind and am responsible for keeping the world in order and tranquilizing the people." [29, II, 91] The Chinese until 1860 used the character meaning "barbarian" to designate foreigners in general [64, p. 98], although states other than intrusive Britain were "the respectful and obedient states." [32, p. 44] The emperor wrote to George III, in reply to a proposal for trading relations, that trade was impossible because foreigners would have to adopt Chinese ways and could not be allowed to travel in or leave the country. [4, p. 323] Subsequently, Queen Victoria was informed that European products were only toys for the Chinese, whereas foreign countries could not dispense with Chinese tea, rhubarb, and silk. [45, p. 44] Foreign traders at Canton, the only permitted port until military action forced open other doors, were long forbidden to enter the city. [32, p. 1] Even when the Chinese were ultimately driven to make concessions, they subjected the "barbarians" to all indignities. Important officials haughtily refused to see foreign merchants. It was made a capital offense for a Chinese to teach the language to a foreigner. [32, pp. 18, 20] A French visitor in the nineteenth century reported that travelers were "imprisoned in closed boats; they are guarded carefully from sight all along the great canal; they are what we may call put under arrest immediately upon their arrival at Pekin." As a British agent related of his high-ranking mission, "They entered Pekin like beggars, staid in it like prisoners, and were driven from it like thieves." [37, I, xix]

3   CAESARISM

States of competitive systems have shown much variety in government, from thorough democracies to more or less oligarchic republics, constitutional and absolutist traditional monarchies, and tyrannies. But they are seldom really comparable to the bureaucratic-imperial despotism unfairly called oriental. On the other hand, the universal empires, through all their variety of culture and conditions, have been uniformly and monotonously autocratic or, to use a stronger term, despotic.

But if the universal empire makes for unlimited government, it may also be that strong government makes for universal empires. In the free-for-all of states, the most sternly power-minded and effectively organized has the best chance of victory; a Prussia among states is best prepared to overrun and rule its neighbors. States more interested in business than bossing their neighbors are disqualified from the outset, as are those governed by debating societies. A single head is usually essential for a strong foreign policy. Republics, more designed to compromise different interests than to forge grand designs of aggrandizement, are unlikely candidates for the crown in competition with states that can mobilize all energies in an aggressive single will. But despotism seems more result than cause of conquest. [542, p. 35] Even if it is true that empires have ordinarily been formed by highly centralized and strongly led states, this of itself cannot explain the regularity and strength of autocracy in empires. For all political systems evolve. As needs and conditions change, governments can change; monarchies and republics that have outworn their day have countless times been permuted into their opposites. Many great empires have lasted three or four centuries or more; after a few generations one would suppose that a government must have taken on the form concordant with its conditions.

There has, of course, been political evolution in the great empires, but it has been predominantly toward the elevation of the autocrat. If a dynamic and driving ruler enlarges his state and eliminates the principal national foes, he immediately enjoys immensely heightened prestige and becomes a vastly more important figure. If previously he was closely restricted by the great nobles, now his own power, as ruler of the enlarged realm, rises far above that of any baron or duke; as conqueror, he can create new dukedoms at will. With his enlarged resources, he can make dazzling his throne and court. He can more freely use the army against the people as it is further from them. Those who might oppose him fear lest eliminating him mean loss or breakup of the empire. Not all rulers will seize the opportunity to make themselves demigods, but most are glad to do so, and if they do not, sons or successors will. Despotism becomes accepted as inevitable if not desirable. Yet empires, while becoming more despotic, lose aggressiveness.

Such an evolution has occurred times without number; that successful expansion adds to the dignity and power of the ruler is almost a tautology. Alexander started on his campaign as little more than the first of the Macedonian nobles; he ended it as a godlike emperor. The Inca rulers became divine despots only as their rule expanded, and the rulership was probably elective until the seventh Inca, the first to rule a really large domain. [173, p. 27] Of the Russian empire, it could be stated simply that extent of territory was, up to the middle of the nineteenth century, inversely proportional to the freedom of the people. [388, III, 3–4] But the best example is Rome, the only republic to create a universal empire. Rome was unique in achieving hegemony under a constitutional order; and the Romans, giving their civic virtues and institutions credit for their unexampled success, adhered to the republican forms with exemplary fidelity, even when they were evidently inadequate. It was to no avail. The political realities of the empire led the constitutional city-state, with numerous checks on power and real elements of democracy, to an eventual totality of despotism in Persian or Chinese style. It was a long road and at times there were efforts to turn back, but progress toward absolutism never halted for long. As soon as the empire had been built, Rome ceased to be a republic in reality; as Sallust said, when Rome still seemed republican, rule of the earth "degenerated into pride and hereditary titles." [*Conspiracy of Cataline*, chap. 3] Something of republican forms and ideas continued for centuries after, however, and the sole universal empire of the West is reputed the most tempered and least repugnant to the individualistic outlook of our civilization.

FROM CITY REPUBLIC TO WORLD DESPOTISM

While Rome was growing up, Italy was permeated by Greek culture. It was once covered with tiny city-states not unlike those of
Greece, with a somewhat similar international life, alliances, common festivals, religious leagues, and countless bloody wars. [285,
p. 34] Like the Greeks, the Italians cast out their kings; having got
rid of their Etruscan ruler, the Romans held the name of king execrated, and they replaced the monarch by two yearly elected consuls. The consuls were advised by the Senate, a body roughly
corresponding to the council of the Greek polis. The several hundred senators were leading citizens named for life by consuls
(later censors) after they had held high and honorable office.
The Senate may be deemed the key institution leading Rome to
supremacy. It was an oligarchic body but not a narrow one, requiring not so much noble birth (the lower classes gained access to
the higher offices and so to the Senate in the middle of the fourth
century B.C.) as demonstrated capacity for leadership. As the magistrates were mostly military leaders, the Senate came to be dominated by senior generals; no other category of citizens could be
counted on so well to maintain the continuity of expansionist
foreign policy and to preserve the republican constitution against
would-be dictators. Like Athens, Rome also showed tendencies to
democracy, and it is said that a Roman delegation went to Greece
about 450 B.C. to study Greek law in preparation for the celebrated
Twelve Tables. As in Athens, the lower classes attained a definite
and honorable part in the constitutional system, and there was a
struggle, largely won by the poorer orders, for relief of debt and
for land distribution. To be sure, equality remained incomplete.
[319, p. 61] The citizens' assembly, the *comitia*, acquired legislative power in 286 B.C., but it never achieved the power to debate,
only voting yes or no on questions put to it. It elected magistrates
and sanctioned laws, but it was more facade than democracy, for
it voted by class sections, among which the poor were hopelessly
outweighed, and its actions could often be annulled by the Senate.

But there were many impediments to tyranny and guarantees of
rights. Magistrates tended to check one another as their spheres
overlapped. Higher officials could veto lower ones. Among officials
of equal standing, anyone could veto acts of his colleague or colleagues; and each of the ten tribunes of the people could obstruct

almost anything. But another tribune might veto the vetoes, and the Senate could exert a great deal of unofficial compulsion, so what had to be done was almost always done despite seeming constitutional obstacles. The clumsy and elaborate constitution worked by virtue of strong civic spirit and because Romans really wanted it to work. [*294*, pp. 120–122]

So long as Roman power was confined to Italy, political development was rather constitutional and democratic. But after the victory over Carthage opened the way to general hegemony, the decay of the traditional constitution was rapid, despite its high prestige [*321*, pp. 364–367], both because expansion raised problems that the old ways were incapable of handling, and because civic dedication gave way to personal greed or ambition. The republic degenerated into plutocracy. The assemblies lost influence and became a corrupt mockery of democracy. Election expenses restricted office to a few families [*294*, p. 242; *321*, p. 152] until the right to rule came to rest on the sword.

The troubles of the Gracchi, less than a generation after the destruction of Carthage and Corinth, made evident the sickness of the state. The questions of the day were no longer to be solved by compromise within the traditional framework, but by violence. In 133 B.C. Tiberius Gracchus, holding the sacrosanct office of tribune, and hundreds of his supporters were murdered; a few years later his brother Gaius, who carried on the agitation for land distribution, was killed with thousands of his party. Never before had Romans killed each other for politics, but thereafter political opponents were treated as mercilessly as foreign enemies. Massacres and proscriptions became regular practice; morality steadily sank in the atmosphere of greed; the courts, which had been turned over to the new business classes of the empire, served mostly to protect villains; and it was dangerous to put the welfare of the republic ahead of personal interests. [*298*, pp. 106–109, 113]

When violence was allowed to prevail, the holders of force, the generals, came to rule; within a generation after the Gracchi, the military servants of the state had become its masters. In better days dictators named for emergencies had invariably laid down their powers without a struggle. Scipio Africanus, victor over Hannibal and savior of Rome, popular and ambitious, as deserving of gratitude as any man in Rome's history, was humiliated and nearly ruined by the constitutionalists, led by Cato. [*321*, pp. 107–109]

But as the republic became increasingly disjointed, long service in distant frontiers made armies loyal primarily to their leaders; and large armies in the provinces gave generals a secure basis for personal power.

Chief maker of the new semiprofessional army was Marius. He began the practice of admitting the poorest men to his ranks and providing for them the equipment that Roman citizens had been expected to furnish in order to be soldiers. [311, p. 110] His army was essentially his own, not the state's; and the Roman soldier always thereafter swore loyalty to his general. [237, p. 193] Hardly less important, Marius deprived the Senate of its vital control over commands and based his authority on plebiscite. [321, p. 162] He also found in confiscations a convenient way of eliminating opponents and filling his war chest.

Sulla, in opposition to Marius, was a conservative, but he carried further the dissolution of the old order. When the popular vote transferred to Marius the command for the Eastern war then being prepared, Sulla occupied Rome like an invader; his troops followed because their chief interest was booty. [298, pp. 117–118] While Sulla and his men were away fighting Rome's battles, Marius returned and butchered the Sullan party with un-Roman vindictiveness; heads of senators were set up for public ridicule. [298, p. 120] Sulla, coming back in turn with his loyal army, made a still greater carnage and set himself up as dictator. He struck coins in his own name as a monarch would, but the traditional forms still had enough prestige for Sulla to try to restore senatorial government. In 79 B.C., after three years of rule, he resigned.

Sulla's successors followed his example, not his wish. The Senate could no longer govern the realm, if for no other reason than that it felt the need to give generals broad powers to pacify the empire [348, p. 15], and those who commanded the troops commanded in Rome. Pompey, returning victorious from an eastern campaign in 62 B.C., rather remarkably refrained from making himself dictator, but he and other political and military adventurers held sway; only lacking was a man of exceptional talents and ambition to arise and snatch sole power. This individual, of course, was Julius Caesar. In his first consulship, in 59 B.C., he passed laws by force, heedless of constitutional requirements. Challenged by those who feared his growing strength, he crossed his Rubicon in 49 B.C., pleading not principles or defense of the state as excuse for his illegal action,

but his personal honor and safety. [*348*, p. 48] Scattering his enemies by superior generalship, meeting no serious or principled
resistance (even Cicero, among the firmest of republicans, thought
it better to yield than to suffer civil war) [*298*, p. 149], he became
sole master of the state.

A man of truly imperial genius, Julius Caesar made a remarkable
record in his brief tenure of power. An instinctive autocrat, he dissolved the associations and guilds, which had become political
clubs, restored the tax on capital, which had lapsed during more
than a century of plutocracy, reformed municipal government in
Italy to establish uniformity with a good measure of self-administration, planned highways and large-scale colonization, and projected a codification of Roman law, accomplished five hundred
years later. [*285*, pp. 235–237] He dealt cavalierly with republican
magistracies, assumed lifetime dictatorship and various other offices, appointed all high officials, and held the sole right to command troops and to control public monies. He replaced with
parvenus the conservative senators who had withdrawn [*351*, p.
64], and bound the senators and magistrates by oath to defend and
support him. [*345*, p. 26] He donned the purple robe of kings instead of the purple-bordered toga of republican magistrates. He
was the first Roman to put his own image on the coinage. [*298*,
p. 159] He traced his lineage to the gods [*347*, p. 55]; his image
was set up in every temple in Rome; a temple was devoted to him
as Jupiter Julius, the chief god of the state. [*294*, p. 415; *285*, p. 234;
321, pp. 192–193]

Wise in many ways, Julius was rash in trying to be a frank autocrat in a Rome still unprepared for autocracy without the use of
terror. Making a mistake his successors would energetically avoid,
he let his enemies live, and they assassinated him in the Senate,
which was that day to discuss making him king in the provinces.
[*285*, p. 239] But the conspirators, who acted in a spirit more of
oligarchic conservatism than of love of fading republican liberties,
could not turn back the tide. The people preferred Caesar to the
oligarchs. The assassins had to flee the city, and there was never
again a real possibility of restoration of the old constitution, even
while Caesar's would-be heirs battled one another.

If the authoritarian Julius had lived, the transformation into pure
despotism might have been rapid and direct. But Augustus was
much more circumspect. He cannot be regarded as a born liberal;

early in his career he was ferocious in persecutions and required
all Italians to swear loyalty to himself as his clients. [298, pp. 166,
169] But after reaching supremacy he was outwardly moderate.
Respectful of tradition or mindful of his adoptive father's fate and
fearful of the daggers of latter-day republicans [321, p. 58], he
prudently disguised autocratic power and made his government in
form a continuation of the revered republic with only such modifications as seemed necessary. Undisputed lord of the empire after
the battle of Actium, he returned to purge the Senate, raising its
dignity while lowering its independence. This body was then
pleased to name him successively Imperator, Princeps, and Augustus, the last title carrying an aura of sacredness. He made a gesture
of returning power to the Senate and people of Rome, and held
himself only the First Citizen. At first he accepted authority not
for life but for ten years, and according to contemporary accounts
he had to be most strongly urged to retain office. But if Sulla yielded
up power voluntarily and Julius would and did not, Augustus probably could not because the Senate was very short of decent and
capable men after the wars and the great proscriptions for which
he had been in large part responsible [348, p. 3], and because he
had to command the armies, which the Senate could not manage.
The legions, loyal to his house and himself, were the basis of his
authority, and there was no doubt who was boss; the people took
a solemn oath to spare not body, soul, life, nor children in his interests. [330, p. 35] But Augustus ruled as constitutionally as possible, not inventing new offices and prerogatives but combining
old republican offices in his own person for long periods, or indefinitely. [324, p. 333] In 24 B.C. he was by senatorial decree released
from the compulsion of the laws [291, p. 352]; but when the packed
Senate offered full powers of legislation and promised to accept
whatever he might decree, he magnanimously declined. [345, p. 71]
He wanted a religious basis for his power, but this he also sought
in terms of the traditional forms. He gave much attention to the
restoration of temples, and when the office became vacant he made
himself Pontifex Maximus, or high priest of the state cult. More
modest than Julius, he refused outright deification in Italy. However, he permitted temples to Roma and Augustus in the provinces,
with local dignitaries as officiating priests. [294, p. 510; 315, p. 615]
The office of Caesar had outgrown the man. Increasingly worshiped
as he became feeble and senile, Augustus was given another ten

years of power when, at seventy-six, he was hardly able to appear in the Senate and had almost lost the power of speech. [*308*, p. 327]

The next Caesar, Tiberius, at first showed consideration for the Senate, even giving it permission to elect magistrates and debate legislation. [*345*, pp. 121–122] He also at first restrained the growing emperor worship, declining permission for statues to be set up to him. With passing years, however, he became more openly autocratic and contemptuous of republican institutions. He demonstrated the firmness of personal power by retiring to semiseclusion in Capri for ten years without loss of authority; the Senate cringed not only before the master but also before his favorite, Sejanus. [Tacitus *Annals*, 4, 74] Toward the end of his reign, Tiberius brought despotism to murderous intensity, executing senators for the slightest inattention.

Through the second century, the government remained fairly close to the form given it by Augustus, called the Principate because the ruler was Princeps or First Citizen of the commonwealth. Power rested in the emperor so far as the troops remained loyal to their oath to him as commander; if they were seriously discontented, his days were numbered. Over private citizens and the civilian government he was absolute, and vicious or depraved emperors used their power viciously or depravedly. Caligula took pleasure in such extravagances as having his horse elected consul and provided with a palace and retinue, and he paraded himself as practically any Olympic god (or goddess) that struck his fancy. He also showed the prevalence of power over mores by planning to marry his sister (whom he may have treated as a wife before her death) in the Egyptian manner. [*310*, pp. 236–237] Upon Caligula's death without an obvious heir, the Senate for the last time debated the restoration of the republic. But the Guard pulled the aged Claudius out of hiding, and good intentions were forgotten. Claudius did little to be held in infamy, but his stepson, Nero, raised to the purple at seventeen, gave absolutism a new turn: men were no longer free to sit back and say nothing, but had to join the chorus of adulation. A leading senator was prosecuted for noncooperation, including inattention to Nero's singing. [*345*, pp. 129–130] This egotist admired himself in a bronze statue more than a hundred feet high; according to Suetonius, he also contemplated renaming Rome "Neropolis." [*330*, pp. 153, 395] Caesars alternated irregularly between extremism and moderation: after the capricious cruelty of Nero, Vespasian was decidedly reluctant to execute his critics; his son Domitian in turn carried on a ferocious reign of terror. Upon his murder there was again a reaction, and the Senate, which had lavished the most fulsome flattery upon him, condemned his memory and ordered his name erased from public monuments. [294, p. 624] The next ruler, Nerva, promised to execute no more senators, and the much-abused law of *maiestas*, or treason, was temporarily shelved. Several sensible rulers followed to give the empire its best period: Trajan, Hadrian, Antoninus Pius, and Marcus Aurelius. As they sought to govern by law and reason and without arbitrary violence, persecutions abated and old forms were maintained or restored. But the son of the philosopher-emperor was the vain and licentious Commodus, among whose many follies was the renaming of almost the entire calendar with his various royal appelations. [282, p. 47] Out of the disorders following his murder there emerged the bearable Septimius Severus, but he was succeeded by the despicable Caracalla; if Nero and Domitian made ravages in the senatorial order, the fury of Caracalla struck at all; that a man be known for property and virtue was cause enough to have him murdered. [314, I, 117–118]

In the trend toward despotism, it gradually became taken for granted that the emperor possessed full powers of legislation, de jure as well as de facto. Late in his life, Augustus provided that decisions of his advisory council should have the effect of senatorial enactments [308, p. 329]; and by the time of Domitian the ruler was quite above the law. [324, p. 329] The empty form of popular approval of legislation died out about the end of the first century. [324, p. 337] Financial and administrative needs led even moderate rulers, like Trajan and Hadrian, to curtail local self-government and to strengthen powers of governors. The Senate continued to enjoy prestige, as it was long felt expedient to make some gestures for the acceptance and sanction of the traditional body; but its powers, limited to whatever the emperor saw fit to concede, gradually withered, and servility was its mode. With little or no voice in the selection of the new Caesar, it automatically ratified the choice of the armies; the power it retained longest was that of refusing deification to a dead master, as when it refused to place such unworthies as Tiberius, Caligula, and Nero among the gods. When Trajan ordered the Senate to be free, a senator, Pliny, commented: "He will know when we use the freedom he gave that we are being obedient to him." [*345*, p. 144] It so fawned on the abominable Commodus as to shout his preferred gladiatorial title 626 times together. [*314*, I, 84] In 217 Macrinus told the Senate that he could compel them to raise Caracalla to divinity but preferred to make this a request. [*282*, p. 57] In the next year Elagabalus assumed the full panoply of titles without waiting for the formality of senatorial recognition. Not long afterward, the relatively decent Alexander Severus, almost the last to seek seriously to cooperate with the Senate [*331*, pp. 7–8], was murdered and succeeded by an all-round barbarian, Maximin; the latter did not bother about senatorial confirmation at all nor did he even deign to come to Rome during his three-year reign. [*338*, p. 76]

The progress of despotism was reflected in the apotheosis of the ruler. It was not difficult for men to aspire to divine honors of some sort, as gods and demigods were numerous and often associated intimately with humans; many people had divine forebears. In the East, divinity was customarily ascribed to kings, and towns made subject to the Romans were as ready to worship the conquering sovereign as their previous ruler. Temples were erected to strong Roman leaders, like Pompey, as soon as they appeared on the scene. [*351*, p. 39] Hence it was inevitable, when Rome became master of the world, that the sovereign should be superhumanly exalted. Julius Caesar achieved a high degree of deification, as men swore by his genius and made public sacrifices on his birthday; he was hailed as "The Unconquered God"; his statue was placed in temples, and a month was named for him as months had previously been named for chief divinities. The Senate, which had the prerogative of introducing new cults in Rome, decreed that as a god he should have a priesthood, but this was not functioning by the time of his assassination. [*351*, pp. 65–68] Those who contended for Caesar's heritage all reinforced their causes by claims of some divine association or ancestry; but the winner, Augustus, was rather reluctant to assume godship. He was sworn to not as a god but as son of a god, and was worshiped only indirectly via his Genius. [*351*, p. 245; *321*, p. 232] Worshiped as a god only in the provinces, he was content to rule as First Citizen on earth, to be translated to the heavens as a god upon decease. This was duly accomplished by the respectful Senate; and the cult of Augustus, which Tiberius enforced with great strictness [*282*, p. 30], enjoyed substantial and supposedly spontaneous popularity. [*35*, p. 77]

Caligula carried self-deification to an extreme, posing as deities of all sorts, prescribing sacrifices to himself and demanding general acknowledgment of his divinity. [*321*, p. 47] Such exaggeration was revolting, but it was at all times much more dangerous to lack reverence for the statue of Caesar than for that of Jupiter. [*347*, p. 114] Not only the emperor himself, but his family, his wife, his parents, or his children, received divine honors; Caligula made his sisters sacred [*310*, p. 229], and Nero deified his mistress. [*282*, pp. 35–36] Before Domitian (81–96 A.D.), emperors claimed divinity mostly as incarnations of ancient deities, like Apollo, Mars, or Jupiter; but Domitian made himself a god in his own right, "Dominus et Deus" [*282*, p. 51], and required that men sacrifice to his image lest they be held guilty of treason. [*297*, p. 42] The better rulers who followed Domitian were less pretentious, but the idea that the ruler was divine became more and more ingrained. By the time of Septimius Severus (193–211), everything connected with the ruler was held more or less holy. Moreover, he was not one of a swarm of gods but identified himself with the supreme sun-god. [*321*, p. 269]

Concurrently the old society was progressively transformed, the empire was brought together into a single body, and there was built up an administrative apparatus to manage it and profit by it. The older aristocracy was gradually crushed or displaced as the republic died. In 82 B.C. Sulla proscribed 2,600 wealthy men and appropriated their property; there was small reason for those who could follow his example to refrain from doing so. The triumvirs, after the murder of Julius Caesar, consoled themselves with the lives and property of some 2,000 of the opposition. Augustus, turned conservative in the exercise of power, rather favored the distinguished families; but he reduced their exclusiveness by easing the way into the upper classes, opening the Senate to knights and knighthood to plebeians. [Baker in *276*, p. 67] His less restrained successors used ruthless and unpredictable terror against the wealthy and prominent. As Juvenal declared, birth and ability counted for nothing compared with money; but to have money was very dangerous, as the emperors always needed more of it.

The economy of the republic had been given over to free enterprise, even taxes and public works being handled by private entrepreneurs; consequently tremendous fortunes were freely made. At first, expansion enriched the capitalists, as opportunities were magnified and multiplied in taxation, contracts, commerce, and finance; and the extravagance of the Roman rich rose to its legendary height under the first emperors. But they could not ride the tiger they had helped to raise. Outstanding prosperity raised such strong suspicions of criminal activities or intent, chiefly treason, that even prudent aloofness from politics gave no safety. Seneca related that it was enough to pick up a chamberpot while wearing a ring engraved with the profile of Tiberius to be accused by a denouncer and lose fortune and life. One man, executed allegedly for incest with his daughter, actually perished because he owned too many mines in Spain. [*334*, p. 201] Nero was especially energetic in such antiaristocratic measures. He also insisted that wills include suitable provision for the emperor. If a will did not so provide, Nero would often confiscate the whole estate and fine the lawyers who had drawn up the ungenerous document. On the other hand, one who had made a will according to prescriptions was likely to face a centurion suggesting that it be put into effect immediately. [*300*, p. 311] Thus by the time of Vespasian (69–79 A.D.) the older wealthy orders had been largely annihilated. [*331*, p. 82] Moreover, opportunities and incentives for enrichment were much diminished in the increasingly controlled and bureaucratic state, and few new fortunes rose to equal those swept away. The census even of senatorial rank sank to only a few tens of thousands of dollars. Rome became less and less a business and commercial society, until under the late empire almost all important enterprises were controlled by the government.

Commercial gave way to political wealth; the new rich were intriguers and climbers. Denouncers shared in confiscations, and large fortunes were made, not by trade or production, but by control of taxes, governorships, handling of public funds, and sequestering of properties. Ex-slaves, or freedmen, were favored by the emperor partly because of their talents, partly because they were felt to be more reliable than aristocratic Romans, who were likely to have more self-esteem and political pretensions; the former were the classless "new men" rising between the fading aristocracy and the declining slavery. A freedman left in charge at Rome by Nero could issue edicts of death against senators without reference to his absent sovereign. [*313*, p. 40] Many such as he accumulated great, though insecure, riches by trafficking in offices and favors; and if they managed by political dexterity to keep their riches, their sons or grandsons entered the new aristocracy.

The Romans also gradually lost in the empire the privileges that had made its acquisition sweet. The republic differentiated sharply between those of Roman rights and those without; but the first Caesar, true forger of empire, extended Roman citizenship widely in Gaul and Spain, especially to soldiers, and wanted generally to reduce distinctions; he intended to give other Italian cities equality with Rome. [*312*, p. 351; *294*, p. 411] Augustus was less generous in granting the privileges of Rome; during his reign the growth in number of citizens was much slower. [*338*, pp. 272–273] But the army did not cease romanizing the empire by its camps and by the settlement of veterans in large numbers on conquered lands; also, many non-Italians, even barbarians, were drawn into the legions and received citizenship as a reward for service. More and more officials who helped administer the towns were given this increasingly cheap distinction, and from time to time contenders for power sought support in the provinces by granting Roman citizenship.

Vassal lands were also assimilated to the common mold, being incorporated as provinces. Vespasian (69–79) particularly, in need of money, annexed several dependent states to the empire and incorporated many free cities. [*338*, p. 41] By 105 all of the empire except Armenia, in dispute with Persia, and the distant Crimean colonies had been brought under a single administration. By the time of Caracalla's famous edict of 212, making nearly every non-slave of the empire a Roman citizen, few remained outside the fold. But then it was hardly a privilege. Caracalla was moved not by statesmanship but by the desire to make more people subject to taxation. The Senate meanwhile changed from a Roman into an imperial body. Under Trajan, it was nearly half non-Italian; by the time of Caracalla, Italians were less than a third, and senators were allowed to reside outside Italy, as aristocrats of the world. [*285*, p. 361] The Caesarship likewise became open equally to all. Trajan (98–117) was born in Spain, as was Hadrian, his successor. Thereafter, the Caesar might as well be a provincial, even a Syrian or an African, as a Roman. There was little reason for a man like Constantine, born in the Danube region, educated in Asia and raised to Caesarship in Britain, to respect Rome's privileged status. [*314*, I, 505] Geographical discrimination thus came to an end, as descendants of conquerors and conquered were on the same legal footing and the old distinctions between Romans and provincials were replaced by a new distinction between commoners and the politically privileged. [326, I, 17]

The empire also implied the building of a complex administrative apparatus. Rome, like other classic city-states, had no bureaucracy. Offices were filled by citizens, serving mostly for brief terms, a government of amateurs; routine seems to have been carried on mostly by slaves. [298, p. 180] Despite the obvious need, little was done to establish a regular service until long after Rome had won a huge domain. Julius Caesar made some moves toward establishing a bureaucracy and installed freedmen as permanent officers of the mint. [302, p. 106] Augustus established a career of public service, but, whereas Julius Caesar was moving toward a uniform imperial system, Augustus kept older forms so far as he could [333, p. 28], and followed custom in naming senators (after their tour of military service) to high posts and knights to secondary ones. [333, pp. 120–121] However, he needed many administrators for large tracts of land taken by the crown. [350, p. 41] In lieu of a ministry, he surrounded himself with informal advisers or "friends," who became under subsequent emperors a regularly appointed council, usually remaining through changes of reign. [313, p. 72] Claudius established secretariats in the imperial household which became virtual imperial departments of state and assumed duties formerly assigned to the Senate [294, p. 527]; while the old republican offices were kept, a new civil service thus emerged from the royal household. High bureaucrats under Claudius and some later emperors were freedmen, but leading posts usually went to men of higher social status as the service became regularized with fixed ladders of promotion. Freedmen, however, largely retained the very important functions of finance, petitions, and correspondence. [313, pp. 53–56] By the second century Rome had a large, highly organized bureaucracy with district administration, graded personnel with promotions mostly by seniority, permanent tenure except near the top [285, p. 348], and standard pay, which had increased enormously in the century after Augustus. [312, p. 481]

The intimate household of the emperor also swelled and became powerful. At first, Caesars lived much as other wealthy Romans did, with a minimum of ceremony; but gradually, as they were surrounded by more and more servants, they acquired the pomp of oriental despots. [313, p. 30] Enveloping the ruler, the court had strong influence over policies and politics, especially when the ruler was weak and vicious. The swarm of mistresses grew to a harem. The numerous attendants acquired formal ranks; court life increasingly required refined etiquette and elaborate classification of dignities. As the sovereign secluded himself, access to him became very precious and his servants intrigued energetically for the prize of influence. A chamberlain of Commodus became so powerful he was able to appoint twenty-five consuls in one year and named most officials next to the emperor himself; another, learning that he might share the fate of many over whose execution he had presided, plotted the murder of his master and helped raise Pertinax to the throne. [*313*, pp. 58–59, 64]

Thus by the first part of the third century the imperial regime would seem to have gone the full way to untempered autocracy. But it was still a bit lacking in thoroughness and system, still burdened with remnants of republican forms and local autonomy. Perfected empire arose out of or as a reaction to a half-century of troubles, 235–285 A.D. During this time civil war was chronic and the Caesarship seemed to have descended to chaos. Of twenty-six Augusti who received official recognition (claimants were innumerable), only one escaped a violent death; barbarians ravaged the empire from end to end and threatened Rome itself; large parts, such as Gaul and Britain, were independent for as much as a decade. When the union was restored it was a little like the emergence of a new dynasty in China after the disordered collapse of the old.

So far as the reshaping of the imperial system had a conscious purpose, it was to prevent the frequent risings, assassinations, and barracks movements that had made a mockery of the Pax Romana. That is, it sought to establish the firm power of the ruler over armies. It was called the Dominate, as the emperor was now accepted as Dominus (master, in the sense of slaveowner) instead of Princeps. Even as Aurelian was reestablishing unity, he identified himself with the Eternal and Unconquered Sun-God, permitting those who approached to kiss not his cheek but his great toe, and informing the soldiers that it was not they but the divine power that made emperors. In his case it was to no avail, for the habit of murder was too strong. But Diocletian, appropriately the son of a slave, endeavored to secure obedience by surrounding himself with still more lofty appearances. A dozen lines were required to enumerate his titles. He withdrew from vulgar contacts and the sight of ordinary men. Early Caesars had usually dressed much like their high-ranking subjects or like generals of the army; Diocletian put on robes of silk and gold, and wore jeweled shoes. He surrounded himself with elaborate etiquette, in part borrowed from Persia [285, p. 440]; as Augustus had once affected modesty, Diocletian exaggerated extravagance. [314, I, 332] Supported by ostentation and ceremony, power was now upheld as sacred. To disobey was sacrilege, for everything about the emperor was holy, and "sacred" became the ordinary adjective to describe that which pertained to him, as the "sacred bedchamber" or the "sacred chariot." [288, p. 337] The acceptance of Christianity, intertwining church and state in ceremonial and religion, little changed these practices. Although sacrifices ceased to be made to the images of Christian emperors, their consecration was not much short of pagan deification in form and went far beyond it in sincerity and effectiveness. [288, p. 311; 321, p. 278] So revered was Constantine that upon his decease the officials continued to pay homage to the corpse as though it were merely a taciturn emperor. [314, I, 577]

The government was also reorganized. Rome was abandoned as a capital, partly because of the constitutional-republican and senatorial traditions which still clung to it like the musty fragrance of departed seasons. With no more claim to power, the senatorial order was enlarged to an aristocracy, admission to which rested on the favor of the emperor. [285, p. 447] The Senate itself was limited to those members invited; it became merely a nominated advisory council. The provinces were redrawn and increased in number to more than a hundred to reduce the independence of any governor, and all were placed on the same level of exploitation as Rome and Italy. Local law was set aside; vestiges of local autonomy, slight for over a century, were abolished, and city officials were named by the central government. [334, pp. 32–33; 303, p. 250] The army was reorganized to reduce its political role; governors were relieved of military command, civilian and military services were completely separated, and the cavalry was detached from the infantry while civilian commissars were attached to the general. [314, I, 537] The empire was surveyed for new taxation, for the new regime needed more money. Control of the economy was strengthened; the government supervised and chose the heads of the guilds, which organized crafts and professions. [570, p. 120] The separate careers of the ever-expanding bureaucracy were merged into a single civilian service of some twenty departments, headed by high officers responsible only to the emperor in a system much like that of Egypt. [*321*, p. 240] The influence of the administrators grew as civilians finally acquired superiority over the military. The emperor's household became incredibly numerous, and court position ranked over public office. To manage the enlarged harem and to prevent inheritance, eunuchs were used; at times they came to dominate the empire. As the ruler withdrew from direct contact with people and soldiers, power went to the court which shielded and insulated him.

Diocletian tried but failed to solve one problem that had caused endless trouble, that of succession to the divine but regrettably mortal sovereign. He set up an elaborate system of two Augusti and two Caesars adopted as their sons; the latter married the daughters of their adoptive fathers in a sort of royal incest. [*309*, p. 95] After twenty years the Augusti were to resign in favor of the Caesars, who would then name two more Caesars as successors. True to his plan, Diocletian resigned in due time and made his partner do the same, but the artificial attempt to establish a quasi-constitutional organization of power could end only in anarchy when challenged by ambition. [*321*, p. 291] The army continued to say the last word as to who ruled, but the consecration of the autocrat was sufficiently successful to keep the succession fairly well restricted to the sacred family.

By the days of Constantine the republican government of Rome had thus been thoroughly transformed into its opposite, an elaborately organized despotism. Compared with the Principate, the Dominate was more refined, more orderly, less bloody, and more systematically oppressive, more organized, and more bureaucratic. It was successful in reestablishing order and reducing civil war. It also saw some economic revival, as the currency was stabilized and production was protected; for example, the Egyptian irrigation system, which had ceased to function in the third century, was restored in the fourth. [*291*, p. 276] But if something was gained, something more was lost. Private freedom and the diversity that once was the glory of Rome were reduced or abolished; it even came to be necessary for men to hold the same faith, an idea utterly strange to the early empire. The Dominate lasted, in the West, only about half as long as the looser Principate, and collapsed in the fifth century before barbarian incursions much weaker than those met and overcome in the third.

VITALITY OF ROME

It is less remarkable that the Roman empire became a full-fledged despotism than that it was so slow in doing so, requiring three centuries and more to run its course. Of all such empires, the Roman seems unique in its long attachment to republican forms and traditions of liberty. After the murder of Julius Caesar, Antony promised to restore the republic, and Augustus professed to do so. Calling himself "Champion of the freedom of the Roman people," he was like the tyrant of a classical city-state, punctilious in observance of constitutional forms. For all his legal powers and immense prestige, he was not quite absolute master in fact. It is said that at times he left Rome to avoid witnessing the continual flouting of his laws [308, p. 100]; he met some difficulty when, in defiance of the traditional Italian exemption from taxes, he introduced a 5 percent inheritance tax with exemptions for close relatives. [334, p. 9] After Caligula, the Senate wanted to restore the republic but had to bow to the soldiers. The latter, however, also felt the strength of republicanism. A legion rising at the end of Nero's reign proclaimed Republic and Senate [338, p. 33], as did the army in Germany, revolting shortly afterward against Galba. [Tacitus *Histories*, 1–56] There were enough antimonarchic critics to annoy Vespasian considerably, and long afterward some Romans remained unconvinced of the virtues of autocracy, although few doubted its necessity. Toward the end of the second century, a commander rebelling against Commodus in Britain sought support by calling for a republic. [314, I, 96] As late as 238 there was a serious effort to recover something of the republican system, as the Senate, in the reaction against the wild Maximin, elected two emperors in the hope that they would restrain each other. [331, I, 21] Even at the beginning of the Dominate, the assassination of Aurelian in 275 may have been in part a reaction by conservatives to his orientalizing. [309, p. 66]

The Senate, the chief embodiment of constitutionalism, retained some prestige down to the very end. In the early empire, its moral standing was restored despite the loss of effective power; as the disorders and abuses of the later republic receded and were forgotten, men remembered the epic struggle against Hannibal and the conquest of the world, achieved by the wisdom and virtue of the Conscript Fathers. The feeling persisted that a strong Senate meant solidity and health, as in the days of Rome's ascent. Senatorial opinion remained a force through the Principate [*326*, I, 5] because it was immensely useful to give legitimacy to the administration in the absence of dynastic tradition. It was not called upon to decide anything, of course, but it was important that the Senate lend its sanction, even if it was necessary to fine absentees to get a quorum. [*308*, pp. 206, 215] Fairly easily controlling its composition, the ruler could well afford to pay it a little deference, giving it some appearance of freedom and authority in return for the moral support of its historical dignity against the caprices of the army. At the time of opposition to Maximin, the Senate, although ultimately unsuccessful, was able to play a real role. In 275, after the murder of Aurelian, the army, weary of seditions, asked the Senate to choose the new Caesar. After much hesitation, it named Tacitus, an elderly senator; but his effort to restore some of the authority of the body remained hollow because it could not command the armies. The next Caesar, Probus, modestly submitted his title to the Senate. [*314*, I, 279, 283] But when he was murdered by mutinous troops, Carus, his successor, simply informed the Fathers that he had assumed the throne.

There was never again any question of the Senate's having a real voice in the government. As the person of the ruler was exalted in the Dominate, it ceased to be fitting for him to pretend deference to any mortals. He even ceased to consult the Senate regarding his choice of colleague and presumptive heir, for the eventual accession of whom the acceptance of influential men would be necessary. But when Constantine set up a new capital at Byzantium, he set up a new senate there, and senates at Rome and Constantinople lived on as shells of the ancient institutions. They seem to have had some prestige [*326*, I, 449], although their chief business was the chanting of endless litanies of nauseating praise for the sovereign. [*298*, pp. 207–208] They even outlasted the empire in the West. In 476 the last puppet Western emperor advised the Senate of his resignation, and in 500 that body received the Frankish king Theodoric. [*509*, pp. 49, 52] Only in the ninth century did Leo the Wise finally end the senate in the East. [*278*, p. 54]

As Rome, in acquiring autocratic government, did not discard the old political structure but imposed a new one atop it, the republican offices also continued to be valued. In the early years of the empire, electoral campaigns were still violent and aroused keen excitement, although nothing was decided thereby. [*308*, p. 41] The consulship, although cheapened by frequent conferral after Nero and eventually reduced to the merest ceremonial functions, continued to be the prized crown of a career as long as the empire stood, and even for decades afterward. [*313*, p. 125] In the East, the ancient titles, as of quaestor, proconsul, and praetorian prefect, were used through the sixth century. [*301*, p. 64] The aristocratic families, those of ancient lineage and the newer ones that aped them, also clung with tenacity to their distinctions, although decimated, powerless, and servile. Emperors were very hesitant to give high social rank to their ex-slave favorites; senators crawled before these, but they could not enter the Senate. [*313*, p. 108] The direct authority of Claudius (41–54 A.D.) was required to stifle protests against the admission of Gauls to the Senate, and few other provincials were brought in until Vespasian (69–79 A.D.), who leaned on them for support. [*313*, p. 102] The old order was truly stubborn.

This was hardly the result of firm character. Romans of all classes groveled before the Caesar, from Augustus onward, with unmatched servility; countless proud Romans kissed the feet of murderers of their sons or fathers. Much more, it must be a tribute to the character of the classic city-state from which Rome sprang. The polis was an extraordinarily effective political form in its Roman as in its Greek varieties, inspiring men as hardly any other form of government has done; and it did not die easily. Most intensely particularistic, it was based upon autonomy of the community and the individual. In it, the scope of the state was restricted while as much as possible was left to voluntary or private action. The economy was especially free of control. The Roman empire itself at first served the greed of private profiteers much more than that of the exploiting state apparatus; and, although rulers like Nero pounced eagerly on attractive fortunes and extortion was a recurrent plague, only slowly did the official apparatus come to manage the economy. Similarly, the classical world was tolerant of belief, and there was no imposed conformity in the empire until the fourth century. Rome had no moral-religious unity, but great diversity of creeds and philosophies, and moral freedom implied a limitation of despotism. Local autonomy similarly was a check on the growth of the central regime. The gradual accretion of provinces, protected cities, and subject allies made it possible for the early empire to be somewhat like a protectorate, a suzerain power satisfied to keep order and collect taxes, while leaving people for the most part to carry on their business under their own laws and, to a great extent, under their own administration. Rome long managed its world with the constitution of a city. [299, p. 3] Native kings, who had been invaluable allies in building the empire, were retained for some generations, much as when England ruled indirectly large parts of the British Empire; provincial towns continued to elect magistrates by popular vote and, through their provincial assemblies, maintained an illusion of autonomy. [320, p. 7; 302, p. 211] The Hellenistic federations and amphictionic leagues were retained for the governance of Greece. [328, p. 110] This made it possible for the bureaucracy to remain small until late in the day. [326, I, 12] Only in the second century did the empire take over much city administration; by the time of Trajan local officials, even when not directly constrained, were finding it necessary to seek approval from the central regime for almost any action. [358, p. 286] In the second century a local leader was punished for saying, "Under the guise of freedom all things happen at Rome's pleasure." [345, p. 105] Nonetheless, there was much more guise of freedom than in most world empires. The disturbances of the third century were required to sweep away the last municipal liberties; not until Diocletian was all local coinage abolished. [354, p. 117] Even then some effort was made to keep up local institutions. Assemblies of local dignitaries were at first permitted and later required, all of certain rank being ordered to attend, partly to register decrees addressed to the provincials and partly as a check on governors, against whom they could complain to the central government. But in the general centralization and advancing decay, the life was gone. [328, pp. 146–157]

Rome was also fortunate in becoming a great empire with a strong and deep republican tradition. It was the republic that had conquered the world and made the foundations of all Caesar's glory, and Roman political theory continued republican even as the empire was autocratic; theory served somewhat to attenuate the reality of power. Indeed, the empire failed to develop a real imperial ideology; hence, if the autocrat would secure legitimacy and the acceptance of the educated, in the absence of an authoritarian philosophy, he had to bow a little to republican traditions and forms. At the same time, opposition was slightly encouraged; one could criticize indirectly by praise of the glorious republic.

If carried too far, such criticism was punished; but during a century or more of autocracy it was possible for Romans to be academic republicans. The continued existence of the Senate and republican magistracies always recalled their past role.

The cultural conservatism of the empire also tended to preserve republicanism, as schools continued for centuries, even down to collapse of the empire, to teach the lessons of the days of Cicero, using the old texts of freer times and teaching the virtues of freedom, unrealistic as they had become. [*314*, I, 72] The bureaucracy was to some extent trained in classic letters and ideals, as literary study was the usual preparation for an official career down to the end of the Western empire; and the prestige of the Senate was sustained by the historians, men of senatorial rank. [*275*, pp. 97, 107] Educated Romans looked back to an idealized republic whose traditions were cherished the more because they emphasized civic and military virtues. [*309*, p. 15] Admiration of the free-spirited culture of Greece persisted most stubbornly in the autocracy; in the middle of the fourth century, Julian was so imbued with the old learning that he sought to restore the old gods. Of course, pretenses became ever more hollow. For example, "free" cities came to call themselves "free and autonomous from the beginning by grace of the Augusti"; and Plutarch advised arranging a little polite opposition for appearances' sake. But the appearances were not without effect. The moral courage and devotion to duty of many Romans of later times, like Marcus Aurelius (161–180), are a fine tribute to enduring traditions.

Fullness of autocracy was also mitigated by insecurity of the empire, without natural frontiers to the north and east and perennially battling for its safety. Between 166 and 395 A.D., barbarians forced their way across the Roman frontiers twenty-three times. [*358*, p. 270] Authority could not lie solely in the palace so long as powerful armies were always necessary and usually a force to be feared. That the rulers shared power with the armies made for disorder but impeded degeneration. Popular feelings could not be ignored, since they easily spread into the army; and the army claimed to represent the people, just as the citizens' assembly of the early republic had been the armed men. Thus the empire at times resembled a military republic, the soldiers being citizens upon whose vote the first magistrate rested. Plutarch warned officials, "Do not have great pride or confidence in your crown,

for you see soldiers' boots just above your head." [*330*, p. 319]
Chosen by the legions, often compelled to keep them busy lest
they turn on him, always dependent on their loyalty and support,
yet unable to reduce their power because of the likelihood of invasion, Caesar could not relax in the sloth of utter absolutism.
The modest and philosophic Marcus Aurelius was less a smug
ruler of the world than an ever-pressed general. He spent most of
his reign in military camp, a situation more favorable for philoso-
phizing than the contrived pleasures and fetid atmosphere of the
palace. The army came to make and unmake Caesars capriciously
and selfishly, but it at least did not give supreme power to stupid
or slothful men; and military politics was probably more whole-
some than palace politics.

Insecurity and military power gave the empire many capable
leaders. The hereditary principle did not become firm, no line of
direct succession lasting more than two generations until the house
of Constantine. This was partly because politics was so murderous
in the imperial family, partly because the Caesars were singularly
unable to produce sons. It was also due to the fact that those born
to the purple usually proved incapable: the worst emperors of the
Principate, Caligula, Nero, Domitian, Commodus, and Caracalla,
came from a lineage of deified Caesars. It was odd that the much
admired Marcus Aurelius should have as son and heir the monstrous Commodus; the Roman system was evidently not suited to
hereditary power. The better scheme was for the emperor to adopt
a successor acceptable to the army; thus, the need to reconcile the
troops led Nerva to name a capable commander, Trajan, as his
heir; and a sequence of good emperors followed by this procedure.
The military also opened the way to the top for many men of
lower-class origins and so prevented Roman society from becoming
stale. On the other hand, the army could get rid of bad rulers, like
Nero or the ridiculous Elagabalus, effeminate boy-priest of a phal-
lic cult.

Republican traditions somewhat impeded the popularization of
hereditary succession; perhaps more significant, the discontinuity
of succession meant that Caesars had to look to traditional and
republican forms for the legitimation of authority. Men were also
freer to criticize the past. Having lived through Domitian's reign
of terror, Tacitus could write bitterly of the abuses of power under
a Caesar who did not mind the blackening of his predecessor.

Caesarship did not seem so sacred when predecessors were often denounced instead of being sanctified as ancestors.

Thus the Roman empire, built as though absentmindedly and unsystematically, to a degree an empire in spite of itself and much of the time under attack, resisted decay through generations of absolutism better than most great empires. But eventually the Western half sank under the burden of the same vices that seem to beset all such mighty states. Only the reduced East, harried and often deeply troubled, was able to carry on yet another thousand years.

4   ORDERING OF POWER

EXALTED MAJESTY

The constitutional law of the universal empire is simple: the will of the ruler is law. His effective power is restricted by tradition, customs, morals, and practical psychology, but by no constitutional limitations. If the autocrat commands something that those around him or those on whose support he rests find repugnant, harmful, or dangerous to themselves, he is likely to be disregarded, deposed (as was the Chinese emperor who in 1898 tried to Westernize his government), or murdered, as were most Roman Caesars. The mightiest despot might encounter difficulty in introducing a new tax or reducing the pay of the army. But in theory, if not always in practice, the pharaoh, emperor, great king, sultan, calif, son of heaven, Caesar, Byzantine basileus, or Russian tsar has had the authority to change any rule, to appropriate any possession, to name or dismiss all functionaries, and to reward or punish any subject. The ruler is the center and focus of the empire, to govern if he is strong, to serve as symbol if he is weak. Even if he is mad or stupid, his approbation is the key to power, and the greatest state is a personal estate. Feudal monarchies and constitutional republican states rest on limited and conditional obligations; the demands of the absolutist empire are unlimited and unconditional. [K. Wittfogel in 409, p. 324] As Ivan III replied to the plea of the men of formerly republican Novgorod for a guarantee of their rights, the imperial autocrat could make concessions but could not contract away fractions of his power. [412, p. 26] A T'ang emperor stated, "All the talents and heroes of the empire are in my bag." [J. Liu in 19, p. 105]

As Montesquieu noted, immense conquests either presuppose despotism or make it inevitable. It seems that the larger the state the greater the concentration of ultimate decision in a single head. "Empire," according to a Turkish sultan, "is a bride whose favors cannot be shared." [433, p. 142] The need and passion of the universal empire, its excuse for existence, is unity and order; these can be guaranteed only by a single uncontested direction, a single will. The empire needs its autocrat at least as a symbol of common loyalty and obedience, preferably as a guide for the whole; the only obvious alternative is civil strife. In the words of Strabo, "It would be difficult to administer so great a realm otherwise than by turning it over to one man, as to a father." [330, p. 97]

Political power commonly gravitates to a single person, and is almost certain to do so unless there is some sort of constitutional delimitation of powers. Leadership is essentially singular. Political parties, movements, or rebellions usually look to a strong individual for positive action and clear policy. Authority is always justified by the need of preventing or resolving conflicts, and the overgreat organization most needs a single will. Division invites dissent and further division; when the Senate in 238 elected two emperors to restrict the autocratic power, the two inevitably quarreled and could not control the Praetorians, who cut down both. [314, I, 163] The essential function of the autocrat is not to administer or to initiate policy but to act as arbiter and final decider of differences. Not only would the regime be paralyzed by opposing agencies or factions; the artificial unity of the universal empire would fall apart if there were no head to overrule the conflicts of interest that inevitably arise. Elevated above the pettier interests and quarrels, symbolic of the state as a whole, and supposedly concerned with its well-being as no one else, with nothing to gain by partiality, the autocrat is the most acceptable, and an indispensable, judge. The mission of autocracy is impartiality.

The exalted emperor is also a moral necessity. The overgrown state can of itself inspire little loyalty or patriotism. However admired, it is too great for love; and its common good becomes distantly impersonal. Men feel themselves less part of the all-embracing order; as it attains its glorious supremacy and no longer arouses a sense of contest, they cease to feel that it needs them. The less the cohesion of a common cause, the greater the need for a cultivated reverence, something men can look up to; and this can hardly be anything but a personality, a sovereign father figure, a demigod to whom all can submit. A dead hero may be useful, as Augustus was to Rome, or a collective body like the Senate, and there may be mingled elements of varying symbolism of power; but these cannot take the place of an imperial will incorporated in a supreme, godlike personage, the most understandable and persuasive of symbols.

Against the tendency of men and nations united by force to seek their own interests, the lofty and distant ruler must seek willing acquiescence, which is achieved through awe and myth, grandeur and symbolism, an exaltation that makes it easier for men to give their wills, not to a fellowman, but to a will mysteriously higher. The greater the veneration that can be inculcated, the firmer the bonds of the state, so that not merely convenience or fear, but conscience, guides compliance. It is best of all if the ruler can be made something like a god, or at least a holy figure, to whom the people can bow with awe and contrition of their souls.

The sublime ruler is thus essential to the imperial system as both center and symbol of government. At the same time, just as the great empire is built not so much because the nations call for it as because a conquering state acquires sufficient might to impose it, its ruler is an autocrat not only because the system calls for leadership but because it is difficult to restrict arbitrary power. His position corresponds not only to a need for unity and order but also, perhaps in the larger part, to opportunities to achieve power and glory.

The greater the state, the easier to dominate it absolutely. Size alone suffices to inspire awe and sentiments of destiny; men tremble before the lord of the world. Even if the monarch is ugly, dull, and ill-tempered, he can be so magnified that at a distance men see a glorious and stately or divine figure to whom they owe everything. Around the world conqueror or world ruler there naturally grow legends of his feats and the portents of his power, tales of uncommon abilities, which not only the credulous believe. [351, p. 6] It is easy or unavoidable for the lord of the empire to believe in the rightness of his will, to suppose that God chose him to rule the universe and perhaps inspires his decisions, hence that his right is divine; it is easy both for those far away and those near and dependent on him to accept this view, and difficult for anyone really to contradict it.

He who stands over the universal empire has countless advantages. Those below find it less humiliating to bow to a single demigod, of whom they cannot be jealous; lesser nobles and men of middle standing have often preferred an autocrat to an oligarchy. The larger the state, the more effective is force in ruling it, as the opposition finds it more difficult to organize and rise. Ten men could hardly rule despotically a town of a thousand, but an army of a million is unnecessarily large to oppress an empire of a hundred million. Force acquires greater potency, and the command of force must be unitary; the fact that the state rests on force precludes any stable separation or checking of political powers. The autocrat is also conscious of his symbolic value and plays upon the need for stability. Any change in rulership, unless the monarch is extremely bad, is disconcerting and tends to shake attachments; hence even a mediocre ruler has to be retained indefinitely, and the longer people look up to him the more natural obedience seems. But security for the ruler requires guarding against rivals; to discourage usurpation or even the casting of baneful doubt upon the position of the ruler, with potential consequences of disorder and weakened loyalties, requires that he be raised as far as possible above ordinary mortals, even to the level of the gods. Nor is it difficult to achieve this; he is rich with the wealth of the empire, strong with its armies, wise with the wisdom of its best men (if he has judgment to use it), haloed with its magnificence, and wrapped in a shining cloud of glory. For these resources, he has no better use than the increase or maintenance of authority, infinitely more important for the true autocrat than any standard of conduct. And authority should swell, not only in the lifetime of the monarch, but through the generations, for it is injurious to any monarch that he should be denied what his predecessors had, while he probably will take more pride in passing to his descendants the fullness of absolutism than the greatness of the state.

For such reasons, the rulers of the great empires have been held or caused themselves to be held above mortal law, essentially superior to other men, even like gods who have title to the earth and all its blessings, on whom the fate of mortals rests and of whom salvation may be begged. To be sure, kings have ever been associated with magic and some touch of divinity, but the more imperial the state the more gloriously sacred the ruler. The pharaohs were gods-in-life in the earliest of empires. The First Dynasty, uniting Upper and Lower Egypt, renounced consecration by the priests of Heliopolis and claimed direct divine authority. [131, p. 97] At first deified after death, like the early Caesars, or merely sons of a goddess [104, p. 7], during the great Fifth Dynasty the pharaohs became living gods [347, p. 22], not gods because they were rulers but rulers because they were gods, responsible for the life and prosperity of the land. [124, p. 192] They were literally sons of supreme Re, who took the shape and assumed the regalia of the reigning pharaoh as he went to the queen's chamber. [*126,* pp. 174–175, 183] In carvings the ruler was always depicted towering far above simple mortals. He was surrounded with abasing cere- mony; everyone approaching the royal person, for example, had to prostrate himself and "smell the ground." The very title of pharaoh was a circumlocution, "Great House," for a being too sacred to be named. It was not enough to be one god; New Kingdom pharaohs had some five names, variously used according to which god they were considered momentarily to embody. [*140,* p. 84] Of Ikhnaten it was written reverently, "One lives, one is in health, when one sees him." [*120,* p. 298] Only in contact with the outside world were pharaohs of the New Kingdom Eighteenth Dynasty some- what humanized, as other Near Eastern monarchs were allowed to address them as "brother." [*94,* p. 351]

The kings of Sumerian city-states were treated as mortals, but the successors of Sargon, the unifier, began prefixing the god sym- bol to their names; Naramsin had himself depicted as greater than life size, and with divine insignia. [*106,* p. 242] The governors were called "slaves of the king," doubtless in hopes that they would prove reasonably obedient. The somewhat smaller empire of the Third Dynasty of Ur continued the custom of the divine prefix and expressed self-esteem in such terms as, "I am the hero, the god of all the lands . . . who possesses the divine strength of heaven and earth, who has no equal." [*125,* p. 40] After the land again be- came prey to division, such pretensions were dropped. But follow- ing conquerors, like the Hittite kings, were incarnations of the sun-god. [*351,* p. 2] The Assyrian rulers set up their statues to be worshiped alongside those of the gods [*127,* p. 600], and, although not exactly held to be divinities, were chosen by gods and conven- tionally called sons of this or that goddess. [*98,* p. 116] In pre- imperial Persia, the king was chosen by the people or warriors, although the choice was usually limited to the royal family; in imperial Achaemenid Persia, he became a sacred, god-descended King of Kings, high priest, and religious symbol garbed like a cosmic ruler, haloed with divinity, though not actually worshiped as divine. At his coronation he assumed a new throne name and put on a robe symbolic of universal dominion. [*249,* p. 95] At ban- quets where he was absent, a table was set up with food and drink for his spirit. [*351,* p. 3] He was so awesome that only seven greatest nobles were said to be entitled to see his face. As a setting for his majesty, there was built a marvelous new capital at Persepolis, which seems to have been forbidden to ordinary men. [249, pp. 98–101]

The Greeks were not immune to such tendencies; a cult was set up to Lysander when he became near ruler of all Greece after the defeat of Athens by Sparta. [351, p. 11] Subsequently, an exemplary conqueror like Alexander could not lag behind the Persians whom he laid low; perhaps to facilitate rule of peoples accustomed to king worship, he found, as soon as he was well on the way to general conquest, that his father had been Zeus, not Philip. Perhaps he accepted deification as much to please his imperious self as from a sense of political need, because he demanded that not only his oriental subjects but also the more skeptical Greeks worship him as a god. Ever after in that region strong rulers have been similarly glorified. For example, the Sassanids strongly revived the old pretenses and added to them, claiming to be brothers or sons of the Sun and Moon, and made themselves as inaccessible as their Achaemenid forebears, if not more so. Centuries later, the Abbasid califs required that subjects approaching them kiss the ground or, by special dispensation, their feet. [452, p. 29]

The Caesars from the beginning tended ever more to distinguish and separate themselves from their subjects, as already noted, until they became eventually quite sacred and remote. Even the relatively temperate Augustus retreated from public view in order to become a better symbol [345, p. 56]; while on an Asian tour he impressed his assembled subjects by mounting an apparatus that wafted him toward heaven and out of sight. [308, p. 11] Caesar's statue could not be set at the level of ordinary men but had to stand atop a high shaft [358, pp. 355–356], and even trivial disrespect for his image was punishable as treason. To dazzle his subjects, Gallienus used a crown with darting rays of the sun, and sprinkled gold dust over his hair, as suitable for the Sol Invictus. [302, p. 618] By the second century the Romans seem to have come to consider the divine spirit of the Caesar as a more effective guardian of the peace than Jupiter; as Tertullian wrote, "It is with greater fear and shrewder timidity that you watch Caesar than Olympian Jove himself." [330, p. 586] The whole apparatus of emperor-worship, with its priesthood and ceremonies, was an important amalgam for the empire. [347, pp. 88–89] The refusal of early Christians to make the required obeisance amounted to rebellion. The Christian emperor of the Roman and subsequently of the Byzantine realm continued quite as holy as his pagan predecessor, an unapproachable being "equal to the Apostles," surrounded by ceremony to stress his superhumanity, resistance to whom was sacrilege. [279, p. 269] Those below him, far from being citizens, were not even subjects but slaves, and they so described themselves. [301, p. 29]

The Chinese emperor was a ritual leader from very ancient times, even during the time of Contending States; but his position was much enhanced after strong and united rule was established. The Ch'in king, having conquered all China, took the new title of "First Sovereign Emperor," with connotations of divinity. He permitted himself to be persuaded that he was a very special being, worthy of immortality, the elixir of which he sought assiduously. He secluded himself in tremendous, labyrinthine palaces and permitted no slightest contradiction even from his eldest son. His dignity demanded that he punish a mountain that had bothered him by having it painted red, the color of criminals. [5, pp. 116–118] The first Han emperor, carried to power by an uprising against the unaccustomed Ch'in tyranny, was less pretentious, but a minister urged, "If the Great King does not possess an honorific title, they will all doubt and not believe in him." [5, p. 131] In time, the Han emperors acquired a duly exalted status and greatly increased the distance between the sovereign and the highest officials.

The dignity of the emperor in subsequent dynasties was unquestioned; even his name was at times tabu, not to be written during his lifetime. [23, p. 12] His character was so esteemed that a later Chinese encyclopedia devoted forty-six volumes to describing his moral qualities. [56, p. 29] Not exactly held divine, yet in some ways more than an ordinary god, he stood in a special relation to heavenly powers and served as a permanent focus even as tides of disorder swept across the land. He was so powerful that he controlled the transmigration of souls and could raise local genii to heavenly rank. [15, pp. 7, 10] Heaven was his father and the earth his mother. [76, p. 308] All had to kowtow before him, striking the ground with their heads nine times; they bowed to his throne even when it was empty. In later times, he seldom left the Forbidden City except for great ceremonies [15, p. 12]; and he was never to be seen except by a few intimates and high officials [54, p. 67], his first maxim being not to show himself to his "children." [3, p. 360] It was a capital crime to remain standing by the road as his retinue passed. [10, p. 68] According to Marco Polo, no one could speak aloud within a half-mile of his palace. [Bk. II, chap. 34] Even his humble representatives, the magistrates, could not appear in public except in official dress and escorted by a numerous retinue. [76, p. 404] A viceroy going down the street was the center of a regular parade of bearers of gongs or flags, holders of placards, riders, men with whips, incense bearers, receivers of petitions, guards, and so forth, to the number of fifty or so. [14, I, 300] Yet when these minions in the provinces received a dispatch from the all-highest, they lit incense and prostrated themselves. [76, p. 314] A British diplomat at the end of the eighteenth century wrote: "In no religion, ancient or modern, has the Divine been addressed, I believe, with stronger exterior marks of worship and adoration than were this morning addressed to the phantom of his Chinese Majesty." [523, pp. 43–44]

Indian emperors received similar adulation. The extraordinary Asoka was modest enough to regard himself as a paternal benefactor, "Beloved of the gods." But the pomp of Mauryan emperors was exceptional. As related by Curtius, they traveled over perfumed roads in golden palanquins garnished with pearls, or, for longer trips, on an elephant all sheathed in gold, with a long train of courtesans also in golden litters. [211, p. 182] Later emperors exaggerated their consecration to the utmost. An Indian treatise on government written in the Mogul period, about 1650 A.D., passed over almost everything the present day would call political science while devoting a hundred pages to the ceremony of coronation. Among other titles, the Mogul emperor was known as "Holder of the Universe." He was also "Shadow of God," although Islamic monotheism forbade outright deification. [214, p. 16] The court form of address came to more than two hundred words of adulation, covering everything from "garland-twiner of spiritual and temporal blossoms" to "second Alexander." [209, p. 30] Surrounded with all conceivable splendor of gold, brocades, and jewels, he sat on a gem-encrusted throne built to demonstrate the quantity of captured treasures. [202, p. 98] As an ascetic Moslem of the strictest faith, Aurangzeb declined to use gold or silver dishes; however, he saw no harm in crystal ones studded with diamonds and rubies.

[*202*, p. 67] So important was his presence that the capital was merely where he located his tent city. [*216*, p. 147] Even a minor servant of the Mogul would ride on luxurious cushions in litters borne by six bearers, with a servant carrying a silver spittoon on one side and two or more on the other fanning with peacock tails, footmen going before and horsemen following. (*202*, p. 91]

Before the Inca unification, the chiefs of warring tribes had enjoyed rather limited status, often ruling only temporarily. [*172*, p. 15] But the Sapa Inca ("Sole Ruler"), as master of a huge territory, became a god incarnate, child of Sun and Moon, divinely begotten, according to the creation myth. So powerful that a slight gesture sufficed to condemn anyone to death, he had to eat alone since no one was great enough to sit with him. [*176*, p. 149] He used gold vessels and never the same ones twice, nor did his dignity permit the use of any garment, even a cloak of delicate batskin, more than once. [*170*, p. 39] He heard petitions behind a screen; it was a rare honor to receive anyone face to face, and no one could approach him without a symbolic burden on his back. [J. Rowe in *180*, p. 259] He went out only in a stately procession, for which a corps of aides ran ahead to warn the people and to sweep the road before him. [*173*, p. 127] So great a being could not really die; and when the breath departed his body, his mummy continued to rule a sort of personal court, in theory indefinitely, fêted, fed, and treated as though alive, carried in processions, and honored along with the mummy of his queen. [*173*, pp. 126, 179–180]

Such pompous mummery has probably been very useful and effective. The most ordinary man becomes awe-inspiring when encased in the riches of a huge realm and all the pomp humans can devise; surrounded by glitter and jeweled trappings, with color and pageantry infinitely beyond ordinary men, the hallowed autocrat seems superhuman to the simple, and tingles the nerves even of the educated. Thus great empire has the power to magnify men; even scholarly historians have waxed enthusiastic over many men who are dubbed "Great" but doubtless would have been quite ordinary if chance had not raised them to a position where moderate ability could do great deeds. Power, no matter how come by, is almost equivalent to greatness in the ordinary estimation; when it is made manifest by a brilliant display, few can avoid being at least a little dazzled. The higher the one stands over the many, the more easily are mysterious powers attributed to him. Ignorant people, and not only the ignorant, find it easier to worship the splendid than the ideal. Certainly the power of the ruler over their lives is apparent and conducive to deep respect. If, then, the emperor can induce the people voluntarily to make even a genuflection to him, their will is partly his; if he can get them to bow low, seeing their bent backs, he raises his head the higher and knows that his word is their law.

Even in Russia, despite contact with the West and awareness of Western philosophies, the glorification of the ruler has gone far. The tsars, from Ivan the Terrible to the last Nicholas, were held to have been "ordained by God himself," and the subjects in Muscovite days called themselves, like those of Byzantine Caesars, his slaves. [Herberstein in *420*, p. 39] To manifest his superiority, if Ivan the Terrible disliked the looks of anyone, he was likely to have him instantly decapitated. [G. Fletcher, in *405*, p. 28] Up to Peter, the tsars were considered holy mostly as champions of Orthodoxy, but the irreligious Peter was treated as sacred in his own right on grounds more political than religious; some even averred that he personally was God on earth. [*367*, p. 78] In the twentieth century, such sentiments had largely vanished, but the paraphernalia of royalty and power could generate quite an aura around the last tsar, Nicholas II, a man not above average in physical appearance, character or ability, and perhaps meaner than most of his subjects. Decades after he had been ignominiously overthrown, a perceptive man could recall the thrill of catching a glimpse of him:

The motionless mass was waiting for Him, that is, the Emperor. . . . Suddenly, like an electric current, . . . on a great dapple horse the rider came slowly. In the distance, His face could not be distinguished, but everyone understood that it could only be He. The wave of ceaseless cheering went ahead of Him, surrounded Him. Something magnificent and thrilling resounded in that powerful roar. In a few moments the rider galloped past in front of everyone, accompanied by a few others on horseback. The troops passed in ceremonial march. . . . Many turned to look where He was, incomprehensible and great, the commander of hundreds of thousands of troops. [*361*, p. 39]

But exaltation of the ruler is not entirely for the good of the state. It amounts to psychological warfare against the independence of the subjects; the higher the one, the lower by comparison the many. This is well when only submission is needed, but spirits frozen in attitudes of passive adoration may become incapable of motion when the emperor needs them. The emperor is everything, but he cannot manage everything; much may remain undone and many decisions untaken because all look to the emperor. And if he fails, the huge headless mass may be palsied. Aurangzeb, even while gravely sick, felt that he had to appear daily in council lest reports of his demise rock the empire. [*191*, p. 266] The Spaniards had only to capture the Inca Atahualpa to capture, in effect, his huge empire. His conditioned people continued to obey him even while he was a prisoner acting on orders from his captors, though by acting with independent vigor they might have saved him. When he had been murdered, there remained no focus of obedience, and resistance to the handful of invaders was virtually at an end. Similarly, when a would-be Mogul emperor, on the point of victory in a great battle for the succession, got down from his elephant to take personal command, the cry went up that he had been killed; and his army panicked and disbanded in a few minutes. [*191*, p. 54; *212*, p. 333] A very similar incident occurred shortly afterward when a Mogul prince, believing the battle won, dismounted to hasten the pursuit of the enemy and soon found himself without an army. [*191*, p. 77] On the contrary, when the brilliant Gustavus Adolphus of Sweden was killed in battle during the Thirty Years' War, his troops pressed forward the more vigorously for vengeance and won him posthumous victory. [*552*, p. 132] The experiences of Xenophon's band of Greek mercenaries in the Persian empire well show both sides of this coin. Cyrus, who had engaged the Greek auxiliaries to help him snatch the Persian crown, was killed while winning the battle of Cunaxa; his Asiatic troops immediately took flight while the Greeks stood firm. The Persian king, Artaxerxes, unable to overcome the tiny band of Greeks in the middle of his domain, treacherously secured the murder of their generals. Far from losing heart, the Greeks elected new leaders, devised new tactics, and fought their way to freedom. [*236*, pp. 21–23]

MONOPOLY OF AUTHORITY

The correlate of the overbearing and exalted central power is the debasement of all else, the fragmentation, reduction, or suppression of independent power; whatever is not useful to the majestic power is useless or harmful, possibly dangerous. Independent churches are brought under control or deprived of vitality so far as this can be done. The tolerance of the Roman empire in its first centuries was unusual, while the complete intolerance of the later empire was better in the imperial logic. Autonomous local government is likewise evil in the sight of the great autocrat, who suffers no legitimate freedom for cities or provinces and little actual freedom except as dictated by weakness or the convenience of an administration incompetent to manage everything. In the great leveling and centralization, the provincial or country towns become places of small account where nothing of importance can be decided. Chinese villages were often left to manage their own affairs, but they had no legal autonomy and no institutions the district magistrate might not alter or dissolve. [*36*, p. 67; *38*, p. 46] The history of a small country like Switzerland deals with many towns and cantons; the history of vast Russia hardly needs to mention any place but the capitals.

The reduction of independent power is best seen in the downfall of the aristocracy of birth and tradition, of the class that has influence by virtue of its hereditary standing. An aristocracy or nobility, conscious of its worth and presumptive rights, accustomed to a share in the government or local power in the provinces, has no place against the overweening prerogative; individual pride is a great sin against absolutism. This is generally true of unchecked government. European absolutist monarchs, though unable quite to crush the old nobility, weakened its position and relied on men of nonnoble origins more fully at the mercy of the ruler. Smaller tyrants, like those of Renaissance Italy or ancient Greece, likewise rightly feared men of established worth. According to Herodotus [Bk. V, 92], the tyrant of Miletus, when a fellow tyrant asked for advice in governing, answered silently by lopping off the heads of grain that overtopped the rest.

Proud aristocrats are much more dangerous than the more impressionable and passive masses. Julius Caesar was adored by the populace of Rome but slain by the men of the finest senatorial families. As Euripides said, "When one man is king . . . if he thinks that any of his nobles are wise, he fears for his despotic power and kills them." [*Suppliant Women*, in *327*, p. 132] The deified or at least sacrosanct autocrat feels justified in cutting down ruthlessly any possible menace, and the most obvious menace proceeds from the great. Even if they represent no danger, they are a probable source of dissension and a focus for opposition. In humbling the overmighty subjects he also further elevates himself, while reaping the gratitude of those of lower birth who view with pleasure the humiliation of the proud. The hereditary principle is out of harmony with the imperial order, so long as this is vigorous. Power seeks totality, and the omnipotence of one will implies overriding all distinctions irrelevant to it; birth gives way to service or favor. It may even be a detriment for a man to be wellborn. The most dependable if not servile servants are those who are nothing of their own right, who have nothing but what the gracious favor of the ruler concedes, who are most zealous and loyal because they have risen from nothing to greatness by their zeal and loyalty, and who may be returned to nothing at any whim.

Thus Egypt, at the beginning of the Old Kingdom, had a great aristocracy which has been called feudal, and, under the first two dynasties, graves of nobles were comparable to those of the ruler; thereafter they shrank to insignificance. Only the clergy, which blessed the deified monarch, retained some standing. [*131*, p. 16] Nobles became his nominated creatures and the governors his servants, as he held full disposition of all property and persons. [*101*, p. 125] Civilians were used as military commanders in the late Old Kingdom [*90*, p. 167], and it represented high rank to be perfumer or manicurist of the pharaoh. [*134*, p. 37] When the New Kingdom restored central power after a long period of disorders, the outcome was similar: the entire country came under a large bureaucracy commanded by the chief minister; all lands were once more the property of the pharaoh; the hereditary rulers of the nomes were again replaced by appointed governors; and the new "nobility" became only his courtiers and servants. High birth ceased to matter much, as many were raised from lowly origins; under Ikhnaten, courtiers even prided themselves on humble birth. [*134*, p. 90; *101*, p. 138; *120*, p. 298] Similarly, imperial unification of Sumeria by Sargon meant the rapid degradation of the aristocratic families and their replacement by appointed governors. After Darius put down the revolt of the Ionian cities, he stripped the aristocrats of their privileges. [*116*, p. 305]

Empire long ago deprived China of a nobility. When the state of Ch'in made itself master of all China and reduced the ancient kings to commoners, some proposed that the emperor's sons be given fiefs; but this suggestion was rejected and the whole land was directly subordinated to the ruler, "to secure peace under Heaven." Only one title was retained, that of court noble; and rank was based on wealth and services, not birth, in the conscious preference for the bureaucracy over the feudal order. [*40*, Bk. I, p. 92; *30*, p. 98] The Han dynasty, founded by a commoner, was at the outset less dictatorial in spirit. Private holdings retained some importance for a few generations. But the feudal lords were soon protesting against the growing control of the bureaucracy; when they rose unsuccessfully in 154 B.C., many houses were extirpated. The sovereign thereafter asserted supremacy by selling new titles, posting a royal adviser to each great noble, and requiring the division of estates upon inheritance. [*30*, p. 107] As a result, the usual life of a noble family was little more than two generations, and soon very few old titles remained. [D. Bodde, in *466*, p. 70] In successive dynasties the civil service became increasingly the chief or sole avenue to advancement. In theory there was perfect justice and equality, as legally inherited privilege disappeared (except for descendants of Confucius), and almost anyone was free to qualify himself, if he had the means to spend years in study, for the imperial service and the highest rank beneath the Son of Heaven.

The great Islamic empires of Turkey and India were more extreme in their denial of hereditary status. In the Turkish empire not only was there practically no privilege of birth; it even came to be a disadvantage to be freeborn, as the Sultan gave all high positions to slaves. [*432*, Pt. I, p. 43] Since Moslem law somewhat limited arbitrary power over believers, he preferred to staff the administration and army with infidel slaves who could be decapitated without complaint. [*439*, p. 22] The Mogul empire in India recognized rank only as granted to its servants and took care lest position become hereditary. The emperor named as his servants and grant holders persons of low birth, even slaves, who would owe him all they possessed and who could be abased with the greatest ease. [*202*, p. 109] There were no territorial titles, because all land was property of the sovereign and royal grants could be revoked at pleasure. [*191*, p. 5] High officials were very well paid, but their wealth was consumed in extravagant display and they were kept indebted; their assets were seized upon their death and nothing remained to give their sons a shred of independence. [*216*, pp. 151–152] It was a fortunate family that could hold itself up for a few generations.

In this respect as in most others, Russia was usually less extreme. But there as elsewhere the reduction, at times extermination, of the older nobility marched with the progress of empire. In pre-Mongol Russia, the boyars had been notably independent and often strong enough to bend the princes to their will; at least, they could quit the service of any whom they disliked. Ivan III, who formalized independence from the Mongols and first created a large and unified Russian state, did much to suppress ancient legal and social institutions, to simplify the feudal system and center it on the tsar [401, p. 24], and to harness the boyars to his state. [377, p. 208] His grandson, Ivan IV, the Terrible, impoverished them and separated them from their political base by requiring that they live at court [K. Waszilevski in 420, p. 63], while allowing them to keep their estates only upon condition of serving him. [388, II, 137] Extremely suspicious, he formed a personal military force, the oprichnina, of as many as six thousand political police, and inaugurated an unsystematic but widespread reign of terror. [404, pp. 163–169] Beheadings and confiscations were numberless as the moody tsar took revenge on ten or a hundred for every one who opposed him or who sought to escape by emigration [K. Waszilevski in 420, p. 64]; and the slaughtered boyars of ancient lineage were replaced by new men, the tsar's unconditionals. By the end of the sixteenth century the will of the ruler was more important than high birth in the making of a boyar. [379, p. 32] Nobility was defined by a set of books kept by the central government, landholding and status being the reward mostly of service to the ruler [359, p. 188]; no offices were formally hereditary. Local government was correspondingly controlled from the center, as the tsar appointed the head clerk of each town. [G. Fletcher in 405, p. 28]

The disorders of the first part of the seventeenth century saw some revival of the nobility, but it again sank when the new Romanov dynasty was firm on the throne. Local institutions were further reduced to mere agencies, unpaid but responsible for tax collections. The boyar council, or duma, became increasingly an advisory, appointed body. [404, pp. 208, 213; 377, p. 271] As a Dutch embassy reported, "All Russians are slaves, except the Emperor. Even the nobles at Court, the Tsar's father-in-law not excepted, call themselves, when addressing the Tsar, his slaves." [457, p. 210] Peter publicly burned the record books of the aristocracy, thus affirming his freedom to appoint anyone without regard to precedence, and swamped the old families by raising tens of thousands of commoners, even serfs, to nobility. [*407*, p. 8; *404*, p. 241] Serf owners at least had the distinction of being called "orphans" of the autocrat, while others were his "slaves," but Peter decreed that all must earn their status by service to the state. Evasion of duties was punishable by confiscation of possessions and outlawry — a penalty perhaps needed, as nobles feigned feeble-mindedness to evade the tsar's demands. [*377*, pp. 418–419]

After Peter, as Western influences grew, the nobles were freed from service obligations on the ground that they were needed to manage estates and collect taxes. [*377*, p. 482] But nobility continued to derive from civil service rank, and nearly all fortunes arose from official connections. [*380*, II, 199] Formal titles, except "prince," were little used, as only court rank counted, and there were few solid benefits of birth. [*370*, II, 320–322] As in China, there was no rule of primogeniture, and estates were divided among the heirs [*419*, p. 268]; consequently, they furnished no firm basis for position, and great families often were reduced to poverty in a few generations. [*380*, II, 210] Contrariwise, men of the lowest origins might come to the acme of society by impressing or charming the autocrat. Menshikov, favorite of Peter the Great, once sold tarts in the street; the consort of Elizabeth had been a cowherd; and Kutaisov, favorite of Paul, was a Turkish orphan adopted by the army. [*313*, pp. 37–38] The old term "boyar" itself went out of use, superseded by "dvorianin," or "courtier." Paul said at the end of the eighteenth century, "There is no one of importance here except the one to whom I speak, and as long as I speak to him." [*419*, p. 280] This remained essentially the situation down to the end of the tsarist regime; position was made or destroyed by a smile or a frown of the sovereign. It was said that, lacking pride of birth or firm sense of superiority, the Russian nobility was not really an aristocracy at all. [*419*, p. 281]

It has often happened, of course, that conquering peoples, acquiring great empires, have set themselves up as hereditary masters over a subject mass. The Persians of the Achaemenid empire, for example, formed a ruling elite, and the conquering Inca nation held most of the higher administrative and religious positions while doing no physical labor. But the logic of empire dictates the erasure of all differences not based upon relation to the ruler, as the privileges of Romans and Italians over provincials of the Roman empire were step by step abolished. Status even in Inca Peru was not so much a matter of race or nationality as blood kinship to the ruling house, meritorious conquered chiefs being rewarded with princesses of the blood. [*173*, p. 137] The invading Manchus re-introduced feudal elements into Chinese society with ranks and hereditary titles, and Manchu overlords had great power during the early years of the dynasty. [Nivison in 55, p. 224] But the rulers gradually deprived the nobility, even the princes, of all substantial influence. Titles could be inherited only with specific authoriza-tion, and they were reduced by one degree each time they passed to heirs [Bodde in *466*, p. 140], so they were brought to nullity in a few generations.

It is useful and rational for the autocrat to overlook distinctions of blood and distribute the rewards of his state according to service and faithfulness; the replacement of inherited or social by political distinction is a prime characteristic of the true and firm imperial autocracy, setting it apart from traditional monarchies and feudal states. It is also salutary, as opportunities are opened to capable men of all classes, and many are doubtless brought to high position who in a more rigid system would waste their talents. But this system has its cost in all the vices of unhindered power.

UNFREE ENTERPRISE

Unlimited government implies control of the economy and the reduction or destruction of private economic power. When there is no restraint, rulers deal with trade, industry, and agriculture as most convenient to themselves. Where there are no private rights there is no fully private property. If the autocrat is weak or inca-pable, or if his apparatus is cumbersome and ineffective, legal or illegal private business may more or less go its own way; and if he is wise, he may find it better to give incentives to producers and to limit controls and exactions. But the imperial state gives private enterprise the same kind of security that a hungry cat might give a mouse.

The first motive for controlling the economy is thirst for money. Much of the drive to empire is the desire to tax and plunder; gov-ernments, like people, find it easier to spend than to take in, and needs always grow. Seldom does any regime feel that it has all the money it can use, and great empires have not been distinguished either for self-denial or sound fiscal management. The demands of pomp and display, of monuments and great works, are infinite; the consuming apparatus, the myriad who live by the public revenues, servants of the state, officials, and sundry hangers-on, are always hungry. There is thus a running contest between those who produce wealth and those who have political power, in which the latter have all the advantages of the state.

Money can be extracted only where it is. The very poor have only labor to give, and the empires have dragooned it in incalculable quantities, although this policy is uneconomic and satisfactory only for gross tasks such as digging canals or building roads. More productive are taxes placed on the land and its produce; they have usually been the financial mainstay. But frequently more alluring is the movable wealth of commerce and industry. The unification of the world, the abolition of frontiers, the establishment of a single currency, and the building of roads and the like are great blessings for trade; but the traders who welcome and perhaps help press forward the universal empire are likely to repent it. They find themselves far more at the mercy of the state, not only because it grows so gargantuan, but also because they cannot shift capital abroad or bargain with competing states. Losing political influence and social standing, they are usually taxed to the limit if not actually plundered. They are the more suitable for flaying as supposedly unproductive elements, speculators, and profiteers; levies on them may be presented as justice. And if a branch of commerce or production seems especially lucrative, the government is likely to take it over and make it an official monopoly. For the governors, private wealth means waste, as it is lost for their purposes. Confident in their capacities to command, they feel sure that they can direct the economy, or at least a large share of it, for the greater benefit of the state or themselves.

There is also political reason for autocracy to be unenthusiastic about private gain. It is an affront that men enrich themselves and rise to substantial station otherwise than by the grace of the ruler; and the wealthy, like the nobles, are always potential stirrers of dissent. Even if there is no fear of private power, tendencies to control are strong, as the bureaucrats assert themselves. The imperial spirit of order extends everywhere, and in the very large state there seems more to gain by control and central direction than in the smaller and less self-sufficient one.

Private wealth, industry, and commerce are also profoundly uncongenial to the imperial spirit, as they represent different and independent values. The marketplace is the image of uncontrol, and the merchant, with his diverse contacts and nonpolitical attitude, is a bearer of heterodoxy and potential subversion in the authoritarian society. Antieconomic and hierarchic in spirit, despising the bourgeois mentality, the empire in a sense represents the victory of the soldier and the politician over the merchant. It is built on militaristic virtues and a sense of command, for which commerce, business calculation, and free choice are hateful. Even if the empire becomes pacific, private property is ever a disturbing element to the perfect order; almost all the utopias banish private ownership. The great empires admit it in practice, but without relish. Likewise, the commercial class, which rests on free disposal of property, is generally demeaned and often made pariahs. If merchants can prosper at all, it is usually by use or misuse of official ties.

There is, then, no reason of principle to refrain from burdening the economy while powerful motives drive the rulers to take much for their own use and to control the rest. The Great Khan expressed this common feeling when he said, "I subdued you by the power of my sword, and consequently whatever you possess belongs of right to me; if you gamble, therefore, you are sporting with my property." [Marco Polo, Bk. II, chap. 34] How fully or in what ways such claims are exerted has varied widely, but ordinarily the sovereign of a universal empire asserts a theoretical right over all and everything. Early in the Egyptian Old Kingdom the concept was laid down that the pharaoh was master of everything the sun went around. Users of land had to pay a rent, for the collection of which a register of taxpayers was set up; and the pharaohs held directly huge estates. In the nonmonetary economy, nearly everyone but the cultivators of the land lived on the royal revenues. In times of disorder and weakness of the central power, land reverted to private ownership and there grew up something of a middle class, which survived through the looser Middle Kingdom. But in the firmly centralized and widely conquering New Kingdom, there were only rulers on top and their servants below, as the pharaohs of the Eighteenth Dynasty again made most or all land their property, either in direct ownership, or as temple holdings and fiefs of favorites. [*134*, pp. 87–88, 93; *113*, p. 598] As was customary in

Near Eastern empires, foreign trade was a near monopoly of the royal house, much of it being carried on in the political form of exchange of gifts with other rulers, and traders were only paid agents of the monarch. [570, p. 255; 117, p. 173; 104, p. 38] Apparently domestic trade was also largely in the hands of the government, and private trade was insignificant, for texts down to the first millennium make no mention of merchants and there seem to have been no laws governing trade. [113, p. 598; 114, Pt. II, p. 28]

Relations of private and commercial property to imperial power appear clearly in Sumeria. In the preimperial city-states, land was privately held except for a fraction belonging to the temple estate; and merchants were important. [122, pp. 74–76] After the rather short-lived Akkadian empire was overthrown, the Third Dynasty of Ur, ruling the entire land, had a regimented and statist economy, with most arable land owned by the crown and foreign trade under the central administration. [135, p. 146] Crafts were organized in controlled guilds as royal monopolies. [100, p. 262] When the power of Ur in turn fell and the region was divided into small states, trade and private property again reached a high development; many traders were able to purchase landed estates and to act independently of the government. However, when the king of Larsin, one of the Sumerian states, gained extensive power and added a god-determinative to his name, the number of private transactions decreased sharply and the names of wealthy families disappeared from the record. With subsequent incorporation in the greater Babylonian empire there were many more administrative records but few mentions of private merchants, as the government took most trade, especially that of the chief commodity, wool, into its own hands. Private trade continued only by government permission; no names of rich individuals come down from Hammurabi's Babylon. [123, pp. 113–122] All land became property of the king, to be neither mortgaged nor sold by individuals. [251, p. 62]

Other ancient empires seem to have sought similarly to control their economies. The great granaries of Harappa have been taken to suggest state control of grain in the presumed Indus Valley empire. [210, p. 138] In Persia, Darius made all land the property of the Great King, which meant that no one was secure in possession of it; there was much interference in the economy [252, p. 193], and the trading community was held in great contempt. [253, p. 175]

The establishment of the Maurya empire in India (325–184 B.C.) saw a particularly violent shift of theory and practice from the previous fairly free market economy to rigorous control and virtual totalitarianism. According to accounts, possibly exaggerated by admirers, all branches of activity were regulated in the empire. The tax on crops was heavy, and cultivators were expelled if they failed to produce properly. [*194*, p. 135] There were state monopolies of salt, mines, and probably shipping; and thirty-two state overseers supervised the manufacture of metalwares, textiles, liquor, and so forth. All prices were fixed, down to the fees of courtesans. Imported articles were taken to a central tollhouse to be auctioned under supervision or bought by the state at fixed prices; foreign traders were not encouraged. Sale of local produce was also limited to authorized persons, with profits not to exceed 5 percent; competition and speculation were supposedly eliminated. [*194*, pp. 166–169; *208*, II, 59; *192*, II, 323–324; *216*, p. 55; *Arthasastra* 4, 3, 2] The once powerful guilds were closely regulated. The huge commercial fortunes of preimperial times, amounting to many millions of dollars in gold [*194*, p. 132], disappeared. Official position became the measure of status, while artisans and merchants were regarded with suspicion, called thieves by the *Arthasastra*, and generally regarded as outrageous profiteers. [*201*, p. 222] Nor was there freedom not to labor. In divided India, there had been multitudes of scholars and teachers; in the empire, to prevent their escaping taxation, men were forbidden to leave productive life for philosophy; only the aged were permitted to become ascetics. [*208*, II, 67]

The Roman empire was remarkable for the stubbornness with which the privatism of the city-state persisted into imperial times, but within a few reigns the old plutocracy was virtually exterminated. Under such emperors as Domitian any fortune that rose above mediocrity was marked for plunder. [*302*, p. 56] Opportunities of private business were steadily narrowed as the state grew, and laissez-faire was in a century turned into its opposite. Credit and banking were hampered by official jealousy, as the emperor himself was the chief banker. [*334*, p. 202] The second emperor, Tiberius, initiated a policy of state control of mines; and the state ran arms, textile, and other industries producing for state needs. [*326*, II, 834] The suspicion with which private societies were viewed extended to large business companies, potentially subversive organizations. [*334*, p. 201] Juvenal treated merchants as very low creatures, and Diocletian berated tradesmen as thieves. Senators were always forbidden to engage in trade. In the late empire the commercial class stood below the humblest landowner. [*303*, p. 247] Exceptionally among empires, land remained in full private ownership, but by the time of Hadrian (117–138 A.D.), it was felt necessary to regulate sternly prices, trade, and occupations. Maintaining this and other Roman traditions, the Byzantine empire fixed prices and wages, controlled shops and trade, and gloried in monopoly and privilege. [*301*, p. 89] Within the confines of the guild-corporations, however, business was given more security and freedom than in most great empires, for the rulers recognized that trade brought in the revenues needed to hire mercenaries. [*311*, p. 422]

In pre-Islamic Arabia, merchants were well regarded; Mohammed himself engaged in trade. But under the Abbasid Califate they came to be despised by the military-bureaucratic elite. [*486*, p. 215] The Turkish empire, which succeeded it, and the Byzantine empire were perhaps more hospitable to merchants than most such polities, as they were relatively prosperous and respected. [*432*, Pt. I, p. 303] But all traders and producers — down to beggars — were closely organized in guilds and thoroughly regulated, prices of all commodities being fixed. [*432*, Pt. I, p. 282] Under Turkish rule, the land of Egypt became again the estate of the ruler, granted in tenancy at his pleasure to those who paid rent or earned his favor, as it had been thousands of years before under the pharaohs. [*134*, p. 93] The sultan had the power, irregularly exercised, to seize patrimonies, which, to be sure, were mostly loot from public funds. After the empire had passed its zenith, the properties of the beheaded became an important part of state revenues. [*431*, p. 133; *432*, Pt. II, p. 30] Since the all-highest set the example of confiscations, underlings were glad to follow, and no wealth was safe. [*439*, p. 55]

The Mogul state was the largest or the only producer of some commodities; it freely engaged in profitable trade, and was likely to take over any business that raised official appetites. [*213*, p. 6; *209*, p. 210] The Mogul owned all land, was legal heir to all fortunes, and was directly or indirectly employer of all except common laborers or holders of his grants. [*199*, p. 222] Shopkeepers might accumulate some wealth, but they dared not let it be seen lest it be confiscated. [*205*, p. 200] It is said that the sight of a rich person without court protection caused in the governors a strange illness curable only by a transfusion of treasure. [*209*, p. 268] In short, all money and goods belonged to the emperor so far as he or his high servants saw fit to claim them. [*202*, p. 85]

The traditional Chinese contempt for trade and merchants is a by-product of the empire and has varied with its fortunes. In the preimperial time of Contending States, merchants were powerful and often reached very high positions; their prestige may have been higher than that of officials. [*21*, pp. 221–223] But the Ch'in empire quickly laid a heavy bureaucratic hand on the economy. Many shopkeepers were penalized or deported, wealthy men were sent to guard duty on the frontiers, commerce was proscribed as the lowest of professions, and the state gave itself a monopoly of salt and iron, and sole ownership of water resources. [*30*, p. 102; *570*, p. 252]

The Hans were at first less totalitarian, but when merchants were able to gain wealth, the officials felt them to be competitors in fleecing the people. [*75*, p. 251] A series of powerful antibusiness measures followed. Iron and salt were again subjected to official monopoly, allegedly to protect the people from exploitation. Merchants had to declare their wealth, which was duly taxed; soon thereafter a price regulation board and state trading companies were set up to eliminate speculation in grain and to garner the middleman's profit for the treasury. [*28*, p. 40] There were ruinous confiscations. [*75*, p. 177] The government objected to any business that employed many workers as a possible focus of subversion. [*570*, p. 328] Merchants were forbidden to become officials; and the middle class, powerful and important early in the dynasty, was degraded and virtually liquidated. [*30*, pp. 114–116; *75*, p. 251; *71*, p. 37] As the dynasty decayed, a powerful minister, Wang Mang (9–23 A.D.), tried to revitalize it by further interventionist measures. He strengthened the state monopoly on salt, iron, liquors, and mining, and had state agencies lend money at 3 percent monthly to protect the people from exploitation. He tried to control prices and stabilize the market by buying and selling. [*52*, p. 109] He declared all land state property, to be shared equally among cultivators. But the empire was no longer strong enough to enforce such measures, and they soon lapsed. [*66*, pp. 84–91; *52*, p. 109] In the Later Han, many merchants prospered by their official and court connections. [*77*, p. 23]

Subsequently, freedom of private enterprise and the standing of

the commercial classes varied inversely with the strength and centralization of the empire, with many fluctuations through succeeding dynasties and periods of division. For example, the Sung
dynasty saw a brief essay in socialism or state capitalism. A great
minister, Wang An-shih, like Wang Mang before him, attempted
again to divide all land equally, part being cultivated for the state,
which handled and stored grain for future needs. According to his
proposal, "the state should take over the entire management of
commerce, industry, and agriculture into its own hands with a view
to succoring the working classes and preventing them from being
ground into the dust by the rich." [29, I, 47–48] His partisans said
that only monopolists and usurers would suffer, but in fact he seems
to have aimed at the destruction of private fortunes. [37, II, 66]
The grand reform was not successful and the dynasty soon afterward lost control of the northern half of the country. Under the
more modest Southern Sung dynasty, merchants improved their
status and were admitted to high circles [39, p. 14]; and revenues
from trade became more important than land taxes.

The Mings, restoring Chinese greatness and territorial integrity
after the Mongol period, turned away from commerce, both internal and external. They kept the old monopolies of salt and iron,
regulated quality and prices, and established government warehouses and shops to make and sell necessities. Taxed and kept
under strict rein, merchants could hope for profitable speculation
only under the protection of officials. [38, pp. 30–32] The merchant
guilds were and remained until the end of the empire largely tools
of the officials. [20, p. 45] A tax of 40 percent on silver and gold
mines reduced them to bankruptcy. [28, p. 199] Even when the
last (Ch'ing) dynasty was rather desperately trying to foster modern industry for defense, it could not rid itself of the idea that the
government, or at least the officials, were entitled to claim any
profits. Whenever they smelled money, great and little mandarins
swarmed around to suck their share; and merchants or industrialists could protect themselves from one set only by buying the favor
of another. [22, pp. 26–27] However, fear saved the wealthy from
the vice of ostentation. [50, p. 160; 43, p. 651]

In China, private property has been a right highly qualified by
social and political exigencies, a concession that the state has re-
tracted at will, just as it has regulated anything or everything in
the life of the people, their building, festivals, music, even manner
of dress. [2, p. 11] Wealth has been acquirable mostly by official

position and has been much less secure than learning. [*65*, p. 132] Merchants have been little esteemed through imperial history, regarded as parasites and lower than peasants. Even when foreign trade was at its best, as under the early T'ang dynasty, it was largely in the hands of foreign merchants. [*40*, Bk. I, p. 203] Yet where they migrated in Asia the Chinese have often proved such capable traders as virtually to monopolize commerce.

The Incas had the socialism that Wang An-shih dreamed of. All land, gold and silver, and anything else he desired belonged to the supreme ruler, the Sapa Inca, divine descendant of the Sun. Since all women were his property, too, adultery was punishable as misuse of his belongings. Production of some articles, as the much desired coca leaf, was monopolized by the state. [*173*, p. 224] As there was no money, taxes were in labor; that is, everyone was supposed to spend his life in the service of the state. Cultivation was partly communal, with much of the crop going into state granaries for general needs. Each ten workers were under a leader, the leaders in turn were under a higher official, and so forth in a pyramid of command up to the divine ruler. [*171*, p. 231; *175*, p. 113] No money was needed; riches consisted in hierarchical position. [*181*, p. 125] Gold was used only for ornament. Trade, which had been substantial prior to Inca rule, radically declined under it. [*170*, p. 170] Goods were exchanged locally by barter, and at a distance by the government, which shifted stores to meet needs. There probably were no merchants. This situation contrasts with that prevailing under the smaller and less united Aztec empire, which had a merchant class, a well-developed commercial system, and, in cacao, a generally accepted currency. [*178*, pp. 86–89]

If, in the isolated Inca empire, political domination was particularly rigorous, the Russian state has in recent centuries been fairly friendly to private property and business. But it was not always so. Ivan IV took nearly half the realm as his personal property [*388*, II, 80], and the Muscovite state generally regarded itself, until after Western influences became strong, as the patrimony of the tsar [M. Fainsod in *391*, p. 240], a natural conclusion from the status of nobles and serfs alike as his slaves. This idea gradually dissipated in the eighteenth and nineteenth centuries; yet as late as 1905 there persisted a feeling that all Russia was personally the monarch's. [*367*, p. 90] Peter carried out large-scale industrialization by state action, making service in industry a public duty for merchants, even as government and military service were obliga-

tions of landowners. He also profited by a host of monopolies ranging from salt and vodka to fish, oil, and oak coffins. [398, pp. 128,
134] Partly as a result of his efforts, Western ideas began to per-
meate Russian society; rights of property were strengthened,
statism retreated, and it became high policy to encourage private
enterprise. But this never really throve or acquired great prestige,
perhaps because it lacked relation to power in the bureaucratic
imperial state; and the role of the state in the economy continued
to be very large under the last tsars. Heavy industry was largely
dependent upon if not controlled by the state, which formed the
framework of the economy. [375, p. 25] At the end of the eighteenth
century, two-thirds of industrial labor was employed by the state;
at the end of the nineteenth, nearly half of the large industrial and
economic enterprises were state-controlled [Mavor in 409, p. 336],
and a large fraction of agricultural land was owned by state or
crown. The Bank of Russia had exceptionally broad powers of
control and surveillance over all aspects of the economy. [368,
p. 50] A nineteenth-century French nobleman wrote, "Russia resembles a great factory, managing in its workshops the activities
and strength of all its inhabitants without exception." [368, p. v]
By corollary, the middle class had neither power, prestige, nor
security; their social standing was low, as was their general reputation. Much of the trade was left to Jews or to foreigners. As
Struwe said in 1898, "The farther east one goes in Europe, the
weaker in politics, the more cowardly and meaner becomes the
bourgeoisie"; or, as Kerensky put it, in treating his failure in 1917,
"The class which accumulates wealth, the middle class, the bourgeoisie, was ever the unwanted child throughout our history." [385,
p. 30]

It is a truism that the political spirit is inimical to the economic,
and the devotees of power and glory look down on moneymaking.
Napoleon, for example, despised commerce and merchants as soul-
less and unpatriotic. [476, p. 60] But it is the universal empire that
can, by virtue of its world rule, best draw the wealth and production of the land to itself. Some generations may pass before control
is made extensive, and its thoroughness has been greater or less,
for reasons that deserve elucidation; but the temptations to exert
political power are overwhelming, and the authoritarian imperial
state is not consonant with an economy wherein men are free to
enrich themselves and wealth is protected by law. On the contrary,

where enrichment is encouraged and moneymaking is more important for status than political position, there one finds a nonbureaucratic, nonmilitaristic, nonauthoritarian, and open society.

The empire gains much by taking over the economy and by weakening or destroying the middle classes or bourgeoisie. A disturbing element is removed, the groups that in other circumstances would be the best support of a republican government. Holders of private wealth can use it to influence policy, thus flawing the perfection of sovereign power. Mastery of the economy also makes available resources that freer states might envy, for the building of canals or palaces, or for the maintenance of a great corps of servants of the autocrat. It is almost a necessity for his stateliness that he be master of productive enterprise as well as captain, judge, and lawgiver. There is also a moral satisfaction in the depression of the middle classes, for this degrades their values. The officials want position, not money, to be the measure of status in the society that is politically, not economically, governed.

There is a certain price, no doubt, to be paid for this exercise of authority, which conduces to no little waste, confusion, and inefficiency. How great the cost has been one can hardly guess, but if it had not usually proved appalling, totally socialized economies would have long since been the rule where there is nothing to hinder the sovereign from taking all to his own management and profit. That even very great empires have usually allowed much or most of the economy to run itself, subject to their skimming off profits, is a confession of incapacity. It may be, moreover, that power over the economy operates eventually to weaken the effective authority of the autocrat. For it opens countless opportunities to bureaucrats and administrators for corruption and private enrichment; harsh laws and controls mean evasion and bribery; political influence guides economic decisions for the benefit of the officials and controllers, not for that of the state. The functionaries may thus use their powers to make themselves really independent of their nominal master.

RULE WITHOUT LAW

To govern the great society, it may be assumed that there must be rules, definite, logical, coherent, and acceptable for their equity, fixing relations between persons and the consequences of actions.

The subjects should have clear instructions as to what they must, may, or may not do. The larger and the more complex the state, the greater need that human interactions be guided by an explicit code instead of custom and informal understanding; that is, the greater the need for law.

But the unhampered rule of a single will is essentially lawless. The imperial society rests on power and position, not agreement, which implies equity. There is no constitution; what are the rules of the game when one player can change them to suit his fancy? Where no fundamental law regulates the political power, there are no real rights, and the decrees that govern the humble have rather the character of commands than of law. Regular rules are necessary to facilitate the decision of nonpolitical matters and to accustom people to certain lines of conduct. But laws, if strictly followed, limit freedom of action; by defining power, they carve out areas of individual freedom. If applied equally and uniformly, they secure impartiality, for which monopolistic power has no love. It desires not that rights and position should be impersonally and legally secured, but that they should rest insecurely upon personal relations. Men should not look to law for help, but to their superiors. The pleasure of the great is their ability to act without constraint. Law impedes the caprice of the bad ruler and the justice of the good.

Hence the attitude of autocratic empires toward law has been ambiguous; they have usually liked to decree laws liberally as manifestations of the sovereign will, but have been wanting in feeling for legality. As was said of the tsarist state, "There are thousands of laws in Russia, but there is no law." [423, p. 440] The laws are less respected because they are too many and can be made or canceled at any time, modified or neglected according to the feelings of the hour. The more difficult to make laws, the higher their prestige; but autocrats often do not take their own laws seriously. And when power is arbitrary, punishment is not a disgrace but a misfortune.

Cicero, as the Roman republic was waning, thought of natural law as supreme and immutable; for emperors generally, law has been little more than the imperial will, perhaps seasoned by custom and the traditions of imperial ancestors. As Darius said, "By the favor of Ahura Mazda these countries showed respect for my law; as it was said to them by me, thus it was done." [249, p. 105] Where the same power makes and enforces the rules, where the emperor is supreme legislator, executive, and judge together, law plays a small part in the ordering of society and receives much less attention than in freer societies.

The empire that most nearly represents an exception is the Roman, unusual in this as in other and related ways. There the legal profession was important during the Principate, and important schools of jurisprudence refined legal concepts to an unprecedented sophistication, eventually culminating in the great codification made under Justinian in the middle of the sixth century. Edicts of a Caesar (which might have been very numerous; more than 1,200 rescripts of Diocletian have been preserved) had particular force only during his reign, but those that seemed useful were picked out and preserved; the accumulated corpus of the civil law came to represent experience and a growing practical response to the needs of the state. [320, p. 14] This it continued to be; through the Middle Ages and into modern times the Roman law represented not only an intelligent solution to many problems of social and economic relations, but also, and more important, a means of strengthening authority. It stood for the rule of princely prerogative over custom and tradition, not the rule of law to protect rights and make free.

The obvious reasons for relatively greater attention to law in the Roman empire are respect inherited from the republic for private property, the continuation of republican forms, and the retention of some local autonomy for a century or more. There was more need for law as relations among different groups called for adjustment partly in terms of traditional ways. Thus an outstanding Roman production is the *jus gentium*, a sort of universal code to harmonize differences among laws of different nations. [320, pp. 12–13] Roman law, however, generally had an imperial character. Even while republican forms were observed, the emperor decreed or decided what he would. In time the sole legal form came to be imperial fiat [285, p. 342], and the lawyers attributed to the ruler unlimited powers, while the law was degraded to an emanation of his will. As Justinian said, "Who is so arrogant as to scorn the judgment of the prince, when lawyers themselves have clearly and precisely laid down that imperial decisions have the force of law?" [301, p. 27]

The jurists of the empire — a number of whom were Greeks —

displayed no great originality, and their work was very largely based on the ever-respected traditions of the republic. From the middle of the third century, Roman jurisprudence was little more than compilation. [*353*, p. 142] Interpretation became narrow and mechanical, until in 426 it was enacted that only five classic jurists could be cited and, if these disagreed, the verdict should be decided by majority vote among them. [*307*] In the empire, moreover, law lost the political importance it had enjoyed in republican days when a great series of statutes helped regulate life and the state for generations to come. The legal profession degenerated to a corps of ignorant and greedy confounders of justice for money [*314*, I, 536], while the officials turned law to purposes of extortion, as testified by the New Testament injunction, "And if any man will sue thee at the law, and take away thy coat, let him have thy cloke also." [Matt. 5:40]

It was the disunited Greeks, not the Romans, who gloried in courts and litigation and cherished the spirit of law. It was a sentiment wholly alien to the imperial spirit that Heraclitus expressed: "The people must fight for law as for a rampart." [*286*, p. 66] Again and again Greek orators praised law as the fundament of their state, and poets sang of law, as Pindar: "Law, sure foundation-stone of cities, dwells with Justice and Peace, dispenser of wealth to man." [*Olympia* 13, in *327*, p. 48] To an incredulous Persian monarch a Spartan explained that the ruler of his people was "law, which they fear more than thy people fear thee." [Herodotus, VII, 104] As Aeschines, a fourth-century B.C. Attic orator, explained, "Autocracies and oligarchies are administered according to the temper of their lords, but democratic states according to established laws." [*327*, p. 134]

Most empires have been much less legalistic than the Roman. Hammurabi's code is famous but probably represents a regression from the legal concepts of the Sumerians; afterward, the law of the Assyrians sank to exceptional crudity and barbarism. [*137*, p. 146] There has been found no evidence of a law code in pharaonic Egypt, and decrees were made simply as the will of the monarch without reference to past practice or enactments. [*104*, p. 44] The Incas ruled their immense domain with only remembered and doubtless elastic rules. Judges punished mostly as they found proper, much as Nazi courts were told to follow not precise law but "healthy racial feeling." In the looser Aztec society there was punishment by fines or forced labor; the more integrated Inca realm, without money and expecting all to serve anyway, had only the primitive physical punishments of beating or death. [*178*, pp. 112–113]

In the Turkish empire, law was largely ethicoreligious, understanding that each case was to be judged not with the impersonality of Western law, but with moral objectives and in the light of the overall interest of the community. [*432*, Pt. II, p. 121] The Sacred Law supposedly stood over the sultan himself, but it was interpreted elastically by the ruler's jurist-theologians or often ignored. For example, it forbade eunuchs, but these swarmed in the palace; it allowed few taxes, but taxes multiplied. [*436*, pp. 158–159; *435*, p. 156] The Mogul emperor often sat in judgment and had his cadis in the provinces; but there was no law code as now understood, and most disputes were left to the parties to settle as they might or to the traditional caste courts. [*213*, p. 9; *205*, p. 233]

The attitudes of tsarist Russia were ambiguous. As Ivan the Terrible expressed it, right conduct for the subjects consisted simply in carrying out the wishes of the sovereign. [*412*, p. 27] But the gradually modernized state required many definite rules; these, although rigorous if literally applied and often perhaps unjust, might always be softened by the paternal benevolence of the ruler. [*368*, pp. iv–v] There was a superabundance of uncoordinated legislation, although tsars from 1649 to 1835, even the willful Peter, tried in vain to codify the great mass, which was of benefit mostly to extortionists and bribe takers. [*402*, p. 18] Nor were lawyers much respected. Nicholas I, holding them responsible for the French Revolution, wanted none in Russia. [*395*, p. 64]

The Chinese empire perhaps best illustrated the incompatibility of law with the well-developed imperial order. The official philosophy of the Ch'in conquerors was Legalism, but this stressed law merely in the sense of harsh rules to manage society for the benefit of power. Confucianists felt that laws were an unsuitable instrument of rule, since the empire rested more firmly on moral authority. [W. T. de Bary in *19*, p. 172] Upright people in any event should follow the emperor's good example without need for instructions. [*20*, p. 85] Under the later dynasties, statutes were numerous, detailed, and carefully drawn; but they were not strictly applied, and no need was felt that they should be. [*76*, p. 307; *20*, p. 96] As law was always subject to change by imperial will, there was no study of its general principles, if these could be said to exist apart from ethical philosophy. No organ of the government was especially concerned with legislation apart from administration. Crimes were given an ethical interpretation, for example as contrary to filial piety, whereas good acts evinced this virtue. [37, I, 105] In dealing with infractions, administrators were expected to use good judgment according to the case, to be guided not by specific prescriptions but by the desire to find a solution serving welfare and stability. [38, pp. 70–71; 20, p. 41] Many persons in addition to the guilty individual might be held responsible for misdeeds, and this was more morally than legally justified; thus, after the horrendous crime of parricide, the magistrate ordered the houses of neighbors torn down because they should have exerted moral influence. [64, p. 229] There was little idea of commercial law to give security to business transactions, so what law there was dealt mostly with administrative and penal matters. All law was in effect criminal, as civil faults were punishable with a bamboo thrashing or worse. [37, II, 246] If there was no cause for the state to intervene, parties, even in criminal questions, were often allowed to settle their differences as they saw fit between themselves. [54, p. 76] Correspondingly, there were no lawyers, lawsuits were infrequent, and disputes were usually handled informally or by arbitration. [64, p. 225] Villagers had a prudent horror of involvement in lawsuits, likely to be ruinous to both parties. Some Ch'ing emperors even urged that justice be made difficult so that the parties would be encouraged to settle between themselves. [37, I, 125]

The universal empire is thus destined to disappoint those who hail its coming as bringer of perfect law. The rule of force is inherently opposed to the rule of law. In the state governed by command, not by adjustment among competing groups and organizations, people tend to be clients or servants of those above them, patrons or masters of those below; impersonal justice shrinks compared with personal relations. An important duty of the ruler, perhaps his most important function, is to act as final judge and arbiter; in this he needs law only to be able to set it aside for political or personal demands. Justice in his realm is assured not by law but by the high virtues of the ruler; to him eyes must be lifted.

Consequently the great empires have emphasized less the strictly legal and rationalistic direction of society than a religious or ideological guidance. Definite rules, which may limit power, are less useful than a looser moral-ethical sense, which can always be interpreted as convenient and which better serves to justify authority. But unhappily, if law ceases to limit the freedom of the supreme rulers, it also loses the respect of the subalterns of the emperor, who like him are set free to please themselves. Thus exaggerated authority undermines itself.

BUREAUCRACY

One man can oversee only a few of his fellows, and the more closely and thoroughly he would control them, the fewer can he personally supervise. The emperor who would manage a huge domain must have an army of subalterns, foremen, managers, and controllers, a great pyramid atop which he can sit in regal command. If an army is necessary to conquer, a bureaucracy is necessary to reap the fruits of power. This does not imply an organization of quite the Weberian definition. It is not necessarily orderly. It must have a regularized hierarchy in which each level enjoys power over those below and in return owes loyalty to those above, but a certain confusion of relations may be deemed politically advantageous. The bureaucracy is quite surely not distinguished for impartiality, a virtue alien to the imperial political spirit and frail when attacked by gold. It need not be specialized, at least in the upper levels. Chosen more for loyalty than for capacity, the higher bureaucrats are likely to be general managers, subject to switching to various departments. The organization may not even be professional if the empire is corrupt and gives great opportunities for enrichment of officials; posts may then be given only for short terms, in order to be given or sold again. But the imperial bureaucracy is democratic-equalitarian in theory and probably in intent of the autocrat; it suits the high power to recruit men of all conditions. The bureaucracy is permanent, probably of complex organization with many grades and involved subordinations; and it is a principal source of power and prestige. It is also as large as the state is swollen, probably disproportionately larger, despite supposed efficiencies of scale, than all the little governing apparatuses displaced by it, and much more important as an avenue of advancement.

This has been the usual story: the ruler seeks reliable men for his service, and there grows up a complicated system of status and divided function, each layer clutching some of the power that flows down from the ruler. Although the smaller pre-Inca communities had been almost unstratified [172, p. 41], the Incas rapidly built up an enormous apparatus, 1,331 officials for every 10,000 men, headed by governors over 40,000 families and viceroys of the four quarters. [178, p. 99; 175, p. 47] The "accountants" were the living law and record books, charged with remembering all manner of rules and traditions, history, and laws. The first empire builder of the Near East, Sargon of Akkad, built up an administrative state; after him, the Third Dynasty of Ur finished replacing the old aristocracy by a bureaucratic elite. An army of controllers swarmed over this state, checking and certifying; the assignment of two pigeons to the kitchen had to be documented and sealed. [100, pp. 253–267]

The pharaohs of the Old Kingdom, setting aside the old aristocracy, established a bureaucracy apparently as elaborate as any subsequent one. Administration was divided into departments, such as justice, taxation, public works, and defense. Almost two thousand official titles were in use; a standard system of ranking them was introduced early in the Fifth Dynasty, as the state was just passing its pyramid-building zenith, so that in the wondrous hierarchy everyone was unequal to everybody else. [89, pp. 11, 300] In the New Kingdom, after centuries of disorder and decentralization, a huge apparatus was again built up to rule the whole land directly under the pharaoh. [95, p. 237] Administrators had the honor of using white garments; they were untaxed and yet enjoyed a secure livelihood. [134, pp. 86, 98] A document of the time asserted: "The scribe is released from manual tasks, it is he who commands" [97, p. 149]; another stated: "The scribe orders the destinies of everyone." [141, p. 151] Officials had broad personal powers rather than circumscribed professional duties [104, p. 36]; the higher ranks of the army, the priesthood, and the palace service were open to them. [88, p. 175] As the New Kingdom matured, position was increasingly dependent on education; even persons of lowly origin, having learned writing, forms of reports, bookkeeping, and the like in the scribe schools, could rise to the highest ranks. [114, Pt. I, pp. 43, 52] The hierarchy was complex; a servant of Queen Hatshepsut had fifteen titles. [462, p. 24]

More gradually than most, the Roman empire grew into a centralized bureaucratic empire. But in due course it evolved a large and highly structured and graded apparatus, open in theory to men of all classes up to the highest ranks; promotion, as it commonly was in such setups, was largely by seniority, except as position was purchased [324, p. 445], with higher ranks approved by the emperor. [279, p. 284] The Byzantine empire seems to have developed an even more elaborate system than the Roman, especially as reorganized in the seventh and eighth centuries. There were eighteen grades, and each official had two titles, one honorary and the other of office. Competence was divided and overlapping, and all important posts were directly under the emperor and responsible to him. [C. Diehl in 292, pp. 729–730]

The recruitment of the Turkish administration was peculiar. The Sultan bought, captured, and especially conscripted Christian boys, preferably between fourteen and eighteen, made them slaves, and cut them off from all previous associations. [435, p. 49] Officials specially skilled in judging boys graded them; some went into relatively menial positions, some went into the elite military forces, some were picked as future administrators. These received special leadership training, being taught Turkish history, arts of war, languages of the empire, manners and decorum, and, above all, Moslem ethics and law. [435, pp. 71–77] So prepared, they could rise, according to faithfulness and ability, to the very highest positions; the vizier and the governing class in general were slaves. [439, pp. 23–25; 435, p. 44] The Sultan's slave family, some 80,000 strong, monopolized positions; it was a privilege to be such a slave, and the Moslem-born were excluded from power in their own empire.

This system was decidedly successful. Drawing upon the subject populations to furnish the staff of government, it well solved the problem of governing a great empire of diverse peoples alien in culture and religion to the small minority of conquerors. Slave recruitment was also a potent method of assimilation, as promising boys of non-Moslem and non-Turkish origin were converted to Islam and Turkish culture. [435, pp. 67–68] But most of all it provided a service wholly amenable to the Sultan's will. Moslem muftis, with some confidence in their religious position, might mildly resist his measures; but the vizier, however rich and mighty, knew that he was as much subject to his master as was a horse. [435, p. 230]

The Turkish slave bureaucracy was in the logic of age-old Near

Eastern autocracy; it was partly built on Byzantine traditions of service, and features were copied from Persia, which enjoyed a minor imperial revival under the Samanid Dynasty of the ninth and tenth centuries. [435, p. 23] It could endure only so long as the autocracy was vigorous. As the Sultanate weakened in the eighteenth century, Moslems secured, at first by bribery, recruitment of their sons as slaves [439, p. 35], and so replaced the Christians in the bureaucracy. [432, Pt. I, pp. 44–45, 56] It then lost its character and usefulness.

In India, the Maurya empire had a highly organized but imperfectly known bureaucracy to carry on its extensive economic controls. [216, p. 55] Akbar, shaper of the Mogul empire, reformed local government, reorganized taxation, and set up a military-civilian bureaucracy with thirty-one ranks, status corresponding to the number of fighting men the official was supposed to furnish. Even such nonmilitary men as poets and cooks were fitted into this hierarchy. [214, p. 104] All were recruited or promoted according to the emperor's fancy or that of higher officials, without formal examination. [214, p. 114] Men of ambition or ability inevitably sought a career with the government; none other was possible. [205, p. 233] Some were wonderfully enriched as a reward for their devotion and political skills, as pay of the officials, or mansabdars, ranged from 1,200 to 560,000 rupees per year, while skilled workers earned 40. [214, p. 137] But they were utterly insecure and could not transmit wealth or position to their descendants. [212, pp. 306–307]

The Russian administration was built up somewhat irregularly after Muscovy became powerful. Ivan the Terrible (1547–1584) reorganized the service and first made it more or less systematic. In the sixteenth century the need for administrators led to the recruitment of many outside the aristocracy, and some civil servants acquired substantial importance by virtue of their usefulness. [359, pp. 209–210] But the departments (*prikazy*) before Peter were rather loosely articulated, without logically delimited functions; each was at once administrative, judicial, and financial. There was no coordination in the confusion of overlaid agencies, each of which worked directly under the tsar and appealed to him. Peter endeavored to copy the ministerial system of the West, and put functionaries on a straight salary instead of fees, in hopes of making them not only more honest but more directly dependent.

[359, p. 223] He also divided the service into fourteen ranks, much like those of the Byzantine empire centuries earlier. [301, p. 298] These were to be the criterion of aristocracy, life nobility being the reward of those who reached the fifth rank and hereditary nobility of those who attained the ninth, with equal opportunities for all to enter at the bottom and to climb by merit. These hopes were frustrated from the beginning, of course, as members of established families filled the high positions and the lowly were rarely able to progress [404, p. 260; 377, p. 421]; but such continued to be the theory as long as the imperial government endured. As Peter strengthened the government, he naturally also enlarged it; in a quarter-century staffs nearly doubled. [359, p. 229] Thereafter the apparatus grew slowly, until toward the end of the nineteenth century an incomplete count showed 435,000 functionaries. [360, p. 178]

The serious weakness of such bureaucracies is that, however fully the emperor may exercise his prerogative to name or dismiss his servants, he can personally know only a few of them. The others have to be selected and rewarded or punished by the selectees of the sovereign, and so on for several degrees down to the humblest. But by delegating authority over personnel, the emperor in effect gives away part of his power; each official who can select his subordinates has a little empire of his own. A partial solution, enabling the sovereign to profit by the assignment of positions instead of giving away this prerogative, is to sell positions; and this has been done to some extent, informally and corruptly, or openly and legally, in many empires. But the cure is worse than the disease, as those who have purchased positions consider them a property to be used. Far better is a regular, objective procedure for selecting suitable and presumably loyal men, whereby status rests upon criteria of effectiveness for the service of the emperor.

The best developed of imperial states, the Chinese, made the great invention of a civil service based on an impersonal, written examination system. This was never the sole means of entry but, after it became well settled, was the most prestigious and the most important; and it did much to give the empire a reliable, efficient, and relatively honest corps of administrators. It also had profound effects upon all of Chinese society and life. The invention was made early. It is reported that about 165 B.C. the early Han emperor Wu, urged by scholar-bureaucrats to test applicants by written examination, asked set questions of men recommended for office. [*39,* p. 4; *71,* p. 33] At first this procedure was sparingly used, but it gradually gained acceptance. In 124 B.C. a college was founded to prepare candidates; its enrollment expanded incredibly to 30,000 later in the dynasty. Teaching Confucianism, it prepared nearly all new officials. [*52,* p. 106; *28,* p. 51] The literati thus succeeded in reserving high office for themselves, and they retained this monopoly or near monopoly through many centuries. It was possible in theory for nonaristocrats to rise in the imperial service; some did so during the Han and later periods, but the need for long preparation made it very difficult. The bureaucratic elite was a rather large one, counting more than 130,000 officials by the first century B.C., although they had little to do but tax and recruit corvée. [*61,* p. 96]

The examination system, like other imperial institutions, fell into disuse during the long disorders after the Hans; but the T'ang and following Sung dynasties revived and perfected it, to form an aristocracy of brains and character. It became in time almost the sole means of entry into the imperial service. [*40,* Bk. I, p. 257] There were also in-service examinations for promotion or dismissal. Great efforts were made to secure impartial grading; papers were even copied to prevent recognition of handwriting. More new blood was brought in than previously, although sponsorship or protection still played a part. [*39,* pp. 67–69] Modest rewards were given to those who failed in order to assuage discontent. The civil service, thus selected for thoroughness of indoctrination in the Confucian system of thinking, tended to become at once more efficient and more pliant in the hands of the ruler. [*61,* pp. 164–166, 202–203] At the same time, it made a tight elite of scholars, landowners, and officials, a more stable and close-knit backbone for society than the West has ever had.

Under the Ming and Ch'ing dynasties, the system was further polished. The bureaucracy was made highly selective, narrowed to only 10,000 to 15,000 responsible officials in eighteen ranks, each with its own fine costume and colorful insignia. These were assisted by numerous low-grade clerks, largely hereditary in status, who swarmed in offices through the country. In the nineteenth century there were only about 20,000 ranking bureaucrats, who commanded some 1,700,000 underlings. [*20,* pp. 37, 89; *570,* p. 307] Everyone was eligible to compete except sons of servants, actors, prostitutes, and ordinary soldiers. [56, p. 147] But the increasing impracticality and remoteness from life of the examinations, which required long years of preparation, practically restricted entry to the well-to-do. It was hard to pay a tutor, and tutoring a peasant was frowned upon; the gentry thus became a theoretically open but practically closed and self-regarding circle. Of those who pored for years over the books, only a tiny fraction were allowed to pass the examinations. Then, having managed to gain entry, officials were periodically reexamined and rated by their superiors to determine whether they should be promoted or demoted. This was no formality; it was seldom possible to make a career without at some time stepping down. [76, pp. 354–356] Official position was thus extremely difficult to obtain and hardly less so to keep. But it was the only way to a successful career and to the improvement of the family, as degree holding gave opportunities to acquire great wealth and land, which meant leisure for sons in turn to prepare for examinations. [38, pp. 15–34; 56, p. 103]

Entry based only on knowledge of the classics became through the centuries increasingly unrealistic, as once fairly practical examinations turned into formal exercises dependent upon memory and imitative skill. There were attempts at reform, as that of Wang An-shih in the eleventh century; he wanted efficient officials and said it was wrong to require youths to spend all their time in literary studies. [J. Liu in 19, p. 113; 28, pp. 154–155] But all such efforts were frustrated by the interest of the bureaucracy in keeping the status quo, and the examination under the last two dynasties degenerated into fantastically stereotyped "eight-legged" essays. But strict classicism was not entirely negative. The system was designed to produce men of the right moral qualities as well as mental capacities, not original thinkers or independent managers, but assiduous imbibers of the Confucianist world view, indoctrinated conformists, men alienated from the people but dedicated to the service of the emperor. These it did produce better than any other.

But however skillfully organized and directed, the bureaucracy is no small problem for its lord. Able to degrade and make more or less impotent the aristocracy, the middle classes, and all independent leadership, the autocrat is driven by necessity to raise up a new and powerful class in his service. This he must do in order to govern, and the better organized his service the more effective his will. But the tool is composed of men with wills of their own; and in raising up a new apparatus, the emperor creates a new power between himself and the country, and in spreading his rule he dilutes it. In part, the bureaucracy is bound to support him by its self-interest as well as the imperatives of command; just as the emperor needs officials to govern, they need an emperor as symbol and center of a firm and settled political order, in which not businessmen nor warriors but bureaucrats find security and power. But the bureaucracy must decide all that the emperor lacks time, information, or patience to decide personally. It is a tremendous repository of knowledge and experience; it controls most channels of information, can often determine what matters are brought before the emperor on the basis of what recommendations, and so may virtually make the decision. And execution is no less important than decision; the bureaucracy can determine to a large extent how or whether the ruler's commands become reality. The autocrat will probably try to drive by fear and seek by creating insecurity to make all more dependent upon himself; to prevent the bureaucrats from combining against him, he may resort to various devices, most commonly dealing separately with different groups or agencies and setting them against one another. But perfect obedience is a dream. Fear begets apathy and irresponsibility; insecurity and short terms of office engender deceit and greed. The bureaucrats have their own interests, different from those of the master; and, whatever loyalty may be engendered, each is more concerned to please his immediate superior than the distant demigod. Hence, so far as the empire has a ruling class, it is the officialdom. The emperor is likely to find his servants sucking away the substance of his power while leaving him the form and the symbols.

INNER COURT

The emperor requires more than a host of helpers to administer his dominions. He also wants a large number to provide for his personal needs, safety, dignity, and pleasures — a royal household. Naturally, the all-powerful ruler surrounds himself with a myriad of cupbearers, fanners, spittoon bearers, hairdressers and manicurists, doormen, cooks, miscellaneous entertainers, and many flunkies who perhaps do little but stand around decoratively. Safety being a prime need, there will be a bodyguard, supposedly of the most trustworthy to be found. And as sexual urges and vanity loom large, there will be girls, numerous beyond the biological capacities of the ruler. They will be maintained largely for appearances of luxury and pride in the ownership of beauty, the most desirable of commodities; they require segregation, the more so as the ruler cannot personally attend to them, and the harem may grow into a second court.

The services any single person needs are small, and capacity for enjoyment is limited. But the personal service of the emperor would expand indefinitely, until it becomes a burden on the revenues of the omnipotent power. It is politically useful, contributing to the glorification of the ruler; the more uniformed and pretentious lackeys at his feet and the more lavish and gargantuan his palatial residence, the greater his elevation over ordinary humans. Yet the lackeys in turn require more staff to provide for them, from cooks to chambermaids, just as more concubines require more eunuchs, guards, attending women, and the like. And the larger the palace, the more persons to fill its rooms and halls and to carry on all the activities and entertainments implied. So as long as money can be found, the household can grow for its own as well as for the emperor's benefit, and possibly more for the former. Those in contact with the monarch like to adopt his standards of self-indulgence and sometimes his laziness, finding this not only humanly agreeable but a badge of status. Those closest to him can most effectively put in his ear the desirability of more luxuries for himself, which profit mostly themselves, while it is impossible to suggest that the ruler of the world should stint himself. Consequently, the household can form a sort of apparatus working for its own improvement, with all the advantages of being nearest to the center of power. It may fill a political purpose, too. All who wish the emperor to govern less himself and to drop the reins for them to pick up will probably encourage him to become engrossed with luxuries and soft dalliances that fill his days and sap his will.

Withal, if the autocrat is quite dispassionate, all the adjuncts of his daily life may have little more political influence than the horses in his stable. But unless he is extremely strong-minded, those who cater to his pleasures are better placed to influence his feelings than those who present official reports at appointed hours. His intimates are for the most part those whose company he enjoys;

probably even barbers are chosen as much for their charming manners as for their special arts of coiffure. Occasionally, a ruler has made very capable men his boon companions; but it is hardly to be expected that, even when weary of wine, women, and lighter diversions, he should choose the ablest administrators to while away the hours. The intimates and toadies of the court are better trained than the civil servants in the subtleties of interpreting and pandering to his moods and whims, these being their chief and perhaps only qualifications. Very likely, also, the autocrat will feel more comfortable in taking their advice, as he knows them better and probably trusts them more; they, moreover, are more totally his creatures than civil servants, who acquire a shred of standing of their own by occupying permanent and recognized positions in a great apparatus which the emperor must feel is something of a power beyond himself.

Thus monarchs of vast empires — if not the iron-willed conquerors of the world or founders of dynasties, their softer successors — have built up large personal apparatuses around themselves. These followers constitute the group most dependent upon the ruler, as they live only by his favor, which is the more constantly in question and the more personal as contact is frequent and close. It also may be the most egalitarian of political groups, the monarch often preferring those who have no pretenses to independent standing, those whose dependence is not merely complete in reality but psychologically total; slaves and ex-slaves, eunuchs drawn from the lower classes, girls recruited from anywhere, are likely to suit the royal fancy and occupy leading places in the household. Nowhere else can one rise so rapidly and so easily erase lowly origins. But if the inner court is of all the most dependent on royal whim, at the same time it can best rule its master. By studying all the tricks and arts of influencing him — and they have nothing else to study — the servants and confidants often rule him who seems to rule, raising up a power of their own until possibly they emerge, openly or almost openly, as the real sovereign.

For such reasons and also no doubt because of changes in values, the inner court is apt to become more prominent as the imperial order ripens toward decay. Two generations after the Egyptian New Kingdom had reached its acme of power, royal favorites, mostly of the harem or harem children, rising and falling precipitously with changes in the atmosphere, played a leading part in politics and helped bring on the great political crisis of Ikhnaten's day. [*120*, p. 268] Two centuries later, Twentieth Dynasty phar-aohs had surrounded themselves with foreign slaves and officials, probably because they were believed dependable. Rameses III was the intended victim of a harem plot, and the punishment of the accused was entrusted to no regular court but to a board of inti-mates, some of them foreign slaves: two treasurers, a fanbearer, a herald, and four cupbearers. [*124*, p. 217; *94*, p. 498]

Roman Caesars preferred ex-slaves and slaves around them, men of the north and the west for the guard, refined easterners for the domestic functions; the lower their social standing in Rome, the less likely that they should aspire to take the throne themselves. [*313*, pp. 36, 56] Freedmen of Claudius became so powerful they were treated as near divine. Hadrian wooed the freedmen of Trajan in order to secure his own adoption as heir; after succession he prudently lowered their status. [*313*, p. 42] Although the Roman empire, rather exceptionally, never knew real mistress rule, from time to time members of the ruler's family, concubines, and female slaves enjoyed sway at court, such as Claudius' wife, Messalina, or Nero's mother, Agrippina, and his mistress, Poppaea. On occa-sion actors and dancers were influential; the frivolous Elagabalus (218–222) enjoyed placing mimes, athletes, and barbers in high positions. [*313*, pp. 59–62; *288*, p. 24] Those who basked in the imperial favor often became very rich, and not infrequently were murdered for it. But servants and courtiers were usually elastic enough to pass indifferently from one reign to another. One high palace official, more fortunate than his masters, fawned impartially on ten Augusti, six of whom ended bloodily. [*313*, p. 43] In the later empire the court swelled enormously, as the Caesar turned to secluded splendor.

The brief empire of the Incas does not seem to have escaped such trends. The first really great ruler, Pachacuti, married not only his sisters but all the many half-sisters of a polygamous house-hold. The seraglio remained modest by Old World standards, with only some two or three hundred concubines [*173*, pp. 123–124], but harem politics and political meddling of the guard were on the rise prior to the arrival of the Spanish. [*173*, pp. 253 ff.] Palace slaves were achieving confidence and authority; this slavery had become sufficiently attractive that nobles sought it for their sons. [*170*, p. 52]

After Suleiman the Magnificent, influence at the Turkish court centered upon the harem, an elaborately organized department including five or six hundred girls, hardly any of whom knew her origin. [433, p. 292] To maintain position, ministers had above all to stand well with harem powers. [431, p. 134] The eunuchs who staffed it, latterly Negroes, were sufficiently powerful that their head was recognized as the third-ranking individual of the empire, following only the sultan and the grand vizier. Discharged girls were much sought in marriage since they were allowed continued access to the harem. [432, Pt. I, p. 76] Its inmates, like the sultans themselves, were largely isolated from the affairs of the world and so themselves became tools of court influences.

Perhaps the logical outcome of overwhelming despotism is, in fact, eunuch rule, wherein the lowest creatures, sons of the poor or of foreign slaves, mutilated for the convenience of the masters, despised by ordinary men and perhaps the more unprincipled for being despised, become in reality supreme rulers. The use of eunuchs is quite natural where a man stands above law. Some rulers, like the pharaohs, the Sassanid emperors, and the Incas, have risen above the prohibition of incest, an almost universal tabu in the most diverse societies; all imperial monarchs hold their dominion over the bodies of male and female subjects. They are probably eager to serve him sexually as well as politically, as any attention from the all-highest is a supreme honor and a potential means of influence. Thus the ruler may freely indulge not only his instinctive drives but his sense of power; and the possession of a harem is one of the most alluring rewards of empireship, even if most of its beautiful inhabitants are never touched. But a harem must be cared for and must be kept exclusively the ruler's, since the monopoly even of what he may not desire is one of its major charms and the girls should be distracted by no other masculine company. Hence, men are tamed, like domestic animals, by emasculation. Then, being admitted to the center of the royal household, eunuchs can influence if not mold the women who dally with the master. They become educators and confidants of young princes, and intermediaries between the inner recesses and the outside world. At the same time, when the worst misfortune is to arouse suspicions of undue ambitions and everyone is distrusted, the eunuchs best deserve the emperor's trust. Of all men, they are most his, because they are not qualified to occupy the throne themselves, because they are of humble, often foreign, birth and have no influential families who might hope through them to step to power, and because they cannot press for inheritable position. They have nothing and can hope for nothing but their position in the favor of the lord.

In the New World, animal husbandry was not sufficiently developed for the discovery of castration. Elsewhere, eunuchs seem to have been prominent in the universal empires, so far as knowledge extends. They were apparently used in the Egyptian New Kingdom; they surrounded the Assyrian kings and played a large role in many subsequent Near Eastern empires. In the Achaemenid Persian empire they were quite influential and sometimes dominant, as in the reign of Xerxes, who was under the sway of his eunuch chamberlain. [252, p. 267] Later, a eunuch who had managed to make and unmake kings and had murdered most of the royal family tried to raise himself to the throne. He was rejected because of his condition; a false beard was insufficient evidence of manhood. [252, pp. 363–364] In Rome, eunuchs were at first held in great repugnance, and early Caesars legislated against them. But they became numerous and powerful from Claudius and Nero onward, members of the imperial entourage, confidants and trusted agents, police, and spies. [570, p. 357] As Rome progressed to unabashed despotism, eunuchs became at times virtual masters of the palace. By the fourth century it was considered proper enough that high dignitaries should be eunuchs, as was usually the emperor's chamberlain. [326, I, 570; 313, p. 35] The Roman empire in the East became a paradise of eunuchs, who formed the chief bulwark against the power of the nobility. [437, p. 237] They were favored as the most trusted advisers; even leading generals and admirals were eunuchs. [277, p. 33] So institutionalized were their functions that they were ordered in eight grades. [C. Diehl in 292, p. 730] Later empires of the Near East and India likewise were overrun with eunuchs; the Mogul emperor in particular had hosts of them.

Court eunuchs were of the greatest historical importance in China. They were known from the eighth century B.C., but became prominent with the establishment of the Ch'in empire. The First Emperor named a eunuch grand master of the palace and instructor of his second son; after the emperor's death, the eunuch contrived to bring his pupil to power and during his reign was virtual ruler.

The great Han dynasty was in due course weakened by intrigues between families of empresses and the eunuch corps; the latter eventually succeeded in making the emperor a puppet, bringing about a palace revolution and the fall of the dynasty. [28, pp. 45–46] In subsequent dynasties eunuchs became tremendously strong, regularly coming to the fore as the dynasty deteriorated in the recurrent cycle. Under the T'angs, they were used as messengers between the ruler and his ministers; this led to a eunuch secretariat, which assumed executive functions. [E. Pulleyblank in 78, p. 80] A leading T'ang eunuch accumulated so much wealth that, when luck turned against him, thirty carts a day for thirty days were required (it is recounted) to carry away his jewels, gold, silver, and silks. [60, p. 235] Others of his kind were able to murder emperors.

Because the Chinese were keenly aware of history, eunuchs acquired an evil reputation for intrigue and avidity for power, and they were credited with the ruin of past dynasties — perhaps without entire justice, since historians are prone to regard the greed of mutilated men as baser than that of the manly. Castration need not imply bad character; and the eunuchs, raised from the least educated classes and divorced from normal aspirations, may have been blamed for a rotting that merely offered them opportunities. The first Ming emperor, studying the errors of the past in the hope of making his dynasty perpetual, determined that eunuchs should be kept very few, illiterate, and excluded from politics. [W. T. de Bary in 19, p. 177] But they again crept in, and had attained tremendous power by the latter part of the dynasty. Some Ming emperors were so fully under their tutelage that they never saw other men. [38, p. 57] At length there were seventy thousand eunuchs in charge of nine thousand women, while the high civil service numbered only ten to fifteen thousand. The eunuchs had a special school to qualify them to compete in politics with the bureaucracy. With an organization of their own, they kept secret records and, with the imperial bodyguard, formed a secret terror police. They not only had the ear of the emperor, but held high positions in their own names; one was in charge of the palace treasury, and another was chief of the palace staff [38, pp. 11–14, 74], and they were able practically to set aside the Grand Secretariat of the literati. [4, p. 68] Under a Son of Heaven who preferred simple and satisfying carpentry to the mysteries of statecraft, a eunuch came to receive honors almost equal to those due the sovereign. [C. Hucker in *19*, p. 152] The next holders of the Mantle of Heaven, the Manchus, were keen students of the problem of dynastic decline and determined to avoid this pitfall. They were fairly successful. The first Manchu emperors cleared the eunuchs out of the palace and forbade their employment. Although they gradually returned, they were never again allowed to rise quite so high. [29, II, 28; 32, p. 186]

Thus the entourage of the autocrat, like the bureaucracy, frequently, perhaps always in times of decadence, transforms itself from mere servants to a power in its own right, perhaps the real master of the sovereign. But if the bureaucracy may well be at least as capable of directing the state as the autocrat, not much good is likely to come of the power of the inner court. It secures itself by playing on the ruler's fears and vanity, and multiplying them. Its cunning encourages and applauds his vices, and the vicious ruler needs worse companions to excuse and season his dissipations. Debauchery, sycophancy, inanity, treachery, deceit, and egoism tempered only by hypocrisy are the natural attributes of the inner court; it is fetid with moral disease; it is the focus of the vices of limitless power; its prospect is rotten impotence.

WHO RULES?

When a man has perfect authority to give or to take away, to raise up or to degrade as he pleases, to make law by the proclamation of his pleasure, it might seem idle to ask who rules. Yet even if the emperor is capable, dedicated, and tireless, he cannot know about and decide everything. So far as he is firm and can count on the execution of commands, one may assume that his is the chief voice and the basic power of decision; but there are always real limits to his choices and his freedom. World-conquering Alexander had to turn back when his veterans tired of campaigning to the ends of the earth. Power and effective decision making are always shared in the organization that is far too great for any single man to oversee and discipline. At best, one may hope to guess, in a particular instance, where the greater share of power lies.

Often it seems not to lie in the person of the autocrat. The builders of great imperial organizations may be counted effectively the masters of their states, like Augustus or Napoleon. They are like builders of mammoth corporations, who do not hope to see all details and whose orders are not necessarily always carried out exactly, but who are really in charge; those who want a decision or advocate a policy go to the boss, whose word is effective. But rulers who follow after seldom fully enjoy such substantial power. The apparatus can best be run by the one who has done most to shape it; once set in motion, it acquires momentum and purpose of its own; and the successors of the great builder are likely to find themselves less driving it than being carried by it. It is twice as hard to reshape as to shape originally, to change a course as to set one. But the epigones are far from twice as strong as the conqueror or the dynastic founder. In the ordinary course, they are almost sure to sink to mediocrity or below it in a few generations. Any hereditary endowment of special talents is virtually certain to be diluted or lost, the more so as wives are apt to be chosen for beauty and gentle charms rather than high intellectual abilities and masterful character. It is also difficult for the pampered palace-bred princes to be as tough as those who fight their way to the top. The ruler's chief asset is will and determination, but ease and luxury do not foster these qualities.

Nor has there yet been devised any suitable means of selecting the man who is best equipped to be autocrat; rather, those who make emperors are likely to prefer a docile nonentity. The designation of a successor is likely to depend upon the favor of the ruler or of sundry characters who have influence with him, not upon any ability in administration or grasp of problems of government; oftentimes, indeed, those who are powerful behind the throne hope to retain their status after the passing of their master by pushing a malleable successor. Moreover, men thirst for that which they lack. Those born to very high station, although certain to resist the slightest infringement of their absolute powers, are likely to be satisfied with the appearances and pleasures of sovereign rule, perhaps spiced with occasional exercises of caprice. To be told a hundred times a day that one is all-powerful and monarch of the universe, to be appropriately garbed and saluted on the dazzling throne, is as satisfying as carrying out some reform of the empire, and immensely easier. Why should the autocrat trouble himself as long as the requirements of the palace are met and his courtiers assure him he is doing his duty? When hard decisions become unavoidable, it is easier for the ruler to let others think about and study the questions and then take their policies as his own.

Weakness also compounds itself. Since many, perhaps most, of those revolving close around the autocrat prefer that he be symbol and figurehead, leaving the actual exercise of authority to them, it is politic to engage the autocrat in endless and supposedly vital ceremonies which agreeably exalt his feelings so that he lacks time and spirit to undertake much else. The servants also encourage the master toward sloth and pleasures that occupy his time and attention. A strong character, while yielding to such pressures, might save his government by making capable men his ministers. Small men on great thrones seek rather to secure themselves by naming men no better than themselves to carry on affairs, by undermining their authority, limiting their initiative, setting them at odds, and keeping them insecure and ineffective by frequent dismissal; the result is that the will of the emperor, if he has any, becomes less effective and power is scattered.

It may well be, then, that the ruler depends more on his tools than they on him; that, despite appearances of glory, the central figure, supposed to be the ultimate authority, has little real control of the affairs of the empire. He is, after all, only a single and probably rather ordinary mortal who holds supreme position because the great union requires someone to stand at its head and because he somehow fits the needs of the system. At the center of all, he has all the strategic advantages if he has the capacity and ambition to use them, but his person is only a wheel in the huge machine.

The powers that potentially stand against him may be classified as three, although they usually or always overlap. First and most obvious is the military force, an ever-present menace and cause of death to numberless autocrats and of insomnia to many more; where the state is menaced or unsettled, the holders of physical force have the last word. In the ideal and truly universal empire this force probably would disappear, as there would be no problem of external security, no need to keep a fighting army, only police and guards, whose influence probably would mingle with that of the inner court rather than represent a power of itself.

China has ordinarily been closest to the ideal universal empire and has best developed its institutions; in China, correspondingly, the military power has been most successfully neutralized. Prestige of the soldiers has been kept very low to discourage their aspirations to replace the virtuous and supernal Son of Heaven, while command has been much divided, frequently given to eunuchs, and checked by devices of rotation and separation. As a result, military rebellions or coups have been infrequent and still more rarely successful.

If the empire is much embattled, the power of the army is sure to be higher. The authority of the Roman legions, overthrowing and raising Caesars, was notorious. The masters of the declining republic, such as Marius and Sulla, rested only on the loyalties of their troops, while the support of the legions gave power to Julius and Augustus. The armies were inclined to respect a hereditary successor, unless he proved outrageously bad, like Nero, or even if he were very bad, as long as he catered to them, like Caracalla. But they demanded huge donatives in return for their support, often amounting to the equivalent of some hundreds of dollars per head, and it pained many a Caesar that the larger part of his revenues went to them while he dared cut neither pay nor perquisites. To take one of a host of examples, when Probus expressed a hope that universal peace might make a standing army unnecessary and ordered his men to dig a ditch on a summer day, they cut him to pieces. [*314*, I, 292] The Praetorian Guard was particularly notorious for its haughty assertion of power over the emperor. Tiberius gave this corps, originally established for the safety of the ruler, a commanding position by assembling it in a strong camp dominating the city of Rome; having acquired this physical power, it claimed to represent the people and so to have the right of legitimating authority. [*314*, I, 91] Septimius Severus (193–211) greatly increased the Guard and filled its ranks with non-Italians supposedly more dependent but certainly not less turbulent. Under him, its commander, the Praetorian Prefect, came to be the second official personage of the realm, heading administration, finances, and the judiciary. [*314*, I, 108] But the aggressive soldiery, a proud elite corps, was dangerous even to its own commander. When the Praetorian Prefect named by Alexander Severus proved unpopular with his men, the personal intervention of the Caesar could not save him from slaughter. [*314*, I, 134] The Praetorian Guard, useless as it became, could not finally be suppressed until 312, decades after Rome had ceased to be the center of the empire. Constantine then vanquished the force led by the Guard in support of a rival Caesar and scattered those who escaped slaughter in battle.

It was a prime purpose of the reforms of the Dominate to secure the supremacy of the Augustus over the armies, but this was fairly well achieved for only a generation or two. From the latter part of the fourth century, generals, usually barbarians, held effective power, especially in the West; after the final division, in 395 A.D., the real sovereign of the Western empire was always the Master of the Soldiers. The barbarian rulers preferred not to occupy the throne but to remain closer to their base of power, the army; for the largely ceremonial dignity of the Caesarship they promoted nonentities. [*326*, I, 327, 342]

In the embattled Byzantine empire the army continued to be a real power, despite all the awesome luster enshrining the emperor. Its assent, both real and symbolic, was essential for the succession, and often enough undid the ruler. [C. Diehl in *292*, p. 729] The Turkish empire, which succeeded to its territories, was likewise insecure, and the army could not be denied a political role. Like the Praetorian Guard, the Janissary corps, organized as the most faithful slaves of the Sultan, became virtually his masters. After the fifteenth century they freely made and unmade sultans, requiring generous payment for the former beneficence. [*432*, Pt. I, p. 179] The vizier of one of the greatest sultans, Suleiman the Magnificent, expressed doubts that he could control them in wartime. [*435*, p. 97] They forced the removal of disagreeable ministers and many times emphasized their displeasure by setting the capital afire. When Selim III tried to reform the disgracefully corrupt and undisciplined outfit, they dethroned him; and they could hardly be contravened until they were destroyed in civil conflict in 1826. Similarly the elite guards regiments of Russia in the eighteenth century, after Peter's Westernization had profoundly disturbed the society, made and unmade tsars until Catherine II was able to restore firm royal power.

The military, and especially those who have the advantage of proximity to the capital and the sovereign, can thus exercise real authority. Consent of the army may be necessary for succession, as in the realm of the Incas, and it holds a potential veto over actions unfavorable to itself. But this power is mostly negative. The Praetorian Guards could murder Pertinax (193 A.D.), then put the empire up for auction and install the high bidder; but they could not govern. The military can take or give power but is not organized to exercise it.

Unlike the army, the bureaucracy can hardly set up an autocrat or cast him down from the throne, but it is potentially more effective in setting the course of government. As remarked above, it has many practical advantages. The officials largely determine what problems come before the emperor, supply information and proposals to him, and may have much control of access to his person. Indispensable, fortified by tradition and expertise, possessing the records and secrets, they command respect; only a bold or determined spirit would find it necessary to go against their recommendations. Naturally, then, the administrative apparatus can become very influential, especially in countless smaller matters that never come before the higher powers, and it may virtually rule as well as administer. In the Roman empire, for example, the apparatus steadily grew larger and more influential; at length the Caesars, accustomed to signing what was placed before them, were driven to decreeing that even acts signed by themselves were invalid if contrary to the laws. [326, I, 605] In the Byzantine empire the upper bureaucracy, centered on the Senate, was even stronger and often was able to check the ruler. [C. Diehl in 292, p. 729] In tsarist Russia likewise the bureaucracy gradually gained influence; much enlarged by Peter, it emerged as a dominant force in the state under Catherine II. [551, p. 145] By the time of Nicholas I, a bureaucratic sea of paper covered the government, and it was said that not the emperor but the head clerk was the real power. [402, p. 21] The Russia of the later tsars was perhaps more a bureaucratic than an autocratic state.

It is in China, however, that the bureaucracy, an elite of scholars, has been most effective. Resting supposedly on proved merit, the civil service was the more aware of its moral authority, not to rebel or depose, but to influence and guide. The civil service gained de facto control of its own entry and promotions, despite the nominal omnipotence of the emperor; even the autocratic and often arbitrary Mings never went over the civil service heads in personnel matters. [38, p. 46] Decisions were often made by a council of ministers, and the emperor seldom saw fit to veto them. The civil service, moreover, had moral checks on the emperor. There was established under the T'angs and kept under later dynasties the position of Censor or "Official Historian," to check misgovernment. The Censor was able to criticize the emperor indirectly by attacking his officials or even directly by calling attention to evil conse-

quences of his actions; with a tradition of audacity some dared do
this. The Censorate also acted as keeper of the ruler's posthumous
reputation. [3, p. 363] It kept secret histories of evil as well as good
deeds for moral effect upon the throne and used the past to check
the present, citing decrees of virtuous dead emperors against contrary pretensions of living ones. The emperor, knowing that his,
reputation if not his power was in the hands of the bureaucrats,
and resting his own authority on tradition, found it hard to go
against precedents cited and the ways of the honorable ancestors
as interpreted by the scholars. Ordinarily, a bureaucracy has much
more power to hinder than initiate, but the Chinese civil service
was of itself able to carry out a significant reform program after the
Taiping rebellion of the middle of the nineteenth century, neither
helped nor hindered by a weak ruler serving merely ritual purposes.
[78, p. 50]

It was a great strength of the Chinese civil service that, by virtue
of fairly uniform and objective recruitment, it acquired a formidable corporate spirit; and as long as the bureaucracy maintains
solidarity, the emperor has no practical means of coercing it. The
chief defense of the sovereign, on the other hand, is to divide it,
to set men and factions against one another so that he can better
exercise his essential role of supreme judge. This means, in practice, that there is no prime minister at the head of a cabinet. The
fear is less that a single chief of the administration might gather
power to usurp the throne — perhaps least of the dangers besetting
the autocrat — than that, by wielding the whole influence of the
apparatus, he might dim the luster of the autocrat and reduce his
freedom of action. This is quite general. For example, when Wil-
helm II came to the German throne determined to rule, he asserted
his authority by dealing directly with the several ministers, so de-
priving Bismarck of leadership of the cabinet. Louis XIV admon-
ished the Dauphin to have no prime minister because it would be
undignified. In tsarist Russia, it was felt that the institution of a
First Minister for coordinating policy would dilute autocracy.
When one was nominated in 1905 it was an important concession
to constitutionalism; and it was not successful as the tsar continued
to have ministers report to himself and named and discharged
without reference to the nominal prime minister. In well-developed
empires it is almost a rule that no one person other than the monarch holds together the reins of administration. The Incas had no

overall coordinator below the person of the ruler, only a traditional council, the vague authority of which decreased as the empire grew. [173, p. 122] At the beginning of the Egyptian New Kingdom the newly strong pharaoh divided the viziership among two [94, p. 236], and the treasurer was more or less independent of them both. [114, Pt. I, p. 49] Around the Grand Mogul there were only informal councils; nearest to a chief minister was the treasurer, responsible for revenues. Akbar even tried to divide responsibilities for the treasury, but this proved impractical. [214, pp. 40, 43] Chinese empires have usually had no real prime-ministership, and none at all from the Ming dynasty onward. The Mings also abolished the Central Chancellery and sought to achieve administrative coordination through a Grand Secretariat with several Grand Secretaries, thereby strengthening the direct control of the monarch. The Ch'ing emperor retained sole power to issue orders not only to ministers but to provincial governors. [45, p. 4; 38, p. 4] In the early Roman empire, or Principate, the Praetorian Prefect gathered substantial authority, but he was not a real chief of administration. Caesars often named corulers, mainly to provide for the succession, and the coruler was usually not associated with the administration. In the Dominate, power was split much more, as the Praetorian Prefects were multiplied and many heads of department were directly subordinated to the Caesar; suspicion, moreover, led him to maintain contact with officials at lower levels. [285, p. 477] Likewise in the Byzantine empire there was no head of the ministry except the ruler, the most prestigious of his servants being the governor of the capital. [C. Diehl in 292, p. 732]

Exceptionally, the Turkish empire had a single vizier in charge of administration. But after it came into maturity with the capture of Constantinople, the office lost much of its previous authority and was occupied by slaves. As long as the sultans were vigorous, the vizier was relatively weak and insecure, his position being as dangerous as it was elevated; the higher he stood, often the nearer to destruction. [439, p. 33] When the sultans became weak and depraved, the viziers at times gained strength; thus, the Kuprili family was able to hold the vizierate for half a century, with intervals, from 1653 until 1702. But power passed mostly to the harem and to obscure figures of the inner court.

By dividing, the ruler can prevent the bureaucracy from emerging as a solid force to challenge him and impose its ideas or take power altogether. But it is much easier to control negatively than positively, to check than to move. The bureaucracy does not rebel, but evades or procrastinates, neglects or sabotages whatever seems hurtful to it. It can defeat almost anything the ruler may propose, showing the difficulty or impossibility of the measure, postponing with many excuses, pretending to execute while doing nothing, waiting for the autocrat to see the light, to change or forget his purpose. By himself, the ruler can hope to strike at only a few whom he may find neglectful or contumacious; alone he cannot budge the mass.

Frustrated by the apparatus, the autocrat turns to his obsequious, servile, and pleasing intimates, those whom he knows to be most utterly devoted to himself, often women whose charms are least resistible. Even if he is tireless, he cannot manage alone; he is distrustful of those who hold imposing offices – the more distrustful as he is dimly aware of his own incapacity – and he turns to men who have no position except his present favor. The Ming emperor who abolished the prime-ministership found himself overwhelmed; in one eight-day period, 1,160 documents and memorials dealing with 3,291 matters were laid before him. He was driven to have personal secretaries attach recommendations, so the Grand Secretary became in effect an irregular new prime minister. [C. Hucker in *19*, p. 138]

Even a rationally minded autocrat like Peter the Great came to rely much less on regular officials, even those installed by himself, than on guards, officers, and sundry friends, whom he charged with all manner of missions, especially securing compliance to his orders. [*407*, p. 136] The chief of his control apparatus became at times the real head of the government machine. [*551*, p. 144] Germans and other foreigners were preferred as supposedly more reliable. Yet Peter, like other autocrats, was regularly deceived and cheated by his friends and favorites, and even by his wife. [*379*, p. 211] Subsequent tsars and tsarinas relied on miscellaneous favorites; Nicholas I, for example, who wanted to be a complete autocrat, regularly looked beyond the ordinary machinery of government to special assistants and advisors. [*404*, p. 362] His unhappy descendant, Nicholas II, trusted hardly anyone but his wife, who, in the hour of darkness, came to select the ministers. She, in turn, placed her faith in Rasputin.

Perhaps every autocracy at some time falls under the influence of a court camarilla which, even if incapable of administering the land, applies the powers of the sovereign for its own welfare. In the words of Diocletian, one of the extremely rare monarchs voluntarily to retire from power, "The best and wisest princes are sold to the venal corruption of their courtiers." [314, I, 337] Early in the Roman empire, Sejanus may have been near to replacing Tiberius as Caesar [338, p. 24], and there were many more or less like him. Under Commodus, a former slave became chamberlain and virtual dictator, able to have senators murdered on charges of treason. [W. Weber in 290, pp. 382–383] On his death, influence passed to Commodus' mistress. Early in the third century, a series of Syrian women, mothers and grandmothers of Caesars, were powers behind the throne. In the fourth century, women of the imperial household or eunuchs of the bedchamber at times held acknowledged power [326, I, 341]; under Theodosius II, the chief will was that of his sister. Likewise, in Byzantine history palace women or various favorites often played leading roles.

While the New Kingdom of Egypt was still vigorous, Queen Hatshepsut, using male dress and a false beard, seized the throne; her steward became virtual coruler. [134, p. 31; 114, Pt. I, p. 8] Later in the dynasty high places went regularly to intimates, to onetime playmates of the ruler, and to relations of palace women. [114, Pt. I, p. 43] A relatively strong Mogul, Shah Jahan, is said to have been ruled by his daughter, for whom, with the encouragement of his court, he indulged an unconventional affection. [191, p. 11] After Aurangzeb, most Mogul emperors were helpless and maltreated puppets of palace factions, and frequently were kept in jail. Chinese dynasties have repeatedly fallen under the domination of favorites of one variety or another. Unhappy emperors had to balance cliques to keep atop the hollow throne, and eunuch power figured strongly in the decay and downfall of dynasties from the Han onward. Even a fairly strong ruler supported by the bureaucracy, such as Wu Tsung of the T'ang dynasty, recognized limits to his power. The eunuch generals of the palace guard politely declined to surrender their seals of office and apparently succeeded in their defiance. [60, pp. 233–237] Typical was the course of the Mings. The Grand Secretaries brought in to take the place of a prime minister gained influence in their own right until they were in turn offset by the eunuchs; the struggle for power came to be waged principally between these two groups. [*38*, p. 53; *61*, p. 299] Late Ming emperors were often mere puppets of the eunuchs and some paid no attention to government at all. [C. Hucker in *19*, p. 133] Sometimes the eunuchs so controlled the machinery that they ruled simply by forging decrees [*4*, pp. 69–74]; only a few of the better-indoctrinated civil servants dared speak out against them. The new Ch'ing dynasty set up a new Grand Council to control the secretariat and tried to exclude the eunuchs entirely from power. But after the middle of the nineteenth century the Manchu emperor was for the most part a figurehead used by a woman and a few eunuchs. [*45*, p. 91] The famous Dowager Empress, for example, controlled by appointments and kept her reigning son practically a prisoner. [*4*, p. 429]

It is one of the great advantages of the intimates of the emperor to stand between him and the world. The guards and attendants monopolize outside contacts and decide what the emperor is to know. When the Han emperor Wu tried to reaffirm personal authority after a series of inactive rulers, power devolved rather to Masters of Writing, who determined what materials reached him and so became powerful over the regular officials. Influence later went to the eunuchs who surrounded the emperor in his apartments. [*52*, p. 106] There is a more dramatic tale of how a great eunuch of the Ch'in dynasty managed his none too brilliant master. He had a deer brought to the emperor and caused everyone to swear it was a horse. The befuddled emperor, doubting his own sanity, was easily persuaded to go into retirement. [*5*, pp. 52–53]

Seclusion helps the autocrat by making his person more mysterious, awesome, and perhaps sacred; it is hard to believe in a god-king unless he is remote. The more ordinary and foolish he is, the more important for his sublimity that he take no notice of ordinary people and affairs, that he be kept out of sight except when exalted by pomp and ceremony when he passes in dazzling state with lofty and immobile mien. The paraphernalia of majesty also separate the ruler, psychologically and physically, from his subjects. The need for a host of attendants, time-consuming ceremonies, and the inconvenience and cost (as of covering the road with gold dust) of elaborate receptions hinder his leaving the palace and insulate him from the country when he does travel. This is all excellent for his self-esteem and surrounds his office with an impenetrable aura. But the greater advantages of secluding the monarch are for his intimates. Screened off from people and affairs, he loses judgment and leadership; he probably also would lose ambition to dominate a world of which he sees little and which, he is assured, is continually bowed in reverence to his majesty. Grappling with reality might only spoil the pleasant picture. If the all-powerful can be persuaded to give himself to pleasures punctuated by colorful and flattering ceremonies, those who control the channels between him and the world become the repositories of his power, the beneficiaries of his glory. Unknown to the people and divorced from the bases of power, he may be turned into a mere tool. His intimates hence seek to make seclusion attractive to him and to impede any attempt to break out and to exercise his theoretical power. The forbidden cities and huge walled palaces and grounds which encompass everything he might desire are a prison for the emperor and a paradise for the parasitic swarm that attaches itself to him as epiphytes sometimes so cover a tropical tree as to smother it.

The influence of the domestics is inversely proportional to the intelligence and character of the emperor. Hence, so far as they have a voice in choosing him, artful courtiers want a dull, vain, and pliable man; no matter how he is chosen, they may do much to pervert him. Intriguers of ninth-century Byzantium favored the rise to power of a drunken groom as companion of Emperor Michael and so brought the downfall of better ministers. [*311*, pp. 177–178] At the Mogul court it was customary to render princes harmless with alcohol and weakening confinement, partly because of paternal fears but also for the benefit of the court. The tyranny of servants over the masters came to its height in the Turkish empire. Confined in the harem since birth, the later sultans had ignorant slaves for companions and received little education beyond basic literacy, but much practice in the arts of pleasure and the refinements of vice. They naturally became utterly depraved, besotted, degenerate, and incompetent. [*439*, p. 31; *430*, p. 34] Although a marble-screened window upheld the pretense that the master might be listening to the deliberations of the vizier and his counselors, the sultans became so captive that they were rarely allowed to leave the capital lest they seize the opportunity to raise a military force against the court. [*439*, p. 57] They were not much respected even as figureheads; of twenty-five sultans following Suleiman the Magnificent, eleven were deposed. Even that outstanding leader allowed a slave girl to make and unmake the vizier and to contribute to the murder of his only two capable sons. [*436*, pp. 183–184] Real power went to women of the harem or shadowy figures in the background. [*431*, pp. 146, 153] The courtiers did not want an honest vizier, as he would check their looting of the revenues, nor a strong one to reduce their privileges; only when the empire was threatened by evident disaster would they have a reformer. The task of the vizier was primarily to fatten the courtiers, and if he failed to do this adequately an intrigue might at any time cost him his office or his head. [*432*, Pt. I, pp. 108–110; *439*, pp. 33–34]

Those around the emperor have another potent weapon, assassination. He needs people to protect him and is inevitably at the mercy of his guards and entourage; the best he can do is to try to select those who are incapable of replacing him, such as foreigners, eunuchs, or slave girls, and those who truly love him. But the more adulation he receives and the more adept his courtiers, the more difficult for him, like King Lear, to be sure of the sincerity of affection; and the most servile guards may be bribed or otherwise led by ambition or fear to desire a change of masters. The underlings who see him daily and at close range see his faults and human weaknesses. They are little impressed by deification, which serves as much their purposes as his. There being no legal means of removing him, those dissatisfied with his person or policies can plot his removal only by violence; and murder is easier and probably safer than civil war. Thousands hate him; a single dagger can end him.

The autocrat is likely, then, to be burdened by chronic terror, from which there is no refuge. Perhaps he can elude danger by movement. The Maurya ruler was so fearful that he changed bedrooms nightly, as did Suleiman the Magnificent [*436*, p. 194], and first Ch'in emperor was always secretly on the move about his complex of palaces. Fear brings precautionary terror, the more ruthless for the loneliness of the autocrat, and terror causes fear and isolation for the one who wields it. Desperately, he may invite informers and strike wherever suspicion alights, not only the guilty but any or all, to instill fear.

But the emperor who permits people near his person cedes them influence and power over himself. Domitian safely slaughtered aristocrats and senators, but fell when his reign of terror extended to his own household; palace officials conspired with his wife to remove the common danger. Likewise Commodus could shed the noblest blood of Rome with impunity, but was undone as soon as he turned upon his intimates; his mistress poisoned him and a wrestler strangled him in his bedchamber. The secretary of Aurelian, learning that he was under suspicion, had only to show a group of generals a fake list of candidates for execution, including themselves. Few Roman Caesars died peacefully, and the effeminate personages of the court were as dangerous as the rough legions. Nor have other empires provided safety for their masters. A eunuch administrator of Artaxerxes III poisoned his master to save himself [253, p. 233], and sundry other Achaemenid rulers, sacred and exalted as they were, fell victims to their servants or guards, as did many Byzantine rulers, Turkish sultans, and the like. Before the nineteenth century, various Russian tsars were done to death by their intimates. The great despotism provides no security for the subjects and very little, except perhaps in a highly refined system like the Chinese, for the despot himself.

Autocracy, then, is checked by the human weaknesses of rulers, their inability to attend to affairs, their susceptibility to seductions, and their vulnerability to daggers or poisons. The empire is seldom guided by a truly united plan and purpose, formed and coordinated by a single will. It lacks form; it is an amorphous oligarchy, wherein the locus of power is often obscure and irregularly shifting. It really has use not for a king but for kingship. A common practice in various great empires has been to bow down before an empty throne. What was important was not the man but the principle of authority, in whose name the despotic system functioned. It is characteristic of the great empires that few people really know who is most influential; power may lie with a female relative, a wife or a mistress, a favorite or an attendant, a secretary or a talented or persuasive minister, or with the autocrat himself. But the very irregularity or lack of fixity of power implies the need for a final arbiter, a single figure with ultimate power of decision, if only to decide between competing cliques and factions. Hence, no matter how freely the monarch may be murdered, another with equal arbitrary powers must be raised to his place.

The Japanese ruler, sacred but impotent, was for centuries a puppet, at one time of the third degree, as he was the creature of the Shogun, who was puppet of a regent, who was manipulated by a warlord. [538, p. 233] Similarly, in early medieval France the mayor of the palace ruled powerless kings. But this implies a semiconstitutional allocation of power; the very great empires seem to have been too much imbued with the sense of unified authority to evolve such institutions. In them, the emperor is always influential, if only by negative example and failure to act. The allocation of power is personal, not institutional. No one else acquires permanent authority, and the emperor has nearly always retained the ability, so far as he sees fit to exercise it, to grant or withdraw power. Sejanus seemed all-powerful in the retirement of Tiberius, but when the latter suspected the favorite of aiming too high, he had him executed without resistance. Turkish sultans treated their viziers with arbitrary violence; Selim I, for example, decapitated eight Grand Viziers in as many years and deposed many more. [431, p. 103] When sultans were feeble and depraved, it was still up to them to turn to this favorite or that and to listen or not to listen when voices insinuated the necessity of dismissing the vizier.

In the lack of fixed relations of power, the highest officials are usually insecure and subject to dismissal and punishment at any time. Men rise and fall rapidly and unpredictably, and it is dangerous to be powerful and successful. Constantine, for example, treated the great men of his government with perfect caprice, raising them, enriching them, then executing them and recapturing their estates; later, he erected statues to some of his favorite victims. [288, pp. 338–339] Ivan IV enjoyed allowing officials to engorge themselves, only to snatch away their plunder and sometimes their lives as well. [K. Waszilewski in 420, p. 65] Under the perfected empire of the Mings, ministers were often flogged to disability or even death for showing the slightest independence. [W. T. de Bary in 19, p. 174]

The Chinese Censorate was a remarkable institution to check the emperor, but it was in fact designed to help him and it cast no shadow on the effulgence of his power. Officials could remonstrate, but their best hope was to persuade an arbitrary lord who did not have to listen. A protesting official would rightly say, "Now in opposing Your Majesty's wishes I have committed a crime worthy of death," and then kowtow, knocking his head violently on the ground. [24, p. 27] Few censors felt compelled to criticize the emperor, and if they did the emperor could execute them. A censor, well knowing the cost to himself, once rebuked a Ch'ing emperor for attachment to actors and alcohol. Called to the presence, he was asked what punishment he deserved. "Quartering," he replied. As the magnanimous ruler found this too severe, the censor suggested beheading; finally he was lucky enough merely to be exiled to the provinces. [76, p. 338] During 240 years of the Ch'ing dynasty forty-two censors were dismissed or killed. [56, p. 95] The censorate, in any event, was highly useful, as it attacked official malfeasance and ferreted out disobedience and corruption. The very existence of the censorate, officially charged with criticizing the highest, inhibited others from doing so. And criticism of the emperor, usually cautious in the extreme, was always in terms of his having been misled by bad advisers; that is, the barbs of the civil service were aimed past the emperor at itself. [C. Hucker in 55, p. 207]

The emperor, of course, is prisoner of his establishment, part of a system that he has little power to alter. But there is little reason for him to seek to change anything of importance in a system so gratifying to him. Unless, exceptionally, he should see the need and practicality of substantial reforms, it is perhaps enough to enjoy the adoring multitude, the splendid palaces, the solemn and sacred rituals of the rulership of the world, and the most sumptuous pleasures empire can provide, all without reproach from without or within. The sense of power can be satisfied by freely disposing of the lives and fortunes of his subjects, rewarding or chastising as he will. Toward him flows obedience and from him, all political power. His is the grand consciousness of infinite authority. Probably nearly all the monarchs of great empires, even those who do nothing at all of their own initiative, would agree with Ivan the Terrible, who thought it a crime that anyone else should aspire to a voice in the government, as though "slaves should possess themselves of power over their lords." [388, II, 69] Time and again he referred to the highest nobles as his slaves: "We are free to reward our slaves, even as we are free to punish them." [404, p. 223] Or with the Ch'ing emperor who in 1749 stated: "Surely, during the fourteen years of Our reign there is no matter, large or small, which has not been decided by Us alone." [Nivison in 55, p. 229] And any true son of empire could appreciate the brash sentiments of the Inca Atahualpa. Although he had never gained full power, even while languishing in humiliating captivity, he proclaimed, "If I desire, no bird flies here and no leaf stirs." [173, p. 313]

5   STRENGTH

GREAT ACHIEVEMENTS

Although the great empire no more asks independent peoples
whether they wish to be conquered and pacified than the tamer
asks the consent of the mustang to the saddle, it promises great
good to its subjects, and in its fold they receive benefits, just as
the wild horse in exchange for its freedom receives a stable and
regular ration, and, giving its labor, enjoys peace and security. If
the empire can be made by force, it cannot be governed by force
alone, nor even by repression of dissent, control of information,
and propaganda. To remain strong it must appeal by virtue of the
blessings it confers.

Most obviously, the empire knits together the world. The people
can only benefit from the breaking down of barriers and the ease
of intercourse over a large area; and this is as impressive to the
mind as it is advantageous to the economy. The first empire builder
of whom we have definite knowledge, Sargon of Akkad, is believed
to have consolidated his conquests by a regular system of imperial communications [253, I, 67]; he also took such unifying
measures as introducing a regular calendar. The Assyrians built
many roads, some of them paved and marked with milestones.
[252, p. 299] The Persians likewise were great road builders; a royal
highroad of 1,500 miles gave swift communication from one end
of the empire to the other. [253, I, 164] Darius, solidifier of the empire, introduced standard weights and measures and made moves
toward a uniform currency. [252, pp. 185–186] The empire became
a melting pot, as scores of nations formed a single army, and imperial builders were proud of using materials and craftsmen from
a dozen lands. [249, p. 100] The Maurya empire, perhaps partly in
imitation, provided itself with a good road system with pillars
about every mile. [215, p. 135]

The Romans, to permit speedy mobilization of their legions,
built tens of thousands of stone bridges and scores of thousands of
miles of well-engineered and solid roads, some of which have

endured to this day. [358, p. 347] With incontestable force, they gave a new security to the world. For the first time, Mediterranean pirates were suppressed, and travel and trade were made safe by sea and land. There was established the simplicity of a single law and uniform currency; barriers to trade were practically eliminated. The panegyrists found much to praise, as one of the middle of the second century: "You have surveyed the whole world, built bridges of all sorts over rivers, cut down mountains to make paths for chariots, filled the deserts with hostels, and civilized it all with system and order." [330, p. 138] In consequence, shipping and commerce throve for a time.

Immediately after securing power through all China, the Ch'in ruler issued a decree blaming the six extinct kingdoms for all troubles and promising peace under heaven. He proceeded to build many roads, standardizing axle lengths to permit carts to traverse the whole domain in the same set of ruts. He also decreed uniform laws, weights and measures, and script, to knit the realm into a coherent whole. The following Han dynasty continued the same work, expanding the road network, improving administration, giving a standard calendar, and so on. In 63–66 A.D., a great highway is said to have required the labor of 766,800 men. [570, p. 39] Similarly in the eighth century the T'angs greatly improved the canal system, the better to transport the grain tax to the capital. [59, p. 33]

The Incas were most remarkable builders of roads, although they had no wheeled vehicles. Their main highway along the Andes, using in part the roads of superseded states, was 3,250 miles in length. Their suspension bridges, spanning abysses 200 feet across, have also aroused undying wonder. These had political utility; the sight of a great Inca bridge was enough to induce a nation to surrender peaceably in the belief that the builders must represent a superior order. [170, p. 153]

Sheer size and the concentrated resources of the world have also enabled great empires to attain unprecedented magnificence. To exalt the ruler and to make visible their might, empires have built the most grandiose monuments, splendid palaces, temples, and the like, with the most dazzling adornment of which masses of men were capable. If there had been no mighty union of Egypt, there would have been no pyramids, mountains of stone that men nearly five thousand years later find, in their dilapidated condition, most awesome; for those of the day, they must have been proof of the divinity the rulers claimed. New Kingdom pharaohs erected perhaps the most spectacular temples ever seen. The magnificent setting of the Persian Great King at Susa was fabled; the Maurya palace was said to be even more brilliant. Although of wood, it had dazzling ornaments, great gilded pillars, and immense golden vessels. [215, p. 122] The Mogul empire graced itself with countless beautiful constructions, such like the Taj Mahal, on which 20,000 men labored for fifteen years. Although it did practically nothing for the people except to provide architectural beauty, and its despotism was foreign, exceptionally cruel, endlessly corrupt, oppressive, and eventually impotent to protect the starving masses from marauders, thanks to its great monuments it retained an air of majesty and sanctity to the end. The Incas built huge palaces, temples, and fortresses; but, perhaps because of Spanish predilections, most celebrated has been the quantity of precious metals with which they dazzled their subjects. They reportedly collected some 7 million ounces of gold yearly, and much more silver; the twenty life-size llamas of cast gold which the Spaniards found were only a small fraction of their treasure. [175, pp. 130, 151]

The Ch'in emperor, Shih Huang-ti, having become master of all China, had built for himself, it is related, a palace for each day of the year [30, p. 39], connected by covered roads, all furnished with canopies, bells, and beautiful women. [28, p. 34] The chief one measured 500 by 2,500 feet and had a central hall that would accommodate ten thousand people. Seven hundred thousand men are said to have labored on it. [29, p. 82] The following Han emperors spent no less grandly on imperial ostentation and court ceremonial, making the palace the prime symbol of greatness. [30, p. 123] It has remained the jewel of empire, and the capital its crown, overawing the great as well as the humble. As all functionaries had to visit the seat of power, no person of importance could escape its spell. Even today Peking is said to be the most impressive capital in the world.

Many rulers of the world have not been satisfied with adorning an old capital, but built new ones for themselves. Sargon of Assyria built himself a great artificial capital [116, p. 116], just as Sargon of Akkad did many centuries before him, and as did Ikhnaten of Egypt's Eighteenth Dynasty and many another. Only a great empire could have undertaken to construct a glorious new capital

like that of Peter the Great on the marshes at the head of the Gulf
of Finland, facing Europe and far from the populated centers of
Russia. The cost in extraordinary taxes and forced labor was fearful, and it was felt necessary for several years to halt all other stone
building throughout the empire and bring all masons to work on
the new capital. But a magnificent city rose as though by magic,
and only two years later it was one of the finest of the world. [379,
pp. 158–159] St. Petersburg remained to shine in the northern
nights, and the work of modernization became legendary, while
the tens of thousands of peasants who died in the swamps and the
millions who starved to pay the taxes are gone and forgotten.

No doubt such glorious works are politically useful. Even if it
were not a device of tyranny to keep people poor and too busy to
plot by putting them to work on splendid monuments, as Aristotle
suggests [*Politics*, 1313*a*], it is a great advantage of the empires
that they are not inhibited from spending freely for uneconomic
magnificence, making incredible displays of the ability to rise above
ordinary standards of utility. The peoples look on their works and
are amazed, and perhaps proud as well to belong to the state that
boasts ineffable riches, which are, after all, a monument to their
sweat. Byzantine glitter was all that ingenuity and wealth could
summon; for state occasions the sovereign was sheathed in gold
and suspended between earth and heaven; such display, an emperor wrote, "compels the admiration of both foreigners and subjects." [301, pp. 31–32] In the distress of the fourteenth century
the court continued to spend its shrinking funds on ostentation
rather than on the impoverished army and navy. [301, p. 197] But
it was not all waste, as the empire rested largely on its image. A
Gothic chieftain viewing the capital said humbly, "Without doubt,
the emperor is a god on earth." [287, p. 17]

There are other and more solid benefits of great empire. At least
when it is new it may represent a rationalized political order,
thorough and systematic; as the overwhelming state, it can do
better whatever the state can do. An eighteenth-century Frenchman wrote, "It seems to me that the Chinese do almost ever sur-
pass us in common and public actions." [43, p. 178] The empire
can, if it desires, found schools, build libraries, subsidize arts, aid
commerce with every sort of facility, and in countless ways promote the general welfare. Emperors usually, as the Hittite king
boasted of himself, are accounted bearers of the welfare of the

people. The Incas, for example, not only opened roads, dug canals, built wonderful suspension bridges, and set up a regular and improved administration, but managed perhaps as thorough a welfare state as has ever been known. They made a complete inventory of people and resources and reshuffled villages, not only to hinder sedition and scatter potential rebels, but to provide all with adequate land. [J. Rowe in *180*, p. 272] They did their best to keep the people busy and well fed. Consequently it is claimed that in their society there were no thieves, idlers, or criminals; houses were left open in complete security. [*175*, p. 100] The state stored large quantities of food and clothing, often sufficient for many years, and supplied these to districts suffering hardship and to the needy, the aged, and the infirm. [*170*, p. 145] It was held a great fault for a governor if anyone in his district went hungry.

The Roman empire offered lavish benefits, at least to the populace of the favored city. Enormous public baths, temples, and circuses helped while away the hours; huge sums were continually expended on games and races, which lasted for weeks and occupied a large part of the year. Thus, under Trajan the festivities of killing some ten thousand slaves gladdened 123 days. [*533*, p. 550] Such amusements lengthened as the empire ripened, until they occupied 175 days yearly in the fourth century; they were halted in the West only in the absolute ruin of the fifth century. [*331*, pp. 103, 179] Nor had the Roman to hunger, however indolent. The dole, a measure of relief in Hellenistic times, came to feed a large part of the population, with handouts first of grain and then of bread from public bakeries. Fed and amused by the state, provided with hot baths, occasionally given a cash handout, as in celebration of a Caesar's accession (which provincials celebrated by paying a stiff assessment), the Roman in the street had little cause to rue the republic or dream of revolution.

Although Wang An-shih's policies of state socialism were abandoned after a few years, Chinese dynasties have constructed huge canals as well as palaces, and have regularly accepted responsibility for storing grain to distribute in famines, for fostering agriculture, and for settling new lands. [*38*, p. 69] There have been many small blessings also; thus, Chinese criminals were grateful to the emperor who spared them transportation during the hot months. [*29*, II, 41] Emperors needing support for unsteady thrones especially sought to improve life, as did the seventh-century Empress

Wu after her usurpation by reducing taxes and military burdens. [*24*, p. 78]

But the greatest blessing of empires, and that in which they have taken most pride, is a construction more impressive than mile-long glittering palaces, the order stretched over the quarters of the earth, the peace of mankind, the tranquillity and harmony of a unified rule. Conquerors of all sorts take credit for saving the people from themselves and ending the petty, fruitless, and exhausting quarrels of warring states. Thus the Incas propagated the belief that before them all was chaos, savagery, and cruel wars [*173*, p. 3; *172*, p. 13]; the Achaemenids were proud of their policies of peace and conciliation of peoples. [*249*, p. 86] The age of Augustus shone as a noble peace after generations of bitter wars, more civil than foreign; and for centuries, even when it degenerated into violent struggles for the succession, Pax Romana was a potent motto, endlessly repeated. For Tacitus, "peace" was a synonym of Roman rule, and to convince the barbarians of the advantages of peace was to persuade them to submit to the empire. [*330*, pp. 360–361] Making war in the name of peace, the universal empire proclaims a great and purposeful order wherein to beat swords into plowshares.

The great and authoritarian empire also brings a social peace. It presents itself as the ultimate simple answer to all political problems, the end of the strife of parties as of nations. This is the rationale of absolutism. As Ivan the Terrible said, "Civil wars will never cease in a country where the subjects do not obey the sovereigns," or even, in his opinion, where the monarch was subject to a senate. [*379*, p. 47] Caesar must be supported because he represents the unity, that is, the peace, of the land. As Hammurabi claimed, in the epilogue of his code,

> I made an end of war
> I promoted the welfare of the land
> I made the peoples rest in friendly dwellings
> I did not allow trouble-makers in their midst
> — I have sheltered them with my wisdom
> That the strong might not oppress the weak. [*125*, p. 63]

All are mindful, or may be reminded, that a house divided cannot stand; united we stand, divided we fall; and few will propose to invite disorder by destroying the central power. Abolishing internal factionalism as well as external wars, the empire erects a logical and planned order and wipes away irrational borders separating peoples and levels false distinctions among them; all the disparate groups look to it to settle their differences. After the fluidity and anarchy of freer states, the empire offers stability and a primitive uncomplicatedness, the security of a seemingly eternal rule, to which men can submit with simple faith in the goodness of the omnipotent ruler. Unanimity is reassuring, while dissent confuses; skepticism is a burden, especially for the less vigorous temperaments. The single order holds life together in fundamental simplicity; belief is always easier to bear than doubt; the monolithic order is solid and straightforward. It stands for freedom from conflicts, and conflicts becloud simple contentment. It upholds stable relationships and frees men from many of the responsibilities with which they are burdened in less ordered and more competitive societies. Reducing change and choice, it relieves people of a freedom onerous to many. If it is essentially mundane and dull, this may represent no loss of felicity; but if it is conventional and unambitious, this gives contentment, as most people find it easier to be conformists. Perhaps the old Russian tsars spoke with truth when they claimed that all were happy in occupying their stations and doing their duty for the state. [379, p. 48]

EQUALITY IN INFERIORITY

The autocratic empire is the supreme embodiment of imposed dominance and unequal rule; yet paradoxically one of its great boons is equality and the erasure of privilege. All participate in the great union; the conquered and the conquerors are set on a level of equal justice. In the Roman empire, the advantages of being Roman or Italian, greatest toward the end of the republic, were gradually diluted and eventually quite lost; and for some functions, like guard duty, non-Romans, even barbarians from without the empire, were given preference. Akbar, wise organizer of the Mogul empire, largely ended distinctions between Moslem and Hindu, opening the highest offices to the latter. His successors turned back to intolerance and thereby went far toward ruining the empire. Pobedonostsev, ideologue of Russian tsardom, justified autocracy as guarantor of equality of the nationalities. [R. F. Byrnes in 393, p. 113] In the eighteenth century the tsars even gave preference to Ukrainians, White Russians, and other minority peoples such as Georgians and Armenians. [425, p. 48] The autocrat has little reason to favor one nation over another, and may well feel that those outside the core community make more faithful and reliable servants.

The mission of peace is also accompanied by and idealized as the smiting down of oppressors and the protection of the weak and helpless under the mighty and benevolent hand of the all-powerful. Power implies responsibility for those over whom its wing is spread; the emperor should be a fountain of all-embracing love and right-eousness. Thus Darius spoke, in words like those of Hammurabi, of bringing justice and law so that the mighty could no longer work their will against the weak: "My law do they fear, so that the strong does not smite the weak." [254, p. 158] For Asoka, "All men are my children" [201, p. 197]; and Ivan the Terrible's virtue was that he ended the oppression of the boyars. [379, p. 47]

Whether or not he was moved by noble sentiments, the ruthless measures of Ivan — removals, confiscations, and executions — have been called democratic and leveling. [K. Waszilewski in 420, p. 62] He himself felt all his subjects were equal, for all alike were his slaves. [412, p. 27] The autocrat, as outlined earlier, is much in-clined to degrade hereditary nobility and any privilege that does not depend upon himself and that stands free of his control; the empires have usually negated hereditary rights. Privileges of wealth are also reduced in great empires. Opportunities for making money, except by official favor, are much restricted by the more or less state-dominated economy; and if anyone can garner riches he is at once highly insecure, politically of little weight, and perhaps kept inconspicuous. The plutocrats, like the aristocrats, are put down; and the masses are probably happy to see humbled those who stood proudly over them. The new master is not only far away, but may be believed more just, as he is sublimely elevated.

If nobles and plutocrats no longer hold sway, only the officials are strong. As the empire has no reason to exclude the poor from its service, and perhaps good reason to favor them, it in theory should open the doors to all without prejudice. The great despotisms have raised commoners, even slaves, to status next to the all-highest and have given at least a taste of the most justified and best-appreciated equality, that of opportunity, the "career open to talents." The equalitarianism of the Chinese examination system was somewhat theoretical, as ordinarily it was very difficult for poor boys to get the years of intensive and wholly impractical schooling necessary, and corruption often undermined the system. But from time to time a few poor boys were able to rise to honor and affluence, as a promising lad might find a generous sponsor or a village would pool resources to hire a tutor. Even if this seldom occurred, the possibility was a profound consolation.

To Westerners, it was a marvel that men rose solely by their efforts in the Turkish administration, so that the son of a poor Christian herdsman might stand next to the Sultan. [*435*, p. 85] Peter insisted on the theory that all should rise through the ranks in army, navy, and bureaucracy, regardless of birth and supposedly by merit only. [*404*, p. 253] The claim was cherished thereafter by tsarist Russia that the doors were open and all could climb to the top. Although there were all manner of special concessions to the nobles and it was impossible for a serf to get a foot on the ladder, the idea remained attractive. An American writer of the nineteenth century found Russia much more democratic than England because it was easier, he thought, for men of the lower classes to rise to high careers in the bureaucratic than in the aristocratic society. [*366*, p. 334] Even non-Russians, except Jews, were in theory equally privileged to advance. [*418*, p. 33]

Conversely, the universal empire is opposed in spirit and to some extent in practice to private slavery; the ownership of some by others is inconsistent with the subjection of all to the imperial master. As Aristotle remarked, it is not in the interest of the tyrant that slaves be disciplined, for it is not they who plot against him. [*Politics*, 1313*b*] It is more dignified for the autocrat, and also safer, that only he should command unconditional obedience. In some empires, like the Turkish and the Mogul, slavery has been important. But where slaves may be elevated to the highest position by a gesture of the autocrat, their status is no longer so utterly hopeless; and in the Turkish state the important offices for a time were filled by slaves. The Maurya empire of India protected slaves and their property by law and forbade large-scale ownership of them in order to keep the state monopoly of basic production. [*201*, p. 220] In Egypt only a few foreign captives were slaves. [*141*, p. 61] In imperial China, slavery was never very important. At its height early in the Han dynasty it comprised roughly 1 percent of the population, mostly personal servants. [*75*, p. 177] Later in that dynasty various measures limited the number of slaves anyone could hold, restricted or taxed their sale, prohibited their killing, and emancipated some. The reformer Wang Mang tried to free male slaves, but the state was then not strong enough to carry through this measure. [52, p. 109] The institution gradually disappeared in subsequent dynasties. [75, pp. 176, 240]

The Roman empire is famed as a slaveholding society, but slavery was an institution of the predatory republic which in the empire gradually melted into a broader subservience. The conservative Augustus restricted manumission in the interest of stability, but he also permitted marriage of freedwomen with all but the senators, gave new rights to freedmen, and made it possible for slaves to testify against their masters. [308, pp. 59, 63, 234] After Augustus, slaves were allowed to form burial societies and to hold some property; coming to be regarded as human, they gained access to the games, baths, and other privileges of the free. [284, p. 306; 302, p. 3] Hadrian deprived owners of their extreme authority, the right to kill their slaves. [345, p. 270] By humane legislation of the second century, the authority of the master over his slaves (and women) was further circumscribed, and slaves gained a position at court nearly equal to freemen. [294, p. 634] Manumission, although legally restricted, was common. Numbers of slaves decreased, partly because there were no more great conquests; but by the fourth century, even when barbarians were captured, they were usually not sold for slaves but made into tenant farmers, subject to conscription. [326, II, 794] In the later empire remaining slaves were mainly personal servants of the rich. Agricultural slavery, mainstay of the republic, had almost disappeared. As the condition of slavery became equivalent to that of the bound farmers, the coloni or tenants were fixed to the land more for the convenience of the taxing state than for that of the proprietors. [326, II, 802]

The Russian empire officially abolished slavery; Peter did away with the already worn-out distinction between slaves and serfs, decreeing that all alike were to serve the state directly or indirectly. [379, p. 131] To be sure, the tsarist regime introduced serfdom, as did the decadent Roman empire, to prevent cultivators from absconding to the unsettled lands and cheating the tax collector. But a writer of Peter's day, Pososhkov, reasoned that serfdom could not be permanent because all alike belonged to the Supreme Autocrat. [388, IV, 103] The idea of slavery was vehemently rejected even while its reality was accepted; and the reality became strongest in the eighteenth century when Westernization was in full swing.

Thus the sway of a single will implies equal treatment, and the wise and strong autocrat can well pursue a policy of leveling, sweeping away all special rights. He has nothing to fear from the masses, but looks askance upon the powerful; he wants neither very poor people, who may be disorderly, nor rich, who may be independent; he has nothing to lose and much to gain from equality, qualified only by the distinctions he bestows for his own purposes. As Montesquieu wrote, "Mankind being all upon a level [under a despotic government], no one person can prefer himself to another; and, as on the other hand they are all slaves, they can give themselves no sort of preference." [*Spirit of the Laws*, Bk. III, chap. 8] Early in the French Revolution, Mirabeau noted and told his fretting king how a level surface assists the exercise of power. [*556*, p. 21] Obedience comes easier, as administration is simpler and more efficient, when all are alike and subject to the same sacrosanct supreme authority. When the great are laid low, it is hard for any to think of standing against the regime; and the satisfaction of equality reduces seditious feelings. Social distinctions shrink beside the supreme distinction between the emperor and his servants, and people feel more equal among themselves as the ruler is projected to the level of the divine. No one is really superior when he towers above all classes and castes, and all are equally at his mercy. China has been praised as the land of natural equality not only because anyone could rise by the imperial examinations, but also because all were equally subject to the will of the Son of Heaven. [*46*, pp. 8–9]

Equality, like peace, is a usual justification of autocratic power; and emperors, like dictators and despots, often claim to be champions of the masses or somehow identify themselves with the humble or make symbolic concessions to them. Kings of the Middle Ages generally claimed to represent the popular interest in their attack on privileges of the few; for example, Charles V, in suppressing the rights of the oligarchs of Ghent, decreed that all the inhabitants should form "one body and community." From Sargon of Akkad, many a great ruler has been graced by a legend of his having lived once among the people, perhaps as a foundling. Pharaohs of the Old Kingdom, although gods incarnate, were "father of the fatherless, husband to the widow, protector of the orphan." [126, p. 215] While European kings have laid stress upon marrying only royalty, great emperors have usually felt quite free to take whom they pleased as concubines or even wives. Beauty alone could make a girl mistress of the Sapa Inca, the Son of Heaven, Caesar, or of most autocrats; when marrying at home, Russian tsars preferred women of fairly humble birth, not of the great families. [379, p. 27] Through the Principate the Roman empire held to a vague theory of popular sovereignty, under which the autocratic power was based on supposed election, the army was considered effectively to represent the people, and the emperor ruled for the well-being of all. Panegyrists called the empire of Hadrian a great democracy in which the more capable were called to govern for the common benefit. [W. Weber in 290, p. 316] The Chinese theory that rulership represented virtue and might be legitimately overthrown by revolution if it ceased to be virtuous also represented a vague acknowledgment of popular consent as the basis of power. The philosopher Hsün-tzu said, "When the people are satisfied, only then is the prince secure." [20, p. 171] Recognizing his duties, a Ming emperor declined immortality when the elixir was presented to him, as there was not enough for everyone. [29, I, 170] Like modern plebiscitary dictatorships, the Chinese empire had some shades of democracy, as villages informally elected a sort of mayor, albeit of slight and uncertain powers and subject to confirmation by the magistrate. Westerners lauded institutions by which it "has been found possible to grant, in the communes, universal suffrage to three hundred millions of men, and to render every distinction accessible to all classes" [37, I, 108, 122], all, however, without in the least curtailing the absolute powers of the sublime ruler.

Many imperial gestures have pleased the people. For example, in 1732 it was ordered that the best peasant of the Middle Kingdom each year be made a mandarin, allowed to take tea with the governor, and inscribed, in death, in the Halls of the Ancestors. [29, II, p. 51] And once a year the emperor graciously stepped down to the level of his lowly subjects by going out with high officials to do a bit of plowing. The Egyptian pharaohs did the same [126, p. 176], as, on the opposite side of the world, the Sapa Inca did with his viceroys. The Inca, while inspecting the realm, would also put on the costume of the tribe he was visiting and ceremonially share their food and drink. [*172*, pp. 50, 59] Aurangzeb, while his government was squeezing India dry, symbolically earned small sums of money by handicrafts [*199*, p. 354], and Moguls sometimes gave away part of their hundred-course dinners to the starving poor. [*199*, p. 139] The Byzantine emperor would in the manner of Christ yearly wash the feet of twelve poor men. [*339*, p. 4] To inspire his soldiers, Peter the Great served in a modest capacity in his own army. [*408*, p. 207] In the same spirit, the emperor may dispense symbolic justice. Byzantine rulers, Turkish sultans, Moguls, and others, have gone out personally to receive petitions and redress wrongs, in fact confessing the inadequacy of their administration, but giving material for tales of their fatherly concern. [*311*, p. 133] The Mogul Jahangir, who enjoyed impaling those who offended him, had a bell in his chamber with a chain leading to a public courtyard, so that anyone could ring for justice. [*199*, pp. 241–242] Who then could blame the autocrat?

Such concessions are the more easily made as they are hollow, just as the citizenship of Rome could be extended easily to all nations in the empire because it ceased to be a privilege, whereas democratic Athens jealously restricted its valuable citizenship. But the masses are pleased with small appearances and have little thought of real sharing in the political power which looms so great and far. They usually believe, even prefer to believe, that their status is natural and inevitable. Tokens of equality are thus precious; and equality, even though insubstantial, appeals more than freedom. The former is a near satisfaction for many who have little ability or opportunity to use freedom; the latter is insecure, demanding, and unequal. A slight hope, even an empty one, of rising, goes far toward satisfying ambitions. For those who have risen, a theory of equal opportunity is the more pleasing as it justifies their position as the result of merit, their own virtue and effort, while those who have failed should blame, not the system or the successful, but themselves. The claims of the empire to represent equality and justice thus satisfy alike those who command and those who must obey.

This logic has sometimes led to real and positive efforts to institute economic equality, as the logical conclusion of the great putting-together is the sharing of property, state socialism if not communism. An extreme example was the celebrated collectivistic paternalism of the Inca empire. Although opinions differ as to how effective it was, certainly little but clothing and houses was held as private property, and there was a strong feeling that the state should provide for all in need. A large part of the product of the land (the fruit of collective labor) went into communal storage, mostly, of course, for the benefit of the elite, but in part to serve needs of the people. Tsarist Russia took pride in a sense of collectivity; Russia belonged to the Orthodox tsar who belonged to the people, all wrapped up in a virtuous togetherness. The great reformer of the Sung dynasty, Wang An-shih, wanting to create something like a communistic state, proposed:

The first and most essential duty of a government is to love the people and to procure them the real advantages of life, which are plenty and pleasure. To accomplish this object it would be sufficient to inspire everyone with the unvarying principles of rectitude; but as all might not observe them, the state should explain the manner of following these precepts and enforce obedience by wise and inflexible laws. In order to prevent the oppression of man by man, the state should take possession of all the resources of the empire and become the sole master and employer. [37, II, 65]

Thus there is an equalitarian sense in total power which overrides all distinctions irrelevant to it and forges the realm into a mighty whole, like a single family; and only the almighty power can do this, for freedom leads to inequality and permits exploitation. Universal empire and the total state, unchecked by private greed, promise equality and so true freedom for the oppressed; it is in the empire that sharing of property or communism becomes a great ideal (see chap. 9). But the dream of total power remains only a dream, and between the ideal and the reality is a chasm that grows wider and deeper as the empire ripens. The efforts of Wang An-shih and others like him, who wished to make the empire like a brotherhood, were defeated by conservative forces. Even the efforts to open the ranks of officialdom equally to all talents have been generally ineffective, despite the fact that this policy would be in the interests of the autocrat as well as of the masses. It would seem that, in the autocratic empire, inequality, even of the grossest nature, necessarily overtakes the pretensions of equality. The empire can no more be equalitarian than an army, wherein subordination is the essential principle of organization, although it might in theory like to treat men as equals. In a framework of strong authority and hierarchical organization, substantial equality is a mirage. It could be made real only if the autocrat were very wise and truly the master of the whole. But if the first is unlikely, the second is impossible. He has to serve the apparatus and the system at least as much as they serve him. Then a horde of persons are in a position to use a share of this power to benefit themselves, just as the autocrat benefits himself. The imperial power cuts down privilege and spawns greater privilege.

POLITICAL CONTROLS

If the empire could fulfill its promises and potentialities of great works, peace, and social justice, it would stand firm as a mountain without need of special devices and the use of force to protect itself. But coercion often comes easier than virtue, and the empire could do with minimal force only if the rulers, not only the autocrat but all who de facto share his authority, were entirely dedicated and always practiced stern self-denial.

Once the momentum and morale of conquest are lost, the empire must struggle to keep up strength and unity. When there are no more external enemies, divisive and centrifugal tendencies grow; many persons would follow their own interests at the expense of the central power or even seek to appropriate it for themselves. Hence it is the major task of the empire, once it has gained full power, to devise the means of holding it entire and pure, of keeping it in the hands of its possessors. As a Chinese student wrote, "Having reduced every part of the empire to submission, and fearing no nations beyond, for all the people surrounding the country were mere barbarians, the government directed its energies to devising ways and means by which peace and order could be preserved." [84, p. 109]

This is a complex task. It is dangerous for the emperor to trust the people; they must be watched, checked, and controlled. The whole country might be heavily garrisoned, but this is expensive and impolitic; armed troops are more troublesome than a disarmed population. Likewise the central power must be very careful of its delegates, much better equipped than unorganized people to take or seek too much for themselves. Hence political controls are needed, and numerous and ingenious systems have been devised. And when opposition of some kind develops, as it will despite all precautions, there must be an organization to root out and punish the malefactors. The autocrat who, like Julius Caesar, allows his enemies to live, invites his own destruction.

A first principle is to permit no organization that might possibly take political action independently of, that is, against, the state. To allow men to organize is to invite them to act together, to unite their strength to the impairment of that of the regime. Aristotle noted even of petty Greek tyrants that they would prohibit clubs, common meals, and circles wherein people might study and debate. [*Politics,* 1313*a*] Cardinal Richelieu wisely advised his king to permit no bothersome societies or communities. [Montesquieu, *Spirit of the Laws,* Bk. V, chap. 11] Universal despots have generally been even readier than French monarchs to follow this advice. An uncontrolled organization may become a focus of sedition, a channel in which opposition may gather and become effective. As Trajan wrote to Pliny, "Whatever name we give them and for whatever purpose, men who have gathered together will all the same become a political association before long." [330, p. 272] But it is not only because they fear movements to overthrow them that rulers hate uncontrolled organizations; local societies usually represent no real threat. They are not so much dangerous as bothersome, potential sources of influence or pressure against officials, means whereby private interests might be partly shielded against state action, and economic power might be converted into political power. In short, they represent, albeit on a modest scale, bits of potentially noxious freedom, means of private action that should be controlled, unions outside the great union — and division of all potential opposing forces is the maxim of imperial rule.

In a thoroughly despotic empire like that of the Incas the question of private organization would hardly arise; but it seems to be a general principle that rigid, strongly and centrally governed societies forbid or inhibit free association. For example, tsarist law and principles (like those of the Soviet Union) banned all unauthorized societies, even small groups meeting regularly to read and discuss. [390, p. 135] The Roman empire from the beginning looked askance at private organizations. Whereas many societies of various kinds had flourished in republican Rome, Julius Caesar prohibited private clubs except for those licensed for professional and religious purposes. [294, p. 408] Augustus banned social organizations as troublesome [345, p. 66]; and the worthy Trajan was so fearful of associations, even for civic purposes, that he refused Pliny's suggestion of a fire brigade lest it become political. Only in burial societies were men permitted to join rather freely. Membership in an unauthorized society was at times punishable as treason. [*330*, p. 271] In the later empire, the state-controlled guilds became compulsory, but they alone survived while other organizations died of impoverishment and regimentation. [*285*, p. 455]

Under successive Chinese dynasties, unofficial associations, assumed to be subversive, were few and severely restricted. Practically the only groups permitted were literary societies, which inevitably acquired a political tinge and were in turn suppressed. [*38*, pp. 36–37; *570*, p. 328] In 1810 meetings of more than five persons were proclaimed seditious. [*29*, II, 78] Practice often lagged behind theory, however; and in times of dynastic weakness, associations for mutual protection and interests became numerous. [*76*, p. 388]

It is almost equally essential to control movement. If trouble can be limited to a single locality, it cannot endanger the vast state. Only if men can move about, send messages, find sympathizers, and concert their actions can they hope to move successfully against the mass of the empire. Hence the regime wishes to assure the best communications for itself, to keep abreast of events throughout its world, while keeping its subjects more or less immobilized. A postal system was one of the achievements of the Assyrians. [*252*, p. 299] The Persians improved on it, with men and horses standing by at intervals; there was also communication by fires on signal towers. But the post was only for official dispatches or strictly censored private communications. [*249*, p. 102] On the fine Roman road network, conveyances were available at regular intervals for officials and messengers, while private use was severely limited. [*302*, p. 206; *313*, p. 278]

Only by excellent communications, a superbly organized fast messenger post, and a visual telegraph system [*176*, p. 70] could the Incas control, with neolithic technology, a very mountainous area six times the size of France. The speed of their runners is legendary; it is said that messages between Peru and Ecuador went faster in Inca times than in the twentieth century. Private movement, on the other hand, was kept minimal. People were expected to stay home and keep at work. Travel, particularly the crossing of bridges, was allowed only for official business, and guards controlled entry into and exit from towns. The gates of Cuzco were especially closely watched lest anyone bring weapons in or take gold out; even persons of royal blood were searched. [170, p. 130; 173, pp. 142, 224] Chinese dynasties have from time to time restrained or prohibited movement from one province to another [76, p. 321], and the imperial post was, into modern times, limited to official business. [20, p. 89]

Passports are an invention of the great empires, which have used them more for their own people than for foreigners. For example, in the Maurya empire, passports were required of anyone who would leave town. [Arthasastra, 2.34.1] In Russia, while peasants were tied to the estates as serfs, the whole population was bound, if less rigorously, by the passport system originated by Peter. By the nineteenth century all Russians were required to have passports, renewed yearly; only peasants remaining in their villages were exempt. Persons without passports were liable to arrest, and police sometimes searched towns or city quarters for violators. [423, p. 443] The state could immobilize anyone simply by taking up his passport. [418, p. 20] It was forbidden to take in an overnight visitor without notifying the police. [390, p. 137]

If the great empires have thus often kept people from moving on their own, they have also moved them for political reasons, to uproot and divide potential opposition, to weaken potential enemies politically by removing them from bases of support, and morally by separating them from traditional associations. Probably the first Near Eastern empire, the Akkadian, relocated large numbers of people [108, p. 34], and the Assyrians mixed the people of that area as never before, sending upper classes and masses to different areas to paralyze both. [116, p. 115] The Persians may have undone some of the Assyrian shifts, as in the release of the Jews; but they also displaced other groups, sending Greeks to Central Asia, Egyptians to Bactria, and so on. [249, p. 110] Displacement was no light punishment for the restive, as not all could expect to survive treks of many hundreds or even thousands of miles. The Roman empire did not use this tactic widely, but the Caesars often exiled inconvenient persons, who, if lucky, might be retired to a provincial estate or some pleasant though unimportant spot. The less fortunate went to small and barren islands in the Mediterranean. [345, p. 161]

The Incas, who carefully studied the arts of governing, resettled disaffected peoples on a large scale, partly to secure the cultivation of idle lands but probably mostly to divide and immobilize. Psychologically adept, the Incas consoled the involuntary colonists by gifts of gold and silver ornaments to the men and clothes and feather adornments to the women [*172*, p. 40]; but the colonists were allowed no commerce with their new neighbors. Representatives of the conquering race were also lodged among vanquished peoples, to teach, inspect, observe, and report. [*170*, p. 133; *173*, pp. 111–112]

The fifteenth-century expansion of Muscovy saw large numbers of dispossessed boyars and other potential subversives brought to the capital, as, for example, the upper classes of Novgorod were removed to Moscow upon the reduction of that free city. One is reminded of the Ch'in emperor, who, upon unifying China, reportedly sent 120,000 aristocratic families to the capital. [*5*, p. 178] A seventeenth-century Russian statute provided for the deportation of suspect persons, and exile to Siberia was common up to the end of the tsarist regime. In the latter nineteenth century many thousands were so disposed of yearly. [*362*, p. 420]

Empires, when strong and efficient, have also reached down to organize all the people or to require them to control themselves. The Mauryans may have kept a register of all inhabitants of the cities. [*217*, p. 115] The Inca population, classed in twelve age groups for control purposes, was arranged in a beautiful hierarchic structure. Fathers were liable for the misdeeds of their children, and leaders of tens were charged with reporting all misdemeanors to the heads of fifties or hundreds, and were themselves subject to punishment (the threatened sentence being death) if they failed to do so within an hour. Such measures, as well as the benefits of the welfare state, helped reduce delinquency. [*181*, p. 19] The Russians had a similar but less far-reaching system of community responsibility. In the sixteenth century, as the state lacked power to keep order, villages were required to elect elders who would answer for infractions if the criminals were not produced. The purpose of elections was to secure general assent and participation, but the nominations were made by the government, and the institution degenerated into a purely bureaucratic and ineffective agency. [*384*, pp. 203–214]

Similar was the *pao-chia* system of community responsibility, old as empire in China. When the state of Ch'in was driving toward universal empire, all persons, even aristocrats and officials, were made answerable for crimes they knew about. [58, p. 135] The organization by which the people should watch over themselves was gradually refined under successive dynasties; Wang An-shih in the Sung dynasty particularly used it to police and tax. [47, p. 58] As the system was finally developed under the Ch'ing dynasty, each household was obliged to display a placard with the names of all adult members, whose entries and departures had to be recorded. Each ten households had a headman, as did each hundred and each thousand; the head of a thousand reported monthly to the district magistrate. [64, p. 231; 36, pp. 43–44] The headmen, named by officials, were responsible for those beneath them and were liable for punishment if lawbreakers were sheltered among their charges. To offset the gentry, headmen were to be commoners. Similarly, the guilds were accountable for the conduct of their members, who were not allowed to move without a passport. [38, p. 32] So strong was the principle of surveillance and mutual responsibility that it was almost impossible to escape the sight of some agent of the government; and any malefactor must have known that his family, kindred, or village would be held to account for his misdeeds. [76, p. 298]

Many other dangerous acts have been *verboten* in various empires. For example, the imaginative Inca rulers forbade hunting; moving out of one's ten-group; the use of precious metals, jewels, feathers of certain birds and various other articles of display by commoners; and the wearing of elegant clothes except on feast days. To facilitate control of movement, each province was required to use its own headgear [170, p. 130]; otherwise, dress had to be identical everywhere. Officials arranged marriages, sometimes uniting the boys of one people to the girls of another for amalgamation. When there was not enough work to keep people busy, useless tasks were invented; and even children of five or six were put to labor to teach them habits of industry. [181, pp. 93, 155, 204; 178, p. 107; 173, p. 134; 174, p. 125] Idle hands could make trouble.

Under the Mauryans, no private person was allowed to own either horse or elephant. [215, p. 134] In the Turkish empire, subject peoples were generally forbidden to ride horses or wear swords, as it was held that they had no business but to pay taxes. [432, Pt. I, p. 158] The king of Assyria alone had the right to hunt. [98, p. 114] Julius Caesar sought to limit strictly the carrying of arms by the

Romans, and his successors firmly enforced this decree. [345, p. 103] The first real Chinese empire, the Ch'in, likewise collected and melted down the weapons in the hands of the people. [40, Bk. I, p. 93] In modern times, the Ch'ing dynasty saw fit to forbid such crimes as religious processions, strange magical incantations, and the gathering of women in temples. [76, pp. 304–305] For the sake of order, a Mohammedan sultan of India prohibited alcoholic beverages and unlicensed feasts, visits, marriages, or hospitality to strangers by the nobles. As he said in this connection, "To prevent rebellions, in which many perish, I issue such ordinances as I consider to be for the good of the people and the benefit of the state." [212, pp. 227–229]

More difficult than keeping a tight rein on the common folk is the problem of controlling those who, by acting as the emperor's arm, share in some degree his power. The ruler must have a huge, highly structured bureaucracy; yet he must keep this mammoth machine amenable and pliable, weak relative to himself, and he must prevent any part of it from escaping his control. The chief strategy is to divide, to prevent any concentration of power that might threaten the center or act independently. This implies, as noted earlier, that there should be no chief minister with jurisdiction over the whole administration, or perhaps not even any minister who stands definitely above his colleagues, except possibly as the favorite of the autocrat. Strong emperors have tried to deal directly with heads of many departments and perhaps with provincial governors as well.

But this procedure is not enough, especially with officials who may be emboldened by distance from the seat of power. The ordinary remedies are to divide the realm into many separate compartments and to split powers between governors and some sort of overseers. Thus the Ch'in empire, immediately on taking control, divided the land into thirty-six provinces instead of the former half-dozen kingdoms. [48, p. 53] The Assyrians cut their empire into more than sixty provinces to make them too small to think of revolt [127, pp. 606–607]; the governors were closely watched and frequently rotated, and were required to make numerous reports. [116, p. 115] Darius redivided the Persian satrapies, corresponding more or less to the earlier kingdoms, to make them smaller and more uniform; and he took care to avoid giving any one man full power in any satrapy. Beside the satrap he placed a general or several generals. There was also next to each a secretary, or police agent, directly under the central power, whose word sufficed for the execution of the satrap. [*244*, pp. 106–107; *250*, pp. 54, 74–75] The provincial financial chief and the commander of the garrison also reported directly to the Great King. Various controllers and inspectors, some called by the Greeks the "King's Eye," also roamed the empire to report evildoing and possible sedition. [*252*, p. 59]

As though copying from Persia, Diocletian, when refurbishing the Roman empire, split up the provinces, allowing the Roman governors only brief terms and separating them from military command. Children of provincial governors were held in the capital as hostages. No one could govern in his native province or purchase slaves or real property or marry there, to prevent identification with the governed. [*314*, I, 102, 532] The Incas sent out trusted delegates, who traveled almost in the style of the emperor himself, to review actions of provincial governors and to overrule them if necessary. They also took sons of chiefs to the capital as hostages and for indoctrination. [*173*, p. 219] The Mogul emperor placed several officials in a single position so that they could check one another; he also moved them frequently, stationed them far away from their own estates, and kept their wives and children at court. As Aurangzeb put it, care was necessary "lest they be tempted to unyoke themselves and slip their necks from the servitude imposed upon them." [*202*, pp. 84–85]

It was probably the Chinese, who, benefiting from experience of successive dynasties, developed the most sophisticated political controls — although all measures failed to prevent power from slipping away after a century or two. Under the last, the Ch'ing dynasty, all appointments down to district magistrate were made from Peking, theoretically by the emperor, and all important decisions were reserved to him. Civil servants were forbidden to form any associations, and long indoctrination managed to convince them it was indeed ill-advised to do so. [Nivison in *55*, p. 221] Officials could never serve in their home provinces, nor were they ordinarily given appointments for more than three years in order that they remain highly dependent. Between posts they were called to the capital to refresh loyalties. [*20*, p. 90] No official was allowed to marry in his jurisdiction or to have any close relative holding office near him. [*76*, p. 353] Every major post was shared by two or more of equal rank and responsibility; yet one high official would hold more than one position, and powers were deliberately made to overlap. [*36*, pp. 4–5] Officials were stimulated to watch their subordinates closely by being held responsible for their misdeeds. The governor-general of two provinces was checked by the governors of each one. [*45*, p. 6] The inspectorate established in the Han dynasty, whereby officials were sent out to observe others of higher rank [*20*, p. 55], had long since grown into the Censorate, an effective inquisition and control agency. Recruited from the top passers of the examinations, kept independent of other branches [*558*, pp. 215–216], to some extent even of the emperor, this organization had great authority. Such devices, often sacrificing efficiency to safety, could not prevent corruption and demoralization, but they were completely effective in forestalling overt dissidence in the civil service.

A civil service may try to gain control of administration for itself, but not ordinarily to displace the ruler; military forces are usually indifferent to administration, so long as their wants are secured, but they may well grasp power for themselves. The problem of controlling the army is hence more crucial than that of keeping the bureaucracy in hand, and even more difficult. If the bureaucracy is tied and immobilized by cross-checks, this is unfortunate but not disastrous; to put the army in a straitjacket is to invite calamities. Such obvious tactics as keeping the top command in the hands of the emperor and splitting field commands were used by the Achaemenids and the Moguls. [*249*, p. 110; *214*, pp. 44, 135] But it is very difficult to have an army that is at once powerful against potential opponents and powerless against the central authority; and this fact must have had much to do with moderating the bellicosity of great empires.

The Roman empire failed to find any means of checking the armies, which became and remained the chief political force. Only the Dominate of Diocletian and Constantine, after decades of very serious military turbulence, concertedly tried to restrain the legions. One means was so to elevate the emperor that obedience would seem a religious as well as a civil duty and the thought of toppling him would verge on sacrilege. On a more mundane level, Constantine entirely divorced military and civilian command, quite contrary to the traditional practice of interweaving the careers, both in the provinces and at the center; command of the infantry was also separated from that of the cavalry. [*302*, p. 341] Withal, the army remained a tremendous power in the state. Finally, in the West military leaders took over entirely.

Although countless Caesars were cut down by the legions, Chinese history knows only one successful military coup, the one that led to the founding of the Sung dynasty. Civilian supremacy was possible partly because China was relatively secure; the barbarians jabbing at the frontiers were much less numerous than those who kept Rome nervous. This meant not only that the army could be relatively small and inefficient, but also that its prestige was low; it was a domestic police force rather than defender of the land. Social and political priority went to the scholar-gentry class, and the soldier was scorned as nowhere else, classed among the lowest of society; it became unthinkable that a soldier should aspire to the moral height of the Son of Heaven. Not content with moral ascendancy, however, the later dynasties used much the same political controls with the army as with the administration. No general commanded more than a small fraction of the forces, and troops and commanders were frequently rotated. Military leaders were rarely given civilian office. Provincial governors were superiors of military commanders in their districts and controlled promotions. All commanders were coordinated and checked by civilian commissars. [38, pp. 44–45] To some extent Confucianist indoctrination, so effective with the bureaucracy, inculcated obedience in the military. Even when rulers became impotent, prisoners of eunuchs or palace camarillas, the armies seldom stirred.

The Turkish sultans were for a time equally successful in guaranteeing a loyal army by education. Christian boys were reared and trained to complete and slavish devotion, entirely divorced from their families and background and forbidden to marry lest they acquire outside bonds. They were not allowed to learn any trade but that of soldiering, or even to buy goods except as provided by the commissary. This Janissary force remained disciplined and very useful so long as it was thus recruited. It became a menace only when relaxed in the general decay. [432, Pt. I, pp. 58, 63]

A more general means of combating disloyalty or disobedience of people – officials and military alike – is the political police, a corps specially dedicated to the protection of the emperor and the state by sniffing out troublemakers and unreliable elements and bringing them to justice. The insecurity of the autocrat and the impossibility of free and frank opposition to his policies imply a political police as a grain warehouse might imply cats. A corps of spies, investigators, and keepers of political purity has probably been a major, though not much advertised, part of all great autocracies, equally to bring the guilty to book and to make the people aware that they are being watched, thus maintaining an atmosphere of respectful fear. The Incas seem to have had secret inspectors as well as overt controllers. [*181*, p. 22] In the Maurya empire, police spies pretended to be merchants, students, even recluses, naturally also prostitutes, to detect crimes and wrong thinking. [*217*, p. 112] Kautilya's *Arthasastra* urged, in much and repetitious detail, the use of all manner of informers and provocateurs to test loyalties of the highest personages. All citizens and property were registered, and everyone from the lowest villager to the heir to the throne was theoretically under surveillance. [*201*, pp. 209, 222]

That agents and spies pervaded the palace, the administration, and the whole life of China hardly requires noting. Although somewhat less despotic in its youth — the Roman republic had no public prosecutor and almost no police force, but depended on the goodwill of the citizens to observe fulfillment of the laws and bring charges if necessary [*310*, p. 152; *298*, p. 29] — the Roman empire was no exception. Augustus himself encouraged informers [*308*, pp. 219–220] and probably had secret agents and police who disposed of political opponents. Under Tiberius and later, even intimate talk among friends was hampered by fear lest some utterance be denounced to the ruler. A secret police corps in civilian garb was detached from the imperial guard sometime in the first century [*345*, pp. 73, 158], and by the second century it had become a strong force. [*302*, p. 34] The later empire was overrun with agents and informers, official and unofficial, who spied on private persons, officials, and one another, denouncing and extorting; there were some ten thousand such agents in government pay. [*314*, I, 548]

The Russian tsars were assisted by a political police at least from the time of Ivan IV. His dedicated and beloved *oprichniki* dressed in black, rode black horses, and carried dogs' heads and brooms to symbolize their tasks of investigation, vengeance, and purge. [*377*, p. 201] Peter reorganized and strengthened the investigatory organs, forming a special department, superior to all others, with authority over all subjects and power to execute its sentences. [*359*, p. 250] He also introduced "fiscals" who were to look into almost everything and encouraged denunciations by giving informers a quarter of the property and perhaps the title and position of the victim. Treason was the only charge a serf could legally make against his master.

Among later tsars, the stern Nicholas I particularly strengthened the antisubversive police to ferret out any dissent and to seal the borders against foreign contagion. [*404*, p. 362] Even schoolchildren were recruited for this service. [R. Tucker in *409*, p. 32] He also set the bureaucrats to spying on one another. [*408*, p. 371] After him the special guard, or Okhrana, gained fame for its often dramatic and sometimes perfidious struggle against the radical movement; but it spied upon the members of the royal family as well as upon students' and workers' unions, infiltrating not only subversive groups but nearly all organizations in the land. If subversive activities were lacking they were invented, since the sections of the Okhrana were rated according to the amount of revolutionary activity they uncovered. [*415*, p. 65] A power to itself, it dominated the ministry of the interior under the last tsars, and had practically unhampered jurisdiction of such cases as fell to it. [*374*] The police in general were so devoted to antisubversion that the protection of the citizens was neglected. The number of police upholding the tsarist state was very large, reaching 104,500 in 1897, plus many rural officials. [*360*, p. 185]

Finally, if the ruler suspected that some persons had failed in their duty of total loyalty, might endanger the public safety by opposing him, or were somehow inconvenient, there was the sword of terror. Sometimes, if the empire was secure and mellow, it could be fairly gentle; for example, the Byzantine empire often only blinded potential leaders of dissent. [*311*, p. 362] In its latter days the Ch'ing dynasty (which slaughtered millions while affirming its power) executed relatively few, although prisoners often died from neglect or starvation [*76*, p. 380]; the laws provided that in case of treason, all male relatives of the culprit and all males living under the same roof, except children, should be executed. [*10*, pp. 71–72] If the ruler is strong and cruel, or feels menaced in his own sacred flesh or dignity, he may murder on a scale befitting his grandeur, and terror multiplies as the friends and relatives of victims in turn become dangerous, and the fear that some may escape makes it more imperative to strike without mercy. The tale of gruesome massacres in the great empires can never be told, but the number of dead must be astronomical, for the divine rulers have smashed humans as a man might step upon a swarm of ants. Those dangerous to the ruler are removed; those who remain tremble, and his state is served. There is little reason for him to hesitate, even if elegance may not require that he, like the Abbasid califs, have executioners with sharp swords standing beside the throne, ready to dispatch offenders. [452, p. 28]

Proscription and political murder were old habits of Rome by the time the republic died. Sulla slew his thousands, and many a Caesar accounted for his tens or even hundreds of thousands. Not only were there executions, but from the time of Augustus many were condemned to the dreaded imperial mines. [345, p. 161] Under despots such as Nero, aristocrats never knew when their time might come, and the best they could hope for was a peaceful departure by opening veins in a warm bath. Capricious murderers like Domitian might condemn a woman for undressing in the presence of his statue. Caracalla (211–217) seems to have outdone his predecessors. On coming to the throne he executed some 20,000 supporters or possible adherents of the brother whom he had murdered [523, p. 90], and many others felt the weight of his wrath. When the Alexandrians irritated him, supposedly by witticisms, he ordered a general and indiscriminate massacre, felling most of the population. [314, I, 118] Gallienus (253–268) wrote to a myrmidon after the suppression of one of the innumerable risings: "It is not enough that you exterminate such as have appeared in arms; the chance of battle might have served me as effectually. The male sex of every age must be extirpated provided that, in the execution of the children and old men, you can contrive means to save our reputation." [314, I, 242] At times ordinary folk were caught up in the network of terror for anything from calling a slave Hannibal to omitting a phrase from public prayer; even when in prison they had to weigh their words, for informers were in their midst. [302, pp. 33–34] When treason was in question, torture was used indiscriminately against citizens and slaves. Nor were the highly placed exempt; Constantine invited informers against the most intimate and trusted members of his entourage. [314, I, 566]

Inca rulers, who had only to raise a hand to sentence anyone to death, prided themselves on mildness to those who bowed without fighting, but rebellious tribes might be wiped out. [173, pp. 95–99] Individual crimes were harshly punished also. The common penalty for even minor misdeeds was death, and any slight offense to any person of royal blood was subject to the most terrible retribution. [*181*, p. 25]

The wild but not purposeless massacres of Ivan the Terrible are renowned. He executed perhaps ten thousand persons of the upper classes, the numbers being known partly from the lists that the gross butcher sent to monasteries for the sanctimonious commemoration of his victims. [*388*, II, 88] Learning of discontent in Novgorod, he massacred perhaps 60,000 citizens. [*419*, p. 189] In connection with various conspiracies or movements of opposition, Peter killed thousands of supposed or real opponents, many with his own vigorous right hand [*377*, pp. 324–325], and deported tens of thousands. Subsequent tsars were less grossly murderous, and caned their nobles instead of lopping off their heads [*396*, p. lvii], but there was never much hesitation in the use of force when it seemed necessary or advisable, down to the cleanup after the abortive revolution of 1904–05. Then the noose, popularly called Stolypin's necktie in honor of the prime minister, claimed many thousand victims.

Other empires might vie for honors in terrorism. Justinian, famous for his law code, killed thirty to forty thousand of the people of Constantinople who had opposed him. [*353*, p. 157] Turkish rulers bowed cheerfully to the koranic maxim, "Sedition is worse than slaughter" [*433*, p. 49], and those who fell from grace were lucky to keep head on shoulders. A high official whose death had been secretly decided was usually dispatched without warning or hearing. Not only the mighty suffered. Selim the Grim is said to have killed forty thousand for heresy, nearly equivalent to political opposition. The first Kuprili vizier brought tranquillity by executing some thirty-five thousand of the unruly, thousands of them by his own hand. [*431*, p. 169; *433*, pp. 221–222] In the Sassanid empire the sword was a powerful stimulant, as a diplomat or a general who failed his mission was likely to find himself headless; and so many of the great families were exterminated as seriously to weaken military capacities. [*251*, p. 93] Similarly, primitive rulers, like the kings of Dahomey, have had many killed merely for pleasure or to evidence their power and wealth. [*264*, II, 55] Many rulers have seemingly enjoyed exercising their power over life as they have beheaded with their own hands or had men slain in their presence; and terror has often exceeded political purpose. When a gang of revelers disturbed Jahangir's peace, he had them immediately executed. [*199*, p. 227] When a noble who had entertained Xerxes on the way to the Greek campaign petitioned that one of his five sons be excused, Xerxes released the young man from the army only to have him cut in two and the halves fastened to the city gates.

Terror may not be indispensable, but it is a very useful pillar of the arbitrary order. It is persuasive evidence of greatness that a man can send hundreds or thousands, as he will, to death; and fear merges into awe. Those who tremble with dread may flatter with sincerity and serve with zeal. Terror is not always unpopular, as many are glad to witness suffering or to see their immediate oppressors fall, and underlings clamber onto the seats of those struck down. But terror cannot be limited to those who are really dangerous. It is more important to strike those who harbor hidden treason than those who show themselves, those who are powerful than those who are weak. The ultimate use of power thus becomes a danger to the most powerful.

GUIDANCE OF MINDS

Terror and force are wasteful and inefficient means of government. They destroy potentially valuable servants and disturb the functioning order. They may deter from rebellion, but they cannot make men fully useful. Slaves can be whipped into digging a canal or plowing a field, but not into doing their best or working faithfully when the controller's back is turned; and force damages or destroys those upon whom it is turned. The more difficult and complicated the task, the less likely it can be done by coercion. When command is felt only as duress, people have no scruples about cheating or evading it. Matching wits with bosses, the subjects take pleasure in getting away with as much as possible. Above all, it is difficult for the ruler to manage by force those directly in his service, the military and administrative leaders. They can be and are rewarded for their labors, but rewards are costly, can never be perfectly apportioned, and stimulate less to service than to seeking of gain. It is far better for the emperor if he can make wills his own, wholly or in part, so that they serve him faithfully and freely, even when they can expect no pay.

Consequently, the control of thinking is a necessary adjunct and continuation of political control for any government that does not rest firmly on the consent and needs of the governed, and especially for the regime that claims fully to command the lives of its subjects. It must seek to manufacture consent and suppress awareness of discontent, to choke off the wrong and implant the right ideas, to avoid blame for evils, and to gain credit for the good that befalls. Dissatisfaction is contagious and must be kept from spreading. The people should be persuaded to accept subjection with equanimity, if not enthusiasm, as a natural, even blessed state, partly because the whole world accepts it, partly because it is superhumanly right. They may be induced to place the values of the empire above their own, and even be led to murmur, in Dante's phrase, "In his will is our peace." Use of the whip is a confession of failure.

Hence, freedom of expression does not mix with powerful empires. Formally or informally, often without systematic censorship but with an understanding of the narrow limits of toleration and grievous punishment for violators thereof, the empires proscribe dissent and attempt to instill correct thinking. Powerful men almost always dislike disagreement, although in freer societies they usually tolerate a degree of it. Freedom of expression can hardly be greater than freedom of action; where there is no room for political opposition and freedom of organization, neither is there a place for free speech. It is self-evident to the strong ruler that contrary opinions are wrong and noxious; they reduce his ability to do good; it is his duty to protect his wards from confusion and perversion. It is a merit in his eyes to punish insults to his name and state or to organize public praise and glorification of his greatness. To allow poisons of dissidence to be spread seems as dangerous as it is unnecessary; it is not control but freedom that requires elaborate justification. The beginning of printing in Russia under Peter was also the beginning of censorship. [423, p. 435] It has never ceased since, except when brief weakening of the government has brought freedom. Illegal presses, not illegal weapons, were the object of the Okhrana's greatest zeal.

Moreover, psychological control is probably the safest and surest of all means of control. Strictly political controls are a hindrance to production and effectiveness. Armies are dangerous, and police forces tend to escape control and often cause as much trouble as they prevent. But censors, teachers, and propagandists, those who dedicate themselves to the praise of the autocrat and the manifestation of his rightness and glory, possibly because they have no means or claim to power for themselves, or because they are persuaded by the formulas they mouth, are probably the least troublesome of all the servants of autocracy. And hardly anyone is immune to the propaganda that fills the intellectual air. If imposed unanimity deadens society, such a problem concerns few autocrats.

Any strong government would like to manufacture favorable opinion, but the empires are most capable of it. Where materials for comparison are lacking, it is far easier to guide thinking than it is in a freer and more chaotic society. In a small state, men know much more of affairs by their own eyes or the testimony of their friends; in the great state, important things are far away, geographically and in their magnitude over the ordinary man; information is mostly indirect, furnished by the regime or through channels that it can control. In a community of states, even tyrants find it difficult to prevent their people from learning of events and ideas abroad. Totality of control is very important; if only a tiny leakage of free information contradicts the official versions, these may be largely discredited, while a censorship that is not fully effective convinces people of the great truths denied them and places high value on smuggled ideas. Thus in tsarist Russia censorship was remarkably ineffective despite the best efforts of the tsars and their police, and the regime's attempts to propagandize were weak and sometimes ridiculous; too many of the educated had knowledge of the more advanced West. But for the truly universal empire there is no consequential outside and no alternative truth.

Censorship and propaganda, moreover, are part of monolithism. When independent powers are destroyed or abased and the economy is brought under control, there is little support for thought contrary to the official pattern; men need only to be brought to accept this reality. In the totality of the imperial order, individuals can with difficulty set their opinions against its grandeur. It sets the standards of success and failure, hence of right and wrong; it suffers no competition, but alone rewards and damns or destroys. Whatever it proclaims has the fundamental rightness not merely of unchallengeable power but of organized society.

Methods of guiding souls have changed through centuries, but the political changes have been less marked than have the material. Many monuments of very ancient empires sought not only to overawe but to convey a message: the emperor speaks on the one hand of his fierceness toward his enemies and on the other of his love and care for his people. When Cyrus conquered Babylonia, he had his scribes compose a long poem on the evils of the previous king and on his own mission as bringer of peace. [252, p. 53] The Egyptians of the New Kingdom had an efficacious program of indoctrination. In the course of extensive conquests, sons of chiefs and nobles were brought to Egypt for training and sent back later to their homelands, where they ruled with the aid of Egyptian advisers and tribute collectors, supported by garrisons. When Egyptian rule was under attack, many of them sided firmly with their masters and educators, even against their own countrymen. [111, p. 246]

The Roman empire in its first century enjoyed some free speech both in governing circles and among the commonalty. Rumors of disasters continually swept the city; Tacitus remarked on the love of the people for the worst gossip. Historians and others wrote critically of almost everything except the reigning Caesar. Although it sometimes seemed that praise for the emperor's mercy and piety was directly proportional to his brutality [275, p. 37], indoctrination was unsystematic. However, games and festivals, chariot races, gladiatorial matches, and animal baiting, which eventually filled a third to a half of the year [285, p. 372], were essentially a form of propaganda, as were many ceremonies, such as grand triumphs wherein Caesars displayed trophies of sometimes fictitious victories. Bothered by the circulating tales, Augustus probably set up a counterrumor factory. There was no regular censorship, but Caesars from Augustus onward kept a close watch over literature and drama. [345, pp. 65–67, 214–215] They regularly patronized the artists and writers who pleased them, assisted cultural activities, and subsidized the theater, which was largely an official institution [345, pp. 93, 96]; but displeasing authors were banished (Ovid's being the most famous case), inconvenient writings were destroyed from time to time, and the law of treason was invoked against offensive writings. [330, p. 93] Circulation of books depended mostly on private copying, and so was not easily controllable. But the relatively mild Augustus burned, according to Suetonius, more than two thousand writings of prophetic or evil character. [330, p. 56]

In view of the emperors' fears, books on magic were always dangerous to own. Augustus severely restricted fortune-telling in his

later years, especially predictions of anyone's death. [*345*, p. 84]
Vespasian expelled from Rome many troublesome talkers, astrologers, and philosophers [*342*, p. 115; *285*, p. 304], but he supported
teachers of oratory. Later Caesars freely destroyed what displeased
them. Valens (364–378), for example, burned many books on law
and arts [*345*, p. 364], and Aurelian contributed to the destruction
of the excellent libraries of Alexandria, finished off a few centuries
later by Arabs, who had the better excuses of primitiveness and
religious zeal. Schools, which had been free and unregulated under
the republic, were increasingly subsidized and controlled under
later Caesars. [*303*, p. 399]

The most primitive of the great empires, that of the Incas, was
as skilled as any in the molding of opinion. While conquering far
and wide, they proclaimed mildness and pity, apparently with
sufficient effect to lead many peoples peacefully to accept their
yoke. Those who preferred the folly of resistance sometimes provided skins for drums used in triumphal processions. For the edification of the populace the emperor trod publicly on the necks of
prisoners. Inca priests went out to spread the worship of the Sun,
which all were required to adopt; conquered deities were transported to the capital. The heads of ten-thousands and conquered
chiefs and their families were also brought to Cuzco for indoctrination in the law, religion, and customs of the empire. For lack of
a system of writing the Incas had men memorize the facts of the
past and put together an official history for general instruction. A
corps of learned men and poets composed and popularized eulogistic ceremonial lays which, under official patronage, largely replaced older accounts; a primitive theater portrayed the deeds of
past Incas. [*173*, pp. 176–178] Perhaps thanks in part to the lack
of written records, this reeducation was so successful that the
conquered peoples seem to have come to accept the Inca version
of history, and nearly all knowledge, even popular tradition, of
independent life a century or less before was erased. [*179*, p. 71]
The Incas also tried to make servitude delightful. Long and colorful
ceremonies culminated in the swearing of fidelity to the rulers.
Forced labor was beautified with singing and bright pageantry,
and the people cultivating the fields of the state sang songs in
praise of the emperor and his god. [*170*, p. 71]

The Chinese were also virtuosos in psychological control, for
which they have in later days given the world the term "brain-

washing." The approach of the first unifiers, the Ch'in dynasty, was rather negative in view of their infatuation with ruthless power and emphasis on punishment over reward, on driving over leading. Even while swallowing the weaker states, the rulers of Ch'in destroyed their records and cultural works as symbolic of their independence. [69, p. 100] When they gained total power they tried virtually to annihilate the whole cultural heritage of the civilization they had overcome and so carried through the most infamous of countless book burnings. It is related that in vengeance against the scholar class, which had regarded Ch'in as semibarbarian, all books except a few, such as manuals of agriculture, were ordered burned under pain of death, "that none within the empire should use the past to discredit the present." The very mention of the previous independent kingdoms was forbidden. Some hundreds of scholars were eliminated at the same time. This purge was in part undone when another dynasty more sympathetic to learning came to power. Many books were brought out of hiding places and others were recovered, more or less, from memory. But it was easier, since so much had been destroyed, for later emperors to have literature rewritten and history reinterpreted as they wished. [5, p. 165]

Subsequent dynasties have inherited a literature suitable for their purposes. Little has been saved and propagated save that which suited successive imperial regimes, and almost nothing that could be called really heretical. There has been little need directly to control schools, since these were necessarily oriented toward civil service examinations. Printing and publishing could then be left formally free; but the printer, vendor, or reader of any publication in breach of good morals, political or social, or which troubled the peace or brought disrespect on authority, was severely punished. [3, p. 393; 37, II, 86] Books have been suppressed, especially under the Ch'ing or Manchu dynasty, which was concerned to secure acceptance despite its foreign origin. The action was exceptionally sophisticated and probably effective. Scholars were set to making extensive literary compilations, collecting and cataloguing all works. For this purpose the government appealed to the loyal people to turn in rare volumes, sometimes paying large prices; there was even canvassing from house to house for the benefit of the imperial library. This gave an opportunity to comb through and do away with literature unfavorable to the Manchus or other invader dynasties. Some 2,320 works were abolished; in 1774–1781, there were twenty-eight book burnings affecting 538 titles in 13,862 volumes. [28, pp. 229–230; 45, p. 3] Subsequently, records were doctored and purged so thoroughly that the Taiping rebellion of the middle of the ninteenth century, which took perhaps as many lives as the First World War, is known almost entirely from Western sources. The literary-ideological purge was also so successful that the Chinese scholar class firmly supported the foreign and increasingly corrupt dynasty against all the risings that threatened to topple it, and that would certainly have succeeded but for the loyalty of the scholars.

From Han times, however, the Chinese preferred persuasion to coercion. For example, officials were sent to read the imperial edicts even to bandits [38, p. 76], who were supposed to bow to the words and examples of virtue. The Hans started schools in annexed areas for the formation of local officials; they also introduced new crops and decreed civilizing reforms of customs. [H. Mujakawa in 78, p. 33] Other dynasties have similarly sought to bolster their order primarily by training administrators and promoting suitable ethics. [W. Eberhard in 19, p. 91] Literary works were subsidized [40, Bk. I, p. 349], and Confucianist themes and morality were injected into popular drama and tales. [78, p. 11] Religious organizations, Buddhist and Taoist as well as official Confucianist, were more or less incorporated into the state structure. Officials gave public banquets for the honorable aged and for those who were successful in examinations. Toward the end of the Northern Sung dynasty there were established "self-indicting study rooms," where those of wrong opinions were to read and think to correct their views. [47, p. 89] Under the Ming dynasty, villages had to hold monthly assemblies, at which they recited moralistic exhortations and repeated the oath of fidelity. [38, p. 26] The Manchus had a corps of lecturers expounding the emperor's maxims to the peasants at such obligatory monthly congregations. They talked of general morality and the love of the emperor for the people, as shown by public works or rice given during famine; and they stressed the corresponding duty to shun false doctrines, obey the law, deliver up criminals, and pay taxes promptly in a filial manner. [36, pp. 185–191] Only the Manchu Bannermen were exempt from attendance, and even they had to memorize the Six Maxims, the Sacred Edict, and the Amplified Instructions. Successful lecturers were rewarded, and the system seemingly had good effects. For children, there was issued a versified form of the Sacred Edict. [29, II, 38] Boards of shame were erected, pavilions in which were posted the names of those who demonstrated by evil deeds their failure to absorb these lessons. [36, p. 186]

While these techniques of spiritual direction were applied to all, the most effective means of securing conformity was the examination system. Since the only lucrative and honorable career was the bureaucracy, this required almost everyone of real ambition — there were literary examinations even for generals [32, p. 24] — to spend years studying the approved classics, soaking up ideas of social order, subordination, and responsibility. While only a small fraction, perhaps 1 or 2 percent by quota under the Ch'ing dynasty [8, p. 11], passed the examinations and entered upon an official career, one could always keep studying and try again or perhaps become a teacher of other aspirants. Those who passed the lower examinations were kept busy preparing for higher ones and so might spend decades indoctrinating themselves. [8, pp. 172–173] Constant immersion in Confucianism, with all its stress on loyalty and service, left little time or mental energy for anything else. No contrary ideas could hope for a hearing, while the Confucianist ethic became, through centuries and successive dynasties, firmer and firmer. Loyalty that had once been tempered by moral judgment became unconditional obedience, whether the ruler was a benevolent autocrat or an outright tyrant, with acceptance of the canon that the "sovereign alone creates blessings and intimidates; to him alone belongs all that is precious and edible." Neo-Confucianism went so far in the exaltation of fidelity that those who had served one dynasty, even in a minor capacity, felt inhibited from accepting a position under another; hence it became difficult for them to countenance revolution even against the most depraved. [F. Mote in 78, p. 232]

USE OF FAITH

It is not enough to punish seditious utterances and to repeat endlessly that the emperor is wise, just, and strong, that his name must be blessed, his commands obeyed, and his taxes paid. To impart a sense of devotion, a habitual, all-pervading sense of dependence, responsibility, and reverence for the supreme power, and to justify authority, a faith or creed is needed. The order of the empire needs to affirm itself upon the deeper feelings, the ideals, hopes, and fears of the people, to make itself part of the transcendent way of the universe. To rule well and completely, the empire should be a universal church as well as a universal polity. Absolute power requires an absolute mission.

If authority is to be efficient and secure, it should be smooth, orderly, and well understood, not violent and obviously arbitrary. A ruler who rests on force alone must always fear force. It is very difficult for an autocrat to be sure of the loyalty and obedience even of those closest to him unless they are profoundly loyal to what he represents; it may always suit the convenience or self-interest of powerful men that he die or be replaced. Dynastic tradition and custom of obedience are helpful, but it is far better if the rulership is strongly related to the divine and eternal order of things; and perhaps all masters of great empires have claimed some sort of divine sanction for their rule. To exercise stable power is difficult for those who have scanty justification, like the Mongols who could allege little except their own appetites and the vague superiority of the free-living steppe peoples over city dwellers. If they had had broader ideals to help assimilate the subjugated nations to their order, their power might have been less ephemeral.

All large, impersonal organizations seek to base their authority to some extent on symbols, ritual, or high purposes. [530, p. 141] They need to idealize their purposes, which are often obscured by size and complexity, even if they need not gloss over the fact that the elite of the organization use it to serve themselves, or that their professed aims differ from their real strivings. [475, p. 7] It has often been remarked that naked power is ashamed of itself and puts on the cloak of an ideal, the garb of duty and faith. This is not, of course, because power has an inborn sense of shame, but because brute dominance, by muscle or guns, is repugnant to the sense of human society, and a rule of sheer arbitrary might is bound to become as corrupt as gangsterism. So far as political and hierarchical relations are not rationally acceptable, they must be explained in mythical, traditional, or mystical terms.

Slavery is more efficient when linked to a persuasive rationale: slaveholders, like any who enjoy a privileged position, know that their superiority is right and natural, that the slaves are better off

in slavery or destined to it by nature and probably happier in servitude, and that there are good and eternal reasons for it all. The
masters are comfortable and more effective in the conviction that
they are doing right, just as the most rational users of power
enjoy feeling that they exercise it only for the benefit of others.
For the slaves, in turn, it is a satisfaction to know that they are
ruled not by chance force but by high principles and the keepers
of ethics, against which nothing can be attempted. Most of all,
the idea of an orderly universe in which they should fill their role
is essential for the middle ranks, who thus feel the rightness of
their obedience to superiors and command over inferiors. It is less
essential to benumb the usually helpless masses than to give the
officials a sense of duty.

Wherever there is a dominant elite, one may expect an appeal to
higher or inscrutable reasons, both because they are useful and
because the elite is in a position to make use of them. Magic is
widely used in primitive societies, especially where the tribal
organization is large and complex, to assure the subordination of
commoners, to terrorize and instill respect, and to transfer wealth
to the fortunate. [532, pp. 137–150] The Spartans, most exploitative
of the Greeks, were likewise the most ideologically inclined. Although they formed a small and close-knit group, ruling for their
own benefit over much larger numbers of serfs and slaves, they felt
it necessary to idealize their constitution as a sacred thing; indeed,
they were able to give many Greeks who had no material interest
in their domination a feeling that it was a sublime expression of
virtue. Of course, they pleased themselves most of all. Empires
similarly need their constitutions or their faiths, perhaps not for
the inculcation of valor and discipline, as in the Spartan case, but
for the sanctioning of subordination.

A faith, or ideal reason for obedience, is the more necessary as
the authority is remote and the need for serving it and making sacrifices to it is difficult to understand. It needs the image of perfection to keep alive belief in the order despite obvious errors and
weaknesses of leaders and subalterns alike; with strong faith the
church can survive many bad popes, while a secular society would
be quickly ruined. As a huge, artificial order without a natural
consensus, the great empire needs, much more than smaller and
better integrated societies, an imposed value system to hold it
together. Lacking the morale of patriotic feeling, it wants a broad

and inclusive creed to cover its diversity and a synthetic moral backbone, as the state loses consistency in ceasing to be a unit in opposition to other units. So far as the men of an empire show patriotism, it is rather ideal or religious than national; they feel that they are fighting, not for something that is their own, but for something that is holy.

A faith or ideology gives validity to the mystique of rulership and the apotheosis of the ruler, as he represents a mission higher than human. It may lend a touch of universality beyond the actual power of the empire; an Assyrian monarch called upon "the gods of the regions to honor him so that none might escape." [466, p. 241] It lends solemnity to discourse and provides a rationale for beautiful and inspiring rituals. It deters change, and change is ordinarily unwelcome to powers that have achieved completion. It acts as a vehicle of uniform instruction, helping to assimilate all to the desired mold. It justifies persecution of dissent, to save souls from their own evil. And it fills minds, serving to a great extent as a substitute for the political activity that occupies many, especially of the elite, in freer and more competitive societies.

The great empire is the more inclined to foster an ideological consensus, just as it is to impose controls on opinion, because it is in a position to do so. In a society where there are many free and diverse currents and where opinions from an independent outside cannot be excluded, the state is less tempted to try to impose a desired view of the universe and society; it usually rather takes lessons from the people than tells them what to think. But where there is a monopoly of power and information, any ruler might be tempted, even if he had no personal interest, to spread his truth. It is, moreover, the easier for the ruler of a great empire to impose the truth that suits him because the people are already convinced of the incomprehensible greatness of the state. Whatever kind of state exists tends to make itself an ideal, even in the freest society; and the people of the empire, for whom the state is all, easily see in the empire the vehicle of all ideals. What it professes is not to be gainsaid.

For the empire, an ethical system is a supplement and partial substitute for law. Autocracy, being fundamentally lawless, has the greater necessity for more general guides to conduct. Broad principles serve better than specific laws to mold the spirit, make positive loyalty, and cover all contingencies. The guidance of a general philosophy or religion is the more needed, also, as the empire tries to control more. When official measures interfere with the economy and overrule the market, when traditional institutions are replaced by bureaucratic ones, no set of rules can be complete enough to secure proper management, even in the unlikely event that nearly everyone wished to follow them exactly. Much must be left to the discretion and judgment of managers and delegates. When formal procedures are complicated and drawn-out, when controllers have large powers of arbitrary decision, everyone — those below in hopes that justice will be served, those above in order to have some plausible basis for their actions — tends to think in terms of broad right and wrong, the ethics of the system. Then it is indispensable for the emperor that he be obeyed, as the tsars used to say, not only from fear, or according to law, but for conscience' sake, or according to religion.

The autocratic empire is thus well ordered if it is like a family in which harmony and dedication to the general interest come less from explicit rules than from the right attitudes of the members toward one another, their love and respect for the father and their complete acceptance of familial roles. The emperor, then, caring for all, acting as symbolic father, expects corresponding filial obedience. Hammurabi, like many others, called himself the "lord who is like a real father to the people." [327, p. 4] Augustus was officially designated "Father of the Country." Not only the Chinese emperor but his officials were fathers of all; even a district magistrate was known as a "father-mother official." [37, I, 125] Probably, in fact, much or most of the respect for authority ingrained in most people is inculcated in childhood, when one learns dependence upon the mother and awe for the overwhelming power of the father. Autocrats are well advised to reinforce family and paternal authority as education for their own. Much of the success of the Chinese empire may be laid to its ability, through Confucianism, to convert filial piety into loyalty for the emperor.

Having so strong an interest in an official religion or a secular ideology, the empire does not incline to favor an independent church. It would be a competitive organization and a political danger, as those who control the supernatural control men. Worse, it would present a source of independent moral judgment, an alternative to the official philosophy, a spiritual refuge from its sway. An idealism is largely concerned with the order of life and the structure of society, so that any group cultivating its own ideals must conflict with the all-embracing imperial order. Hence the empire seeks full conformity and the inclusion of all in an official church. Free states in a competitive system tend to be more or less tolerant; the imperial order is intolerant.

Very old empires took it for granted that temples and priesthoods should fully support the state and the divine or near-divine ruler, albeit much more in ceremonial than ethical ways, providing more magic than philosophy. In ancient Egypt the independent authority of the priesthood varied with the strength of the pharaoh, low in the great times of the Old Kingdom, larger in times of decay when the temples, with huge tax-exempt landholdings, became semi-independent fiefs. In the renewed New Kingdom, high priests apparently were seldom men of ecclesiastical vocation, but mostly courtiers, and the temple was part of the royal estate. Only as the pharaoh happened to be weak did the priesthood enjoy relative independence. [*114*, Pt. I, p. 17] Ikhnaten was able to introduce a new religion of his own and impose it on the land, although his successors went back to the older gods. The loss of independence of religion in imperial unification was quite marked in Mesopotamia. As long as the city-states were independent, the priests were rivals of the civil authorities; after the Akkadian conquest, in the successive empires, they were only servants, appointed and controlled by the rulers. [*125*, p. 60; *106*, p. 252]

More sophisticated and more ethical religions have probably been more useful. After Asoka had completed the violent conquest of India, he turned to nonviolent and passivist Buddhism and the moral law of Dhamma, which should make a perfect and pure order, and which made it a capital crime to kill animals. He was able to reduce substantially the power of the Brahmins, but not to break it entirely, for they were able after him to return and eventually to banish Buddhism from India. The authoritarian spirit of Islam has served many grossly despotic empires, like the Turkish and the Mogul and various califates and sultanates; under it the church was always closely meshed with the state, if not a part of its apparatus, and lacked an organized priesthood of its own. The theory of the califate as a heritage of the Prophet was developed only under the imperial-minded Abbasids and for their benefit. They liked to stress the religious nature of their rule and on ceremonial occasions literally wore the mantle of Prophet. [*452*, pp.

27–29] The greatest of the Moguls, Akbar, not satisfied to be head of church as well as of state in Moslem tradition [213, p. 14], undertook to establish an eclectic religion of his own, a blend of Islam and Hinduism in which the sun was symbol of divinity and Akbar himself was worshiped as its representative. [199, p. 158] This religion faded after him, but it left something of a halo around the imperial person. [216, pp. 132–135] His less statesmanlike heirs, especially Aurangzeb, retreated to Mohammedanism, clashing with the Hinduism of the majority of their subjects. The Turkish empire was tolerant in permitting sundry creeds, but the sultan asserted his control not only of the Moslem but of the other religious hierarchies, like the Greek church. [436, p. 158]

In its first centuries, the Roman empire was remarkable for the variety and freedom of its creeds. The official cults of Jupiter, Mars, and their fellow gods had long been associated with the aggressive city-state of Rome; but they fell into decay in the last generations of the republic. Augustus sought to revive them as support for the larger rulership and as moralizers of society. He became Pontifex Maximus, or chief priest, rebuilt temples, filled vacant priesthoods, and made the emperor the central figure of veneration. His successors emulated him in performing the rites, fostering piety, and at the same time placing themselves among the Olympians. Deified Caesars and the old gods long remained popular despite their lack of emotional appeal and the crudity of many myths and ceremonies [302, pp. 533–536], as the subject peoples lightened their subservience by making it a religious duty.

Later emperors patronized not only the old pantheon but various imported oriental gods. Local cult prophecies were used to suppress sedition, and Vespasian paraded miracles allegedly performed by himself. [345, pp. 93, 138] But the great change came when Constantine, an ostentatious despot and murderous egotist from whom only his mother was safe, had the merit to see the utility of Christianity and adopted it as the state cult. Decreeing observance of Sunday, he called it "the day of the Sun." [437, p. 253] Each of the first seven Christian emperors also became Pontifex Maximus upon accession and continued to use remnants of paganism [303, p. 34], but Christianity rapidly prevailed under imperial auspices. Julian the Apostate tried to turn back to a universal pagan church with reformed liturgy and priesthood; but Christianity, with its call for resignation, acceptance of worldly

authority and suffering, and transfer of hopes to the next life, was
much more suitable than a refurbished pagan mishmash.

The breakup of the Western empire enabled the bishop of Rome,
become pope, to escape political control; but in the Eastern or
Byzantine empire the church continued at the service of the state
and contributed to its unmatched stability. The ruler was absolute
in spiritual as in lay affairs. [C. Diehl in 292, p. 726] He nominated
and dismissed bishops, chose the patriarch, and could force abdica-
tion or deposition; on occasion patriarchs were imprisoned or executed. [311, p. 59] Through managment of synods, he could do
much to fix dogma. [301, pp. 33, 165] The monasteries, however,
accumulated wealth and had some independence; and in times of
imperial weakness the ecclesiasts could assert themselves, as in
390 Bishop Ambrose was able to bring Theodosius to public pen-
ance for an evil-tempered massacre. [285, p. 437] In 491, upon the
accession of a minor figure, the patriarch secured a written promise
that there would be no ecclesiastical innovations. [353, p. 102] But
stronger rulers were not so troubled, and they were fortified as
the state was churchified. Of the latter-day Caesars it was officially
proclaimed, "The Lord who giveth life shall lift up your hands,
O Masters [or Lords] above the whole universe. He will make of
all peoples your slaves." [301, p. 29] Court life became an endless
and intricate religious ritual. Imperial edicts were "celestial commands," and taxes became "the divine delegation." In justification
of the innumerable mutilations used as punishment there were
cited words of Christ about cutting off hands and plucking out
eyes. [437, pp. 241, 253] Bishops were expected to watch over the
conduct of officials. [353, p. 160] Theology became the intellectual
meat and drink of the empire, keeping minds in changeless and
harmless channels.

The marriage of the Orthodox church and the autocracy continued in Russia. In 1393, as rising Moscow was taking to ways
of absolutism, the patriarch of Constantinople wrote to the grand
prince, "It is impossible for Christians to have a Church and not to
have a tsar, because the Church and state are in close alliance and
it is impossible to separate one from the other. . . . Listen to Peter,
the Apostle, who said, 'Fear God, honor the tsar.'" [377, pp. 140]
Ironically, the Russian church had freedom and immunities under
the domination of the heathen Mongols, for whom empire meant
little more than the collection of taxes, but was curbed and sub-

jected by the Christian rulers of unified Russia. [*416*, p. 110] In
the fifteenth century the prince exercised decisive influence over
the election of patriarchs and sometimes deposed them. [*377*, p.
142] Ivan III, as a great unifier, went further. Sometimes acting as
head of the church, he firmly asserted his own superiority over any
metropolitan, and boldly confiscated formerly sacred lands of
monasteries. [*416*, p. 119; *377*, p. 167] Ivan IV (the Terrible) removed various immunities and privileges of the church, such as
the right to acquire land. [*359*, p. 40] He held that any attempt to
oppose him as a man necessarily led to opposition to God. In the
looser Kievan Russia, princes had usually been elevated to saint-
hood unless they were quite impossible [*367*, *passim*]; now the
tsar became holy ex officio. In the seventeenth century, his every
act was a religious ceremony, his life was a drawn-out ritual, and
his right was that of the champion of the church. Rightly could
Tsar Alexis upbraid a prince as anti-Christian for slowness in
sending forces, because he hurt the cause of Christ's defender.
[*367*, pp. 63, 69]

Peter, as a strong monarch, did a great deal to make subservient
the church, which had regained much authority in the Time of
Troubles early in the seventeenth century. Finding the orders to
be parasitic, he curbed religious landholding [*407*, p. 149], placed
church properties under surveillance, and decreed that no new
church buildings should be erected without permission. [*377*, pp.
410, 415] Most important, he decapitated the church. The Patri-
archate of Moscow had been established in 1589 to complete the
picture of that holy city as the Third Rome, but Peter found it no
longer necessary. When it became vacant, he declined to fill it but
set over the church a synod of bishops appointed by himself and
ruled by a layman, the Over-Procurator. [*404*, p. 257] His purpose
was explained in an official proclamation: when the church had
a single head the people were prone to see him as equal to the
ruler, another sovereign who might lend support to sedition. [*379*,
p. 145] He also gained close administrative control of the church,
which was made into almost a branch of the state; one of the duties
of the office of the Over-Procurator was to spy on the clergy. [*377*,
p. 413] The church at the same time should help control the people.
Although Peter was highly irreligious, he required regular church
attendance, partly that everyone should hear official pronouncements in religious surroundings. He also imposed the duty of

auricular confession while freeing the clergy from the obligation of secrecy in order to uncover opposition. [*377*, p. 416; *379*, p. 146]

So little liking was there for religious independence that in the eighteenth century the popular idea of Holy Russia came to have rather an antistate flavor; for the tsars and officialdom it implied an entity larger than themselves and a standard by which they might be judged. [*367*, pp. 116, 230] Catherine completed the work of Peter by closing many monasteries, secularizing most remaining church properties, and giving in return a government subsidy. [*377*, p. 549] The church hierarchy was partially assimilated to the bureaucracy and given similar official honors and decorations. [*402*, p. 91]

As a result, the church shared in the discredit and decay of its patron in the nineteenth century. The ecclesiastical career became unattractive for the educated and ambitious, and the intellectual level of the church, never high, sank. Poor and ignorant, the priests became mere custodians of ritual, virtually without spiritual influence, forced to bargain for ritual fees, as impoverished as the peasants among whom they lived, social equals of the blacksmith. [*410*, p. 74; *418*, p. 151] Church courts were apparently quite as venal as civil courts. [*419*, p. 55] Still, the church served its political masters. The slogan of tsardom was "Nationality, Orthodoxy, Autocracy"; its ideologue, Pobedonostsev, stated: "The Church and the Church alone has allowed us to remain Russians and unite our scattered strength." [R. Byrnes in *393*, p. 113] The catechism taught in state and church schools until 1917 included the following question: "What does religion teach us as our duty to the tsar?" with the answer, "Worship, fidelity, the payment of taxes, service, love and prayer, the whole being comprised in the words worship and fidelity." [*423*, p. 440] The people learned the virtue of suffering. As was said in a time of great hardship, "Who are so noble, so true-hearted as they? Instead of rebelling against the Lord's anointed, they ascribe all their sufferings to the will of the Lord." [*390*, p. 5] In 1915 a metropolitan, to justify the administrative chaos, indicated that not only the tsar but his ministers as well had the Holy Ghost upon them. [*367*, p. 87] Ever faithful, the Russian church continued to offer public prayers for the last tsar well after he had been overthrown.

For the Incas, the worship of the sun served as justification for conquest, a duty imposed by the deity upon his elect. It also facilitated acceptance; peoples bowed not to a mortal like themselves but to the Son of the Sun. The priests served as missionaries and upholders of the Inca order, and native chieftains were incorporated into the priesthood. [*172*, p. 35] The conquered were deprived of support of their own gods, as their idols were carried off to Cuzco. [J. Rowe in *180*, p. 272] Upon all the people was laid an obligation of confession, after which they received penitential punishment and were plunged into the river. [*173*, pp. 57–58]

The Chinese have probably best fortified empire with a coherent and sophisticated, yet understandable and persuasive ideology, Confucianism, the most effective philosophical support of autocracy yet invented. Yet Chinese emperors have always used or managed other creeds and churches as well. Long before Confucius, the weak Chou emperor was head of the traditional state cult, a sort of pontifex maximus of the Chinese, and this he never ceased to be. As such, he was so powerful over the pantheon that it was believed he could promote or demote gods in the celestial hierarchy, just as he dealt with his earthly servants. [*40*, Bk. II, p. 135] The emperor acted as head of the recognized Buddhist and Taoist organizations as well. Sometimes quite crass use was made of religious beliefs, as when in 1005 a Sung emperor, having suffered defeats in the northwest, tried to restore his prestige by fabricating and appearing to find suitable heavenly revelations.

Chinese rulers were also careful lest religious movements exercise independent strength. The Hans probably forbade entry into monasteries. [*29*, p. 127] The Sui-Tang restoration of empire in the seventh century harshly repressed Buddhism and other sects that had flourished during the centuries of disunion. As a minister stated shortly after the accession of the dynasty, Buddhism led people to disobey and escape taxes, "to defraud the sovereign of his prerogatives and power, and appropriate his exclusive rights to lead humanity toward reformation for good." [*31*, p. 37] Although the founder of the Ming dynasty was a Buddhist priest, he proscribed the most active Buddhist groups. [*28*, p. 200] Monks were required to have certificates, temples could be built only by permission, and proselytizing was restricted. [*77*, p. 68] Later there came violent persecutions, directed less at beliefs than at the wealth the temples had been able to accumulate by their relative freedom to trade. Some forty thousand Buddhist temples and many thousands of monasteries are said to have been destroyed in the ninth century. Later in the dynasty Buddhism was threatened with abolition and Taoist books were destroyed. [29, p. 172] Such measures ended independent religions, including Mazdaism, Manichaeism, and Nestorian Christianity, as forces in China. [28, pp. 130–131] The place of religion has declined through successive dynasties. Although the emperors closely regulated monasteries, ceremonies, and clergy [31, *passim*] and named high priests of Taoism and of some Buddhist groups, while carrying out official rites as well [40, Bk. II, p. 28], they have been generally unfriendly to transcendental religion. The Sacred Edict of the Ch'ing dynasty exhorted the people to shun Buddhism, Taoism, and Christianity alike. [40, Bk. II, pp. 125–126] While the masses held to harmless ancient superstition, the emperors usually favored only Confucianism as support for their authority and way of life for the governing class.

They have been well served. The Ch'in dynasty, first imposing strong centralized empire, sought a merely despotic rule of force. The attempt failed. To say frankly, as did the Legalists of Ch'in, that the people exist for the benefit of the ruler, is foolish, however realistic. The Ch'in dynasty fell; the wiser Hans emphasized a traditional order of accepted rights, precedence, and ceremonies, and the conservatively authoritarian philosophy of Confucius, mixed with elements of other schools, gradually gained acceptance [40, Bk. I, p. 139], and was proclaimed official doctrine in 136 B.C. Under it, the rule of the emperor was founded on the moral order of the universe, the need for stability in society, and the respect naturally owing to parents and elders, all entwined in ideas of hierarchy, harmony, and the unity of the universe.

During the long post-Han disunity, Buddhism became, practically, the religion of China. The founder of the reunifying Sui dynasty tried to use it to promote the ideal of unity and to make death more palatable for soldiers; he also vaunted his Buddhist messiahship. [W. Eberhard in 19, p. 88] His dynasty was brief, however, and the T'ang, although founded by a Buddhist, preferred Confucianism. All subsequent dynasties made it the moral basis of their authority, its popularity rising and falling with the firmness of the empire. Refashioned into Neo-Confucianism during the Sung dynasty, it was made a state cult, although a pallid one, as well as an ethical system; Confucianist temples were established with occasional ceremonies and commemorations but no religious hierarchy that might faintly trouble the imperial power. Neo-Confucianism exalted the harmony of the universe as the manifestation of a Supreme Ultimate standing over and beyond all things. Harmony in turn implied a noncompetitive and static world based on virtue, moral self-discipline on the part of the ruler, and loyalty and conformity on the part of the ruled. [20, pp. 61–62] The essential relations were all of inequality: the subordination of children to parents, of wife to husband, of ministers to the emperor. To prevent chaos, everyone stood under someone else. [53, p. 7] The authority of the emperor was that of a father, just as governors and magistrates were fathers of their provinces or districts; while strengthening the habits of virtue and obedience in family relations, Confucianism borrowed them for the support of the whole imperial structure. Law, then, became the order of the universe as discovered by the paternal ruler, keeper of universal right. "The father and mother of the people" was duty-bound to control the activities of all who depended on him. [E. Zürcher in 12, p. 58] Full moral authority blessed political power for the perfection of despotism. [Nivison in 55, p. 23]

This supremely effective Confucian vision of harmony and social order made other religions superfluous. Even in times of decay and demoralization, it remained a stabilizing element; and emperors may thank it that, through many disorders, hardly any in recent centuries have been assassinated. Deeply inculcated by the examination system, it gave stature to the civil service and the literati as possessors of the philosophic-ethical heritage. Identified with the regime, they did their duty with a profound sense of rightness and satisfaction of station. Without the sincere idealists it produced, the imperial regime could hardly have functioned. The good Confucianist was the perfect civil servant, completely loyal to his superiors and yet dedicated to the common good, a devotee of the classic motto, "A scholar should be the first to become concerned with the world's troubles and the last to rejoice at its happiness." [J. Liu in 19, p. 111] The people had to assume, when a magistrate was bad, that he was acting contrary to the intent and tradition of the empire, while the good Confucianists were more truly loyal to the principles of imperial authority than the fallible men who happened to occupy the throne.

HIGHER DISCIPLINE

If ideology may, by giving a rationale for selfless obedience, powerfully buttress the authority of the ruler, it helps in another and subtler fashion to make the imperial order workable. The ideal nexus between ruler and ruled binds him as well as them; by making the autocrat part, even an instrument, of something greater than himself, it serves to guide him who is subject to no human control. Calling on all to obey in the name of something holy, he is caught up in the expectations of virtue. Mentors can speak to him in terms of traditional and superhuman values which he himself accepts as salutary for the empire. So far as the authority claims to rest upon moral superiority, it helps to maintain some sort of moral standards for those who recognize no human law; and without standards of some sort, it is almost impossible for the autocrat to preserve sane decency or for his government to function. If power comes from above, as Bossuet wrote for the benefit of Louis XIV, "Kings should not believe that they are its masters and may use it as they wish; they should exercise it with fear and restraint as a thing which has come to them from God, and for which God will demand an account." [464, pp. 5–7] If the title to absolutism is virtue, the monarch, so far as he is aware of human limitations, must feel some need to show himself virtuous. Supreme and total power, moreover, is a very heavy burden, and if it is complete, its possessor is deprived of purpose in life; when all is his for the wishing and nothing remains to desire, only a higher idealism can give purpose and direction to his deeds.

The father-ruler enjoys feeling that he is sacrificing himself, that the use of power is for the benefit of his subjects and painful to himself; and this is much better for him than merely to gloat in the bully's mastery. Charged with the welfare of his people, the emperor is the shepherd who boasts of loving his sheep, although unworthy; and as he seems to love them, they are obliged to obey him. The symbol of unity, he is the high priest or demigod who represents them before the mysterious higher powers of the universe. This implies mostly exercising a divinely conferred authority but it also, and equally flatteringly, means that the emperor takes upon himself a high responsibility for his children, even expiation of their sins. More important as a symbol than an active personality, he is guarantor, by his holiness, of the prosperity of all. [487, p. 28]

It is therefore the more important that he be virtuous himself. Moreover, impersonal moral imperatives should give the ministers a basis for criticism even of the most high, and courage to utter it, albeit with great tact and care; and such criticism is the more vitally necessary as there is no political check upon his folly or caprice. An idealism should not only give the apparatus a better purpose than self-interest but also should keep the ruler from injuring himself and his system.

The idea is powerful: what mortal should pity himself and complain when the supreme and semidivine master of all suffers like a messiah for his children and for a divine cause? The ruler, too, may find better satisfaction in self-denial than in indulgence. Consequently autocrats have not always been nearly so evil as one might expect from the lack of restraints. After the unbridled Domitian brought his own downfall by his excesses, the Caesars for a good century fairly well accepted the philosopher's ideal of the dignified ruler and his moral duties, to the benefit of the empire and themselves. [345, p. 148; 343, p. 87] Many rulers, with the revenues of the world at their disposal, have lived simply and modestly in accordance with their sense of morality; thus, seventeenth-century tsars furnished luxurious meals to thousands of drones at court but themselves ate frugally. [379, p. 26] Even a foul-tempered man like Ivan the Terrible felt obligations to do right as servant of God. "A tsar," he said, "must not only govern the state but save souls"; and he had fits of piety and repentance. [363, p. 7] Like his subjects, the Sapa Inca was supposed on occasion to make confession, although he had the privilege of speaking directly and privately to heaven. [173, p. 182] In the extreme, the monarch might be called upon to give his life; it seems that in times of famine Old Kingdom pharaohs were sent to heaven, with what will is not known, by snakebite. [126, pp. 175–176] In the religious-ideological climate, although there is generally nothing to prevent the autocrat's decreeing innovations to suit his fancy, he may do so sparingly. The existent law usually suits his interests well, and he can often see or be shown that to go against tradition is wrong and bootless. In the Turkish empire, for example, Moslem law, based on revelation, was held sacred; the sultans seldom tampered with it, and they had little to gain by doing so, as it was an excellent framework for despotism. [439, p. 23] Under it, all were bound to obey the divinely appointed sultan, no matter how abusive, so long as he did not transgress the Sacred Law, as determined by the ulemas whom he named. [435, p. 233] If sultans were pious, as Suleiman became late in life, and ate from earthen instead of silver dishes, it was no hurt; if they had heeded the prohibition of alcohol, they would have prospered better.

It is in China that ideology has been most effective as cement and mortar of the imperial order. Indeed, the ideology of social order has been felt to be so important that advantages of policing have been sacrificed to it, it being accounted a great crime to accuse one's parents, even if justly. [10, pp. 80–81] As far back as the early Han a scholar told his master, "The Prince knows that he who is in power cannot by evil methods make men submit to him. Therefore he chooses the six teachings [of Confucianism]." [77, p. 14] Thoroughly imbued with their heritage, the conviction of Confucian justice, the best bureaucrats sought to uphold their principles of government against palace intrigues, eunuchs, or any caprice, as well as to inculcate the Son of Heaven with the virtues of his ancestors. Some, as outstanding Censors, would accept disgrace and death in the humble effort to correct the favorites or the emperor himself; that some, in the general atmosphere of sycophancy, were ready to speak bitter truths did much to check the degradation of the court.

It suited the literati to have the emperor as symbol and father figure, rather than active administrator; it equally suited the emperor to be held up as a moral example. As he called for filial obedience, he himself must be dutiful. Since his was the sublime duty of keeping heaven and earth in tune, he should study well his conduct. As his heavenly mandate rested on his virtues, and as he was so powerful that his failures would bring on natural disasters, it behooved him to be an example of rectitude. When drought or flood occurred it was his duty to suffer for the woes of his people, to examine his conduct, and make open confession. [76, p. 368] Moreover, each emperor knew that upon his decease he would be subjected to a kind of trial to determine the honor due him. [37, I, 107] Chinese histories told countless stories of noble deeds and sayings of emperors and of their love for the people, largely, perhaps, for the edification of the people, but partly that emperors should strive to be no worse than their predecessors in upholding the harmony of Being.

Ideology has thus served the weak and powerful alike, making servitude more bearable and more effective. But it rather beautifies and softens in appearance the power structure than changes it. The most humane religion has seldom checked atrocities. Tsarist rulers, sincerely believing in divine law, easily confused themselves with God. The responsibility of the Chinese emperor to Heaven relieved him of responsibility to the people; if he was evil, it was up to Heaven to remove him. It is far better for the ruler, for his authority and his sanity, to represent some sort of higher right or law than to hold a merely arbitrary and earth-based power; but this means no freedom for the people and no immunity from decadence.

GRIP OF EMPIRE

As the state grows, it gains in political capacity (unless its area should become too large for its means of communication and control), just as by defeating and annexing its neighbors it becomes stronger internationally. The empire that has come to full hegemony over its world and so is infinitely strong in relation to other powers is also totally strong at home. Its sense of limitless power lends conviction to its claims. The universal empire stands above the world, overwhelming, inescapable and unassailable, the master of each body and mind, the essence of power, glory, authority, and right.

Sheer size is an immense advantage. The individual shrinks and feels himself shrunken in the incomprehensibly huge realm and against the gargantuan and complex state, which is infinitely greater than himself or anything he might do. The more massive the organization, the harder to hope to move it, much less to overturn it; wisdom dictates fitting into it and making the best of whatever it offers. Distance helps to sanctify the autocrat and to make hopeless any thoughts of opposing him. Emperors are the more godlike the farther away; the divinity of Alexander, for example, found favor everywhere except in his own Macedon. [351, p. 27] The outspread state makes force more effective for government; the farther from home an army, the more subject to its commanders and the better usable against the people. A few thousand men in the capital can decide the rule of many millions, while a massive potential opposition is scattered and impotent. As the state expands, it becomes more difficult for individuals to observe and understand its workings, as they must to curb its power. Its weaknesses become less visible and its power more so. A town can fairly easily concert a rising against a tyrant, but in an empire the ruler can summon distant soldiery to smash local disorders. The government is everywhere; opposition, unless it can elude the police, is unorganized, incoherent, and at the mercy of the forces of order anywhere it might show itself. Size discourages dissent and suffocates rebellion.

The complexity of the state also makes it the harder to envision alternatives. Elaborate structure and multiplicity of functions, along with size, are the central facts of the imperial apparatus; the more complex, the more awesome and even magical in its workings; unable to judge for himself, the individual is compelled to take the general view and to seek confirmation in consensus; humans are always prone to accept a group verdict or an authoritative version of facts even though contrary to the plain and immediate evidence of the senses. [530, p. 161] Complexity demands special knowledge and professionalization and gives the experts the right to decide. The idea that the wise should govern appeals to ordinary men as much as to Plato, and there is little need or means of questioning the wisdom of the far-off men whose rightness is sealed by power. Heterodox views are quixotic and bring only anxiety, which conformity cures. It is lonely and naïve to set one's views against those of the authority, which has seen and studied all. This is the iron law of oligarchy: the larger the organization the more concentrated its real government and the harder for outsiders to interfere. [530, p. 41] It is true alike of legislative bodies [as noted in *The Federalist Papers*, nos. 48–52], large corporations, private clubs, and political parties; it is truer of the monopolistic state.

The rulership of a great state has less need to be capable or popular than that of a small one. Beneficent or oppressive, the empire is like a power of nature; puny men bend before it and hope for mercy. With the prestige of mystery, distance, and vast resources, it bedazzles and overawes. It is like the ocean, boundless, eternal, and majestic in its quiet or its furious moods. It is greatness incarnate — important, marvelous, and universally valid. Great states and great power imply great men, men of infinite capacities, whom ordinary mortals can only envy and admire. Power excites feelings far beyond mere acceptance. When the individual is so small and helpless against the gargantuan order, it is not only difficult for him to rebel but even to hate. Unless they are well schooled in self-respect, men instinctively cringe before the power above them.

All life is tied together in one nexus under the single rule outside of which or against which there is no bearable life; it is bootless to hate the empire, and civilized men would rather die than to abandon everything and flee to the barbarians. The tyranny of the Mogul empire was somewhat tempered by the possibility that exasperated people might escape to the territory of an independent rajah [*191*, p. 232], but in the fully universal empire there is no hope but to make the best of the system. As Cicero wrote to an exile, "Wherever you are, remember that you are equally within the power of the conqueror." [*314*, I, 73] Nor can the dissenter look to foreign models to support his idea of right, possibly to lend him support if he should rise in opposition to it. It is hard even to imagine that there could be a different sort of state when one knows no other; and the image of itself which the state projects is the only one.

The totality of the state at home means that only with it can one progress or achieve anything. Official position comes to mean everything, standard of living, reputation, power, probably self-respect as well. The necessities of living mold to conformist attitudes. Deference and flattery are sincere, so far as they are necessary and appropriate. Compliance, bodily and spiritual, comes easy when there is nowhere else to go, no competing claims for loyalty, and no other career to dream of. Altruism also benefits the state, as its welfare is the welfare of all. Those who would serve the people can do so only through the constituted authority; no improvement is conceivable except through the state power. The idealistic Chinese scholar-bureaucrats whose integrity could not stomach a bad emperor saw no way but retirement. In the Russia of the nineteenth century, many students turned radical, largely under Western influence; after graduation and faced with the need of living in the imperial system, they would become bureaucrats, submissive, harsh, and corrupt as their colleagues. [*360*, p. 183] Goncharov, who wrote eloquently of the moral depravity of Russia, took a post in the censorship.

It is less important that the empire is good or bad than that it is unavoidable; but those who bow in conformity feel that this is just. Power sanctifies itself and makes justice. It is a far better persuader than pale reason; many adore it, nearly all respect it, and all must heed it. The mass of men usually accepts the political order in any event, even though individuals may detest certain holders of power; but in the empire the authority of the autocrat is incontestable, too great for simple men to consider him responsible. No one has any rights against the empire, because rights rest ultimately upon some power. Nor is there personal dignity against the master of the universe, however unjustly he upbraids, lashes, or imprisons. Maltreated Greek leaders could go over to another city-state, but the emperor's hapless ministers or favorites hope most of all to be recalled to his service. Upstanding men find it not unworthy but noble that they sacrifice their individual feelings and integrity on the altars of the rulership of the world.

Great organizations of any kind become something of an abstraction, not a mere group of mortals working out their purposes but somehow an ideal, a larger entity with its inherent purposes, giving a direction to those who share in it and answering, in its way, their questions of why. Far better can the universal empire equate itself with a value system. Virtue is obedience to socially accepted norms, which are, in the tightly ruled society, whatever is sanctioned, used, and upheld by the great and admirable. All must measure themselves by those to whom they look up, and none can make a real ethic of his own. The values in the empire can only be the values of the empire.

The chief values of the empire are universal. Its holiness, like that of God, is benevolence and justice, omnipotence in wrath and mercy. It is the greatest dream, the limitless order of all, the harmony precious to the mind. Agreement is as good as disagreement is noxious; the glory of unification is simple for the untutored and alluring for the sophisticated, while the benefits of division are subtler and as though paradoxical. Instead of the wearisome uncertainties of hateful disunity, the waste and toil of men and nations at odds, the empire brings the priceless boons of firm government, cooperation, and the security (or the illusion) of universal law. Its gifts are visible and material — peace, efficiency, great works, and power — while its costs are spiritual and intangible. The Russians are supposed to have called in Scandinavian adventurers in the ninth century, saying, "Our land is great and fruitful, but there is no order in it; come and rule over us." A poet of nineteenth-century tsardom had the same sentiment: "Wild peoples love freedom and independence, civilized peoples love order and tranquillity." [N.

Karamzin in 382, p. 192] Especially for the weary and timorous, a calm despotism is a welcome refuge from the storms of liberty.

The imperial order appeals to philosophers, also, however ill philosophy fares in it. Thinkers like the clear-cut and absolute, the image of totality and final truth, the simple and complete answer; all these qualities the great empire claims to embody. The mind needs to put things in order, to comprehend in general terms and see great wholes; the universal empire is as intellectually and aesthetically pleasing as the chaos of competing states is repugnant. The empire, regarding itself as the end of history, induces a soothing feeling that life, politics, and society are the result, not of chance and conflicting forces, but of great design, the work of a supreme will, human or divine, with purpose and meaning, perhaps inscrutable but beneficent.

The universal government pleases not only the greedy and ambitious but also pacifists and platonists, not only those who would profit but those who would give themselves. The divine ruler calls upon men to rejoice in being his slaves; and many do, finding deep satisfaction in being an instrument, if they can believe in the cause they serve. There is so much admiration for military glory that thousands will sacrifice themselves, not merely to die upon occasion but to suffer all manner of hardships for an infinitesimal share in the glory of some conceited and morally barbaric commander; there is a fulfillment in giving, as though to God, in submitting heart and soul to the great state or its ruler. The men of the Byzantine empire chanted to their lord, "Our souls have no duty but to look toward you." [301, p. 34] The empire believes that everything should have clear utility for itself, or for the community; it hence stands for the submergence of egotistic impulses, for unselfishness against the selfishness and unhappy individualism of looser societies, which it righteously despises; it gives contentment by calling for dedication. The firmly organized society relieves of lonely freedom and responsibility by giving everyone a place and a duty. If the empire is indeed well ordered, it gives the sweet freedom of perfect obedience.

The empire trains to passivity. The more ponderous the mass weighing upon him, the less the individual can hope to strike out independently; and the empire, treating people as politically incapable, makes them so. Where there is no independent organization, there is no practice or training in political activity, no leadership to rally, guide, and organize the discontented, no habit of self-reliance. Practice, moreover, makes submission easier; having once bent the knee, men learn to prostrate themselves. The Athenians murmured at Alexander's demand for divine honors, but after him they willingly raised altars to second-rate kings like Demetrius and Antigonus. [*351*, p. 28] There is a story that an oak tree once stood high and unbending. When a storm came, the proud oak was toppled, while the modest rushes, instead of vainly resisting, bent with the wind. Men find security in bowing, some gladly, some reluctantly, before the mighty, and placing their will beneath a higher will; obedience is a simple and comforting way of life.

Compliance is easier as the superior will is far away and more than human. As a French philosopher would have it, it is better to be ruled by a lion of good family than a hundred rats of one's own species. [*419*, p. 285] The much maltreated Russian boyars spoke in similar tones to constitution-minded Polish nobles: "If the Tsar himself takes it into his head to act unjustly, it seems to us easier to put up with his transgression that with that of one of our brothers, for he is master of us all." [*379*, p. 48] Dante, suffering from the disorders of free Florence, likewise longed for a master: "The human race is most free when it is under an autocrat." [*De Monarchia*, Bk. I, chap. 12] Even convinced republicans are often fond of kings and queens, creatures at once human and mysteriously superior to ordinary humanity, with their palaces and crowns and age-old gaudy ceremonies, symbols of order and stability. The idea that the supreme will, the splendid father figure, might be evil is too discouraging to be admitted. If he has faults, they are the other side of greatness; if he fails, the blame is for bad men near him. Just as Russian peasants believed the Little Father loved them but wicked officials suppressed his manifestos, high ministers assured themselves the tsar meant well but was misled by intrigue. The very existence of the state seems to rest upon him. When Ivan the Terrible withdrew to a monastery and pretended to abdicate, shock and uncertainty gripped his sheep, the people of Moscow. A deputation of leading citizens went to fling themselves at his feet and beg him to return and rule them as he saw fit. [*388*, II, 76]

Not only dogs lick the hand that beats them; mankind bestows more liberal applause upon great destroyers than upon benefactors.

[*314*, I, 6] The majestic music of the empire says, "Bow down humbly, be ye proud or lowly, before the ruler of the universe." Few resist. Those who have had the divine privilege of kissing the hem of the king's robe lose the power to think objectively about royalty, although they may come inwardly to hate the king. Even in rationalist, individualist western Europe, the king's touch has healed until recent times, and the awe surrounding imperial despots has been indescribable. Those of the court, whose chief virtue and qualification is loyalty to the autocrat, are usually more royalist than he. But even of those who have little to gain, he generally does not have to command adulation; most are glad to give it freely.

After Julius Caesar was assassinated, the people cast out the would-be restorers of the republic and rushed to worship the dead master as a god. [*282*, p. 8] Not only the dull and depraved masses but the most cultivated intelligences join eagerly in the adoration of the omnipotent. Cicero, great defender of the republic and the Senate, thus addressed Julius Caesar: "It is for you and you alone, Gaius Caesar, to reanimate all that you see lying shattered. . . . it is all these wounds of war's infliction which you are called upon to heal and which none but you can treat." [*345*, p. 21] If the men of recently free Rome viewed the autocrat in these colors, it was easy for Asians about 15 A.D. to speak of the "greatest good and bringer of benefaction, the emperor Augustus, the father who gives us happy life, the savior of all mankind." [*345*, p. 59] There was no pricking the bubble of illusions except by foolishness; Nero hurt himself not by massacres but by undignified public singing. [*302*, p. 74] As a modern German saw it, emperor worship "expressed the longing of a yet unconverted mankind denuded of its own dignity for the union of a finite being with the Absolute — a union through which all might attain to redemption and the consciousness of freedom." [*509*, p. 30] In the later Roman empire, the people took for granted that the state was ordained by God, and it would have been a waste of breath to suggest alternatives. [*278*, p. 32]

Such was the awe of the Inca ruler that breaking his commandment was felt as sacrilege; those who had been led into lawbreaking by passion were driven by conscience to confess. [*181*, p. 21] The good Russians, we are informed, were proud of their political police. "The real honest Russian has always had respect for power that was power, and he bowed before it, without asking questions or meditating upon the reasons there might be for commands given." [*415*, p. 97] True awe of the monarch is the conviction that life could not prosper without his presence and blessing. [*487*, p. 30]

Even when the empire is shattered, devotion lives on. A century after the real power of the Moguls had vanished and while the land was split and in turmoil, that alien and tyrannical dynasty was still regarded as rightful sovereign of all India. [*216*, pp. 135–136] For Atahualpa, a rather poor character, overthrown and executed as he had executed so many, a dirge was sung: "O Inca, my father, Now in Heaven thou seest me, How I am unfortunate and wretched. . . . My heart is torn from my bosom, Yet I live on." [*176*, p. xii] The vast majority of the Chinese literati remained loyal to the Mongol dynasty, a harsh barbarian rule, even as a peasant uprising was sweeping it away. [F. Mote in *78*, p. 206]

Submissiveness was probably most complete in China. To an English visitor at the end of the eighteenth century it seemed that the feelings and actions of the people were entirely molded by and completely under the sway of the government. [*3*, p. 359] Even men of gentry rank were so terrified of a district magistrate, the lowest representative of the Son of Heaven, as to be unable to speak in his presence. [*64*, p. 238] The literati under the later dynasties were taught and came seemingly to believe that it was inconceivable to criticize the monarch, that even a critical thought was a moral lapse. The ministers who might have held themselves colleagues of the sovereign in serving the people came to think of themselves as his slaves. Troubles, in the Neo-Confucian ethos, could come only from failings of the officials, not the shortcomings of the sage-emperor; the former often felt guilty even when ignorant of their fault. [Nivison in *55*, pp. 16–22] With the utmost servility and few exceptions, the court exalted the most degenerate Son of Heaven as a paragon; and his victims were convinced of their unworthiness. Officials were required to accuse themselves of misconduct and request punishment, and they complied. [*76*, p. 354] Those capriciously condemned to die sometimes abased themselves with confessions of utter badness. A servant of the Mings, tortured and sentenced to death for political reasons, wrote with evident sincerity to his son: "My body belongs to my ruler-father. . . . I only regret that this blood-filled heart has not been able to make recompense to my ruler." [C. Hucker in *55*, p. 208]

The universal empire has also shown its potency by its ability to impress upon numerous and diverse peoples a common pattern. The ruler of the world has no reason to discriminate among peoples, but he would erase national differences and cultural divisions of all kinds. Nationalities may recall an independent existence and provide the basis for dangerous separatism. Uniformity is a great convenience for administration and indoctrination, and also a sign of submission. The centralization of the empire, concentration in the government and the capital, and the anemia of provincial and independent life make it easier to level and assimilate; and it is in the autocratic spirit to make all alike.

As soon as the Chinese expanded beyond the original center of their civilization, they set about educating their new subjects to Chinese culture and so brought about an extraordinary degree of cultural unity over a vast expanse. Probably the early Near Eastern empires, with no compunctions about the removal of peoples, did much to mix and amalgamate. The Hittites took the conquered into their armies. [101, p. 160] The Persians likewise made a multitude of nations into fighters in their service, while they drew workers from all parts of the empire and themselves spread out everywhere as administrators and landholders. [249, p. 108] Systematically and successfully, the Incas imposed their universal religion, their architecture, and even their style of dress. [171, p. 220] They established schools to teach Quechua, ordered their new subjects to learn it, and preferred those who became fluent. [181, p. 204] This energetic policy, skillfully pursued without arousing significant resistance, was successful enough that when rebellions occurred most of the subject peoples sided with their masters. In less than a century the Incas erased most of the preceding Andean cultures and imposed on the region an imprint that has endured to this day. [J. Rowe in 180, p. 273] Similarly, the Spaniards were much more successful in giving their ways to American natives than were the more highly cultured but freer English; even zealous Puritans were only mildly interested in converting the heathen.

A poet wrote of Rome at the beginning of the fifth century, when the empire was breaking down in utter sterility, decadence, and impoverishment: "She alone has received the vanquished into her bosom like a mother, not like an Empress, and protected the human race with a common name, and called those whom she conquered to be her citizens, and linked far-off peoples with bonds of loyal affection." [*354*, pp. 182–183] In a few generations, provinces were Romanized by the armies, administration, literature, and culture of the empire. [*300*, p. 51] Many of the natives were killed or enslaved while Roman colonists settled in the conquered lands; at the same time, the natives were gradually taken into the fold and assimilated to the Roman status. As local traditions died out or survived only among the lower classes, provincials were proud to hold themselves Romans [*326*, II, 1022]; and Roman citizenship was a high honor until it was given to everyone. The barbarian chiefs learned to ape their rulers, in using Italian pottery or oriental fabrics as in erecting useless public monuments. [*308*, p. 127] Even the Roman pantheon, lacking as it was in the ordinary attractions of religion, spread widely in the West. [*299*, p. 20] Care was taken to extend the Latin language, the use of which was inflexibly required in the administrative and military services [*314*, I, 33–35] and which was necessary for all who wished to rise in the world. Languages derived from that of Rome, or Romance languages, permanently displaced native tongues through a huge area of the Western empire. By contrast, linguistic islands have persisted for many centuries in the nations of the West: Welsh in Britain, Basque in Spain, Breton in France, Romansch in Switzerland, and Sorb in Germany. Similarly, the Russian language is much more uniform over a huge area than English or French in the relatively small expanse of these countries.

For these reasons, the universal empire, incarnation of political power, is normally very stable; rebellion is almost unthinkable so long as the empire can maintain reasonable efficiency. Even if its justice can be questioned, acceptance rests more on prestige, and the prestige of the monopolistic state is total. The holders of power have every conceivable advantage, and their chief purpose is to maintain their position, which to them is a god-given right. People are much more aware of threats to their power than of possible gain by upsetting the order; hence defense of the status quo is inherently better motivated than attacks upon it, which can succeed only if the defenders of order are grievously weakened. This is the more true where, as in the universal empire, the opposition must start from nowhere. In destroying independent authority the imperial autocracy also destroys alternatives to its rule. There is no one with strength, character, and prestige to forge a different kind of government. The aristocrats are discredited, demoralized, rendered impotent and corrupt by dependence on the supreme power. The populace, become a mob, degraded and characterless, has neither inspiration nor a basis for political action. The bureaucracy, hated if any group in the empire is hated, is the victim of revolutionists, not their hope. The army can, like the inner court, at best replace an unbearable autocrat.

Against the great machine and the custom of awe and obedience, dissension can succeed only if the ruling apparatus is ready to fall apart. Only palace coups, which usually change nothing and satisfy only a few ambitions, are feasible. It is difficult to organize a broad movement, even a sizable conspiracy, since there are traps everywhere. Any opposition is driven to illegal or criminal means, the only ones available to it, and is thereby discredited or incapacitated as potential political leadership. Rebellion must be against the whole fabric of society, the whole web of power which runs through all aspects of life. Those who rejected the Russian tsar as the antichrist in the eighteenth century rejected the entire state; their recourse was to flee into the forests. [367, p. 88] Popular revolutions against well-established empires are virtually never successful, even in times of decay, except perhaps against foreign domination. In China, Confucianist doctrine conceded that the mandate of Heaven might pass from a bad emperor, and there were as many peasant risings as years of history. But the only successful popular rebellion was that against the Mongols, which led to the Ming dynasty.

After the middle of the first century, there was no practical republican thinking at Rome, the most republican of imperial cities [345, p. 135], although republican forms endured. In weakness and civil war, there was no important rebellion against the empire itself, no move to recover national independence. As the empire ripened, liberty came to mean merely economic security; and the official view was that liberty and autocracy were the same. The spirit of men moldered, too. In the early empire men cringed servilely from fear or greed; in the full-blown empire they genuinely accepted the authority of the autocrat and their dependence on his mercy and goodness. [345, pp. 148–149] Even those few spirits who regretted the loss of freedom had no solution; Plutarch doubted whether the people could use or stand more of the freedom that he saw they missed. [345, p. 105] In this spirit, Dobroliubov, despairing at the evils of tsardom, wrote, "We are thirsting, waiting, seeking for someone to tell us what to do." [375, p. 7] The people may even forget what freedom is. The very expressive Chinese language has no word for this concept, the nearest equivalents carrying a connotation of laxness or depravity. [2, p. 247]

Only the grossest abuses of a decrepit tyranny and extreme desperation can drive men — without assistance or encouragement from abroad, with little morale and no resource, without tradition or training, and virtually without hope — to rebel against a powerful empire. But the tragedy of the rebels is that, even as they march out to die against the regime, they have nothing different to put in its place; they accept its fundamental values and claims. Combating the oppression, they develop an organization like the one that has dominated their lives, tightly controlled, secret, hierarchic, and intolerant. Just as the imperial regime blames not the system but bad people for its shortcomings, the revolutionaries strike not against the system, perhaps not even against the person of the ruler, but against bad officials, the hated bureaucracy — not the principles but the exponents of autocracy. They would purify of vice and corruption a regime that they can regard only as necessary, find better ways to express the values of the empire and to fulfill its promises. Unlike foes of European absolutist monarchies or of the tyrannies of Italian city-states, they are usually unconcerned with freedom and the basic form of government. They wish only a transfer of power to a better emperor or a divinely sanctioned messiah. If they should be successful they can do little more than renovate the state, inject new life for a century or so, not slackening but strengthening state authority, set up new oppressors, and carry on in the old manner.

In the Roman empire even peasant jacqueries raised up presumptive Caesars. In the disturbed Russia of the Time of Troubles, nearly all the peasant movements marched under the banner of the tsar [367, p. 70]; a revolutionary like Bolotnikov attacked not the tsar but the bad landlords, and had a pretended tsarevitch at his side. [413, p. 41] Stenka Razin massacred serf owners and nobles as traitors to the tsar, to whom he proclaimed fealty. [A. Shestakov in 420, p. 110; 377, pp. 285–286], claiming that the tsar was really on his side but was prisoner of the boyars. [408, p. 171]

In the eighteenth century Pugachev claimed to be the missing Peter III, invested by God; to act the part of the monarch, he repeated his imperial titles to a tedium and insisted on calling his adherents his faithful slaves. [*386*, pp. 390–393] He promised to right wrongs, to give freedom from serfdom, conscription, and taxation, to restore the old faith and allow beards and traditional dress; and he appealed to forced laborers, fugitive serfs, escaped prisoners, and outcasts in general. [*377*, pp. 588–589; *404*, p. 288] But he was so concerned to seem the proper autocrat that his courtiers took the names and titles of those in Catherine's court. [*367*, p. 99] Even in the nineteenth century, as Western political ideals were creeping in, Russian revolutionaries agitated, not against the autocratic system or usually even the person of the tsar, but against the evils of the bureaucracy. In 1895 Lenin wanted to attack not the tsar but capitalism, lest the workers be repelled. [*376*, pp. 30–31]

Chinese rebel movements usually began in opposition to local officials, remaining nominally loyal to the emperor until forced into total opposition. They were often led by would-be officials embittered by failure in the examinations. Sometimes they claimed to represent defunct dynasties, Sung pretenders against the Mongols, Ming against the Manchus, thus borrowing legitimacy from the past. Challenging not the divinity of the throne but only the current occupant, they aspired not to less but more perfect empire, in which promised justice and equality should be a reality. [Y. Muramatsu in *78*, pp. 256–257] So far as they have had a doctrine, it has usually been a religious creed with foreign roots, Buddhism, Manichaeism, or, in the nineteenth-century Taiping movement, Christianity. Recently the Kuomintang and Communists alike felt the necessity of borrowing from Western republicanism, socialism, or Soviet Marxism to support claims to power, just as Russian revolutionaries did against tsarism. But the authoritarian essence has remained.

This essence of empire has a most powerful, practically unshakable grip. But strength makes weakness. The ability of the empire to impress itself upon its subjects does not prevent but abets its intellectual, economic, and ultimate political failure.

6 INTELLECTUAL FAILURE

GLEAM OF GRANDEUR

The great empire, proud beyond compare, would excel in all visible things. Not only roads, canals, palaces, temples, and incomparable monuments should proclaim its glory; it would grace power with beauty, painting, sculpture, and fine crafts. Moreover, the better-ordered empires, like the Roman and the Chinese, have taken pride in literature and scholarship to crown their political glory and wealth with the greatest achievements of mankind.

It is a poor state that has no architects and painters to beautify it, no poets to praise it, no writers to entertain its people; a vast empire, commanding the world's resources, is the best patron. It can turn the world from strife to peaceful arts for the release of creativity. Trade and travel may be set free, so that fertilizing currents can flow. The special attainments and knowledge in every part of the huge area become everywhere available and, flowing into the common fund of culture, may add to the enrichment of all. Dangers and impediments to commerce are removed. Trade and industry should flourish, producing the extra wealth that supports the less immediately productive pursuits of art and scholarship. The government, lavish on an unheard-of scale, can support schools, libraries, and academies beyond the capacities of petty states, and may do so not only to adorn the state with learning but also to train administrators. And the glory and confidence of the imperial order is itself inspiring, calling upon men to think in grand terms and celebrate the great achievements around them.

Consequently, empires have done wondrous things. The first centuries of Egyptian unification in the Old Kingdom and of re-unification in the New showed exceptional brillance and productivity. The Great Pyramid, of most admirable workmanship if not precisely beautiful, is the essence of the monumental; its area at the base is about five times that of the Milan cathedral. Many such works inclined (and still incline) people to bow before the profundity of Egyptian ways. Imperial Egypt also is credited with impressive technical achievements, such as the construction of ships hardly to be surpassed in length until modern times. [90, p. 105]

Of all the imperial civilizations, probably the Chinese has most excelled in art, technology, literature, and philosophy. Not only did various dynasties build on a memorable scale, conscripting millions of laborers for works magnificent beyond all previous conception [28, pp. 117–118]; Chinese scholarship may be held even more creditable. Beginning with the great university of the Hans, to train men for official service, Chinese dynasties repeatedly sought to foster learning; compilation and scholarly description rose to towering heights, especially during the latter dynasties, the Ming and the Ch'ing. Like the scholars of eleventh-century Byzantium [301, p. 250], and of the Turkish empire in its great days [436, p. 199], the Chinese literati gave much labor to the making of encyclopedias; the *Great Standard Encyclopedia* of the fifteenth century in 22,937 volumes is a monument as outstanding as the Great Pyramid. Like the Romans, the Chinese have given the world lengthy, detailed accounts of their past: the twenty-five standard dynastic histories would require some 45 million words in English translation, yet these are only a small part of the accumulated records. [A. F. Wright in 484, p. 37]

Chinese science excelled in practicality in contrast with the Greek bent for speculation. The first two centuries of the Han dynasty were remarkable for advances in astronomy, such as the establishment of a calendar that remained basically in use until 1927, discovery of the ellipticity of the moon's orbit and the period of its revolution, and a primitive seismograph. [28, pp. 47–48] Sunspots were recorded from the first century B.C. [J. Needham in 468, p. 146] The Later Han saw advances in such branches of technology as the making of paper, ceramics, and textiles, as well as in the fields of astronomy and alchemy. [52, p. 111] There were important developments in medicine under various dynasties, even the Ming, in most respects intellectually dead. [J. Needham in 468, p. 171] The resources of the empire may well support important scientific investigations, as in the eighth century there was sent out a Chinese geodesic survey to traverse some 2,500 kilometers, and an expedition sailed far into the South Seas to observe the constellations of the Southern Hemisphere. [J. Needham in 468, p. 132] No small state could afford so large an investment in knowledge.

Among the most brilliant periods of Chinese history was the

Sung dynasty (960–1127), a time when culture and science flourished. Although China was already so archaistic that it was impossible to teach anything without claiming to rest on the classics, and disputes could take the form only of varying interpretations, there was speculation and innovation. Opposed schools of philosophy flourished despite official dislike for controversy. There were schools established by the state and also many private academies, scholarly retreats free from government interference. [28, p. 155] Printing, invented about the beginning of the period, came rapidly into use and made education more widespread than ever. [39, p. 19] Artists were fruitfully encouraged by official patronage. Poetry, the glory of the preceding T'ang dynasty, was imitative; but Sung writers were masters of a reformed and simplified prose; and the painters, especially of landscapes, rank among the world's finest. [28, p. 155] There were many treatises and not a few technical innovations, including the use of gunpowder. [52, p. 134]

Yet there were certain limitations to the Sung achievements. Intelligent men devised a program of scientific investigation, questioning nature; but this good intention was not followed by the suggested inquiry and experiment. [28, p. 160] Neo-Confucianism, the philosophic glory of the times, contained nothing very original but cleverly drew elements of Buddhism and Taoism into a useful synthesis. [40, Bk. I, p. 258] Literature and art were much more refined than spontaneous or original; and much of the new artistic expression, as in painting styles, had its origins in the preceding Five Dynasties period. [62, p. viii] Scholarship was mostly compilation of older works.

Of all the great Chinese dynasties, the Sung was least qualified to consider itself a universal empire. Pacific from the time they achieved power, the Sungs never tried to conquer the whole Chinese sphere, and were almost always being pressed by peoples of the north. In time half the country was lost to them, and the latter Sungs were even compelled to pay tribute and accept subordination to the semibarbarous Kin rulers as their "uncles." [40, Bk. I, p. 243] For them, foreign commerce was especially important. [28, pp. 151–152] They thus could not well isolate themselves in grand complacency as stronger dynasties could. In its insecurity and incompleteness, the Sung empire was like tsarist Russia of the eighteenth and nineteenth centuries, which likewise saw a fair amount of intellectual creativity.

Many other examples could be mustered to show how the empires, especially in their youth, added to our intellectual and cultural heritage. The museums are full of their works. But the imperial way, as already sketched, cannot be very favorable to creative and inquisitive impulses. It is axiomatic that freedom is essential for innovation. It would hence be surprising if the work of the empires had not been more to perfect and expand than to create, more to harvest than to plant. Their colors are not of the rising sun but at best of a bright afternoon, and more often of a dull twilight. The remainder of this chapter endeavors to show how and why this has been.

POVERTY OF ROME

Despite countless notable works, from Egyptian pyramids to Inca roads and Chinese palaces, there is a certain incompleteness or superficiality in the achievements of the empires. They are most striking for show and size, as though the grand state could most easily excel in mass. Rome had a hundred statues for one of the Greece of Phidias; there are said to have been hundreds of thousands in public view in the city. [358, p. 352] Emperors commissioned images of themselves scores of feet in height. The most ambitious was that of Gallienus; unfinished because of the uncertainty of Caesarian tenure, it was a godlike figure 200 feet tall, crowning the highest point of Rome. [288, p. 231] Roman buildings dwarfed the best the Greeks could do; for example, it is claimed that the Circus Maximus held more than 300,000 spectators. [358, p. 347] Even the late empire was ornamented with buildings as magnificent as ever, such as the giant baths of Diocletian and the basilica of Constantine.

But the vaunted marble city of Augustus has been called the "mausoleum of the Roman spirit." [298, p. 196] Size indicates more concentrated effort than it does genius, and the cultural creativity of the imperial societies has lagged far behind their promise and has been disproportionate to their material potentialities. The sublime union of mankind has not witnessed a glorious release of intellectual energies, a springtime of the arts and sciences. Rather, the imperial society has seemed capable of doing little more than completing an edifice already begun, building upon intellectual foundations laid in more disordered and freer times, adding little that is original. The great empires have generally stayed close to old patterns. By corollary, their better times have, so far as the record appears, come early in their lifetimes. After a few generations or at most a century or two of development, the great empires have been overcome by sterility in the meaningless repetition and elaboration of worn and lifeless motifs, with a dreary and purely ornamental art alien to the life of the people, a literature become rhetoric or mere entertainment in old styles, and very little serious exercise of intelligence.

That the cultural road of empires is downward justifies a belief that whatever initial brillance and creativity they may boast is not fully of their making. A nation subjected to arbitrary authority can live for a time on its intellectual capital, as Benjamin Constant pointed out. [465, p. 91] Unless an imposition of authority is totally brutal and demoralizing, people will continue for a time to think and do more or less as they did before; in particular, the values of the imperial society will only gradually come to prevail over all. The effects of the imperial order upon human creativity are clearly to be discerned only in mature empires which have, so to speak, exhausted the moral and intellectual heritage of a freer order; so judged, the universal empires have been utterly disastrous.

The example of Rome is particularly instructive, as the reins of control were for a time slacker in the Roman empire than in most such empires, and for this reason presumably gave more latitude for creativity. At the same time, Rome took over the heritage of a civilization as profusely creative as any. Yet Rome, building great, was intellectually dwarfish. Virgil wrote, "These be thy arts, to impose the customs of peace"; and Rome truly shone in no art but that of domination.

In its inception, Rome took over the achievements of the elegant Etruscan civilization of city-states which preceded it; expanding Rome borrowed from the Greek culture, which flowed around it; imperial Rome, while building the highways, aqueducts, and legal codes required by the world state, was usually satisfied to draw upon the achievements of the conquered. Even the celebrated and often striking Roman architecture owed much to foreign sources. The Etruscans, who originally made Rome into a city, were masters of the arch and vault. [283, pp. 102, 165] Many foreigners, mostly Greeks, contributed to Roman building [533, pp. 527–528], which lost inventiveness after the empire was established. In sculpture, it was easy to carry away Greek statuary or to send orders to Athenian bust factories. What modest originality there had been declined rapidly after Augustus. In the second century even technical finish began to decay, falling to incompetence in the third. [358, p. 353] When Constantine took Rome, he could find no artists to make even a hackneyed victory monument, and had to borrow parts, inappropriate as they were, from Trajan's. [314, I, 366–367]

The Romans preferred wonders to science, and in this domain their contribution was singularly poor, consisting of almost nothing but uncritical and unsystematic compilation of Greek sources, as in the work of Pliny. In mathematics, the Romans created nothing at all; it was always easier to enslave a Greek. [458, p. 79] Quintilian thought youths should learn astronomy, but for no better reason than that poets used the rising and setting of constellations to indicate time. [330, pp. 289–290] Fond as they were of butchery, the Romans never thought of studying anatomy, which had advanced very far at the hands of the Hellenistic investigators. Unlike Greeks and Phoenicians, the Romans bothered with no explorations, content to remain in ignorance of the world outside their sphere. [314, I, 16] Such science as there was in the Roman world was the fruit, not of the Roman West, whither tribute flowed, but of the Hellenized East which logically might have been thought the more decadent. Although Alexandrian science and mathematics practically ceased with the Roman conquests, there arose a few lights in the general darkness of the following seven centuries, such as the astronomer Ptolemy, the algebraist Diophantus, and the physiologist Galen, the first two of Alexandria and the last of Pergamum. [458, p. 55] But even in these few glimmers, the scientific spirit was weak. Ptolemy, although he assembled more data than his predecessors of three centuries or more before, was less critical and original. Galen ascribed cures to divine intervention [Sandbach in 290, p. 707]; Hippocrates, six hundred years earlier, had searched for natural causes.

Technology prospered little better than science. Although the supply of slaves decreased, there was a retrogression of mechanics. Interest in invention was almost nil. Vespasian refused a mechanism for conveying columns, allegedly because he wanted to employ the idle. [300, p. 321] According to Pliny, when an artisan found a way to make better glass, his workshop was destroyed to prevent competition with ornamental metals; by another account, this man, so unfortunate as to attempt an improvement, was put to death. [*330*, p. 298] The crafts decayed as the empire aged, and industry and commerce fell away after the plateau of the second century. [*345*, p. 236] Agricultural methods saw no improvement through the whole course of the empire [*326*, I, 767]; only when it was shattered in the so-called Dark Ages, did men begin learning to farm better. Despite its great importance for imperial trade and communications, maritime shipping did not progress at all. [*338*, p. 211] The Roman empire might well be blamed for the fact that not until about the fifteenth century did civilization reattain the level of the Hellenistic world of 1,700 years before.

Although something of ethics was respected, the Romans always looked down on Greek metaphysics, which they regarded as unmanly logic-chopping. After Augustus, even the pedantic teaching of philosophy nearly vanished from the curriculum; only a mysticized Stoicism held on for a time. More rationalistic and skeptic schools of Greek philosophy disappeared. [*294*, p. 588] Systematic metaphysics was replaced by an eclectic hash; speculative philosophy gave way entirely to consideration of moral problems, seeking not truth but laws of conduct; and moral philosophy had to be quite divorced from politics. In the second century, Marcus Aurelius was a belated devotee of moral Stoicism; writing in Greek, he showed that elegance was still possible, but not original thought. One of the best philosophers was the Stoic Epictetus, who taught that a man might call his soul his own no matter what the ruler wished. The Eastern empire in the fourth and fifth centuries produced a few minor thinkers, like Iamblichus and Simplicius, but the most important innovation was Neo-Platonism, the work largely of Plotinus of Alexandria. Not only was this teaching as unoriginal as indicated by its name, but it was essentially mystic-intuitive, filled with magic, superstition, mysticism, and empty verbalisms. Greek philosophy became for the Romans a mere source of literary allusions, like the old myths, devoid of meaning [*303*, p. 411], while astrology and the grossest magic reigned supreme. [*330*, pp. 568–570]

Political thinking shriveled to nothing. In republican Rome, Cicero wrote elegantly, although without originality, of politics; under the empire, a man like Pliny could only comment on literature and nature. Even in the days of Augustus the themes of oratory avoided contemporary events, problems of the day, and the rulership, venturing only slight and veiled criticism by implication. In their debates the senators more and more attacked not real issues but one another. [345, p. 82] When Trajan introduced a secret ballot in the Senate, some members saw no better use for their ballots than to write obscenities, so completely had they lost the sense of politics. [H. Last in 290, p. 418] Not even legal studies showed much depth, although Rome had what Greece lacked, a professional legal class interested in systematizing and transmitting the law. Most of the leading lawyers were Greek or at least had a Greek education. [528, p. 191] There were two great contending schools of Roman jurists, but there seems to have existed no difference of principle between them. [324, p. 389] The empire came to an ahistorical frame of mind; time seemed to have stood still after the end of the republic. Writers did not even compare the present with the past, which was used only for literary illustrations. [345, p. 257] Even the ruler seems to have ceased to think seriously of present times; Marcus Aurelius in his *Meditations* failed to refer to contemporary events. Conservatism, however, kept republican forms alive; in the fifth century the administration still used forms and titles of the republic.

Literature was only slightly more creative, as the modest originality of the republic evaporated in the empire. While the Romans liked to scorn the Greeks as weaklings, they did not mind copying indiscriminately from them. Spelling, pronunciation, and vocabulary were much influenced by the Greek, while form and substance were copied unabashedly. The first Latin author of note, Livius Andronicus, was a captured Greek; the first two Roman prose writers wrote in Greek [294, p. 270], and the early Roman historians (like the last historian of the empire) [326, II, 988] were Greeks. Most productions of the late republic and early empire — the great times of Roman literature — were little better than free translations of Hellenistic works. [533, p. 532] Whereas early Latin verse was based on stress, as natural for that language as for English, the Greek influence led to the adoption of Greek meters based on syllabic length. Only when the empire broke down did Latin poetry revert to stressing meter [295, p. 180], as exemplified by such medieval poems as "Stabat mater dolorosa."

In the time of Augustus, Latin literature enjoyed its golden age, but native inspiration was neither deep nor lasting. The celebrated poets were court entertainers, skilled and talented but not vital geniuses, imitators of Hellenistic style rather than Hellenic genius. The greater figures of the age — Livy, Virgil, Horace — were products of the dying republic [298, p. 196], and the latter two predeceased their emperor. For all his graceful appeal, Virgil was a pallid follower of Homer. The heroes of the Iliad are true and upstanding men, ready to do battle against odds for their honor; Virgil's are witless tools of the gods whose destiny turned on miracles and portents, just as the poet looked to the nod of one whom he called a "winged god who deigns to don a human frame." In the best time of Latin literature, students perfected first their knowledge of Greek [294, p. 462]; and for Horace, who turned out elegies at the suggestion of the monarch, it was originality enough to be the first to introduce a Greek form. [318, p. 45] After Augustus, with less patronage and fading spirit, Latin literature entered the silver age of writers like Seneca, Tacitus, Juvenal, Martial, and Petronius.

The later empire showed scant talent in either poetry or prose. The empire reportedly boasted twenty thousand stone theaters [358, p. 349]; together they elicited almost no dramatic art. Gore and repetition were the heart of tragedy, and there was always a danger that the ruler might see some unpleasant characterization as applying to himself. Domitian was so sensitive that he forbade actors to appear in public. [M. Charlesworth in 290, p. 36] Form and elegance prevailed over sense; as early as the second century it was a sign of genius to be unintelligible. [345, p. 245] The strongest genre was satire or criticism of customs, not of the social order. Poetry was eventually given to such precious conceits as verses that could be read backward, made shapes like an altar, or had the most artificial and elaborate arrangements of rhythms. Likewise, the schools of oratory paid extraordinary attention to details of form, such as the folds of garments, stance, and gestures, and poetic meters of sentences, while quite ignoring content. [288, pp. 237, 241] Even imperial edicts degenerated into a language of obscure floweriness. [275, p. 110]

There was some esteem for learning as long as the empire was reasonably prosperous. Many schools, even for the poor, existed by the third century [304, p. 43], although in the fourth century education was reverting to the family [311, p. 6]; and a fairly high degree of literacy apparently obtained for some centuries, many books being copied and sold. Rich Romans of good taste kept Greek philosophers as household pets. [*343*, p. 78] But teachers ranked low and scholarship was modest. Stressing form from the beginning of the empire, schools taught mostly grammar and rhetoric, how to express instead of what to say; the heart of education was oratory on hollow, set themes. Greek culture was officially encouraged from the time of Trajan, sums of money being given to cities to establish chairs of philosophy and promote rhetoric; but no impulse to intellectual life resulted. [F. Sandbach in *290*, p. 706] Pliny, in the first century A.D., recognized that love for things of the mind was waning. [*302*, p. 163] After him, the Roman empire came more and more to feel itself as old, regarding the dim past as the height of civilization; rhetoricians of the fifth century declaimed with pseudo sentiment on themes from Homer, Virgil, or the history of the republic. [*303*, p. 392] Down to the end of the Western empire and after it, education continued to be based on the same worthy old classics. [*326*, II, 1006] Largely because of this tendency, much Greek literature was preserved. But for four centuries or so literature decayed along with other arts like architecture and sculpture, and the Roman mind lay paralyzed and torpid. The chief employment of intelligence in the fourth century was to contrive ways of escaping the obligations of the state. [*275*, pp. 29–30]

In this as in other respects the Byzantine empire carried on the Roman tradition after the West had been lost to the barbarians. Beauty was a matter of show, of empty phrases, idle and flowery forms in literature, of glittering display, gold and jewels in tangible works. Painting was incredibly conventional, as practically every stroke of the brush was prescribed. [*353*, p. 374] Byzantine thought was pretentious and formalistic in rhetoric, given to hairsplitting and extreme conventionalism, and feebly creative only in historical writing and theology; productive of hymns, breviaries, and dry treatises on moral perfection, it turned in gilded circles for century after century. [*301*, pp. 241–257] Games, races, and public executions occupied minds and passions to the exclusion of most else. [C. Diehl in *292*, pp. 758–759] Despite several attempts to start a university, none ever prospered in the Byzantine realm. [*277*, p. 16] The cultured persons of the eleventh century spoke as well as they could the classic Greek of the fifth century B.C.; and quotations from Homer were common currency. [*278*, p. 23] The latter dynasties of the Byzantine empire cultivated the classical heritage and emphasized pure Hellenic speech more assiduously than ever; in their purism, geographers would use no names not mentioned by Herodotus nearly two thousand years before. [278, p. 42] But in a thousand years the empire added not a single great work to the storehouse of world literature. [437, p. 245]

Perhaps writers could not be expected to give better than their audience wanted. Horace complained that the people would rather watch a tightrope walker than a new drama [533, p. 530], and the popular heroes of the people were gladiators and jockeys. [294, p. 572] Classical drama, which required some serious attention, was a complete failure; some liked simple pantomimes; upper and lower classes alike swarmed to the races and the spectacles of blood and gore, which seem to have become the chief delight of the masses, thirsting for the excitement not to be found in civic life. [308, pp. 10, 217] Ironically, Augustus held gladiatorial games in honor of Minerva, goddess of wisdom and study. [308, p. 189] The ordinary folk of Athens applauded the stately and often slow-moving tragedies of Aeschylus and Sophocles; to stir the Romans, the hero had to be actually burnt or crucified. [331, p. 180] Values had shifted from the literary to the sadistic.

Some perceptive Romans saw fairly clearly their failure, yet they could make no suggestion for remedying it. Lucian showed how bad the historiography of his time really was but could not himself write better. [345, pp. 260–261] Tacitus stated baldly, "By the operation of the great imperial system a hush has come upon eloquence as indeed it has upon the world at large." [298, p. 196] In the first century, as Rome stood near the pinnacle of its might and glory, Pliny made a commentary on the inexplicable barrenness of his land:

More than twenty Greek authors of the past have published observations about these subjects. This makes me all the more surprised that, although when the world was at variance and split up into kingdoms, that is, sundered limb to limb, so many people devoted themselves to these abstruse researches, especially when wars surrounded them and hosts were untrustworthy, and also when pirates, the foes of all mankind, were holding up the transmission of information—so that nowadays a person may learn some facts about his own region from the notebooks of people who have never been there more truly than from the knowledge of the natives—yet now in these glad times of peace, under an emperor [Vespasian] who so delights in the advancement of letters and science no addition whatever is being made to knowledge by means of original research, and in fact even the discoveries of our predecessors are not being thoroughly studied. The rewards were not greater when those ample successes were being contributed by many students, and in fact the majority of these made the discoveries in question with no other reward at all save the consciousness of benefiting posterity. Age has overtaken the character of mankind, not their revenues, and now that every sea has been opened up and every coast affords a hospitable landing, an immense multitude goes on voyages—but their object is profit not knowledge; and in their blind engrossment with avarice they do not reflect that knowledge is a more reliable means even of making profit. [*Natural History*, II, 117–118; *330*, pp. 298–299]

That Pliny remarked on this unhappy contrast at least indicates some use of intelligence. But the remnants of critical thought were eventually dissolved in superstition and abysmal mental poverty. In the fifth century it was held blasphemous that a doctor speculated that foul air might have some relation to plague, for this could only be by the will of God; in the sixth century a commentator, rejecting the Aristotelian explanation for an earthquake, said: "It is enough for us to know that all things are ordered by the divine mind and a will we cannot fathom." [*278*, pp. 36–38]

STERILITY

Intellectual movement was the life of Greece; the Roman mind stood still and gradually sank to rest. Fixity in forms and institutions, and aridity, often utter sterility, seem to be the prime traits of all universal empires. According to Montesquieu, "A nation in slavery labors more to preserve than to acquire; a free nation, more to acquire than preserve." [*Spirit of the Laws*, XX, 4] Seeing little need for progress, resting its authority upon a fixed and traditional position, the empire fears change as potentially threatening. A seventeenth-century Spanish lexicographer defined "novelty" as something new, noting that "characteristically, it is dangerous because it sullies traditional usage." [*478*, p. 65] The Russian empire, to be sure, was driven by the persuasive argument of military setbacks to acknowledge the need to borrow, and an autocrat like Peter could shake it vigorously and impose drastic reforms. Even so, it could generate little of its own; and Peter said of his state,

"Anything that is new, even though it is good and needful, will not be done by our folk without compulsion." [*407*, p. 162]

It is an ancient and oft-repeated story that the great empire exhausts the mental energies with which it began. The creativity of the Sumerian city-states was fabulous, but after the end of their independence, art was unified and change became slight over centuries. [*130*, p. 254] Literature showed little further development in style or subject matter for a millennium or more, as long as the basic culture endured. Sumerian literature and religion were good enough for the Babylonian empire, which found it necessary only to add details and change names, the spirited epic of Gilgamesh becoming world-weary in reworking. [*125*, p. 34] So large a part of subsequent Near Eastern civilizations has been found to be derivative from the Sumerian that much of the rest might also be found to be of Sumerian origins if these were better known. [*125*, p. 59] The Hittites made advances in military and political organization, but in literature and art were primitive and imitative. From the Sumerian-Babylonian past they borrowed mathematics and medicine, even the antique epic of Gilgamesh and forms of worship for Hittite gods; far from improving on their heritage, the Hittites were unable fully to profit by it. [*110*, p. 215; *96*, pp. 68–70; *555*, p. 75] After them the Assyrians, inventing practically nothing, looked back to styles and texts a millennium or two old. [*97*, p. 150; *125*, p. 91] Their carvings were unoriginal though forceful, and their literature consisted of copies of the ancient classics and commentaries upon them, texts of astrology and magic, lists of conquered cities and the like. [*249*, p. 59] Their records, as the empire was declining, became so formalistic that the sense was quite buried beneath the flourishes. [*462*, p. 33] Unlike the Assyrians, the Persians were a new people entering the sphere of civilization, but the originality of Achaemenid art consisted in the size and ornateness of their buildings and the proportions in which borrowed elements were mixed. [*250*, p. 87]

In Egypt, the Third Dynasty, after crushing the great rising in the Delta, attained a cultural level hardly surpassed by all the succeeding millennia. [*126*, p. 14] The Fourth Dynasty, still experimenting with forms and materials, made the big shift from the graceful step pyramid to the monumental forms of the great pyramids; but the subsequent decline was nearly as rapid as the amazing rise. The pyramid of Khufru [Cheops] was slightly smaller, and poorer in craftsmanship, than the climactic one of his father, while the next represented more marked deterioration. The works of the Sixth Dynasty are numerous but in no wise comparable to those of the Fourth two hundred years before. [*90*, pp. 125, 131, 156] Through subsequent centuries, the Egyptians prided themselves much less on innovation than on the copying of antiquity. As one of them wrote, "Every word [of the ancestors] is carried forever in this land." [*134*, p. 134] Literature is best known not from the glorious imperial days of the Old Kingdom or the New Kingdom, but from the relatively weak and decentralized Middle Kingdom. [*134*, p. 20] Even borrowing was extremely slow. The empire having been formed without benefit of the wheel, this useful invention of the ancient Sumerians was not taken over until about a thousand years later, in the times of domination by the Semitic Hyksos. [*97*, p. 101]

The Eighteenth Dynasty, at the beginning of the New Kingdom, after a long time of weaker government, showed vigor like that of the Fourth Dynasty, building such memorable works as the vast temple at Karnak, some 1,200 feet in length, with ornate halls, although of inferior workmanship. Afterward was decline. Learning was by copying, memorization, quotation from the classics, and repetition of formulas. [*134*, pp. 86–87] Even pride of new construction vanished; Rameses II played havoc with the monuments of his predecessors, appropriating their materials on a huge scale. He was often content merely to have his name placed on statues of his predecessors. The records of his wars were composed in the dry verbiage of fawning scribes, a few facts buried in a mass of conventional phrases, old hymns, and songs of praise used and reused. [*93*, pp. 488–489] Sculptors of the Twenty-sixth Dynasty spent their time copying the works of 2,000 years earlier, never tampering with age-old conventions [*126*, p. 262], while courtiers received titles and ranks of their Old Kingdom predecessors. [*116*, p. 133]

The ageless conservatism of Egypt, where the Greeks found the priests proud of the stereotypes of their distant ancestors, is proverbial. But apparently the most static society ever known was that of the Indus Valley, with styles and techniques kept unchanged for perhaps seven hundred years. During this time, so far as appears, nothing at all was added. The script, highly developed as first known, continued unaltered through the whole span. Mohenjo-

Daro was rebuilt at least nine times without change. [*210*, p. 139]
Such inability to improve was cause enough for downfall. Through
centuries of high civilization the Indus people retained a primitive
type of spear and axe, failing to copy the Sumerian shaft-hole axe
of which they must have known. Their conquerors, whom they
doubtless regarded as barbarians, had horses and better tools and
weapons. [*190*, p. 28]

Almost as striking was the stagnation of the Byzantine empire,
for a thousand years insisting that there should be nothing new
and expending its feeble intellectual energies on theological quib-
bles. In the Turkish empire, which followed on the same ground,
innovation was likewise virtually nil, and processes and manners
remained the same century after century. In the eighteenth century
the Copernican theory could hardly be mentioned. [*432*, Pt. I, pp.
215–216; Pt. II, p. 154] Education for military and administrative
positions included little history, no geography or natural science.
Literature was extremely artificial, intended not to convey meaning but to show command of rules and proper expressions [*437*,
pp. 312–313]; poetry was composed of conventional ideas and
artificial conceits woven with great elegance; prose was bombastic,
ingenious, and trivial. [*433*, pp. 302–303] Conservatism was such as
seriously to hedge the powers of the sultan; even minor changes in
accepted practice were difficult for the autocrat to put into effect.
[*439*, p. 22]

The Mogul empire brought to the ancient Indian land considerable elegance and vigor in art, especially painting and architecture;
but the sober sandstone buildings of Akbar, at the beginning of
the empire, gave way to the lavishly adorned and inlaid marble
monuments of his grandson, Shah Jahan, and in about a century
vigor was lost and styles became frozen and formalized. [*216*, p.
140] The court was the sole cultural center of the great land, but it
produced not a single first-rate genius. [*213*, p. 73] Intellectual
rigidity was such that an outstanding and relatively enlightened
prince, Akbar, seeing Portuguese domination of the sea in the
sixteenth century, made no move to meet it with a navy of his
own; being shown printed books, he did not inquire into printing
for his own use; receiving clocks from Europe, he did not have his
artisans copy them. He even refrained from training experts in
artillery, but was content to rely on foreigners. [*207*, p. 258] Astrology was a serious preoccupation; no one would think of purchasing

a slave or putting on a new cloak without consulting the stars. [*191*, p. 161]

Despite the recognized need to learn from the West at least the arts of defense, Russia was extremely conservative until and even after the times of Peter. In the seventeenth century, medieval authorities ruled, and geometry was held sinful. [*413*, p. 19] A printing press was introduced in 1553 but was laid away until 1615. Arabic numerals were not used until after 1641, and afterward remained something of a rarity. [*379*, pp. 44–45] The theories of Copernicus and Galileo were generally anathema in the eighteenth century. [*377*, p. 412] Mental torpor was most obvious in the Orthodox church, virtually changeless for centuries, totally bound in ritual and impervious to ideas; it never produced any original theology [*419*, p. 432], and down to the present it has been notorious for inordinate attention to form and neglect of the spirit. In the seventeenth century people would rather die than eat eggs in Lent, but they did not mind beating priests after respectfully doffing caps to them. [*379*, p. 42] Millions were so imbued with the importance of strict ritual that they withdrew from society, and thousands immolated themselves rather than accept minor changes, such as crossing with three fingers instead of two and adding a letter to the spelling of "Jesus" — changes themselves introduced in the name of return to true ancient ways.

China saw a great reversal from the intellectually exciting times of the Hundred Schools and the Contending States to the conformity and sterility of the unified realm. In the Han dynasty there remained some diversity of thought for about a century until Confucianism was made canonical; but this and eventually the still more formalized Neo-Confucianism became the only acceptable mode. Scholars could do little more than comment and interpet the old classics, and the more steeped in Confucianism they became, the more impervious to change. The frank Confucianist motto became, "Transmit but do not create." Especially after the thirteenth century innovation was ever less, scholasticism more arid, and traditional forms more barren. Philosophic and political originality was almost nonexistent. A few penetrating observers were able to analyze troubles of their times, but they could suggest remedies only in terms of Confucian virtues. As a Ming authority said, "Ever since the time of the philosopher Chu, the truth has been made manifest to the world; no more writing is necessary, what is left to us is practice." [*40*, Bk. I, p. 317] It is said that, to describe the Chinese imperial government, one might take almost any time from the beginning to the end, for it hardly changed during two thousand years. [*67*, p. 291] Even the organization of the village sought only to conserve and uphold the ageless order. [*82*, p. 240]

So important was it to do as in classic times that a T'ang minister, Fang Kuan, reverted to the style of warfare of a thousand years before — chariots drawn by oxen — thereby inviting a rout. [E. Pulleyblank in *78*, p. 99] Respectable literature in the later dynasties was inconceivably empty; the anonymously composed drama and novel of Ming times were the work of the unscholarly, much below the dignity of the literati. [*40*, Bk. I, p. 320] Education was entirely based on the changeless classics. The *Thousand Character Classic* was standard fare for schoolchildren for 1,400 years, up to 1912. Such was the emphasis on rote memorization that children would commit to memory an entire book before the teacher began to explain, one by one, the meaning of the ideograms. [*54*, p. 64] Scholars eventually became generally ignorant even of their supposedly favored subject, history, except as given in the age-old classics. [*65*, p. 98] Such was the reluctance to touch upon current politics that in the schools of the later Ch'ing dynasty the study of history ended with the founding of the dynasty, more than two centuries earlier. [*65*, p. 83] By consequence and because of bureaucratic secrecy, there were few studies of practical administration, useful as this subject would have been to the empire. [C. Yang in *55*, p. 144]

The civil service examinations, which determined the character of education, reflected and partly caused the intellectual drought. In early Sung times they were not yet entirely based on the classics, some contemporary writings being used. Although the examinations in history and law depended almost entirely on memory, those in literature in particular called for originality and skillful reasoning in discussion of contradictory passages; and there was some effort to make them broader and more practical. [*39*, pp. 61–64] But conservatism, fortified by the bureaucratic mentality and the desire to have easily graded tests, prevailed; and under the Ming and Ch'ing dynasties the examinations decayed into the most barren formalism. The central part was a stylized eight-part or "eight-legged" essay. Based on a quotation from the *Four Books* or *Five*

Canons, this consisted of (1) two sentences of preliminaries, (2) three sentences of introduction, (3) introductory paragraph, (4) paragraph of not more than three sentences on the subject, (5) short rhythmic paragraph, (6) long rhythmic paragraph, (7) preliminary concluding paragraph, and (8) concluding paragraph. The essays consisted mostly of a series of homilies. [76, p. 431] Sentences alternated with fixed numbers of syllables, and each thought was presented with an antithesis. [56, pp. 147–148] It is not to be wondered that candidates preferred to enter the cubicles with prefabricated essays in minute characters up their sleeves. They had also to write a poem of six five-character couplets and to reproduce by memory some hundreds of words from the *Annotations of Sixteen Imperial Commandments* or the long *Sacred Edict*. [54, p. 58] Only the highest grade of examination required discussion of current problems of government, and even then the form was prescribed in most minute detail. The papers were graded more for form, including rhythm and calligraphy, than for meaning; examiners in the nineteenth century would disqualify a paper for abbreviating a single character. [76, pp. 443–444] The civil servants produced by the system were above all backward-looking; in the 1880's they thought that the way to protect Peking was to reconquer Sinkiang, ancient gateway of nomad invaders. Despite the pressing need for competent generals, the military examinations were hardly more practical. In the nineteenth century they comprised mostly horsemanship and archery, with nothing of firearms. [14, I, 439; 54, p. 61]

If one might generalize from such evidence, the autocratic empire is most of all prone to worship form, the correct and elegant way, the properly formalized and impressive means of expression. This may be partly in compensation for lack of content; gestures take the place of real feelings in the general advance of hypocrisy; proper flourishes do much to cover or make up for the intellectual vacuity which descends upon the fully ordered world. Perhaps in greater measure, formalism is a direct response to the needs of the imperial regime. Its great virtue and longing is stability, which requires unquestioning adherence to traditional patterns; and these are developed in appealing elegance and detail. Ceremonies of all kinds, to be performed simply because they are right and proper and with no need of explanation, tend to smother independent thinking and to increase respect for an authority that is right and proper per se, a priori, as it were. To be conventional is to be obedient to authority. Irrational institutions rest more easily on memory and habit than they do on an ideology; the less the practical utility of the structure the more fearful it is of change, because change opens the door to questioning and more change.

Pomp and solemn formalities reinforce the extraordinary position of a man who probably is innately very ordinary; everything about the autocrat must be surrounded with a maximum of ritual and endlessly impressive ceremonies, which capture the spirit and transfix the mind, giving him a kind of legitimacy an elected president does not need. The maintenance of the authority of all his minions requires similar support, and nothing is so important as status and the tokens that evince it. Hence symbols of deference, regular procedures, and attention to form are the hallmark of the highly structured regime.

Consequently, the imperial order is permeated with formalism, from the manner of addressing superiors to the proper gestures at dinner. Court society everywhere is enormously concerned with form and protocol, and in the empire the court is model for all. Tokens of prestige become the height of glory and ambition's crown. A lady of the court of Louis XIV would faint with joy if her name on her bedroom door was prefixed with the preposition *pour*, a mark of distinction. [523, p. 225] Preoccupied above all with status, Chinese officials distinguished their rank by a multitude of such details as buttons, embroidered emblems, the color of umbrellas, and the number of flounces. [14, I, 298] The Chinese made a sort of game of the rules of etiquette, in which the adept could enjoy embarrassing the novice who did not know the proper response. Such attention to form and show took precedence over more substantial concerns. In the middle of the fourteenth century, the Byzantine court, nearly penniless and back-to-the-wall against the Turks, gave its attention to the utmost detail of court formalities as in the grandest times. [301, p 197]

An incidental result of this fondness for correct form is a divergence between the written and spoken languages, between the proper and the vulgar speech. Fond of elegance and fine distinctions, the court and bureaucracy favor conventional, refined language in traditional patterns, not only for its own sake but also because it is a mark of superiority and distance above the ignorant herd. Education maintains and strengthens the artificial forms, while the popular speech, without cultivation or educated leadership, continues to evolve and probably becomes simpler. Something like this seems to have occurred often, perhaps in all the very strong empires. A series of Near Eastern empires kept or developed special languages for administrative or religious purposes, such as Sumerian, Akkadian, and Old Persian, kept as written languages for centuries after they had passed out of general use. The written language of the Achaemenid empire seems to have been quite artificial. [252, p. 176] Under the Sassanids there arose the curious situation that reading was in effect translation, as though our writing were composed of French words, to be read as their English equivalents. [253, p. 467] In Egypt, ordinary speech more than once broke away from the conventional, written in hieroglyphics, and finally the demotic became a separate language. The court Incas spoke a tongue forbidden to commoners. [172, p. 30] Classic Chinese, encumbered with a tremendous number of learned allusions and subtle and indirect styles, became completely incomprehensible to the uneducated. An exclusive treasure and cherished key to authority, requiring long training and careful exercise of memory, it solidly reinforced traditionalism and the status of the elite. Something like the common speech remained unacceptable for purposes of writing practically until the dynasty was overthrown in 1911. Only with the loss of power by the bureaucratic elite, the scholar-gentry class, could the vulgar tongue come into literary use.

Most important has been the separation of Latin from the dialects that became the Romance languages. In the late republic and early empire, the legions were spreading the language of Caesar through the world. But as the empire ripened and the ruling elite drew apart from the masses, the court and government kept to a language that was artificial not only by conservatism but by stylization; for example, the précieux poets after Augustus avoided vulgar words like "ship." [E. Sikes in 290, p. 712] In the increasing alienation of governors and governed, the people of the provinces, who had given up their native speech for Latin, began speaking less and less like their rulers until their dialects became precursors of the Romance languages. Meanwhile, official, learned, and religious circles kept as close as they could, in the general cultural decline, to the tongue of Cicero, using their mastery of the difficult language to assure their superiority. [275, p. 111] Similarly, the

Byzantine empire, after giving up Latin, held to classic Greek while spoken Greek became a separate language, having a literature of its own and a vitality missing in the official literature. [*301*, pp. 249–250]

States of modern Europe have shown such tendencies. The court of Louis XIV used a highly refined French as distinct as possible from the crude speech of the middle and lower classes. [*510*, p. 256] While the French court preferred an artificial version of the national tongue, many princes, especially in Germany, went further. To support their somewhat synthetic claims to autocracy, they adopted French, often to the virtual exclusion of the native speech. In Russia, Church Slavonic, a foreign language for Russians, was the ordinary literary medium until Peter the Great; not long after him, the court and most of the aristocracy communicated in French. In less authoritarian England, the Norman ruling classes, despite links with French possessions, fairly soon gave up their own tongue. In 1362 Parliament decreed that all lawsuits be in English, and by 1385 English was the medium of instruction in all grammar schools. [*461*, p. 48]

THE NONCOMPETITIVE WORLD

If Pliny had explored more widely that larger part of history during which there has been little or no material progress and the human spirit has grown only inward, he would not have found unaccountable the mental decay of his age in the face of material advantages. He might even have seen in the great peace a detriment to the flowering of genius. Storms are movement, but in the great calm the ships would stand with slack sails. The very tranquillity, smug and superior, of the great empire, and the idealization of peace and harmony, are the death of creativity.

In part, the empire stultifies itself by reducing diversity within. Instead of a number of sovereign states, each important within itself, it contains only provinces looking to the capital and the ruler. The vibrant life of many centers is suffocated. As Plutarch observed, "Fortune has left us [Greeks] no prize for contention. For what dominion, what glory is there for those who are victorious? What sort of power is it when a small edict of a proconsul may annul it or transfer it to another man and which, even if it last, has nothing in it seriously worthwhile?" [*330*, p. 320] In the great centralization, very few persons are in a position to propose novelties even in nonpolitical matters; hardly anyone dares think for himself. As the imperial capital is the center of authority and wealth, dictating modes and fashions from its eminence, it would be an impossible presumption for a provincial city to attempt more than emulation. Building, art, literature, and science in the universal empire are all centered on the capital and royal patronage. In the Mogul empire, for example, even the more modest crafts prospered only in the shadow of the court, from which all blessings came. [*202*, p. 93]

The logic of the system and administrative convenience demand homogenization of laws, institutions, and language throughout the empire. Perhaps more important than the actual uniformity achieved is that only a single pattern, the received and official way of thought and action, is consequential and worthy of attention. This seems all very fine to the empire, but it sharply reduces the potentialities of free development and the mutual stimulation of parts. The imagination is aided by variety; minds and ideas grow from contact with diverse influences. In the uniform mass it is hard to think or do differently from the surrounding multitude; awareness of differences is the strongest encouragement to innovation. The more society is of one piece, the harder to make comparisons and criticisms; the only standards are the sanctioned practices and tradition. But criticism of the present by reference to ancestors' ways serves only to keep patterns, not to improve them; and conservatism sees little need for reason.

The more firmly bound the whole order, the less latitude for change, as the inertia of the huge monolith holds back all parts. If cultural growth may be compared with invention in biological evolution, the conversion of the various environments of the state system into imperial uniformity is like the replacement of a varied landscape of valleys and islands, with their possibilities of divergent development, cross fertilization, and progress, by a level plain. In the featureless environment, as in the inert homogeneity of the empire, there is little stimulus of variations meeting and interacting, and if novelty should arise it is likely to be overwhelmed by the great mass.

No less serious is lack of external friction to warm intellects. It is difficult indeed for any organization to remodel or seriously to criticize itself wholly from within; an external stimulus is almost indispensable. For the most part, men think and invent because they have to; and in competing systems they have been compelled to undertake this most reluctantly undertaken activity — one that they can, however, become hardened to and with practice even find agreeable. If ambitions are fulfilled and security is achieved, it is very easy to stop thinking entirely, or to be content to rehearse the past forever. Likewise, a man alone for a long time on a desert island should expect to have no profound meditations but to concern himself merely with the business of keeping alive and, in hours of leisure, to contemplate only the facts of his own existence. Creativity rises from interaction.

Such is the situation of the universal empire. Competing states, none of which can be certain of victory, are always spurring one another and demonstrating, in the most convincing possible way, the need to keep learning. However much we love peace, there is nothing like a contest to stir our energies. The universal or near-universal empire has limited contacts with anything outside; and these are of little effect, as the empires commonly wear pride and arrogance as armor against foreign influence. The rulers of the world cannot bring themselves to learn from the barbarians. Even if they could perceive the necessity, they do not want to, as borrowing is an acknowledgment of inferiority. Turks, Romans, Incas, and all such world conquerors could only despise the heathen, infidels, or barbarians without. In China, the T'ang and Sung dynasties, with relatively good cultural records, were most open to foreign trade and intercourse; nonetheless, the traditional policy was that Chinese ships should not leave Chinese waters. Early in the Ming dynasty, there was a series of great naval expeditions to Araby and Africa in 1405–1433, just about the time Portuguese navigators were creeping down the African coast; but the Chinese expeditions came to nothing. Curiosity satisfied, the Mings withdrew almost entirely from foreign contacts; near isolation remained the rule. Until gunboats forced open the doors in the nineteenth century, the regular response to European invitations to trade was that China needed nothing from without.

Late in the nineteenth century, when Western power was impinging so strongly that it could no longer be shrugged off, a Chinese minister recognized the relation between lack of external contacts and the traditional order: "Scholars of a unified world can be created by examination on formalized writings; scholars of a world of many countries cannot be created by examination on formalized writings." The old system, he contended, could not stand, with foreigners disturbing tranquillity and order. [8, p. 203] The fixity and uniformity of the imperial system could not mix with the diversity of independent states.

To make firmer its rule, the great empire proclaims and convinces itself that it is not only immensely superior to the barbarians but near perfect; it is complete and its truth is immutable and final. This conviction is a useful asset in the affirmation of rule, discouraging any ideas of alternatives and inhibiting foolish notions of change. It is hard to deny; men enjoy being told that theirs is the perfect order. It is easy, then, for those in authority as for their subjects to come to believe that they or their ancestors must have already learned and invented everything worthwhile, and that no real improvement is possible except by refinement of the past.

At one time the masters of the world proved their superiority by laying low all who stood in their path, and the greatness of the past weighs heavily upon the present. Pride of success is a heavy impediment to new thought. Even small and relatively open states, like Venice, tend to become ingrown and complacent if their past has been especially glorious; far more is the universal empire subject to stagnation. Any apparently successful solution inhibits the finding of other solutions. The mind, having filled itself with an answer, resists beginning anew the search; it must be jolted into recognition that a better insight is needed. Creativity requires not only the necessary faculties, knowledge and education, but also some sense of uncertainty and potentialities unattained, a drive to find new answers, and a mixture of tension and hope. These are common property of the competing states, but the empire represents an incontestably successful and therefore exclusive set of solutions for the principal problems of society. With the end of questioning, searching, and progress, greatness more and more belongs to the past. Hence the empire clings to antique models the more desperately as it feels itself losing strength, and seeks to recover lost virtues until, as in archaistic times, in Egypt, Byzantium, or China, it would live practically in a dreamworld.

The universal empire, feeling its completeness and enjoying the finality of its simple answers, needs administrators, not thinkers; fearing change and looking always backward, it can hardly admit even one new thought in each century; closed upon itself in dull smugness, it prefers autosuggestion to inquiry, policing to improvement. Such attitudes have again and again made the greatest polities into magnificent collective idiocies, unable to absorb even childishly obvious lessons most vitally necessary for their own survival. For example, the Chinese were entirely unable to learn the military arts that the West thrust upon them. In the 1620's they were led by curiosity to seek Western firearms but regarded them with disdain and completely failed to master their use and manufacture. Their perennial attitude was well expressed by the emperor writing to George III in 1790: "I set no value on objects strange or ingenious." [4, p. 325] In the nineteenth century, when the Western superiority had become much more marked and dangerous, the Chinese were badly shocked by defeat. Yet learning was still extremely difficult. Chinese scholars tried to prove that Western sciences, even geography and mathematics, were derived from the Chinese classics. [51, p. 75] European clocks were regarded with incredulous amazement, for there could be no good artisans outside the Flowery Kingdom. [43, p. 124] British warships were disdained as only slight improvements on Chinese inventions. [32, p. 42] In the latter part of the century, as Chinese technical inferiority became glaringly evident and searing defeats cost humiliation, treasure, and territory, the government feebly and halfheartedly sought to initiate the manufacture of modern arms. It even cautiously tried to introduce some Western learning. Yet, despite official approval of the study of Western methods, only about four hundred copies of translated Western technical books were sold yearly in the thirty years before defeat by Japan in 1894. [8, p. 205]

WEIGHT OF THE STATE

Monotony and exclusiveness are perhaps less profoundly suffocating to creativity than are the uses of power, of which forcible suppression or censorship in the conventional sense is only the most obvious. It is very difficult for creative endeavor to thrive in the politically ordered environment of the great empire: all the countless measures taken to check independent power, to foster an orthodox philosophy, to make opposition impossible, and keep control in the right hands tend to suppress initiative of all kinds and to make men servants, not independent doers and thinkers. The ease with which power can be abused profoundly discourages all endeavor; not even simple crafts could really prosper in Mogul India, where the arrogant omrahs paid artisans by caprice or not at all. [*191*, p. 288] In the imperial order, there is security and prosperity only in conformity. Individualism is negated and penalized, yet it is as individuals that men reach for the new; art and literature are essentially individualistic and antiauthoritarian in their higher expression. Ideological bent and the sense of totality inhibit flexibility and thought, even if the empire consciously wished to encourage them.

Probably it does not. Reason is dangerous and corrosive of official truths; real freedom of expression is hence impossible. Sooner or later the most seemingly innocent of arts, if it aspires to any depth or originality, acquires political implications as an undesired interpretation of life. Where all else is made to conform, whatever is left free may become an outlet or symbol of nonconformity. To think for oneself implies that authority is incomplete if not misguided. The irreverent answer is most often nearest to truth, but absolute power demands absolute reverence. Uniformity of thought symbolizes obedience and makes people more docile, while diversity bespeaks disobedience. Ever suspicious of spontaneity, the autocrat asks first of all about the motives of any new departure. Holders of authority are usually dubious of changes, not only in the power structure of society, but also in styles and culture. Anything that implies a breakdown of the accepted is regarded with horror; only order and uniformity are reassuring. Art has stronger feelings of criticism than of praise and thrives on clash and conflict, but the sublime order admits no genuine differences.

Easily convinced of his own wisdom and his duty to guide his sheep, the ruler can hardly refrain from repressing false, subversive, and immoral productions. It is worse if, instead of being lazy and careless, he is idealistic, like the stern and intolerant Aurangzeb. Signs of discontent are to be repressed for the good of all; yet to be discontented and seek improvement is a worthy function of the mind. Objectivity is an impediment to loyalty; it and its cousin, neutrality, become praiseworthy only when there are balancing forces and a need to find common ground. The political is intrin-

sically at odds with the intellectual, and the empire is the consum-
mation of political success. As John Dewey said, "If we once start
thinking no one can guarantee where we shall come out, except
that many objects, ends and institutions are doomed." Many freedoms to think and do the empire finds inconvenient; and, although
many rulers would like artistic and intellectual luminaries to adorn
their state, it is more important to keep all under control.

Under the Maurya empire, places of amusement and musicians
were forbidden, that men should spend their time working for
the king [*318*, p. 166], and entry into the ranks of teachers and
ascetics was closely regulated, men being permitted to devote
themselves to scholarly pursuits only when deemed no longer
useful for production. [*208*, II, 67] The stupidity of life of the
masses was carefully fostered to keep them at work. [*201*, p. 219]
The ideology of the conquering Chinese state of Ch'in, as trans-
mitted by the empire, was explicit in this regard: people should
remain dull and uneducated so that they would be content to work
and obey. "Sophistry and cleverness are an aid to lawless men," and,
"Indeed, the people will love the ruler and obey his commandments, even to death, if they are engaged in farming, morning and
evening; but they will be of no use if they see that glib-tongued
itinerant scholars succeed in being honored in serving the prince."
[*16*, pp. 177, 192–193, 206] In the religious controversies of the
ninth century, the Byzantine empire forbade exercise of its only
substantial art, painting. [*311*, p. 55] The Turkish empire forbade
the importation of books, purged texts of doubtful ideas, and prohibited printing until the early eighteenth century; and the colleges
after the middle of the sixteenth century were restricted almost
entirely to theology and law. [*432*, Pt. II, pp. 150–151] The stifling
of Russian thought was concomitant with the establishment of the
empire. [*388*, II, 242] Tsardom never lacked a censorship, of varying stringency but constant stupidity; in the nineteenth century it
forbade mention, among other things, of bureaucracy and trade
unions. [*418*, p. 97]

The Chinese empire hardly needed censorship as it made the
education, or indoctrination, devised for civil servants the only
useful one. A single philosophy led to advancement; for two thousand years there was practically no opportunity for study except
for the examinations and under official auspices. [*84*, p. 102] In that
time, only two or three non-Confucianists succeeded in entering

government service, and they were soon driven out. [*56*, p. 15]
Yet the only real scholars were those who managed to secure educations outside the official establishment. Regulation of the thoroughly Confucianist and conformist intellectuals tended to increase from dynasty to dynasty until under the Ch'ing they were forbidden to publish their own works, to organize factions, to argue unreasonably, to meddle in political and judicial questions, to petition the government regarding the welfare of the common people, to instigate lawsuits, or sometimes to meet even for harmless purposes. [*36*, pp. 240–242]

It need hardly be mentioned that serious political or philosophical inquiry is almost impossible in the imperial order. Political study is seldom more than a rationalization of political positions; it can flourish only in an atmosphere of maximum freedom, like that of classic Greece. Any serious inquiry into the nature of society, the purposes and justification of power, the bases of conduct, and the criteria of truth is potentially an affront to the sovereign and universal power. The supreme state may not desire even a controlled discussion, for it may always turn into undesirable channels. Best is that the citizens simply ignore things political. Catherine II told her subjects that, as concern for their welfare kept her sleepless, they need not trouble themselves about politics and were forbidden to do so. [W. Richardson in *403*, p. 151] Turkish newspapers of the nineteenth century amused their readers with all manner of faraway stories, but carried hardly a word about events at home. [*418*, p. 97] The incapacity for self-examination is such that the empires have not even been inventive of ideologies to suit their own purposes, but have always had to borrow the fundamentals from freer societies; even an antirational philosophy can be originated only in a clash of contending views. In the set imperial order, to delve deeply into anything is dangerous and pointless. But when the state and fundamentals of the social order are beyond discussion, all thinking is inhibited.

Natural sciences are less impeded than are studies of more direct political implications, but they also sicken. Science has probably fared as well in the Chinese empire as in any; yet even there so apparently harmless and unworldly a science as astronomy suffered only a little less than history and philosophy, which were mere handmaids of authority. The Han astronomers gathered, as mentioned earlier, an impressive body of data; but they were interested in developing neither scientific theory nor technical applications. They sought merely to study portents for political significance or to calculate the length of dynasties. The regime used a semilunar calendar which was suitable not for agriculture but for festivals and rites, serving not economic but political needs; and changes made to accommodate symbolism were as often as not directed toward less accuracy. Astronomical instruments were at times kept secret lest they be used for some subversive purpose. [J. Needham in *468*, p. 132] A prime duty of astronomers of all dynasties was to foretell eclipses and to rescue the sun or moon when one occurred. [*14*, I, 309–310] But failure of these to occur on schedule was motive not for correcting the astronomers but for rejoicing that Heaven, swayed by imperial virtue, had withheld an ill omen. [*50*, p. 126]

In general, the government sponsored science only so far as it did not develop new and therefore dangerous ideas, for ideas might be made a tool of political struggle; and what scientific achievements there were came mostly from the work of hobbyists. [W. Eberhard in *19*, pp. 63–68] But independent progress was very difficult. About 260 A.D. one Ma Chün made many remarkable inventions, including a differential gear; but having no classical learning, he could obtain no position of importance and was unable to get his inventions applied. [J. Needham in *468*, pp. 130–131] Scientists were usually civil servants, often lodged in the palace and employed in the imperial workshop; they had only to please the masters. [J. Needham in *468*, p. 124] The Chinese built escapement clocks from the eighth century, about six hundred years before western Europeans, but they were only for palace and primarily ritualistic use. [*6*, p. 848] China is the land par excellence of unapplied inventions.

As the Chinese did with astronomy, the overbearing state cleverly chokes independent creativity not only by repression but also by setting minds to artificial and harmless tasks, at once taking up energies, winning support, and buying intellectual ornamentation for the regime. The endless ceremonies and amusements of the court of Louis XIV were designed to occupy the upper classes and keep them out of mischief, such as had culminated earlier in the disorders of the Fronde. [*523*, p. 224] Lest the elaborately trained literati find time to fall into independent thinking, various Chinese emperors put them to work revising the repeatedly revised classics.

This occupation required a great deal of erudition but little originality; under the later and more tightly organized dynasties, the only literature of significance was the work of nameless popular storytellers and entertainers. In the same spirit, the Russian empire fostered the study of Graeco-Roman classics. A minister of Alexander II proposed that teachers of the classics should, like the police and the Orthodox clergy, support the state by turning minds to innocuous pursuits; Greek and Latin composition was made the heart of secondary education and a prerequisite for entry into universities. [402, pp. 131, 163]

As Tacitus remarked, everything became focused on the supreme power [*Histories*, 2.38], and, "After the conflict at Actium, and when it became essential to peace that all power be centered in one man, these great intellects passed away. Then too the truthfulness of history was impaired in many ways; at first, through men's ignorance of public affairs, which were now wholly strange to them, then, through their passion for flattery, or, on the other hand, their hatred of their masters." [*Histories*, 1.1] An exiled writer at the beginning of the empire commented: "When what one writes is adapted to what one guesses to be the feelings of another, and not to the expression of one's own judgment, you may be sure that I appreciate the difficulty of emerging unscathed." [345, p. 23] The poets of the Augustan era were, like those of T'ang China, court poets; Maecenas was engaged by Augustus to find literary talent to ornament his reign. [354, p. 208] Writers like Virgil, Pliny, Martial, and Lucan flattered their rulers, whom they saw in the flesh, not merely as gods, but as greater than gods. [347, pp. 100–101] Criticism had to be cautious to the point of servility. The respected Pliny, writing to the tolerant Trajan, permitted himself only the mildest criticisms through his eulogies. [334, p. 46] Later writers became more and more accustomed to pleasing the ear of the autocrat; and the less secure they felt, the more fulsome their praise, rising to a height under the tyrannical Domitian. If Tiberius frowned on flattery, the literature of his reign was, nonetheless, nearly as unctuous. [345, pp. 212–213] When Nerva and Trajan relaxed the controls of Domitian, it was felt as an era of great freedom; but habits of conformity were well set and no great rebirth of culture followed. [345, p. 143] An unknown writer of this time commented: "Today we seem in our boyhood to learn the lessons of a righteous servitude, being all but completely swathed in customs and observances when our thoughts are young and tender, so that we emerge in no other guise but that of sublime flatterers." [298, p. 199] In the second century Lucian was able to recognize and discuss the need for speaking out truly and freely; yet he felt obliged to write a panegyric on the emperor's mistress. [345, pp. 259–260]

Such courting of favor is sickening for genius; as Benjamin Constant remarked, "When the human soul has been debased, the artist . . . loses the ability nobly to depict the human form." [465, p. 93] Not only the supreme ruler must be pleased, but all his underlings. The servant — and all men but one are servants — weighs statements not for truth but for their effect upon relations to his superiors and presently comes to think as he speaks; the heart follows the lips. The more smoothly and effectively hypocrisy drips, the more poisonous to intellectual integrity. At length, where there is no danger of contradiction, the most palpable absurdity may be taken as truth. As the Persian proverb went, "If the monarch says that the day is night, Reply, 'The moon and stars are bright.'" [191, p. 264] In the Mogul empire, flattery was so general and so hyperbolic that anything could be believed. When a sycophant said that the earth trembled beneath his lord's footsteps, the latter replied quite seriously that for this reason he traveled in a palanquin. [191, pp. 264–265]

The effects of the subordination of some to others are not usually so extreme, but the hierarchic-bureaucratic order itself makes an arid environment. The big organization puts all in a single mold of solemn formalities, obligations, and more or less synthetic values; it also breeds its own traits of personality by raising up and rewarding the politician-executive over the specialist-thinker. Successful maneuverers, manipulators, and managers are inclined to be antiphilosophic; and to rise in the empire means thoroughly to accept its ways and values. Cramped in a framework that neither expects nor rewards brilliance, the most brilliant mind becomes dull. Successful and self-satisfied, bureaucrats have little cause to exercise their minds even if their energies are not engaged in improving or maintaining status, and their mentality is not shaped by the fact of having risen by the arts of pleasing and conforming. Those who have climbed the ladders of power are dubious of innovation or essential change in principle, since change is likely to be injurious to them; and they are hence apt to be conservative in all spheres, even those of no immediate concern to them, like art and religion, while they distrust thinkers, who are less than totally loyal to any claim and whose passion for reason is the enemy of authority. The authoritarian structure arrests the growth of individual character; that is, it raises the authoritarian personality, which is the opposite of the creative. [489, p. 97] Almost no personality of history has been very successful both organizationally and creatively.

Men rise in the imperial order by loyalty and usefulness, not by initiative; success comes not from originality but from the favor of superiors. Novelty is a disturbance of routines and mental habits if not a threat to established positions. Individual inquiry is a prideful sin; questioning creates feelings of insecurity in bosses and subordinates alike. The official wants those below him to be cooperative and obedient rather than brilliant and creative, much less self-willed. Probably not distinguished himself by high intelligence, except in the mastery of practical psychology and intrigue, he does not want the capacities of inferiors to show up his own deficiencies. If the subordinate would progress, he seeks to please by thinking in the same way as his superior; he should even be discreet in his achievements lest he annoy by showing up his betters. To do or propose anything unconventional is to cause trouble for the system and himself. To get along, traditional ways are best and far safest; there is least risk in going with the herd in the trodden paths. Communication and exchange of ideas prosper only between equals, but inequality is the essence of bureaucratic order. To differ with superiors or to make it necessary for them to justify their opinions is most hazardous and unlikely to be rewarding. It is far better for one's career to be wrong with an acceptable opinion than right with a maverick or disagreeable one; if events should vindicate the dissenter, so much the worse. Obedience, the worse as it is sincere and wholehearted, becomes the instinct. It is best to study the rules, accepted procedure, and higher views, for whatever is outside their framework implies criticism if not subversion. Ideas must be safe and near to accepted truth; there may be brought forward clever tactics or adaptations, but never a notion that might disturb the established order or the rationalizations that support it. Orthodoxy calls for loyalty, and loyalty is to the organization and the men who represent it, not to truth.

Subordinates are thus driven rather to repress than to express, paralyzed in their own personalities as they depend on arbitrary wills above them, unable to be honest with themselves and society, and so condemned to mediocrity. But practically everyone is a subordinate. If a few at the summit have a broader view and feel heavier responsibility, they, too, can hardly escape the servility of spirit by virtue of which they have climbed to greatness. And if, by some chance, they should perceive the need for some new departure, the conformist mass below is probably too much for anyone, even the emperor, to budge.

THE DISPIRITED SOCIETY

Despotic power crushes souls, and in the wake of glory the supreme and universal order brings not only peace and security but stagnation and stultification, apathy and dismal drabness. The fuller the central power, the less room for any shred of initiative; the more dominant the top, the feebler all below. The very grandeur of the order deadens independence and individual thought. Even in a small group it is not easy for anyone to set himself against the prevalent opinion; the larger the group that is doing and thinking alike, the harder for sane persons to go against the suggestion of the whole, even in their secret thoughts. Against the state, too complex and distant for comprehension, against the truth of the universe, who can set his own notions? When man is caught up in an organization beyond his comprehension and compelled to act for reasons he does not understand, his mind falters. The overwhelming mass dehumanizes and devitalizes. When things are fated or arbitrary, one is better off not thinking or striving. The ego of all, as the rulers desire, is lowered; and the people are led, in the face of unlimited power, to accept the authority over them as necessary and salutary, or at least unavoidable. Total power for a few means resignation for the rest.

In the face of the imperial power, men are happier if they do not try to be in any way different or original. Insecure, uninformed, knowing themselves to be weak and sinful, men seek the safest and simplest way, which is the way marked out by custom and authority; for the subjects of the great empire, it is only wisdom to attach themselves to convention and their superiors, to obey and to conform. Thus, when Nero showed a passion for rhetoric, that art became the rage of Rome. Later, Marcus Aurelius made philo-

sophic expression or posturing the mode; less sublimely, all the rich
had to take the same potion as prescribed for his aches and pains.
[302, p. 31; 313, p. 32] Once having accepted the pigtail, a badge
of servitude imposed by foreign conquerors, the Chinese became
attached to it as an ancestral custom. So little did convenience
weigh against conformity that from subtropical to subarctic China,
men changed from winter to summer dress on a day fixed by imperial decree, irrespective of the weather. [64, p. 121]

Genius, however, requires self-confidence, a belief in improvement, and a will to act on one's own and set out on uncharted ways.
Thinkers, especially scientific discoverers, are inevitably individ-
ualists; and the great are lonely. They need to feel that their wrestling with nature and their search for new truth and interpretation
are important; yet in the great empire all is allegedly well-regu-
lated. Genius is deeply honest and essentially unselfish [482, p. 22],
alien to politics, impassioned for its work, not for control over people; the urge to mastery of men is the enemy of artistic and intellectual creativity.

The more efficient the empire, the more unimaginative and conventional are its people. Yet genius is always somewhat, and usually
decidedly, maladjusted in terms of the mediocre milieu. In the
great empire, moreover, the idealism that energizes genius is lost.
Even if one does not groan under oppression, he fails to feel himself a political participant. The sense and purposes of patriotism
are missing in the universal state, where men need only to bow to
the higher powers. There is no call to make the most of whatever
gifts one has, as in the more demanding atmosphere of a competitive society; and the more one is subject to command, the more
passively he limits himself to what is commanded. It is enough to
do the appointed tasks, pay taxes, and rear children to do likewise,
to survive and enjoy the blessings that fall, without questioning or
aspiring. Education and knowledge are to be sought only in the
accepted manner and as means for advancement. Self-assertion is
folly in the perfect order; or, if one aspires to rise, it should be attempted only through prescribed and conventional channels. Least
of all is there reason that anyone should risk his little happiness
by attempting more than the custom-bound society demands of
him or sacrifice anything for the common welfare; but progress
almost always implies sacrifice. Genius thinks not of security or
personal gain but of its bright hopes.

Intelligence is almost equivalent to invention and search for improvement; instinct suffices for conformity. Intelligence, the ability to form new patterns, rejects habit, tradition, and pure command as sufficient bases for actions. Discouraging or repressing questioning and change, the empire in effect represses intelligence. But the intellect cannot stand still; restrained from advancing, it falls back. [465, p. 95] Nothing need be done to close minds; men use their faculties as they are driven to do so, usually with reluctance and often with anguish; unless there is a will to apply the brain, there is no intelligence; and the empire discourages all but the minimal thought of immediate utility. In the late republic, as exigencies of rule were leading Rome toward imperial forms, audiences lacked intellectual stamina to follow a detailed plot, and even older Roman plays had to be cut down for duller intellects. [294, p. 463]

To sift truth from error at best requires an effort; where there is no great advantage for the former, the latter often prevails, as errors are infinite, simple, and attractive — and many a fancy lends support to established position — while truth is one and often stern. The imperial order, itself irrational and hence distrusting reason, excels in credulity and superstition. The free Sumerians sought to cure disease by natural process; the physicians of the Babylonian and Assyrian empires, a thousand and more years later, prescribed magic. When the Ionian Greeks came into contact with varied Eastern superstitions, they compared and questioned. But the many lands conquered by Rome added to its spiritual burden rather than lifting it; when all manner of creeds and practices were brought together, there was no inclination to inquire into their validity, but rather to roll all into a marvelous eclectic hash. [302, p. 445] Instead of laughing at Egyptian myths, Plutarch found reverent rationalizations for them: "The legends are to be interpreted in a pious and philosophical manner." [343, p. 58] In the fourth century, Rome was so fearful of magic that the copying of spells was punishable by death. [275, p. 65] Weary old empires have been buried in a jungle of credulity, fearsome superstitions, geomancy, astrology, and magic of all descriptions such as would appall a simple animistic savage; and their few intellectuals strive rather to glimpse mysteries than to grasp facts.

With exaltation of unreason come dullness and stupidity. Impatience and distrust of intelligence have a cumulative effect as con-

formity sees itself rewarded and placed in a position to demand
still more conformity. Education is favored only as it fits into the
official pattern, and perhaps more asphyxiates intelligence than
nurtures it. The autocratic ruler has usually more to fear from,
learning than from ignorance; the illiterate masses represent no
danger. Lack of written records probably helped the Incas wipe
out traditions of independence in a very short time, and thus secure
a remarkable degree of acceptance for a highly exploitative regime.

Despotism, as de Tocqueville remarked, freezes the soul. The
poor find it enough to keep alive, the educated show only a little
less indifference and apathy, and all lose the capacity to wrestle
with new thoughts. Curiosity limits itself to the near and personal,
beyond which it is unfitting to inquire. Repression of thought
comes to be accepted willingly, as relieving of the need to think.
The philosophers, then, may be the more suitably abolished, if
any should aspire to this occupation, as they have nothing to say;
it was no scandal when a relatively enlightened emperor (Vespasian) chased them like dogs out of Rome.

In this condition, all enterprises except the state shrivel. Much
of writing degenerates to pomp and bombast, dull, wordy, and
empty. Industry and diligence cease to seem virtues when they
are no longer important ladders for success and when their fruits
may be seized by a greedy subdespot. Invention is not quite zero,
because the state cannot control everything. But even if discoveries
are made, lack of incentive and entrepreneurship prevents their
utilization. Just as important Chinese inventions have again and
again been applied for magic or symbolic purposes, Hero's very
ingenious devices were used, in Roman times, for the most trivial
purposes, such as an engine for mysteriously opening temple doors
when a fire was kindled. The clocks that fourteenth-century Europe
found curious and useful were used in Byzantium to mystify and
inspire awe. [569, p. 125] And if material improvement ceases, its
stoppage contributes to the general immobility of society. Like
change, stagnation feeds upon itself, as poverty makes it impossible
and stability renders it unnecessary to reconsider anything; and
the more ignorant men become, the more confident that they have
nothing to learn.

It seems that the people of the great empires themselves find life
dreary and monotonous. Many Russian writers of the nineteenth
century complained bitterly of the land where "generations live

and die without leaving behind a memory or a lesson for their children." The later Romans saw their own world as senescent. [322, p. 223] Without the clash of rival powers, there was little in it to catch the imagination. The free or nonofficial writers of the second to the fourth century largely ignored the world around them, except when they satirized its shortcomings; all preferred to speak of events up to the end of the republic, whose heroic deeds, and those of classic Greece, were endlessly rehearsed. Only apologetically would they touch upon the affairs of their own times. [288, p. 217] They found no real drama in great events, intrigues, and plots; desperate contests for supremacy were merely mistakes, preferably to be forgotten when order was reestablished. There were not even consequential accounts of the history that men endured with resignation; it seems more interesting to modern scholars than to those who existed through it. Fact became quite unimportant and what passed for intelligence was at best sparkle. [345, p. 82] There was room for little more than propaganda, ornament, and light entertainment, mixed with much pretense and pedantry. The once animated classical world fell into apathy and mental torpor capable of producing almost nothing of note. The superstitions that had never ceased among the lower classes enveloped all. Credulity, if not gullibility, became a virtue called faith. Forgetting commerce and manufacturing, the Romans gave themselves so far as they could to sensuous sloth.

The dullness of the late Roman empire continued in the Byzantine, which was not only incredibly conservative, but exceptionally uncreative. Through its long history of violence, intrigue, and murder, almost no principles were involved and few memorable or romantic characters. [287, p. 350] The tremendous interest in theology and religion had no relation at all to conduct. The extreme incapacity of the people was shown by their weakness against the traders of the Italian city-states. With small numbers and far from home, Venetians and Genoese fought over the passive body of the pretentious empire and at one time held the best parts of it. The Byzantines complained much of their exploitation by Italian traders, but they should have lamented their own incredible incapability. By the end of the fourteenth century the port of Galata, controlled by the Genoese, was producing seven times as much revenue as the traditional center, Constantinople. [301, p

195] The Venetians regarded the proud Byzantines as an inferior, slave race; one cannot say that this haughty attitude was unjustified.

Similarly the Chinese empire of modern times showed a mental rot and cultural deadness much beyond mere adherence to past and consecrated ways. Uninterested in precision, latter-day scholars abridged and corrupted the records of their supposedly revered ancestors, to the serious inconvenience of modern investigators. [J. Needham in 468, p. 137] The massive encyclopedic works virtually went out of circulation and became quite inaccessible to ordinary scholars. [65, p. 100] At the end of the sixteenth century the Jesuit Ricci found in Peking astronomical instruments superior to anything he had seen in Europe, but they were out of use because the court astronomers had forgotten how to work them. [10, p. 149] Astrology was a prime guide for peasants and emperors alike. [4, p. 135] Innumerable ceremonies and superstitions, often of the grossest sort, prevailed everywhere and in all aspects of life, even in the highest circles. For example, men would go without hats and umbrellas to help clouds turn into rain. [14, II, 120] In the latter nineteenth century the official gazette called for the erection of "lucky towers" to remedy the shortage of adequately prepared examination candidates. [65, p. 314] European missionaries found much that was exasperating in the Chinese mentality: curiosity was blighted; horizons and interests were narrow and strictly bound by material concerns; an impoverished monotony was accepted as the natural condition of life; excuse and pretense covered anything; it was almost impossible to get a direct and factual answer to questions. [64, *passim*] The Flowery Kingdom was the "Land of make-believe." [15, p. v]

Thus the great empires seem to do little better than utilize the intellectual capital they receive from freer societies, perhaps polishing but inventing little that is really new. Worse, they are incapable of sustaining the cultural heritage with which they begin, for a power-oriented and exploitative empire is inherently contrary to the use of intelligence. Under it, the qualities that elevate and ennoble humans atrophy; and these are the qualities that give strength to any order. Eventually this mental anemia becomes a serious sickness. The fossilized society gets further and further out of touch with reality, more irrational and less capable of amending itself or even of accomplishing its supreme task, holding itself together. According to Andersen's tale, the emperor, charmed by the melodies of a nightingale, acquired a bejeweled mechanical imitation, which sang the same song endlessly over and over. He and the court much preferred this tame imitation. But eventually it wore out, and only the wild bird could revive the ailing emperor's spirits.

7   IMPOVERISHMENT

BURDENS OF EMPIRE

Universal empire brings most favorable conditions for strong economic growth, just as it seemingly does for cultural development. Trade is made secure and barriers are broken down over a huge area, so that goods can be freely interchanged much more extensively than before. There are all the advantages of scale, and producers can count on an almost indefinitely large market. To be sure, there may not be large economies of series production with relatively primitive techniques, but there should be some; and a higher degree of specialization becomes possible when makers of pots, knives, ships, and the like can cater to the whole empire. The potentialities of very large-scale production should also encourage men to improve their techniques and to work toward mechanization of production, the more obviously profitable as output requires enlargement. And competition should stimulate producers in the empire to a new degree, as they are no longer sheltered monopolistically in the markets of petty states but have to meet prices and qualities of wares brought from anywhere. Moreover, the economy is mostly released from the burdens of war and defense, as these are removed to the far periphery and occupy a much smaller share of human energies. Men are no longer distracted from their businesses by the need to take up arms, nor is capital taken for the internecine wars of competing states. Politics ceases to occupy time and attention, and men are freer to devote themselves entirely to the peaceful pursuit of material welfare.

This glowing promise is not realized, or not for long. The universal empire fails economically as it does culturally, although perhaps not so rapidly, as the positive factors are more solid. It is a dismal economic failure apparently for many of the same reasons; indeed, incapacity to apply intelligence is as deadly in the long run for production as it is for writing. A central trouble is that the almighty state can no more refrain from controlling and oppressing the economy than it can refrain from censoring the arts and suppressing free expression.

The imperial economy is made anemic by continuous bleeding; ruinous taxation is probably universal. In competing states, official greed is ordinarily checked by the fact that producers may remove themselves from an oppressive state, and capital seeks refuge abroad. More importantly, it may be moderated by the openness of the society, the constitutional or possibly republican order, and the incompleteness and insecurity of tyrannies. The empire knows nothing of such restraints; the autocrat is free to appropriate such of the property or labor of his subjects as his tax gatherers and police can extract for him. He may be restrained by moral conscience, which is likely to be elastic, or by fear of rebellion, for the suppression of which he has every advantage. He may think of the long-range benefit to himself and the realm; as Trajan said, the governors should shear the sheep, not flay them. But the officials never have enough money; and, if sometimes emperors have reduced taxes and sought to spare their peoples, oftener, taxation has grown more and more rapacious as resistance is worn down, special demands become permanent burdens, the needs of the apparatus steadily increase, and the people merit ever less consideration as they become more degraded. Taxes, labor service, rents, and various official and unofficial tributes are the heavy cross that bends the children of the empire to the ground.

Thus it was in the beginning. The Egyptian pharaoh, when strong enough to do so, owned most of the lands and had serfs working them, either directly for himself or for his partisans; and all was strictly controlled that he might garner the product. [94, p. 237] Orderly taxation requires censuses, and the pharaonic empire was efficient in this regard; early in the Old Kingdom note was taken of all the property of each household. [462, p. 12] In the New Kingdom none but officials, not even priests, were exempt from taxes. Peasants received only a small fraction of the harvest and were beaten [114, Pt. II, pp. 16, 21], just as when Egypt groaned under the Turkish empire three thousand years later. [134, p. 97] Almost all labor was more or less forced, with no pay beyond subsistence. [114, Pt. II, p. 15] Countless monuments, from the pyramids to the awe-inspiring temple of Karnak, well bespeak the exploitative capacities of successive dynasties in that land of limited population. But needs inevitably outgrew resources. In the Nineteenth Dynasty there were grave troubles and complaints of abandoned fields as the collectors used their most ingenious methods to gather to themselves the produce; yet the royal granaries were empty. [*120*, pp. 73–74]

The most primitive form of taxation, after the gathering of plunder and tribute, is forced labor, such as was mobilized to build the pyramids. In the ancient Near Eastern empires it was comparable in importance to exactions of crops or goods, and possibly more burdensome as it took men away from production. It was also widely used as punishment for the seditious or unruly. The only compensation was that the empires popularized their labor service and tried to make the slaves proud of their works. [*117*, pp. 176–178] While regular imposts were sometimes not excessive, they were commonly outweighed by irregular levies for the needs of armies and court, and compounded by multifarious corruption. Officials and imperial delegates were not regularly salaried but compensated themselves through the perquisites of position; they had every temptation to acquire riches as best they might. As a man of ancient Babylonia lamented, "You can have a lord, you can have a king, but the man to fear is the tax collector." Taxes in the Assyrian empire were severe enough to cause a serious decline of the agricultural population. [*128*, p. 168]

After the Assyrians, Darius was reckoned moderate in rationalizing taxation and adjusting the burdens to the ability to pay. [*462*, p. 55] But Persian rule was not gentle. There were taxes on animals and trades, inland customs, forced gifts and confiscations, and a head tax, which was inevitably abused as it was flexible and so an invitation to bloodsucking. [*117*, p. 172] Surveyors every year estimated the probable harvest, and corresponding levies had to be paid even if there had been a drought. [*249*, p. 113] There was much forced labor, and the satraps, obliged to deliver only a fixed sum to the treasury, extracted what they could. [*250*, p. 76] As a result, with omnipresent government interference in the economy, production had already begun to deteriorate in the time of Darius, shortly after the empire was formed. Prices rose and incomes fell; presently free workers were more to be pitied than royal slaves [*249*, p. 116], while the monarch gathered yearly the equivalent of many millions of dollars in precious metals. [*252*, p. 298] Egypt alone paid an annual tribute of about 40,000 pounds of gold, plus grain and the maintenance of officials. [*253*, I, 163] Centuries later, the Sassanid monarchy taxed not only land but heads, fruit trees, and so on. It is told that a mother once beat her child for picking a bunch of grapes, saying that nothing could be touched until the king had had his share. [*253*, I, 462] Grain had to stay on the threshing floor, even at the risk of spoilage, until the collector came. Once the monarch asked his dignitaries in council their opinion regarding new taxes. When one councilor ventured to inquire whether the taxes would be permanent, the king ordered him beaten to death with a writing case (as he was a secretary), and the others chorused their approval. [*250*, p. 148]

Great empires have laid crushing burdens on India. In pre-Maurya times the peasants paid a land tax of only about a tenth of their crops. [*189*, p. 307] The merchants also waxed rich in relative freedom. But the Mauryas instituted crop taxes of a quarter or a third, a sales tax of one-sixth, and a multitude of other levies which must have been oppressive, as the penalty for evasion was death. [*215*, p. 128] The Moslem sultan Alauddin (d. 1316) set out deliberately to impoverish the Hindus to hinder their rising [*212*, p. 227]; it may be assumed that he was successful, as were his Mogul successors, who spent lavishly on marble palaces inlaid with semiprecious stones while mercilessly squeezing peasants, artisans, and merchants alike. Akbar, who took a census of all inhabitants, set the standard assessment at one-third the crop, and tried without great success to end extortionate collections. [*199*, pp. 171, 151] His less principled descendants raised the norm to half and opened the door to all manner of unbridled extortions. [*205*, p. 249] Akbar left the cultivators enough to keep agriculture going; Aurangzeb let them be squeezed nearly to death. [*205*, p. 256] It is said that officials would take everything they could find beyond the dry crusts necessary for existence. [*216*, p. 155] The chief, sometimes almost the entire, business of the administration was taxation, which was farmed out to concessionaires to exploit ad libitum. [*205*, p. 235] Even though irrigation was neglected, villages were assessed a lump sum that the collectors thought suitable; crop failure brought not remission but famine. Farming ceased to be remunerative. Akbar had decreed that all arable land should perforce be cultivated; it seldom was except by compulsion. [*191*, p. 226] Much good land was left untilled, as peasants fled to foreign lands if they could, sought a living in towns, or attached themselves to the retinues of officials. [*191*, p. 205] Hordes were hauled into forced labor to work on the splendid monuments, or to satisfy any official caprice. If a mansabdar wanted work done, he had men dragged from the bazaar. [191, p. 256] Commerce was also bled at every turn with tolls and imposts; those who managed to gain a little wealth sought to hide it by living as meanly as possible. The farmers were famished and the weavers went naked, while mansabdars gloried in the most ostentatious displays of opulence. [212, p. 340] But the bloodsuckers were likely to be victimized also, as sometimes zealous treasurers made audits of tax collections by means of torture, racked many to death, and plundered the plunderers. [219, pp. 44–45] Thus far had the Moguls come since the beginnings of the dynasty as a modest power of Central Asia. When a rich caravan was overcome by the snows, Babur's father held the goods two years until the owner's heirs could come from China to claim them. [199, p. 57]

When the Turkish empire was beginning, people welcomed it for relief from Byzantine levies. [433, p. 32] As it reached its climax under Suleiman the Magnificent, the treasury was full, sustained by booty of conquest, and taxes were relatively light. [431, p. 130] But this unnaturally happy situation could not endure. Taxes grew irregularly until they were up to half the crop in some provinces, plus a host of dues payable to the landlord, collector for himself and the government. Most taxation of agriculture fell into the hands of tax farmers, who delivered as little and extracted as much as possible; at the height of the empire the government received perhaps half of what was collected. [436, p. 163] Taxes were wrung out forcibly; in some parts, peasants were so accustomed to being beaten that it was thought shameful to pay voluntarily. [432, Pt. I, p. 215n] The situation was somewhat improved by letting contracts for life, so that the contractors had an interest in keeping the peasants alive and producing. [432, Pt. I, pp. 240, 255] To assure payment, peasants were bound to the soil as virtual serfs. Despite this, in the seventeenth and eighteenth centuries many villages were deserted as men absconded to better areas, took up banditry, or went to city slums. [432, Pt. I, pp. 242, 257] A minor burden was the right of pashas, traveling with large retinues, to demand subsistence along the way. As a result, villages practically disappeared along the important highroads. [439, p. 50] The rich, too, had their woes, as confiscation was an important source of revenue even under the most considerate sultans. [436, p. 162] In return, the government paid practically no attention to the needs of the people. [*435*, p. 149]

The Incas were efficient in taxation, as they were in other aspects of empireship. The general and apparently well-applied principle was that everyone (except perhaps a few of the elite) should spend his entire life, after providing his own subsistence, working for the state. Although persons of royal blood were free to expropriate anything in the kingdom [*181*, p. 25], taxes were labor, primarily agricultural. Land was divided into three sectors: as much as deemed necessary was left for the people, and the remainder was cultivated for the benefit of the state and the official church or cult of the Sun. [*176*, p. 56] The people also kept the llama flocks of the state, and worked on and kept up roads, bridges, and monumental buildings. Each ten-group usually furnished a servant for the officials [J. Rowe in *180*, p. 268], and men did military duty while women spun for the state the wool from the state herds. Where land was less than enough to keep the population busy, more labor service was demanded. [*170*, p. 141; *178*, p. 51] Officials visited the villages yearly to select promising girls approaching puberty, some of whom were taken to work for the state in convent-like institutions; a few were picked for sacrifice or service to the Sapa Inca himself. [*174*, p. 125; *173*, pp. 149–150]

No close estimate of the proportion of the total product taken is possible, but it may have been about two-thirds in normal years. [*172*, p. 43] A share was returned in welfare services. The granaries fed those who had no one else to care for them and stood as a guarantee against famine. Thanks were given to the ruler for other benefits, also; for example, each man on his wedding day was given two garments. [*170*, p. 98] But the strongest emphasis was on duties. Everyone had to work as a matter of principle: women were supposed to spin while they walked anywhere; children of five or more helped their parents on their assignments (inspectors being assigned to make sure that they did); children under five were set to catching lice. [*170*, pp. 100–102, 148; *176*, p. 62] If there was not enough to be done, work was invented; an Inca is said to have ordered a hill moved to keep people from sloth. [J. Rowe in *180*, p. 268] Even princesses were expected to knit while visiting. [*170*, p. 101] And those who possessed nothing else had to give a tubeful of lice to the governors to show that what they had belonged to their betters. [*181*, p. 122]

The case of Rome is especially interesting because of the contrast between the city-states, where taxes were light and almost entirely indirect, and the empire, which crushed itself under unbearable taxation. From the beginning, the purpose and utility of empire making had been financial, to acquire lands to plunder and then to tax. All provincial land was held, in a sense, to be the property of the conquering state; its use had to be paid for. [*346*, pp. 136–138] At first it was the practice to levy officially only the same dues to which the people had been accustomed; if this policy had remained in effect, there would have been no serious cause for complaint, although the sucking away of a large and steady tribute to parasitic Rome would have threatened commerce and industry. But the provinces suffered much more from abuses and irregular levies than from the official taxation, which was limited by Rome's lack of an effective bureaucratic apparatus. [*308*, p. 335] Armies stationed in the provinces requisitioned and confiscated freely; there were heavy contributions for special occasions, such as the accession of new Caesars. Variably in different provinces there were taxes on the product of the land, duties on goods entering or leaving, taxes on crafts and professions, little-known local levies, and rents for lands taken over by Rome. [*342*, p. 515; *294*, pp. 231–232] There were also head taxes. [Luke 2:1–5] Even the postal system established by Augustus could be burdensome, as towns on the way were required to furnish horses, hostels, and so forth. [*330*, p. 148] And there were such sundry extortions as ingenuity devised; according to Tacitus, the manner of exaction could be worse than the tribute itself. [*330*, pp. 360–361]

These exactions, rather chaotically extracted in mostly unknown amounts, tended to get harsher, generation by generation. Even when the empire was young and vigorous they must have been severe; in 103 B.C. the king of Bithynia answered a Roman request for military assistance by saying that all the men had been sold to satisfy the Roman tax gatherers. [*332*, p. 8] In the days of Augustus, the western provinces were in a ferment because of taxes; but when a proconsul was accused by the Gauls of immoderate extortion, he absolved himself by showing Augustus a large room full of gold and silver. [*308*, pp. 125, 115] In the first half of the first century A.D. overtaxation was already making agriculture unprofitable in Judaea, driving many into brigandage. By 60 A.D. it had led many villages in Egypt to refuse to till their fields, which had to be assigned to them compulsorily; the hardship was such as to cause a serious decline of population in many parts of the province. [285, p. 367] With some exaggeration, it was said that Rome turned province after province into desert by merciless exactions. [344, p. 223] The Italians, supposed beneficiaries of the empire, long remained exempt from most regular taxes and levies, but not from the abuses of officials and soldiery nor from the confiscations. There was a certain pressure in favor of the ruler: from the time of Augustus it was common practice to will one's property to Caesar, a fashion less to be attributed to patriotism than to the fact that wills were public. [308, p. 254] Even a measure designed to afford relief could become a burden, as when large sums were put out as nonrepayable loans on Italian land; the money having been consumed, the interest was a perpetual tribute. [312, p 440]

Disorders caused taxes to be raised, as the military needed more and more; Caesars could not afford to economize at the expense of insatiable armies, which conferred and took away the purple. According to Dio Cassius, Caracalla extended citizenship only to increase revenues; he said, "Nobody in the world should have money but I, so that I may bestow it on the soldiers." [330, p. 429] In the hard times after Commodus, taxes rose sharply, as supplementary levies were introduced and many duties formerly limited to Rome or particular provinces were made general. But there were better days as well as worse. Alexander Severus is said, rather incredibly, to have reduced the weight of tribute to a thirtieth. [314, I, 144] Diocletian, restoring order and unity after fifty years of civil conflict, tightened taxation through surveys, made Italy subject like the rest, and decreed the most fearsome penalties for evasion. [331, p. 18; 294, p. 746] He collected the chief tax, that on agriculture, not in cash (the currency having become much abased) but in kind, a wasteful and inefficient method; the rate was not fixed, but was decreed each year by the emperor according to his needs, which grew as court luxury and display became more mandatory. The irregular levies were not eased, although commuted to money when the currency was stabilized under Constantine, but became much heavier as the autocracy developed into the Persian style. [326, I, 68]

The trouble would have been far less had the people been required to support only the emperor, his swollen entourage, and the purposes of government; but land was consumed by a swarm of

insatiable locusts. Taxes at first were given over to private partner-
ships, which vied for the privilege and compensated themselves by
collecting, under limited controls, what they could. Exploitation
was the more brutal for being restricted in time; whatever the
interests of the exalted ruler, the publican wished only to mine
his territory and carry away his loot. At first the tax farmers were
often natives, but they were displaced by Romans with greater
political and financial resources. [294, pp. 231–232] Predation was
scarcely limited except by the governors, who themselves saw their
assignment as a chance for enrichment. By degrees the empire instituted direct collection by its own servants, but even after Tiberius some taxes were given over to publicans for collection [321,
p. 247], and officialdom represented small improvement. Ironically,
the government became so greedy in its own right that tax farmers
had to be conscripted in the latter part of the first century. [330,
p. 370]

Most early emperors took some interest in the general welfare,
and governors were placed on a regular salary in hopes of keeping
them more or less honest. But there was no checking the arbitrariness of officials, who were the less restrained as the disarmed provincials were defenseless and came to lack military and political
experience as their shoulders became accustomed to the yoke. Proconsuls not only taxed, but sold exemptions from their depradations
in gangster style, demanded special contributions, speculated in
grain, and impoverished by usury. When an emperor, possibly
Nero, confiscated an estate in Greece the procurators simply swept
away all livestock and other movable assets; years later, a few
rustics were squatting on the abandoned land. [312, pp. 437–438]
Requisitioners for the army sometimes so ravaged the population
that the emperor on occasion removed them from entire provinces
even at the cost of needed supplies. [303, p. 274] Only a fraction of
the takings went into the treasury. By instituting honest collection
in his province of Gaul, Julian the Apostate could reduce the tax
rate to less than one-third. [326, I, 120]

By the fourth century, agriculture hardly paid in Italy and sometimes was rather a luxury to be indulged. [303, p. 260] Peasants
petitioning Commodus for relief ventured to threaten, "We will
flee to some place where we can live as free men." Much land went
out of production, and much more became useless as drainage was
neglected and good farming practices were forgotten. [278, pp. 84–

85] Farming was difficult in any event because the army took all the horses. [285, p. 453] As Lactantius wrote at the end of the third century, "Because of the enormous assessments, the resources of the tenant farmers were exhausted, fields were abandoned, and cultivated lands were converted into wilderness." [330, p. 459] Many decrees intended to compel cultivation showed that in the fourth century it had become unprofitable. This was the reason for the ominous influx of barbarians, large numbers of whom were invited to take up deserted lands. While tax collectors tortured, men sold their children to slavery to pay. [331, pp. 174–175] Voracious officials sometimes emptied whole villages. When from time to time generous emperors remitted uncollectable arrears, hordes of peasants emerged from hiding. There was no little truth in the exclamation put into the mouth of a British chieftain by Tacitus: "They rob, butcher, plunder, and call it 'empire'; and when they make a desolation, they call it 'peace.'"

Overtaxation also brought serfdom. Agricultural labor was perpetually in short supply [326, II, 817–818] as peasants abandoned their holdings because of rising taxes and declining yields, and the response was to hold them by compulsion. By 275 A.D. those in arrears were bound to the land until they should, hypothetically, liquidate their debts. As landowners were being pressed for taxes, it was necessary that men be held to work for them [300, p. 244], and ascription to the soil was steadily strengthened, especially under Diocletian, great affirmer of autocracy. It was sternly forbidden for agricultural slaves to be sold off the estate, and tenants who ran away could be recovered like slaves and had no standing in the courts. Constantine permitted landlords to chain tenants suspected of contemplating flight. [326, II, 796] Thus the condition of small farmers and slaves converged, as the position of the latter was somewhat improved while the former descended to serfdom and there remained.

The rural masses were thus frozen in hereditary servitude, not only burdened but fixed in status for the benefit of the state. Something similar happened in the towns, which in the early empire had enjoyed a certain autonomy. By the third century interference had become overwhelming, municipal treasures were being confiscated [314, I, 151], and freedoms had been lost, until the towns became unpaid agents of the government. Duties without rights were piled on local officials whose opportunities to make money decreased as autonomy shriveled; the position of local councilor, or curial (member of the municipal curia), formerly a coveted honor, became a cross to bear, mostly because the local officials were made responsible for delivering taxes to the government. [285, p. 239; 302, p. 246] How the taxes were collected within the municipality, the empire cared little; and it was simpler to require the wealthier men, those entitled by their possessions to belong to the curia, to hand over the assessed amount. It was charged that they used the position of tax collectors to enrich themselves; not to be cheated, the empire raised the assessments. [303, p. 251] Hence the position of curial, laden with both imperial and local obligations, had to be made obligatory; as early as the middle of the second century respectable men were sufficiently oppressed by municipal duties to be driven to outlawry. [330, p. 375] Curiales were forbidden to aspire to the senatorship lest they escape; the doors of the army, government service, and eventually the church were closed to them; they could neither sell their property nor travel except with special permission; if they fled they were to be hauled back; if they defaulted they were subject to torture or death [278, p. 29] and their relatives were held responsible. [303, pp. 255–256; 285, p. 367] Local office thus became virtual slavery.

As the state pressed its demands, commerce and industry became unprofitable. But administrative convenience and fiscal needs required that everyone stay in his slot, and his children likewise; if anyone wished to move, it was presumably and probably to escape obligations. Merchants were inscribed in corporations and compelled to transport goods for the state and to give it first option to purchase at fixed prices, at least from the first part of the second century. [342, pp. 386, 524] This practice led to a decline of once-flourishing commerce and its withdrawal from the larger centers where regulations were most strictly enforced. [303, p. 247] The remedy was to impose controls; workers and managers alike became bound to their trades. Under Alexander Severus professional guilds, organized and supervised by the government, were virtually a part of the state apparatus. [285, pp. 369–370] Tied to his profession by birth, no one, from the baker to the shipper, could escape his burdens even by giving away all his property. [278, p. 61] So castelike did the imperial society become that even the gladiatorial calling was hereditary. In the Dominate the senatorship, too, became at times burdensome, because of expenses attached, and could not be refused. [*324*, p. 448]

Within a century or two each great Chinese dynasty experienced financial trouble, greed grew with mounting incompetence [*61*, p. 118], and burdens on producers became unbearable, until impoverishment and revolt undermined the foundations.

In the period of Contending States, about a tenth of the crops went as taxes, or land was so allotted that one field in nine or ten was to be cultivated for the government. [*46*, p. 171; *84*, p. 104] But the Ch'in empire raised taxes twenty times over, according to reports of unfriendly chroniclers. [*44*, p. 54] Corvée labor was conscripted on an enormous scale for the great public and imperial works; and the people groaned the louder, as such oppression was unprecedented. Subsequent Han rule at first ameliorated these burdens and nonetheless had in its early decades a vast surplus in the treasury. [*61*, p. 95] But within a century and a half the nominal rate of taxation of one-thirtieth of the crop had swollen in reality to about one-half [*75*, p. 202], and half the farmers were subject to forced labor. Under pressure of taxes, usury, military service, and corvée, many were forced to sell land and children. [*66*, p. 5] Taxation became quite unbearable on the poor while great estates, steadily growing despite contrary decrees, had gained exemption. In the face of consequent revolts a minister, Wang Mang, tried to repair the empire by various reforms, including nationalization of all land to end tax exemption. But such measures were rescinded within three years. [*61*, pp. 120–121] After an interval of disorders, which seriously reduced the population, the Later Han dynasty again eased tax burdens and helped the needy [*44*, p. 61], but relief was ephemeral. Before the dynasty collapsed, corrupt palace cliques were pitilessly squeezing and squandering [*74*, I, 780], and many peasants had again been forced to banditry or semislavery under the great holders. [*77*, p. 19]

After the long period of division, the Sui dynasty reunited China and celebrated victory with great public works and splendid palaces; the burdens became so heavy as to lead in a generation to rebellion and change of rulers, much as in the Ch'in dynasty. [*44*, p. 65] The T'ang dynasty at first reduced taxes and ended arbitrary exactions; the population grew and the empire expanded. [*44*, pp. 67–68] But the grain tax was raised fivefold and more in a century. [*59*, p. 33] By the middle of the dynasty, or after about

150 years, taxes had become so crushing that peasants often preferred to pay 50 or 60 percent of the crops to private landlords rather than pay the state levies. [*61*, p. 188] This situation led to an attempt to tax all cultivable land, with the result that eventually large areas were abandoned despite an open invitation for anyone to cultivate them. To swell the revenues, monopolies were established on such products as salt, tea, and liquor; but extravagance led to bankruptcy, risings, and the end of the dynasty. [*44*, pp. 71–74]

The subsequent Sung dynasty sought, as usual at first, to help agriculture. Always pressed by barbarians, the Sungs had less opportunity to fall into slothful extravagance; but they were shortly beset by the old problem of rising costs and failing revenues. After a century, troubles led to the socialistic reform program of Wang An-shih, very like that of Wang Mang under the Hans. Wang An-shih sought to equalize landholdings for the benefit of taxation (to which this advocate of state socialism gave priority in the distribution of the harvest [*40*, Bk. I, p. 254]), to eliminate privileges and exemptions, to restrict luxury goods, to lend money to the indebted (at 40 percent interest instead of the usual 100 percent or more), and practically to control the entire economy. Like his namesake of earlier days, Wang An-shih was frustrated; the reforms were sabotaged and undone. [*61*, pp. 206–207; *52*, p. 138; *44*, p. 80] No administrative remedies were of avail; the ancient Square Field system of land allotment was three times tried and abandoned. As the dynasty aged, the people became so exhausted that they offered little resistance to the barbarians who occupied the northern and more populous half of China. The latter established the Kin empire, which quickly found itself in similar straits. It began rather favorably with much free land (because the population had been massively slaughtered), but soon fell into the usual financial swamp. Taxes were raised and as much as half of all the land was taken to support the army, but production declined until famine and inanition gripped the land. [*44*, pp. 91–92]

The Mongols swept aside the enfeebled Kin empire and the remnants of the Sung as well, and reunited the country. Having dealt energetically with the population problem, they furnished farmers with seeds and oxen and at first exacted only 10 percent of the crops. But taxes rapidly rose and tax farmers followed their instincts; even in the relatively brief life of this dynasty, about a century, there came concentration of ownership, declining production, famines, and uprisings. [*44*, pp. 93–96]

Peasant risings led to the Ming dynasty, which relieved the peasants of most of their burdens, only to become as oppressive as its predecessors. Larger estates began to gobble smaller ones as taxes were increased. In the decline, foreign troubles and inefficiency multiplied needs for revenue, leading to exhaustion of both the soil and its tillers. Expenses near the end of the dynasty were more than ten times as high as at the beginning. [*28*, p. 199] Land was taken for "Palace Farms" to yield income for the court. These led to abuses and corruption; attempts were made to abolish them, but court influences were able to negate the decrees. Finally the government became so desperate as to free criminals for a payment of grain, and the last years of the dynasty were bedeviled by almost constant famine. [*44*, pp. 101–105]

Founders of the Ch'ing (Manchu) dynasty took to heart the lesson that overtaxation was ruinous, promised never to raise land or poll taxes [*70*, p. 201], and curtailed the extravagance of the court. They also encouraged settlers of land, much of which had been left vacant by disturbances supposed to have carried away half the population. [*44*, pp. 109–111] But good intentions were undone; the dynasty, like its predecessors, gradually weakened, and the easy prosperity gained by returning wastelands to use faded as population increased. Expenditures again multiplied tenfold. [*56*, p. 200] Public monies were drained into private pockets, and the chief business of the government, the collection of revenue, became its worst failure.

By the nineteenth century all the old evils had returned in full force. Various levies, like the farmed-out salt tax, were all subject to abuse. The land tax, though nominally moderate, became in practice extremely onerous. Usually required to deliver fixed amounts, the magistrates collected what they could. They imposed all manner of surcharges and capricious penalties, added to assessments, failed to give receipts, and so on; in consequence, the peasants paid three to perhaps ten times the amount due. [*70*, pp. 208–210; *57*, p. 83] A memorial of 1885 described the collectors as "living on the blood they suck from the peasants," almost a literal statement, as peasants were frequently beaten until they bled. [*70*, p. 207] Toward the end of the dynasty, as though in recognition of realities, governors were authorized to place surcharges on the land tax at will. [70, p. 204] Collection of taxes was very unfair, also. Since villages were collectively responsible for payments [37, I, 108], the more powerful could shift much of the burden onto the weaker. By a variety of tactics, the gentry secured partial or total tax exemption; their tax rate was estimated at a third to a quarter of that of peasants. [70, p. 215] As most large landholdings escaped taxation, the burden on the peasantry was heavier; the more the poor were squeezed the more defenseless they became. Taxes and rents drove peasants into indebtedness, tenancy, banditry, and rebellion. The collapse was delayed until 1911 only with Western support.

Although the Russian empire never could fall into such degradation as overtook the Roman and the Chinese empires, the people were hardly less afflicted. Ivan the Terrible, great consolidator of empire, imposed taxes with such vigor as virtually to wreck the economy [K. Waszilewski in 420, p. 65], and made the communities responsible for collection. Succeeding tsars saw little reason to ease exactions, but imposed on everyone over fifteen the duty of serving the state in some capacity. [377, p. 195] It is typical of the attention of the state to its own needs that early in the sixteenth century backward Russia had a general census every two or three years, whereas most countries of western Europe did not begin to take censuses for economic purposes until the eighteenth century. [K. Wittfogel in 409, p. 335] To facilitate taxation the tsar attempted to centralize trade, and burghers were attached to their towns. The weight of taxes drove the peasantry to run away to the south and east, and the central regions were partly depopulated [359, p. 49]; to keep the peasants as taxpayers, they were step by step fixed to the soil and serfdom from the sixteenth century. [377, pp. 216–218; 388, II, 219 ff.] Such restrictions were less effective in land-rich Russia than in densely populated empires; but in 1642 representatives of the provinces lamented to the tsar, "Your Majesty's governors have reduced people of all stations to beggary and stripped them to the bone." [377, p. 270] Since many sold themselves into slavery to escape exactions, the regimes in the sixteenth and seventeenth centuries forbade this; those who preferred to be slaves objected strongly to compulsory freedom. [377, pp. 278–280]

Peter strengthened the state in taxation as in other respects. He instituted a head tax, which became the most lucrative source of revenue, and gave the landlords the task of collecting it. [407,

p. 160] As a result, a large majority of the nation were placed in uniform bondage. [398, p. 114] Almost everything, from bath-houses to beards, was taxed to the limit. [377, pp. 359–360] Forced labor was used on a colossal scale, with payment of a copper or two, or perhaps nothing at all. The official attitude was stated by one of Peter's underlings: "It is unheard of for the Tsar's treasury to pay people to carry out certain work; there are enough sticks in Russia to thrash those who refuse to do it." [379, pp. 152–153] Such policies sufficed to reduce the number of Peter's subjects. The census of 1710 showed a 20 percent decrease over a span of thirty-two years, mostly of Peter's reign, with increases only in areas of recent settlement and decreases of more than half in some districts. Part of the decline was due to prudent evasion of the census takers, but a remedial census in 1716–17 showed further decline. [377, p. 361] This was a remarkable achievement in a huge land with a population only one-tenth of that supported by the same area today.

Succeeding centuries brought limited improvement. Evasions continued, despite much legislation and the best efforts of the police to capture fugitives. Some 27,000 peasants ran away annually in the years following 1727. [359, p. 265] In 1735 it was officially reported that more than half the peasants had absconded, leaving the remainder to pay their dues. [377, p. 487] In much of central Russia peasants strove to be assigned as little land as possible, because the additional taxes were less than the return. [419, p. 133] An official inquiry of 1871 showed that many peasants paid taxes equivalent to all or more than all of the net produce of their land, their subsistence (about equal to or somewhat larger than their taxes) being derived from crafts and outside work. [406, pp. 44–46] To extract taxes, some collectors would take away grain, cattle, and tools, thus ruining future production; the wiser ones flogged on a large scale. [406, p. 92] Such methods were successful; it is said that in times of famine the first concern of the peasant was not to feed his family but to satisfy the tax gatherer. [390, p. 379]

It can hardly be estimated, especially for the older empires, what part of the income of the realm or of that of particular producing classes, particularly the farmers, went to nourish the government. Official rates, even when known, mean little. Assessments might be capricious and unfair; officials often collected arbitrarily for their own benefit; there were all manner of official and semiofficial extortions. Land rents, moreover, were often inextricably mingled with taxes, the landlords acting as collection agents of the regime. But we can be sure that the great peace of the empire has usually or always been very expensive, at least for those less able to defend themselves politically, those lacking some connection with the levers of power. Our sources are mostly writers of the empires, usually biased in favor of the existing splendid authority and not deeply moved by the troubles of the vulgar masses unless they inconvenienced the government or upper classes. There is every reason to discount glowing descriptions of imperial prosperity, just as one discounts panegyrics to the emperor or travel brochures.

It seems practically a rule that the more perfect politically the empire is, the harder it squeezes; as Kluchevsky said, the state swells and the people shrink. Contrariwise, free states, despite their wars and troubles, have been less exacting. Greece, which under Roman rule was half depopulated and largely reduced to rusticity, in freedom knew only the most moderate taxation. In Attica the land tax was 10 percent in the sixth century B.C., later reduced to 5 percent [289, p. 195], and there was little or no graft. Dues on commerce, the chief reliance of the fisc, were a trifling 1 or 2 percent. The Athenians regarded direct taxes as undignified for free men, permissible only temporarily for special needs. [462, p. 125] The freedom-loving Swiss until modern times paid scarcely any taxes, and no direct taxes. In most of the free cities of medieval Europe taxes were very light and unoppressive. In an extreme example, the burghers of republican Hamburg in the eighteenth century assessed their own property taxes, paying what they felt they owed, with no questions asked; this was possible because the rate was at most only half of 1 percent. [535, p. 91] Although empires, at least since the Old Kingdom of Egypt, have been demanding to know the number, whereabouts, and holdings of subjects in order to learn what could be taken from them, the British Parliament in 1753 rejected the idea of a census as an invasion of liberties; the first census, an incomplete one, was taken in England, then the most advanced country in the world, in 1801. [465, p. 4]

It may not be exactly true that lowness of taxes corresponds to the degree of freedom in a land, but it is difficult indeed that an all-powerful government should restrain itself. It is much to expect officials wholeheartedly to check one another when all profit from the same abuse of power, and little more than fear of almost impossible rebellion checks the government. Prudent rulers may look to the needs of the future and their reputations, but power is almost invariably exercised until it meets resistance, and the people of a strong empire are little able to resist the power to tax.

Worse, the burden of taxation usually increases; short of a breakdown of government, taxes are seldom lightened in the course of imperial evolution. Precedents are accumulated, and custom leads the children to accept what would have been unthinkable for their fathers. As a Roman rhetorician of the middle of the second century told Caesar, the people come to enjoy paying taxes: "Moreover, all people are happier to send in their tribute to you than anyone would be to collect it for himself from others." [330, p. 137] Rulers impose extraordinary or emergency levies; such taxes, if paid, will probably be imposed again and become regular and permanent. The growing corruption and license of the officials, seemingly a regular feature of universal empires, increases the burden enormously. Always more disposed to flay than to shear gently, officials become butchers, cheating alike the producers and the state; to compensate itself, the central power may raise rates. Then the more the taxpayers try to cheat their oppressors, the more justified the latter feel in squeezing them; and those who know they are despised or hated in their turn despise and hate. As the people become more impoverished and degraded, the gulf grows between them and the rulers, who look down on the dirty and ignorant masses; the people seem to have been born for nothing better than to support the higher classes. The upstanding and honorable Roman farmer of the republic became the worthless and despised serf of the late empire. The ordinary Chinese were once decent people; the half-starved ragged tillers of decaying Chinese dynasties were regarded as subhuman by the refined scholar-official class. [77, p. 19]

Depressed and robbed, with no incentives to improvement of any kind, the peasants may flee, try to find other means of livelihood, become parasites themselves, or simply reduce production. Exactions of the tax gatherer quickly discourage thoughts of improved farming practices and conservation of fertility for the future. If peasants can hope only for subsistence they do only what is immediately necessary to subsist; works of drainage, irrigation, or soil conservation, which a prudent agriculturist might undertake for his own benefit, he is unlikely to sustain for the benefit of those who wring out his substance. Even if he wished to improve his estate, the impoverished and probably indebted farmer is in no position to make the necessary investment. Under the Moguls, for example, no one would repair canals, and much land fell out of use for lack of water; indeed, hardly anyone cultivated except when compelled to. [205, p. 202] Loss of productivity, capital, and skills thus contributes to the general ruin.

But as production declines, needs of the government remain the same or rise. The citizenry having become debased, the empire probably relies on mercenary troops. But payment of these indispensable and powerful minions is a matter of life or death; it comes to seem that the more than can be sucked from the people, the securer the regime. At the same time, the weakening and rotting empire is more than ever driven to keep up at least the appearances of power and grandeur; hence the ebbing life of the land must be bled the more.

This vicious circle must come to an end. Taxation defeats itself by making men desperate. Revolt, unthinkable while the great empire is in health, becomes inevitable in its sickness; with or without invasion, the end of the grand order is at hand.

LANDLORDISM

Closely related to exhausting taxation is the concentration of land-ownership in a more or less parasitic elite. The exactions of the autocratic state are unequal, as a few can better defend themselves and the vulnerable many are the more burdened. Those who can resist or escape official depredations through status or special favor build up private power; voluntarily or under compulsion, the afflicted put themselves at the service and under the shelter of those who can protect them. The latter thereby become stronger and still better able to resist the tax gatherers, probably men of their own class. Men also use their positions to build up large landholdings, which are more attractive because land and official connections, often coincident, are the securest form of wealth. In times of uncertainty, land is the safest investment and the last to be stolen. Transportable goods and money are the natural booty of the strong. The state cannot consume the land, which, if taken, can only be laid waste or placed under the administration of someone more favored; and if confiscations are frequent, no one will be eager to buy it.

Even if not related to officialdom, the large holders are best able to resist or bargain with the tax collector and to protect themselves and their clients against banditry. But landholding commonly has a political basis. There is no easier way for the ruler to reward faithful servitors than to assign tracts to them. Those enriched by official connections have no better use for their earnings than the purchase of status-giving land; and political power is used in many ways to dispossess smallholders or the disfavored, thus at once increasing concentration of holdings and joining the official to the landed interest. In circular effect, the fact that the elite are big landholders makes land a safe and prestigious investment. The landholder is hence likely to be an ally or agent of the regime, helping to keep order and to collect the produce of the humble cultivators in repayment for his privileges. In mentality, also, a landed aristocracy is much more congenial to the imperial order than is a commercial one; the former represents order and stability, but the latter is a possibly disruptive force alien to the imperial system.

A landlord power seems to have grown up in all vast empires that lasted long enough. The Egyptian Old and New Kingdoms in their ripeness had many large semi-independent estates. In the Assyrian empire, as production fell under the weight of taxation, feudalization progressed. Similarly, in the empire of Xerxes, taxation, debts, and usury (40 percent being charged on loans secured by land) enabled a few great proprietors to gather most of the land to themselves. [252, pp. 298–299] When Alexander marched into the realm a century later he found huge semifeudal holdings ruled by nobles in castles and worked by serfs. [357, p. 733] Estate building likewise marked the Mogul empire, as the rulers lost power to prevent it; peasants, it is said, were better off in permanent serfdom than under transitory officials who cared only for the golden harvest of the day. [205, p. 238]

Each Chinese dynasty saw a growth of estates leading to private and disintegrating power, parasitic, unproductive, and antiprogressive. Under the Later Han, many relatives of leading court families and high eunuchs were able to acquire huge holdings. Harassed peasants fled to them to become slaves, tenants, and retainers of the local lords who ruled largely self-sufficient, small, nonmonetary economies protected by their own soldiery. [61, p. 136; 77, p. 18] In succeeding dynasties political power was similarly converted by various tactics into private power and vast estates, despite the efforts of many emperors to halt or reverse this dilution of their authority. The T'ang dynasty tried to impose the "equal field" system, but after about a century it broke down in the face of rising inequality, corruption, falsification of records, and large grants to favorites. [61, p. 163] Estate building was carried on semi-legally through moneylending and pressure of local officials, or illegally through seizures. [59, p. 29] Energetic attempts to check it failed entirely. Peasant proprietors became extinct and rents took at least half the harvest. [79, p. 40] The Ming tax system, which set appropriate rates for different classes of land and households, was undermined by fraud, as the wealthier gentry connived with the taxing officials. The poor could recur only to the rich, officially or de facto exempt, for shelter, while court personages obtained estates of hundreds of thousands of acres. [28, p. 199] The position of landholders was so strong that they were able to reduce their dependents to virtual slavery. The labor service was also corrupted; a few benefited, many absconded, and the rest were the more oppressed. [61, pp. 337–338]

Such afflictions began to trouble Rome as soon as the city found itself swollen into an empire. Latifundia first appeared in Italy, to spread thence over the Roman world. As early as the Second Punic War, Rome's longest step to general dominion, there was a substantial increase in large holdings as influential persons found themselves able to acquire lands abandoned, conquered, or confiscated. Enactments to check the trend were futile, as land was the securest asset in civil strife, and the yeomen were drawn away to the armies if not ruined by debts. Declining profitability of grain made it more difficult for smallholders to maintain themselves. Land was the prime basis of social standing. In the late republic eager landowners were using fraudulent and illegal means, as well as purchase, to expand their domains. [285, p. 155]

Early emperors tried to curb the progress of the latifundia; and Pliny and Seneca, in the twilight of the Augustan age, blamed them for the disappearance of the sturdy farmer class of old Rome and the already evident decline of the empire. "Latifundia perdidere Italiam," Pliny wrote: "Latifundia have ruined Italy and soon will ruin the provinces as well. Six owners were in possession of one-half the province of Africa at the time when the Emperor Nero had them put to death." [330, p. 166] By such procedures, the Caesar personally came to hold a large part of Italy and North

Africa, to the benefit of the stewards but probably not of productivity. The evil of the estates can hardly be measured, but it is suggestive that slaves usually served as overseers for often absent and careless owners, whose luxuries were supported by half to three-quarters of the tenants' crops. [300, p. 243] While many hungered, some suffered from overeating. [304, p. 42]

But Pliny could not envision the ills to come, as the ailment was progressive until the end of the empire. Not only were the small farmers undone, but the more modest estates were harder and harder pressed to sustain themselves [303, p. 262], while the larger ones were better able to stand off both bandits and officials. [294, p. 753] The ruin of the cities and the curiales left the landowners as the sole remaining nonofficial power. By the time of Constantine, many were immune to local authorities and answerable only to the emperor himself, who was hardly in a position to move against them or to transfer the land to someone else. [331, p. 129] Ensconced on their estates, colluding with local officials, the landlords were able to commit all manner of abuses, against which the godlike emperors fulminated in vain. The local lords could further enlarge their domains as taxes fell heavily on the small, lightly or not at all on the great; and those without official protection were cheated by incomplete receipts, false weights, and doctored assessments. [303, p. 273] When officials collecting arrears descended like wolves on the sheep, with soldiers to torture, imprison, and murder, there was no remedy but to surrender and become a tenant or a serf of the powerful. Occasional remission of taxes helped those who had been able to avoid payment. Debts were used, with the aid of venal officials, to swell estates; only the wealthy could bid for auctioned properties. [303, pp. 276, 264–265] To maintain production, the empire allowed free take-over of abandoned land [285, p. 456], thus providing an additional incentive to ruin weaker neighbors. If other means failed, sheer terrorism was used.

With little desire to produce vulnerable visible wealth, the great estates became ever more self-sufficient, providing their own needs, with their own processing industries. [291, p. 274; 342, p. 524] The fine villas became the centers of aristocratic life, and the decaying towns were increasingly driven to follow the small cultivators and seek the protection of the local lords, who, amid the failing forces of the empire, kept their own armed forces and prisons. [331, p. 130] Feudalism entered the empire even before it was broken.

The imperial economy thus came to rest upon plantations farmed by serfs, as small farmers were ruined and the supply of outright slaves dried up, except for children sold. The economic effects were no less grievous than the social. Capital went not into industry or commerce (which in any event were paralyzed by state controls), but unproductively into land, the only safe investment. It is not to be wondered that by the fifth century the empire was socially and economically as well as culturally degenerate.

In the eastern, Byzantine half of the empire, conditions could hardly worsen; neither, however, did they much improve. Officials were ordered to be fathers to the Caesar's subjects and at the same time to extract money energetically [353, p. 159]; forced to pay many times the legal rates, peasants were left barely enough to perpetuate themselves and perhaps not even that. [311, p. 359] The countryside became depopulated in some areas at various times, but saw some restoration under sager and stronger emperors. Estates, with their attached retinue and many serfs, slowly grew, although emperors fought them with every weapon from special levies to confiscations and false accusations of treason. [353, p. 158] In the tenth century the central regime won a bitter struggle against the rising barons, but they were only briefly checked and the empire in its decrepitude turned into something like the feudalism of the West. [301, pp. 92–93, 153–160]

As in Rome, taxation in Russia led to the virtual elimination of the small, independent producers and the fixing of the peasants in serfdom practically indistinguishable from slavery. In the sixteenth century, laborers, it is reported, worked six days of the week for their masters [v. Herberstein in 420, p. 40]; in the seventeenth century, as flight was outlawed and the government undertook to recover fugitives, the serfs became simply slaves; the very clothes on their backs were the property of the landowners. [398, p. 93] If there was not enough work for them at home, they were rented out. [I. Pososhkov in 386, pp. 78–79] After the middle of the eighteenth century the landlord class declined politically and economically in the face of Westernization, although the grand manors swarmed with mostly shiftless and useless house serfs. [394, p. 33] After the emancipation, the old nobility sank rapidly, and the peasants acquired more and more of the land.

The contribution of landlordism to the ruin of great empires is less obvious and direct than that of overtaxation, but it must be esteemed substantial. It stiffens the political and social system, reducing mobility to near zero. It makes for a caste mentality, uneconomic and unprogressive. It raises essentially parasitic values. More concretely, sharecropping and tenant farming are generally detrimental to agriculture. The feudalistic plantation is more a political than an economic institution, with a spirit of domination and social position rather than of production. Since monetary rent becomes impracticable, one-crop farming is virtually necessary so that the owner can easily garner his share; livestock raising and mixed cultivation are too complicated. But one-crop farming strongly tends to soil depletion, unprogressive practices, and backwardness. There is little incentive to build up the soil for the future or to improve oneself in any way, and when men cease to think of going forward they slip backward. Wheat yields in Italy dropped spectacularly after the empire was established, and the size of allotment held necessary for a husbandman increased sevenfold and more. [*344*, pp. 206–214] In Egypt, where fertility was automatically sustained by the Nile floods, population was maintained while it declined elsewhere in the empire.

The ruin wrought by concentrated political landholding has been widespread. Much like the Roman latifundia were, for example, the haciendas of prerevolutionary Mexico, a society shaped by centuries of Spanish imperial rule. Prior to 1910 almost all the land was held by very large owners who, uninterested in improvements or mechanization, satisfied with ancestral ways and the wooden plow, preferred to spread out rather than to intensify production, and to exploit labor rather than technique. Their ambition was a monopoly of land for political and social ends, "pride of proprietorship, a minimum of toil, the leisurely oversight of an estate . . . unlimited opportunity for the exercise of authority . . . for the display of fine horses." [*485*, p. 132] Consequently they often accumulated both peon-serfs and land beyond the economic use made of them. Through tax discrimination — large holders paid little or nothing, small holders were heavily assessed — loans, and various other legal and partly legal means, they swallowed up their less influential neighbors.

Landholding in Mexico became ever more concentrated through the nineteenth century, until 1 percent of the families held 85 percent of the land, and 97 percent held none; a large majority of the villages were on haciendas, the virtual property of the owners and completely at their mercy. [554, p. 192] The result was economic disaster. The agricultural nation became an importer of large amounts of food. By one estimate, yields of the chief crop, maize, dropped during the century from an average of 75 hectoliters per hectare down to 10. [485, p. 132] Peon earnings fell correspondingly. Taken at 100 for 1797, they sank gradually through long years of civil conflict to about 60 by 1891. Thereafter, as the building of estates took almost all remaining small holdings and brought the peons into complete subjection, their earnings fell sharply to 30 or 35 in 1908. [469, p. 15]

OVERPOPULATION

A different kind of problem which has beset universal empires is the difficulty, perhaps impossibility, of balancing numbers of mouths and food resources. This problem has recurrently troubled humanity since the dawn of history. The poem *Cypria*, roughly contemporary with the Homeric epics, has the Trojan War started by Zeus to relieve earth of excess numbers of men. But pressure of population on the land is peculiarly a difficulty of pacific and static societies. A dynamic society of competing states is more likely to benefit from compensations and checks. The advance of technology and improved production should enable a growing population to maintain or raise its standard of living. Higher aspirations and more active social interests in the open and more cultured society may check the birthrate. Frequent wars certainly play their part. And various centers of rising civilization, like classic Greece, China in times of its superiority over surrounding peoples, and western Europe in modern times, have been able to send large numbers of people to less developed lands. For such reasons, various of the freer peoples have probably lived fairly comfortably, even if not all could boast the luxury that made such Greek cities as Sybaris a byword.

For the most part, universal empires have lost these means for keeping population proportional to production and have suffered accordingly; unless the food supply contracts to squeeze the population (as in the Roman empire), the population expands to the limits of the food supply (as in the Chinese empire), destitution resulting in either event. Arts of production are probably static or regressive. The peace of the empire largely or entirely ends battle casualties and to some extent protects life. There is no emigration. In the dullness of existence and disinterest in social concerns, people turn inward to the family and family values. The attitudes and policies of the empire are probably natalist, also. A surplus population helps despotism and the despotic spirit by reducing the value of individuals, lowering the educational level, and forcing men to spend their energies in the struggle to keep alive. Rulers want more subjects, taxpayers, and workers, numbers to reflect and magnify their glory. The laws by which the Roman empire, from the days of Augustus, sought to encourage reproduction are familiar, although they do not seem to have been very effective. More significantly and more generally, the authoritarian philosophy and social order are favorable for large families, as stability, coherence of the generations, conservative values, and strong parental authority combine to encourage parents to rear as many children as they can. This is particularly true of Confucianism, according to which sons were almost the highest desideratum.

The Russian empire was spared many troubles by its abundance of land, but even so many districts were overcrowded with a large surplus of rural labor before the end of the tsarist regime. The Inca empire, in its short life span, could promise subsistence to everyone and could freely settle people on vacant land. As there was apparently no improvement in agricultural technology, this condition could have resulted only from massive slaughter in wars preceding or during the establishment of the empire, assisted by reprisals against unruly tribes. But so far as appears from often fragmentary data, most great and stable empires have suffered severe crowding. Landholdings of the creative Sumerian times, when there was a good deal of equality, were often 200 to 300 hectares; but in the Babylonian empire, 90 percent of all private plots comprised less than 8.5 hectares. [*101*, pp. 98–99] According to an Assyrian epic, the people so increased that the gods had to strike with famine, plague, and flood. [*136*, p. 406] It is some indication of land shortage that, according to archeological data, a peasant of Cyrus' time earned the price of only two pounds of wool per month [*252*, p. 80], and wages continued to decline under Persian rule. [*252*, p. 274] In the Mogul empire, the population of already crowded India increased about 50 percent during the seventeenth century [*216*, p. 153], which doubtless contributed to its impoverishment and debilitation. In times of bad crops, the people were driven to cannibalism and to searching manure, like pigs, for undigested grains. [*205*, p. 202]

In China, every prolonged period of peace appears to have brought a crowding of the land, which helped destroy prosperity and peace. Subsequent times of disturbance, contrariwise, have brought death to hosts, perhaps a majority. An agricultural economy requires a settled order that men may sow in confidence of reaping; and the stronger the pressure on the land, the greater the need for security from those who would feed themselves by robbing neighbors' crops or stores. Even more do the cities require protection for markets and sources of supplies and foods. The livelihood of the masses and their existence thus depend on the political order; consequently, the population, which grows because of stability, must decrease in times of instability; swelling and shrinking of numbers (with a long-term tendency to growth if techniques of production improve) are the natural accompaniment of the establishment of firm imperial control and its disintegration.

In the time of the Contending States, there seems to have been little population pressure and land was rather freely available. [*84*, p. 104] Under the Hans, numbers grew and a land shortage developed. Registered taxpayers rose to 59 million in 2 A.D., but subsequently declined because of weaker government as well as decreased population: in 57 A.D., with the advent of the Later Hans after an interlude of disturbances, there were only 21 million on the registers. The figure climbed back up to 48 million in 140 A.D., but a century and a half later, after much turmoil, there were only 16 million registered. [*61*, pp. 120, 130] Numbers swelled again under the T'ang dynasty, only to shrink in the ensuing time of troubles, as millions of bandits overran the land, robbing, burning, murdering, and destroying cities. [*28*, p. 143]

By the early Sung, so much land was unoccupied that many inducements were given to take it up; in some places, nine-tenths of the arable land had reverted to waste. [*44*, p. 77] The Ming dynasty saw a very large increase in population; and the disorders attendant upon its fall, although lasting only a few decades, again removed the excess. A rebel movement at the end, according to the chronicles of outraged officialdom, killed 600 million. [*61*, p. 344] Extensive cutting of the dikes and their disrepair in the disorder also meant widespread starvation. [*4*, p. 91] Under the Ch'ing dynasty there was a spectacular growth of population, supposedly from 50 to 350 million in a century and a half. The gain was made possible partly by new crops, like maize, sweet potato, and sorghum, and partly by an expansion of cultivated land. But this expansion meant movement into the unproductive margins of the deserts and onto the denuded hills and terraced slopes of the southern uplands, ultimately to the detriment of farms below. [44, p. 120; 28, pp. 220–221] The standard of living inevitably sank; famines began toward the end of the eighteenth century and became chronic; thereupon population growth tapered off. Uprisings also took a huge toll. The most destructive of these, the Taiping, cost some tens of millions of lives, mostly of noncombatants. The rebel forces sacked and burned villages; the imperial forces burned villages and put the men to the sword. [34, p. 65]

In the Roman empire, depopulation rather than shortage of land was lamented by Latin writers from the early days of the empire. Augustus, worried by the trend, legislated to require marriage, penalize childlessness, and reward fertility; a mere three children sufficed to entitle a man to privileges. [294, p. 489; 344, pp. 234–236] Not many of the upper classes, it seems, could show the qualifying number. But citizen population rose, partly by reproduction, partly by extensions of citizenship, from 4 million in 28 B.C. to 5 million in 13–14 A.D. and 7 million in 47–48 A.D. [294, p. 489; 285, p. 296] It is probable that the population of the empire grew for a century thereafter, except in Italy and Greece. [338, p. 337; 357, p. 730] Some of the loss of Italy was the gain (in this sense) of the provinces, for many Italians went out to exploit the subject lands. The founding of many new cities into the third century may indicate continuing growth, at least in favored regions; and about 290 A.D. Tertullian thought the empire was in danger of overpopulation. [313, p. 270] If there was a shrinkage in the later empire — the city of Rome itself began to decrease in the third century — the causes were not the epicureanism of the affluent but the hunger and despair of the poor. Only extreme poverty and oppression could have led to a general practice of limitation of births, crude abortion, or infanticide by a diverse agricultural population, who, at least as long as land was available — and it was abandoned on a grand scale — must have found children helpful and desirable. If the rural masses of the Roman empire failed to reproduce to the limits of the land, they were left hungry by their masters. [326, II, 1043]

Whether the degradation of the masses is the outcome of pressure on land resources, exorbitant taxation and extortion, parasitic landlordism, or declining productivity of agriculture, or all together, the results are calamitous. Poverty, ignorance, and hunger lead to further deterioration of agriculture, which declines because of poor farming practices, carelessness, erosion, and mining of the soil. When people are overabundant and valueless, the masses lose both dignity and the ability to assert rights. If land becomes scarce, rents rise and the privileges of ownership increase. For the more fortunate, it becomes all the more essential to maintain superior status over the near cattle, to emphasize the differences and make deeper the gulf between humans and subhumans. It becomes easier to think of ordinary men as depraved and by treating them as worthless to make them still baser. As the importance of status is accentuated, the whole society becomes more rigid, less productive, and less capable of breaking out of its shell.

THE BANKRUPT SOCIETY

These fairly tangible ailments — the rapacious demands of the state, the concentration of land in the hands of a nonproductive class, and the pressure of population — might suffice to explain much or most of the decay of empires, the seemingly inevitable fall that constitutes the grandest of historical tragedies. But there are other causes of economic decline or, it might be phrased, aspects of the incompatibility of political monopoly with economic progress.

The atmosphere of the imperial order is usually antieconomic. Intellectual sterility and distaste for innovation are reflected in a static or declining level of technology and lack of forward-looking enterprise. Economic progress is disadvantageous to many holders of political power and privileged position. Like the Spartan oligarchy, and for the same reasons, the great autocracy is apt to look askance at broader enlightenment and movement, essential for economic growth but politically suspect. Thus the finance minister under Nicholas I opposed the building of railroads because they would increase restlessness. [402, p. 51] The values of the empire are essentially political, not economic; a career is to be made by power over people rather than by producing something cheaper or better. Wealth is much less a means to power than power is a means to wealth. Although trade was fairly important in the early

T'ang period, there is record of but a single person of merchant origin who became an official, and merchants were always insecure unless they enjoyed official connections. [59, p. 41]

The official classes, the only ones with influence in the empire, think in terms of politics and position rather than of production. It is enough for them to be able to extract from others; and like the emperor himself, they are likely to delight in conspicuous waste and display (unless it should be too dangerous) as a token of power.

The omnipotent state extends monopolies, controls, and interferences of all kinds over the economy. These are potentially stifling enough to undermine the entire structure. [352, p. 329] Those who have power are easily convinced that they should use it to see that right is done; to refrain is an admission of weakness and of lack of vision. There is a general feeling that the all-knowing and all-powerful state should guide the economy for the benefit of the community and of itself, that all economic activity should serve not personal benefit but political ends. If some branch is conspicuously lucrative, its profits obviously belong to the empire, so various commodities have been made state monopolies, like salt, alcoholic beverages, tea, and so on. T'ang merchants in the eighth century, well before the Italians, devised payment by draft, but the government, sensing an opportunity, took a monopoly of draft transfers, charging a fee of 16 percent and stifling the development of financial methods. [2, p. 42] Financial stringency, an inevitable woe of the unrestricted state, leads to the feeling that the state is being cheated and so must be protected; the remedy for an economic trouble is the issuance of decrees or the use of force. The officials like to control and manage: this justifies their status, gives the pleasures of wielding power, makes more positions in the services available to relatives and clients, and opens up countless possibilities of minor and major graft. The controllers do not consider the inconvenience of regulation and rarely admit that their intervention is bad or useless; if it proves ineffective, it should be sharpened, possibly reorganized, and reinforced with greater powers. An example is the administration of the copper mines of southern China in the eighteenth century. At first, the state took only 20 percent of output as a tax. But as this share did not seem enough, it was decreed that all had to be sold to the state at low fixed prices. So much evasion and smuggling followed that free sale was again permitted. When production thereupon tripled, the officials restored controls and practically took over administration of the mines, which supported a large staff of controllers and a management much more occupied with policing than producing. [2, pp. 46–48]

As mentioned earlier, the Roman economy came increasingly under the wing of the state, although Rome grew up with a tradition of extreme private enterprise. The more compulsion was exercised, the more became necessary; and voluntary cooperation failed as burdens were increased and coercion came to be accepted. To prevent private gain, Diocletian in 301 A.D. decreed the prices of all major commodities and professional services, to be enforced by a penalty of death, as others before and after him sought to do, without positive results. [285, p. 427] The collegia, or guilds, convenient agencies of control, gripped all professions and were gradually amalgamated into the official apparatus. Many factories became state enterprises with bound workers. [342, pp. 524–525] As in agriculture, the condition of industrial free workers merged into that of slaves. The only large-scale manufacturing came to be that of the state for its own requirements, such as imperial factories of arms and textiles or the huge public bakeries at Rome; most production beyond that for local use (except for luxury goods for the elite) was for the state and was moved by state transportation. [331, p. 75; 285, p. 450]

For an autocratic empire to encourage free enterprise would be more anomalous than for a king to turn democrat. But possibly one should not assume that state enterprise is necessarily inefficient. It has advantages of large size and all the benefits of planning and coordination which the bureaucracy can give it. At best, however, it stands in the way of economic calculation. Under conditions of monopoly of power, bureaucratization of the economy easily leads to the death of initiative, to confusion and inefficiency. State control of transportation facilities was crippling to trade in the Roman empire after the first century. The autocratic will is often extravagant; for example, Diocletian's remedy for lowered production of grain was to decree the uprooting of half of the vines in the provinces. [M. Charlesworth in 290, p. 38] Only if criticism or internal or external competition keeps the administrators on their toes should one expect efficiency from state operation.

Another frequent result of financial stringency and indifference to commercial values is the depreciation of the currency, an effortless taxation. Beginning with Nero, Caesars abased the currency until it became nearly worthless, the "silver" coin being copper with a silver coating. Diocletian tried to restore sound money but had limited and temporary success. Rome was hence driven back to a nonmonetary economy; taxes and rents were collected and payments were made in kind. [*285*, p. 366; *331*, p. 59] Trade was nearly paralyzed. To be sure, Constantine stabilized the currency with the gold solidus, but the economy could not be reactivated.

Other empires have similarly undermined their coinage. Prices rose very sharply in the Achaemenid empire. The Turks after the sixteenth century met deficits by reducing metal content. [*432*, Pt. I, p. 189] Russian tsars like Peter likewise sought to make money by depreciation. [*398*, pp. 135–136] The Hans debased their currency before the empire was ripe, and most Chinese dynasties have followed their example, sometimes driving money to worthlessness. [*40*, Bk. I, p. 117] Under the last, the Ch'ing dynasty, silver coins went out of use, and silver for payment had to be weighed and even assayed. [*20*, p. 46]

Many governments other than universal empires have shown the same weakness, especially in modern times. But the omnipotent regime that does not value free foreign commerce is much less concerned with soundness of money than are trading nations. Thus, maltreatment of the currency was habitual in China, but during the period of fragmentation under the Five Dynasties (between the T'ang and the Sung), the proposal to use iron instead of copper coins was met with the argument, "The old currency will all flow into neighboring countries. . . . Merchants will not travel, and produce will not circulate." [*62*, p. 75]

Apart from official policies of interference and control, the universal empires have created decidedly unpropitious conditions for business and commerce. The prestige of mere merchants and moneygrubbers in the splendid empire is as low as their political power. Merchants of free states, such as England, Holland, or the Italian republics, have regarded their calling as almost holy, a dedication to employment and prosperity. In the empires, they have regularly been considered parasites, almost pariahs, even if rich. Even the Assyrians despised merchants, despite the relative freedom of commerce in their empire. [*127*, p. 609] Russian merchants of the nineteenth century, regarded as rather loathsome, were notoriously crude and ignorant, many of them illiterate except for the barest essentials of reckoning; if they made money enough to educate their children, the young people would leave for more dignified professions. [*419*, p. 179]

The merchants suffered not merely low social status; they had no security and often had to be careful not to become very rich or at least not to show it, unless they had official protection. The unpredictability of arbitrary power is profoundly discouraging to enterprise. [*467*, p. 355] As Euripides wrote, "What use to build a fortune, if your work promotes the despot's welfare, not your families'?" [*Suppliant Women*, in *327*, p. 133] When men have managed to garner wealth in the great autocratic state (usually by illicit means), they have been struck down by greedy or envious rulers or their subalterns, often losing not only estate but life as well. The attack on commercial property in the Roman empire greatly contributed to making inevitable the statist economy. Under a tsar like Ivan the Terrible, there was no safety for anyone; according to the English ambassador, people were so fearful of being deprived that they had no incentive to work more than was necessary to keep alive. [*405*, pp. 61–62] Under a more civilized ruler like Peter, the squeeze was less violent but still detrimental to the economy. Officials made endless trouble for traders until they were paid off, and all manner of fraud was perpetrated at the expense of commerce. [*403*, p. 73] Those who made money took care to hide it. As an English visitor remarked, people were idle much of the time [J. Perry in *403*, p. 57], and Muscovy was overrun with beggars. [*405*, p. 151]

Nor was it necessary to be rich to be penalized for industry. Mogul grantees had nearly absolute power not only over their peasants but also over artisans and merchants; the only remedy against extortion or dragooning was to appear poor and useless. [*191*, p. 225] Likewise in the Russia of Peter the Great it was dangerous to be known as skilled, lest some lord send for the craftsman to do a task and reward him only by not having him beaten. This was almost a matter of principle. Like Peter, autocrats commonly have doubted the necessity of rewarding subjects for doing their duty. [J. Perry in *403*, pp. 59, 61] The propensity of empire is force, that is, more stick than carrot. In the late Roman empire landowners drafted as shippers were ordered to convey goods without consideration of profit and were expected to make up losses from the revenues of their estates. [*326*, II, 771]

The merchants, of course, respond by making what they can

however they can, paying the officials and compensating themselves in higher prices, and in so doing confirming the low opinion held of them. Trade cannot thrive in such an atmosphere. The highly organized Incas apparently eliminated private trade altogether, although even among primitive peoples there is ordinarily a fair volume of exchange. In Russia the tsars and bureaucrats so molested the towns that men fled from them instead of to them as in western Europe in the Middle Ages, and people had to be legally fixed to towns as serfs to the land. [*419*, p. 169] Wealthy men had to be forced to live in Roman towns, likewise, even though they owned estates. [*326*, II, 772–773] The Roman empire began to show signs of falling apart economically even in the first century, almost as soon as it had been properly put together under the Pax Romana [F. Oertel in *291*, p. 232], and quite early the great estates began to show a tendency toward self-sufficiency. [*291*, p. 253] Economic specialization, with all its concomitant advantages, was lost, and cities withered as the countryside reverted to primitivism; industry, like agriculture, sank to cruder ways. [*357*, p. 742]

Troubles reinforce one another. Waste is built into the system as officials gain prestige and influence, not by saving, but by spending as much as possible of the public funds. The endless needs and power of the state make it rapacious, and rapacity leads to waste and indifference; according to Pliny, crops were snatched away to rot in granaries. [*326*, I, 30] An atmosphere of insecurity, control, and monopoly discourages individual effort in any direction. The ordinary Byzantines, like most people of the empires, felt that by no diligence could they materially improve their lot. [*311*, p. 245] Capital is invested not in productive enterprise but in land, concealable valuables like gold and jewelry, and official status, or in the luxury of the hour: faced with confiscations and the difficulty of transmitting wealth to their children, fortunate Turks would waste with abandon. [*436*, pp. 204–205] Decreasing trade and purchasing power reduce the scale and quality of manufacturing. Failing production and impoverishment breed ignorance and apathy. Undernourishment reduces strength and productivity; it has often been found that people of poor countries of today can be enabled to do twice or three times as much work merely by proper nutrition. [*New York Times*, Aug. 19, 1963, p. 6] Poorly fed children reach neither their physical nor mental potential, and the elite feel justified in treating them as congenital inferiors. Those who feel unjustly treated are relieved of the obligation to do for themselves, as they ascribe their misfortunes to injustice. Where oppression is fated, so are the woes of nature and poverty; why struggle? Unless those who are robbed become robbers in turn, their hope for improvement lies in becoming an official or a bandit, preferably both. Insecurity at the hands of the desperate as well as the powerful weighs heavily on commerce and agriculture. Thus uncontained power exhausts itself, until it can no longer stand.

8   POLITICAL FAILURE

The universal empire can excuse its failure to fulfill its cultural and economic promises because, while it claims the control of the whole of life, these are not its purposes. It is designed first and above all to govern its world strongly and effectively, and to its sacred power it sacrifices all else.

Thus it is ironic that the grand empire, a political creation for primarily political ends, is also a political failure. The regime turns out, as the autocracy comes to its equilibrium, to be the opposite of what it would be, infirm, ineffective, and ultimately unable to defend itself. The failure is general: at the summit, in the selection and character of the autocrat; in the apparatus, which comes to serve itself better than the regime and the empire; in the control of the people and the land; and in the defense of all from disturbances and invasions.

SUCCESSION

The central contradiction of the hierarchic regime, in which each has a superior to direct and coordinate his activities, is that the superior of all has no regular or formal restraint. If the autocrat is evil, deranged, stupid, or lazy, only by disorder — a coup or murder — might one hope to return good order. There is no suitable and feasible way of replacing the autocrat. Likewise there is no good way to decide who is to be emperor, the symbol of unity and ultimate arbiter. The founder of a dynasty has valid title through his effective leadership, tested in struggle and proved by success. But the consecrated or deified lord ages like other mortals, and in departing raises an unsolvable or at least unsolved problem. There is no real or fixed rule of succession, and there can hardly be one. Unless law stands over men, there can be no orderly transfer of authority.

One might suppose that the regular procedure would be to mark the eldest son (or in his absence another close relative) as heir apparent, train him carefully, crown him in due course, and hope that he turns out reasonably competent and well intentioned, as has been customary in European monarchy. Thereby the father should cherish the kingdom for the sake of his son, the son should strive to be worthy of his forebears, and uncertainty should be avoided. This system is not feasible, however, for the autocratic empire. Sooner or later, and likely sooner, power would devolve upon someone quite incompetent to handle it. In a more constitutional kingdom, it is less crucial that the sovereign have high qualities, and his incapacity is less damaging; the government of the kingdom can continue on its fixed lines. But it is much harder to train an absolute than a limited ruler, and it is harder for the born autocrat to be good; the knowledge that one is sure to be all-powerful is corrosive for the best character. Yet a bad autocrat can be disastrous for the great empire, which depends so much on the quality of top leadership; as there is no limit to his power, there is none to his abuses. Even if he is merely negligent, his power is likely to fall into the hands of the worst of men.

More decisive from the autocrat's viewpoint is the fact that a fixed succession would mean a serious restriction of his powers and a danger to his authority. A designated successor, especially if he is irremovable, is a potential equal; as the autocrat ages and his departure looms, the successor becomes a superior, an insult and a danger to the sovereign. He is likely to thirst for the sublime delights of rule, to feel that he is being cheated by the longevity of his worn-out father of what belongs to him, to listen to those who hint that he is better than his parent, and possibly to yield to the temptation to hasten the change of rulers. Even if he is more modest and dutiful than the heir of supreme power can be expected to be, he is always a potential center of opposition. Careerists, intriguers, and all manner of dissatisfied politicians look to him as their hope and seek to set him against his father. As soon as there is some prospect of the demise of the aging monarch, the opportunists see the heir as representative of future power, and he can draw men to himself by promises of favor upon his near accession. This means a division in the government, an unbearable situation. An example of the manner in which the inability of a king to control his heir undermines his position is the experience of the first Hanoverians, George I and II, both at odds with their presumptive successors; the conflict between father and son, wherein the first was stronger but the second was bound to win in the end, greatly helped the parliamentary and cabinet system to evolve.

The question is apt to be complicated in the great empire for another reason, that the sons are more numerous. In many or most cases the ruler has had several or numerous wives or concubines and correspondingly numerous offspring. As they are many, he feels less special affection for any of them but more easily regards them simply as rivals and dangers. They, in turn, with less attachment toward their father, are the readier to conspire against him and to attack one another in a contest for the goal of goals.

If it is not practicable to give a fixed heir an indefeasible right to the succession, the more suitable practice is that the autocrat should designate whom he desires, probably but not necessarily a son, reserving the right to alter his choice whenever he desires. Even so, emperors have often been reluctant to name a successor. This may be in part because of human aversion to face the eventuality of their own demise and the fact that the state which is nominally theirs should continue without them. Moreover, the naming of an heir implies recognition of the potential equal. Once he has been recognized, cliques have a powerful interest in the early disappearance of the ruler, the more so because he may change his mind. The selection, a matter on which hang the careers and perhaps the lives of the most influential members of the regime, is the center of the fiercest internal struggles and intrigues, which may exhaust the best of energies and tear the court and government. Even if the emperor makes a choice and dies, the question is very likely not settled. He cannot command from the grave; there may be many disappointed against one victorious claimant, and civil strife is likely, the more desperate since eligibility for the throne means danger to its occupant; the choice is victory or death. If the autocrat is really autocratic, the beginning of a new reign is a more or less bloody purge as rivals and all those associated with them must be swept away.

The all-powerful ruler is apt to have trouble with his family and close entourage. They are unlikely, seeing him close at hand and in all his human frailty, to have the absolute respect he feels is due him and which he is accustomed to receiving from his humbler subjects. Tension grows as confidence in a long tenure of power is lost on both sides. Those qualified by near relation to replace the ruler are always suspect. As Kautilya wrote, the ruler "should guard against princes right from their birth. For princes devour their begetters, being of the same nature as crabs." [*Arthasastra*, 1.17.34] The remedy he proposed was to render them harmless with idle pleasures. Sometimes rather extreme measures have been taken against near relatives, such as the blinding, killing, or imprisonment of sons and brothers on principle.

The autocrat is thus beset by conflicting desires and needs, to prevent the emergence of an alternative center of power, to keep the court more interested in his continued presence than in his departure, to prevent excessive internal conflicts, yet to secure the inheritance of his blood and, if he is concerned for the welfare of the empire, to provide for orderly passage of authority to a capable heir. A policy often followed is that the royal blood is held sacred and the succession is confined to members of the dynasty. Most commonly, a favorite son has been revocably nominated, probably not the eldest, who is at some disadvantage as the most apparent rival. This gives the holder of power satisfaction in continuation of the blood line, while no one in particular is in a position to threaten him. A logical consequence is that the autocrat should marry his own blood, and several empires have resorted to incest.

Practices have varied. The pharaoh designated a successor, normally a son by a sister or perhaps a daughter, and sometimes tried to assure the succession by naming him nominal coruler; there were a good many contests. The Assyrian monarch nominated his successor, ordinarily his son. [98, p. 118] Succession in the Achaemenid Persian empire was usually disputed and often the cause of murder or civil war. One of the later Great Kings, Artaxerxes III, inaugurated his reign by killing all the remaining princes. [253, p. 231] In the Sassanid Persian empire, because a law of succession was considered inconsistent with autocracy, the ruler named whom he desired within the sacred family. Brothers of the heir were in grave danger of murder or at least blinding; many of them consequently raised a standard of revolt, either with a party at home or with the aid of foreign enemies. [251, pp. 37–38]

Roman Caesars tried to designate their successors but often failed. Those who had sons would seek to keep the crown in the family, and the legions were much inclined to favor offspring of any emperor who was not unpopular. In the Principate, however, sons often turned out very badly; the empire got its best rulers when, as fortune dictated, there was no carnal issue. Then the

Caesar had to adopt a man of capabilities acceptable to the army; an able successor in sight dampened the ardor of the legions for lifting up a new contender. This practice gave Rome an extraordinary series of good emperors after the killing of Domitian, one of the worst. The good series ended with Marcus Aurelius, who had an atrociously bad son, Commodus. But the practice of adoption could not be regularized. Sometimes Caesars failed to choose, and sometimes the choice was unacceptable. The legions acquired the vice of making and unmaking Caesars with abandon. Death of an Augustus or dissatisfaction meant that commanders raised their banners or were thrust forward against their will. Nomination could not be refused; having been proposed, one could only fight his way to victory or be killed. Diocletian tried to set up a sort of constitutional arrangement with supposedly equal corulers; but he was sufficiently the boss to make his fellow sovereign, Galerius, follow the royal chariot a mile on foot as chastisement for defeat. [314, I, 321] The semiconstitution worked only under the firm control of Diocletian, and broke down in civil war when he withdrew. Subsequently there was a tendency to hereditary succession conditioned by the need for military support. But sons still came to the purple less by virtue of their birth than by their fathers' will. [285, p. 440]

The practice of the Byzantine empire was similar. The ruler named whomever he wished and hoped that his favorite would be able to gain acceptance. Usurpation was frequent; only after the ninth century were hereditary dynasties able long to maintain themselves. [301, p. 37] Of 107 sovereigns between 395 and 1453, only 34 died peacefully on the throne. Eight fell to war or accident, but 65 were swept away by revolutions, riots, or military coups. [301, p. 128] Potential rivals were blinded with hot irons, or worse. [430, p. 27]

The Turkish empire, which took over the area of the Byzantine empire, as well as many of its practices, had no less difficulty deciding who should be sultan. Despite an old rule that the legal heir should be the eldest male of the ruling house, all sons had an equal right, and title was simply possession; whoever could get himself proclaimed and on the throne held it of right. [430, pp. 5, 9] The passing of a sultan was consequently an invitation to a scramble, and the practice of giving princes provinces to govern facilitated uprisings. Hence unity and tranquillity seemed to require elimination of potential rivals. Bayezid I began the practice of putting brothers to death on the very battlefield of Kossovo, 1389, which first gave the empire the stamp of real greatness. [*436*, p. 10] Mohammed the Conqueror, who essentially completed the empire by taking Constantinople, decreed that his successors, upon coming to the throne, should kill all their brothers. [*432*, Pt. I, p. 36] As the sultans abandoned formalities of marriage in favor of the freedom of the harem, offspring were usually fairly numerous; successive rulers for their own security cheerfully obeyed the mandate, giving their brethren the privilege of strangulation instead of decapitation. Sultans also sometimes did away with unfavored or dangerous sons to clear the way for the preferred. [*430*, p. 25] At the end of the sixteenth century, the ascending sultan disposed of nineteen brothers and fifteen women pregnant by his father. But, as each potential candidate for the throne might better die trying — perhaps seizing the throne from his father, as did Selim the Grim — than wait for the cord, the rule made for the fiercest contest and for infinite intrigue.

The uncertainties of succession contributed to a shift of power to court camarillas, which largely decided the issue. If possible, a camarilla would keep the death of the ruler secret for some days until it could raise its candidate to the sanctity of the throne, if necessary fetching him from a distance. [*430*, p. 37] The monarch consequently owed his elevation to the camarilla and was hardly in a position to oppose it. The inner court, in any event, gained the upper hand and weakened the nominal autocrat still further by confining the princes in a building without communication with the outside world, appropriately called the "Cage." There they lived among slave girls and eunuchs, vitiated in body and mind; as a further precaution, their concubines were sterilized or their offspring were slain at birth. [*432*, Pt. I, p. 36] Raised to sloth, vice, and the philosophy of the harem, the princes posed no more threat; primogeniture was restored [*435*, p. 94], and fratricide was no longer necessary. But for the government, degeneracy was worse than murder.

Somewhat the same spirit prevailed in the Mogul empire. When an early Mogul, Humayun, refrained, in obedience to his promise to his father, from murdering or incapacitating his brothers, the result was prolonged civil war which nearly cost him the empire. [*199*, p. 99] Thereafter destruction of rival princes was a matter of course for the winner; or they might be blinded, imprisoned, or drugged. [*214*, p. 23; *209*, p. v] Princesses were not to marry — as Turkish sultanas were often married to eunuchs [*436*, p. 77] — lest their husbands aspire to the throne. [*191*, p. 12] Shah Jahan trembled for his safety as four sons intrigued for his throne; afraid to imprison them, he gave them distant provinces to rule. [*191*, pp. 14–15] One of them, Aurangzeb, by shameless and perfidious maneuvering, defeated and did away with his brothers and imprisoned his father; he kept his own sons jailed.

Inca chieftainship was elective until the empire was well established [*173*, p. 27]; it then became irregularly hereditary. Also, instead of political matches, brother-sister marriage was instituted to preserve the purity of the royal line. The most competent or preferred son of the first wife might be named; he was seldom the eldest. [*175*, p. 116; *173*, p. 83] As at Rome, the heir had to be acceptable to the army; and one of the greatest Incas, Pachacuti, gained power as a military leader when the designated prince remained inactive during an invasion. [*173*, pp. 82–98] On another occasion, the Sapa Inca nominated a new heir when the army found his first choice too pacific. [*173*, pp. 104–105] Conflict was frequent. A disputed succession greatly facilitated the Spanish conquest, as Atahualpa had just achieved victory over his half brother, a victory he celebrated by killing all his many brothers and perhaps some thousands of his royal relatives. [*181*, p. 94]

In the Muscovite tsardom there was no formal law of succession, although custom fixed it in the royal family. In 1722 Peter issued a ukase setting forth the sovereign's authority to designate whom he would [*404*, pp. 209, 264], but during the eighteenth century the palace guard usually had the last word. Definition in accord with the practice of West European monarchy came in 1797. [*377*, p. 614]

In the Contending States of China, rulership passed by primogeniture [*13*, p. 301], but in the empire the monarch named or unnamed his heir presumptive, whose mother became empress. There were occasional atrocities, and the existence of potential candidates for the throne was often as unenviable as it was precarious. The Han emperor Wu destroyed all maternal relatives of his heir designate, and the T'ang emperor Wu Tsung on his accession allegedly killed four thousand intriguers. [*60*, p. 233] But the imperial system became sufficiently smooth so that after 960 the throne was never usurped in the palace, although it was at times the prize of invasion or rebellion. After the rising of a Ming prince, the members of the royal family were entirely separated from the administration and placed under close supervision. The palace women, who were taken from undistinguished families so that they would lack aspirations and powerful connections, were similarly secluded from outside contacts to prevent participation in politics. [38, pp. 42–43] The Ch'ings similarly kept the princes outside the capital city, but prevented their acquiring territorial standing. [20, p. 81] On occasion it was held treasonous for one son humbly to plead on behalf of another lest they make combinations. [4, p. 265] The designation of the heir apparent was delayed as long as possible, and the nomination was kept sealed, to be announced on the deathbed. The emperor also somewhat fatuously claimed the right to bind his successor's conduct. [4, p. 317] The lucky one under this dynasty was never the eldest son. As the dynasty weakened, succession came to be decided by a council of the imperial family, largely influenced by the women. [40, Bk. II, p. 27] This method implied, of course, a substantial shift of power from the ruler to the household.

The question of choosing the new autocrat has thus brought grave troubles. Each time an emperor dies, the autocratic power briefly lapses and the empire is tested. It may fail; the difficulty of agreeing upon a new ruler in short order broke up the oversized Mongol empire, with various power centers far from the capital. It may fall into civil war, which fearfully tore the Roman empire and plagued many others from time to time. Even if there are no great battles, the struggle for succession, in the absence of accepted rules, is profoundly divisive and detrimental to the imperial power. Clever courtiers use their subtlest arts to win the crown for the candidate most beneficial to them, and the character most pleasing to the autocrat is seldom of the strength and will requisite for ruling the empire. The more capricious the choice of the ruler, the readier others are to think that fortune might have smiled upon them, the more inclined to intrigue for the prize before it is awarded and to hope for a chance to retrieve it afterward if the autocrat should be weak, unpopular, or unlucky. The atmosphere becomes clouded with suspicion and distrust. For his safety, the autocrat must be ruthless; and the more dangerous it is to be an unsuccessful candidate, the fiercer the struggle for the crown.

A contested succession represents a temporary breakdown of the autocratic system, as it creates a vacancy of power where others can assert themselves. Hence, the fiercest despot may feel the need for an element of constitutionalism, calling upon a council of leading men to sanction the transfer of power, to assure the fulfillment of his will. At a succession crisis the Praetorian Guards or Janissaries can make themselves felt as never else; then all the maneuverers of the palace are at their busiest and the lackeys become lords. It is best for the aristocrats or court figures, of course, if reigns are brief and interrupted by minorities. Thus, in the absence of a strong ruler after Ivan IV, Russia became briefly something like a constitutional monarchy until the Romanovs were firmly seated on the throne. Likewise after Peter the Great, who killed his son, a series of irregular successions and a minority rule permitted the aristocracy to recover a good deal of power.

Thus it is preferable for many that there be no definite right to the throne, but more or less a free-for-all, whereby the title of the emperor derives from the consent of some group or clique. Of course, he cannot be expected to remain grateful for many years; but when a ruler has put himself in the power of a camarilla, it requires no little determination, acumen, and political purpose to fight free of it. Not many emperors are willing to go to the trouble of really changing things. In any event, those who can influence the succession do not want a ruler who is likely to hurt them, but a slothful and inactive one who will serve as public symbol, in the name of whom they can rule.

It is hence impossible for the great empire, wherein the ruler is all-powerful, to assure itself a good master. It is most likely to get one when it is much embattled and concerned for military power, as were the Inca and Roman empires; then many people, especially the soldiers, can agree on the necessity of a strong leader for the general safety. But in the complete security of the universal empire, cumulative degeneration of character is more likely, with effects felt through the whole of the government and society.

THE INEFFECTIVE APPARATUS

As the imperial order has no means of assuring competency at the summit, neither is it able to make and keep its apparatus an efficient tool for its high purposes. The bureaucracy should be characterized by fixed rules equally applied to all, by fair opportunities, competent administration [566, p. 224], honesty, impartiality, and devotion to the interests of the state. It is more likely, in the overgrown state, that the virtues turn into vices: predictability of action becomes rigidity and conservatism; fixed lines of authority mean that inferiors do nothing without orders; devotion to the state becomes narrow self-serving. Such faults as lack of initiative and avoidance of responsibility, slowness, excessive attention to precedent, a formalistic approach to problems, the stupidity of routine, remoteness from and indifference to people, waste of manpower, and corruption are commonplace in the apparatus of freer states [551, p. 43], but in the great empires bureaucracy comes beautifully into its own. Little has been written of the administrative machines of the great monopolistic empires, and their inner workings remain mysterious to us as they must have been to the people of the time. But from all indications, the tangle of bureaucratic vices in the monopolistic empires grows into a great jungle.

The bureaucracy, as the heart of the imperial state, enjoys the advantages of the great organization and suffers its defects. When order and obedience are the prime virtues and independence is subversive, there is no room for initiative. When there is little protection of law and the prime consideration is not to offend a superior, judgment means choosing the least offensive course and doing nothing out of the way. A maxim for scribe-officials of the Egyptian New Kingdom was, "Never question an order, never speak out of turn. Then you will not lack for food." [134, p. 86] The best way to make no errors is to do nothing positive; the first rule is never to stick one's neck out; the way to succeed is to guess what the superior wants. The tsarist Russian bureaucrats knew it was safest to do nothing without instructions, and so waited for higher orders, indifferent to the needs and petitions pressed upon them. [423, p. 447] Taking a firm stand risks alienating someone. It is hazardous to tell superiors disagreeable facts. Officials of the Ch'ing dynasty who sent in unpleasant reports were likely to be at least degraded; the extreme of frankness in their memorials seemed deceitfully servile to Westerners. [32, p. 41] To be original or unconventional in the bureaucratic setup is to be visionary, uncooperative, or downright troublesome. As failures are seen as the result of disloyalty and blame is to be shifted to inferiors, responsibility is a danger to be shunned; hence decisions are passed upward or to committees, where they are diluted or lost, while each tries to find cover for his actions. [*519*, p. 13] It is hazardous even to excel. A courtiers' saying was, "Do not seem wise before the king." It might be ruinous to do great services, as powerful men do not like to be indebted. [*564*, p. 136] Best of all is to be regular, loyal, and conventional. The bureaucracy thus envelops itself in routine and wastes motion in procedures. Difficult decisions are evaded and long delays are preferred to possible errors; novel situations and new ideas cause only confusion. For such reasons, it commonly occurs that administrative agencies function well only for their first few years, afterward becoming hidebound and inefficient. [*558*, p. 176]

Forms are a substitute for thought, and the bureaucracy, winding itself up in forms, becomes devoted to them. The Roman imperial service, for example, was hopelessly addicted to papers and files, or what has come to be called red tape. [*326*, I, 602] Under the Moguls, a payment order had to be approved by a dozen scattered officials, signed twice by the emperor, and passed through ten stages from entry in the diary to issuance of treasury draft [*209*, p. 52], and such elaborate procedures were common in various branches. Likewise the structure of imperial bureaucracies, wherein nothing except position is important, can become a forbidding maze. Perhaps none has excelled the earliest, that of the Egyptian Old Kingdom, where almost two thousand titles were in use, with strict conventional rankings in an enormously complex status system. [*89*, pp. 11, 38] Some officials recorded as many as fifty titles on their tombs. [*89*, pp. 19–20] After Diocletian the Roman system of ranks became so elaborate that civil servants spent much of their time studying and enforcing the minute distinctions. [*519*, p. 63]

In view of stress on form and status, the infinite inertia of the mountainous organization, the regularized procedures, and the fact that the safest course for anyone is usually to do what was done in the past, the strongest tendency is to follow routine. Progress and change are threatening, or at least cause discomfort by necessitating adaptations; these not only require new and unpleasant mental processes, but hurt the position of some functionaries. Indisposed to inquiry, the bureaucracy finds it hard to perceive a need to change, while the fixed order becomes more and more ingrown. Hence patterns may be extraordinarily conservative; it has been said that there was no important change in the form of Chinese government for two thousand years, from the Hans until the twentieth century. [*84*, p. 109] Until 1834 the British Exchequer continued to keep accounts on parchment scrolls, using Tudor script and Roman numerals. [*571*, p. 89]

Since the bureaucracy desires to operate by rules and there is no penalty for dullness, promotion is probably by seniority; this in turn contributes to the stiffness and mediocrity of the whole. The static heirarchic order ordinarily favors patience and the ability to sit tight, even where there is more or less pretense of judging and rewarding service, because promotion by seniority gives security, permits relaxation [*566*, p. 203], and is the simplest means of selection, the most understandable, and the least controversial. Thus even legislative bodies, like the American Congress, allot positions of importance according to the length of time a legislator has kept his seat. Real judgment of performance in the bureaucratic system, as in a peacetime army, is difficult and hardly desired by most officials. Such seems to have been more or less the rule of the great and mature empires. In the Roman apparatus, for example, although the ruler was supposedly absolute boss, status came to be hereditary and strictly by seniority, fixed periods being required in grades, except as graft enabled some to step along faster. [*326*, I, 602; *321*, pp. 358–359] But if one can progress merely by routine and inoffensiveness, boldness or originality is folly.

An alternative to seniority as a criterion for advancement might be impartial examinations to rate ability; but this plan is much more feasible for entry than for promotion, and only the Chinese seem to have attempted it. Seniority, however, cannot be applied to the higher and more important ranks, which are filled by favor, by cooption, in which the high officials choose one another, so far as the emperor does not inject a personal preference or decide between rivals. Thus, in the Chinese civil service, as elsewhere, there were strict rules for the lower ranks, while relations among the higher functionaries were flexible. [*56*, p. 100] So far as a career is not automatic, as it may be to a large extent on the lower levels, it hinges on persuasion, friendship, perhaps purchase, usefulness not to the people or even the state but to certain individuals; often manipulation and playing upon weaknesses are most useful. As Lord Shang wrote, "To strive for promotion by serving superiors with sincerity is like wishing to climb a crooked tree by holding on to a broken rope." [*16*, p. 187] Even in large American corporations it is said that managers would rather advance those who can be relied upon to uphold authority than those who know their job well. [530, p. 139] Brilliance is more apt to be offensive than pleasing, as it shows up the many who are mediocre from caution if not from lack of ability.

The moral results are deplorable. Those who rise either by negative virtues of amiable timeserving or careerist maneuvering are likely to carry such attitudes to whatever position they may occupy and to make their values those of the apparatus. Good slaves, it is said, make bad masters; but everyone in the apparatus has to act the slave much of the time. Sincerity and faithfulness to one's convictions surely cause trouble with one's superiors; the organization thus selects against moral rectitude. [558, pp. 71, 22] In the organization, thinkers have little status, and conviviality is more important than intelligence. It is important to know nothing deeply but to be adept at personal relations, wise in the ways of ingratiation with superiors and of management of inferiors. Quarrels hinge on power, seldom on policy. The staff ponders less what should be done than what the chief wants and how he should be approached. There is little interest in facts contrary to his preconceptions. [558, p. 70] Each man is demoralizingly at the mercy of his boss; humiliations from above are compensated by contempt for those below. In the upper spheres, where relations are less formal, the bureaucracy merges into the court of the autocrat; there it is still less likely that the honest should prosper over the slimy. The great autocrat, and the little autocrats below him, are less likely to take to their bosom men who correct their shortcomings than those who share their lusts and vices. But the servants cannot be expected to show more virtue than their masters, and the vices generalized through the great organization become its morality.

Success in the bureaucracy is position, which means power, prestige, and probably wealth as well; and there is no other avenue to fortune. With the prizes so dear, there is a continual wrangle; the climbing of place seekers grows more desperate as the ladder narrows toward the seat of all authority. Outwardly, the bureaucracy may seem solid and united; inwardly, it seethes. Some advance, others are checked; and each higher functionary clambering up or slipping down carries with him a coterie or clique of family, friends, and clients. When the Ch'ing dynasty was in its youth, a European noted that the officials were most occupied in studying one another's character. Dissembling their true feelings, they used a thousand subtle means to injure their rivals. [43, p. 239] Their insecurity and the fact that, with no alternative to turn to, office meant honor and economic standing for their extended families as well as themselves, made them extremely jealous and status-minded; it is a credit to their education that the merciless contest did not turn into murder in the Turkish style. [76, p. 356] In this underground and underhanded competition, principles have little or no place; and the ethics of the power struggle is that of the court. Sycophancy is the safest posture, honesty is naïve, indirection is the rule. The hurt of rivals is often the easiest advantage, and a common tactic is to accuse of disloyalty and to persuade the puissant that others are dangerous. Politics becomes intrigue in a network of special privileges and influences.

There is also a more or less covert struggle among departments for jurisdiction, power, and positions. As in the Roman apparatus, loyalty of the bureaucrats was primarily to their division, to which they were permanently fixed, and each section tried to advance its own interests at the expense of others. [326, I, 602] In the lack of common purpose, such internal squabbling, whereby each strives to expand its own sphere while otherwise shirking responsibility, goes on among local offices as well as great departments. [519, p. 27]

The bureaucracy develops its own goals [474, pp. 11–12] and is more inclined to care for its own interests than those of the lofty master or the people without. Aware that they are indispensable, the officials cannot but take advantage of the fact to promote individual and corporate welfare. Wrapped up in their organizational procedures and purposes, thinking only of status, the functionaries easily become engrossed in bureaucratic values and fond of regulation for its own sake. They grow careless of the real world outside, callous and supercilious toward the people, outwardly deferential and servile to the higher powers but inwardly indifferent to them. Even in open societies, the administrative apparatus often tends to hold itself somewhat aloof, as superior, not servile, to society, and it is viewed with misgivings by the people, distrusted and distrusting. In the imperial society, the apparatus, as arm of the all-powerful, can truly regard itself as a caste above.

Because of inefficiencies, rivalries, internal empire building, and the desirability of positions, the apparatus tends to enlarge itself at the expense of people and emperor as well; a prime goal of most large organizations is the protection and aggrandizement of the organization itself. [*474*, p. 12] The departments can always make work for themselves. The larger the staff, the more referrals upward and downward, with corresponding delays, equivocations, and justifications, the more consultations per decision and the more interoffice communications to coordinate the unwieldy structure. Each official who can do so tries to make his own position more important and possibly more lucrative by getting more subordinates, while rivalry of bureaus leads to duplication or multiplication of offices and positions. Most of all, perhaps, the bureaucracy tends to grow because there is no other suitable career; and officials at all levels are under tremendous pressure to find jobs for sons, relatives, and friends. The official class thus has an enormous interest in making the apparatus as large as possible, until it submerges the whole state. Probably all the great empires have seen such a proliferation of officialdom and hangers-on of the regime, until, as was said of tsarist Russia in its twilight, "Everything seems to be under the blight of the bureaucracy." [*418*, p. 87]

The emperor, and probably his chief ministers, may be disturbed that the machine supposed to serve them goes its own way and serves itself, but they have no remedy. The larger the organization, the smaller percentage of its activity represents the wishes of the sovereign, as his authority is diluted. [*558*, p. 167] Political controls designed to reduce independence — the dividing of responsibility, the setting of one to check another, the establishment of multiple and interlocking chains of authority — make for more irresponsibility and inefficiency; and the more people are tied by controls, the less responsibility is felt by anyone, including the controllers. Officials bypass their immediate superiors or inferiors and go across regular lines of authority [*558*, p. 77], but such procedures raise new conflicts and confusion and cloud responsibility. The creeping stupidity and corruption of the great organization are almost incurable, and complexity of structure insulates from improvement. When the apparatus waters down policies that it finds hurtful and sabotages their execution, it is a herculean labor to try to enforce compliance. The autocrat's servants, after all, are more necessary to him than he is to them.

It is not easy for the sovereign even to know how far he is being obeyed. An administrative apparatus usually unites against all outsiders [*558*, p. 40]; it hides or disguises its defects and protects itself by secrecy and the mystique of professionalism; it can checkmate the most absolute monarch simply by not informing him, or perhaps by overwhelming him with detail. [R. Merton in *474*, p. 55; *566*, pp. 233–234] The chief is told what he should hear; and control agencies, even if competent, join hands with the controlled on a common ground of advantages. Obedience is primarily to the immediate superior, not to the remote authority. Solidarity is a bureaucratic instinct, natural where the higher ranks govern advancement and the lower are the basis of their superiors' power; loyalty to the corps is a prime virtue and disloyalty the chief sin. The officials are accustomed to applying the law as they see fit and often for their own benefit; it is hard to expect them to apply it against themselves, or to do more than pretend compliance while waiting for higher powers to change or to forget their reformist urges.

Regulations tend to defeat themselves. Stronger controls make the apparatus more cumbersome, increase paper work, and further reduce initiative. Fear makes for worse shirking of responsibility. Command that is felt to be unreasonable breeds dissimulation and deception. It is as rewarding to pretend as to comply, and the prestige of a ruler and the safety of his servants combine to require falsification. Distrust of local authorities and of subordinates leads to centralization in theory and paralysis in practice, with complications of jurisdiction, delays, and confusion. This distrust hinders as much as helps the aims of management, just as the emperor, by trying to look into everything himself, makes himself incapable of seeing anything. Strictness of accountancy, where there is no helpful spirit, makes for hypocritical pretense, as the rules are accepted for appearance's sake. The nineteenth-century Russian bureaucracy, for example, was notoriously corrupt and equally rule-bound. When the governor's stove required a minor repair, the need had to be attested by an official commission and certified by the procurator; the estimate of costs, although only a couple of rubles, was similarly processed and then checked by another commission, an architect, and a procurator, whereupon authorization was issued. This was all waste paper, as the stove was repaired with due haste and the forms filled out at leisure. [*419*, pp. 206–207] The effects were not to maintain high standards but to keep paper pushers busy, to indicate to all that they were distrusted and so might as well cheat when they safely could, to keep the controllers occupied with trivia, and to satisfy higher powers by close control of details — while eyes were closed to grossest venality and extortion. The efforts of tsars from Peter onward to cleanse the bureaucracy were no more successful than attempts to make it equalitarian with promotion only by merit; it continued to stagnate, hardly changing until the shock of defeat in the Crimean War. [M. Fainsod in *391*, p. 244] Even in the second half of the nineteenth century, the bureaucracy, accustomed to seeing fads come and go, shrugged off the intellectual movements sweeping the country. [F. Morstein-Marx in *391*, p. 76] Under pressures of modernization, it tended to become rather more corrupt and defensive, resisting any moves toward diminution of authority [M. Fainsod in *391*, p. 247], venal, incompetent, and jealous of prerogatives.

Problems of administrative control are omnipresent, of course; but it is in the autocratic empire that they become unmanageable. It is the woe of the great empire that its enormous differences of rank and privilege inhibit communication, provoke antagonisms, make status the prime goal, and tempt to the exercise of privilege for its own sake. [*455*, p. 107] Worse is the monopoly of power. Independent controls are needed to prune back the burgeoning defects, to criticize and press for reform. Only outside the official structure is there reliable and objective criticism of it. Open competition makes honesty more useful, requiring men to measure themselves and their subordinates by their performance. [*558*, pp. 23, 80] Only when they feel a strong purpose exterior to the organization can officials be expected to stress results over charm or compliance. When power at the top is arbitrary, irregular, and self-justified, the delegates of power cannot be impartial and self-restrained. The despotic master ought not to expect his slaves to be upright men of virtue.

PARASITIC HORDES

Heavy taxation and squeezing of the economy would not be ruinous if resources were transferred to productive purposes. It is possible that the state might aid capital formation and consequently raise productivity by checking consumption and redirecting resources where they are most useful. But if the universal empires ever thought seriously of doing this, they did not succeed.

The exactions of the great state, together with endless graft and extortion, represent rather a transfer of substance from producers to nonproducers, leaving the former without resources for investment, discouraging enterprise and initiative, and encouraging cheating, manipulation, and thievery. The chief ambition of the victims must be to join the ranks of their oppressors, while the parasitism of the fortunate makes bitter the shrunken fruits of labor. Those who mulct, swindle, and extort tend to encourage and support one another, while the masses in becoming poorer lose their moral and political resistance to exploitation, until there are practically two classes, those lucky enough to live by their relation to power, and the unfortunates who labor. The way of those above is waste and show; the empires have excelled in the production of luxury articles, not necessities. The way of those below is dull backwardness. Making some rich by making others poor makes all poorer.

The exploitation of man by man is doubtless as old as human society, and primitive peoples have known enough of it. But to a large extent it is the disease of the great state, for it is mostly power that gives one the means of taking from another, and power is the attribute of political organization. Official status and economic privileges protected by the state give men the opportunity systematically and permanently to profit at the expense of their fellows. The sovereign who disposes of lives and property can take without return, and he confers on his subalterns and a host who attach themselves to the prevailing order the power to do likewise. Kautilya listed forty ways in which ministers robbed the fisc [*Arthasastra*, 2.8.21]; he might have listed another forty means apiece whereby the emperor, inferior despots, and sundry parasites stole from the people, and all possessors of power looted one another.

The earliest empire seems to have been as exploitative as any. By the end of the Old Kingdom the swollen capital was teeming with officials, courtiers, and lackeys of the pharaoh, growing more numerous as his position weakened, a class of rich living off the state while the starving poor were given to banditry. [*134*, p. 8] The New Kingdom also appears to have been grossly wasteful and thoroughly corrupt. Fief holders extracted as much as possible and paid into the treasury as little as possible [*114*, Pt. I, p. 21]; inspectors connived with tax collectors and shared their plundering of the peasants. [*134*, pp. 99–100; *462*, p. 11] The scribes contemned all manual labor, especially agriculture. [*124*, p. 103] In the latter days of the Assyrian empire, while its military defenses were crumbling, palatial expenditures continued to consume enormous resources. [*462*, p. 33] In the provinces of the Achaemenid empire, the officials who seem to have bought their posts had more or less carte blanche to exploit [*253*, p. 163]; in the capital, fifteen thousand are supposed to have fed at the tables of the Great King [*462*, p. 59], more likely hangers-on of the palace than devoted servants of the people. The Abbasid Califate kept up the Near Eastern imperial tradition by spending nearly all its revenues on the royal household and court. [*486*, pp. 161–162] The Inca empire apparently had not lived long enough to become thoroughly rotten when it was cut down; but its most striking achievement, at least in Spanish eyes, was the accumulation of enormous amounts of purely ornamental gold and silver. How bloated the court had become may be judged from the Inca's taking two thousand women to keep him company on his travels. [*172*, p. 51] The households of the royal mummies were also becoming excrescent burdens, which one of the last Incas tried in vain to curtail. [*173*, p. 180]

The Turkish empire, although it had no aristocracy of birth, evolved from a strong military order into a vast system of corrupt holdings. Membership in the once heroic Janissary corps was purchased as a title to immunity from taxes and payment for doing nothing, and the tickets were bought and sold on the market as an investment [*439*, p. 41]; yet the privileges could not be abolished because too many officials shared in the graft. [*432*, Pt. I, pp. 182–186] Provincial governors were judged by their remittances and permitted to profit as they could; in the general cynicism, the offices were put up for auction. [*432*, Pt. I, p. 207] Tax farms were sold and resold, with a profit each time, until the entrepreneur had to plunder to repay himself. [*439*, p. 50] Judges became wealthy in their term of office of a single year. [*439*, p. 53] The vizier, like other officials, was the more avid for quick riches as he could not expect to last long. Some of the sultan's slaves accumulated fortunes equivalent to many millions of dollars [*435*, p. 87], as a lucky few, living in the shadows of the court and enjoying enormous influence, skimmed the cream of the graft. [*439*, pp. 34, 51] Even education was venalized, as degrees, entitling one to a teaching position, were conferred by favor or sale; lacking inclination and ability to teach, the degree holders hired substitutes and merely drew the pay. [432, Pt. II, p. 150]

The Mogul empire bled India to anemia for the benefit of the luxurious court, a swarm of grasping officials, and huge, perhaps beautiful, but certainly useless monuments. [212, p. 339] It was unconcerned to justify its existence by pretense of benefits to the population, who saw the authorities only as police and tax or rent collectors and were otherwise left to themselves. [213, p. 11] Virtually none of the public works were of any practical utility. The only important exceptions were a waterworks undertaken for military use and a canal started by foreign inspiration. [205, p. 195]

Akbar, founder of the empire, set up the bureaucracy as a military organization, with thirty-one ranks corresponding to the foot or horse soldiery they were supposed to maintain from their allotments. But differences soon arose between the nominal and actual number of troops, and under Shah Jahan the mansabdars were permitted to muster only a third or a quarter of the command for which they were paid, or perhaps none at all. [214, p. 129] They thus came to have princely salaries: governors received from 12,000 to 30,000 rupees monthly (partly required for expenses and staff), and the highest civil servant, the treasurer, was paid about 250,000 rupees, while a skilled laborer earned about 3 rupees. [214, pp. 43, 108] The payroll grew from approximately 1,650 mansabdars under Akbar in 1590 to 8,000 in 1637 and 11,456 in 1690, partly through the absorption of local rajahs' administrations but mostly from bureaucratic proliferation. [214, p. 110] Waste was splendid: under Aurangzeb, the royal perfumer received 20,000 rupees yearly, the superintendent of goldsmiths, 50,000, and others in like proportion. [214, p. 112] The officials felt entitled or obliged to emulate the royal way of life, with harems and households as large as they could afford, or sometimes ruinously larger. Great trains of servants were kept for show; no worthy mansabdar would appear in public without a hundred or so foot and mounted retainers. [214, p. 124; 209, p. 70] But the satisfactions of the mansabdar's life were not perfect. Unless he could conceal assets, he could not pass them on to his descendants or found a family fortune, since all or nearly all were seized at death by the emperor, who considered himself proper heir of his servants, as of any wealthy subjects. [191, pp. 164–167] Hence, money was spent extravagantly and unproductively as rapidly as it was received.

[*205*, p. 303] Although they were subject to no regular taxes, officials had to make costly presents to the emperor on many occasions, such as birthdays, New Year's, and any audience, if favor and status were not to be imperiled. [*213*, p. 125] Governorships, even if bought for cash, always required the protection of some high personage at court or in the royal harem. [*191*, p. 230] As each level in the hierarchy, seeking to make the most of its insecure carte blanche, squeezed those beneath, only the peasants had no remedy but to pay the imperial taxes plus forty to eighty taxes formally abolished by the beneficent Mogul, but extracted nonetheless by his minions. [*213*, pp. 57, 60]

The Roman empire is reputed not to have succumbed to quite such shameless robbery even in its darker days; yet there, too, the parasitism of the powerful lay heavy on the land. The big fortunes of the early days of the empire rested upon the least productive branches of the economy, farming of taxes, investment in land, lending at usurious interest, and politics; the huge cost of a political career meant that one had to expect even larger returns. Magnates and officials used the soldiery to collect their usurious loans [*338*, p. 257], and many Romans settled in the provinces in occupations related to the collection of revenue. [H. Last in *290*, pp. 441–442] Despite well-intentioned laws, governors of provinces were virtually unchecked. They usually expected to become rich in the single year of office, the brief term of which checked the affirmation of independent power but made avarice more frantic. [*300*, p. 19] There were many ways to use authority; a privilege for which the cities were especially willing to pay was that of not playing host to the army.

A lucrative profession, somewhat repressed under the more statesmanlike emperors and correspondingly rampant under the worse, was that of informant. Under the law of lese majeste, one-quarter of the estate of the victim went to whoever disclosed intended treason. Since three-quarters went to the state, accusation was nearly equivalent to conviction. [*300*, p. 189] Even the laws of morality promulgated by Augustus were turned to the purposes of the blackmailers. [*302*, p. 35] In the first century it was reported of Alexandria that the "city has become practically uninhabitable because of the multitude of informers." [*330*, p. 378] While delation prospered, Tacitus assures us, "virtue ensured destruction." [*Histories*, 1.2; *349*, p. 420]

Official position was a better avenue to fortune. Some freedmen early in the empire acquired the equivalent of tens or scores of millions of dollars by virtue of their relationship to the Caesars [*313*, p. 44]; even favored slaves often grew extremely rich. Lesser officials likewise profited in countless ways; one reason that men had to be frozen to their professions was that government careers were so attractive. [*326*, I, 69] In the later empire, most positions were held only for short terms, usually a year or two, because of pressure to share the graft. Children were enrolled to get them on the promotion ladder [*326*, I, 586], and posts, even governorships, were salable, usually less for the benefit of the treasury than for that of the higher officials. [*275*, p. 35] Posts were multiplied, many carrying no duties but entailing salaries, fees, privileges, or tax exemptions. [*326*, I, 576, 581] Nothing was done unless palms were greased. [*275*, p. 30] There were many ways of turning an extra penny: court attendants took fees at every turn, which, originally quite irregular, became fixed by custom; palace doorkeepers became especially wealthy by closing or opening doors; employees of the mint struck coins light and pocketed the difference. [*326*, I, 496, 582, 436] Justice became thoroughly corrupt, as vividly reflected in the New Testament: "Agree with thine adversary quickly, while thou art in the way with him; lest at any time the adversary deliver thee to the judge, and the judge deliver thee to the officer and thou be cast into prison. Verily, I say unto thee, thou shalt by no means come out thence, till thou hast paid the uttermost farthing." [Matthew 5:25–26] So expected did it become that officials would make good use of their prerogatives that in the time of Diocletian the regular pay had dwindled to near insignificance. [*326*, I, 51]

The state grew enormously wasteful. From Augustus to Vespasian, a span of half a century, revenues increased sixfold, with no expansion of territory and only a small rise in prices, yet the treasury was empty. [M. Charlesworth in *290*, pp. 13–14] Caligula (37–41 A.D.) in a single year wasted in luxuries the equivalent of more than a hundred million dollars. [*302*, p. 32] Although some rulers, like Marcus Aurelius, preferred simplicity, the luxuries of others knew no bounds. Elagabalus' banquets were graced by huge bowls of nightingales' tongues powdered with pearl dust. [*523*, p. 97] The imperial household grew, until by the time of Julian (361–363) there were many thousands of cooks, cupbearers, table servants, barbers, eunuchs, and the like, most of them probably defrauding and pilfering, some making great sums in the handling of imperial moneys. [*313*, p. 66] In the time of Constantine, there are supposed to have been a thousand barbers at the court, and one barber had twenty servants and as many horses. [*314*, I, 747] According to Lactantius, writing of the end of the third century, the number of those receiving from the state was much larger than the number of those paying taxes. [*330*, p. 459]

While the middle classes were ground down, the upper and official classes, growing more selfish as they grew more oppressive, used all manner of corruption, exemptions, bribery, and perverted justice to swell their wealth [*303*, p. 246] with the assistance of the soldiers: the armies of the early empire were drawn from the people and had some feeling for them; the professional armies of later times bullied without compunction. The chasm between rich and poor widened ever more, and servility toward the one increased together with tyranny toward the other. [*303*, p. 228] Men of the lower classes were put to death for the most trifling transgression, while the great robbers were praised. [*275*, p. 46] While the poor were becoming serfs or brigands, the new senatorial class had practically a monopoly of high office, almost automatically becoming prefects, governors, or consuls [*303*, p. 254], and had powers that Caesars could hardly touch. Enjoying great privileges, exemptions, and judicial power [*285*, p. 456], ruling vast domains from their castles, they, like everyone else who could, engaged in every imaginable abuse of position. While there was a serious shortage of labor for all productive purposes, such as mining, agriculture, and crafts, trade in luxuries held up better than that in necessities. [*342*, p. 524]

In the capital, oddly enough, not only the great and the officials were parasitic, but multitudes of the poor licked the gravy of the empire. An outgrowth of the buying of votes and popular support in the later republic, the dole became a regular feature of Roman life, and the emperors, theoretically sovereign by popular election, did not see fit to curtail it. Grain was furnished to about 200,000 people, the number fixed by Augustus and continued until after Constantine, who gave the populace of his new capital, Constantinople, similar benefits. Not only grain, but bread, olive oil, wine, and bacon were handed out, and occasionally money, so that idle citizens should share in the benefits of having conquered the world

[*338*, pp. 249–251]; in the middle of the fifth century, when the empire was moribund, there were still about 120,000 recipients. [*326*, I, 687] For the bored there were spectacles and games, lasting all day a large part of the year, massive exhibitions of skill, daring, and, above all, blood; in 114 A.D. more than 23,000 gladiators took part. [R. Longden in *290*, p. 215] Provincial cities were also given to luxuries, games, and imposing edifices in imitation of Rome; their inhabitants remained for a time well fed while the peasants in the countryside starved [*326*, I, 10], and while the villages were being deserted, the larger centers were swelling with idle rabble and mendicants [*309*, p. 58], until the cities, too, withered in the late empire.

The story of a hypertrophied officialdom growing up to overburden and exhaust the realm has been played out many times in China, as each major dynasty has built up a vast apparatus standing over the people and growing in size and worthlessness, like a swarm of locusts infesting and consuming all. Early in the Han dynasty strong efforts were made to bring the economy under control; in the words of a Chinese chronicler, "No one troubled any more to accumulate and increase his patrimony. But the provincial officials, thanks to salt, iron, and levies on acquired fortunes, had abundant resources." [*30*, p. 116] The inscription on a lacquered box of 4 B.C. shows seven artisans supervised by five administrators [J. Needham in *468*, p. 125] when the Han dynasty was only halfway through its life. The senile dynasties might all be characterized as was the Ming dynasty: "Scions of the Imperial blood, eunuchs, court favorites, panders, and harpies of all descriptions fastened like vampires on the peoples' throats and the whole country, in hollow-cheeked despair, thus became an easy quarry to the robust and at that time physically and mentally healthy Manchus." [*57*, p. 25]

The Manchus made a serious effort to forestall decay, but their physical, mental, and moral robustness faded away in due course. Corruption became omnipresent and exaggerated. The emperor once found that he paid seventy-five times the market price for eggs. [*4*, p. 337] One outstanding peculator, Ho-shen, allegedly appropriated as much as nine-tenths of the tribute flowing from the provinces. [*4*, p. 356] He put in his pocket property more than ten times the annual revenue of the government [*45*, p. 7], an

amount calculated at about £ 280 million at the end of the eighteenth century, equivalent to much more than a billion current dollars. [*4*, p. 364; *61*, p. 392] As long as his master lived, he was
immune; when an official charged treasury deficiencies, Ho-shen
had the investigation entrusted to one of his own men. [Nivison in
55, p. 234]

Many devices were used to cheat the state, such as classifying
old land as newly cultivated (and so tax-exempt), pocketing taxes
and reporting them uncollectable, describing farmland as waste,
and all that mandarin ingenuity could invent. [*36*, pp. 106–107]
The mandarinate became an association of petty tyrants and insatiable thieves, effective only in oppression and pillage. [*37*, I,
357] Vague criminal laws gave endless opportunities for profit by
the magistrate judges; for example, rules against popular diversions, like gambling, served as grounds for minor blackmail. [*10*,
p. 82] One might be threatened with eighty strokes of the bamboo
for "conduct that offends propriety" [*37*, II, 249]; and justice was
close to legalized extortion, prosecutions being encouraged by a
regular scale of fees for relief from punishment; for example, an
official of the 4th rank was expected to pay 12,000 ounces of silver
as the price of not being strangled. [*10*, p. 65] Unpaid police —
thousands in large cities — lived by victimizing the unprotected,
often joining with bandits and outright criminals for mutual advantage. [*76*, pp. 378, 401]

Salaries and antiextortion allowances did not begin to meet the
needs of officials, who had to provide their own secretaries and
flunkies [*20*, p. 92], but the usual three-year term of service could
repay all the costs of education and establish a family fortune.
There was no scale of fees for services, but all charged as they
pleased. [*14*, I, 304] The provision that they serve only three years
and never in their home districts made them more careless of local
feelings, indifferent to improvements, and more eager to gather the
harvest quickly. [*37*, I, 367–368] Local clerks and aides, however,
seem to have been quite as rapacious, despite some efforts of the
more dignified magistrates to control them. [C. Yang in *55*, p. 136]
They skillfully used their meager authority; for example, the door-
keeper required large donations for permitting any nonofficial to
see the magistrate, smaller tips to pass in calling cards. [*14*, I, 323]
The emperor repeatedly circularized the magistrates against
abuses; they would dutifully give orders to clerks, attendants, and

police to treat the people with heavenly justice; and all would go on as before. [76, p. 382]

The magistrates exerted themselves minimally. One who took the trouble to preside over trials in person, instead of sipping tea on a divan, was held quite extraordinarily dedicated to duty [37, II, 94]; a just official was a freak to be made the hero of popular fiction. [51, p. 65] Fingernails several inches long and cumbersome sleeves to impede activity were symbols of proud uselessness. Even the lowest grade of the scholar-gentry class would avoid any physical effort, like lighting a fire or carrying a small bundle. [65, p. 93]

The government gave the villagers little more than the privilege of paying the taxes that the gentry evaded [36, pp. 124–125], and the "father-mother" officials had little contact with their children except through tax collectors and police. [57, p. 83] Village headmen were disliked, even though more or less elected by the villagers themselves, because they were associated with the government. [82, p. 174] Left generally to their own devices, the villages were expected to look after their own needs for public works, schools, and relief. Irrigation and water control projects were largely left to the local gentry. [8, pp. 59–61] The empire did not even keep local order; this the people were supposed to do for themselves through the *pao-chia* system of group responsibility and the local militia. The granaries traditionally maintained to relieve famine became a source of speculation, of little interest to the state except perhaps to reduce banditry. [76, p. 397] It was well that welfare was not handled by the officials, for money allotted to relief largely disappeared short of the intended goal. When such funds were privately managed, 70 to 80 percent went to proper purposes; when they went through the hands of the lower officials, 80 to 90 percent disappeared. [8, p. 62] When late in the century funds were with difficulty collected for a navy, the Dowager Empress spent them for a new palace. [70, p. 204]

The Russian empire suffered not a little from the same sickness. All the tsars were aware of the national malady; some struggled vainly against it, and others resigned themselves to the inevitable. [380, II, 295–296] In old Muscovy, before the reforms of Peter, revenue-yielding posts were regularly given as a reward for military or court service. Administrative position was regarded as little more than a fountain of wealth, for impoverished officials could recoup their fortunes in a year or two as governors. [388, II, 250–

251] The commonest means of extortion was criminal accusation with threat of torture. Judges paid heavily for their posts and had no salary, but came out rich after a three-year term. [J. Perry in *403*, p. 46] Local officials were the greedier because they knew they would be squeezed at the end of their year, and district governors for the same reason freely allowed them to fatten. [*405*, p. 42]

Peter tried to remake the administration on the Swedish model, imported advisers, established training schools, and broadened recruitment. [M. Fainsod in *391*, pp. 242–243] But he had little success in transmuting the system; the new men he brought in were apt to prove even more grossly corrupt than the old aristocrats [*407*, p. 133], and they saw to it that nothing of importance was done without bribery. [*388*, IV, 263] In despair, Peter proposed at one time to hang everyone who stole from the government. "Your Majesty desires to reign alone, then, without subjects?" was the rejoinder of the attorney general. "We all steal, the sole difference is that some do it on a bigger scale and in a more conspicuous manner than others." [*379*, p. 142; *377*, p. 384] The worst villains, of course, were the favorites of the tsar. The inquisitor appointed to root out corruption was himself convicted of extortion. [*379*, p. 141]

Not only was it impossible to purify administration in an atmosphere of widespread profiteering; it was difficult to advance the economy very far despite valiant efforts and huge expenditures. Many industrial companies were formed at government urging; but their purpose was much less to work and produce than to use the subsidies, bounties, and privileges; and they usually collapsed when official support ended. [*398*, p. 127] Trade, of course, was strictly controlled by the government and as much victimized by the officials.

After Peter, court figures continued to accumulate great wealth. In 1760 Elizabeth complained that corruption was the rule in the courts and all branches of the administration [*377*, p. 494]; it was no less so before and after her day. Catherine II said, "There is hardly a judge who is not affected by this disease," that is, bribery and corruption. [*551*, p. 152] Because of manifold demands, the treasury was chronically empty during the eighteenth century; the currency had to be devalued, and the pay even of the palace guard was in arrears; yet court luxury and the building of palaces continued. [*377*, p. 489]

The nineteenth century and increasing Westernization brought little improvement. The military was gravely weakened by misappropriation and graft of all sorts, from officers' drawing pay for nonexistent troops to the notorious sale of naval supplies. [*380*, II, 295, 302] Supplies were stolen, funds melted away, and entire shipments disappeared en route. [*423*, p. 444] Moscow trading houses had regularly to pay off officials to avoid molestation. [*396*, p. cxlvii] Great men profited on a great scale, little men on a small one, and lower officials regularly had to pay the higher. [*389*, p. 7] Like the Chinese, the tsarist government economized on pay by letting the officials victimize the people. [*389*, p. 6] Only a small fraction of the horde of functionaries received a living salary, so peculation of some sort was taken for granted. [*360*, p. 182] The police used any small infraction of the law, real or supposed, to extract a tip. [*397*, II, 443–444] Laws were designed to help the authorities; for example, if a murderer was not caught, they could fine the district where the body was found; bodies might be judiciously located for this purpose. [*389*, p. 6] The passport system was used to extract money. [*418*, p. 19] It was the more difficult to attack the evil as officials were usually exempt from the regular courts and responsible only to His Highness. [*423*, p. 443]

Venality so pervaded the judicial system that even the Minister of Justice had to bribe to get legal action taken. [*389*, p. 5] As a British physician put it early in the century, "The whole system of administration in Russia is like the tissue of a decayed spider's web, or rather like the center of an immense wheel held together by rotten spokes; corruption supports corruption, rottenness props rottenness." [*397*, II, 439] The tsar himself felt helpless. Once Nicholas I ordered a bejeweled watch given to a court painter, but it was received minus jewels. The stern tsar complained ruefully, "You see how they rob me? If I tried to punish all the thieves in my empire according to the law, Siberia would be too small and Russia would be made a desert like Siberia." [*395*, p. 62] The peasants joined and fleeced where they could; if a former villager was making good pay in town, the commune to which he belonged might require his return unless he paid a suitable amount, which was usually spent frivolously. [*419*, p. 122]

In all states there are temptations to profit by political position. There are personal preferences and favoritism even in the best-ordered administration, and some get ahead more by playing up to superiors than by doing good work. But where criticism is free and the state is limited and constitutionally ordered, parasitic and degenerative tendencies can be kept in bounds; they grow wild where monopoly and unlimited power are the principles of government. Athens had informers, like those of Rome, hungry for a cut of the property of their victims. But in Athens they had to convince not a greedy toady who might share the loot, but a popular jury. While juries might be swayed by demagogy, there was a public defense; delation was open, and juries often punished the falsifiers. [325, p. 60] In the Roman empire, where political difference was treason, where the autocrat was commonly in fear of his life, and where the discovery of plots was the profession of a large number of police and spies, it was a piece of fortune if a sensible emperor restrained the terror.

The freer the society, the more the state represents a common effort for the general welfare; especially in a small and intimate community, government is public service. But an imposed imperial regime is essentially alien and parasitic; Rome, drawing rivers of gold and silver from subjected lands, imported not only its foodstuffs but almost everything it consumed, textiles, metalware, and all manner of manufactures, and exported only authority. [358, p. 189] The lion takes the lion's share and elevates leonine virtues: the universal empire is the most successful and profitable use of force.

The empire is the embodiment of success by political rather than economic means, that is, by taking rather than by producing, and consequently encourages a political mentality. The prestige of force, manipulation, and ingratiation is high, while that of honest toil is correspondingly low. Landlordism in the great empire is pernicious not because agricultural units are large, which up to a point might well be economically advantageous, but because the holding of land, like nearly everything else, takes a political and nonproductive bent, representing position and command, superiority over the farmers instead of productive farming. Imposition, like freedom, grows on itself, as the atmosphere of acceptance of inferiority, reverence for power, and general credulity withers the sense of independence.

The example of the highest is itself highly prejudicial. The autocracy makes a great play of splendor and wealth to evidence and glorify its power, and, as the great setter of styles, sets the mode of conspicuous waste. As it pretends to limitless power and riches, no one need scruple about siphoning what he can from the public trough. The extravagance of the ruler makes extravagance incumbent upon his minions, while his freedom to dispose of the property and self-respect of his subjects gives his servants moral freedom to take for themselves whatever they can — a freedom strongly reinforced by obligations to family and clients. [489, pp. 82–83] It is in any event easier to let officials compensate themselves at public expense than to pay them from the treasury, and the usual insecurity and brevity of tenure oblige them to reap energetically. Since officials must keep up an appropriate style, and those who steal are uncomfortable in the presence of real honesty, it might be ruinous to be honest, and it is more politic to follow the general mode than to attempt to correct it. Usually the great empires have turned a half-blind eye to official stealing, perhaps denouncing but hardly trying seriously to extirpate the evil, which is in any case irradicable. As long as the thievery is not too blatant and the thief is amiable, it may be ignored. It is undesirable to punish officials, who should be held in awe as representatives of authority. Severity is for political offenders, who represent a personal insult and danger to the sovereign; stealing from the people is a venial matter. When Nicholas I set up a corps of controllers to check defalcations, they concerned themselves only with careless talk and petty political dissent. [419, pp. 207–208]

There is more parasitism also where the state has a larger role. Control and management of the economy, with political decisions substituted for those of the market, multiply opportunities for influence, favor, and graft. When taxation is very high, people seek to escape it so far as possible by political means; a point is reached at which it is cheaper to bribe one's way out than to pay levies legally. Economic and political controls imply a numerous police, and police are everywhere tempted to profit by the violations they are called upon to prevent, the more so when the citizenry have little sympathy with the enforcement of the law, the police feel themselves disliked anyway, and the political power is remote from the community. The secret police especially revel in opportunities, as they can cause endless trouble for anyone, fabricate conspiracies, or cooperate in real ones (as police agents cooperated in several assassinations in tsarist Russia, including that of the prime minister, Stolypin) in order to make themselves feared by the people and indispensable to the rulers. As the exiled Napoleon said from his experience, "The police invents more than it discovers." [239, p. 341]

The successful efforts of the elect to prosper by the weakness of the rest are corrosive of the whole fabric of society. Parasitism suffocates enterprise and initiative. It prevents the formation of capital and penalizes effort, since visible wealth is an invitation to plunder. It diverts resources, intelligence, and energies from productive to wasteful uses. Those who snatch political wealth are little disposed to apply it to production, although they may buy land for security and status. It is morally impossible for them to think in economic terms; as their harvest is garnered without plowing and sowing, it is not replanted but hoarded or carelessly consumed. The insecure loot may better be reinvested in political influence or the enjoyment of the fleeting day. Tacitus tells how the beneficiaries of Nero's largesse were ordered, after his downfall, to return all but a tenth of their takings; but they had left little more than the memory of their vices. [*Histories*, 1, 20]

The parasitic order is also profoundly unprogressive. Those who profit by their relations to existing institutions find any breath of reform a threat to their standing, their way of life, and their very existence; and they are likely to be powerful to block what seems dangerous to them, the more successfully parasitic the more powerful. For absentee landlords, usurers, political and military bosses, monopolists, and all who enjoy special political or official privilege, progress spells ruin. Unless there are international competition and a foreign danger, perhaps not even then, it is hard for them to be intelligent, broad, and flexible enough to see a need for change and to adapt themselves to it. Their status is the sweetness of life: soft white hands that know not toil, untroubled ease and luxury, the bearing and manners and all the marks that set them off from the plebeians, are dearer than life itself.

Moral ravages are likewise grievous. The parasites and bloodsuckers, being successful, impose their values, which become the accepted standard of morality and conduct. No matter what ideology may be mouthed, when deceit and cunning use of power give an easy and respected life, while honesty and industry are for the poor and stupid, all will prefer the former. The whole atmosphere then becomes putrid, and the miasma infects equally those who enjoy and those who have to work. When corruption is systematized, to be honest is to be naïve and silly. Those enriched by injustice have no care for justice, while the impoverished "are hardly capable of any virtue, because their poverty is part of their servitude." [Montesquieu, *Spirit of the Laws*, Bk. XX, chap. 3]

Generations then grow up with the awareness that improvement is to be sought at the expense of others, and the longer this opinion prevails the truer it becomes, the more futile and naïve to oppose it. The dignity of labor sinks along with the condition of the toilers. The meaner the passive masses, the higher the prestige of idleness and privilege. Rulers and ruled draw apart, opposed in their interests, like butchers and cattle. In the world state, the human community is destroyed, and grand empires become hollow shells.

THE DILAPIDATED STATE

The ruler desires that no one except himself be above the law and enjoy irrational privilege. The last thing he wishes is that unproductive persons and classes fatten on the economy and the state, that his minions become independent and self-seeking, exploiting the people for themselves. Overtaxation is more the fault of countless uncontrollable little bosses and bureaucrats than of the great emperor, better situated than any other to take into account the broad interests and needs of the state. The central treasury may well be empty while the people are being squeezed to exhaustion.

The whole apparatus should obey like a well-lubricated machine or like the disciplined army that the state may once have resembled. But armies can conquer more easily than they can govern. The emperor can rule only so far as hundreds and thousands below him are minded to obey, and those on whom the imperial power rests have their own interests and desires. Indifference and self-seeking pervade and incapacitate the state. Decrees are issued and forgotten, and spasmodic attempts to revitalize have at best a temporary effect. Faults and fissures threaten the whole edifice, but no one can repair them, and perhaps few really care. The supposedly omnipotent monarch finds himself nearly or entirely a figurehead, unable really to direct the apparatus which is supposed to be his alone. The weakening of the levers of government is a general disease of empires, enfeebling their maturity and bringing decrepitude to their old age.

Each universal empire has seen such erosion of the central power. About 2700 B.C., having crushed the remnants of local independence, the pharaohs became absolute god-kings and built up their own administrative machinery to replace the old nobility and to control closely the entire country. In the glorious Fourth, the great pyramid-building dynasty, the pharaoh was everything. But as the court grew and the bureaucracy expanded, high functionaries managed to make their own positions secure and hereditary. Temples gained exemption from taxation, and peasants began seeking the protection of local lords. [*131*, pp. 17–18] In the Fifth Dynasty, as the pharaohs' pyramids became smaller, tombs of the ministers became bigger and better. [*89*, p. 301] Toward the end of the dynasty, the entire administration of nomes, or districts, was placed in the hands of single nomarchs. [*89*, p. 297] These were able to inscribe their names alongside that of the ruler [*90*, p. 150], and to build impressive tombs, not clustered like satellites around the pharaoh's, but in their own provinces. In the following dynasty, primogeniture had returned, and inscriptions speak more of nobles and less of pharaohs, who had descended from being gods to being sons of gods. [*88*, p. 90] A nomarch could send his own forces on a southern campaign [*101*, p. 128], and some took royal titles. [W. Edgerton in *466*, p. 126]

Thereafter, with the power of the pharaoh almost gone, some towns regained the autonomy of predynastic times; nomes were independent and fighting among themselves, and famine came as irrigation works fell into disrepair. According to writings of the time, highborn ladies were reduced to rags, there was violence everywhere, and farmers wore armor while tilling their fields. [*130*, pp. 58–59]

After a long interlude of the less centralized Middle Kingdom and the foreign Hyksos domination, the New Kingdom arose to great power and glory under the Eighteenth Dynasty. The pharaohs were again absolute masters of a reunited land. But again power gradually disintegrated. In about two centuries, even very high bureaucratic positions were becoming inheritable, remaining in one family for generations. [*114*, Pt. I, p. 43] In time the land came to be held by an uncurbed nobility. Powerful priesthoods stood apart from the state, and tax-exempt temples owned much of the wealth. [*94*, pp. 473–474, 492] Organized gangs looted temples and tombs with impunity, and lawbreakers, supported by officials, stood almost above the law. [*124*, pp. 259–267] The army decayed into mercenary bands, local potentates behaved like independent sovereigns, and the kingdom broke down in general disorder. [*102*, p. 163; *131*, p. 19] An energetic pharaoh might be able to pull some order from the anarchy, but final collapse and foreign subjection could not be long delayed.

In the more turbulent Near East empires were not so free to rot in peace as in isolated Egypt. The greatest one, the Achaemenid Persian, was unusually quick to fall apart. Although royal secretaries, visiting inspectors, and other devices were used to keep the satraps entirely obedient, in less than a century they were reaching for independence [*251*, pp. 62–63] to the extent of making war on one another. [*116*, p. 148]

Roman emperors similarly lost control of their domain. Early Caesars largely made the quality of the government and, within a pseudoconstitutional framework, effectively set policy. As the armies became more unruly and professional, they increasingly made all but the stronger emperors their creatures or their victims. The civil service also acquired greater authority and independence. Despite the theoretical freedom of the ruler to choose his servants, official position became largely an inherited or purchased possession, and fixed status meant independence and authorization for pursuit of self-interest. [*294*, p. 743] As abuses multiplied, there were more and more edicts against them, but the dead weight of officialdom, general indifference, and the bureaucratic instinct for mutual protection rendered all nugatory. The most violent legislation, threatening beheading and burning, banishment and torture, failed to move violators from accustomed ways. [*303*, p. 267] The attempt to give redress was almost given up. When the empire was young, there had been some possibility, albeit a slight one, of bringing miscreants to account; Cicero, for example, prosecuted the governor of Sicily. The late empire confessed impotence to give justice; if a defrauded taxpayer could secure no help from local authorities, he was permitted the comfort of posting his complaint publicly [*303*, p. 275], a dubiously useful if not dangerous act.

The increasing volume of regulation multiplied opportunities for graft and peculation and depressed the economy. The result of Diocletian's decree of death for violators of price controls was a general rise of prices. [*352*, p. 328] When merchants were commanded to proceed straight on voyages to designated ports, making no detours and carrying only the prescribed goods, inevitable evasions brought more decrees and more opportunities for illicit gain. [*303*, p. 234] When the cost of fulfilling a duty became more than the bribe required to evade it, no one could be held to his post. A new set of officials was charged with controlling the controllers, but the more supervisors the more bribery.

As a result, the apparatus worked mostly for itself; by the fourth century, bribery and cheating were universal. Delation became a common business, even of the court. [*331*, pp. 176–177] Army supplies were grossly peculated and lists were padded, to the detriment of military capacities and morale. [*303*, p. 27] Some revenues were entirely consumed by the apparatus of collection. [*312*, p. 440]

Political controls also failed. When associations were permitted for funerary purposes, they became a front for other activities; the regulations had gradually to be abandoned. [*302*, p. 255] The oppressiveness and weakness of the government drove the wealthy to set themselves up as local lords and enabled them to do so. Those who fled the tax gatherers in effect banded together under the aegis of the more potent, offering themselves as supporters in return for shelter. Peasants in some places paid soldiers for protection and put themselves under captains, who gradually turned into feudalistic landlords. [*326*, II, 775] Soldiers also let themselves out to landlords as retainers and rent collectors, with the same results. [*326*, II, 791] Attempts were made to compel division of inheritances, but without effect [*570*, p. 189], and against the patronage of rich over poor the Caesars legislated repeatedly and vainly. [*345*, p. 367] After Constantine, land of the imperial household was given out on permanent leases and became practically private property. [*326*, II, 789] The local magnates became the more intractable as they piled up riches in the midst of the general penury. By the beginning of the fifth century some country estates had incomes of a thousand or fifteen hundred pounds of gold. [*313*, p. 115] The empire no longer even attempted to curtail the privileges and exactions of the aristocrats. [*326*, II, 1045]

By the time of Herodotus, it was unnecessary for men to go about armed, but in the Pax Romana, insecurity returned as in the dark ages before Greek civilization. Brigandage created problems in Italy during the late republic and in the time of Julius Caesar;

Augustus found it necessary to establish armed garrisons in towns to keep outlawry in bounds. [305] Despite continual efforts at pacification, by the second century large bands of robbers were rampaging in Italy and Gaul. [285, p. 327] Under the philosopher-Caesar, Marcus Aurelius, so many peasants fled to the swamps of Egypt that they set up a sort of government in defiance of Rome; and deserters in Gaul and Spain started a small civil war against Commodus. [342, p. 374] The compulsory service laid upon the curiales included antibandit action. In the third century, the bands swelled, as army deserters mingled with refugees from taxes, and efforts to suppress them were unavailing. [330, p. 432] Aurelian felt it necessary to build walls to protect Rome itself. A province of Asia Minor, rebelling against Gallienus, defended itself desperately — as well it might in view of the fate of vanquished rebels — and successfully, remaining independent for many years in the heart of the empire. Unable to reduce it, the Caesars surrounded it with a fortified line. [314, I, 244] Diocletian ended the civil wars, but under his rule peasants were goaded to desperate uprisings; a jacquerie in Gaul, proclaiming a rustic as emperor, was crushed only by much force after many years. [288, p. 73] And Diocletian was compelled to recognize the independence of a naval commander who rebelled and set himself up as ruler of Britain; he lasted for ten years. [314, I, 309] In the fourth century the lines between bandits and officials, between deserters and mercenaries, were often blurred, and travel in the country districts of Italy was highly unsafe. Deserters from military service continually harassed the people; emperors piled penalty on punishment for desertion and outlawry, only to be led by helplessness to pardon those who would return to order. [303, p. 242] Attempts to combat banditry led to further oppression, as when in 399 shepherds were forbidden to own horses. [303, p. 241] The towns generally fortified themselves in self-defense; but in the fifth century, while the barbarians were making hash of the empire in the West, the country districts probably suffered more from brigands than from invaders. [303, p. 379] Even the sacred imperial principle of unity was lost, as the later Caesars had to admit that they could not manage the great empire the republic had put together. In 285 Diocletian handed over the rule of the West to a coemperor, despite the danger of allowing a possible rival to administer large areas; the empire had become unmanageable. By dint of much campaigning, Constantine managed to reunite the empire, but he proceeded to divide it among his sons and a nephew. Thereafter, it was only briefly under a single head, and usually was divided among several ambitious Caesars. Rome did not so much fall as fall apart.

Despite its severely autocratic principles, the Turkish empire encountered equal difficulty in controlling its servants. As it rolled on to conquest, leaders were expected to present booty to the autocrat; when expansion halted, they brought gifts instead, and there soon developed a system of payment for offices and promotions. [432, Pt. I, p. 178] Terms of office were made yearly to provide as many jobs as possible to sell or give to relatives and friends. But the purchased position was a private right, in effect a license to make as much money as possible during the time paid for. [432, Pt. I, p. 196] In the provinces, governors managed, however, to prolong their period of office to life or hereditary tenure, with great slave families like that of the sultan. [435, p. 58] Local landowners came to control the civil and financial administration in many places, and those who could better protect their adherents grew still stronger. [439, p. 42; 432, Pt. I, pp. 198, 256] Revenues from the land were almost entirely consumed by the collection apparatus [432, Pt. II, p. 1], ipso facto virtually independent. Many of the class supposed to do military service took to brigandage, which became irrepressible. The Janissary corps became a power to itself, which the sultan dared not touch lest it overthrow him. The sultan himself, debilitated by his peculiar upbringing, became weaker and weaker and more capricious as he lost authority. The wonder of wonders is that so rotten a structure held together as long and as strongly as it did.

The Mogul empire began coming loose before expansion was completed. Even as Aurangzeb was rounding out the conquest of India, his servants were setting up their own authority and marauders were undermining the state. The governors were practically absolute in their realms, checked by little but the frequent shifts which served to increase their rapacity [202, p. 113]; eventually they secured hereditary authority in successor states. [214, p. 136] There were numerous informers and inspectors, but they usually conspired with the governors to deceive the monarch. [191, p. 231] Banditry was so prevalent and the highways were so dangerous that there was little travel. [209, p. 70] The abused peasants benefited slightly from the mounting disorder, for they were needed as armed retainers to protect the wealth of the great. [213, p. 53] The Great Mogul, on the contrary, became a maltreated and pitiable figurehead.

The drama of decay of power has been played out to its melancholy finale at least half a dozen times in China. Each dynasty, entering with effective centralized control, drifted toward weakness, with ebbs and flows as strong personalities or favorable conditions stemmed the tide or as weak emperors or great troubles sent it rushing onward. Control passed irregularly from the nominal ruler to those around him; many a Son of Heaven became the creature of such men as licked his ancestors' boots. Various groups then waged a struggle for power atop him, like the eunuchs and the literati, the former enjoying advantages of nearness to the imperial person, the latter having control of the administrative apparatus. Officials and favorites grew wealthy although the treasury was near bankruptcy. The civil service became corrupt, like everything else, as positions were put up for sale and so became a species of property. Authority broke down in the grossest manner, banditry taking over the countryside, until larger-scale rebellion or barbarian invasion hardly mattered.

Such troubles are best known from the writings of Europeans in the long twilight of the last dynasty. Under the early Ch'ings, the civil service system was entirely honest and was based purely on merit [43, p. 281]; toward the end, it approached a complete breakdown. The purpose of ideological formation was lost to sight as the examinations became excessively formal, even by imperial Chinese standards, emphasis shifting from classical learning to calligraphy and prosody. [8, p. 203] Worse, money rather than scholarship became the chief means, legally or illegally, of obtaining position. Myriad ingenious ways of cheating were devised, from the purchase of essays, the forging of diplomas, and the hiring of stand-ins to the use of prepared essays, written in minute characters on fine paper, secreted with an index in the scholarly sleeve. [65, p. 122; 76, pp. 450–451] Or the candidate might pay the emperor instead of an underling; sale of office was fully legal and increasingly common as financial needs mounted [56, p. 106], until perhaps half of the positions were filled by outright purchase. [15, pp. 32–33] Methods might be combined; a cash payment served to raise the ranking of examination papers. [*14*, I, 334] Advancement was also for sale, and it might be said that payment was necessary to retain office, as each rank was required by custom to give valuable presents to its superiors. [*14*, I, 322]

Those who rose by study and by honestly passing the examinations were likely to be idealistic followers of Confucian ethics and faithful servants; those who entered by favor or purchase were not. They naturally felt entitled, if they might not have otherwise, to recompense themselves freely for the cost of their positions. They also came to think of high office as personal and then family property. Even within the examination system, they were able to assert some hereditary title to office, as papers of near relatives were graded separately and more favorably. By a typical perversion, the separate grading that helped to preserve privilege was originally instituted to favor poor boys. [*8*, pp. 184–185] At the same time, the civil service itself lost status. Connection at court became more important than official position, and landlords increasingly found means to stand up against the magistrates. [*70*, p. 215]

Schemes of control became worthless. The Mings set up a corps of spies to watch over untrustworthy governors; subsequently the spies had to be abolished because of excessive corruption. [*43*, p. 211] The Confucianist emphasis on filial duty and loyalty to superiors, designed to assure loyalty to the emperor, backfired in nepotism, as each official had the duty of maintaining a tribe. [*20*, p. 93] Frequent shifting of the mandarins hindered their putting down roots anywhere, but the permanent subalterns became real and irresponsible bosses. [*37*, I, 369] The *pao-chia* system of headmen responsible for the tens below them was never fully effective; when the Ch'ing dynasty was a century old it had already degenerated to a formality, ineffective in the face of unchecked criminality. The better men evaded headmanship, while scoundrels sought it for blackmail. [*36*, pp 46, 79] The lecture system, once useful for indoctrination, lapsed into hollow routine or was neglected entirely; on the appointed day the mandarin would walk in, have a cup of tea, and walk out. [*37*, I, 358] Sometimes assemblies to hear the emperor's maxims turned into subversive gatherings. [*36*, pp. 192–195, 201] The placards supposed to be hung in front of each house, listing the inhabitants, seldom appeared, except perhaps when a new magistrate arrived. [*64*, p. 231] The imperial command carried less and less weight in the provinces. A governor who was assessed 1.5 million piculs of rice might deliver only a sixth of this amount, yet suffer no punishment. [79, p. 152] When belatedly the empire wished to introduce Western industry for defense, it was hampered by inability to do away with provincial levies on the movement of goods. [22, p. 13]

Taxation became a contest between officials collecting as much as possible and the people trying to evade entirely. The monopolies of commodities such as salt and tea led to large-scale smuggling or bootlegging; salt inspectors themselves were often smugglers. [65, p. 218] A large part of the currency was counterfeit; this was so common that it was accepted, in conventional proportions, as normal in trade. [64, p. 141] The proverb ran, "Heaven and emperor are far away," and of all Chinese, the Son of Heaven was most freely cheated. [64, p. 111]

In the disorder, as provincial governors gained more or less autonomy, the suffering people also gained a little freedom. If they became so enraged as to beat up an unpopular magistrate, the governor might take the easier course of considering his punishment just. [37, II, 79] Generals and mercenary forces went their own way, as occurred in the fading of various dynasties, and rude and starving soldiery often merged into the troops of deserters and peasant bandits who ranged the country, fleeing taxes or military service. [77, pp. 26–27; 59, p. 26] Bandits were "as numerous as hairs." Some areas the government did not attempt to police; travelers ventured into them only with large escorts. [37, II, 83] The many rebellions were failures, but they sapped the moldering foundations. Tax registers were often burned, and fiscal embarrassment resulted. To protect the officials, each city was required by law to be girt with a wall. [64, p. 243] So far as it could, the regime closed its eyes and ears to all such troubles; and the officials outside ignored them, since to report unpleasant happenings was only to cause embarrassment and possible disgrace. [45, p. 49] Even attempts to suppress rebellion caused trouble, as the troops murdered and robbed [45, p. 51], and generals were not anxious to pacify when they profited mightily from the disorders. [4, pp. 347–348]

The universal empire thus descends into a contradiction: men welcome the firm hand that establishes peace and ends disorder;

yet strength and unity turn into weakness and disorder. Probably disorder is inherent in arbitrary and unlimited authority. It cannot assert a real legal basis, as its constitutional law is a human will. When the rule is force, the instruments of force and the apparatus of control have their own right to rule for themselves. Compulsion cannot succeed without some voluntary cooperation and cannot bind everyone. To combat the abuses, laws may be made infinitely rigorous; while it was a nearly universal practice, bribe taking in China was punishable by death. [*10*, p. 82] But overstrict laws only increase opportunities for extortion and disrespect for laws in general. Contrary to the mores, they cannot be enforced because too many people profit by and sympathize with their nonenforcement. If the basis of the law is violence, anyone who can grasp a shred of power has a right to make law. Under the despotism, many ape the despot: the serf owner, the police captain, and the judge would all, like the emperor, have their arbitrary will. [*419*, p. 93]

It is impossible to keep all powers pulling together unless they share a common cause, and the veneer of ideology can hardly hide the fact that there is little common purpose in the universal empire. When the empire is the world, no one, neither ruler nor ruled, identifies his fortunes with its welfare. As soon as a regime has settled down to enjoy possession of the world and tensions of conflict slacken, the political will turns flabby. The aims of government diverge from those of the people, the former seeking secure and profitable dominion, the latter wishing mostly to be left alone. The interests of the apparatus at the same time diverge from those of the emperor. He wants fullness of power and security for himself; they want the same for themselves, but their security is his weakness and their gains are his loss.

Thus there is inevitably a contest, the one or few on the top trying by all devices they can invent to keep control, all those below who have any sort of position trying to fortify it. In this struggle, the monarch and his immediate coterie have the great advantage of standing over all, acting purposefully, and dividing the adversary by setting one group to offset or control another. The apparatus as a whole can neither formulate positive policy nor act coherently, and any individual in it is at the mercy of the supreme power. Yet the victory seems largely, in the long run, to go to the many small authorities. Deification of the emperor practically requires that he keep out of sight, that is, out of touch with his government. His character probably declines as power gravitates to a loose group of favorites, members of the entourage or royal family, harem favorites, or masters of palace politics. Loss of firm unity at the top means a loosening of authority through the whole system. The court gives no clear direction, and ministers become accustomed to making their own decisions under looser reins. The high figures expend part of their energy and power against one another, leaving more freedom and responsibility to the lower ones. The departments are less coordinated and tend to oppose one another, and the discontented may find support from powers at odds around the less assertive throne. Down the line, lower officials find more latitude to do as they see fit; and the idea of strict obedience fails as the only one really entitled to demand it, the monarch himself, becomes more a figurehead and less a pilot. Weaker emperors, preferring outward loyalty to ability, lean on ministers too weak to threaten them but also too weak to manage their own subordinates. Feeble autocrats distrust those next to them, and the distrust pervades and enfeebles the system. Moreover, as his real power decreases, the emperor or those around him feel the greater need for ceremony and seclusion; thereby his ability to govern lessens, as he accepts honor instead of power.

As the court becomes less capable of forming and exerting a definite will, it must let the apparatus carry on the government of the land; as the apparatus grows by natural process, it becomes more unwieldy and independent. In the ubiquitous conservatism, the bureaucracy turns rigid like everything else and comes to represent an accepted and supposedly unalterable order, strengthened by tradition, ritual, and formality. Official position and innumerable privileges become prescriptive right. There is not much the empire can do against this, not only because it lacks power and drive to hurt its powerful supporters for a doubtful gain, but also because it, too, desires stability above all. The empire likewise becomes a prescriptive right to rule, and disturbance of any kind is anathema. The victorious apparatus then becomes secure and self-governing, stores power for its children, and makes itself hereditary. Thus returns the principle of inheritance, deeply antagonistic to absolute power.

Fear lest ministers become too strong is a reason to give more rein to subordinates. In the general arthritis of the system, it is easier simply to let things go, to let them manage who are on the spot and can hope to meet the exigencies of the hour. In the hostility of the people to the extortionate power, the autocrat finds it as well to shift responsibility to those directly in charge, while he remains holy and apart, probably ignorant of evils that he could hardly repress. And as he loses control of the middle layers of government, as the whole machine becomes stiff and unresponsive, and as the localities become more isolated by the reduction of movement, the autocrat can do little better than allow the local powers to free themselves to some extent from their immediate bosses.

But independent standing permits officials, especially those in the field, to use their strength to enrich themselves, and their riches to strengthen themselves. Those who gain by dishonest practices thereby acquire an economic basis for power, to hire their own retainers, to protect themselves by bribery, and to make their influence felt at higher levels. The treasury is left empty and the authority of the center is as low as it is bankrupt. Without money, it can command little force and lacks means either to reward or to coerce. The peculators, on the other hand, use their growing authority to reinforce those aspects of the system which make peculation easy. Driven by financial need and desirous of sharing the graft [275, p. 35], the regime probably weakens itself further by selling offices, exemptions, and privileges, in effect issuing licenses for private predation. Not receiving enough from taxes, it may raise rates, thereby giving more openings for illicit gain. The oppressed turn bandit, or help and shelter the bandits who harass the oppressors. [494, p. 23] And if one can cheat with impunity, a hundred others feel entitled to do no less. There is little moral compulsion, if officials feel such a drive at all, to turn due taxes over to a corrupt and wasteful court or to call upon a dissolute emperor to act as supreme judge. From the graft of the great to the banditry of runaways, all varieties of venality encourage one another, just as the lawlessness of the sovereign sanctions the amorality of those below.

Incapacity to rule means that the regime becomes useless, and the chief occupation of officials is a continual half war with the people. They have, after all, an immediate and personal interest in robbing, only a vague and distant interest in helping. The autocrat himself would perhaps like to see the people prosperous and to give them justice; but, as the Russian proverb had it, "Heaven is high and the tsar is far away." Even if they could bypass the officials to petition for redress, he could do little to chain the multitude of harpies; and it is much safer to keep quiet. The bureaucrats, moreover, have a positive interest in the unpopularity of the regime, although they may not be conscious of it. As the government is more disliked, bureaucrats become more essential and hence untouchable in the eyes of the enfeebled authorities.

Thus there are various facets of decomposition, the autocrat losing capacity to govern, the agents of the regime setting themselves over the people, local magnates setting themselves up as more or less autonomous and for a price sheltering people beneath them, and the boldest of the poor escaping into disorder and brigandage, revolting not in hopes of improvement but from despair, not against the ideal of the empire but its evil representatives. In different ways, individuals and groups seek to profit at the expense of others or to protect themselves against the profiteers, while insecurity and disorder in turn increase distrust and drive people inward and back to the elemental groups of family or clan. Having brought the world together, the empire lacks a unifying principle. The great would-be universal order turns into disorder, and union brings disunion.

CRUMBLING DEFENSES

If universal empires are intellectually torpid, if they decay in productivity and are riddled with corruption, all this is not ordinarily enough to bring destruction. The immediate cause of downfall has usually been simply lack of will to fight for life. The Persian empire was not toppled because it lagged behind Greece in civilization or because it became impoverished; it still had gold to pay for mercenaries when it had no good fighting men of its own. The ordinary story of great empires is of declining military strength until collapse in the face of relatively minor forces.

The apologists have often spoken of "barbarian hordes" as though the forces of usually unsettled and smaller nations were vastly numerous, overwhelming the empire by their weight. But the numbers of the barbarians are multiplied manyfold by fear and shame; those who vanquish the omnipotent empire must be like the sands of the sea. Rome, when a mere city of moderate size, put great kingdoms to rout, and the civil convulsions of republican times did not halt expansion. [*309*, p. 56] After conquering all the world worth having, when Roman citizens were numbered in scores of millions, Rome trembled before the barbarians of the outer fringe. As early as 6 A.D., when the empire was in its veriest youth, a revolt in distant Pannonia panicked the city that once stood firm in the face of gravest danger from men like Hannibal at its gates. [*237*, p. 202] Even more shameful, the troops with which Rome opposed invasion were themselves mostly barbarians, without whose support the life of the empire must have been much shorter.

The end of expansion itself betokens enfeeblement. Although the conquering empire has grown ever greater and supposedly mightier in relation to the powers remaining around its borders, it becomes less capable of vanquishing them or loses the will to victory. It suffices simply to hold what has been gathered. But as peace is idealized, men lose martial spirit. As the masses are degraded, they become incapable of determined fighting, and the oppressed have little desire to die for their oppressors. There are no remedies but only half helps, like lashing men into battle, hiring foreign soldiers, and buying off the barbarians.

Sometimes empires have so decayed that they fell apart quite of their own weight. The Hans succumbed before the barbarians entered, and the demise of the Egyptian Old Kingdom could apparently be laid to internal causes. Usually, however, some power or powers are ready, when the time is ripe, to rush in and carve up the moribund body; or at least incursions of cruder but more vigorous peoples heighten the disorders. Military capacities ebb from generation to generation, with occasional resurgences under good leadership, until the marauders knock down the gates. For example, the Egyptian New Kingdom began about 1570 B.C. as a great uprising against foreign occupants, the Hyksos, and went on to conquer far afield. But after a century or more, the army was becoming professional and hereditary; by 1380 it was largely composed of foreign mercenaries, who were hired to hold what Egyptians had once taken. [*88*, p. 148; *94*, p. 496] The bureaucracy came to regard the soldiers with utmost contempt, although they were politically potent, and school texts contain many diatribes against the military profession. [*114*, Pt. II, p. 11; *140*, p. 92] After a time, the extra-Egyptian empire, which had been acquired to produce tribute, was held together by subsidies to princes willing to accept its suzerainty. [*111*, p. 265] Foreign incursions increased, outsiders settled in Egypt, and eventually the mercenaries or raiders — categories not always distinguishable — took over the country.

The magnificent Assyrian army likewise decayed and became foreign as the empire aged. [*127*, p. 604] The Persians came out of their mountains to overrun in a brief time the effete Near East, but within a century gold and diplomacy became their strongest weapons. The memorable repulse of the hordes of Darius and Xerxes by small numbers of Greeks, divided among themselves, is a familiar epic. In 345 B.C. the rebellion of Egypt against the Persian empire was mostly a fight between Greeks helping Egypt in order to weaken the traditional enemy, and Greeks, not only troops but generals, hired by Persia to suppress the rebellion. [*249*, p. 125] Artaxerxes had in his army plenty of cooks, cupbearers, and porters, but few fighting men. [*252*, p. 410] Alexander set out to conquer the East with no more than 30,000 infantry and 5,000 cavalry from the Macedonian hills; against him, Darius III depended mostly on foreign hirelings; the great battles of the campaign were of near Greek against Greek over the moribund Persian kingdom. The last Achaemenid had tried in vain to train Persians to fight in the style of Greek hoplites. [*237*, p. 87]

Military decadence should hardly have been much advanced in the Inca empire, as it was barely a century old and was still expanding up to the advent of the Spaniards. But it is no sign of vigor that a well-organized state of some 6 million souls and immense wealth could have been mastered by 130 foot soldiers, 40 cavalry, and one small cannon. The strangeness of the invaders and their horses helped to demoralize the superstitious Incas, and the Spaniards' diseases had helped prepare the way for them. But the much less tightly knit Aztec state offered far stiffer resistance, which was overcome by Cortez only with the assistance of discontented subjects and allies of the ruling Aztecs. Of all the American civilizations, the disunited Mayas presented much the strongest defense, holding off the conquistadors for many embattled years.

Into the India of the sixteenth century Babur marched down from Afghanistan with only 12,000 men, and he overthrew the Sultanate of Delhi with a population of tens of millions. Like Pizarro, he beat armies overwhelmingly larger than his own partly by technological superiority, as he provided his forces with the fire-

arms the Indian rulers neglected [*216*, p. 120], but he owed victory
mostly to discipline and will. Typically, when his army was en-
camped in the snow, Babur refused to take shelter, but stayed
out to shiver with the men. [*199*, pp. 82–83] A century and a half
after Babur's feat, the Mogul armies were chaotic assemblages,
nominally under a single commander but guided by the almost
uncoordinated chiefs of separate units, without discipline or training. [*214*, pp. 131–141] The nobles went to war in palanquins [*199*,
p. 319], attended by countless followers and immense baggage
trains carrying the luxuries of the court [*212*, p. 356]; the emperor
took his harem along and the chief officers followed his example.
[*214*, p. 155] Even common soldiers brought wives and slaves to
ease the hardships of campaigning. [*191*, p. 221] There was little
organized supply, and pay was often in arrears. Horses and soldiers
were branded to make them easier to recover. [*214*, p. 130] Not
without reason, the foot soldiers were regarded with contempt,
and only the cavalry was esteemed. [*199*, p. 348] Such forces might
charge with some blind impetus, but had no steadfast discipline;
checked, they would panic and turn into a runaway mob. [*191*,
p. 55] They were incapable of coping even with robber bands and
tribal intruders. In 1762 at Plassey, Clive needed only 3,000 men,
including 950 Europeans, to put to flight a host of 50,000 infantry,
18,000 cavalry, and 53 guns. British losses numbered only 22.
[*211*, p. 356]

The Turkish empire in its inception was a magnificent fighting
machine. At its heart was the famous, later notorious, Janissary
corps, made up of Christian slave boys selected for strength and
intelligence and trained to severe discipline and absolute loyalty.
Allowed neither to marry nor to own property, they were completely devoted, and often saved the day for less elite Turkish
armies. [*431*, p. 41] But their rigorous order was gradually
loosened. Moslems were admitted, and the members were allowed
to marry, as the slave levies were discontinued. Membership
eventually became little more than a patent for privileges of a horde
of nonsoldiers, too strong to be abolished, but virtually useless for
war. [*432*, Pt. I, pp. 182–186] The corps evolved into its opposite,
privileged instead of slave, Moslem instead of Christian, numerous instead of elite, with membership hereditary or purchased
instead of conscripted; and of the hundred thousand or more Janissaries in 1825, only about 2 percent were trained soldiers. [*439*,

pp. 40–41] The territorial armies similarly decayed. As the empire approached its climax in the reign of Suleiman, soldiers sometimes had to be driven into battle with sticks, and the army could not be held together through the winter. [436, pp. 68, 74] Fief holders of the empire furnished more than 200,000 troops in the sixteenth century, but only 25,000 in the eighteenth. [432, Pt. I, p. 190] Many fiefs, including the more desirable military ones, came to be sold to the highest bidder; they were often held by slaves, eunuchs, or sundry creatures of the court. [439, pp. 43–44] More and more the great martial state had to depend on irregular and barely organized bands, in effect hired for the campaign. Lured by bonuses and the call to glory, they deserted as quickly as they joined; pillaging as they went, they were often more dangerous to the peasants of the realm than to the enemy. [432, Pt. I, pp. 194–195]

China has repeatedly gone through the cycle from matchless strength to utter impotence. The Contending States before unification, although quarreling among themselves, were not menaced by the barbarians without, but expanded at their expense. The armies of the first empires, the brief Ch'in and the Han, marched boldly afield, carrying their banners and their law far beyond the original Chinese homeland into the Yellow River valley, to the tropical jungles of Vietnam, and across Central Asia to Afghanistan. But then the tide halted and began to recede. Eventually the ruin of the peasantry brought the ruin of the old army, which had to be replaced by professional forces. As in Rome, barbarian auxiliaries were brought in and became adjuncts of disorder. Finally, after the regime had collapsed, nomad intruders rode in without resistance. Subsequent dynasties similarly conquered broadly at first, only to lapse in a century or so into feebleness; as was said of the Sungs, "The incompetence of the eunuchs entrusted with command was rivaled, if not surpassed, by the cowardice and aversion to battle of the men." [7, p. 278] In decline they would hire barbarians to defend them against other barbarians and their own subjects, as the T'angs hired Korean and Central Asiatic generals and troops. [40, Bk. I, pp. 200–201] In due course the Chinese again would find themselves victims of a far less numerous people.

How effectively the empire could soften is shown by the experience of the Mongol conquerors of China. Outnumbered about a hundred to one [416, p. 131], meeting little resistance although they came with rapine and mass slaughter, these formidable warriors smashed all Chinese opposition and then swept on even beyond the greatest Chinese conquests. But in less than a century of easeful mastery over the Celestial Kingdom, they quite lost ferocity; the once invincible world conquerors were beaten by bands of despicable peasants and had to ride away to their native plains.

After expelling the Mongols, the Ming dynasty as usual pressed the frontiers far out in all directions. It in turn became effete and rotten. The last Ming increased already unbearable taxes for the army but had almost no soldiers. [4, p. 98] His regime was overcome by a mere bandit troop and then displaced by the Manchus, backed by a population less than a thirtieth of the Chinese. The Manchus then strove more systematically than their predecessors to keep up martial virtues, but they could only postpone the rot. There appeared no new threat from the steppe, but the Manchu forces grew so weak that to keep order they were compelled to resort to local militias, despite horror at such a threat to their power. [45, p. 8] The militia was sent ahead against disturbers of the peace while the regular government troops remained back out of danger; the latter, while consuming three-quarters of the revenue, were unfit to cope even with bandits. [56, p. 204] Most of the soldiers had, in fact, become civilians; they might appear sometimes for a review, but even for this duty they could hire substitutes for a few pennies. [37, I, 397] It was not only by superior weaponry that small European contingents easily beat the Chinese in the nineteenth century.

The spirited civilian armies of Rome similarly gave way to unruly and self-seeking bands of mercenaries. There were not many or strong calls upon patriotism after the climactic struggle of the Second Punic War. In subsequent wars, Rome steadily prevailed — despite stagnation of military technique and gradual decline of morale — through weight, determination, and the absence of military genius in the ranks of the opponents. But from the time of Augustus, popular dislike for military service grew as civic feeling continued to diminish. Augustus himself had no fondness for fighting; he led troops in person only so long as he had to, and then, having secured his position, delegated command as had no Roman leader before him. His army made no such bold dashes as had those of Julius, but relied on equipment and numbers, and sought as much to overawe barbarians as to defeat them. Hadrian, early in the second century, felt compelled, for lack of martial spirit, to assign legions to the defense of their home provinces. [*321*, p. 244; *285*, p. 349] In the shortage of volunteers it was necessary to conscript soldiers; landowners were required to furnish quotas of men. [*320*, p. 27] This meant that military duty was punishment and servitude, from which exemption might be purchased; the army got the dregs, and the prestige of soldiering fell ever lower. Slaves, once subject to death if they tried to enter the army of free citizens, were first used as soldiers in Augustus' day [*308*, pp. 310–311]; increasingly they were offered bounties and freedom for joining. As the most wretched folk were dragooned into the legions, they were branded to keep them there; deserters had to become bandits or seek shelter with great landholders. [*303*, p. 236] In the fourth century, self-mutilation, such as the amputation of thumbs, was a serious problem. Terrible penalties were used to drive men into the army, and burning alive was the punishment for sheltering evaders. [*326*, I, 156, 312] Nor were the upper classes interested in military command; the senators, excluded from officership by a jealous Caesar, made no effort to recover their ancient prerogative.

As a result of such unwillingness, it became difficult to raise armies. After the defeat of Antony in 30 B.C., Augustus had about 500,000 men in his service. [*285*, p. 270] But from the fourth century onward the empire probably could not muster, from a population greater than 60 million, more than 20,000 fighting men. [*331*, p. 96] In 356 Julian had only 13,000 troops, few of them veterans, to face the Alemanni. Even then, the imperial troops were better organized and led than the barbarians, although their equipment was hardly superior; when the Romans could muster a sizable force, even in the fourth century, they could ordinarily beat the enemy in pitched battles. [*303*, pp. 287–289; *311*, p. 27]

As wars ceased to be felt as defense of the homeland, and civilians grew averse to fighting, this was left to professionals. The only interest of the legions became plunder abroad or pay at home. The many civil wars were fought mostly for money, the prospect of a fine donative when the candidate was installed as Caesar. Obedience hence depended on good pay and became correspondingly dubious; aware of their power to extort, the armies made and toppled Caesars freely, even frivolously. By the reign of Alexander Severus (222–235), even a capable and generally accepted emperor could not manage the independent legions. To provide home comforts, they brought their wives with them; the children were first expected and then required to follow the profession. As early as Hadrian's day, one-third to one-half of the army recruits were born to the life, and the proportion rose thereafter. [*326*, I, 22] Many had their own slaves, and they were sometimes more eager to capture slaves than to beat the enemy. [*326*, II, 851–853] Naturally, they were more devoted to amusements than fighting and were better clothed than armed. [*330*, p. 511]

Late in the third century, as pay was much reduced by the incapacity of the state, the soldiers were being allowed to compensate by robbing the people on whom they were billeted. [*326*, I, 32] Under the Dominate, the army was divided into two chief parts, the troops stationed along the borders to oppose barbarian invasions, and those in the interior. The former were degraded and neglected; the latter, hardly ever called upon to fight a foreign enemy but only to keep the people cowed, were pampered. [*314*, I, 539] They consequently forgot martial virtues and, fierce as they were against the peasants, stood in terror of foreign enemies. After Constantine, there were hardly any more tactics and training; and the centurions, tough disciplinarians of the old army, disappeared. [*338*, p. 309] The soldiers even discarded armor and helmets as impediments to flight. [*337*, chap. xviii] The cavalry, a somewhat elite service for which discipline was less important, remained relatively strong, as it did in other decaying empires like the Achaemenid [*249*, p. 131], the Sassanid, and the Mogul. Free peoples of high morale, like the Greeks, the early Romans, or the Swiss of the Middle Ages, were victorious on foot.

The army also became alien. Barbarians were incorporated from the time of Augustus, and their numbers ever swelled. They were sometimes hired to remove a menace and at the same time to acquire a guard, as though thieves were employed as watchmen; sometimes they were captives forced to choose between army service and slavery. [*303*, p. 292] They came to be positively preferred; in the later empire, the more barbarian, the more esteemed as a soldier. [*338*, p. 315] Whole barbarian armies were also called upon to defend Rome. When Hadrian beat the Sarmatians, he did not annex them as earlier Roman rulers would have done automatically, but paid them a subsidy to defend the frontier [*342*, p. 363], and his successors did similarly. Eventually whole peoples were invited or allowed to enter the empire; such groups as the Goths, permitted to keep their arms [*320*, p. 29], became virtual states within the Roman state, with their own military and political organization. [*326*, I, 157] The empire might have succumbed sooner had not its guests also become soft and effeminate.

The barbarians, however, coming to represent the real power, made themselves rulers. In the third century, Gallienus conferred consular ornaments on a barbarian chief [*287*, p. 16], and it became more and more expeditious to name the heads of hired or invading bands as Roman commanders. By the second half of the fourth century, many Germans were generals, consuls, and senators. [*320*, p. 28] They increasingly dominated Roman political life until in 392 the German Arbogartes assumed the title of "Master of the Soldiers" and replaced the emperor Valentinian II with a puppet. [*320*, p. 29] It was an anticlimax when in 476 another chieftain thought an emperor no longer necessary even as a figurehead, and so brought the Western empire officially to a close.

This was the celebrated fall of the empire. There was never a coordinated barbarian attack, and the intruders entirely lacked the purpose of destroying the respected Roman state, but fought against one another for dominance. The final battles were mostly between those in the Roman service and their cousins seeking to displace them. The empire was dissolved, not by defeat, but when foreign armies, none being able to establish clear supremacy, ceased even nominal obedience and set up their own kingdoms.

The Byzantine extension of Rome mustered strength to preserve itself, although Byzantine diplomacy preferred to buy barbarians off so far as possible. [*301*, p. 62] From the first it depended largely on mercenaries, as they were considered more reliable than native levies [*301*, pp. 41–46, 201]; the emperor's personal guard, too, was foreign. [*311*, pp. 360–361] All citizens were supposedly subject to service, but they mostly desired to run away. Hence a tax was substituted for conscription and foreigners were hired — Slavs, Latins, Arabs, Armenians, and so on. Men of western Europe were most esteemed; Catalans in particular were offered double pay. The Turks, too, were called upon to help; in its extremity the supremely pious empire did not scruple to lean on heathens. The mercenaries were good fighters, sometimes inspired with the defense of the millennial Christian empire [Diehl in 292, p. 738], but they were usually greedy and mutinous, ready to loot and despoil, or sometimes to abandon campaigns at their pleasure. Fewer than six thousand Spaniards, having quarreled with their employers, besieged the capital for two years in the fourteenth century, defeating all forces sent against them. [301, pp. 203–205] Twenty thousand assorted West European crusader-adventurers quite overcame the empire at the beginning of the thirteenth century. [311, p. 12] More afraid of tax gatherers than of invaders [353, p. 161], the peoples of the frontier provinces practically invited the Turks to come and rule them. [438, pp. 31–32]

Imperial Russia suffered some of the same disease. The unification of Muscovy extinguished most of the martial spirit of earlier centuries, as the former warrior-aristocrats became administrators, landlords, and courtiers. The peasants, although physically strong, had little stomach for battle, showing some impetus in attack but no solidity in defense. A contemporary commented of those whom Peter was desperately striving to forge into a fighting force that they preferred to hide in the bushes or they "offer prayers that God will grant them a light wound which will allow them to be sent on leave or win some compensation." [379, pp. 37–38] In later times, the prestige of ordinary service continued low because this type of service was often used as a punishment, and the army was filled with vagabonds, pickpockets, gypsies, and the like. No one with money had to serve, for substitutes could be hired. Officers profited by exploiting the labor of men in their command, while neglecting their training. In the early nineteenth century the people seemed to a German to be essentially pacific and devoid of military ardor. [380, II, 315–318]

Military failure has resulted partly from cultural failure; unprogressive in all other areas, the empires have been unprogressive in armament as well. Peter met defeat at Narva partly because his army was ill-equipped; after a few years of energetic modernization he could stand much better against the Swedes at Poltava. In Rome, classical culture once gave a margin of excellence, as Roman armies could meet with good steel and strong shields the soft iron weapons and leather or wicker shields of the Gauls; the latter could win only by overwhelming attacks or wild courage. But Teutonic warriors gradually improved their armor while Rome stood still; in a few centuries they had come approximately up to the Roman level and by skill in cavalry swung the balance somewhat in their favor. There was a similar evolution in China, as the peoples of the steppe were not slow to learn the arts of war and then to apply them against the lagging Chinese. Much more radically, the Chinese in their millennial lethargy fell far behind the progressive West, as did the Turks and Mogul India; nor could they learn when the lessons were painfully pressed upon them. Courage comes harder when one's weapons are manifestly inferior.

But far more than poor weaponry, the empire suffers a failure of manpower despite a large population and high organization. The decline of the soldierly profession means that it is drawn, at least in the lower ranks, from the dregs of society, the poorest, most ignorant, and most miserable. Physical weakness may well be added to moral. It is said that the Spartans laughed at the poor bodies of captured Persians; they probably suffered less from lack of exercise than from undernourishment. Perennial Indian weakness before northern invaders, from Afghanistan or Europe, has apparently been due partly to lack of protein if not sheer hunger. [212, p. 212] The people of the Roman empire in its later days are said to have shown considerable physical degeneration, presumably because of poverty and inadequate diets. Under such circumstances men have little spirit to resist the rude but healthier barbarians.

More generally significant are the fears of the rulers, who tremble more before their own people than before distant and despised foreigners. Absolute monarchy finds security in the disarmament of the nation, itself a potential enemy [232, p. xvii], and monarch, courtiers, and bureaucrats alike are extremely apprehensive of military forces; weakness and effeminacy seem safer than manly spirit and potential rebellion. Julius Caesar limited the carrying of arms by Romans, and subsequent rulers strictly enforced the prohibition. [345, p. 103] The military ardor of Roman citizens died more completely as they were disarmed. As the external threat was growing at the end of the second century, Dio Cassius argued against arming the people for fear of sedition [237, p. 236], and even when the empire was collapsing under the barbarian incursions, security seemed to require the prohibition of military training by local bodies. [345, p. 103] Similarly, army command had to be divided for safety, and authority denied to potential usurpers.

Augustus limited the dignity of an official triumph to the emperor alone, lest generals gain a high opinion of themselves. To weaken the small remaining prestige of the Senate, men of the senatorial class were practically excluded from military service by Maximin (235–238), although the military career was once the only way to enter its ranks.

The first unifier of China, somewhat like Julius Caesar, collected and melted down the arms that had been in the hands of the people. [*40*, Bk. I, p. 93] Subsequent emperors were usually more fearful of internal opposition than concerned for external defense. The former danger was near and visible, and many measures were taken to check the military commanders. A mandarin of the nineteenth century expressed the trouble by a parable: a master was so afraid lest his servants steal his treasures that he had them tied up; when thieves came, there was no one to resist. [*8*, p. 204]

When the empire settles down to mere possession, the military force becomes rather a burden and a threat to the ruler. So far as the empire is truly universal and successful, war becomes remote, unimportant, and uninteresting. Defeat is no longer thinkable, and few concern themselves with the protection of the far frontiers; there is no more engagement of body and soul for the homeland. The pretense of imperial omnipotence relieves men of the responsibility of exerting themselves for it. Religion and ceremonial may be called upon to replace waning patriotism, as they were from early days of the Roman empire. [*314*, I, 10] A historian of the fourth century wrote that men did "brave deeds for truth rather than country, for piety rather than dearest friends." [*353*, p. 119] But to be willing to risk life and limb, to stand firm in the sight of gore and death, men need a sense of personal involvement, an identification with a cause, and a deep respect for their fellows. In an empire no political participation stirs spirit and interest; the people, separated from their rulers, are loath to fight for themselves.

As patriotic violence recedes, war sinks out of souls. In the great order, there is no legitimate forceful contest to harden men; fighting becomes merely disorder or crime. The Spartans shrewdly carried out frequent little butcheries of helots to keep their men in trim. As Bacon said ["Of Greatness of Kingdoms and Estates"], "In a slothful peace both courages will effeminate and manners corrupt." At the same time, the docility that the empire inculcates is not a suitable virtue for soldiers. The levies may march by command and the whip, as they have learned to obey; but they do not know how to hold against an onslaught or to stand against force. Knowing only how to follow orders, they shirk responsibility and fear danger. Taught to bend before their superiors, they bend before the enemy as well. As Demosthenes said, "Though absolute governments dominated by a few create fear in their citizens, they fail to awaken the sense of shame. Consequently, when the test of war comes, everyone lightheartedly proceeds to save himself." ["Funeral Speech," in *327*, p. 137] "If the people of a realm are enslaved," Peresvetov wrote in the time of Ivan the Terrible, "they are not courageous, for an enslaved man is not afraid of shame, nor does he gain honor for himself." [*412*, p. 30] On the contrary, a Spartan said, "We are warlike, because self-control contains honor as a chief constituent, and honor, bravery." [Thucydides, I, 84]

In the hierarchic society, aggressiveness is repressed; one strikes only at weak inferiors, whereas toward strong superiors one learns passivity and submissiveness. Virtue then is not self-assertion and steadfastness, but compliance and suavity, the qualities of those who live in dependence. Manliness and masculinity consist of doing for oneself; the way of the subordinate and beaten, like the whipped dog, is effeminacy. With anarchy and lawlessness go meekness and servility. Nonviolence is better than daring, when the power above is a fate perhaps to be appeased but foolish to oppose, and this is the psychological defense of the defenseless. Many philosophies of patient suffering have served subjected people, from Tolstoyan or Gandhian nonresistance to Chinese Moism, Buddhism, and Christianity. The subjects of the empire not merely become less willing to bleed for their unloved masters; they do their utmost to avoid it. "Now where men have no power over themselves nor are autonomous," Hippocrates said, "their concern is not to train themselves for war but how *not* to seem to be fitted for fighting," since only the rulers profit by their death. With very little to defend and nothing to gain except possibly some loot, peasants of the later Roman empire went indifferently with the imperial or barbarian armies or preferably stayed home. Men can be driven to plow or mine but not to be courageous, dragged into the army but not made warriors. Well known is Herodotus' picture of Persian forces being whipped into battle against Greeks, who knew for what they were fighting. In the early Roman republic, military service was a privilege limited to those who could equip themselves [298, p. 25]; in the later empire, the legions had to be driven into the fray at swords' points. Only the aristocrats, who have a stake in the imperial order, may continue to fight tolerably well — which deepens their contempt for the craven masses — although many of them also prefer to enjoy their ease at home, and the imperial generals usually lead their troops from the rear.

For such reasons, the universal empires are essentially unmilitant; their philosophy is pacifistic, their humble commoners loathe fighting, their despised soldiers are weak, incompetent, and more loyal to their generals than to the distant state. The rulers find it better to rely on foreigners, who have no interest but their pay, than upon their own "children."

Therein lies a strange contrast. While the masses of great empires have often seemed unwilling to strike a blow for their homelands or even for their poor lives, the men of open and contentious societies, like the Swiss or the Greeks, have fought valiantly and usually honorably for money or adventure in far lands. The broken and oppressed hordes hardly think of raising a hand to defend their own skins; men of a different style of life would rather die than turn tail. Xerxes thought men should fight because they feared their master, but a renegade Spartan told him that his countrymen held fast in battle from fear of no man but of law, that is, the sense and self-respect of the community. [Herodotus, VII, 101–105] According to Herodotus, the Athenians became brave and consequently victorious when they became free. [V, chap. 78]

THE AMORAL SOCIETY

If the great empire is lethargic and economically stagnant, if it cannot get its people to defend it, these and other troubles result in part directly from shortsighted actions, especially the stifling of free activity for the ease and security of the regime. But they are deeper than merely ill-conceived policies. The disease of diseases is a creeping demoralization, a loss of community feeling and of the sense of responsibility to something greater than the self or the immediate circle to which one belongs, a loss of purpose in existence. The empire can tell men, in its accepted ideology or style, that they should give of themselves, but it strives in vain to make them feel why. Without good spirit, which omnipotent regimes have been unable to synthesize, there are no good armies, for men look out only for themselves; there is little cultural creativity, because men are not inspired; there is no economic progress, because there is no urge to improvement. In their spiritual fiber, empires rot even while the tapestry is outwardly splendid. When the Roman empire was in its springtime, Pliny spoke of the ills of latifundia but Horace lamented moral decline. The two aspects cannot be set apart, but Horace looked deeper.

Spiritual failure is a product of the basic axiom of empire, the dominion of those who are on top, the rule of power for the sake of power. The empire should be a beautiful utopia, with perfect controls and infinite strength, if it were only held together and administered with complete honesty and goodwill. But imperial dominion itself is a contradiction of these qualities. Where there is no fixed law but an arbitrary will, there is no fixed right but that of power. Wherever power exists, it is likely to be a little misused; where it is unchecked, it is sure to be much misused. In the best of states the police are a little inclined to take a lofty view of their functions and indulge a bit of human arrogance; the unlimited force of the empire is a pressing invitation to abuse. The imperial glory is mastery over people, supposedly for their security but without their consent or control; and if some governors would benefit their charges, many more are open to temptations to profit themselves; plundering of some sort, taking much with little or no return, may thus become the main business of the government and the value of the society. Arbitrary power destroys security and hence morality [465, p. 85]; the corruption of authority shrivels the idealism and generous impulses of ordinary men.

Where there are no rights, there is no moral basis for duties. In a system without fundamental respect for justice, all ethical feeling is sapped. The aim of empire is control over people; and in it the means of advancement is the use of people, the making of others instruments of one's will. Position represents power to dominate and ability to please. With demoralization setting in after Augustus, Tacitus reported, the readier men were to be slaves the higher they were raised, and the "higher a man's rank the more eager his hypocrisy." [*Annals*, I, 1–2] As those above are overbearing, those below are servile, and cynicism and sycophancy invade all. Descendants of those Romans who would sooner kill themselves than betray a secret kissed Nero's toga on learning of the execution of a father or son. [*302*, p. 48] The people fawned so doglike that they insisted on the deification of vile favorites of the emperor, as courtesans, and even Hadrian's beautiful boyfriend, Antinous. [*347*, pp. 105–106]

Where there is no law, a man requires exceptionally firm character to restrain himself. Without an anchor, the personality is set adrift. He whom none can call to account for wrongs and broken promises forgets the meaning of honor. Mendacity, bad faith, shameless arrogance, selfishness, and violence come naturally to strong autocrats of all lands and all ages. Even if they had no such inclinations, ministers or favorites are probably ready to encourage them to set themselves above the people, to indulge in all manner of sport, dissipation, or vice, in order that the autocrats be less capable of interfering with the effective use and doubtless misuse of power by the underlings. But the rotten apple spoils the barrel, and whom should officials and commoners more admire and copy than the highest of all? The atmosphere of the imperial court is usually fetid and corrupt; at best it is servile and infused with falsity; the atmosphere of the imperial state and society cannot be much better.

The imperial order demoralizes also because inequality is its essence, whatever its pretense, as a few are in a position to take advantage of the many. In a state of moderate dimensions, as Tacitus said, equality could be preserved, but when the world was subdued, conflicts between patricians and the people were inflamed. [*Histories*, II, 38] In the conflict, the people, of course, are losers. So far as they are a conquered and beaten folk, they must be expected to behave accordingly, and the masters are more justified in despising them as they grovel. As the masses are impotent, the great care little for their feelings; and as they are ground down, the worthlessness of ordinary humans becomes glaringly evident. There is neither urge nor hope to raise them, and the differences are more humiliating as they are emphasized. The dazzling luxury of the mansabdars made the ragged and starving common folk appear subhuman. Roman aristocrats were afraid for themselves but haughty and pitiless toward the servile masses, and in tsarist times even the lowliest clerk regarded the peasants as near beasts.

The rulers thus acquire a poor idea of human nature, as they perceive the generality of mankind to be so much worse than themselves, creatures of basest fear and greed. This pleasing conviction in turn justifies the use of power and violence. Pobedonostsev, ideologue of tsarism, thought government should be by an "aristocracy of the intellect," because "every man is a lie, weak, vicious, worthless, and rebellious." [R. Byrnes in 393, p. 114] But morality means regarding other humans as worthy of consideration and essentially equals, not merely tools or objects of one's pleasure. The power of one over another impedes trust and communication; and where a few stand high over the dull and passive masses, there can be no general standards of conduct; nor, in reality, can the character of the elite be much better than that of the despised populace. The general rule in China was, be weak to the strong but strong to the weak [37, I, 29], and the district magistrates were mice to their superiors but tigers to commoners. [64, p. 230] Self-indulgence and luxury go with hardness and cruelty, frustration makes personalities harsher, and the incongruity between pretenses and reality of rule makes only for falsity everywhere.

The imperial government, which has ceased to be an expression of the community, becomes its enemy, a visible and feared antagonist. It became the Chinese instinct to avoid contact with officials, as they ordinarily meant trouble. The district magistrate, on the other hand, would ride haughtily through town in his palanquin, barely glancing at his subjects while his bullies compelled everyone to dismount and uncover in his presence. [37, I, 180] The ordinary Turk's feeling for his government was, "You might complain of its lack of understanding, just as you cursed the hailstorm which destroyed your crops, but you were in no way answerable for it, nor would you attempt to control or advise it, any more than you would offer advice to the hail cloud." [G. Bell, quoted by 470, p. 279] But the state, and especially the strong state, largely makes right and wrong; when it is only a collector of revenues and driver of bodies, morality decays except as men feel the need of a code for their immediate and personal affairs.

In the city-state, love of homeland means love of the state; in the empire, they are virtually opposites. For the Greeks, individual welfare was identified with that of the community. But the empire raises conflicts between conformity to the official order and devotion to one's own. Patriotism, a powerful and generous stimulus, fades away in the vast state that has accomplished its mission of general dominance, so ending its great purpose; men have little love for the universal and feebly identify its fortunes with their own. In the second century B.C., when Rome had barely made itself mistress of the Mediterranean, Polybius was attributing the moral decay (which would seem high virtue to a more depraved age) not only to wealth but to undisputed sway [298, p. 86]; and the historians have harped again and again on the selfishness, indifference to civic needs, and love of luxury of the Roman upper classes from the early days of the empire.

Group solidarity is directly proportional to feelings of hostility to or difference from outsiders. Although men may enjoy the prestige of the omnipotent state, they do not feel its troubles or work with enthusiasm for its prosperity. A smaller group, feeling itself in contest with powers outside, evokes unselfishness and makes for better relations among its people; where there is no contest and no mission except the enjoyment of power, apathy follows. The solidarity of the universal empire is facade, propaganda, and resignation.

"It is a bitter thing," a Decembrist wrote from prison to Nicholas I, "for a Russian not to have a nation and to terminate everything in the Sovereign alone." [367, p. 136] All responsibility belongs to those who hold all power, and the people can only let the mighty manage. Politics has no interest for those who have no voice and share; no questions of principle remain, but at most fickle personal followings, like the attachment of the Roman mob for favorite gladiators and charioteers. When the Chinese emperor died, the gabbers in the teahouse would not trouble themselves to speculate on the succession, for it was the affair of the mandarins. [36, I, 117] Indeed, indifference is desirable. To have an interest in politics is subversive; the government decides in secret, veils its workings, and wishes no pressures from outside.

In the great structure, only a few can feel themselves more than cogs in the machine, the ends and inner workings of which are obscure; even the officials below the highest have little participation. Those who might have been leaders in smaller states find themselves, in the great order, mere local functionaries; their victories are no more exciting than the building of a new temple. When the great issues of politics had been wiped away by the Roman conquest, only a petty race for titles fired ambitions of town officials, who had to be content with erecting another monument to Caesar. [345, p. 105] Even in the days of Augustus, Romans were becoming apolitical, as aristocrats shied away from public service and senators absented themselves from the Senate. [*345*, p. 70] After unification, the Russians had no more local history. There were only provinces and capital; everywhere, towns were remarkably alike, and men moved indifferently among them without local pride. [*418*, p. 95]

Only a handful can see themselves as responsible and important in the making of the future of the community whose needs are not theirs. Civic spirit means involvement in something, responsibility before equals, a sense that our world needs us to help make justice and prosperity. [*514*, p. 176] Men work better than strictly necessary and respect the standards of society when no policeman is looking largely because they feel they have a stake in the future and the social order. They rise to the awareness that their and their children's futures are not fated or made by a capricious will but depend partly upon their own good work, that they are not helpless pawns but are capable of actions of broad significance. This was the feeling of the Athenians. As Pericles said [according to Thucydides, II, chap. 40], "We alone regard a man who takes no interest in public affairs not as a harmless but as a useless character." But the empire is or likes or claims to be a practically fated order in which men are dependent midgets. And when the people are treated as mindless, they become so, indifferent and careless of what should not concern them.

A few at the top who have powers of decision, and especially those who are publicly responsible for the direction of the state, may be more inspired. Many Roman emperors, alive to the needs and responsibilities of the world state, strove valiantly to improve their world; even as the empire was becoming monstrously corrupt, occasional Caesars tried to be the statesmen they thought Rome needed. While the common run of bureaucrats were lazy and venal, and backstage influences were sinister, tsarist ministers were often hardworking, honest, and idealistic within the limits of their vision. In the miserably rotten Mogul state, where lower officials were uniformly thieves, higher ones were frequently just and statesmanlike. [*213*, p. 55] Many Chinese ministers were honest and devoted to duty. Some from time to time fought selflessly for reforms; and while petty mandarins were as indolent as sloths, higher officials were busy from predawn to late at night. [*64*, p. 32] This is a rule of large organizations in general: the men who are most responsible are almost certain to work harder and with more spirit, while those at the bottom do more or less what they have to do. But the empire is nearly all lower grades, with a minute top. The best Caesars were powerless to purify their society, and the strongest reformers of the Chinese courts were cast aside. When all authority is sucked to the center, the roots shrivel, so that the best intentions are impotent.

The mass of the empire swallows, and wishes to swallow, the individual in isolated helplessness. Most people need the stimulus of competition to exert their best efforts or to do much beyond the necessary. Idealism is most of all produced by the competition of groups in which individuals feel themselves participants; the team calls strongly for the dedication of its members and justifies self-sacrifice. But the monolithic society dissolves, so far as it can, combinations and free organizations; it is unfriendly to the notion of men getting together for their mutual benefit, lest the totality of the state be impaired. Not even to help the government should men combine. In the dire emergency of the First World War, when local government unions were formed to assist the tsarist regime with supplies, they presently came under suspicion; persecuted by the police, their meetings dispersed, and some of their leaders arrested, they were thoroughly frustrated. [378, p. 132] The state, after all, is supposed to be complete and perfect, and the necessity for spontaneous action is a reflection upon its competence. The only independent groups that prosper are more or less illicit, like palace cliques and robber bands.

For such reasons the imperial societies, so far as one may judge, seem to have suffered a serious lack or weakness of standards of conduct. They have suffered not so much from lusty sins and remarkable perversions as from indifference, less bawdy immorality than apathetic amorality, likely covered with pretenses of virtue. To be sure, Rome at times, as under the colorful Elagabalus, reached a depth of degradation and vice hardly surpassable anywhere; the annals of such courts as the Mogul and Turkish are not for the squeamish, and the grossest sexual indulgence, breaking the deepest prohibitions in human society, has seemed natural for extreme autocracies.

But generally there is little excitement of defiance in the sins of the empire; there is no great inspiration even for evil. Those without ideals are not driven by positive bad motives; they are simply amoral. With apathy comes fatalism, a belief that life is a lottery, or a destiny over which it is not worth exerting oneself very much and which may be influenced more by mysterious influences than by one's own efforts. There is a fondness for superstition, magic, and general credulity, together with a skepticism of ideals. Truth and falsehood are spoken with equal earnestness or indifference, and lying is no burden for the conscience. People learn from childhood to be smooth, probably deferential, perhaps charmingly diplomatic, usually cunning or sly. Laziness is common; Russian peasants, doubtless like all men in such circumstances, saw no point in exerting themselves when anything was liable to be snatched from them. [*396*, p. cxxxv] The working day of the tsarist bureaucracy was only four to five hours. [*360*, p. 183] Work is a demeaning necessity for the poor, and the best hope is to rise to a situation where it is avoidable. Honor does not go far; it is much more important to be clever.

Such seems to have been the atmosphere of the Roman empire in its ripeness. Likewise its half successor, the Byzantine empire, was a murky realm of intrigue, utter selfishness, and treachery, relieved by occasional passionate devotion. [C. Diehl in *292*, p. 775] The advice of one of its leading statesmen was to trust no one, neither friends nor wife, but always to beware! [*301*, p. 151] This was sound advice, for, while the people were fickle and bloodthirsty, the ruling classes were generally unprincipled and capable of any meanness, servility, or double-dealing. Their habit was deceit; their love was for intrigue; their character was as weak as their intelligence was often sharp; their only law was fear and self-interest. [*311*, p. 311] In a contemporary saying, "They are formed of three parts: their tongue speaks one thing, their mind meditates another, and their actions accord with neither." [*433*, p. 35] Not without reason, the Byzantines were regarded in the West as wily and untrustworthy. Gregory the Great wrote of them: "We have not your finesse but neither have we your falseness." [*301*, pp. 146–150, 212] The most theological of peoples, the Byzantines were, in the opinion of their contemporaries, most given to whoring, blasphemy, gambling, and drunken brawling. Westerners were brought in as soldiers, administrators, and diplomats for their fidelity and capacities; despite religious and linguistic barriers, they were given the most difficult and honorable posts. With its excellent situation, Byzantium was a great emporium; but its trade was in the hands not of natives but of foreigners, first mostly Syrians and Armenians, then Italians, who quite took over. [*301*, pp. 220–221; C. Diehl in *292*, pp. 760–762; *529*, p. 34]

Many foreigners observed such spirit, or lack of spirit, in the Russian empire after the sixteenth century, when Hanseatic cities forbade merchants to sell on credit or lend money to Russians. [*390*, p. 147] At that time, it was reported, when Moscow merchants "begin to swear and protest, you may know for a certainty there is some trick underneath, for they swear with the very intention of deceiving." [*381*, I, 113] It was said of the subjects of Ivan the Terrible that no man's word was of the slightest account [*405*, p. 152], and that the tsar commented, as he charged an English goldsmith with making some plate, that all Russians were thieves. [*405*, p. 20] An Englishman in the service of Peter avowed that he could as soon find a Russian with hair on his palm as honesty in his heart. [J. Perry in *403*, p. 35] Another remarked that the Russians, unable to rely on the future, were entirely oriented to the present. [Richardson in *403*, p. 137] When Peter copied the Swedish administrative organization, he failed to copy the local units of government specifically for lack of capable men. [*408*, p. 212] Brigandage and violence were the order of the day, and bandits found shelter and protection with both nobles and common folk. [*408*, p. 248; *384*, pp. 201–202, 220] About a century later a German student reported that the merchants were not to be trusted; that good-hearted peasants, turned merchants, automatically became hard-fisted rogues; that artisans took no pride in their work but were concerned only with appearance and sale, not reputation; and that the "Russian in any enterprise looks only to immediate and rapid result." [*380*, I, 45, 53–54] Facts were turned to suit convenience so freely that it was no insult to tell someone he was lying. [*390*, pp. 51–52] Making a purchase was a duel of wits, usually prolonged, between buyer and seller, the latter commonly enjoying the advantages of false weights, counterfeit and adulterated goods, wares shoddy except where visible, and the like, while the former had only the wisdom of experience dearly bought; and the merchant exposed in trickery would be annoyed, not ashamed. [*396*, pp. 287–292] Merchants in their organizations were hence quite lenient with cases of fraud, having themselves usually risen by dubious means. [*419*, p. 576] Because of general unreliability, they could not buy goods on the basis of samples, but had carefully to inspect the entire lot of merchandise. [*418*, p. 64] In the nineteenth century the merchant guild of Moscow was more than half foreigners; and of 132 export and commission houses, 92 were non-Russian with non-Russian personnel except for menial positions. [*390*, p. 349] Foreign directors were preferred even though they could hardly speak Russian. [*371*, p. 15] Government clerkships in the first part of the nineteenth century were largely filled by Germans, preferred as industrious and reliable. [*380*, II, 197]

A British physician resident in Russia early in the nineteenth century noted that their government had made the Russians servile, obsequious to superiors, and haughty to inferiors. As later characterized by a Frenchman, the nobles were empty and conceited, the clergy cringing, the merchants mean-spirited, and the serfs deceitful and thriftless. [*394*, pp. 1, 33–34] Appearances were everywhere served up for realities, as in the villages Potemkin set up for his mistress, Catherine. After the burning of Moscow in 1812, the Russians made more haste to erect facades than to rebuild. A fake hospital was run only for occasional visits of high authorities, with healthy peasants bandaged and put in the beds to groan. [*396*, pp. vii, xciii–xcvii] The Russians were famed for indifference to promptness, indiscipline in everything, and a sort of casual amorality [*423*, pp. 262–263]; they were typically characterized as sensual, thriftless, fond of display, unmethodical, and unreliable. [*396*, p. viii] At the end of the nineteenth century a British observer speculated that, if the bonds of autocracy should ever be snapped, the Russian masses would "vie in lawlessness and savagery with those of the pre-Christian era." [*372*, p. 89]

Such strictures may be discounted as the superior reactions of persons who did not sympathize with an alien culture, but these persons were no mere tourists; most of them loved Russia and the Russians for all their faults, and had spent many years studying them. One can hardly doubt the correctness of the judgment of a British ambassador to the court of Catherine the Great: "The form of government certainly is and will always be the principal cause of the want of virtue and genius in this country, as making the motive of one and the reward of both depend upon accident and caprice." [*403*, pp. 136–137] And some have noted even more directly the relation between morals and form of government. The free commercial republics of Novgorod and Pskov were widely known for an integrity sharply in contrast with the character of the Muscovites. [*397*, p. 293] Herberstein wrote of Novgorod early in the sixteenth century, not long after the merchant republics had been annexed, "The people used to be very courageous and honorable; but now, doubtless by the Russian contagion introduced by the people who emigrated thither from Moscow, they have become most degraded." [*381*, II, 27] Likewise, after Ivan the Terrible abolished the liberty of Pskov, "it followed that in place of the more refined and consequently more kindly manners of the people of Plescov [Pskov] were introduced those of the Muscovites, which are more debased in almost everything. For there was always so much integrity, candor, and simplicity in the dealings of the Plescovians that they dispensed with all superfluity of words for the purpose of entrapping a buyer, and briefly stated the case exactly as it stood." [*381*, II, 29] Industry had been a powerful support of free Novgorod, the great productive center of northeast Europe [*364*, p. 18]; but state-supported industrialization languished in tsarist Russia. Peter's costly program of Westernization produced some 200 large plants for the manufacture of textiles, iron, glass, and other products; yet inferior Russian goods cost twice as much as imported goods, and most of the plants were compelled by inefficiency to close as soon as government subsidies were ended. [*377*, pp. 390–391] After a century and a half of experience and intermittent efforts at industrialization, and despite low wages, the cost of making many common articles in Russia was double or more that of western Europe. [*390*, p. 352]

In China, tyranny undermined all confidence and drove men to moral isolation, passivity, and indifference to progress [*76*, p. 298], and made them indifferent to ideals and the sufferings of others. [*49*, p. 15] In the handling of money, private as well as public, small sums as well as large, squeeze was taken for granted. Some went so far as to say that all Chinese were thieves and liars [*50*, p. 105]; and all found that the Chinese, trained by generations of dealing with a hostile government, had attained a high level of evasiveness and deviousness. As a Jesuit of the seventeeth century wrote, "Their essential quality is to deceive and cozen, when it lies in their power; some of them do not conceal it but boast of it; I have heard of some so brazen-faced that, when they have been taken in the fact, they excuse themselves by their simplicity." Moreover, "If the Chinese have been deficient in excellent mathematicians, they have at least had perfect astrologers; for it sufficeth to be an able deceiver and to have a knack of lying handsomely, which no nation can dispute with China." [*43*, pp. 237, 223] Indirectness went with suavity, the Chinese, even of the lower classes, being perhaps the politest of people. [*50*, p. 196] If the houseboy reported that his aunt was gravely sick and that he had to take a few days off to care for her, he might possibly be speaking the truth; but it was much more likely that he had quarreled with the cook and would be seen no more. [*64*, p. 66]

A literatus would take joy in slipping a momentarily lent book into his pocket; merchants and customers made sly sport of cheating each other of a few coppers. [*64*, p. 281] False weights, false prices, false goods, and false money were all part of normal trade. [*64*, p. 279] Many carried little scales with them to weigh the coins. [*37*, II, 147] The mutual suspicion of merchants usually required the presence of a third party to make bargains, as has been common in the Near East. The interest rate was 2 or 3 percent per month, but for lack of trust there were no investment funds. Building workers would come late, stop often for tea, pilfer tools and materials, and go home early. [*64*, pp. 254–256, 44–46] All crops required guarding, not only fruit and melons but even grain, which would be snipped in the night with a scissors; many slept in the fields at harvest time. [*65*, p. 162] With no encouragement for excellence, manufactures decayed, those of the nineteenth century being much inferior to those of earlier generations of the dynasty. [*37*, II, 120] But even in the seventeenth century fine wares had been scarce because purchase was reserved for the palace at fixed prices, which discouraged effort and pains. [*43*, p. 158] When late in the nineteenth century the government anxiously sought to foster industrialization for national defense, it was almost impossible. Since officials would grab any profit incontinently, managers would siphon off as much as they could themselves and appeal to the government for subsidies. [*22*, p. 27]

The greatest deficiency was in what Montesquieu called the essence of virtue, the preference for public over private interests. Not in a position to work for social goals or general aims, not encouraged to do so, people forget all but personal needs. No property is secure. Indifference more than poverty makes banditry ungovernable. Hardly anyone thinks of serving the state; public office is either an imposition or a source of enrichment. The autocratic power has no means of getting its servants to feel concern for the property entrusted to them. To be public-spirited seems officious and ridiculous. In times of the Contending States, a Chinese prayer ran, "May it rain first on our public fields, and afterward extend to our private ones." [64, p. 107] Under the empire, the poor had enough to do to keep themselves alive and stave off the harpies; the rich could not afford to be honest and simple, but had to be corrupt, cruel, and avaricious lest they lose their fortune to men sharper than themselves. There was no feeling for mutual help; one would be reluctant to pull a drowning man from the water or to help quench a conflagration [76, p. 382] lest he become involved in complications, just as when a Muscovite was being murdered in the street, people would only watch from their windows. [405, p. 151] Life for the Chinese had meaning only in the narrowest context; for most people it was only a series of mostly disagreeable facts; concern for anything outside the immediate material sphere was wasted effort. [64, p. 89] Missionaries in China met their greatest obstacle not in pagan beliefs but in moral indifference and concern only for immediate and material benefit. [37, I, 179]

In the early days of Rome, as in the Greek city-states, men gave of themselves and their estates to the community. By the early empire Roman citizens had become selfish and indifferent. In the later empire, the horses of the imperial stables were weak because their feed was stolen; private persons appropriated public buildings to their uses or hauled away their stones. [303, pp. 239, 243] Similarly, in the latter generations of the Ch'ing dynasty, paving stones of roads and bricks of unguarded walls would disappear to private use. [64, p. 111] Russians of tsarist days were irresponsible and careless with private and public property alike. Hotel furniture was broken, park gardens were plucked or trampled, and library books were freely torn or lost. [390, p. 98] Uncivic behavior was accepted as normal.

Such demoralization may be ruinous. In the society without direction or purpose, parasitism runs amok, and parasitism in turn kills any remnants of idealism. So far as efforts are turned toward profiting from others, they are wasted from the point of view of the community; if everyone tried to live by graft, all would starve and go naked. But it is more than a waste of energies; it means a breakdown of the better part of society. The useful functioning of human institutions requires that men to some extent look beyond their own and immediate interests and accept impersonal or social values. Humans cannot effectively work together unless there is mutual trust and feeling of common purpose.

If there is much of these qualities, little command or direction from above is necessary; if there is little or none, no system of compulsion is effective. Joint actions can be either cooperative and voluntary, as in a frontier camp, or compulsory and commanded, as in a conscript army; but the better the spirit, the more effective the command. No government can operate without the positive support of a large number of persons; no emperor can work his will unless there are many whom he can trust. If no one is reliable, networks of inspection, spying, and control are worse than useless. The autocrat may enjoy the fact that the officials mistrust one another and find it difficult to join against him; but the less he can rely upon duty, the more effort must be expended upon administration; waste and friction grow, as the substance of the state is consumed by those who are supposed to serve it.

A well-disposed society is easy to govern, because good order is made mostly by the people. Taxes can be low because they are easily collected and the money reaches the treasury and is economically used. But as waste, graft, and evasion increase and become accepted, rates must be raised or the treasury suffers; and incentives to bribery and evasion increase to the further detriment of public attitudes and respect for law. When men desire to assist the common defense, they are ashamed to stand back and the army is easily disciplined. But avoidance of military service reduces the prestige of the army, which is left with those who cannot buy or secure release. Such an army can have little worth; and the more despicable the recruits, the less effort is expended upon them and the less reason there is not to peculate their supplies. It is easy to enforce generally accepted laws; crime is ordinarily kept within bounds by the feelings of the community. With general indifference, crime comes to be profitable, uncontrollable, and prestigious, while those charged with combating it join in profiting by it; as the rulers resort to greater severity, they only increase hatreds and opportunities for extortion. Amorality raises the need for all manner of controls, yet makes the controls unworkable. When no one is to be trusted, precautions must be everywhere. The physician to the Moguls had to take every remedy he prescribed for his sovereign patient [202, p. 83], and the king was ever on the move to escape potential assassins; everyone else, except the poorest who had nothing to lose, doubtless had similarly to be wary of all around him. Yet mistrust and controls fearfully undermine efficiency. Even if it really wishes to improve the lot of the people, the empire may be unable to do so in the face of distrust and cynicism. The Chinese government in the latter part of the nineteenth century could not reform the hopelessly tangled currency, or excused itself for not doing so by saying that the people would regard any innovation as a new scheme to defraud them. [*64*, p. 259]

But idealism does not perish entirely; rather, it changes its focus. According to Pushkin, a gang of Russian peasants locked up the district officials, set fire to the house, and gloated at their screams, but went to great lengths to rescue a cat from the blazing roof. [*413*, p. 70] Indifferent to the official society and the larger community, people turn inward to family, clan, coterie, village, sect, or perhaps a group in moral if not political rebellion, with whom there is felt a community of interest and moral fulfillment, toward whom there is loyalty, sincerity, and dedication, and with whose help oppression may be resisted or at least made more bearable. [*496*, p. 62] Sun Yat-sen compared his people to a sheet of sand [*20*, p. 291]; and the typical village was divided into clans, neighborhoods, religious groups, and socioeconomic classes, quite incapable of joining for any cooperative purpose. [82, p. 241] But within the smaller group relations were very close and adherence was often total; dedicated only to their intimate relations, men were quite honorable toward these, and willingly suffered the greatest hardships for their families.

Russian peasants were oblivious to social interests and intensely suspicious of outsiders; they often killed doctors trying to help them in epidemics, not merely from ignorance but because they were different and seemed to be agents of the regime. [*360*, p. 89] Yet they had great solidarity within the commune, managing their own affairs democratically and accepting responsibility for sustaining the needy. And the large family, uniting several generations, was most firmly integrated, nearly everything being considered collective property. Earnings, even of grown sons, all went to the head of the household. But when autocracy was softened by the abolition of serfdom in 1861, these bonds began rapidly to loosen. [*394*, chap. 2] It seems probable that the tightness of endogamous professional groups in the late Roman empire was due not only to compulsion but to the weakening of broader loyalties. On the other hand, as the Greek polis grew up to absorb the lives of the citizens, the old family and clan bonds were greatly loosened. [*116*, p. 267]

In a somewhat different way, people of morally depressed societies may shake off many weaknesses by leaving the old milieu. As a minority abroad, they gain cohesion; separated from the politics and values of the host people, they develop a sort of internal freedom and sometimes corresponding prosperity. At home, the Chinese suffered moral anarchy; abroad, they found great solidarity. Foreign trade in China was largely left to foreigners, but when Chinese emigrated to Southeast Asia, they were able to acquire a near monopoly of commerce. Much more industrious than the peoples among whom they settled, the overseas Chinese were envied for their prosperity but needed for their contribution to the economy. [*73*, pp. 93, 53–55] Similarly, such peoples as Indians and Arabs, upon settling in Africa or Latin America, have developed capacities for trade and industry which one would hardly have suspected in the homelands.

More striking are the outcast groups that emigrate spiritually. To set themselves apart from the uninspiring mass, youths are likely to seek identification with secret societies or outlaw gangs, much as slum boys give intensest loyalty to their gangs, which have norms of conduct different from and more exacting than those of society at large. Secret societies, concerning which little or nothing is known unless they become successful revolutionary groups, run through Chinese history; and China's stirring tales of dedication and heroism are seldom of respectable citizens but of the blood brothers of bandit troops and outlawed secret groups. [*51*, p. 127] Dissident religious groups, millenary sects seeking a purer life, trying to cut themselves off from the imperial society at heavy material cost, similarly may rise to moral superiority. When Christianity was a persecuted or at best a disliked sect in the Roman empire, the believers puzzled their neighbors by abstention from ordinary pleasures, shows, and public festivities and by their disciplined and modest conduct. [*330*, p. 586]

Such movements are best known from tsarist Russia. Dissenter sects were often puritanical in contrast with the more or less dissolute society around them, socially dedicated, often better educated, given to sober and demanding codes of conduct; and persecution was sometimes intensified precisely because the sectarians were too good an example and were too prosperous. Most numerous were the Old Believers, those who refused to accept the state-imposed liturgical reforms of the seventeenth century. Many, retreating to the northern forests, lived practically a monastic life. More literate than the average Russian, better artisans, much more prosperous despite discrimination, they seemed to be morally and psychologically the strongest sector of the population. [*425*, pp. 52–55; *413*, pp. 26–27] Sundry other peasant groups developed a morality of their own. The "Christs" of the eighteenth century despised most worldly pleasures and particularly renounced alcohol and tobacco; they were modest in dress, careful of money, and generally restrained in conduct. [*387*, pp. 41–46] The Khlysty ("Flagellants") lived in brotherly communities with very strict rules, infractions of which were expiated by striking the head on the ground and fasting. No one was allowed to suffer want, yet the barns were full and the stock was sleek; peasants sometimes said they had a magic of turning stones into grain. [*387*, pp. 80–82] Another group, the Dukhobors, so strongly wished to keep apart from the evil world that they developed their own folkways and style of dress, just as though they were a separate ethnic group. [*387*, p. 89] By good farming methods, they had higher yields than their Orthodox neighbors, and on the average were easily twice as wealthy. [*387*, p. 92] Vaguely pantheistic, pacifist, and quite unorthodox in their beliefs, they were hated by the government, which felt compelled to remove them from their homeland because the good order and prosperity of their villages too effectively advertised their sect. [*369*, p. 269] When a large part of the sect was transplanted to Canada toward the end of the nineteenth century, they retained their attitudes toward government; Mounties were regarded as Cossacks, and census takers as conscription officers; one of their own kind trying to register births was called Caesar and Satan. [*424*, p. 420] No longer oppressed, the Dukhobors lost their raison d'être; communal enterprises languished, their leadership became corrupt, they learned to steal and to distrust one another, and their prosperity evaporated as the group disintegrated. [*424*, pp. 414, 427, 436–437]

Even more remarkable was the economic success of a puritanical sect called Molokane ("Milk Drinkers"). In Siberia, toward the end of the nineteenth century, they were called "Russian Americans" because of their big barns, mechanical equipment, and substantial houses. In one area where land was abundant, they cultivated twice as much land per household as did their neighbors, and sold fourteen times as much grain. Known for their high level of education, they were also outstandingly successful as merchants. [387, pp. 151–162] Such sects were not large, comprising only a few tens or at most hundreds of thousands, and they preferred to live in self-contained villages; if they had been large enough to be hierarchical and powerful, they must have lost their character. They were somewhat like the Huguenots of the autocratic and imperialist France of Louis XIV, who brought persecution on themselves largely because their wealth, acquired by hard work and despite much discriminatory regulation, aroused the envy of less dedicated Frenchmen.

Thus, as the great political order brings political disorder, it turns hearts loose while subjecting minds. Failing its task of ethical justification, the great moral union brings moral anarchy. When the empire is more efficient and better able to dissolve groups and to make all hang from the center, it probably deprives its people more effectively of social purpose.

FAILURE OF REFORM

Various troubles, like overtaxation, pervasive corruption, stagnation, and rot are all too evident even in the fragmentary knowledge we have of such empires as the Egyptian. The records permit their documentation in detail from better-known empires, like the Roman, or the Chinese of recent dynasties. Moreover, these woes could not fail to strike intelligent men of the times, as they compared past with present. And it is eminently in the interests of the autocrat, for his own good name and security and to assure the strength and prosperity of his realm, to treat and cure the disease. Evidently there have been intelligent and well-intentioned autocrats of decaying empires; why have they not been able to use their unlimited powers to reform and restore the state to strength and health?

Some have been superficially or partly successful. At least, empires that seemed about to collapse have rallied to new life. For example, the New Kingdom under and after Ikhnaten was quite weak and had lost much of its external empire, but the new Nineteenth Dynasty recovered much of the old glory. The end of that dynasty saw a worse breakdown of the pharaoh's authority, but the Twentieth Dynasty restored a fair semblance of power. The Achaemenid empire came close to complete disruption under Artaxerxes II; twenty years after his death, Artaxerxes III could congratulate himself on ruling as much as Xerxes held at the maximum, 150 troubled years before. Yet the revivals of Egyptian power under the Nineteenth and Twentieth dynasties were largely the work of Asiatic or Libyan mercenaries, for which the empire furnished the organization and framework of effective action. The recovery of the nearly lost Persian empire was accomplished by hired Greeks. Such restoration is hollow; the renewed Egyptian empire was quickly shattered, and the expanse that owed allegiance to Artaxerxes became the booty of Alexander less than a decade later.

More impressive was the recovery of Roman power under Diocletian and Constantine, after several decades when it seemed to be almost shattered in the middle of the third century. The revival was not only political and military; the economy recovered in the fourth century from the depths of the third, although it did not again reach the earlier level, and fairly soon sank back. After the fall of the empire in the West, the Eastern or Byzantine empire may be regarded as a great rallying or series of rallyings. Justinian, for example, strove to be a worthy heir of Augustus and reconquered much land that had been lost. Several times the Eastern empire seemed near death, only to convalesce to fair health. Various Chinese dynasties have likewise recuperated from grave illness to at least a slight renewal of vitality. The Han dynasty came to grief and lost the throne; after a generation of disorders, it came back (as the Later Han dynasty) and ruled for another two centuries. Subsequent dynasties have enjoyed less marked revivals; thus, the Manchus had a minor reinvigoration after the Taiping rebellion, when, from 1862 to 1874, the administration was somewhat rectified, schools were started, and the government adapted itself to the need for conducting foreign relations. [79, p. 8]

Such rejuvenescences are not entirely heartening. They have never been very strong and full-blooded but have been more like an Indian summer, an afterglow during which the fundamental demoralization and decay continued. [79, pp. 46–47] The Later

Hans never enjoyed the vigor of the first two centuries of the dynasty. The Ch'ing revival was brief and shallow; soon the dynasty was again on the road to degradation and ultimate ruin. The Dominate of Diocletian pulled together the Roman empire only to straitjacket it; and the fundamental dissolution proceeded more rapidly than before, carrying it to impotence, at least in the West, in little more than a century. When it was again overtaken by disorder, no salvation was possible.

Such revivals are unsatisfactory also because they seem to be much more an outcome of disorders than of reforming will. It is as though power must be partly broken in order to be rebuilt, and the system must be badly shaken to be solidified; each of the mentioned restorations was preceded by long and fearful civil wars. Although capable individuals must have been necessary to take advantage of opportunities, the respective empire apparently earned a new lease of life through its convulsions. In upset times, the parasitic apparatus is knocked down, men gain the independence of anarchy, easy and slothful ways are lost, people are put upon their mettle, realism returns, and the air turns healthier. Men are faced with obvious dangers and the need for change, while the structure of order and control falls partly to the ground. By this token, one might say, the fuller and longer the breakdown, the cleaner the slate for a renewal of the empire, while a brief or partial breakdown permits only a partial revival. Otherwise expressed, within the sphere of the universal empire there are naturally fluctuations between order and disorder; if the realm swings far in one direction, it is likely to swing correspondingly back. As vested interests and entrenched powers are swept away by turmoil, the stage is prepared for a strong rule to impose itself again; vice versa, as a strong rule removes independent powers, it paves the way for eventual fuller breakdown. Similarly on a smaller scale, disorder at the center often leads to a reaction; after the fears and revulsion aroused by a Nero, a Domitian, or a Commodus, there came the relative decency of Vespasian, Nerva, or Septimius Severus. Contrariwise, complacency or perhaps boredom engendered by a time of fairly decent and orderly government may facilitate the ravages of a capricious despot.

Thus the empire can be reformed or made reformable by a breakdown, much as an earthquake might facilitate slum clearance and rebuilding. Conscious order and policy can also seek to amend the ills and set the power aright, but success is not conspicuous. Usually the reforms, even if intelligent, fail to alter the bases of the regime and are shortly frustrated by conservative forces. For example, Pertinax in 193 A.D. tried to restore honesty and frugality to the state nearly ruined by Commodus. An eminent and respected soldier, he was in a better position than anyone else to attempt this purification; but he was overthrown in less than three months by the Praetorians, beneficiaries of the customary extravagance. [314, I, 88–89] The hard-fisted Septimius Severus had then to fight many battles to restore order to the state. Even in the rankly corrupt and fetid Turkish court there was sometimes a realization that the courtiers must sacrifice momentarily a bit of personal interest to permit the state to live; but substantial reform was impossible. Early in the eighteenth century a treasurer presented a detailed program of salutary changes which, if carried through, should have made Turkey a new power. He was involved in intrigue and executed. [439, *passim*] The Janissary corps often checkmated attacks on corruption, resisting violently any reduction of its perquisites. Early in the nineteenth century, Sultan Selim III extirpated this cancer, slaughtering more than 100,000 [434, p. 274]; but there was no salvation. The rot went on for another century until radical defeat, loss of imperial possessions, and revolution shattered the old order.

Chinese ministers, soaked in Confucianist doctrines, have often proposed great reforms for the salvation of order; usually purged for their pains, they have never been remarkably successful. The reformer who has left the clearest mark on Chinese history was Wang An-shih, who tried to save the declining Sung dynasty at the end of the tenth century. His proposals, inspired in part by the ideas of Wang Mang nearly a thousand years earlier, were implemented over a period of sixteen years with the help of a sympathetic sovereign. They included various measures of state control of the economy, the regularization of local government, the refurbishing of the *pao-chia* system of responsibility for the keeping of order and payment of taxes, the reform of taxation, the state trading system, loans to farmers, state granaries, and the modernization of the examination system to make it a test of real ability rather than merely of classical learning. [47, pp. 5–6] The aim was to strengthen the state and improve the bureaucracy while regulating the people for their benefit. The results left much to be desired.

While Wang proposed to ameliorate the lot of the people, he helped the treasury more by the stringency of tax collections. The lower officials failed to carry out measures as intended but used them rather as means of gain. [47, pp. 115–116] And the reform depended on personalities in the palace. Decease of Wang's patron led to an antireform of eight years; afterward many of Wang's measures were restored for several decades, but they were decided by personal intrigues. [47, p. 96] Worst of all, the reforms were shortly followed by the fall of the dynasty, just as the earlier and similar measures of Wang Mang had been the prelude to years of conflict. In fact, the reforms fortified the vices of power. Strict conformity and intolerance of dissent replaced the relative tolerance that had graced Sung China, as dissent was held to be sabotage to the movement. The secret police was strengthened. A single interpretation of the classic books was made obligatory, and in the atmosphere of conformism all examination papers came to read alike. It became impossible even to hint at faults in the state lest criticism be implied. [47, pp. 88–90]

The more famous reforms of Peter the Great, which did much to modernize the antique Russian state and bring it into the West, suffered the same vice of increasing state power. He accomplished much; for example, after his defeat at Narva by forces only a fourth (some say a tenth) as large as his own, he built a disciplined army and an artillery quite up to the standards of his day. [379, pp. 134–135] He also managed to overcome much of the old prejudice against commerce and industry. [398, p. 121] But while superficially Westernizing, Peter was hardening the non-Western essence of the state. He reverted to the older view of the realm as his personal patrimony, contrary to the slightly more liberal tendencies of the weaker regimes of preceding generations; he strengthened or restored the service obligations of everyone; he unified and extended the bondage of serfdom. [398, p. 150] Moreover, his reforms were made for power under military necessity and external stimulus only [388, IV, 60]; he had only one year of peace in a thirty-five-year reign.

After Peter, Russia continued the salutary habit of borrowing, but lessons were difficult to absorb except when the need was driven home by defeat. Victory, on the contrary, was stultifying. Thus, after the great achievements and high prestige gained in the Napoleonic wars, Alexander I gave up the notions he had been fondling of amending the state, and turned to mystical visions of destiny. After him, Nicholas I made stern efforts to exclude foreign and liberal influences in his garrison state. Devoted to the military, he attempted to clean up corruption while operating a personal despotism; he particularly tried to perfect the army, and was credited with success. [*380*, II, 303] But the humiliations of the Crimean War showed that the rot had only gone deeper. Defeat then brought a decided improvement of public morality and made substantial reforms possible. [*419*, p. 212] In rapid sequence, Alexander II carried through the emancipation of the serfs, establishment of organs of local self-administration, remodeling of the judiciary, and modernization of the army.

Obvious foreign danger is a much more effective argument for change than insidious internal malfunctionings. Indeed, a foreign enemy is sometimes used to unite society and to make possible measures otherwise unacceptable. But rigidity has often been such as to inhibit the most necessary changes in the face of the greatest clear and present danger to the very life of the state; or, as soon as the need recedes a bit from view, the half measures taken are apt to be withdrawn. This occurred even in an empire as relatively receptive to foreign influence as the Russian. In practice, emancipation was so managed that the Russian peasants were little improved economically and were left tied to the villages. The self-government organs, the zemstvos, as soon as they began to assert themselves, aroused the hostility of the regime and were more and more hamstrung; the bright hopes of progress with which they were inaugurated came to almost nothing. The liberalization of the court system conflicted with the need for political prosecutions and was neutralized by giving more powers to the police. A half century after the Crimean War, defeat at the hands of the insignificant Japanese again showed fearful rottenness and weakness; this time the tsar was compelled to concede a semiconstitution and an elected representative body. This, however, was soon made highly unrepresentative to make it compliant and conservative, and was allowed only limited powers of debate. The essence of the bureaucratic structure could not be touched. Defeat in the First World War, two revolutions, and years of civil war were necessary to smash the old order and to permit a new and stronger one to arise on the wreckage of the old.

Successive Chinese dynasties have showed complete incapacity to adapt in their decline, or, it might be said, have declined and fallen because of inflexibility. As the Mongols were knocking on the gates, the Sungs continued to quarrel over academic precedent. After the Mings had been driven out of the capital first by bandit-rebels and then by the Manchus, they might well have ejected the invaders if they had only mobilized the still considerable national forces. But they thought mostly of keeping up the luxury and pomp of the court, and spent their shrinking revenues on revels, dramas, and banquets instead of supplying the army, while the habitual intrigues prevented support for energetic generals lest they become strong. [4, pp. 167–170] The Ch'ing dynasty equally failed to turn back on the downward road. After humiliating defeat by Britain in the Opium War (1842) and great and dangerous uprisings, there was a short reform period, as already noted; and minor efforts were made to take over Western technology; but these passed with little trace. After a still more humiliating defeat by Japan in 1894, the emperor tried seriously to Westernize, decreeing many reforms, most importantly the basing of the civil service examinations on Western learning. The people obediently turned to Western stud-ies, and Western books were briefly much in demand. [65, pp. 134–135] But the Dowager Empress and the reactionary court ended the reformers' Hundred Days by proclaiming the emperor ill, set-ting him aside, and arresting the reform party. [51, p. 12] The dynasty then continued blithely on the way to degradation. Only after nearly forty years of disturbances and fifteen of invasion and war could a new and stronger state arise on the ashes.

It is difficult for any state to recognize that it is deeply imperfect and in need of fundamental change, but the difficulty is vastly com-pounded for the inherently conservative, closed, and pompous empire. The regime is too accustomed to taking pretense for reality to make great sacrifices to improve itself. All the influences that conspire to reduce intellectual inquiry and make for cultural and social rigidity operate likewise to hinder perception of evils, analy-sis of causes, and adoption of improvements. Unless men see clearly what can and should be done, there can be no useful reform; a few men at the top, even if enlightened, cannot do this alone. It re-quires open and frank criticism, something excessively difficult for the imperial order, which can neither permit opposition nor com-mand truth and sincerity. Any society tends to screen its basic faults, and they are easily kept hidden unless oppositions can freely operate; and realism comes especially difficult for a failing society. In the empire, the elimination of rival powers leaves only the emperor and his immediate servants able to introduce, or perhaps even to suggest, reforms. But the ruler is largely relieved of the necessity of thinking, certainly of thinking deeply about anything but the maintenance of his personal station, and many persons have an interest in his thoughtlessness, for ideas are disturbing to prerogative.

Nor is there any suitable group to execute reforms if they are decided and decreed. If the attention of the ruler must move things, the area of success can only be as large as that which he can personally oversee. Those who would have to change things are the beneficiaries of things as they are, and they soon manage to bury reforms or learn to negate them. In the fourth century a Caesar, to combat the fearful corruption of justice and to protect the weak, established the post of public defender in each city; as this official had to be chosen from the official class, nothing was improved. [326, I, 145] Good policies administered by the corrupt classes are turned to ineffectiveness, or become bad policies. The puritanical laws of Augustus were almost a dead letter within a decade except as they were useful for extortion. [308, p. 218] The T'ang set up a fund to normalize grain prices by buying in good years and selling in bad; this salutary measure became another means of squeezing the peasants, who were compelled to sell grain at low prices, while the capital was employed in extortionate loans. [59, p. 36] Effective implementation of policies requires personnel interested in their implementation.

In the same way, reform is impeded because it implies a change in the power structure, a sacrifice by the elite. If a wise emperor should be found willing to surrender some authority for the greater good, a host of people are likely to murmur the agreeable message that he must conserve the fullness of power, some on principle, some because they enjoy wielding powers nominally his. And no ruler can go strongly against his supporters. Romans recognized that the decline of agriculture was due mostly to overtaxation [326, II, 812], but too many influential people profited and no cleansing lasted. Russian tsars held back from clearly needed reforms, as the granting of legal equality to the peasant majority, because they feared injuring the gentry class upon which they rested. The monarch is not a free agent but part of an apparatus with which it is dangerous for him to tamper seriously. He is part of an elite, but no elite can check itself.

Reform is the more difficult for the aging autocracy because it is inherently irrational and rests upon habit. When the foundations are shaky, any disturbance is dangerous, and opposition becomes revolutionary. As the structure grows more brittle, it cannot bend for fear of breaking. If change is admitted in principle, there is no surety that it can be held within desired limits. At best, innovations are justified by some tradition or accepted value. When Ivan IV was crowning himself tsar, he claimed to be upholding ancient rights, whereas he was introducing gross novelties. [373, p. 179] The legislation of Suleiman, dubbed "The Lawgiver," professed to be, and mostly was, restoration of old ways. [435, p. 160] Especially do rulers of an outworn empire find it necessary to uphold the well-worn and accustomed; reformers of late nineteenth-century China tried to base their proposals on Confucianist doctrines. When the dam is near bursting, injudicious repair may loose the flood, like the summoning of the Estates-General (itself called up from the distant past) by Louis XIV. The weakening empire lacks the strength to make measured changes and fears that any admission of inadequacy will call more policies into question until perhaps the whole order comes tumbling down. As the aging state becomes more conservative from long habit, it may even reassert the more emphatically the value system that is threatened; the less sure it feels of itself, the less inclined to admit serious examination of its fundamentals.

More basically, the imperial order cannot really reform itself from within because of its intrinsic nature. As a system of rule for the sake of ruling, it cannot make the interests of the regime correspond to those of the generality, nor can it restrain its own power. To the contrary, the reforms it makes are directed toward fortifying the central power and so strengthen the fundamental vice and illness of the overgoverned and overcentralized society. The ruler cannot be expected to think of improvements except as carried out by himself and basically for his power. The regime regards its strength and welfare as equivalent to those of the whole people, and troubles can be attacked only by new decrees or reorganizations, not by granting real freedom. Great reforms, like those of Peter or Wang An-shih, were designed above all to give the regime better means of action, externally or internally. While

complaining of bureaucratic abuses, the ruler reinforces bureau-
cratism by his determination to control. Peter, as an intelligent
Westernizer, wanted his people to have virtues of self-reliance and
initiative; still more, he wanted them to be totally obedient. He
would have slaves with the virtues of free men, but the slavery was
essential and the freedom incidental. Hence he sought to improve
only by force and failed to purify the vitiated state. [*388*, IV, 44;
407, p. 135] When Turkish sultans tried to curb abuses of pashas or
Janissaries, it was above all to restore the autocratic power. Early
in the eighth century, the T'ang emperor set about eliminating
the waste and corruption of the previous reign and regularizing
taxes; while some graft was eliminated, the main effect was more
centralized control of the economy, more taxes for the treasury,
and soon greater waste than ever. [*59*, p. 26] Ironically, it was the
relatively sensible and moderate successors of Domitian who made
or permitted big inroads on local freedoms, which the tyrant had
left alone. [F. Oertel in *291*, p. 259] Under the mild rule of Nerva,
provincial governors got out of hand [R. Longdon in *290*, p. 204],
to the misfortune of the towns. When Hadrian subsequently sought
to restore their finances, the result was further loss of autonomy.
[*330*, p. 343] There is salvation neither in relaxation nor in the
fullest use of power. To save itself, the sick empire needs new
purposes beyond rule and exploitation; but this change requires
that it should cease to be itself.

If the sick empire is unable to undertake a radical cure, nonetheless it might be possible for a young and healthy one to do the
necessary to guarantee its health. But it is hard to bestir oneself
to repair the roof in sunny weather; and perhaps only the Chinese,
acutely aware of the mortality of preceding dynasties and assiduous in the study of history for the benefit of politics, have done
much consciously to avoid the fatal mistakes of the past. Especially
the latest dynasties, the Ming and the Ch'ing, studiously tried
to make themselves immortal by analysis of the vices of their
predecessor, drawing lessons that were more cogent as the culture was stable. In the result, these dynasties lasted 276 and 267
years, respectively; it is hard to guess whether they lasted longer
than they would have without consciously taking lessons from
history. In any event, the most emphatic reform was not successful. This was the elimination of eunuchs, conspicuously asso-

ciated with the ruin of earlier dynasties. The founders could not bind their successors; as these grew up in the palace atmosphere and mentality for which eunuchs were suited, the latter returned to service and to power. Later in the dynasty, historical comparisons may have actually proved more demoralizing than instructive, as scholars, cognizant of the classic symptoms of decadence but unable to bring improvement, despaired and sometimes saw no better course than withdrawal of support from a sinking regime.

So far as the central problem of the empire is demoralization, this suggests a theoretically simply answer: engineers of souls should systematically use the imperial power to indoctrinate, to give right attitudes and sound values. The great empires need ideologies or faiths in order to function tolerably well, and it is reasonable to suppose that if the ideology were perfect or were perfectly propagated, it would solve the problems of corruption and independent self-seeking and keep the empire happily integrated. If all were good Confucianists, or Stoics, or Christians in the sense of Constantine's church, most troubles would vanish. Indeed, it is inconceivable that Chinese dynasties could have lasted as long as they did and retained so much vitality but for the Confucianist morale. Giving philosophic reasons for obedience and loyalty, Confucianism was driven deep into men's minds by unending education for the examinations; its thorough assimilation was a prime means to success, and men who rise by mastery of a doctrine are likely to be sincerely devoted to it. Consequently, one of the most striking facts of decadent dynasties has been the persistent foci of exemplary dedication in the midst of general putrefaction. Augustus, feeling morality already much lowered in the empire, which had only recently reached its full extent, revived old rites, dedicated new temples, and did whatever he could to restore the values of the republic. Moreover, classical education then and until the fall of the empire stressed vigorous political traditions incongruous with the imperial society. Perhaps the long vitality of Rome owes much to such factors; and if education had been more thorough and better managed in the Roman as in the Chinese empire, the imperial structure might have stood yet firmer.

Thus it might seem possible in principle that a wise empire could better study the basic causes of decline and eliminate them permanently while using its monopoly of power to mold character and develop the morality necessary for the smooth functioning of the machine. The central power might even educate itself to the need to limit power, prevent abuses, and permit enough freedom of groups and individuals for social health, fostering active competition in salutary ways while teaching the people not only to be submissive but to be positively desirous of the public good.

Even if such self-education is possible, it is supremely difficult and, of course, has never been done with more than partial success. It is much easier to inculcate outward subordination, habitual obeisance, or passivity than unselfishness; stamping out dissent, the emperor makes cynicism. The individual is much more influenced by the effective than the proclaimed values around him; fine but empty words produce not virtue but duplicity and hypocrisy. Indoctrination is ineffective where it clashes with experience. The people may be absolutely convinced that they must adore the emperor, but when they see others helping themselves at his expense they do likewise, even while bowing to him. The spirit is shaped much less by formulas and sermonizing than by circumstances. In the fourth and fifth centuries the Christian church, backed by the Roman state, preached vigorously a new and stricter standard of morality supported by the most fearsome sanctions of eternal retribution; but there was no visible improvement. [326, II, 979] The most theological of empires, the Byzantine, has been reputed as among the most dissolute.

The most difficult to moralize are probably not the people at the bottom, usually submissive, aware of their weakness, and humbly incapable of doing much harm, nor those on top, who are more engaged in the success of the system, feel its fortunes as their own, and are grateful for the rewards it has given them, but the great middle layers upon whom administration rests. They lack the satisfactions of real participation, yet have opportunities for predation which the populace lacks. For the empire to function well, they must use their positions of subleadership for the general as well as their private good. But it is easier to train men to passive than to active obedience. Rulers can purposefully make character only within narrow limits; as Theognis said, "It is easier to beget and raise a man than to put good sense in him. . . . You will never make the bad man good by teaching." [327, p. 40] At the same time, training can never be separated from the relations of the trainee to his teachers and to his fellows; and the emperor can hardly make others much better than himself. His position is essentially an assertion of the superiority of power; he is fundamentally a poor example even if he tries to do good, and he cannot really indoctrinate himself. The official is more influenced by the example of those above and around him than by anything they say, and when some start to help themselves — as can never be entirely prevented — others cannot resist doing the same. The monarch who sees the realm as his estate may wish wise laws to secure its well-being, but he cannot keep his servants from feeling that it might as well be *their* estate.

Perhaps, then, the empire could be healthy indefinitely if it could only guarantee itself a higher inspiration and purpose. But this is like asking that turtles improve themselves by flying. Purpose relates to something outside or above. When the state is complete, unchallenged master of its world, the purpose of the powerful within it is to gain for themselves as large a share of its power and benefits as possible; that is, to advance at the expense of their fellows. The motto of the ruler, as stated by Gibbon, is: "Divide what is united, reduce whatever is most eminent, dread every active power" [*314*, I, 540]; and those who exercise power in his name have corresponding drives for themselves. It is logically contradictory for power voluntarily to limit itself; limits are accepted as imposed by necessity or opposing forces. Caesar may want the appearance of a free Senate supporting him, but even more he wants a tractable one. Political systems grow out of circumstances; they do not purposefully make or remake themselves, and the autocrat cannot fundamentally change the autocratic system of which he is exponent and beneficiary. As Montesquieu said, despotic government "is ruined by its own intrinsic imperfections, when some accidental causes do not prevent the corrupting of its principles." [*Spirit of the Laws*, VIII, 10] The universal empire can really reform only by ceasing to be itself.

DECLINE OF EMPIRES

Having eliminated all real enemies, the universal empire claims totality and immortality, and those over whom it holds sway may well imagine it as broad as the sky and as eternal as the stars. Stability is its aspiration and vaunted virtue; having achieved all power, why should it not live forever? Whatever its vices, it holds massive resources and an organization none can challenge. It has immense prestige; the barbarians could not conceive the destruction of the Roman empire, and to this day men have shared some of the amazement of the Romans that Rome should fall, as though this were a visitation of divine wrath. Like those of St. Augustine's day, modern scholars have been much more impelled to seek explanations of the downfall of the grand empire than to account for the end of Greek independence and creativity; yet the latter was indeed a calamity for civilization.

The great united state is unstable; and the declension of Rome seems mysterious mostly because of the mystique and fascination of great power, the people's and historians' awe of the only universal empire of the West. Less amazing than the fall was the length of life from the sack of Carthage and Corinth in 146 B.C. until the sack of Rome by Alaric in 410 A.D. or the deposition of the last Western puppet emperor in 476, a longevity of 555 or 621 years. All such empires have similarly rotted and become too feeble to defend themselves or have simply collapsed, and almost all more quickly than the Roman. Among universal empires, only some of the most ancient seem to have lived longer. The Indus Valley civilization is credited with having endured in stability, and supposedly in imperial order, for some six or seven hundred years, from about 2400 to 1800 B.C. The span from the unification of Egypt until the breakup of the Old Kingdom may have approached nine hundred years, but unification was incomplete during the first part of this period. Others of which more is known have been less nearly eternal. The New Kingdom lasted a fairly normal half millennium, much of it occupied in disorders and weakness. Perhaps because of much greater exposure to invasion from all sides by large armies, the most successful empires of the ancient Near East — Babylonian, Hittite, Assyrian, and Achaemenid Persian — have had much briefer lives, hardly passing, in their high glory, two centuries. The period from the victories of Cyrus, establishing Achaemenid greatness, to those of Alexander, destroying it, was only some 220 years. Yet the Persian empire was not merely overcome by a strong new power; it was thoroughly rotten when Alexander stabbed through it as an axe goes through punky wood. The Turkish empire subsisted in fair strength for nearly three centuries from the taking of Constantinople in 1453 to the serious defeats of the first part of the eighteenth century, and it lingered on until the First World War, an almost unbelievable record for an empire lacking geographic advantages and superficially seeming arbitrary and poorly organized. The Mogul empire of India was much less resistant. In less than two hundred years after the founding by Babur (1526) it had fallen into extreme debility; the British and French came in the eighteenth century, not to overthrow a vital state, but to take advantage of its disintegration.

The solid mass of China has seen a sequence of great empires, but none has approached immortality. Although the sublime dynasties of China reputed themselves millennial, they have in fact not held authority so long as the royal houses of France, Austria, or England. The longest, the Han, held out 442 years, but it was practically two dynasties with an interlude of decades of chaos between the Former and Later Hans, much like the interval of strife in the middle of the third century which separated the Roman Principate from the Dominate. After a long division and a brief unifying dynasty, the T'angs held power for 280 years, only to collapse in the usual administrative incapacity, impoverishment, famines, banditry, and rise of local powers. [61, p. 193] No dynasty after them sustained itself so well. The Sungs, emerging after sixty years or more of disorders, within a century were suffering the same old administrative and financial troubles, with a swollen and corrupt bureaucracy, large landholders avoiding taxes, and peasants fleeing to them for protection. In less than two centuries nomad peoples occupied the northern half of the country, while the Sungs held on to the southern part for more than a century until the Mongols swept all before them. The Mongol (Yüan) dynasty became utterly weak in less than a century and was expelled by a native uprising, and the Ming and Manchu dynasties fell into degradation somewhat more rapidly than the T'ang long before them. Western powers pressing against China in the nineteenth century found only a shell. None being in a position to make China its sole colony, they sought rather to preserve this shell than to complete its destruction. Only the help of Britain enabled the dynasty to survive the great Taiping rebellion of the 1850's.

There is no regularity in the life span of great empires. By the examples mentioned, two to five hundred years might seem normal. But the grandchildren of Genghis Khan, who conquered more widely than anyone before or since, could not hold his heritage together; and the failure was not only family dissension and distance from the capital to the provinces, but corruption in the administration and in the intriguing court. One might suppose that there was simply too much empire for too few Mongols, but it is not clear why those who could conquer should not be able (with foreign advisers, especially Chinese) to administer, except that they had a drive for victory but no ethos for management.

The opposite extreme is the Byzantine empire, which continued nearly a thousand years after the fall of Rome in the West, in a continuity much more remarkable than the breakup of the Western empire. It may have survived at the time barbarians were marauding over the West largely because it was less exposed to incursion and had a solid base in Asia Minor. [278, p. 95] Yet, beginning from a low level of vitality, the Byzantine empire repeatedly mustered new strength; and it was more absolutist in theory than in practice, with some appreciation of the importance of trade and a good deal of party strife garbed as religious controversy. [311, *passim*] One source of strength seems to have been a constant influx of new blood. The empire always relied on mercenary troops recruited abroad; after finishing their service, these troops were not sent away but were given landholdings and thus incorporated as fresh elements into the life stream of the empire. This system was, of course, similar to the old Roman practice; the Byzantines simply managed better to keep the newcomers from asserting independent power.

Another and perhaps more important factor for longevity was the fact that the empire was neither universal nor securely tranquil; it continually faced severe troubles and had many refreshing defeats. Although able to gather enough strength to sustain its pride, it was usually too pressed to behave quite like a universal empire. Despite continuity of institutions, the famously long-lived empire may practically be called a series of empires, each one building anew around the old core. Even as Justinian in the sixth century was trying to reconquer the West, he was beset by invasions of Asia Minor and had to pay tribute to the Persians. [353, p. 139] In the first part of the seventh century, the Balkans and Greece were held by Slavs and others, while most of Asia Minor was overrun by the Persians; there was thought for a time of removing the capital to Carthage. But the anarchy brought relief from imperial officials and tax gatherers, the economy was released from some of its old shackles, and the towns had to learn to look to their own protection; the people responded with renewed spirit. [*311*, p. 21] Most of the lost lands were recovered fairly soon; but presently the Arabs came, amputated large parts of the empire permanently, and in 674–678 and 717–718 besieged Constantinople. Again there was recovery and expansion to a new maximum in the eleventh century, followed by decline until Constantinople was taken by a small force of Crusaders early in the thirteenth century, and the realm was split into three states. When once more restored, the empire was no longer large, holding only a corner of the Balkans plus part of Asia Minor, until its demise. As the Turks were battering at the gates in the fifteenth century, there was some inclination to draw away from empireship. The ruler was urged to call himself "King of the Hellenes," and inspiration was drawn less from the Roman and imperial past than from the struggle of Greeks against Persians for freedom 1,900 years before. [*301*, p. 21] There was also some release of the intellect as the world state dwindled to a city. In its last years of near impotence, Byzantium produced works of unaccustomed warmth and naturalism; then, too, lived the greatest philosopher of Byzantine history, the bold thinker Plathon. [*437*, pp. 259–260]

Empires have thus rotted at different tempos; seemingly the rot has been abetted in some instances and retarded in others by special conditions, but it is universal, just as men must eventually become senile. Possible causes are many and various. For Rome, writers have cited the decay of customs, infection by Greek and oriental vices, supposed dire effects of Christianity (a charge of pagans of the time), overuse of the soil and its consequent exhaustion, large landholdings, slavery, racial mongrelization from slaves, diseases (especially malaria), and plagues; the great pestilence of 166 A.D. is said to have marked the beginning of the downturn. [*358*, p. 292] A noted scholar has hypothesized that the decay of classical civilization was due to the changes in class composition and to class struggles, which rent the Roman world. [*342*, p. 535] Nor is it entirely unreasonable to hold the fall to be belated punishment for sins of pride.

Witnesses of the decline have sometimes had a rather good understanding of it. Turkish writers attributed the weakness of their state, among other causes, to the withdrawal of the sultan from political leadership to the harem (whereby obscure influences gained dominance), to the naming of unqualified men, especially eunuchs, to high positions, to the sale of offices for the short-term benefit of the treasury, and to the enrichment of court favorites. [431, p. 132] Chinese historiographers, with the benefit of repeated experience of imperial decline, came to a sophisticated understanding of the dynastic cycle. According to the interpretation developed in recent centuries, a new dynasty, entering with fresh spirit and competent officials, would expand to the natural limits of the empire. There would follow a time of stability and tranquillity during which the governing class would become enervated and lose its dedication and will to adhere to the code. Increasing luxury of the governors would reduce their capacities while straining the treasury, and funds needed for flood control and defense would be turned to private use. Taxes would rise beyond the endurance of the peasants, and the cost of suppressing uprisings would further increase the burden and weaken the government until its overthrow and a thorough cleansing became inevitable. [79, pp. 44–45]

One should hardly seek any single general cause of decay to fit all; least of all should one expect to find a simple answer. One does not ask medicine for a one-sentence statement of the cause of hardening of the arteries; far less should one look for a brief and illuminating explanation of the arthritis and collapse of something so complex as the universal empire. There is, nonetheless, a perceptible sameness in the great empires; and there is a predictability about their decline which one misses in freer competitive states. No one can peruse accounts of their woes in senescence without a feeling of *déjà vu* as one again and again meets the symptoms of rigidity, formalism, corruption, overtaxation, ineffectiveness of administration, and the like. The imperial illness is not strictly a trouble of universal empires, of course; to some extent autocracies great and small are susceptible. But it is an affliction more marked in the great than in the weak, in the Spain of the Hapsburgs or the France of the Old Regime than in medieval Italian despotisms, and most marked in the universal empires, wherein autocracy comes to its finest flowering. The imperial rot has no relation to the decadence of civilizations in freedom, if this is really a meaningful concept. Rather, the illnesses of free and servile states are opposites: decadence in the context of Hellenistic

Greece, perhaps the China of the Contending States or Buddhist India, or the modern West means, if anything, that society is cut loose from its moorings to suffer an excess of uncertainty and change, of doubt and individualism, evident weaknesses beneath which dwells no little strength. Imperial decadence is the staleness and incapacity of an overrigid hierarchic society, and it is a rotting at the heart which may remain long hidden behind the facade of order, conformity, and power. [392, p. 222] The one is more freedom than men know how to handle; the other is the choking of thought, spirit, and enterprise under overwhelming power. Great empire itself signifies decadence.

It also appears that decay is essentially a single disease, although the symptoms are diverse, because there seems sometimes to be a marked turning point from vigor toward loss of vitality. For example, under Augustus the life curve of the Roman empire leveled off and began its long decline in many ways mentioned earlier. More striking were the changes that overtook the Turkish empire under Suleiman, who raised it to its apogee. He began the practice of absenting himself from meetings of his council, thereby inviting the erosion of the sultan's real authority [436, p. 173]; his viziers became directors of the administration instead of heads of a board as previously [435, p. 164]; by delegating command he broke the precedent of the sultan's always leading the army in person to inspire if not direct it. [436, p. 157] He instituted the practice of raising favorites irregularly, without requiring them to climb the administrative ladder [439, p. 30]; he began the admission of sons of Janissaries to the service, thereby altering the character of the corps [435, p. 120]; and, under him, the chancery was opened to the Moslem-born. [435, p. 186] He greatly increased the splendor and thus the expenses of the court, and in compensation began the sale of offices, a practice that soon spread until all officials were selling the posts they controlled. [435, p. 115] In his time the charging of private fees for official services was just beginning to become vexatious, and taxation, later to become a destroying scourge, was becoming burdensome. [435, pp. 187, 144] He was the first sultan to allow himself to be guided by a woman of the harem. He was the last of a series of eight strong sultans [433, p. 78]; after him there was only one really active sultan. For another century or more the Turks garnered many victories, but after Suleiman the empire that had spread irresistibly over the Near

East and much of Europe could at best hold its own. The fulfillment of empire was its adversity.

If the empire is power incarnate, it is a truism that its decadence is the corruption of power. As unlimited power is the prime and perhaps only essential trait common to the universal empires, so far as their failings have anything in common, they must derive from the excess of power and its consequent misuse. According to the widely known dictum, absolute power corrupts absolutely; and the universal empire represents absolute power as does nothing else on earth. The basic vice seems to be the impossibility of power ruling itself. According to Plato, political wisdom was reserved to Zeus alone. The fuller one's power over others, the more difficult to rule oneself. Unrestricted power is almost always, perhaps always, overused if not misused; even with the best of intentions, omnipotence cannot restrain itself from trying to do too much. Inevitably, if princes were measured by ordinary standards, they would be rated as meaner than the less favored; as Lord Acton said, "Great men are almost always bad men." [Quoted in 522, p. 219] Many a man who might have been decent or at least harmless has been converted into something of a monster by the experience of infinite adulation and unbounded authority. Emperors from long before Tiberius and down to Napoleon and Stalin have grown arbitrary and careless of human values as they accustomed themselves to seeing a world at their feet. The better the ability to impose a will, the less need to make it rational or ethical.

Not only the use of power but the structure of authority tends to pervert the supreme ruler. In order to become and remain an autocrat, it is no asset to be modest. Ignorance of one's limitations or a willingness to ignore them are valuable qualifications for strong leadership; and if one were not disposed to overestimate himself, a thousand bootlickers urge him on. Even democratic presidents and prime ministers sometimes lose good judgment when they are surrounded, as they easily may be, by agreeable yes-men whose principal object is to please; and the greater the power of the leader, the more severely is his character tested. Violence, pomp, pretense, and bad temper which would disgrace an ordinary man are entirely pardonable in the emperor; they may even be part and parcel of his greatness. It is well for him to be careless of others' rights and feelings, to know how to ride over people, to use them and cast them aside when useless, perhaps to have a strong disposition capriciously seasoned with kindness. If he is vain, unjust, even cruel, it is little matter, for all will be forgiven as long as he is strong. Power is intensely self-righteous; it will not be measured by others' standards, but makes its own. Where there is absolute power, no standards remain but the needs and the will of the autocracy. The will of the despot is character-istically unpredictable; typically he will be fierce at times and again demonstratively mild and generous to those who strike his fancy. A cook once let a drop of sauce fall upon the hand of a Persian monarch; the irate king ordered immediate beheading. Thereupon, the cook poured the kettle over his master, as he explained, to save him from committing an injustice. Laughing, the monarch forgave him. [*251*, p. 39]

The logic of the imperial system is obedience, as men have superiors and inferiors to obey and to command; but at the top the logic fails, because no one can relieve the emperor of the burden of an unchecked will and freedom above law, which is more likely to be a freedom to be evil than good. Nor can the em-pire train men to responsibility and moderation in supreme power, for its motto is only obedience and it cannot educate wills in the use of freedom. Men rather, as Tacitus wrote, act the slave to become the master [*Histories*, I, 36], but the slave turned master is worst of all.

Nor can much better be expected of those immediately around the autocrat. So far as he is only a figurehead, those who wield his power may do so obscurely and irresponsibly, without even the sense of belonging to the empire and to history which may actuate and inspire the formal head of state; and the processes by which men and women become powers behind the throne and in palace or harem corridors are among the least edifying. Little better can be expected as the ruler chooses his own helpers. Even a brilliant man (as the autocrat is unlikely to be) is often irritated by very intelligent servants, whose ideas compete with his own; he is likely to feel that his own basic thinking is sufficient and to desire only administrators and clerks to handle details. And commonly, the less men know the more confident they are in the general rightness of their opinions, especially when they are assured of heavenly guidance and are flattered from morning to night. Com-fort and security require the removal of potential equals, an affront if not a threat to exalted majesty; and the stronger a servant becomes, the less secure; eunuchs, despised and incapable of taking the throne, may be allowed to rise the highest. As noted by Bacon, fear is the more intense as the despot finds all his desires satisfied; and it gnaws more keenly when one is dimly aware that he is not big enough for his position. Anxiety for loss of power rises as power becomes more complete, and the autocrat fears relaxation lest it indicate weakness, strong men lest they displace or over-shadow him, and intimates lest they betray him. Frequency of conspiracies leads to the habit of doing away with potential con-spirators, that is, men of real character and independent minds, and makes an atmosphere of servility in which decency dies and enterprises shrivel. There is little room for honest men around the autocrat, whose misfortune it is perennially to be deceived. Sin-cerity is not subject to command.

By unhampered exercise, power cripples itself. The very meas-ures the autocrat takes to safeguard his authority — division of responsibilities and authority of those around him, multiple con-trols, exclusion of outside influences, suppression of criticism, and destruction of independence — bring on paralysis. The habit of power, which corrupts rulers, makes the people craven; when some have arbitrary mastery of others, they abase their inferiors. Fear then leads to death of initiative, to apathy, and to incapacity. Those in charge try to decide more than they are competent to, and they are led to command the more by the passivity of those below.

For the sacred end of maintaining, strengthening, and using position, no means are bad; deception and force are easier than the attempt to satisfy the needs of the people. Policy is thus de-flected from the creative and positive, actions being judged — usually without vision or much intelligence — in terms of the needs of the rulers. There is always a potential contradiction between measures to please the rulers and measures to improve the wel-fare of the land, and usually a real conflict; lacking a necessity to do better, the governors prefer their own interests. Proclaimed equality and justice turn into their opposites.

Such faults, vices, and abuses of position are to be found in some degree in any state. Graft, overtaxation, confiscations, unjust enrichment, intolerance of criticism or dissent, bureaucratic rigid-ity, formalism, and other evils are never absolutely to be avoided. But where there are competing states, power is ipso facto checked.

The ruler must think seriously of the strength of his country if it is continually measured against other states; he must think more of the welfare of his people if they can compare his government with that of neighbors, flee from his jurisdiction, remove their wealth from the grasp of his agents, or hope for foreign sympathy and help in rebellion. The mentality of the state must be different; so far as all are aware that most of the world is independent, there is no point in claiming omnipotence; when ideas flow from abroad, the government does not seem omniscient even to itself. Thus decay really begins for the empire as it approaches its great goal, the end of its career of conquest, eliminating competition and the vitalizing freedom of independent states. Then, with no more need for sacrifice, the empire has only to maintain its grip internally and can freely indulge the vices of unchecked power, the poisonous sweets of riches, prestige, display, and all the delights of the flesh, but most of all the gratifying mastery of man over his fellows.

Power is checked by contrary power. Perhaps it might also be checked or at least directed by higher purpose. But it is difficult that an earthly goal should be sufficiently inspiring to overcome the contradiction between the welfare of the elect and that of the generality. It is hardly possible to focus on the good of all. It is not easy to agree just what this is and to define it, and in the absence of objective criteria it will be interpreted to the advantage of those who interpret it. Moreover, whatever their professions, many or most of the elite, particularly in the lower layers, have little or no interest in the improvement of the people's lot. Their greatest satisfaction is superiority to the common herd, and much of material enjoyment lies in having what others want; the poorer the coolies, the richer in effect the mandarins. A supernatural goal, a relation of the autocracy to divine purpose, is perhaps more feasible; and the great empires have sought to use faiths not only to instruct the people but also to guide the otherwise uncontrolled sovereign. But the dictates and values of even the best-developed religions are somewhat vague and subject to varying emphases and interpretations. With a little rationalization and help from his lackeys, the autocrat can easily convince himself of the rightness and divine sanction of almost anything he does.

Thus the power that overcomes all its enemies is subject to a wasting disease. Utter omnipotence would imply not only amorality but incompetence. As soon as the great order is set up, its decay commences; and the universal empires have been reasonably vigorous and lively only a small part of their lives. To be sure, there is a compensation. Like order and power, growing disorders and troubles tend to check themselves, as graver needs bring more realistic responses. With ebbs and flows, the universal empire may last for what seems an eternity to mortal men. But it eventually becomes so helpless and useless, as bad habits and parasitic institutions fix themselves, that many men remove themselves from its grip by becoming bandits; local magnates set themselves up in defiance of the central power, and the end comes from rebellion, invasion by despised barbarians, or mere dissolution.

The universal empire at its acme fails to extend itself indefinitely, despite its potential strength to do so, because the lure of additional conquest and prospective gains at some point are more than offset by the reduction of purposiveness and potency. In fact, the great empire begins to decline, in terms of the ratio of military power to population and territory, even as it expands. When the outward thrust is exhausted, it seeks only to maintain itself; but this, too, eventually fails. For the forward movement of humanity, it is fortunate that the greatest empires are mortal; otherwise, all the world would remain permanently sealed in universal empires and civilization as we know it would have long since come nearly or entirely to a halt. The stability of absolutism, like that of freedom, is finite; there is a release from the strongest shackles.

The fall of the empire is, withal, the greatest of human tragedies. It is more sickness than drama, more drab decay than exciting struggle, a degradation without art or glory, infused not with heroism but with futile stupidity and cynicism. But it is the supreme tragedy of flawed character, the chasm between what ideally might be and what, in poor human nature, in reality exists. It is bread turned to ashes, almost the death of hope.

The universal empire dissolves but does not die. It is so appealing and so useful, and so deeply shapes society, that it cannot
simply be forgotten; upon its collapse, it is as though the roof
of a house fell, leaving the walls standing in the way of any new
building. An empire may have gathered up many independent
states into its one great body, but when that body falls apart the
pieces cannot easily resume independent life. The institutions of
free states can be submerged in the imperial order much more
easily than the institutions of the empire can revert to those of
the open society. In the decay of empire, men recover a degree
of freedom, but it is a dead freedom, mostly the autonomy of lesser
tyrants in a poor and static society, or the freedom of an incapable
dictatorship, until there emerge new powers capable of new departures. In the wreckage of the Roman empire, new life came
first in the towns that grew up outside, and in opposition to, the
established order, some five hundred years or more after the breakup of effective imperial rule. For full-fledged nation-states to be
built required approximately a thousand years. It seems almost
impossible for a community of free states to reemerge where a
universal empire has once stretched across the land and fixed its
ways and symbols of authority.

When the imperial regime loses the capacity to make itself
obeyed and to keep order, when economic and administrative
unity breaks down in an agricultural economy, something like a
feudal order develops. [466, pp. 7–9] This might be described
as a system whereby the central authority, lacking military
strength, seeks to retain something of the prerogatives of empire,
while the lesser powers, having largely ceased obedience and
probably engaging in more or less violent conflict, but acknowledging superiors in a formal and ceremonial order, are unprepared to assert complete independence. By custom, the vassal
may owe certain dues and conditional military support to his lord,

who in turn sanctions and guarantees the position of the vassal and his fief and adjudicates between him and his rivals. The fief holders in turn exercise limited powers over those below them, and government is largely local. Fighting is the business of a professional class; the bulk of the people plow and reap. The feudal society has in lessened degree the chief traits of the ripe empire, hierarchy and rigidity: political position is the basis of wealth and is itself a piece of property [466, p. 5]; pride of status is everywhere, as superiors display great disdain for those who humbly bow to them, the lords despise commerce and the merchant class and fear their influence; convention and formalism prevail in manners, art, and religion.

It is characteristic of feudalism that the distant ruler receives more honor than obedience. In contrast to a loose tribute-paying empire, which arises from conquest not translated into full dominion, feudalism comes rather from the decay of a respected central power. In the breakup of a great empire, whose prestige outlasts its strength, there arise local powers largely uncontrollable by the center but incapable or undesirous of asserting full theoretical sovereignty, perhaps combining reverence for the sovereign with opposition to his rule, much as medieval adversaries of the Pope did not cease to revere him as head of the Church. The barons go their own way, the more satisfied to hold the monarch up as symbol and source of legitimacy as he is unable to interfere with them; religious institutions enjoy wealth and independence with the sanction of the imperial authority; municipalities and other bodies acquire fixed rights, often looking to the supreme ruler for protection from local magnates.

The best-developed feudalism and the one that has impressed itself upon our culture is that which arose from the breakup of the Roman empire. By the fourth century something of a feudal order was emerging, as great estates became self-sufficient economically, acquired political powers with their armed retainers, and often obtained legal immunities. As kingdoms arose from the general wreckage and barbarian rule, kings largely took the place of the emperor; still, the universal powers of the Papacy and the Holy Roman Empire presided over the Middle Ages. Much the same order emerged eventually, although much more slowly, in the Byzantine realm. From the ninth century, small holdings were disappearing into the vast estates, which could protect the people, and large landholdings were given in return for defense of the frontiers. It was attempted to make holdings conditional upon service, but they gradually became personal and hereditary, while the mercenary troops on which the state increasingly leaned were more loyal to their own leaders than to the emperor. [E. Kantorowicz in *466*, pp. 157–164] The barons largely prevailed after the tenth century; with their own armies, they regarded themselves as nearly independent, fought and raised revolts, and held courts like little emperors. [C. Diehl in *292*, p. 771]

Much the same must have occurred in many an empire, from the time when the Egyptian Old Kingdom fell into disorder and the nomarchs became nearly free hereditary rulers. The satraps of the later Achaemenid empire were nearly autonomous and were able to make much trouble for their overlord. [B. Brundage in *466*, p. 110] The Seleucid state, which inherited the Persian part of Alexander's conquests, similarly became a loose feudal conglomerate. The semi-independent territorial lords had only to furnish troops on occasion and to pay fixed dues; and many of the Greek and Phoenician cities were practically independent under their communal administrations [*281*, pp. 412–414]; the empire formed a remarkable parallel to the medieval Europe of feudal lords and partly free trading towns.

China had a feudal period after the rather weak Chou emperor lost power in 771 B.C.; the feudatories long continued to recognize his ritual and theoretical supremacy and to seek investment from him; only after several centuries and countless wars did the one-time vassals, reduced in number and increased in power, assert themselves as sovereign in their own right. Again after the Han empire fell, a sort of feudalism emerged, as military commanders and local magnates set themselves up and various dynasties claimed the mandate of Heaven; but imperial institutions were now more strongly fixed. [D. Bodde in *466*, p. 83] Better developed and longer lasting was the feudal system of Japan, rising strongly after the central authority had been eroded in civil conflicts in the twelfth century. With modifications it endured until Western penetration brought the Meiji Restoration.

Something of the universal empire can continue in the institutions and hierarchic loyalties of feudalism; more often, the empire itself has been reborn out of the crucible of disorder, like a phoenix arising from its ashes. The aspiration and the ideal of absolute and overreaching power are hardly lost where they have once soaked, so to speak, into the earth. Especially in China, the most imperial of lands, the throne has not been left long vacant. This may be ascribable partly to the excellent ethical-ideological basis of the Chinese imperial order, but probably more to the fact that the Middle Kingdom is a natural geographic unit and, unlike the Roman realm, relatively lacks internal barriers and divisions. The borderlands from which invaders have come are arid and capable of supporting only a sparse population; hence, they have looked to China as the only center of civilization, while the rulers of China never had to doubt their absolute preeminence. Germanic intruders into the Roman empire regarded themselves not as enemies but as aspirants to Roman dignity; Turks, Tibetans, Uighurs, Khitans, Mongols, Manchus, and others have even more admired Chinese culture and have often come to think of themselves as Chinese while fighting over the Chinese land.

Since the great unification of 221 B.C. China has usually been gripped by a general empire, and intervals of disunion or disorder have grown successively shorter up to the latest dynasty. The longest disruption came after the Later Hans. From the beginning of the third to the end of the sixth century there was much disorder in the exposed north while the south was more tranquil, a little like the Byzantine empire after the fall of Rome in the West. In something like an insecure state system, Chinese society became much more open, and cultural and technical advance was steady and impressive. Despite political division, the Chinese cultural area was expanded. [40, Bk. I, p. 163] Individualism revived and birth replaced bureaucratic rank as a title to authority. [W. Eberhard in 19, p. 75] There were clear signs of a nascent capitalism, as never afterward in China. [2, p. 30] An exceptional number of scientists and inventors were able to rise from lowly status. [J. Needham in 468, p. 129] The first Chinese map makers appeared, and there were explorations of the Indian Ocean. [28, pp. 64, 78] Cultural importation flourished as never before, with much mathematics, medicine, architecture, and music coming from India. The old manners and morals were widely abandoned even among the upper classes. There was considerable ferment and free controversy among philosophies. Confucianism was subject to critical scholarship in an atmosphere of eclecticism. Some independent thinkers, looking down on the antiquated codes, even called for complete liberty. Buddhism also entered and flourished, and native Taoism developed into a substantial religion.

Throughout this progress and deviation from tradition, however, imperial grandeur was not forgotten, and independent states gained no real stability. Looking to the precedents of the past, many rulers studied Confucianist political ideology and statecraft and aspired to reunite their universe. [78, p. 64] At length one succeeded and established the militant but short-lived Sui dynasty. It was followed by the brilliant T'ang dynasty, outstanding for its refinement of Confucianism, perfection of poetry, and improved examination and civil service system.

After the decline of the T'ang dynasty, China was fragmented for somewhat more than half a century in the Five Dynasty period. Although imperial ideas of government continued within each kingdom, there was substantial change from the imperial pattern. Chancellors acquired real power [62, p. viii], and civil service position was made frankly hereditary, with only nominal examinations. [18, p. 105] Merchants traveled freely among the various states and were used for various official missions, as they were more welcome than officials; the latter sometimes passed themselves off as merchants. The rulers gave much attention to trade, including that from overseas, as necessary for revenue. [62, pp. 76–78] At least in some of the states, Buddhism and Taoism were freed from control and given such favors as exemption from taxation. [62, pp. 91–94] There were many cultural advances, including perhaps the invention of printing.

The succeeding Sung dynasty had control over most of the land only rather briefly, about a century. During the following century and a half China was split into northern and southern halves. This was a time of some freedom of thought and cultural development.

Since Sung times, the imperial order has been more effective and times of disruption between dynasties have been briefer. The intervals between Yüan, Ming, and Manchu dynasties were only a few decades of fighting, which perhaps sufficed to remove a large part of the population, but offered no opportunity for cultural renewal or political development. By corollary, conservatism became still more extreme, until European disturbers of the established order took the place of the nomads, who had lost effectiveness because their numbers did not increase, though China became

steadily more populous. Only confrontation with the more powerful Western culture and a long series of military defeats partially
discredited the old ways and broke the spell of Confucianism.

The repetition of universal empires in China was unique, although in Egypt the New Kingdom stood to its predecessor, the
Old Kingdom, somewhat as the T'ang dynasty stood to the Han.
The intervening period of some six hundred years was occupied by
a century and a half of chaos, some two and a half centuries of
the rather feudalistic Middle Kingdom, and two centuries of new
breakdown and foreign (Hyksos) rule. Although the New Kingdom
made technical improvements, it took over the old institutions
with a minimum of change. Upon its decline Egypt came permanently under alien rule.

The region of Persia and Mesopotamia has seemed possessed
with the idea of despotic empire since Sargon of Akkad, as suc-
cessive rulers ever after dreamed of regathering the lands. The
Kassites in the sixteenth century B.C. inherited the Babylonian
empire, adopted its institutions, restored ancient monuments,
and built a temple on a plan then 1,500 years old. [*130*, p. 316]
After the Hittites came the Assyrians, and after these, the Persians.
The latter, under the Achaemenids the most successful of Near
Eastern imperialists, became models for a long line of successors.
Alexander's heirs, the Seleucids, who ruled only about a century,
were semideified, although not very powerful, kings. The native
Persian Parthian dynasty, which took over their disintegrating
realm, was, like the Seleucids, imbued with Hellenistic culture,
fond of the Greek language, and tolerant of religions. Their state
was less than absolute; the king was checked both by a royal family
assembly and by a council of nobles, and conquered lands were
left largely autonomous. There was no standing army. Palace
women and eunuchs had little political influence. [*253*, I, 365–370]
But the Parthian rulers, calling themselves "King of Kings" and
tracing their ancestry to the Achaemenids, tried to live as grandly,
with palaces and harems, as their predecessors. [B. Brundage in
466, p. 113]

Early in the third century, after a long but precarious rule, the
Parthian regime was overthrown; and the new Sassanid monarchy
consciously sought to revive the empire and ways of Darius seven
hundred years before, claiming his inheritance from the Indus to
Greece. Much strengthening the state, the Sassanids curbed the

feudal lords, reducing their landholdings and bringing them to court. They built up an elaborate bureaucracy and established an exclusive state religion. [B. Brundage in *466*, p. 114] The ruler's title rose from "Lord" to "King," then "King of Kings of Iran," and finally "King of Kings of Iran and non-Iran." [*249*, p. 208] He claimed world dominion, as Xerxes had once done, although in fact he held little non-Iranian land and not even all of Iran. As splendid as any in history, the Sassanid monarch sat in a display of precious stones and metals on a curtained throne which even the highest noble could approach only when summoned. [*321*, p. 277; *253*, I, 465] The crown was so heavy that it had to be supported from the ceiling by a chain during the rare state audiences. [*250*, p. 146] The king was God's representative and took the title of a god, discordant as this was with the official religion of Zoroastrianism. [*254*, p. 297] Altogether it was quite a thorough despotism, with arbitrary and violent rulers, effective control over the provinces, serfs treated like dirt, and many titles, uniforms, and distinctions for the proud and cruel official classes. [*250*, p. 167]

The Sassanid state lasted more than four hundred years and showed the ordinary symptoms of imperial decay. It is said that lying and hypocrisy were so prevalent that no one could be sure of anything. [*251*, p. 39] Culture became frozen and formalistic, and the Zoroastrian worship became arid and ritualistic. Fighting was largely the business of the cavalry and the aristocrats, as the unpaid and disorderly foot soldiery was worthless. [*250*, p. 150] Toward the end, power slipped away from the autocracy to the nobility, bureaucracy, and priesthood. [*249*, p. 225] Depopulation became acute, and prisoners were taken in to occupy idle land. [*251*, pp. 105–106]

In the seventh century the Arabs easily crushed the Persian monarchy, but Persian political ways conquered the less pretentious desert people. The Arabs soon laid aside tribal manners to copy, in the Abbasid Califate, Sassanid seclusion, their splendid eunuch-infested court and great harem, and refined etiquette. According to the inherited theory of absolutism, subjects were duty-bound to obey even a bad ruler. [*432*, Pt. I, pp. 29–30] After the Abbasids, Persia suffered many invasions, including that of the Mongols, and great and little despotisms, all as pretentious as their resources possibly permitted. Finally, in the sixteenth and seventeenth centuries, the Safavid dynasty tried once more to restore the greatness of the Achaemenids and partly compensated the small number of victories by the pomp of the court.

Of all empires, the Roman has enjoyed the most extraordinary life in death. From the time of Augustus, all accepted it as an undying reality; as Tacitus wrote, "The good fortune and order of eight centuries have consolidated this mighty fabric of empire, and it cannot be pulled asunder without destroying those who sunder it." [330, p. 411] During the disorders of the third century there was little or no idea of departing from Roman universality, so firmly had Rome imposed itself upon the spirits of men. In the fourth century, Lactantius, like men generally and Christians in particular, thought the end of Roman dominion would be the end of the world. [287, pp. 20–21] Rome had to live on because it was impossible to believe in its demise.

The economic and political center of gravity of the Roman empire shifted steadily toward the East, possibly because Eastern societies (except for Greece, which remarkably decayed) were long hardened to empire and more resistant to its ravages. Long after Italy and the Western lands had fallen under barbarian kings, a New Rome lived on in the East; it suffered many grievous setbacks but was at times great and powerful enough to nourish the best dreams; in the sixth century Justinian almost succeeded in re-creating the old world rule by reconquering Italy and much more in the West. Resting on its Roman past, the Byzantine realm kept as close as possible to Roman forms and ways until the end. Its central political doctrine was that there could be in the universe only one emperor, whose mission was to reunite all Christian lands. Until the thirteenth century it never deigned to conclude a formal agreement with a foreign power, and the concessions the emperor was compelled to make were "gifts" of grace. [339, pp. 5, 10] No new start was ever possible and no political theory but Caesarism. The only idea of the state was divinely appointed absolutism. The only conceivable recourse against a bad ruler, as in classic Rome, was assassination or rebellion, whose success indicated, somewhat as in China, the passing of heavenly favor. [279, p. 273] The politics of dagger, poison, or military rising continued as in Rome's evil days, with a note of decadence as the eunuchs contested with the bureaucracy, the landed aristocracy, and the military. Treason, murder, and corruption were normal; labyrinthine amorality gave the word "Byzantine" its connotations.

Power and territory shrank until at length nothing was left but a bit of land around the city of Constantinople; yet the "Autocrats of the Romans" never let facts interfere with pretensions of world mission and sovereignty. While the Turks were tightening the final siege of the capital and the Byzantines went begging for help from the Russians, they still insisted on full recognition of their sovereignty. [342, pp. 8–9] Even the small daughter realm of Trebizond, which was split away when the Crusaders temporarily captured Constantinople, would be no less. Lasting until Turkish conquest in 1461, it did its best to maintain imperial pretenses, with court and government in despotic style, as magnificent as it was powerless. [437, p. 411] Its ruler called himself "Emperor and Autocrat of the Romans"; when forced to retreat from such pomposity, he became, modestly, "Emperor and Autocrat of All the East, the Iberians and the Transmarine Provinces." [336, pp. 27, 29]

In the West, barbarians who overcame Rome militarily were conquered spiritually. They invaded with respect, not to conquer but to procure military commands and position for themselves; it never occurred to them to seek destruction of what was supreme and eternal. [287, p. 19] An able Gothic chief said, "When experience taught me that the untamable barbarism of the Goths would not suffer them to live beneath the sway of law, and that to abolish the laws on which the state rests would destroy the state itself, I chose the glory of renewing and maintaining by Gothic strength the fame of Rome, desiring to go down to posterity as the restorer of that Roman power which I could not replace." [287, p. 18] When Rome had fallen, men refused to believe it; a few years after the sack by Alaric, the leading poet was predicting its everlasting sway. [303, p. 147]

Formal extinction of the empire in the West came in 476 when the barbarian leader Odoacer deposed Romulus, the last puppet Caesar at Rome, and declined to appoint another. This was a gesture of reverence to the imperial authority, as Odoacer said that one monarch sufficed for the world and asked the Byzantine emperor to entrust him with the rule of the Western provinces; formally, it was rather a reunion than an extinction. [287, p. 25] For many generations thereafter the sole Roman emperor exercised from Constantinople a shadowy world sovereignty, grandly conferring titles to lands over which his control was nil. [353, p. 111] At Rome, there remained a shell of the old administration, with

Senate and consuls; and coins continued to be struck in the name of the empire not only in Italy, but in Spain, Gaul, and North Africa. [320, p. 32] Rome was never long under barbarian rule, and reverence for Rome saved the independence of the bishop of Rome and the papacy, as Franks and Lombards shrank from subjecting it. Nor was Roman law ever entirely out of sight; favored by kings, as it suited them much better than tribal customs, it continued widely in use through the darkest ages. [287, p. 32]

The most curious continuation of the state of the Caesars was the Holy Roman Empire. This phantom was evoked by the Pope, who had to call in one set of barbarians to protect him from another, and who had no better means of rewarding his friends than the conferral of a glowing title. When the Frankish ruler, Pippin the Short, was summoned to preserve the pontiff from the menacing Lombards, he received a Roman consecration and the high distinction of Patrician to legitimate his somewhat dubious title. [287, pp. 39–40] A few years later, the Pope, still needing Frankish support, crowned Charlemagne as Roman emperor. This nominal revival of the Western empire seemed permissible because the Byzantine throne was then occupied by a female usurper, but those who supported her regarded it as a rebellion. [353, p. 267]

The Holy Roman Emperor, crowned in Rome by the Pope, proceeded to claim universal authority, which Charlemagne fairly well justified by vast conquests. After him, there was much anarchy in Italy; not until a century and a half later could Otto the Great refound the Empire that filled the Middle Ages. The emperor that the Pope had evoked sought to become his master, and there ensued the perennial battle of temporal and spiritual claims to world dominion. But while the kings of the new European nation-states were consolidating their sway, the Holy Roman Emperor was enfeebled by archaic traditions and the ceaseless contests arising from the passion for universality. [287, p. 431] Still, as he became impotent and limited to his German base, he did not stress any less his dignity of eternal power, unlimited prerogative, and rightful rule of all Christendom, above law and answerable only to God. Frederick III thus esteemed himself while abjectly begging his way from castle to castle. [287, pp. 277–278]

Especially in Italy did the afterimage of Rome's glory fill men's minds. Dante gave it eloquent expression; afflicted by the disorderly politics of the Italian city-states, he called for a new Caesar to impose peace, and hailed the efforts of Henry VII, legitimate successor of Augustus and Justinian, to dominate the flourishing free cities, including his own Florence. The argument was convincing: human fulfillment requires peace; peace needs a single rule and justice a supreme judge; history proves that the Romans were chosen to give order to the world. After Dante, students of Roman law were equally enthusiasts of autocracy. A senator of Padua in 1318 said, "If the whole universe were under the command of a just king, one could see carnage, war, rapine, and all shameful actions cease. . . . Let us choose a prince from among us." [544, p. 260] At that time, although the Holy Roman Emperor had failed to come to Italy for three generations, his image rather waxed than waned because of the revival of Latin studies and the work of the lawyers. To the fifteenth century, the idea of independent states would still have seemed shocking anarchy.

The Reformation virtually ended the authority of the Holy Roman Empire, because the universal church stood for the universal empire. In 1530 Charles V became the last Holy Roman Emperor to be crowned by the Pope. But the increasingly outmoded institution lived on until Napoleon, world conqueror in his own right, dissolved it in 1806. After the overthrow of Napoleon, some wished to bring back the good old empire, but it was replaced by the Germanic Confederation. Still, the unifiers of Germany in 1871 called their ruler Caesar; and Roman law remained in force in much of Germany until 1900 unless contravened by modern statutes. [320]

Napoleon himself thought of his realm as a renewal of the empire of Charlemagne if not of Augustus, and at one time he intended to be crowned Holy Roman Emperor [287, p. 411]; his son he had crowned "King of Rome." His laurel crown and his standard, capped by an eagle, were pure Roman. His first constitution took over Roman terminology wholesale, with consuls, senators, tribunes, and prefects; in due course and in acknowledgment of victories, Napoleon crowned himself emperor and called himself "Emperor of the West," like the ruler of the Western half of the Roman empire. [509, p. 214]

Something of the Roman empire has thus lived on and traveled far. Distant Moscow claimed for centuries to be a Third Rome, and early tsars (or czars) sought legitimacy by a myth of descent from Augustus Caesar. [367, p. 41] In the middle of the seventeenth

century, Byzantine law codes were used for the codification of
Russian law. [*408*, p. 175] Turkish sultans called themselves "Caesar." The hero-king of Mongolian and Tibetan epics was called
Kesar. Mazzini, leading the unification of Italy in the nineteenth
century, thought in terms of Roman unity. In the 1930's a new
Caesar, Benito Mussolini, paraded as restorer of imperial glories
and boasted of Mare Nostrum.

The language of the empire likewise continued, not merely as
popular speech and reshaped into the Romance languages, but
also in canonical form, as near as men could keep to the speech of
Cicero and Virgil. Despite its difficulty and complex grammar,
Latin was the lingua franca of the Middle Ages, of Germanic and
Scandinavian lands as well as those of Roman, or Romance,
tongues. If Newton and many after him wrote in Latin, if Latin
is still widely used for scientific purposes and is extensively taught
in secondary schools in Europe and America, this is a noble tribute
to the immortality of the only universal empire of the West.

IMAGE OF AUTHORITY

Amazing in the aftermath is the strength and permanence of imperial ideas and forms. The universal empire is the grandest of
human creations, the mightiest and most impressive structure
known to man; it never ceases to possess the mind and remains
indelibly imprinted upon society. It weighs on all subsequent life
of the peoples upon whom it has impressed its unforgettable glory.
It is an addiction which, once acquired, is not to be rid of without
an age-long period of abstinence. It is like the urge to power which,
although it brings no happiness, never leaves those who have tasted
it. The Near East has been gripped for four thousand years; southern Italy to this day is under the effects of Roman and Spanish
imperial rule.

The empire, which began in splendor and promise of a new
dawning, ends in darkness and impoverishment; the grand state
above all states becomes a morass of despair and apathy. Very few
love the dying empire sufficiently to fight for it, as mercenaries and
bandits struggle over the near corpse. Perhaps with some exaggeration, Salvian wrote in the dying days of Rome: "The one wish of
all the Romans there [in the Visigothic kingdom] is that they may

never be obliged to pass under Roman jurisdiction; the one unanimous prayer of the Roman common people there is that they may be allowed to live the life they lead with the barbarians." [326, II, 1061] But however bad the decadent world state, it is remembered as good in the anarchy that follows its breakup; and those who had no love for it mourn its passing. The misery, starvation, corruption, and tedium are forgotten; in retrospect it seems an age of order and tranquillity, the natural state of mankind, which must be restored to the land divided against itself. Its failure is seen as an unnatural disaster, brought on not by its inherent wrongness, but by human errors. Its vanished greatness and eternity are exaggerated. Legend had it that the Assyrian empire lasted more than five thousand years, and the Persian, more than eight thousand [St. Augustine, *City of God*, Bk. XII, chap. 11], instead of the few centuries of reality. In disorder, the vision of fixed authority is more entrancing than ever. Invading barbarians think of themselves as heirs, not executioners of the sacred order, even if they are incapable of managing it. The decayed edifice falls of its own weight, but to those who view the ruins it seems a magnificent temple wrongly smashed.

Welcomed at birth, accepted in maturity, unloved in senility, mourned in its demise, the empire has the fortune that its good is memorable. Building roads, opening commerce, giving uniform laws and sound administration, it earned gratitude. It put an end to the bickering of nations, the pointless and never-ending wars of competing states; it gave peace and security. It spread its culture over its whole world and built monuments that astounded or stupefied all who looked upon them. It little matters that its achievements were mostly expropriations and its order was the annihilation of competitors.

The empire has resources to glorify itself, and its tremendous temples stand out over many slighter ones; the riches of the imperial capital are incomparable. Moreover, the great works of the empire are concrete and visible, works of wealth and display of the state, not the achievements of inquiring minds. But respect for the empire is much greater than its works. It is designed to impress and to overawe. Its servants are employed in celebrating its majesty and convincing the people of the rightness of respect and obedience, and they have been successful. If Ramses II made as many and as huge images of himself as possible, mankind has rather marveled at the magnificence of his advertising than at the baseness of his vanity. Hence the empire, which has glorified itself in life, is venerated in death. It is hard to believe that it is really gone; it will be or must be brought back to govern mankind.

The grandiose empire bespeaks power and glory as nothing else. To the simpleminded, power is proof enough of rightness, and of the empire as of men, great glory raises above the standards of ordinary humanity. The empire, like the emperor, is forgiven a thousand wrongs if it is strong. Nothing excites the imagination as much as the man who stands high above his fellows, upon whose whim the fate of the multitude hangs, or who lays low great hosts and many nations. Alexander showed his temper by annihilating Thebes for venturing to rise for Greek freedom, but his brief dominion over his world was so spectacularly charming that bards of medieval Europe sang countless lays to him; kings of Sumatra traced their ancestry to the hero dead a thousand years before and thousands of miles away. [560, p. 47]

The imperial mentality persists in political leaders, the common people, and the intellectuals alike. Unity is a natural goal for all rulers. Universal empire is the perfect and complete use of power and so appeals to seekers after power, while the people will support whoever reintegrates the divided land. In the shadow of a bygone universal state, any chief who finds himself rising feels encouraged and entitled to aspire to the universal hegemony; it is an undying inspiration if not a duty to restore the natural and harmonious order. Illiterate barbarian rulers during the post-Han time of division would have the classics read to them and dream of reconquest of the whole empire. [W. Eberhard in 19, p. 76] This legitimacy impedes the acceptance of the legitimacy of independent sovereignties and excuses aggressions. Hence it is extremely difficult for a stable community of states to grow up on the rubble of the broken empire. There is no basis for peace or understanding among candidates for the supreme throne, and where there is no peace there must be a supreme ruler.

If the empire has taught the great to aspire to rule the world, it has equally taught the humbler folk to accept passively their lot, and, like their betters, they retain the lesson. Obedience and inferiority are understandable principles of society, and those who have learned them continue in passivity when the power above has faded away. The people of the late empire are steeped in apathy and indifference; they can do no better than bend before the ruler divinely placed over them. Molded to acceptance of the fixed order, however alien and distrusted, they cannot imagine breaking away to anything different or openly opposing. All the patterns of life are permeated with the principle of authority. A change of rulers matters little, for the government means only self-exalted distant splendor and the present burdens of oppression. Invaders are no more to be resisted than tax collectors. The Egyptians after the New Kingdom were indifferent as Cushites, Assyrians, Libyans, Greeks, and Persians fought over the kingdom. In the vast area of North Africa and Asia conquered by Alexander's small army it was easy for a tiny Greek-Macedonian minority to maintain its rule, even while the epigones were fighting among themselves after the conqueror's death. For generations, the only rebellions the epigones had to face were those of Greeks — of Greek soldiers in Bactria and Greek cities in Europe. [293, p. 4] Similarly, after the Turkish conquest of the Byzantine empire, its longtime subjects adopted the religion and ways of the conquerors with little hesitation and became faithful supporters of the crescent as of the cross, in contrast with the Balkan peoples who kept stubbornly their Christian faith and national languages and customs, eventually to rebel. Those who have surrendered their souls are slaves forever.

The intellectuals also cherish the glories of the empire. Even to scholars, grandeur is more striking than originality. The empire is immodest and is readily believed because it leaves behind the mass of records. The histories of the great empires are written by themselves, and contrary views are seldom heard or are forgotten if not expurgated. Eulogistic inscriptions have been taken by serious students [320, p. 15] as proof of the sincere love of the people. Some, reading Roman historians, are persuaded that the building of the empire was reluctant self-defense and largely an innocent response to aggression. Roman chroniclers wrote of prosperity under the wise and benevolent empire, light taxes and concern for the people; in the absence of contrary accounts, one is disposed to accept now the version that was then acceptable. We want to believe that great leaders, then and now, can do miracles and bring happiness to the world in a short time. Moreover, peace and order are generally accepted conditions of bliss, and there is no more lauded merit than that of the empire that brings them. Unity is good; unifiers must be forgiven possible incidental brutality, the

eggs broken to make the omelet. They are not regarded as destroyers of fertile open societies but as builders of the new order, Pax
Romana or Sinica. Greece and Rome are mentioned together, as
though the latter had been cobuilder instead of stifler of classical
civilization. Even the relative simplicity of politics in the empire
— the tangled contest for power having been thrust behind the
scenes — is a relief compared with the jumble of competing states.
Law and fixed order appeal to the intelligence; so the scholars or
scholastics zealously guard the traditions of the empire when it is
dead and put them back into practice when the opportunity arises.
This was true, no doubt, of the scribes and priests of the Near East
for all the intervals between empires, as of the conservative sacer-
dotal orders of Egypt through millennia. The Middle Ages lasted
in Europe as long as the universal powers born of the Roman empire, the Holy Roman Empire and the Papacy, held sway over
minds, impotent as the two often were; and as they were coming to
an end, the scholars worked for a restoration of the forgotten
Roman forms of government. The Chinese literati dutifully polished the ideology of empire and cherished its traditions in intervals between dynasties. Ready to worship Confucius they, like the
Master himself, looked to a perfectly ordered society in which
neither Confucianism nor any other major philosophy could have
arisen. Modern writers almost invariably accept the establishment
of a great imperial unity as a very fine thing indeed. Even archae-
ologists, removed from political drives, have seemed enchanted by
empire to the extent of seeing empires wherever they found imposing ruins. Thus, students of the Mayas have designated their periods of florescence as Old Empire and New Empire without a
shred of evidence that any Maya empire ever existed.

In the vitality of imperial ideas, forms, and institutions, one can
only guess how much is due to their attractiveness — to the appeal
of glory for adventurous spirits, of grandeur for those who wish to
look up, of order for those weary of strife, and of stability for those
who long for certainty — and how much to social or political utility.
Charlemagne, we may assume, took the Roman crown not only
because many people found it proper that there should be a new
Caesar and because he was personally pleased to pose as ruler of
the world, but also because it was useful for his government to
cultivate this idea of sacred universal rulership incorporated in

himself; and no doubt his underlings did their best to promote reverence for the Roman ideal not only for aesthetic reasons but for his benefit and their own. Roman law was revived in the dawning of modernity not only because of its beauty or abstract justice but because it was highly favorable to the authority of princes who were in a position to patronize and foster the studies that pleased them. Generally, the patterns of the empire, its basic principles of subordination, its ideology, its concepts of honor and status, its religiosity, and its whole way of thinking are useful for the holders of power, standing as they do for hierarchy, submission to authority, and firm social order. The empire promotes uncritical acceptance of the given, loyalty to simple ideas integrating society, not inquiry or challenge of tradition. The admiration for imperial authority, transformed and simplified, becomes the idealization of strict legitimacy. Even simple respect for past achievements is conservative in effect as it binds men to old patterns and makes the present see itself as poor heir to lost splendor. Elites, the greater part of whose life revolves around the maintenance of superiority, and who by their thinking and example very largely make the values of all because they embody success, hold sacred the values that are nearly synonymous with the maintenance of their status. And it is a great strength of the stratified order that in it everyone has a position of some prestige and authority over inferiors, and so a stake in the hierarchic social order — except the poor and ignorant common folk who do not matter; nor is anyone to blame for his station.

Because the patterns and ideas of the imperial order serve to stabilize and stiffen society for the benefit of those in great and small seats of power, something of the empire can drag on its existence practically forever. The nobles and aristocrats continue, as in the feudal society, to bow to a lord to whom they render scant obedience, and demand that all should bow likewise. The throne that is empty or filled by a puppet is still useful, as men rest their own status on the sacred authority of an invisible or factually impotent king as well as upon that of an energetic master. And if storms have dashed the throne entirely, whatever can be upheld of the habits and ideals of the great empire, and reverence for authority and acceptance of the social order serve to lend rigidity, organizedness, and deadness to society. This goes on from generation to generation as power and position perpetuate themselves and parents form their children in the patterns of authority in which they were formed. [489, p. 144]

CELESTIAL EMPIRE

The universal empire may immortalize itself in yet another way, by its profound and enduring influence on religion. The omnipotent authority on earth makes it easy for men to accept the divine authority above, the single will ordering the entire universe. This conception, like that of a universal monarch over all the earth, does not come easily. It is a very sophisticated idea that the great forces of the universe are ruled by a single authority when their conflict and perpetual antagonism are much more obvious than the essential harmony. The sun struggles against the storm clouds or the wintry blast; the ocean pounds against the land; pestilence destroys the fruits the good earth has given; death carries away life; the light strives against the darkness. It is a philosophic tour de force to perceive behind this apparent contradiction and chaos the single entireness of ultimate purpose.

Religion deals with authority or rulership on a higher than human level, and humans see their gods somewhat in terms of the powers in the society they know, as they are or as they rightly should be. Ideas of the governance of heaven are much influenced by the governance of this world, just as men normally have credited deities with some aspects of earthly creatures, usually human but often animal features, and essentially human feelings. Monotheism is an abstruse and difficult concept, not only for those who perceive the turbulence of nature but for those who see society as fragmented, with no supreme ruler but many groups, each with rightful leaders and at odds with one another. Independent coexisting tribes, as in early Palestine, would look to their own tribal gods, the supernatural chief or patron of each owning no subordination to any other. Similarly, city-states of the Middle Ages, while acknowledging the supreme God, as they acknowledged the ultimate sovereignty of the Holy Roman Emperor, cherished and relied on their individual saints, as they relied on their own forces for self-defense. In a different way, the utterly tolerant and fantastically multiplied polytheism of the Hindus corresponds to the extreme division of their society, in which through centuries of near anarchy innumerable castes and other groups were tolerant of one another and largely autonomous within their own little sector of society.

The classic polytheism is that of the ancient Greeks, divided into many independent city-states. Just as no man was supreme in Greece, neither was any god absolute. The tentative monotheism of some philosophers was impersonal and uninteresting to ordinary people, abstract, not devotional, akin to pantheism. Zeus, as sky-god, was only the head of the loose divine family; Aphrodite at times had power over him, just as a beautiful woman bends a strong man to her will; and he, like the other gods, was subject to the impersonal command of Fate. [343, p. 4] Different cities looked to their special protectors, and these had their alliances and intrigues like the city-states, and often opposed each other, as in the Trojan War, where sundry deities helped either side. The gods in Homer, like the limited kings, urge as much as they command. And as the state was little developed, likewise there was little of an organized priesthood. Most of those who carried out divine functions were citizen-amateurs, like the managers of the state. Nor was there any official creed or catechism, no scriptures but much poetry. The oracles did not command but upon request gave advice, often ambiguous.

Like the state, the gods did not have much to do with conduct. The Greeks concluded from the mess and disorder of human affairs that the gods were not seriously concerned with earthly doings. [343, p. 16] Usually they left men alone to go their own way, intervening only if called upon or to punish conduct that was especially offensive. They represented no justice and required no worship, only offerings. [116, p. 189] There was no general code of conduct, no real duty to superhumans, and no particular demand for loyalty. [343, p. 14] Sin was a mistake, not a state of mind, a wrong to the community more than an infraction of divine will. [116, p. 189] Good and bad souls alike went after death to a shadowy and unimportant Hades, nor was the vague immortality of the philosophers much more moving. The gods themselves had no pretense of being very good and in fact, according to the legends, engaged in many unedifying adventures, especially amours with attractive mortals. They were not overly dignified; a smith, Hephaestus, was a major Olympic deity. On the other hand, there was no extremely bad god or devil. By corollary, humans were on their own. They could hardly blame a malignant deity for their misfortunes (unless they transgressed some convention), and if they raised themselves it was not by divine grace but by their own efforts and rather to the annoyance of the Olympians. [343, pp. 11–12] Sophocles glorified the wondrous deeds of man, and Heraclitus said that a man's character was his destiny. [116, p. 281] In the words that Thucydides put in the mouth of a Spartan, "For we, that must be thought the causes of all events, be they good or bad, have reason also for tranquil inquiry to foresee them." [I, 83] It was the great virtue of Greek thinkers very early to seek to interpret nature as a regular order, in which divine intervention was exceptional.

The Phoenicians, who had small city-states like the Greeks but enjoyed less freedom and were much more influenced by the great empires of the Near East, had a somewhat similar polytheistic outlook but emphasized more the chief god, Baal. [91, pp. 57–58] There were many local and special gods for cities and aspects of nature; especially important was Astarte, the fertility goddess, an approximate counterpart of Hera plus Aphrodite. The priesthood was not important and ceremonies were simpler than elsewhere in the Near East. [133, p. 345] Like the Greeks, the Phoenicians paid no great attention to the afterlife [118, p. 138], and they sought favors of the higher powers not by contrite submission but by the sacrifice of valued things on the altar, such as virginity or an infant son.

Much earlier, the Sumerians likewise had a pantheon reflecting the political order of their small states. There was no supreme autocrat among the extremely numerous gods, who met to debate, quaffed deeply, discussed freely, and came to agreement under the leadership of a senior god, chosen king by the assembly. [520, p. 33] Moved by all the human passions, they could be wounded and even die, that is, go to the Underworld. [135, p. 85] According to one myth, Enlil, the chief of the gods, was banished by a divine assembly to the region of darkness for the rape of a virgin goddess. [122, p. 253] They were human enough, in the tale, to be terrorized by the Deluge they had evoked, as they "cowered like dogs, crouched against the outer doors. Ishtar cried like a woman in travail, there moaned the mistress of the gods." They were, like the most obvious forces of nature, essentially unfriendly to mankind, with no pretense of fatherly affection, but they did like the sacrifices offered them, and the other gods rebuked Enlil, the chief, for nearly exterminating mankind in the great flood. [*109*, pp. 76–80] Some gods were local, others general [*135*, p. 85], and the great temples were for the local gods. [*100*, p. 23] Each city-state was the estate of its own god, or comprised the estates of several gods, while Enlil was leader of all [*136*, p. 338], much as one city usually held a sort of leadership over the whole community of city-states. The Sumerian ideas of an afterlife were rather vague and confused, but even the greatest heroes went to a gloomy abode below, and everlasting life in the light was the rarest of blessings. [*135*, p. 91]

After more or less united empire came to prevail over Mesopotamia, religion changed. Under the Third Dynasty of Ur, the priests were made part of the state apparatus, and the theory grew that humans existed only to serve the gods. [*100*, p. 261] Hammurabi and his successors elevated the leading Babylonian god, Marduk, to be a general governor of the universe, a supreme lawgiver ruling the stars and all below. [J. Needham in *468*, p. 135] In following centuries, he formally assimilated many other gods, including Enlil of old Sumeria, became full king of all gods, and was called simply "Bel" or "Lord," with a solar aspect. With the elevation of Marduk also came the growth of a large and broadly organized priesthood. [*136*, pp. 339–345] When the Assyrians subsequently marched to dominion over the Near East, they carried their onetime local divinity, Ashur, to corresponding supremacy. The conquered nations were made subject not only to the Assyrian monarch, who was a "faithful shepherd" of all peoples and "shepherd of the four world regions," but to his god Ashur. Likewise the other gods became subject to the omnipotent will of this towering and perfect deity; there remained only Ashur and minor spirits. Marduk, god of Babylonia, was admitted as a manifestation of Ashur. [*127*, pp. 609, 613–614] Late in the empire, there seems to have been a revolt against Ashur and an attempt to replace him by Nabu: "Thou shalt follow after, trust in Nabu, trust not in any other god." But Ashur was soon restored. [*127*, p. 165; *137*, p. 172] A standard Assyrian prayer ran,

> O God, I do not know how great thy punishment will be,
> I pronounced lightly your august name,
> I neglected the law which you gave,
> I committed many sins, I know not where, everywhere!
> My God, abate thy wrath! [*137*, p. 173]

Early in Egyptian history there were strong tendencies to assert the supremacy of a single deity, or at least the real identity of major ones. [*140*, pp. 142–143] In the Old Kingdom, worship of the sun was instituted by the Third Dynasty or early in the Fourth, but it was rather the religion of the pharaoh than that of the people [*126*, pp. 14, 163]; while he worshiped Re, they worshiped him. [*138*, p. 8] When they sacrificed to lesser gods, they were in a sense still adoring the pharaoh, as he was held the incarnation of all local deities and all temples were his [*126*, p. 182]; as the pharaoh represented all deities, there was not much need for formal monotheism. But there was a monotheistic essence, as the Egyptians often wrote simply of "God." [*95*, pp. 24–29] By the Fifth Dynasty, as the state was entering its decline, Re had become a lord of gods, perhaps equivalent even to such ancient and revered deities as Osiris, perhaps a sole god in his own right. [*138*, p. 50; *89*, p. 296] The pharaoh, whose tomb came to be built in the form of a Sun temple [*141*, p. 129], at the same time was degraded from a god in his own right to mere Son of the Sun. [*138*, p. 8]

The empire restored in the New Kingdom gave supremacy to Amon, "King of the Gods." Associated with the liberation of Egypt from the Hyksos domination, he promised dominion over all the earth. [*114*, Pt. I, p. 33] As the New Kingdom came to the end of its expansion, however, Amon ceased to be a great war god and was regarded rather as a cosmic creator and universal ruler, largely identified with the solar disk. [*114*, Pt. I, p. 14] Theologians consciously tried to unify the pantheon under his rule and rites generally were brought into a common pattern. [*126*, pp. 125, 182] A hymn of Amenhotep III's reign speaks of the sun as "Creator of all and giver of their sustenance," and "Sole Lord taking captive all lands every day." [*92*, pp. 275–276] Although a god of dread aspect who felt no human passions and had no unseemly adventures, he listened to the prayers of the poor and protected the humble from rapacious officials. [*138*, p. 16; *126*, pp. 126–127] The priesthood of Amon, highly professionalized and hierarchically organized, claimed jurisdiction in his name over all the temples of Egypt. [*114*, Pt. I, pp. 14, 17; *88*, p. 177] Meanwhile the divinity of the pharaoh, representative and son of the supreme god (who physically consorted with the queen), was emphasized and somewhat justified by the impressive figure of Thutmose III, perhaps the most renowned conqueror of Egyptian history.

Thus the groundwork was well prepared for Amenhotep IV to go further, seeking not only to elevate the sun-god above all others but to do away with all rivals. In the glorification of Aten (an old name for the solar disk or sun-god, which had come into use during the preceding reign [138, p. 19]), the names of Osiris and other ancient gods were erased; references to plural "gods" were hacked from old monuments; the worship of the newly universal god was decreed not merely for Egyptians but Asiatic and Nubian subjects as well [140, pp. 72, 207], and the pharaoh changed his own name to Ikhnaten ("pleasing to Aten"). There was also a shift of tone from the mechanistic-magical to the personal-moral; Aten, the benevolent father of all (a hymn ran, "Thou settest each man in his place, thou carest for his wants" [140, p. 207]), was to be approached above all with humility and prayer. [92, p. 301] However, the pharaoh did not neglect himself. Such was his glorification that everyone was portrayed with the homely features of Ikhnaten, and tombs of the time show not the private life of the deceased, as had been customary, but the splendors of Aten and Ikhnaten. [140, pp. 217, 219] The two were hardly separable, as the pharaoh was the sole mediator with Aten, perhaps the sole god in person. [134, p. 191]

The religious revolution was something of a political revolution as well. Ikhnaten, son of a commoner wife, was supported by new men, a court party of his own [134, p. 187], including a large Asiatic element. [138, p. 31] Perhaps for this reason there was much resistance, and the new religion hardly outlasted its founder. While Ikhnaten was attending to the worship of Aten and himself, much of the empire was lost, and his successors faced troubled times. The succession was broken, and the conservatives prevailed. Ikhnaten's capital was abandoned, and his works were execrated. But much of the spirit lived on. The universal qualities of Aten were attributed to Amon, now become more beneficient and lonely [138, pp. 152–153], called "Father of gods," and "Sole and only One, maker of what exists." In the heightened piety, men saw it was appropriate to confess sins, acknowledge unworthiness, and beg for mercy and help from the Supreme Being. [92, pp. 310–319]

Strong rulers, like Aurelian, who restored the unity of the Roman empire, and Louis XIV of France, have ever found the sun a fitting symbol of their splendor. Likewise, great empires have often been disposed to adore that brilliant and potent orb. But most dedicated to the sun was the empire of the Incas. According to legend, the Sun created the first Inca to propagate his worship, and the Inca army marched with the duty of spreading the cult of the sun-god. The first obligation of a conquered city was to erect a temple to him above the temples to their local deities; the latter were often carried away, put on trial, kept as hostages, or sometimes smashed. [*173*, pp. 161–164] An integral part of the imperial apparatus, sun worship required elaborate and splendid rituals, a large priesthood and many diviners, sacrificers, and caretakers of shrines. [J. Rowe in *180*, pp. 293–298] The priests served also as guardians of morals; those with burdened consciences went to them lest secret sin bring woe on all. After hearing confessions, the priests imposed penances corresponding to the offense, perhaps a whipping by assistants stationed nearby, possibly even death. [*173*, pp. 57–58]

Before the Incas, the sun had been only one of many worshiped objects, along with a wide variety of spirits and oracles reminiscent of the local gods and spirits of Greek religion. [*173*, p. 43] The early Incas who founded and consolidated the empire called their supreme god Viracocha, or simply "Lord" — the same title having been taken as the name of one of the great conquerors. Viracocha was commonly considered equivalent to the sun. He was, however, also identified or confused with the old-time Inca family god, Inti. [*173*, p. 165] In another aspect he was held superior to the sun and all else. It is said that Pachacuti, consolidator of the empire, postulated a higher god because the sun was not always present and even in his glory could be thwarted by a cloud across his face. [*173*, p. 163] Thereupon Pachacuti worked out a theology and revised the ceremonies appropriately. However considered, Viracocha was fitted for an imperial destiny, as he would tolerate no equal gods, and his worship justified expansion in the eyes of both conquerors and conquered. [J. Rowe in *180*, p. 329] When the Inca empire perished, his worship, not yet deeply inculcated, quickly vanished, while the older local deities lived on. [*178*, p. 26]

Zarathustra, who lived in the time of Cyrus or earlier [*246*, p. 57], elevated Ahura Mazda ("Wise Lord") from being merely the greatest of numerous gods to sole rulership, omniscient and omnipotent source of all being. His seems to have become the monotheistic religion of the Achaemenid empire. Although the Prophet's name is not mentioned in the various and lengthy inscription of Darius, Ahura Mazda appears in every other line and neither Darius nor Xerxes mentions any other god by name. [254, p. 154] As appointee of Ahura Mazda, Darius regarded himself as called upon to repress evil, the Lie, which was equivalent to rebellion. [254, pp. 157–158] Xerxes, who called himself the "Savior," whose advent Zarathustra had foretold, claimed to have expelled the old sky and weather gods opposed by Zarathustra. [246, p. 171] Somewhat later, the calendar was reformed to correspond to the Zoroastrian canon. [254, p. 155]

After the downfall of the Achaemenids, Zoroastrianism fell apart. With recentralization, the Sassanids gathered and canonized the old writings in the Avesta, restored Ahura Mazda to full glory, and made his the state religion. [254, pp. 179–191] The founder of the dynasty said, "Religion and kingship are twin brothers, and neither can dispense with the other. Religion is the foundation of kingship and kingship protects religion." [254, p. 284] By corollary, he repressed other faiths, such as Christianity, Judaism, and Buddhism. The Sassanid empire thus institutionalized intolerance at about the same time that the Roman empire did the same with the establishment of Christianity. The priesthood, large and hierarchic, was part of the governing apparatus and a strong support for it. [250, p. 153] But monotheism was not quite consistent. Ahura Mazda, or Ormuzd, was a supreme deity served by many inferior gods and tutelary spirits. [250, pp. 171–173] It was also recognized, as it seems not to have been in earlier times, that he was limited by a force of evil. [254, p. 55] Although there was some uncertainty, he was usually conceived as struggling against the Satanic figure of Ahriman [254, p. 179] with his army of rebels, who would in the fullness of time be overcome, a dualism that would come easily to the state that claimed world dominion but found itself usually sorely beset by heathen and evil forces. Ormuzd demanded the assistance of men in the shape of morality, purity, obedience to his commandments, and dedication to assist against Ahriman, the prince of darkness; in return, he rewarded with the bliss of paradise or threw into hell. The principal sin was aggressiveness. [254, p. 53]

This was the official religion, whose sacred fire was symbol of the King of Kings; indeed, the founder of the dynasty wished to extinguish all holy fires except the one at the royal residence. [247] But various heresies, officially opposed, showed much the same tendencies or an intensification of them. One preached a higher god than Ormuzd and Ahriman, and so moved to logically complete monotheism. [*250*, p. 177] On the other hand, Mani, a prophet arising early in the dynasty, stressed the fundamental dualism of the universe, not so much as good spirit versus evil spirit as good spirit versus evil matter [*254*, p. 183], the light-spiritual and the dark-earthly parts being organized much as the Persian kingdom was. Man, between the two worlds, was rather evil and could be redeemed only by strong faith and strict adherence to the law and with the aid of the Redeemer. In the elaborate organization of the Manichean church a class of "perfects" followed high monastic standards of abstinence from pleasures. [*250*, pp. 180–182] An early Sassanid was tempted to try to make this the catholic and unifying religion of the empire, but the strength of the orthodox establishment deterred him. [*254*, p. 184] Persecuted both in Persia and the West, Manichaeism yet managed to spread through much of the Near East, North Africa, and southern Europe, where it became alloyed with Christianity. A derivation of Manichaeism, Mazdakism, exalted more the Ruler of Light as Lord of Heaven, surrounded by vassals and ministers like rulers on earth. [*251*, p. 188] It required that the people be nonviolent, vegetarian, and mild and merciful. They should share worldly goods in brotherly fashion and perhaps their women also, because God placed good things on earth for all alike and inequality resulted from violence. [*245*, pp. 343–344]

Such a religion is the complete antithesis of the worship of the frolicking beings of Olympus, just as the Persian priest, courtier, or serf, or the hereditary official or bound tenant of the later Roman empire was a polar opposite in his political and intellectual outlook to the free farmer or trader of classic Greece. The peoples of the free states and those of the great empire live in worlds far apart, politically, economically, socially, and morally, and no less, religiously.

If the world of the great empire is to be consistent, it must profoundly alter the religious outlook. The universal empire implies that the universe is strongly ordered, and a monotheistic religion bespeaks firmer rule than a polytheistic, just as an autocratic society is more governed than a pluralistic. National or local gods, often of limited jurisdiction, are superseded by a god corresponding to the whole empire; when men lose attachment to their state or city, they are ready to turn away from deities associated with its aspirations. For those taught to revere the supreme earthly monarch, near-human and fallible gods are unacceptable. For Philo, God was the "King of Kings," and there was no more point in honoring lesser gods than provincial governors. [*340*, p. 25] In the imperial unity, bringing all within a single compass, unity of religion becomes a positive value, to erase differences between peoples and to put all in a common mold. The universal creed, grander and more compelling than any local one, convincingly sustains universal power, whereas particular gods might lend support to rebellion. And it is not fitting that the dissident should be able to appeal to another god than the one whose representative the emperor is; such a deity of the wrong-spirited must be a devil. Just as there is a single great political power permanently established and unassailable, to which are owed blind loyalty and obedience, there should be a single faith to overspread all differences of race or nation, to overcome all prejudices and divisions, that peace and charity reign over the single sheepfold under the one Shepherd. There should be a single great truth, a truth already known and unquestionable. Philosophic dissent, a fundamental questioning of reason for authority, is banned, of course, as potential political dissent. The splendid ruler of the universe requires complete submission; fearful of hidden movements, he looks not only to the deeds but to the thoughts and motives of his subjects. Unlike the leaders of freer states, the great autocrat feels the need to peer into men's consciences; and no punishment is too harsh for the disloyal.

The empire represents itself as the Kingdom of God on earth. The emperor is easily credited with doing more than is humanly possible, and he represents something incomprehensibly great, the organizing, ordering principle of the world, surely worthy of adoration. Who but he can fill the longing of the peoples for a savior? [*296*, p. 219] As an inscription of 9 B.C. put it, "The birthday of god [Augustus] has brought to the world glad tidings that are bound up with him. From his birthday, a new era begins." [*335*, p. 4] The appearance of the emperor is an epiphany. A new reign is a promise of salvation, and the years were dated, in the Roman empire, from its beginning. [*487*, p. 29] Worship of the emperor, or of the god from whom he is descended or by whom he is chosen and consecrated, tends to crowd out worship of others, because failure to subscribe to it is disloyalty and competing cults are ipso facto suspect, because participation in it is socially and politically advantageous, and because a large, centrally controlled and state-supported priesthood desires to make its own sway exclusive. Because of the importance of ceremony and ideology, the state must concern itself with religion, which, like all else, should serve its purposes, guiding conduct in general instead of answering individual needs.

The political structure and ideals of the empire furnish a model, not the only one but certainly among the most important, for conceptions of divine power. The mind proceeds from the known to the unknown, perceiving the hidden or dimly perceptible by analogy with things at hand; and the great heavenly power can hardly fail to be conceived analogously to the earthly power. As the empire subordinates all lesser nations in a great union, monotheism subordinates all the lesser spirits to a single ruling will. The imperial power, which accepts no rivals and demands universal obedience, for which minor disorders are insignificant, suggests, if it does not actually impose, belief in an absolute god standing in lonely omnipotence, an all-transcendent majesty, a personally directed ultimate order above the apparent clashing of natural and social forces. Tertullian frankly held the Great God to be like the Persian King of Kings or the Roman emperor, all-powerful above his many satraps or governors; should not honors go, he asked, to the Supreme Power instead of to the subordinates? [340, p. 49]

The bureaucratic structure of the empire is similarly a model for the universal church. Like the empire, the church would make itself exclusive, absorbing or suppressing all rivals, and universal, spreading its message everywhere, whereas polytheistic believers are little concerned whether others share their gods or not. Likewise, as in the imperial order independent forces are anathema, so in the heavenly order all not conforming to the divine will are considered demons, the category to which early Christians relegated pagan gods — the new monotheism does not deny the existence of older gods but relegates them to an inferior class. The character of the emperor may also be attributed to the ruler of heaven: sometimes wrathful, yet just and merciful, capable of fearful anger, yet loving his sheep or unworthy children, looking into consciences to be sure of utter loyalty and faith, and jealous of the worship given him. Political terror suggests divine wrath. A deep cleft between feeble and sinful humans and the almighty benevolent God above corresponds to the gulf separating the exalted and dignified emperor from his mean subjects. The tolerant gods of polytheism might concede benefits in a more or less commercial spirit in return for sacrifices made; they looked more at the gift than at the heart of the giver. The Ruler of the universe, however, too lofty to bargain with his subjects, calls rather for total submission of the will than for material gifts, and in return promises not so much a material benefit as peace and rest for the soul. It is a token of this projection of earthly to celestial rulership that the supreme deity loses individuality, being called Lord or an equivalent, like Dominus, Ahura Mazda, or Viracocha, more or less leaving behind a personal name, like Jehovah, as his individuality (implying the existence of others) is dissolved in majesty.

The imperial order also profoundly affects the values of people and, accordingly, their religious ideas. In the stress on exclusive loyalty and obedience, faith becomes a prime virtue, and mental passivity is better than insolent inquiry. The power-ridden society is pious, as the essence of piety is deep respect for power. Religiosity is increased by differences between rulers and ruled, for the former a support of status, for the latter a consolation. The empire is inherently pacifist; compliance with the powers that be is much wiser than yielding to anger; self-denial is better than courageous self-assertion; asceticism becomes a prime virtue. In the face of provocation, humility is best. Pride is a cardinal sin, as the empire teaches self-depreciation. There is no room for individuality. One should leave things to the Supreme Ruler and give all to Him. All elements of authority, from the stern father up, increase the propensity to respect for higher powers. Ptahhotep, early in the Old Kingdom, offered such precepts as "Put thyself in the hands of God, and thy tranquillity shall overthrow [thy enemies]" [*104*, p. 67]; "If thou abasest thyself in the service of a perfect man, thy conduct shall be fair before God"; "What is loved of God is obedience; God hateth disobedience" [*95*, p. 27]; "Give way unto him that attacketh." Success and wealth, according to the wise vizier, are given by God, and the unfortunate should humbly honor their masters. [*104*, pp. 66, 70]

The empire teaches people to look for salvation, not to their own efforts, but to the mercy of superior beings; the litany of the empire, endlessly repeated, is "Lord, have mercy on us." By corollary, woes come from doing ill in the sight of the powerful, and attitudes are nearly as important as deeds, as for the emperor intentions are nearly as criminal as acts. In the same way, the welfare of mankind depends not so much on human efforts as upon the love or anger of the supreme Authority, and the universe itself is not something as it were natural, but the result of and ordered by a great Will. Differences of standing must be divinely ordered in the divinely ordered universe; and poverty is not a fault but a burden inescapable on earth to be borne with patience, as the ruler gives and takes by his inscrutable will. Or it is a virtue, while wealth, which comes from cheating or oppressing the people contrary to the will of the supreme Ruler, is very sinful. The humble masses see with glee that those proud of material goods are cast down, if not materially, at least spiritually; perhaps they look to a sharp reversal when they will be redeemed and their oppressors tormented. Cherishing the ideal of equality in the sight of the divine Ruler, a promise defaulted by the earthly emperor, they look in their depression more longingly to the Father-Master above. Downtrodden and without hopes of raising themselves, men are held to be bad by nature, as they are ordinarily regarded by the rulers of the empire, and weak, capable of redemption only by grace falling from above. Religion then relieves a dull if not unhappy present and is a refuge from demoralization for those overtaken by powers they cannot match [504, *passim*], a profound comfort for those who give sincere devotion.

A strong and effectively governing empire has less need of a transcendental religion, because it is of itself a church and a religion, total and sufficiently capable of managing society, punishing and rewarding; and a single great religious establishment may represent an unmanageable competitive power. The emperor of China felt himself to be an adequate intermediary between earth and Heaven. Augustus seems to have been sufficient savior for most people of the Roman empire. But after generations of decay it is no longer possible to hail the accession of a new Caesar as the beginning of a new era. As the factual power of the emperor ebbs, he can no longer usurp the rule of a heavenly god; hopes of salvation must be transferred from the failing earthly potentate to a higher sphere. The perfect order, which has failed on earth, is projected to heaven, while emperorship is more idealized as the emperor is more secluded from actual rule, an unseen being without human failings. When the emperor is no longer able to chastise and reward effectively, justice requires that sins be requited and merits recompensed by the deity, and as the bases of morality shrink there is more need for preaching.

Burdened by their sense of inadequacy, failure, and sin, people look for a new and true savior to lead them away from oppression and despair, a better Ruler to whom to give a higher loyalty. Thus Ipuwer, in the breakdown of the Old Kingdom, wanted Re to come and reign over Egypt. [252, p. 7] As he wrote, the redeeming god "shall bring cooling to the flame. Men shall say, 'He is the shepherd of all the people, there is no evil in his heart. If his flocks go astray, he will spend the day to search them. . . .' Verily he shall smite evil when he raises his arm against it." [94, p. 205] Jewish messianism turned from hopes of national liberation to the promise of a divine new age; and many a millenary movement since has hoped for a better empire of peace, order, justice, and harmony by divine command.

As the social order decays, more need is felt to turn to church and heavenly powers for the security and stability the empire can no longer give. The clergy as well as the bureaucracy gain independent authority in the slackening of central power. In the latter generations of the Old Kingdom and of the New Kingdom, as in the troubled times of many Near Eastern empires, the priesthood became a major force in the state. The rise of religiosity in the Roman empire is especially striking. Similarly, in the Turkish empire, the power of the Moslem establishment and its material position and influence grew steadily, reign by reign. [435, p. 234] The weaker the temporal empire, the more necessary to fill in the spiritual realm the functions that had been filled by earthly power, perhaps to promise that the lord of light will in due time return to scatter the hosts of darkness. Feeling the need of guidance, trained to faith and reverence for the universal power, but without an effective emperor on earth, the postimperial society gives itself to the worship of the great heavenly Lawgiver; and religion is an essential part, if not the very skeleton, of its traditional order. Then religion, which may alter rapidly in fluid situations, as a buttress of the social order acquires its marvelous conservatism, meticulously retaining usages through centuries or millennia.

It may be because postimperial societies especially need a sustaining faith that the Near East, land par excellence of broken empires — which one after another came to proclaim their aspirations, infuse the people with their image, and leave nostalgia upon their departure — has been the birthplace of so many great religious movements. A people such as the Hebrews, always under the cultural influence of the empires and usually subject to their rule, but without a universal monarch of their own, were particularly well equipped to evolve religious ideas. Their monotheism gradually evolved; Jehovah was held sole sovereign of the universe by the time of their release from Babylonian captivity. [322, p. 87] Satan was conceived of originally not as the antagonist of Jehovah but as an agent looking around for misbehavior, the counterpart of the Persian inspector-general, the King's Eye [472]; he became the counterpart of Ahriman, the incarnation of evil. [253, I, 113] But Judaism was only one of a multitude of faiths arising in the land from Syria and Egypt to Persia, from ancient cults of mother-goddesses, like Cybele and Isis, down to the Bahai movement of nineteenth-century Persia.

It was also under Persian influence that the idea of the dead rising for judgment and reward appeared in the latest parts of the Old Testament. [520, p. 274] Previously, the Hebrew Sheol had been, like the Sumerian underworld and the Greek Hades, a place of little religious significance. Zoroastrianism also probably looked at first toward the achievement of justice on earth, but in time transferred attention and hopes to the future existence. [254, p. 58] According to the developed beliefs, all souls would come onto a narrow bridge over a deep chasm; the wicked would fall from it into a hell of eternal torments, but the righteous would cross to an "abode of song, with no night, no cold, no sickness." [253, I, 112; 254, p. 57] This emphasis seems to have been very common in the faiths of the imperial order. The Egyptians were so impressed with the importance of the future life that they paid much more attention to their tombs than to their houses [124, p. 1]; perhaps it was their chief preoccupation. [95, p. 10] Incredible exertions went into the task of providing a permanent home for the pharaoh, whose presence should bless the land forever. [141, p. 49] The Egyptians also elaborated the idea of the trial of the soul and the weighing of its sins and merits. The heart was placed in one pan of a scale and a feather in the other. If the heart, burdened by guilt, outweighed the feather, it was thrown to an obscene beast to be crushed and consumed; if not, the deceased was sent to a delightful residence with Osiris in the sun. [*141*, pp. 73–74; *557*, p. 38]

The Christian stress on postmortal existence has been at times almost equally strong; the Byzantine church especially dwelt upon resurrection and immortality. [*412*, p. 6] Buddhism, which in India promised the bliss of extinction, in China acquired a complex of heavens and hells. Taoism, in a more specially Chinese vein, stressed rather longevity or earthly immortality; and if one went to heaven he might return to sojourn on earth. [*1*, p. 110] Chinese alchemists sought elixirs to preserve the body, as Western ones sought the magic of making gold. [J. Needham in *12*, p. 250] Ancestor worship and belief in the continuity of spirits in the family have also filled some of the same needs. Similarly in Russia, Orthodoxy made much of the continuation after death; Russian scientific and pseudoscientific thought has turned to the indefinite prolongation of life, as it has not done in the West. [*422*]

This turn of religion or psychology comes easy to the empire. For the man who has achieved all power, the most painful of facts is ineluctable death, the mockery of all pomp and praise. Any absolute ruler is likely to think much of his own survival. The pharaohs' tombs became gigantic as their power became complete at the beginning of the Old Kingdom. The founder of Chinese unity, Shih Huang-ti, having conquered all there was to conquer, was obsessed with using his limitless power to escape death. He put multitudes of magicians and philosophers to seeking the drug of immortality, and sent a corps of youths and maidens to find the legendary abode of immortals. [*30*, p. 39] As a last resort, he had, it is said, 700,000 men construct him an immense and elaborate tomb, at the center of which was an artificial universe with painted sky, rivers, and an ocean of mercury. [*40*, p. 97; *30*, p. 40] If the ruler cannot retain life in reality, he may do so in appearance, as the Inca mummies continued to preside over their personal courts [see above, p. 85], a matter of utmost importance for the ruling Inca; Atahualpa was willing to profess Christianity in the feeble hope that, by avoiding burning, he might become a mummy. [*173*, p. 313] Immortality is essential for total dignity.

Immortality also promises that no wrongdoers escape even in death. Unhappily, the ethical law of the empire is often cheated;

evildoers escape and many fail to receive justice; all should be requited by the Great Judge. The law of Darius went so far as to prescribe the punishments to be suffered in the hereafter [252, p. 131], while Xerxes promised happiness in life and blessedness in death to those who followed the path of Truth. [254, p. 158]

The people, too, long for immortality. The felt need is greater as society is atomized and civic feelings are weakened. When there is little hope of betterment in this life, they need the promise of relief; when there is no justice on earth, they are consoled by the future, wherein the cheated and the oppressed, the deserving and the faithful, should dwell in a paradise like the emperor's palace, while the unfaithful and the breakers of the good law must be cast into unspeakable dungeons.

The sense of the empire, its claim that all should be ordered and justice must be complete, thus calls for immortality. The great organization itself is immortal and its conservatism and adherence to the past encourage a sense of permanence of men, also. It is supposedly perfect, officially optimistic; it does not admit doubt or tragedy, which is suffering beyond deserts, an evil from which there is no escape. Individualism means the essential loneliness of humans in an often capricious and unfriendly universe of finitude and futility.

CHINESE BUDDHISM

China, unlike the more agitated Near East, has been notably unproductive of great religions. The philosophy of the Chinese state and the upper classes has long been rather secular, or at least has given little attention to supernatural questions; Confucianism is much more a social philosophy than a religion. The uncultivated masses, on the other hand, have been immersed in a tangle of superstition; no monotheistic church in the imperial image stands out.

At one time, however, China saw a religious development somewhat parallel to that of Christianity in the sinking Roman empire. In the weakening of the Han empire, nearly contemporary to the Roman, there was a sharp rise of religious belief, both popular and philosophic. Taoism flourished; and Buddhism, introduced from India but adapted to Chinese ways and needs, became strong. The latter dominated Chinese culture for some four centuries after the Hans. Only with the reestablishment of universal empire was it pushed into the background, eventually to recede into insignificance.

Buddhism seems to have entered China in the second half of the first century A.D., as the Han dynasty was heading toward decline. Although at first little noticed, it spread as the land became torn by disorders, the peasantry was driven to desperation, and scholars increasingly looked for better answers to the serious questions of existence and society. Taoism also became a significant religion at this time. In 165 A.D. the emperor of the declining dynasty ordered official offerings to Lao-tzu and dedicated a temple in his honor; he was formally apotheosized as "Emperor of Mysterious Origin" and provided with a heavenly court. [524, p. 332] After the fall of the Han dynasty at the beginning of the third century, Neo-Taoism enjoyed about a generation of high prosperity. [77, p. 30] Buddhism for a time seemed more like a Taoist sect than an independent religion. However, with its better philosophic basis and broader spiritual appeal, Buddhism prevailed generally and was widely established by 300 A.D. [77, p. 33; D. Bodde in 466, p. 84] It gained firmest hold in the north where conditions were most disturbed by continual incursions from the steppes. By 381, nine-tenths of the people of the northwest were said to be Buddhists [33, p. 56], and the high tide came in the fifth century when in the midst of much upheaval there swelled the longing for spiritual salvation. [2, p. 255] The progress of Buddhism was not much less in the south, where an emperor of the first half of the sixth century embraced Buddhism, repressed Taoism, and had himself named Emperor Bodhisvatta, that is, near-Buddha. [77, p. 51] The Buddhist church, never so firmly organized and united as the Christian, was much more tolerant and less clearly set off from competing beliefs. Consequently it never suppressed its rivals, and its dominance was not complete; but China seems to have been fairly describable as a Buddhist land from the third until the ninth century. Similarly in Japan, where many Chinese patterns were reflected, Buddhism gained great influence as the central power shrank, until in the fourteenth and fifteenth centuries it dominated Japanese culture. [E. Reischauer in 466, p. 41]

The framework of Chinese Buddhism was taken from Indian philosophy, translated with difficulty into the very different Chinese idiom. However, beliefs underwent such changes as virtually to make it a new religion, especially in the most popular sect, that of Pure Land. Started about the end of the fourth century, this school sought salvation not in the classic Buddhist manner through mental discipline and the gradual accumulation of merit, but rapidly by prayers, ceremonies, and complete faith in the grace of a Supreme Ruler, the Amitabha or Buddha of Infinite Splendor. [33, pp. 62–63] The Buddhist philosophical Absolute became a personal God offering redemption to all. [26, pp. 188–189] The idea of reincarnation in successive lives lost importance; instead, the soul should fear a hell or series of purgatories, or aspire to the Pure Land, the place of bliss. This was no Nirvana of merciful extinction as offered to Indian believers, no mere release from suffering but something fully as alluring as the Christian heaven, with music, limpid lakes, bright birds, and marvelous jewels. [83, pp. 132–133] The good Buddhist should be charitable, meek and non-violent, accepting humbly the evil blow without striking back in anger; like the Christian, he should hold the world's goods to be unimportant and should overcome earthly desire to please the Deity. [83, p. 135] In various observances, Chinese Buddhism resembled the Christianity of Rome, as in a tonsured and celibate priesthood, monasteries, fast days, and the use of a rosary.

Christianity succeeded and became permanent in the West; Buddhism in China shriveled. The reason for the decline of Buddhism probably lay mostly in the strength of the state, which found another ideology more suitable. But it is not obvious that Buddhism had necessarily to conflict with authority. It always and even with great humility accepted the superiority of the state. Much as early Christian fathers called for loyalty to the powers of the state, the founder of the Pure Land sect had affirmed obedience to temporal rulers: "They who rejoice in the way of Sakya invariably first serve their parents and obey their lords." [77, p. 50] The reunifier of China was a onetime Buddhist monk, who favored the religion, even while opposing sects that might serve as foci of sedition. Under his Sui and the following T'ang dynasties, Buddhist ritual was an important support of the empire, while Buddhism continued to play an important part in the life of aristocracy and common folk alike. [77, p. 70] Buddhism was also useful in inculcating courage in the army. Traditional belief and practices required burial of the body entire at home where it would be served by rituals of the descendants; Confucianism implied no other immortality. Buddhism, with its view of a detachable soul and future paradise, was much more consoling for those dying far from home and family. [77, p. 74]

Despite the inoffensiveness and utility of Buddhism, the traditional Confucianism better suited the emperor. The reunifiers of China were at pains to restore Confucian rites in order to transfer the legitimacy of the gloriously remembered Han dynasty to the new. Confucianism also had theories of social and political control which no rival could match. [77, p. 66] Nor did it offer any threat of independent power; unlike Buddhism, it did not stand as a movement outside the state. The chief argument against Buddhism was that it encouraged withdrawal from state service, which Confucianism held up as ideal. [*31*, p. 51] Even if conventional Buddhism was passive enough, it was continually proliferating independent sects which were always a potential menace, especially when they looked for the early arrival of a messiah, who might spring up to head any peasant uprising. [77, p. 69] Moreover, it was some reflection on the authority of the emperor that Buddhism offered a personal salvation instead of perfection of the social order. [E. Zürcher in *12*, pp. 58–59] For these reasons, even while tolerating Buddhism, Sui and T'ang rulers kept tight reins on temples and monasteries, strictly regulating and limiting their activities.

But the supremacy of Confucianism probably owed most to the examination system. Since entry into the civil service continued to be based on proficiency in the Confucianist classics, for which Buddhism offered no substitute, they dominated education and gradually reduced Buddhist influence among the gentry. With the support of the official classes, later T'ang rulers could attack Buddhism as an independent power wasteful of money; great repressions in the ninth century dealt it blows from which it never fully recovered. [77, p. 83]

The Sung dynasty, following the T'ang after two generations of disorders, effectively ended Buddhism as a power in Chinese life. Neo-Confucianism was developed in part to meet within the Confucian framework problems raised by Buddhism; it also assimilated elements of Buddhist philosophy and so reduced its appeal. The strong Sung state likewise undercut Buddhism by taking over the charitable and social functions of its temples. Printing strengthened the preferred Confucianist philosophy, as the new abundance of books enabled many more persons to study for the examinations and so to indoctrinate themselves. The Sung and subsequent dynasties also developed more effective social controls in propaganda, the direction of schools and scholarship, and the censorship of undesirable writings. [77, pp. 93–96] Buddhism was thus deprived of its intellectual basis and lost its attractions for the elite. Its priesthood ceased to be a desirable career, and its theological level sank. The intellectuals became vaguely agnostic concerning powers above the Son of Heaven. The peasantry remained primitively religious [77, pp. 95, 97]; in the general intellectual numbness, the chief means to redemption was endless repetition of the holy name. [31, p. 229] Buddhist deities became more and more confused with native demigods, and Buddhism and Taoism, close together when Buddhism first came to China, tended again to fuse. But the order of heaven was still patterned after that of this earth: a supernatural bureaucracy ruled the afterlife under a celestial emperor, with functionaries keeping the records of souls, assigning them appropriate status, and issuing permits as needed. [77, p. 102]

NEW FAITHS AT ROME

The Roman domain, evolving from republican city-state to despotic world empire, likewise went from a loose polytheism, with cults of many independent deities little concerned with conduct, to a stern and exclusive monotheism under an exacting God. Power-bent Rome did not start from so democratic a constitution as Athens; and early Roman religion, concentrated in state cults, was much more centralized than the many colleges of priests and independent temples of Athens. But empire led Rome from countless divinities, great ones corresponding to the Olympic gods of Greece and minor ones inhabiting hearths and groves, to a universal church.

As mistress of the world, Rome clung tenaciously to the old traditions and cults; but they no longer sufficed. Degraded by being made subsidiary to emperor worship, they gave little or no moral guidance, which had been largely supplied by the intense patriotism of the city-state. In the empire, a better faith was needed. Human life had become a frail bark tossed by great and inscrutable forces, sadly in need of direction and support. Denied participation in the life of the state, the people longed for a new belonging and a finer promise, something more comforting and inspiring than the old rituals, which became hollow as the city-state lost meaning. With declining individualism and intellectual curiosity, if not intelligence, men needed ready answers for the riddles of the universe, especially how and why one should conduct his life. Some turned to the moralizers, who tried to find a philosophic substitute for the stimulation and focusing of energies of the old political life. The conservatives tried to adapt the old religion and fit it to the new mentality. Those who needed stronger emotional comfort turned to new creeds from the East, which taught resignation and promised mercy to those who humbled themselves and prayed with faith.

Philosophy itself, ceasing to inquire into objective reality, merged into religion. In Hellenistic times, as the Greek city-states lost authority, interest in things spiritual grew, and philosophy began to fit itself to the new temper and aspect of the world. Turning inward, it became partly mystical and partly skeptical as it renounced truth seeking in favor of moralizing, concern with reality in favor of concern with conduct. Rome continued and affirmed these trends of half-subdued Greece; Roman philosophy, like Chinese, was above all ethical. Zeno preached and Romans adopted the doctrine of the world state of universal equality, in which men should be brothers under a Supreme Power, who acted as the highest official of the world city, thereby justifying and spiritualizing the universal order. [287, p. 6] Life being no longer very promising, Roman Stoics taught self-mastery, renunciation, and equanimity in suffering; anger should be met by kindness. [343, p. 34] Their most marked difference from Christianity was the retention of a good deal of spiritual pride and moral self-sufficiency, holding man fundamentally strong and capable of finding spiritual truth by reason. [343, pp. 39–40] Giving philosophy an ever more religious cast, Seneca's monotheism called for recognition of the triviality of earthly life and for service and gratitude to the Almighty, fountain of reward and punishment. In this vein Marcus Aurelius wrote: "There is one universe, made up of everything, and one God who pervades everything, and one substance, one law, one common reason." [*Meditations*, VII, 9] Believing in no afterlife of consequence, he resigned himself: "Everything is right

for me which is right for you, O Universe," and "On every occasion
a man should say, 'This comes from God.'" [*Meditations*, IV, 23;
III, 11] As Apollonius said, "My prayer before the altars is, grant
me, ye gods, what is my due." [*302*, p. 347] The Cynic philosophers,
like the Stoics, were monotheists and believers in fate, preachers
in the spirit of Christian monks and of ascetics, which many of
them eventually became. [*302*, p. 361] In the later empire, pagan
moralists preached love and forgiveness, indifference to wealth
and obedience to the earthly powers, hardly differing from their
Christian counterparts except that the latter laid heavier stress on
the evils of sex. [*326*, II, 971–972] Philosophic acceptance of the
empire was well expressed by Dio Chrysostom: the monarch is the
shepherd of his people, appointed by God for their good; his power
rests upon virtue and divine favor, but he knows less pleasure than
anyone else.

This philosophy doubtless helped to reconcile men to the empire
and even the uncertainties of existence under a Nero or a Domitian,
but it was too impersonal to save from loneliness and loss of purpose. Worship of the imperial person, on the other hand, lacked
conviction and was discredited by evil and unbalanced rulers. [*347*,
pp. 82, 99] The cult of the ruler, however, was the biggest religious
organization, from which it was treason to remain aloof. Flooding
over local gods as the Roman empire flooded over small states,
emperor worship brought together large numbers of temples and
priesthoods and prepared the way for a single church. Indeed,
Elagabalus would have liked to proscribe all other worship, while
Alexander Severus tried to bring all religions of the empire, including those of Abraham and Christ, into his chapel. [*338*, p. 75]

In the general eclecticism and under the influence of emperor
worship, the old Olympian deities changed character; the gods of
Virgil are midway between the near-human figures of Homer and
the abstractions of a philosophical religion. [*308*, p. 46] Subsequently they lost individuality and were merged into a common
faith of the universal Father and Guardian, somewhat remote but
morally perfect and omnipotent. [*302*, p. 5] Thus was formed a
loose but essentially united religion, with a heavenly king presid-
ing over lesser deities; Zeus became a principle of animation [*343*,
p. 10], and other gods and spirits were to be honored as emanations
of the Great Divinity. The ancient myths were given moral interpretations; and sacred ceremonies promised happiness in the here-

after. [299, pp. 202–210] So adapted, the old religion showed much vitality. Awakening late to the challenge of new faiths, it strongly affirmed its whole inheritance, including animal sacrifices and miracles; oracles poured from every rock. [278, p. 15] This paganism retained great vitality, especially in the hearts of the conservative upper classes. It was the old pagan gods that Christian writers attacked, not the mystery religions [329, p. 29], and in the last days of the empire there was some inclination to turn back to pagan rites, as Christianity seemed to have failed.

Many, especially of the lower and less tradition-bound classes, moved on to creeds imported from Eastern lands that had been brought under Roman rule. The several oriental religions alike evoked an omnipotent Ruler who demanded full and wholehearted service and in return gave a sense of dedication in this life and bliss in the next. They offered hope in a world from which hope had faded, the unburdening of sins, and contact with the Master of the Universe. Their divinities were subject to human passion and suffered as the emperor suffered for his people, yet they were ever victorious. They had a much more elaborately organized priesthood than the nonbureaucratic old Roman or Greek religion. Bearing no relation to the classic municipal and social institutions, the new religions were above all universal, uniting men everywhere without distinction of nation or class. [299, p. 27]

The first important importation was the Phrygian Great Mother, riding in a chariot drawn by lions. She arrived in 204 B.C. but dwelt in obscurity until near the end of the republic. Her rites centered on her mourning for a fair youth slain by a boar, and his subsequent resurrection. [302, pp. 547–559] An essentially monotheistic Egyptian worship [557, p. 475] syncretized under the Ptolemies, that of Isis and Serapis, followed not long after. By the time of Julius Caesar their tonsured priests were common on the streets of Rome, and the cult spread widely through the empire. Isis was the Universal Mother, the Mater Dolorosa and Mother of God of paganism [322, p. 54]; Serapis was Lord of all the elements. They left Egyptian zoolatry behind and stood for ascetic purity, the judgment of merits after death, and a future recompense; their mercy, especially hers, embraced all who laid their hearts before them. They used an impressive ceremony, perhaps as regular and complicated as that of the Catholic church, to which it bore marked resemblances. Serapis, like many deities of the Near East, suffered death but was resurrected on the third day. The clergy held apart from worldly things, upholding purity and abstinence. [*302*, pp. 560–584]

Various other religions gained importance in the ripening empire. Elagabalus briefly tried to establish a Syrian god at Rome, and Aurelian built a temple to the Sun, as Rome seemed to draw toward a solar monotheism. [*302*, p. 443] There were eclectic movements and mystical philosophies, like Hermeticism, which gathered pieces of Judaism, Stoicism, and Greek metaphysics into a promise of redemption and immortality by asceticism and a qualifiedly monotheistic revelation. [*329*, p. 30] But the faith that offered most competition to rising Christianity was Mithraism, which came to Rome from Persia (where nothing is known of its practice) about the end of the republic and was spread rapidly by slaves and soldiers. Unlike other imported religions, it seems never to have been persecuted, possibly because of its popularity in the army. It was not favored by the upper classes, however, and is consequently better known from archaeology and inscriptions than from literary sources. From the beginning of the third century it was associated with the worship of the emperor as Sol Invictus, and Diocletian recognized the youthful god Mithra as protector of the empire. [*299*, p. 143] Its doctrines centered on adoration of the sun as source of light and life. It also taught the slaying of the bull, from whose blood new life sprang up. Among its ceremonies was baptism in a shower of bull's blood; it also had holy meals of bread and wine. The adversary of Mithra was Ahriman, the old Persian personification of evil. At the end of time Mithra would raise all from the dead, give blissful immortality to the good, and annihilate the evil and Ahriman himself. [*299*, p. 159]

Mithraism lost out despite favor shown it by various emperors. Among likely reasons are that it had little place for women and that it did not have a well-organized clergy. It was also unfortunate in being strongest in the northern regions most exposed to barbarian inroads. It came back briefly, however, under Julian the Apostate and later, and its worship lingered in some places into the fifth century. Most of its doctrines, such as purification, the final judgment, the wrestling of good and evil, rituals and festival days, including December 25 and Sunday, were close enough to Christianity that men passed from it to the newer faith with ease. [*322*,

p. 66] Its teachings went on in Manichaeism, another Persian religion in the lineage of Zoroaster, which had a long and influential life in the Near East and in Central Asia.

THE ROMAN CHURCH

The looseness of the imperial fabric of Rome, unlike that of China, permitted the rise of new religions; but for nearly three hundred years, Christianity made slow progress. However, it grew as life became increasingly wretched and insecure, and during the disorders and breakdown of the third century it became a real force in the empire. [329, p. 163] As the more vigorous Roman traditions were abandoned in the reshaped Eastern-style empire of the fourth century, it won out over its rivals. An obvious reason for its victory was the relative purity of its ethics and its freedom from the grosser superstitions and practices that encumbered other religions. It offered a morally perfect God against those of whom many a lewd tale was told. [329, pp. 121–122] More broadly appealing than Stoicism, more coherent and satisfying than the pagan cults, the Christian message also fitted very well the imperial social order. Universal harmony in brotherly love is the dream of world empire; Christianity proclaimed the peace on earth that Rome promised but failed to produce, and the universal love that dissolves lesser groups. Deprecation of riches was the more acceptable as they were insecure, and commerce lacked prestige. The preference for the faith of babes over the learning of wise men [Matt. 9:25] and scorn for the traditional philosophy [Col. 2:8; I Cor. 8:1] went with the currents of the age. The distinguishing moral of Christianity – the injunction to turn the other cheek when smitten – has for an individualistic society the nobility of ordinary impracticality. But for the subjects of the despotic empire, it had the practicality of good sense: if the tax gatherer or official strikes in anger, do not provoke but mollify him by mildness and meek humility, perhaps turning a hurt to advantage by eliciting sympathy and embarrassing the one who resorts to illegal violence. The teaching of the impossibility of earthly help must have increasingly appealed to the masses, for whom it was all too true, as inadequacy and impotence drove men to long for a savior. [343, p. 88] Christianity stressed the sinfulness of human nature, which was notorious in the empire, but vouchsafed the compensating love of God. Perhaps most cogent of all, while the Roman Caesars usually sadly failed to conform to the ideal image of the sublime ruler who sacrificed himself for his children, the Christ, who, being Pilot of the Universe and Ordainer of all things [as expressed by Clement of Alexandria, quoted in *343*, p. 99], yet became human and suffered the most shameful death, inspired deep love and gratitude. It was a great joy and solace that men became like God by meek and passive suffering. Doubtless in part because of its insistence on sexual morality, Christianity seems to have appealed especially to women, the wives and mothers. Ladies of the upper classes and even of the imperial family were drawn to the faith long before their menfolk were prepared to accept it. [*313*, p. 257] After Constantine, too, women were the chief support of the newly established religion, to which the men usually turned only after two or three generations. [*275*, p. 83]

It was a strategic advantage that Christianity, in the Jewish tradition and unlike the pagan cults in general, was radically intolerant. Its most striking difference from Mithraism and other competitors was its firm refusal to compromise with pagan gods. [*322*, p. 67] Although heathen customs were adopted rather readily, Christianity even looked askance on mixed marriages. [*313*, p. 259] This brought persecution but was doubtless a point of long-term strength. Its conversions were solid and its defenses strong; its truth held the confidence of a new revelation. Victory, when it finally came, could be complete, whereas a tolerant religion would always be subject to the waves of the day. A great deal, however, was owed to the patronage of the state. Although there had been only occasional repression until Diocletian, Christians were still but a small minority, perhaps as few as 5 percent of the population, certainly less than 10 percent, early in the fourth century [*320*, p. 20; *353*, p. 47]; after a few decades of imperial pressure, most had been turned from the older faiths.

Although the upper classes still mostly scorned it, Constantine was wise enough to adopt the religion against which Diocletian struggled in vain. As Constantine saw it, Christianity promised spiritual stability. [*356*, p. 157] Teaching peace and humility, future salvation and resignation to worldly ills, it was at once a consolation for the oppressed and a better support for monarchy than any of its rivals. Church writers made every effort to assure the

Caesars of their obedience; Justin, for example, wrote: "Everywhere we are more ready than anyone else to pay your taxes, both ordinary and extraordinary." [*First Apology*, 12] Tertullian claimed that Christians were the best subjects, never plotting against the emperor nor raising riots. [329, p. 131] There were cited many passages of the New Testament suggesting submission, including the dictum of rendering to Caesar the things that are of Caesar, and Christ's saying of Pilate, "Thou couldst have no power at all against Me, except it was given thee from above." [John 19:11] As Saint Paul wrote, "Slaves, obey your earthly masters with fear and trembling, single-mindedly, as serving Christ. Do not offer merely the outward show of service to curry favor with men, but, as slaves of Christ, do wholeheartedly the will of God. Give the cheerful service of those who serve the Lord, not men. For you know that whatever good each man may do, slave or free, will be repaid him by the Lord." [Eph. 6:5–8] Or, in the words of Romans 13:1: "Let every soul be subject unto the higher powers. For there is no power but from God: the powers that be are ordained of God. Whosoever therefore resisteth the power, resisteth the ordinance of God." The Beatitudes bless not the courageous, the energetic, or independent spirits, but the meek, the poor in spirit, and the peacemakers, the good subjects of the empire. Rome turned away from the canonical virtues of Greece, fortitude, self-control, and justice [343, p. 98], to prefer the new triad of faith, charity, and humility.

Although early Christians had a low opinion of Rome and Roman rule [323, p. 105], the Church Fathers soon came to recognize the place of the Roman empire in the divine scheme. Eusebius spoke of "Two roots of blessing, the Roman empire and the doctrine of Christian piety." As he saw it, "Two mighty powers, starting from the same point, the Roman empire swayed by a single sovereign and the Christian religion, subdued and reconciled all these contending elements." [353, p. 65] The monarchy was used in teaching as a model to make understandable the rulership of God. [340, p. 58] Augustus was held the earthly counterpart of Christ; the single monarch of earth corresponding to that of heaven, the "Lord and Savior appeared together." As the ancient kings were swept away by Augustus' empire, so Christ drove out the old gods [340, pp. 75–82, 73]; despite some trouble with the Trinity, it was sought to Christianize Augustus and romanize

Christ. At first depicted in the catacombs as a shepherd or a fisher, Christ soon took on the aspect of a king and the "Maiestas domini" of the Ruler of the world [487, pp. 29–30], and Jehovah became Dominus, like Caesar. When pagan critics in the first part of the third century objected that insistence on a single deity amounted to an attack on the separate nationalities for which the empire then still had some respect, as though to impose a single law on all the diverse peoples, Origen replied that it was indeed possible to bring all together and to preach universal love, since men no longer were separated by national rivalries. [340, pp. 58–67]

After Christianity became the state religion, it naturally supported the imperial power that favored it, both implicitly by calling on all to be good, patient subjects, and directly by recognizing the divine vocation of the empire. Emperor worship was not ended, only modified. [326, I, 93] As a writer of the fifth century put it, "He serves God faithfully who faithfully honors him who rules by the authority of God," and "Faithful devotion must be given to the Emperor as a present and embodied God." [347, p. 129] St. Augustine, whose lifetime spanned the crumbling of the empire in the West, likewise called for submission: "With cheerfulness and good will: to the end that, if they cannot be made free by their masters, they may make their servitude a freedom to themselves, by serving them not in deceitful fear but in faithful love." [*City of God*, Bk. XIX, chap. 15] If slaves are miserable, he wrote, it is because they are sinful; and it is wrong to champion the subjected because this means subverting authority. As the empire went to pieces in the West, barbarian kings, desirous of consecration for themselves and a basis of order for their unruly peoples, usually led or drove their subjects to baptism. [492, p. 27] Christianity is even credited, in the Nestorian form, with inspiring Genghis Khan to universal empire. [559, p. 360]

Not only were the Caesars converted to Christianity; they in return converted Christianity from a faith of the oppressed into an intolerant state creed with official dogma. Constantine gave presents to converts and privileges to cities that destroyed their pagan temples [314, I, 655]; in 324, only eleven years after the Edict of Milan decreed toleration of Christianity, he expressed the desire that all his subjects embrace that faith. The next year the Council of Nicaea began the persecution of heresy; already it was considered necessary that men not merely worship the Christian God and follow His ethical mandates, but subscribe to exact interpretations of the relation of Christ to God and the nature of the Trinity, obscure as this was to the untutored. Pagan sacrifices may have been banned about 337. [*326*, II, 938] In 341 the persecution of paganism was started, a decree of that year demanding, "Let there be an end of superstition. Let the madness of sacrifices be done away with." [*343*, p. 218] Julian (361–363) tried energetically to restore a somewhat purified and elevated paganism, with promise of eternal rewards and punishments and with an organized priesthood and public charities in the Christian manner. [*353*, p. 72; *343*, p. 215] His reign was too brief to shake seriously the Christian position, but for thirty years toleration remained the rule. However, Theodosius (379–395) abandoned the old title of Pontifex Maximus, made Christianity the sole official faith, and began in earnest the suppression of dissent. It was not easy to establish conformity in lands long accustomed to great diversity of beliefs. By a decree of 380, only followers of the Nicene Creed were acceptable citizens. [*353*, p. 80] The old faiths persisted stubbornly into the latter part of the fifth century, as laws continued to be passed against their temples and rites [*326*, II, 938; *320*, p. 20; *322*, p. 198]; Justinian in the sixth century tolerated pagan philosophers. [*353*, p. 150] But the idea became more and more accepted that men should be burned for rejection of the official doctrine, which amounted to rejection of the universal order.

It was also hard to secure agreement on just what Christians should believe, but it gradually came to be accepted that a deviant interpretation of Christ's divinity was a mortal sin. For example, Arianism, especially popular with the Goths, held that the Son was not coeval with the Father but had been created. The Nestorians contended that the divine nature of Christ was essentially distinct from the human flesh. The Monophysites, who were mostly of the lower classes, regarded the divine nature as absolutely predominant. [*353*, pp. 98–99, 155] All such variants were anathematized and, after many a clangorous controversy, were defeated and suppressed in favor of the doctrine that the human and the divine in Christ were entirely fused — the view that best upheld the dignity of the semidivine emperor while implying his moral responsibility.

Becoming official, Christianity, like all successful movements, gained power at some cost in purity and virtue. The Church, which had exalted poverty, rapidly became wealthy and subject to the corresponding temptations. It was no longer clear whether men embraced it from conviction, fear, or self-interest. Standards changed; early Christians had held it sinful to be a soldier or official of the state; and doubts lingered regarding the compatibility of Christian duties with state service. Many preferred holy orders to a share of power. [*326,* II, 983–985] Christianity was also transformed from a brotherhood into a bureaucratic organization. The early Church had been decidedly anarchical; so far as bishops came forward, they were equal among themselves and lacked an overall hierarchy. [*304,* pp. 310, 381] But when taken over by the state, the Church reproduced within itself the imperial system. Forms, names, and insignia were borrowed from the priesthood of emperor worship. [*347,* p. 83] Greek was replaced by Latin as the language of the Roman Church. [*356,* p. 5] The provinces were subordinated to the capital, with a hierarchy of powers corresponding to those of the imperial government [*287,* p. 11] as the bishop of Rome claimed supremacy over other bishops. In the middle of the fifth century it was declared that "Everything which the Apostolic Chair has sanctioned, or shall sanction in the future, shall be considered as law for the Church." [*320,* p. 51] When the emperor renounced the title of Pontifex Maximus in 375, it was assumed by the Pope. [*356,* p. 21] The Church was ready to fulfill the role assigned to it by St. Augustine: when the temporal world empire had to perish for its sins, the City of God should survive as its better counterpart.

The destiny of the Church differed in East and West according as earthly power weighed upon it or left it to carry on the heritage of Rome. Where a Caesar continued to rule, the Church remained subordinate to him and closely meshed with the political power. The primate of Constantinople was never elevated so high over other bishops as was the Roman Pope, and the Eastern Church to some extent escaped the corruption of wealth and power which afflicted the Western Church during the Middle Ages. But it suffered servitude to the state; weaker rulers gave it more latitude; stronger ones, like Justinian, acted firmly as head of church as well as of civil administration, even deciding doctrinal questions [*287,* pp. 337–339]; and the more willful emperors did not hesitate to depose patriarchs or humiliate them. Particularly in the campaigns of Iconoclasm in the eighth and early ninth centuries, emperors, seeking to restore or strengthen monotheism against worship of the saints and the Virgin, attacked monasteries and asserted imperial control over thought and education. [353, pp. 252, 261–262] The hold of Orthodoxy upon men's minds became firmer and firmer, even as Byzantine temporal power declined. Literature became discussion of church affairs, theological disquisitions, and Biblical exegesis; church questions outweighed political differences, or these were formulated in terms of theology. [277, p. 13] Subsequently in the Russian empire, Orthodoxy followed its Byzantine ways with dry dogma, extreme conservatism, formalism, and pompous ceremonies adorned with glittering vestments and incense. [396, p. xi] In Constantinople itself the Eastern Church was overthrown by the Turks, yet the pattern of church-state relations continued basically the same in the Turkish empire: a church that was beneath and fused with the temporal power, yet was something of a force in its own right, resting on a sacred law which the sultan could not easily change, but which suited him very well.

In the West, the mission of the Church to uphold the universal order rose as the empire tottered; and the end of the Western empire in 476 left the field open for the Papacy to claim the heritage of the Caesars, the universal empire in the name of Christ. [287, p. 100] Bearer of the ideal of a single people united under a single power and with a unifying world mission, so that to be a Christian was thought the same as to be a Roman [287, p. 13], the Church became the chief link with the imperial past. As the empire faded in growing disorder and ignorance, the Church, the chief remaining repository of classic culture, kept up traditions of literacy and supplied lawyers and administrators for the Dark Ages. The Peace of God feebly substituted for the Pax Romana.

The awe of the barbarians for Rome, ancient capital and titular, though not administrative, head of the empire, enabled the Pope to remain independent after the fall of Roman power. But the Church perforce had to share sovereignty, unable as it was to muster large armies. Oppressed by the Lombards, the Pope called in the Franks to save him [320, pp. 69–70]; Pippin and then Charlemagne, respecting the Pontiff as a superior ruler, set him up as the temporal sovereign of a substantial territory. [301, p. 214] In return, Charlemagne and a succession of Germanic rulers through the Middle Ages received from the Pope consecration as legitimate heirs of Caesar. Their Holy Roman Empire was the temporal side of the world empire of Christ, its purpose being largely, down to Charles V, to maintain the unity of the Church. The emperor was Defender of the Faith and had an ecclesiastical role: he claimed a voice in the selection of the Pope and convoked a council in case of a disputed election. [287, p. 111] The Catholic Church, it was accepted, required a universal Roman state in order to continue to exist. As an abbot wrote about 1310, "The state of all Christians is only one, therefore of necessity there will be one single prince and king of that state for the spread and defense of that faith and the Christian people." [287, pp. 47, 99]

Standing over the chaos left by the departure of the power of Caesar, the Pope asserted something like universal sovereignty. Administering the Church patrimony and the city of Rome, Gregory the Great fortified the temporal power of the Papacy; in 1073 he asserted sovereignty over Spain on the ground that it had been an ancient Roman province. [562, p. 93] By the fictitious Donation of Constantine, the Papacy claimed that that monarch had bestowed upon the Pope the dignities of imperial Caesar, the diadem, scepter, and the like, and legitimate sovereignty of the West, as emperors long named coregents. In 1075 Gregory claimed that only the Pope should be called universal, that only he should wear imperial insignia and only he should make new laws, that all princes should kiss his feet and he should be supreme judge on earth. [543, p. 140] When Adrian came from the Netherlands to assume the papal seat in 1522 he exclaimed, upon seeing the Vatican, that it was fitting for the successor not of Peter but of Constantine. [553, p. 345] Popes of the Middle Ages, such as Innocent III, held that the Church had been entrusted with the government of the world and all earthly kings and princes were subject to them as the sole universal power, and they affirmed the authority to deprive monarchs of their states if they proved to be unworthy vassals. [320, p. 314] Claiming a sort of lordship of the world, the Pope in 1155 authorized the king of England to conquer Ireland. Pope Boniface in 1300 sought to place himself over a confederation of European powers; arrayed with sword, crown, and scepter, he boasted, "I am Caesar, I am Emperor." [537, p. 104] Levying taxes, administering schools, hospitals, and countless convents, holding a large portion of the lands of Europe, receiving revenues far greater than those of any king, demanding and accepting the obeisance of earthly rulers and peoples alike, the Church was indeed like a universal empire.

The claims of papal sovereignty were abated only on the threshold of modern times. In 1455 the Pope gave Portugal permission to seize much of the non-Christian world. [526, p. 24] In 1493 he assigned most of the New World to Spain, and Africa and India to Portugal, at the same time forcefully reasserting his own supremacy. But the Spanish and Portuguese rulers, good Catholics as they were, rejected his authority. The Middle Ages were ending.

The Reformation, undoing the universality of the Church, did not end its political role. Protestants might find texts in the Old as well as the New Testament to support monarchical authority, but kings soon perceived that Catholicism was better for thrones. It was not sheer religious idealism nor pure foolishness that led the Stuarts to seek from Rome sustenance of their Divine Right, even at a cost of antagonizing most of their subjects. On the other hand, Calvinism, propagated from republican Switzerland and Holland, not to speak of more radical sects like the Anabaptists, made monarchs shiver. The essence of the anti-Roman protest was individualistic and subversive of control; it was bound eventually to culminate, when the mentality of universal authority was laid aside, in religious toleration and demands for popular participation in government. It was like a reversion to the ways of antiquity, when the right of all to believe as they like was taken for granted, before the Roman empire laid its authority and creed upon the world.

Thus the Roman Church upheld something of Rome's sway many centuries after the empire lay outwardly shattered in the West. And it has done well; to this day, the lands of Roman dominion in the West (except North Africa, overrun by another imperialism from the Near East) have remained Catholic. The Church was more vulnerable where there were no roots of the Roman empire beneath it; the lands lost to Protestantism are those that were proselytized only long after the fall of Roman power, like England (lost to Rome before the Church was implanted there and perhaps more thoroughly lost to Roman culture because the Church was missing), most of Germany, and Scandinavia. (Elsewhere it has remained strongest among peoples held in inferiority, like the Irish, French-Canadians, and Poles.) Nor was the Church much weakened in the lands of Roman dominion by the Reformation. The caliber of its leadership having been greatly and permanently raised by the challenge, it reinforced doctrines and organization and kept as much as possible of the past. Ruler of a sizable territory around Rome until 1870, the pontiff of the Roman Catholic, or Universal, Church still sits upon a throne in regal garb and with a great crown under a gorgeous crimson canopy [323, p. 3] to preside over his stately court. He performs many ceremonies reminiscent of those of the Augusti, and his state speaks and writes their tongue, even as the Orthodox Church uses the neoclassic Greek of the Byzantine empire. It was a matter of indifference, perhaps desirable, that ceremonies were unintelligible to the mass of worshipers. The Pope addresses his pronouncements, as did the Caesars, "Urbi et orbe." Like the Caesars, the Pope is a nonhereditary but absolute monarch. The senate or curia he selects is dominated by Italians, although the Church is worldwide. The Church has found very little to add to the philosophy that Thomas Aquinas worked out when it was near the zenith of its power. It has continued to claim the minds of its members, prescribing beliefs over a large area; and papal infallibility was formally asserted in 1870 after the loss of nearly all temporal power. In smaller ways, too, the Roman Church has kept up the ancient modes. When the men of the Renaissance dug up classic statues, they admired the restrained perfection of unadorned white marble. They could have learned better about classic statuary from the Church, whose artisans, handing down antique tradition, decorated their images in gilt and bright colors, blue, red, and green, like the ancient works before the elements washed away the paints. [358, p. 353]

ETHICAL COMMUNISM

The imperial order bespeaks the idea of a universal church under a universal and omnipresent God, and it develops and reinforces the idea of requitement of earthly merits in an afterlife. It also leads to demands for a fuller justice on earth, to feelings that inequality of property is wrong and that sharing as much as possible is a great virtue. Such ideas are a natural reflection or extension of the imperial promise of equality [discussed in chap. 5], and they have been strongly cherished by many of the dissidents from the imperial society. [discussed in chap. 8]

Equal sharing has never been found practical in large-scale society which always found it necessary to give individuals title to goods and to permit some to acquire and accumulate much more than others. It is also a political absurdity, because those who possess regard the idea with no little aversion, and property corresponds more or less to power and authority. It is hence remarkable that the clamor for economic equalization could ever be more than the envy of disgruntled individuals.

But conceptions of justice must arise from a social reality, and the partial or complete denial of individual ownership has various roots. One is the family background. There is always some community of property among man, wife, and children; this is obviously called for in view of their different roles and is made practical by the intimacy of their existence and the closeness of their bonds. Those who are accustomed through formative years to viewing many or most things as equally available for whoever needs them may well keep such attitudes, extend them, and in times of crisis and trouble revert to them; each one may claim an equal right to eat in days of famine, just as the children are all entitled to be fed from the common stores. If the family remains together after children become producers, the sphere of joint ownership enlarges. Land, livestock, crops, furniture, perhaps almost everything may be simply family property of a group of a dozen or so adults. The great families of the South Slavs, for example, and the Russians at one time, have had such arrangements.

Many primitive groups have operated more or less as extensions of the family, with extensive sharing or limited ideas of individual property rights among members. For example, the Eskimos, living in villages rarely of more than a hundred and with no fixed authority or leaders except those recognized as superior hunters, held all natural resources free and common; an individual's property was subject to others' needs, and if he accumulated too much it was likely to be taken from him. [495, pp. 67, 82, 69, 81] Bushmen of South Africa would customarily divide game and gathered foods among members of the band, but this practice was more expected generosity than collective right. [271, p. 148] The Hottentots, living in independent tribes of a few hundred to a thousand or so, similarly expected everyone to share freely and expressed contempt for stinginess. A hungry man was entitled to help himself from another's flock if he duly informed the owner. [271, pp. 319–321]

The very democratic community, like a large family, may insist that those who have share with those who have not. The state is the ultimate guarantor of property and has sovereign powers over it; to share in control of the state means to share in the ultimate sanction of everyone's property. Equality of political rights may imply economic leveling, as the former comes to seem illusory without the latter; and the plebeians, like the patricians, find it just that political power be turned to economic benefit. There consequently are many demands that the rich be taxed if not expropriated to pay for benefits of the masses, from free recreational facilities and emergency relief to a general dole. Aristophanes, in the *Ecclesiazusae*, mocked even more radical ideas circulating in Athens, that the state should maintain all equally in free abundance without money. However, the democratic order, as best seen in classical Athens or rural Swiss cantons, has hardly led to a deprecation of private property as wicked per se, but rather to calls for better and wide access to it, for equality, not communal use. If Euhemerus in Hellenistic times proposed collective ownership of the soil, his idea came not from Athens but from Egypt. [315, p. 320]

Heavy stress on common effort and organization also implies more or less denial of individual property. For this reason, in military establishments as in pioneer camps, men commonly live and eat together and use collectively owned equipment for common ends. The citizens of Sparta tried to maintain nearly propertyless equality for the sake of military strength and solidarity against their far more numerous subjects; calling themselves "Equals," they took meals in collective messes and lived much like soldiers in camp. [116, p. 231] Similarly, Plato deprived the elite of his *Republic* of property so that they should dedicate themselves wholly to the ideal government. Alexander I organized part of his army in communal settlements, which combined collective farming with regulation of all aspects of life. [404, p. 354] Cossacks of eastern and southern Russia had a good measure of collectivism, equality, and common property as long as they were engaged in frontier warfare, only to go over to private property when disorders moved away and their military vocation was finished. [394, pp. 110–111] Collectivism is inherently hostile to individual property and its free use.

Conversely, communism implies an organization to handle the common property, which must be the sovereign authority. But in relatively small or free states, the role of government is ordinarily not so great that men easily envision assigning to it all possessions and replacing economic with sociopolitical controls. Hence it is in the opposite political order from the democratic, in the great and autocratic empire, that one finds the best seedbed of communistic sentiments. The empire does not hesitate to intervene, and it fosters an ethos of control and management. It is equalitarian in its outlook or claims, as everyone in it is equal in submission to the autocrat, himself so elevated as to be incomparable. It is unfriendly to merchant interests and scornful of commercial calculation. In it, there is little place for private wealth.

Since the emperor is father of all and his children are naturally equal, the only justification of the greater riches of some is their better service to the state. This might be a plausible excuse in a well-ordered empire. But, as officials grow richer and the poor poorer, and as the former obviously gain much more by squeezing than by serving, the contradiction between ideal and reality becomes too strong; theirs, the most conspicuous possession, comes to seem simply wrong. Wealth is indeed detestable when it is based, not on production or service, but on political superiority, the right of the stronger; and to condemn their property is to condemn robbery. Nor is the standing of commercial property much better; the officials, whom the people know to be mostly scoundrels, consider the merchants to be low and useless creatures; no wealth is really respectable. It is dangerous unless accompanied by political influence, and that which is dangerous is easily taken to be bad. Wealth does not promise power, which would make it acceptable if not virtuous; what has to be hidden, like a shameful blemish, cannot be good. The notion of private right to goods is weak not only because property is insecure, but because the autocrat, who represents the state or the people, is residual or theoretical owner of everything, or at least of all land. This means that those who hold much wealth for their own and not the emperor's benefit do so wrongfully; not only does all belong to the lofty ruler, but all economic activity should serve his or, equivalently, the general welfare. The strictly private in the despotic empire, whether intellectual or economic, smacks of subversion.

The ideal of sharing also fits very well the sense, though hardly the reality, of autocratic rulership. For perfectly strong government, people should not look to their own estate and permanent holdings but, enjoying only as far as and as long as they merit, should remain dependent on the ruler. They should work for the state, not for themselves, nor should they store up treasures for their children. Distinctions between men should be based on position occupied or rank conceded, not on riches accumulated. These make false and invidious differences from the point of view of the supreme power. Only in complete equality and property-lessness is there complete subordination to the superior command; the anti-individualism of communism harmonizes with absoluteness of control. Moreover, unequal wealth makes for envy and disharmony, for the pride of some and the jealousy of others; peace and concord demand that all stand so far as possible on a level. The ideal empire, perhaps the ideal state in general, like the utopias of the philosophers, would banish private ownership as an imperfection in the perfect society. Contrariwise, an autocratic power is essential to any dreams of full sharing, as it requires an omnipotent organization to administer all property and production, and only a very strong government could keep the stronger from getting more than the weaker. Aspirants to full communism commonly presuppose a power to make it work, and the well-managed autocracy, with state control of all resources, justice for all and no special privilege, is approximately a communistic order.

The utopianism of the empire, its promise and vision of a perfectly organized society of peace and justice, encourages dreams of social perfection. Messianism is always equalitarian. Particularly when past their peak of effectiveness, however, as the reality of controls weakens, empires seem to have stimulated a feeling that private possession is per se evil. Such doctrinal repugnance, associated with the religiosity natural to the aging empire, is a reaction to the growing gap between pretenses and realities. The discontented long for the fraternity that the empire fails to give. Claimed equality and justice are made more desirable by the real background of inequality and parasitism, and growing insecurity

strengthens the demand that the community assure the sustenance
of all. If the emperor becomes more remote and no longer effectively has the use of the realm that is his, as rulership goes over
to divinity and the emperor shares ownership with the deity he
represents, the way is open for the people to feel that they also
have a right to the domain. For what belongs to the god is for
everyone to use but for no one to take as his sole possession. Then
groups that would rebel against or withdraw from the rotten and
false imperial society are inspired with an ethical vision of brotherhood and equality to build a better order. In part, this is a call
for fulfillment of scandalously broken promises; in part, it is like
an extension of the tightly bound family to which men may have
spiritually retreated, to abolish the hatreds, distrust, and parasitism
with which the empire reeks. Then they would generalize the
familial virtues for the happiness of all; without coercion or command, as among true children of one father, all would work for
the common weal in the great brotherly union to bring the reign
of heaven on earth.

The logic of imperial power, though usually not its practice,
thus favors the communistic ideal. It is almost beyond guessing
how frequent and strong such sentiments may have been. In fact,
empires have allowed great inequality and have been dominated
by aristocratic elites; passionate cries for real equality could be
expected only from the usually voiceless masses, who may hardly
dare protest the extortions of an exceptionally greedy functionary.
Only under unusual circumstances, when the intelligentsia is
markedly dissatisfied or when discontent grows into rebellion,
might one expect undercurrents of communistic feeling to come
to the fore and become articulated. But usually education has been
well enough controlled that intellectuals, so far as there are any,
are close to the elite. Generally the great empires have taken little
note of the sentiments of subversive groups and have seen no reason
to remember the ideologies of equality and sharing.

It is only a wild surmise that there may have been in ancient
Egypt or early Near Eastern empires movements to share the
wealth that belonged to the monarch or to the great gods and their
servants. Even for the Roman empire, information is meager. In
the general tenor of many sayings of Jesus, possession is reprehensible and salvation may be better sought in renunciation of worldly
goods: "Woe unto you that are rich! for ye have received your con-

solation. Woe unto you that are full, for ye shall hunger" [Luke 6:26, 27]; "Give to every man that asketh of thee; and of him that taketh away thy goods ask them not again" [Luke 6:30]; "Consider the lilies, how they grow. . . . If then God so clothe the grass, how much more will he clothe you, O ye of little faith?" [Luke 12:27–28] "Sell all that thou hast, and distribute unto the poor, and thou shalt have treasure in heaven. . . . how hardly shall they that have riches enter into the kingdom of God" [Luke 18:22–24]; "Lay not up for yourselves treasures upon earth"; "Ye cannot serve God and Mammon," and so on. To comply with such injunctions, to demonstrate their mutual love, and no doubt partly to prepare for the imminent return of the Christ, early Christians seem to have shared more or less of their possessions, although how generally and to what extent is unknown. Acts 2:44–46 records: "And all that believed were together and had all things common; and sold their possessions and goods, and parted them to all men, as every man had need, and they, continuing daily with one accord in the temple, and breaking bread from house to house, did eat their meat with gladness and singleness of heart." Likewise, Acts 4:32, 34–35: "And the multitude of them that believed were of one heart and of one soul: neither said any of them that aught of the things which he possessed was his own; but they had all things common. . . . Neither was there any among them that lacked: for as many as were possessors of land or houses sold them, and brought the prices of the things that were sold, and laid them down at the apostle's feet: and distribution was made to every man according as he had need." The expanding church advocated rather charity than communal sharing for ordinary men, but for a time it was customary for the brethren to have the main meal of the day together, an important part of Christian fellowship which was in time reduced to a sacrament. [355, pp. 57, 67] Early Christianity, however, was more a way of life than a dogma [335, p. 124], and late in the second century Tertullian wrote, "All is common among us — except our wives." In another connection, however, he said that Christians kept a treasury of voluntary offerings for the needy, a procedure hardly necessary in a fully communal society. [330, pp. 588–589] If communism for the generality was soon given up, there remained propertyless monastic communities for the dedicated; and the total renunciation of private possession has continued to be an ideal for some Christians to this day.

The Christians were not alone in this respect; sundry other religious communities in the Roman world likewise more or less renounced property. For example, according to Philo, the Therapeuts gave away their possessions upon entry and lived virtuously in community. [335, pp. 67, 76] Of the Essenes, Josephus wrote, "Whoever joins the sect must place his property at the disposal of the society for its common use. . . . they all like brothers share only one common property." [355, p. 69] All were equals in every way. They were also pacifists who refused military service. [335, pp. 131–136] The nearby Qumran community, which believed, about the time of Christ, that the last battle of good and evil was at hand, also worshiped, lived, and ate in common. [306] There were also ascetic and communistic inclinations in Gnosticism, a religion akin to both Christianity and Manichaeism; one sect in the second century held that private property was the origin of all woes, and that divine justice could not be satisfied except by equality and community of goods, including husbands and wives. It is not known how far this extreme communism was practiced. [251, pp. 209–210; 335, pp. 234–235]

More successful was the Mazdakite movement, which arose from Manichaeism in Sassanid Persia late in the fifth century. [249, p. 222] This came to the fore after the empire was disastrously defeated by the White Huns, humiliated and forced to pay tribute to them. The land was gripped by hunger and want; the power of the throne was shaken; it is small wonder that the gross inequality, whereby nobles and clergy stood far above peasants and craftsmen and enjoyed all the fruits while the poor starved, should have troubled many, even of the upper classes. [251, p. 239; 245, p. 358] That God favored the poor was a teaching of the established religion [251, p. 61]; Mazdak went on to preach that God gave wealth to all men to share equally for harmony and brotherhood, that no one had more rights than another, and that goods, like water, fire, and pastures, should be used in common. [251, p. 131; 245, p. 343] It was also proposed that the possession of women be equalized, or at least that the great harems be abolished. For a time Mazdak was supported by the autocrat against the opposition of most of the nobility and the clergy; but it is not known to what extent his program may have been put into effect. [248] Harems were probably restricted, and there was at least much looting of state granaries by the hungry, despoiling of large estates, and seizing of lands.

[*251*, pp. 239, 138] But disorders become more a political and social revolution and less a religion. [*245*, p. 358] The heir to the throne accepted the plausible argument of the traditional priests that if the Mazdakites prevailed there would be no more place for the highborn. The movement was then severely repressed, and its writings were destroyed. As a secret sect, however, it survived the fall of the empire and lasted well into times of Arab rule. [*245*, p. 362]

The Chinese empire had peasant uprisings of some sort on an average of nearly one per year, and many bandit gangs and secret societies grew into political forces. Ever ready to denounce and expropriate the riches of their enemies, the official and possessing classes, secret societies usually tried to broaden their appeal by more or less promising communism or equalization. [Y. Muramatsu in 78, pp. 256–257] In the fading of the Han dynasty, as eunuchs contended with literati, and great landowners and private armies were going their own way, a formidable peasant uprising, the Yellow Turbans, tried to set up an equalitarian society. [78, p. 47] Mystical Taoists, they propagandized everywhere a New Era of universal peace [74, I, 773–774], and organized communities with communal eating and public confession of sins. Spreading like a great storm over most of China [2, pp. 192–193], they were repressed only with severe bloodshed. In this tradition, particularly since the middle T'ang, peasant uprisings have rather regularly sounded notes of equality. [34, p. 101] A peasant leader after the fall of the Northern Sung dynasty proclaimed abolition of rank and equalization of wealth [2, p. 157], confiscating property of the rich for the benefit of the poor. Late Ming rebels fought for equalization of landholding [34, pp. 102, 104], and the Yellow Turbans continued to inspire movements of rebellion through the Boxers of 1900. [74, I, 773]

Best known, although only from Western sources, is the Taiping rebellion of the mid-nineteenth century. It sought to perfect the religiously inspired Heavenly Kingdom, the antithesis of evil Manchu rule, with an explicit program of communism. Its leader, the Heavenly King, declared that the "empire is God's empire, not that of the barbarian Manchus; the people, their clothing and their food belong to God rather than to the Manchus." [45, p. 64] All, being children of God, had equal right to the earth and its fruits; the commander of the Taiping forces spread the word: "We will all eat together as members of one family." They called one another brothers and sisters. [45, pp. 57–58] In agreement with ancient strains of Chinese collectivist thought, each twenty-five households were to form a communal unit with their treasury, storehouse, and church. [20, p. 137] Land was to be distributed equally according to the number of mouths in the community and should be farmed collectively. According to the program, "All lands under Heaven shall be farmed jointly by the people under Heaven. If the production of food is too small in one place, then move it to another where it is more abundant. . . . Land shall be farmed by all; rice, eaten by all; clothes, worn by all; money, spent by all. There shall be no inequality, and no person shall be without food or fuel." Moreover, "In the empire none shall have any private property, and everything belongs to God, so that God may dispose of it. In the great family of Heaven, every place is equal, and everyone has plenty." [9, pp. 39–40] How far these extreme proposals may have been carried out in the large share of China controlled at one time by the Taipings is doubtful; it probably was of limited practical effect except in the military organization [20, p. 137], although serious attempts were made to enforce the public ownership of money, a particularly suspect form of wealth. [45, p. 64] The system soon broke down in nepotism and dissolute living; there were intrigues and bloody purges around the Heavenly King; favorites accumulated great wealth while the poor paid higher taxes than they had paid to the Manchu government and were driven to eating grass. [45, pp. 65, 72, 81–82]

The poor, however, had no monopoly of ideas that might be called socialistic or communistic; ideas of collectivist leveling have come to the fore again and again, as in the earlier mentioned reforms of Wang An-shih, and they run like a red thread through Chinese political philosophy. In the ideal state of Chuang-tzu, "All things grew in common and were neighborly." [80, p. 104] There were socialistic tendencies in the thinking of Mo-ti, whose call for universal love somewhat resembles that of Jesus. He seems to have been a monarchist, but in the preachings of later followers equal love for all humans meant pure communism, with equality of possessions and status for all, and dissolution of the family. [25, pp. 368, 393, 401–402] More important, Confucianism, in writings probably of the Han dynasty [27, p. 592], idealized a utopian "Grand Union" in which family ties should be swept away, with no marriage or hereditary relations, and there should be no private accumulation. [*67*, pp. 45–46]

Modern thinkers have had a similar message. For example, T'ang Chen, writing in the first decade of the Ch'ing dynasty, advocated equality and sharing of the world's goods by all; antimonarchic, he accused the rulers of robbery. [*27*, p. 494] These were hardly more than vague aspirations, but Kang Yu-wei, seeking in the latter part of the nineteenth century to save the ailing and defeated dynasty by thorough reform, spelled out the social implications of total power in logical detail. Believing that Confucius was really a reformer whose meaning had been distorted by the conservatives, he visualized a new empire in which everything should be public and united. In his "One World" he wished to abolish independent states, as makers of war; the world should be redivided into artificial administrative districts. To end all distinctions of nations, separate languages should be amalgamated into a new universal tongue. [*68*, pp. 39, 53, 99–101] The races should be mingled; differences between people based on family, occupation, and class must be erased in the general equality. [*68*, p. 138] Women should enjoy complete equality in education, political participation, and occupation. Marriage should be free and temporary. As the family causes discord, inequality, selfishness, private property, and corruption in government — indeed, it is the principal obstacle to peace and equality [*68*, pp. 179–183] — it should be entirely dissolved. Women would go into special institutions when they became pregnant, remain with their children only as long as needed to nurse them, and turn them over to state nurseries and schools; children would receive names from state organizations. [*68*, pp. 184–195] Almost all needs would be publicly provided, agriculture, industry, and trade being managed by the state, which would assign men to the fitting employment. [*68*, pp. 218–223] To prevent the demoralizations of tranquillity, there would be competitions in production, arts, and knowledge. The scholars would study the perfecting of the utopian order and the achievement of immortality, in the Taoist tradition. [*68*, p. 41] The antisocial and lazy would have to be consigned to penal colonies [*68*, p. 200]; but Kang believed in the indefinite perfectibility of human nature, and ultimately all mankind would progress from love of kin to total love of all creatures. [*68*, p. 266]

The most authoritarian states of the West have also shown communistic impulses. In the sixteenth century, as Spanish grandeur was at its apogee, theologians of the Inquisition attacked riches as evil per se and favored sharing of wealth for social harmony. A monk proposed a communal society on the model of the beehive. [494, p. 77; 573, pp. 103–104] In later centuries, Andalusian anarchists advocated living without money, all working together and drawing needed goods from common stores. [494, p. 81] Similar impulses appeared in the waning and breakup of the Old Regime of France. Louis XIV, the Sun King who spread his rays over Europe, had a little the character of a universal autocrat, as he ruled much the most populous, richest, and strongest country of Europe. Claiming to make law by his fiat, setting aside many of the old independent powers, he held that the realm was his estate and gave France the tone of a strongly centralized regime. As the state decayed in the eighteenth century, some sought to draw the logical conclusions of absolutism and improve upon it. When the philosophes descanted on the achievement of peace and happiness through the law of nature, the bringing of a utopia of order and justice, they were seeking fulfillment of failed promises of the benevolent sovereign. Rousseau, who was enormously popular and more than anyone else the ideological father of the French Revolution, held that private property was unnatural and idealized the free life of the primitive in a manner to encourage thoughts of abolishing false distinctions and differences. If Rousseau did not spell out consequences unpleasant for the aristocracy whose salons he frequented, some others were more radical. Mably held that "Inequality is degrading and sows division and hatred." Therefore, "Our first law is that nothing is to be privately owned. We should bring to the public storehouse the fruit of our labor: that would be the Treasury of the State and the inheritance of every citizen." Men should work not for gain but by inspiration. [460, pp. 182–183] Even more explicit was the obscure Morelly, who drew up a detailed blueprint of a communist society, which he practically dedicated to Louis XVI. According to Morelly, it is self-interest that causes insubordination and revolts in the monarchic state; without property there would be no private aspirations and hence no discord; and it is the spirit of property, the chief vice, which causes the decay of empires. [517, pp. xv, 15, 48, 51] Therefore, and because the happiness of the people is the glory of the sovereign and their welfare is his prerogative [517, pp. 46, 54], he should achieve the perfect unity of the propertyless community and inaugurate a new order in which men, stripped of selfish possessions, would follow the laws of nature. The people, as religion taught, should give all to the poor, and the monarch should be the dispenser of charity. [517, p. 46] The first rule should be: "Nothing in society shall belong to any one person, except the things he actually uses for his needs, his pleasures, or his work"; and the second, "Every citizen will be sustained and employed at public expense." [517, p. 85] Morelly's dream was equalitarian, not libertarian: everyone was to be required to marry upon attaining the prescribed age, and all aged ten to thirty should wear uniforms; after the age of thirty, they should have a pleasure outfit but without particular adornment. [517, pp. 95–99]

One who dedicated his life to ideals of sharing with the fervor of a martyr was François ("Gracchus") Babeuf. A surveyor of land titles who became convinced that the claims he was called upon to support were mostly based on force or fraud [V. Daline in 453, p. 66], Babeuf looked to the reestablishment of what he believed was pristine equality. At first he advocated giving life possession to cultivators, with residual ownership in society as a whole. [M. Dommanget in 453, p. 46] By 1786, perhaps influenced by some traditions of communal land use in his native Picardy, he was advocating, not the division of estates, but their cultivation by "brotherly communities" in which all would work better and more diligently for the common welfare. [V. Daline in 453, pp. 55, 60–61] Equality was to be the key to happiness: "Progress, I believe, is only equalization." [453, p. 70] By 1787, as winds of revolution were stirring, Babeuf was looking for concrete means of making his equalitarian society. How many may have nourished similar dreams at the time cannot be guessed, but it is noteworthy that Babeuf, a man of lower middle-class origin, found sympathetic correspondents in the aristocracy, with whom he shared ideals of the state of savage equality, graced by comforts of civilization, where men "ought to possess nothing private but enjoy everything in common." [473, pp. 203–205]

If the French regime had not been overthrown by a pathbreaking revolution, whose strongest emotion was equality, Morelly would be forgotten and we would know nothing of Babeuf and such dreamers. But in the breakdown of the old order, unconventional ideas came to the fore and into the light of history. Not a few peasants shared the conviction that land titles were immoral and that (in the words of Babeuf) the "land belongs to nature," and so to all, and demanded not only an end of feudal dues but sharing of the land. In 1790–1791, in some parts of France, there was considerable but confused and mostly leaderless agitation for the "agrarian law" of confiscation, advocacy of which was enough feared to be prohibited under pain of death. [M. Dommanget in *453*, pp. 47–48] The Parisian sans-culottes also had rather strong ideas about equality, although they seem hardly to have contemplated living together as brothers. The General Council of the Paris Commune decided, for example, that "Wealth and poverty must disappear in a world based on equality," and some Jacobins demanded nationalization of supplies of food and consumer goods in general. [*545*, pp. 57, 61] Hatred for wealth, if not love of poverty, was widespread, and merchants, held guilty of speculation, suffered particularly fierce attack. Extremists like St. Just uttered such sentiments as, "We must have neither rich nor poor. . . . opulence is infamy." [*490*, p. 228] But the clearest expression of the communistic urge was the Society of Equals headed by Babeuf, which, in the waning of the Revolution, planned a coup to overthrow the Directory and set up an equalitarian republic. Babouvism was not a major current in the great upheaval, but neither was it insignificant. In 1795 the clandestine Babeuf paper had a circulation of 2,000 to 3,000, and the group was joined, as the Directory became more conservative, by remnants of the Montagnards, former Jacobins, and Robespierrists. The conspirators thought they had 17,000 adherents ready to leap into action when the call went out, but the leaders were arrested as they were writing out a victory proclamation. [*473*, pp. 248, 262, 299]

In the Russian empire, esteem for private property was rather low for the familiar reasons: extensive state intervention in the economy, weakness and low prestige of the middle and merchant class, strength of the state and the feeling that it was responsible for everything, the claims of equality and fundamental Christian justice along with awareness that much wealth was illicitly acquired in terms of the standards outwardly maintained. Several rationalistic heretics of the sixteenth century called for equality and renunciation of property [*412*, p. 114]; one Yermolai-Erasm, depicting an ideal state under a benevolent master, held that "All riches . . . are gathered only by force or intrigue." [*411*, p. 105]

Dissident movements and attacks on established privileges took a more or less leveling or communistic bent. In the eighteenth century Pugachev started out pretending to be the assassinated tsar and so the upholder of legitimacy; in the course of rebellion he perforce became a scourge of possessors and a general equalizer. [388, III, 10–11] Late in the eighteenth century Radishchev wanted the land to be divided equally among those who worked it [412, p. 66], and the slavophils of the nineteenth century laid great stress upon communal ownership of land. Of sundry other oppositionists and revolutionary currents of the nineteenth and early twentieth centuries, some of the less radical held out to the peasants only the prospect of dividing land equally among those who watered it with their sweat. This was a congenial idea for the peasants, who regarded officials and merchants as parasites [399, p. 56], who cherished vague ideas of the land belonging to God or to no one in particular, and who enjoyed a good deal of sharing and mutual aid in the village commune — an organization much strengthened by serfdom and collective responsibility for taxes and the maintenance of order. [394, p. 85] Some in the nineteenth century spoke of the "agrarian communism" of the Russian peasant; Western thinkers were surprised to find in backward Russia institutions of their socialist utopias. [394, p. 81]

More radical populists sought to bring justice by making all society one great family, or a confederation of little families, wherein no taint of private ownership should poison brotherhood and harmony; the right to the world's goods, they held, was like the right to life, and "Everything belongs to everyone." Or, as their propagandists said, "Down with bureaucracy and government, live to yourselves in the villages, work together as an artel [cooperative], eat together, and you will be happy." [414, p. 11] Anarchism, reflecting hatred of authority and entirely negating rights of property, has had capable leaders, like Bakunin and Kropotkin, and has been more popular in Russia than in any other country, except perhaps Spain, also a land of authoritarian tradition. And the anarchism that has found favor in Russia has not been the individualist variety known in America, but communist or collectivist anarchism. [497, p. 49] After the Russian Revolution such tendencies found expression in the equalitarian-communist regime of Makhno in the Ukraine. [494, pp. 184–186]

The Russian Dissenter groups mentioned earlier, as they tried to make for themselves a more perfect society, usually found private property more or less wicked and advocated or carried out some sharing among brothers and sisters. Following the example of the early Christians, some Old Believers lived in communities with common ownership of land and buildings, collective farming and cooperative handicraft industries; keeping separate households, they worked together and divided the product equally. [*413*, p. 26; *369*, pp. 215–219] Numerous deviant sects, mostly small and ephemeral, were at times still more communistic, holding that covetousness of material things was the beginning of corruption, even that communism of goods was more important than faith in Christ; for them a godly world order meant primarily equality. [*421*, pp. 70–71] An eighteenth-century sect of "Runners" taught that God made all things common, and private ownership was but oppression. [*412*, p. 115] The Khlysty ("Flagellants") of the nineteenth century had communes with two or three families per house, owning everything jointly except clothing, doing all productive labor collectively, and dividing the product equally. [*387*, pp. 60–61] The Dukhobors believed that "People should hold property in common and freely give to each other because they are brothers." [*387*, p. 86] Ideally, they lived in communal villages, working together for the common storehouse from which all drew according to their need. [*387*, p. 87; *369*, p. 269] The Molokane were inconsistent in their application of the general tenet that love and equality required that the goods of each be those of all. Some satisfied themselves with charitable support of needy brethren, that none might suffer; others found release in communal living. One group, called Obshchii ["Sharers"], lived in large houses for thirty to fifty persons, within which even clothing was common property; these groups formed villages that owned collectively land, livestock, tools, and the like. They farmed as a whole, to the accompaniment of hymns and sermons, and shared the product equally. There was a joint fund from which members borrowed as they needed; if unable to repay, they could cancel the debt by fasting, one day per ruble. Positions of leadership and management were shared by rotation. [*387*, pp. 137–140]

Such institutions seem to have been a good deal like those of the widely known Israeli kibbutzim, which have applied the principles of equality and sharing on a large scale perhaps more successfully than any others; and the idea of the kibbutz grew from the fertile soil of the tsarist realm. The founders of the first kibbutz were Russian Jews, endowed by persecution with a powerful loyalty to the group and with a fervent hope for the new and better order, and much influenced by Russian socialist ideas or by the same atmosphere that evoked them. [459, p. 13; 549, pp. 4–7] Like most Russian peasants, they believed that only manual, preferably agricultural, labor, was good; like some Russian peasants, they made a fetish of equality in all things and felt that life would be much purer and happier without money and commerce and the corresponding jealousies and worries. Much more than Russians, they were injured by discrimination, the more painful as it came from persons they felt to be cultural inferiors; they called for justice and generalized this yearning to a passion for equality and the community of right. With or without a religious frame, the ethos of the kibbutz represents the reaction of the outcasts in the authoritarian society, who justify themselves and restore self-respect by fulfilling and overfulfilling broken promises. When they could withdraw entirely by emigrating to Palestine, and even more when they faced exceptional difficulties and dangers of a truculent foe in the new country, their groups cleaved with most extraordinary firmness. In the proper kibbutz there is no ownership at all, but all needs, even for travel money, are cared for by the community; members take turns in management posts, less esteemed than manual work; children are raised in communal nurseries and schools. [549, 547, 456, 568]

These movements are thus, in effect, rebellions against the failure of the empire to give the justice and equality it promises. They also represent attempts to find in the smaller or outcast group the values of sympathy and humanity missing in the atomized and psychologically oppressive imperial society. As such, they can hardly hope to succeed on a large scale. If success should perchance come, as has very rarely occurred, they fall into more or less the same vices as the authoritarian system they opposed. An anarchistic or communistic community, grown great and powerful, has no better means of escaping despotism than any other great state. Likewise Christianity, on becoming the official church, forgot most of its equalitarian convictions or left them to a few dedicated souls on the margin of society. The kibbutzim, thanks to their strong dedication, their considerable success in separating themselves from alien influences, and the compelling need for cooperative endeavors in Israel, have retained their purity much better than most groups; but the relative prosperity and tranquillity of recent years are a severe trial for them. Why should we yearn to share, why should all consider themselves responsible for the community, when there are justice and good feeling outside the community as well as within it?

Moreover, the appeal of the communistic movements has been inherently limited. They are for the discontented, those who feel cheated; they have little attraction for those in positions of power. Hence they have remained utopian. They have not arisen from broad political and economic experience, but are reflections of the aspirations and pretensions of the supreme empire starkly set off by its sordid realities. Despite attractiveness in times of imperial weakness and injustice, the equalitarian movement can hardly hope to be successful on a large scale and for long. It is too impractical and inexperienced, and the degraded masses on which it must rely are too incapable. If it should manage to overcome the central power, as the Taiping forces came near doing, it can perhaps renovate and rejuvenate the empire, giving it new strength, but it cannot replace the autocracy with anything basically different.

EFFECTS OF DOMINATION

There is a broad spectrum of societies from the freest to the most rigid and controlled. At one end is the small or divided state in competition with many others, with an open and flexible society of many autonomous or protected segments, freedom of organization and political action, social mobility, and values rising from below. At the other is the self-contained world state, with a single ruling center over a rigid social order inhibiting independent organization and movement and upholding an artificial or manipulated legitimacy. [541, p. 40] In the past the autocratic or imperial order has prevailed usually and in most lands; even today, when no state on earth can think of itself as a universal empire, most societies would seem more characterized by control than by freedom. Societies suggestive more of imperial Rome than of democratic Athens largely fill history and our own world. The imperial order is very persistent and it appeals to elites and leaders, the people who count. It surrounds and supports itself with a whole range of ideas and institutions. It has the advantages of definiteness, positiveness, and unity; freedom implies doubt, variety, and division.

Much of the imperial order has spread by imitation and borrowing, as suggested earlier [see chap. 1]. For example, Japan, otherwise isolated but pervaded by mainland influences, has emulated and idealized Chinese emperorship and at times has suffered similar decadence. Thus the Tokugawa Shogunate passed through something like the classic Chinese dynastic cycle. Symptoms were evident in little more than a century of rule: decline of martial virtues, heavier costs of court and administration, financial troubles, inefficient government with laxity and corruption, higher taxes, recurrent famines, and pressure of population on food supply. Attempted reforms from time to time proved futile or further damaged the economy. [61, pp. 621–622] Like Japan, probably all small states on the fringes of great empires have been at least a little influenced by their imposing example.

In other instances, without becoming nearly universal empires, states have attained sufficient greatness to take on many imperial ways and much of the imperial mentality. Louis XIV tried to make France a full-fledged despotism and came tolerably near success; examples might have been drawn much oftener from his state for the theses of the preceding pages. After him the power, though not the pretensions, of kings declined markedly, and France took on some appearances of a decadent empire. As French hegemony receded and foreign influences became important, however, there was much loosening of society prior to the revolution of 1789. Such middling empires, often with inflated pretensions, have been very numerous indeed: Hapsburg Spain, Arab califates of the Middle Ages, several partial empires of India, and the Aztec rule of Mexico have been mentioned in earlier pages; and many might be added to them, such as successor states to the Mongols in Central Asia and various sizable empires of sub-Saharan Africa.

Broadly speaking, wherever national power has been greatly extended, one might expect to find some of the effects of universal empire; in modern times the greater part of the world has been either imperialist or colonized. There are, to be sure, sharp differences between colonial empires, even the largest, and the type of empire discussed in this book. The overseas empire is hardly thought of as amalgamable into a single grand unit, nor does it comprise a politically self-contained world. In acquiring colonies, distant and noncontiguous, a state does not eliminate its rivals or bring international relations to an end. While ruling a large part of the globe, England remained very much a member of the European state system; the maker of a universal empire pushes the boundaries and the competition so far away as to be more or less lost to view. Withal, rule over alien territories has probably always had a stiffening effect on government and society, raising the prestige of the leadership, offering more political means of advancement, and justifying strong prerogative and imposed authority.

Even countries of a great liberal tradition have been led toward illiberal ways by dominion abroad. The Holland of the eighteenth century, enjoying the rule of the Indies, was much less free and democratic than the nation struggling for independence a century earlier. Likewise the great empire of England has undoubtedly operated to stratify British society, although this tendency has been minimized by industrial development at home. Economic development freed Britain from dependence on colonial exploitation; wealth was gained mostly by production, only to a minor degree by political position, and empire was more a result than a cause of British prosperity. But empire gave great glory to the monarch and placed many prestigious and lucrative positions in his gift. Officers returning with tales of adventures in pacifying natives and nabobs loaded with a colonial harvest gave England something of an imperial mentality. Dominion in Ireland, too, worked for illiberal forces in England. In 1914, when the question of Ireland's future was most acute, there was a real threat that British army officers would refuse to obey the civilian government, and some conservatives wanted the king to resume powers that had lapsed for centuries.

Much more striking was the effect of empire upon Spain, whose national life was dominated for some three hundred years by the wealth and glory of American possessions. Overwhelmed by riches from conquest and immensely inflated in self-esteem, Spain became in the sixteenth century not a little like a universal empire, nourishing fantasies of world mastery and settling into a rigid and exceptionally unproductive social structure. This was so firmly implanted that it endured hardly changed through loss of empire, invasions, defeats in war, and revolutions down to our times. Portugal, a much smaller country but possessing (or possessed by) an imperial position in Asia and America even more important relative to the metropolis, also took on much of the appearance of the grand imperial state, with consequent oligarchy, class division, and cultural and economic stagnation.

If the exercise of power by one nation over another thus affects the rulers, it serves even more strongly to shape or misshape the society of the ruled, and nearly all of what is now called the underdeveloped world has a heritage of colonial status. Somewhat paradoxically, the effects upon exploiting and exploited peoples are similar, as oppression is oppression with basically similar effects at all levels. Sometimes the colonial regime, overriding traditional native despotisms, may have imported the ways of the liberal-individualistic West and helped to open and modernize a backward society. But rule by an alien democracy is always at least a little tyrannical, and rule by an alien despotism is doubly despotic. It has often been observed that foreign rule tends to bring an increase of crime, disaffection and apathy, and widespread corruption; natives who are treated as inferior beings must be expected to act the part. The people of an exploited colony may thus find themselves in a situation like that of provincials of a universal empire, or worse as they are held frankly unequal to the people of the ruling nation.

An example is Mexico, which in three centuries of Spanish rule acquired a class structure and a tradition of lawlessness and moral anarchy which prevailed for a century after independence and have not been completely overcome to this day. The Spaniards respected the land for little but the ability to produce silver, the chief bulwark of the greatness of the Spanish king; and if the king had his share, thousands of lesser parasites took theirs through taxes, monopolies, various restrictions, and many imaginative extortions. Nothing was permitted to Mexico which was faintly competitive to Spanish interests. The only legal exports were precious metals and vegetable dyes. [527, p. 101] Although policies vacillated, manufacture of anything that could be supplied from Spain was generally prohibited; the making of permitted commodities, such as textiles, was severely restricted and regulated. [485, p. 19; 477, chap. iv] Crops that competed with Spanish exports, such as olives, grapes, hemp, flax, and tobacco, were forbidden or limited. [477, p. 144] So shortsighted were restrictions that the prohibition of local production of mercury caused serious hardships for the silver mines, the chief revenue producers. [527, p. 103] Commerce was, so far as possible, restricted to Spain; coastal trade and trade with other Spanish colonies were more or less forbidden, and Americans were not allowed to own ships. [477, pp. 86–87, 96] These restrictions on commerce were gradually lifted (despite opposition of the smugglers) after 1768, but then duties were correspondingly raised, and there was a maze of quotas, shipping was limited to certain ports, and legal monopolies were sold for high prices. As a result, goods were extremely expensive and smuggling flourished with official connivance; the greater part of trade was illegal. [477, p. 90] Governors tolerated or encouraged illicit commerce because the regulations were so forbidding and Spain was so incapable of providing the needed goods. [477, p. 113] There were many internal legal monopolies also, including articles of prime necessity; monopolies were leased out, the holders squeezing the consumers as best they could. Merchants were organized into monopolistic chambers aiming at the tightening of privileges. There were also

many de facto monopolies that produced nothing for the government, but cost the people dearly; for all these, the only relief was
contraband. [*477*, pp. 92–94]

Lawbreaking of all sorts thrived not only on the excessive number and the unreasonableness of laws, but also on the cumbersome-
ness and weakness of administration. All business had to go through
the office of the viceroy, and local government was made a nullity.
[*477*, p. 266; *531*, p. 117] Everything was buried under a mass of
papers; minute instructions were issued on every subject and forgotten. Even direct royal orders would be held up for years or
sometimes quite ignored if inconvenient to the officials or if, as
was usually the case in later generations, the viceroy was weak.
[*477*, pp. 265–266, 307] Lesser posts were auctioned to seekers
after social standing and enrichment; judgeships were salable
and transferable as valuable pieces of property. [*485*, p. 20; *531*,
p. 194] District governors received no salary but emerged very
wealthy from a five-year term by virtue of their prerogatives as
judges and tax collectors and their broad powers over the Indians.
[*477*, pp. 267–268] There were many regulations against peculation, and clever schemes for setting one group to control another,
but these produced little but an atmosphere of intense suspicion.
[*477*, p. 208; *531*, p. 130] The government was cheated as much as
the people; although the colony was administered for the purpose
of gathering revenue for the crown, the treasury was usually in
distress. [*531*, p. 134] Merchants and officials combined to deprive
the customs of the benefit of its innumerable charges. The farming
out of taxes, with consequent abuses, grew in the eighteenth century as taxes came to be more often in arrears and collection was
difficult. [*531*, pp. 132–133; *476*, p. 194] It was also necessary to
resort to forced loans and such arbitrary procedures. [*477*, p. 202]
Yet very little was done to foster production. No roads were built
until the end of the eighteenth century, and the many minerals,
other than silver, in which Mexico is rich were scarcely touched.
[*527*, pp. 102–104]

The Church was practically a branch of the administration.
Taking a tenth of the product of the land as tithes [*477*, p. 225],
owning a great deal of real property and always receiving more
by pious, especially deathbed, wills, it was extremely wealthy, but
its wealth was concentrated; a bishop received from a hundred to
a thousand times as much as a village priest. [*477*, p. 217] Exempt

from ordinary law, the clerics, like the military, enjoyed the delights of the flesh, much concerned for fees and little concerned with abstinence or celibacy. [527, p. 110] There was serious preoccupation, however, with purity of doctrine. The Inquisition, its zeal fired by the authority to confiscate property of heretics, functioned virtually to the end of Spanish rule; it managed to consume in flames its last victim, a priest turned revolutionary, in 1815. [485, p. 188] It was apparently quite successful, as the authority of the Church was unquestioned on the eve of independence. [477, p. 257]

The Holy Office controlled publication, even excluding from Mexico some books permitted in Spain. In the growing twilight, the Church taught and the people believed that earthquakes, epidemics, and similar catastrophes were divine chastisement for their sins. [477, pp. 68, 216] Almost all education was administered by the Church and religiously oriented, and it did not prosper. Early in the life of the colony, a worthy beginning had been made toward educating the Indians; but the attitude grew that learning was not good for the lower classes. A college founded by Franciscans to teach Latin, rhetoric, medicine, and other subjects slowly degenerated into a primary school and then died altogether. [527, pp. 154, 96] The University of Mexico went its benighted way through the eighteenth century, uninfluenced by the new knowledge of that age. Literature was dry and artificial, dedicated to religious reflections or the glorification of the king. The sole outstanding and lively writer, Juana Ines de la Cruz, was put into a convent and condemned to frustration. Only religious painting and church architecture flourished. [527, pp. 112–113]

When profit and status were to be found in monopoly, graft, and privilege, the gulf between classes was immense and unbridgeable. [485, pp. 18–21] While Spain pretended full legal equality, there was an infinite distance between proud, elegant Spanish lords and the practically subhuman native lower classes, dirty, drunken, ignorant, almost propertyless, and often enslaved. [477, pp. 15, 51] The Spanish-born, only about 1 percent of the population, held almost all important positions in government, Church, and legal commerce (illegal commerce being in the hands of foreigners) to the exclusion of those of the same race born in the New World. They claimed that the latter were indolent, undisciplined, and scornful of labor [477, p. 19], traits not lacking in the Spanish-born. In the words of a viceroy, "The colonists were born to be silent and obey, not to proffer advice on the higher affairs of government." [*485*, p. 17] Although demoralized by exclusion from the higher positions, the natives of Spanish blood, or Creoles, filled the second ranks and especially swelled the legal profession, which made trouble for business by endless and often ruinous litigation. [*477*, p. 300] They also held most of the land in a sort of feudal system transplanted from Spain. Great haciendas, as self-sufficient as possible, served as the basis of local political power; these primarily political holdings were so extensively left unused that it was recommended that cultivation be made compulsory. [*527*, p. 102; *477*, p. 155] At the bottom were the Indians, many of them landless laborers tied by debts to the large estates. There they were de facto slaves, often locked up to prevent flight, freely punished by overseers, and worked to the limit of endurance. Factory workers similarly were kept and treated as actual slaves. Regarded by their betters as shiftless, deceitful, and without honor, the Indians, it is said, rarely spoke truth even when it was in their interest to do so. They seem to have preferred being poor, and even when they had abundant land they cultivated only the minimum necessary to pay tribute and remain alive, because if they had possessions these were likely to be taken for debts, Church dues, or taxes. [*477*, pp. 159, 46–48] Many were vagabonds or robbers.

Very far from uniting against oppression, all classes were jealous and distrustful — Spaniards, Creoles, Indians, Negroes, and sundry mixtures. The Spaniards, little interested in Mexican affairs and usually desirous of amassing enough to retire suitably at home, despised all the rest. The Creoles resented the special status of the Spaniards and compensated themselves at the expense of the other sectors. The mestizos, or those of mixed blood, trying to make their way into Creole society, had their own little monopolies of the more profitable occupations as exclusive guilds, from which Indians were excluded. [*531*, p. 145] The Indians, with no group below them to look down on, hated and feared everyone else, regarding the mestizos as allies of the oppressors. [*485*, p. 24] The Spanish government, of course, favored rivalry and division among the various groups. [*477*, p. 122] So little union was there that the movement for independence was weak, more like a civil war than a general rising against rule from overseas. It was unsuccessful in its own name; separation from Spain came only as a result of grave troubles started by the Napoleonic invasions of Spain and a decision by leaders of the elite to transfer allegiance to a local monarchy. Independence was followed by chaos, so well had Mexicans of all classes learned to hate one another and the government, and so habituated had they become to lawlessness. Political and ordinary banditry were uncontrollable, and rude dictatorship alternated with civil war for generations. Stability was achieved only in the 1920's after a terrible and drawn-out revolutionary storm annihilated most of the upper classes. Even thereafter, Mexican society, at least in the more backward sectors, retained many of the old characteristics: wasteful government, graft and public indifference to it, political apathy, formality and detachment in personal relations outside the family, isolation and suspicion, the acceptance of deception as normal, more interest in magic and sorcery than in the higher religion. [508, *passim*]

Portuguese rule has left a similar imprint upon Brazilian society. The Portuguese government, so far as it could, extracted gold and diamonds; worse for Brazil were the limitation of trade to Portugal and the almost total prohibition of manufacturing. There was fastened on Brazil an exploitative colonial regime not unlike that of Mexico, with government by a very small elite, and great landholders reigned like little despots over their domains and slaves of African origin. [502, p. 50]

Unlike Mexico, Brazil became independent in 1822 without fighting, and remained officially an empire until 1889. It has never been through the purgatory of a social revolution. On the other hand, Brazil has received much more European immigration than Mexico, and largely through the efforts of the immigrants there has been substantial industrialization in parts of the country. Consequently, while Brazilian cities have been modernized, much of the old style of life persists in the countryside, especially in the northeast. More than half of the farmland is in properties of more than 2,500 acres each [550, pp. 302–303, 309]; a tiny fraction, perhaps 2 percent, of proprietors own the larger part of the land, and most persons are landless laborers. [498, p. 19] Planters, who resorted to armed retainers after the slaves were freed in the 1880's [502, p. 53], are still bosses. Most people of the lower classes find it necessary to stake their welfare on a patron, landholder, or political boss, who gives small favors and protection in return for the support of his clients. [561, pp. 106–107]

The people who count are separated from the masses by customs, manner of speech, dress, and etiquette [561, p. 99]; the former would not, of course, think of soiling their hands with work. Divisions are not only of class but of factions of all sorts based on personalities and politics, not on policies or principles. [491, pp. 195–196] In one small town, a barber would cut hair only of the partisans of his group, while opponents went to another barber. [491, p. 198] Such divisions make cooperative endeavor difficult or impossible; community spirit is hardly to be found except in small neighborhoods of perhaps twenty or forty families, which sometimes have their own saint and a common general store. Only within the neighborhood is there mutual help, with men joining together to prepare the fields and to bring in the harvest. [561, p. 150]

There is a desperate struggle for political influence even in small towns, as government positions are very numerous and important, providing income for at least a fifth of the population. [561, p. 154] Salaries are not large, but work involved is not usually enough to prevent one from holding another job also. [491, p. 194] It is impossible to undertake anything injurious to the officeholders. In the lack of local initiative, there is a strong feeling that all improvement should come from the government; but the government spends its resources for salaries and occasional showy rather than useful public works. [491, pp. 182–183] The farmers, on the other hand, see the government only as a taker, collecting taxes and conscripting without return. [491, p. 206]

Such social relations imply a power structure of dysfunctional status groups impeding progress. [498, p. 279] The Brazilian economy has notoriously suffered from uncivic and predatory attitudes toward people and resources. Family or kinship groups remain important, largely to the exclusion of other loyalties. [C. Wagley in 513, p. 188] The native and Portuguese Brazilians have displayed relatively little entrepreneurial capacity, as business and industry have been promoted mostly by persons of other backgrounds, such as Italian, German, or Lebanese immigrants. [499, p. 526] Government is notably ineffective; in 1965 an aircraft carrier would not be put into use because both navy and air force insisted it was their prerogative to operate the planes. [*Newsweek*, Jan. 25, 1965, p. 46] Although higher education has been fostered, there has been little urgency in building schools for the masses, and illiteracy remains very high, especially in the northeast. Conventional religion tends to be limited to formal observances, while magic and spiritism, partly of African inspiration, are very popular. Mixed with all is a certain almost unshakable faith in the greatness of Brazil, proved by territorial immensity, a conviction that God is Brazilian and that, whatever the murkiness of today, Brazil is the land of the future.

If studies were available, one might draw a recognizably similar picture of many countries or regions, all different yet in basic outlines a good deal alike. One may suspect that differences arising from historical circumstances and environment (and the differing stress of observers) are less fundamental than the similarities. Evocative is a nineteenth-century characterization of the West Indies: "There has been romance, but it has been the romance of pirates and outlaws. The natural graces of life do not show themselves under such conditions. . . . There are no people there in the true sense of the word, with a character and purpose of their own." [Quoted by 521, p. 1] An Indian author found this society, while not without color and charm, to be generally coarse and gross, greedy, cruel, ignorant, and uncreative, with no community but only races, religions, classes, and cliques, where the eminent despised the poor; and the poor, always resentful of success, held their superiors to be crooked and contemptible. [521, pp. 28, 41–43]

On the fringes of the great European cultural center, one finds an illuminating example in southern Italy and Sicily. When the Lombards invaded the peninsula in the sixth century, the south remained under the Byzantine empire. The Normans took over in the eleventh century, and while free cities were sparkling in the north during the Middle Ages, the south, held by usually strong monarchies, knew little of the Renaissance. [467, p. 360] But the character of Sicily and Italy south of Naples, with its unquestioning respect for the past and customary forms, its world of transcendental values, fondness for aristocratic titles and distinctions and outward deference to superiors, came down from times of Spanish rule, from the beginning of the fifteenth until early in the eighteenth century. [450, pp. 13–14] Bourbons of the least progressive stripe upheld the ways of Spanish autocracy until the Italian unification of 1860. Even then the government, although more beneficent, remained half foreign, and the people saw as the forces

of order men who knew little of the local language and mentality.
[*479*, p. 69]

At the beginning of the nineteenth century, nearly all the land
of Sicily belonged to the Church and to the barons who dominated
the antiquated parliament, paid little or no taxes, and exercised
almost absolute power over their subjects by authority conceded
by Spanish kings of the seventeenth century. [*479*, pp. 100–103]
During the Napoleonic Wars a British army of occupation tried to
impose a constitution based on the British model, but it was unsuccessful and was largely rescinded. The fact that serfdom was
legally ended made little difference, as the peasants remained dependent for their livelihood upon the few great landholders. [*479*,
pp. 115–117] The middle class was insignificant, commerce was
almost nonexistent, and only land represented wealth and status.

Fearful of outside influences, the Bourbons kept the kingdom
almost entirely cut off from Europe by prohibitive tariffs and restrictions on travel. [*479*, pp. 123, 130] In this static isolation, the
government sought only to keep power by the means it deemed
most effective, arbitrary violence and suppression of any movement among the people; ambitions were reduced to a struggle to
acquire position and wealth, not by producing anything, but by
taking through cunning, foul play, or open violence. Society became more than ever divided into discordant cliques and feuding
factions striving to get the upper hand by political or forceful
means. Much influence went to a class of lawyers, schemers, and
wire-pullers. [*479*, pp. 123, 135] Still more went to the irregular
wielders of force, the ruffians and bandits.

The most striking characteristic of southern Italy and especially
of Sicily in the nineteenth century was the phenomenal prevalence
of organized and half-organized banditry and general criminality.
Something like private war was an accepted institution, as in
medieval Europe, while formal abolition of feudal rights strengthened the position of hired bullies [*479*, pp. 124–125] and the corruption of the police and the worthlessness of the courts compelled
people to look to their own strength. [*467*, p. 365] Violence was
an instrument of the upper classes; just as the government found
it easy to enroll the criminals in the police force, powerful men
kept them as clients or hired them as a private armed force. Monopolistic associations were based on intimidation and murder.
[*479*, pp. 21, 5–8] Attempted land reforms were frustrated or

turned to the benefit of the large landholders by gangsterism. [*450*, p. 28] It was dangerous to undertake a program of social improvement, even something as apolitical as assisting an orphanage, because the better classes might fear the activization of the inferior strata and send an assassin. [*479*, pp. 3–4] The more organized gangs, loosely called the Mafia, represented a highly conservative force at the service of respectable people, whom they protected for a price [*467*, p. 373]; reputable murderers wished to be assured of the standing of their clients before undertaking assignments. [*479*, p. 6]

But lawlessness is a two-edged weapon. While the government tried to use the criminals, the latter probably more effectively used their prerogatives as agents of the government, and public revenues were the booty of whichever faction managed to get its hands on them. [*479*, p. 354] The life even of a great city like Naples was run by an association of big and little thieves, who controlled and coordinated thievery. [*467*, pp. 363–364] If the landowners used ruffians to keep the peasants in their place, the servants turned their guns on their masters. [*471*] When the bandits or *Mafiosi* needed money, they extorted from those who had [*467*, p. 378]; it was perhaps not too much to say that the brigands ruled the countryside by right of arson, killing of livestock, and murder. For such reasons, the rich complained bitterly of the insecurity of life and property, and called upon the government to repress brigandage by arbitrary violence [*479*, pp. 58–59], while many, especially of the lower classes, saw nothing wrong in brigandage, viewing it as a tax on the rich or almost the only escape from serfdom. [*494*, p. 38] Notorious thugs were often regarded as heroes, and boys of fairly good family would join the bands for excitement and prestige. [*479*, p. 57] When the bandits on the mainland, unlike those of Sicily, were rooted out and destroyed after unification, they were long afterward remembered with affection. The peasants greeted the ballyhooed Abyssinian war with dull indifference and hardly thought of the First World War, in which many had died, but instead recounted legends of the brigands of earlier generations as those who had stood for them and for the defense of Calabria [*494*, p. 50] against the noxious state. [*507*, pp. 134–135]

Because of public indifference and because the alien government, based on a liberal ideology, did not employ the panoply of despotism, lawlessness was uncontrollable. Most of the people ignored civil authority or regarded it simply as a more alien and more evil bandit organization [*494*, p. 36], and any cooperation with it was not only an invitation to be murdered but was felt to be dishonorable. [*479*, p. 17] In the Sicilian contempt for law it was practically a civic duty to assist or conceal a criminal. [*467*, pp. 366–367] Victims might appeal to the heads of the Mafia, which was more a web of understandings of leadership and affiliation than a set organization, or, more likely, try to avenge themselves, or endure with resignation. There was no concept of lawbreaking because there was no idea of law, only bonds of personal advantage and loyalty. [*479*, p. 60] Hence the police, recruited from among the criminal elements (if one may call criminal what was not generally reprobated), was ineffective: bandits were killed by other bandits, not by the security forces; there was large-scale contraband with the knowledge of everyone and the connivance of many; those out of power would not denounce the stealing of public funds because they hoped in turn to do the same. [*479*, pp. 48–49, 92, 354] In short, government entirely failed to keep the peace, and the power of one gang, like that of a feudal lord, was limited only by the power of others.

Not only was there no respect for authority; there was no collectivity at all except for narrow self-interest. Criminals stood together in defense of the freedom of their profession and the merciless suppression of traitors to it. Those on top were united in their determination to keep others down. There was no notion of public but only of private interests, and no one thought of improving the miserable village, or, if one did, he was checkmated by overriding indifference and distrust. [*450*, p. 22] As seen by a contemporary investigator, everyone's motto was to maximize immediate advantage and assume others were doing as much; it was regarded as abnormal, even improper, for anyone to take an interest in anything not strictly his own business. [*454*, pp. 85–87] The upper class was most intensely jealous of power and privileges, which meant wealth and reputation, and, keenly sensitive to any injury, was implacable in hatred and vengeance. [*479*, p. 10] The elite were convinced that the more one did for the people the more ungrateful they became, while the peasants, too brutalized to find a place in the power structure, thought of themselves as more animal than human, victims, not participants. [*480*, p. 218; *507*, pp. 62, 3] They had no share of power, belonged to no party, and regarded the state as farther away than heaven and much more menacing, something it was right to cheat as it cheated them. Failing to pay taxes or tithes, they were regularly squeezed by local police. [507, pp. 17, 76, 129] Even the local doctor, holding a semihereditary sinecure, regarded the peasants as good only to pay fees for his standard prescriptions. In recent years, peasants were intensely suspicious of outsiders and felt sure that officials were cheating them, whether they were or not. [454, pp. 33, 101; 480, p. 221] The officials might readily enough victimize the poor, as no one would take the burden of acting against malfeasance. Locally elected officers had no powers, and the municipal council seldom bothered to meet. Abstract political principles were of no importance at all, and a man could turn from communist to monarchist with perfect ease. [454, pp. 19, 99] Even routine services of local bureaucrats were handled according to personal relations. [450, p. 65]

In such circumstances, ambitions were limited; no one hoped to advance by work or thrift, or even by a stroke of luck to rise from the lower to the upper class [454, p. 65], although one might hope to wangle favors. [480, p. 226] All but the basest classes had utter contempt for manual labor; the principal satisfaction was not to have to work, and the ordinary aspiration of the upper classes was to enter the bureaucracy. [480, pp. 223, 227] Horizons were circumscribed; many peasants never traveled as much as a day's walk from home. While some of the upper classes acquired considerable learning, it was strongly academic, literary, and impractical; intelligence turned to subtlety and religion to bigotry. [450, p. 25] In a world of superstition and magic, where time had come to a halt, the old books could molder in the dust. [507, p. 93] Even in the 1950's, with the need for knowledge pressing everywhere, children went to school for only a few years and forgot most of their learning soon after leaving. Secondary education, for the few going away to seek it, was wholly classical or rhetorical and excluded scientific and technical subjects. [454, p. 23; 480, p. 226]

Only personal relations were strong. People would gather under the powerful patron upon whom they depended, and within a narrow circle, a coterie, clientele, or the family, there were honor and friendship; outside, indifference or hostility prevailed. [479, p. 61; 450, p. 65] There were few or no social enterprises; churches were formalistic, inactive, except perhaps in rivalry among themselves. [*454*, pp. 16–18] The area was and to this day largely remains miserably poor, with a lack of public spirit of any kind and an inability to cooperate on any scale much larger than the family. Yet the educated generally were convinced that fundamentally all was rightly ordered. [*450*, p. 32]

Like southern Italy and Sicily, Sardinia has long been a breeding ground for banditry and lawlessness; so has Spain, especially Andalusia, land of latifundia, smugglers, and anarchists. Such ailments are widespread in differing form and degree. But they are not universal. Scandinavia has been exempt for centuries, and so have the Low Countries, and England since Tudor times. [*494*, chaps i, v] One may surmise that material progress improves the social order. But the reverse is probably truer. Where men find tremendous difficulty in using the cornucopia of ideas available to expand human capacities, that is, in much or most of the world, economic advancement seems to be retarded most of all by moral, institutional, and political incapacity, or an inflexible and ineffective social order generated by misuse of power. A society may be unfree not only because it is formally despotic but also because it remains tied up in a whole web of authority of family, class, landholders, castes, and so on, whereby some dominate and exploit and others react with hostility and suspicion. Inherited status means superiority by virtue of what one is, hence scorn for inferiors for what they are and repugnance for marks of lower-class status, especially working with one's hands; for those below, the superiority of the elite implies the hopelessness of their own efforts. [*489*, p. 81] Ambition dies, indifference and disorder prevail outside the narrow and intimate sphere. Hostility and suspicion in turn isolate people and hinder their improvement, as society is divided into antagonistic groups, classes, or castes, which are not competitive yet are unable to cooperate. The more outworn, irrational, and exploitative the authority, the more resistant it is to change. For those who happen to be on top — perhaps for everyone — the structure of society is not to be questioned.

These are traits that are more easily acquired than lost, just as character is more readily perverted than perfected, and once acquired they are shed only under heavy pressure or over a long time. They are, of course, the opposite of the virtues of a free

society, civic dedication, modesty, and frank straightforwardness.
It is good order and honest dealing that make production, especially large-scale production, possible. Pericles spoke proudly of
the Athenians' "Freedom from suspicion of one another in the
pursuits of everyday life" [Thucydides, Bk. II, chap. 37], and this
must have been a great part of their success. A large fraction of
the material possessions of western Europe were destroyed by
the Second World War. Yet, with the catalysis of American aid,
it had much more than restored itself in fifteen years and had gone
on to extraordinary prosperity. This achievement may be credited
partly to technical skills, but it must be mostly due to morale or
social order, the ability of people to work constructively together.
The society that encourages unselfish effort, that rewards approximately according to real contributions, and that gives a sense of
participation in a worthy enterprise progresses even if its natural
endowment is of the poorest. Progress rests mostly upon virtue.

People cannot get together to make their future when each person is chiefly anxious lest he give a bit more or receive less than
his due. An Italian writer tells an anecdote of the penalty of in-
civism: when a group of workers had to carry on their shoulders
a heavy metal beam, one would bend a little to relieve his back;
others would follow the example, stooping lower and lower until
all were on their knees and could do nothing. [534, p. v] It is not
surprising that many countries remain nearly or quite stagnant
despite tolerable supplies of natural resources, cheap labor, and
no little assistance from without. Governments are unable to tax
effectively because of evasion, which is justified by the usual corruption of the government itself. Bureaucracies are inflated, lazy,
and self-seeking. Influence and official connections are more rewarding than good work. Neither talent nor capital, so far as they
exist, go into production but into more promising or safer pursuits
or perhaps wander to a better home abroad. Squeeze is omnipresent in one form or another. Cheating is not dishonorable, only
an embarrassment if one is foolish enough to be exposed. Insecurity
is costly, and an excessive share of the national income goes to
pay for policing. [481, p. 52] Transportation, especially of valuables, is hazardous and expensive; goods are damaged on the way
and pilfered at stops. Thievery makes it necessary for traders to
raise prices. Warehouses leak. Crops must be guarded; in many
places it is not worthwhile to have a fruit tree, as one does not

care to feed the neighbors. The Orient, a traveler has remarked, begins where one has to start watching his luggage. [*206*, p. 13] Productive facilities are carelessly used; monopoly serves profits but not efficiency. Libraries are hard pressed to keep their books from being stolen. Communications are slow and unreliable. All manner of dealings are made difficult because men have little reason to trust one another. Polite dissimulation is the rule and prevarication becomes instinctive. Everywhere the emphasis is on show rather than substance. Learning is impractical and superstitions of all varieties are omnipresent. Community welfare is the least of concerns; people would burn down a public forest to fry a private egg. A large part of the population lives on the rest. It has been said that even in Italy, a fairly effective country by world standards, at least two nonproducers — speculators, monks, landlords, controllers, dealers, bureaucrats — live on each producer. [*534*, pp. vii, viii] Progress under such conditions is necessarily slow; if there were no special stimuli, like the urge to catch up with the vastly richer and stronger nations and the international competition for power, it might well be negative, as it is in some countries and may become in others.

ISOLATION: HAWAIIAN DESPOTISM

If a corporation enjoys a monopoly of its market, it is likely to become conservative, careless, and unresponsive, more concerned with what may be called the political, the maintenance of position, than with improvement of production. A monopolistic church easily becomes formalistic, authoritarian, inflexible in doctrine but perhaps flexible in moral standards. If it has to accept a likelihood that souls will drift away to a competing body, if there is a challenge of a rival theology, it can much better keep up a vital spirit and lively organization. If the livelihood of workers depends upon a single labor union, the organization is much less constrained to heed the wishes of the rank and file than if there is an alternative, and much more subject to manipulation by selfish cliques. Organizations need the stimulus of competition and a check or control from outside. Reform seldom comes from within, and holders of authority fall into habits of arbitrariness and postures of infallibility unless they must stand up to equals. This basic principle is as general as human society and prevails even in so small a group as the nuclear family: when a family is isolated, parents can easily impose strict rules on the children, who will not complain of impositions; when families live in close contact, the children-subjects feel entitled to as much freedom or luxury as the neighboring children enjoy. The autocratic father would do well to remove his family to a farm.

A crafty autocrat will seek to separate his people from the outside world so far as he can — by checking trade and travel and improving self-sufficiency, by reducing the flow of information not useful to his regime, by generating suspicion and hostility. It is politic to hold up foreigners as enemies and to persuade one's own people of the superiority or special virtue of their culture and social order. Foreign contacts and respect for foreign ideas tend to check domestic authority and to increase freedoms in numerous ways, many of which have been discussed in previous chapters. Contrariwise, if the world without is of small importance, the ruler can much better think of himself as a demigod and behave as one.

A realm can best be isolated and made a world to itself by conquest, pushing out the frontiers, and annexing the neighbors, that is, by making itself a universal empire. By raising the power of the state far above that of others, its superiority is manifested; hence men feel little need to learn from without, and foreign examples are uninstructive; the distant barbarians are little encouragement for political opposition. The farther away the frontiers, the more the empire seems to the mass of citizens like the world and its law like a thing of nature; foreign influences shrink, economically and politically. The futility of alternatives is made apparent by the annihilation of rival states. While love of country diminishes, reverence for the rulers of the grand state increases. Political energies, less demanded by the contest of nations, turn inward; the problem and preoccupation is less defense than policing, and the monarch of the world is entitled to treat his subjects as he will.

The most effectively isolated states are the very great empires, for whose peoples outside contacts were slight to nil; although their distant campaigns may loom large in the histories, they would seldom affect the tenor of life. But even for smaller states, a relatively high degree of geographic isolation lends itself to a despotic and rigid, one might say imperial, social order. Perhaps the best example is the most isolated sizable realm in the world, the kingdom of Hawaii, 2,000 miles and more from such small neighbors as Tahiti and the Samoas. Here, where bountiful and gentle nature encouraged an easygoing and simple life, as unspoiled men plucked the abundant fruits and fished the thronging seas, there grew up a first-rate despotism much like its larger cousins of Inca Peru or even imperial China. Its development need not be laid entirely to isolation; but one can hardly doubt that this played some part in the intensity of tyranny and its shape. It is most suggestive that a few years of contact with foreigners of different persuasion sufficed to make a shambles of the whole elaborate system of social controls.

Of the archipelago, seven or eight islands were inhabited when Europeans found them, but only four were of importance. Perhaps half the population, which was in the neighborhood of 150,000, lived on the one island of Hawaii, comprising two-thirds of the total area. In earlier times there had been travel and migration from other parts of Polynesia, principally Tahiti; but for several centuries before the arrival of Captain Cook in 1778 isolation had been nearly total. There had been at that time a number of separate kingdoms, usually at least four, although the whole may have been at times more or less under a single authority. [*154*, pp. 40–41]

Government was despotic, but kings were insecure, rebellion was frequent, and tyranny was mitigated by the ability to migrate to other islands. [*157*, p. 21; *161*, p. 20] Hawaiian kingship was brought to its height by a great conqueror, Kamehameha, who in 1790 set about uniting the whole group of islands under his sway. Thanks in part to guns acquired from the European ships beginning to appear, but perhaps more to his energy and driving personality, Kamehameha, with his 16,000 warriors, in a few years put together a little empire of the Hawaiian world.

Having thus conquered all in sight, Kamehameha dreamed of sailing to claim possession of distant Tahiti, but was prevented by insurrection. [*156*, p. 153] Like other great unifiers, he then set about organizing his realm. He appointed governors, for the first time, to administer the several islands. [*159*, p. 53] He brought great chiefs to the capital and required them to accompany him on his travels. [*159*, p. 52] Brigandage was suppressed, and law and order were firmly established. Kamehameha made court etiquette stricter, enforced all the old rights and prerogatives of chiefs, which had frequently been neglected, and added new ones. [*150*, p. 150; *156*, p. 157] He strengthened religious institutions, made uniform laws, and even brought together the dialects of the different islands. [*153*, p. 61] As conquerer he claimed all lands as his property, dividing among his followers on conditional tenure what had been held as hereditary possessions. More, he made himself the source of all ownership and position. [*150*, p. 149; *156*, p. 155] For his glory and the welfare of the people, he undertook spectacular public works, such as splendid temples, and more utilitarian projects, such as ocean fishponds. [*156*, p. 178] In the fullness of his kingship, Kamehameha was hardly inferior to the greatest of the great.

As established by Kamehameha, the Hawaiian monarch was the incarnation of all law and authority, religious as well as secular, master of lives, property, and souls of his subjects. [*153*, pp. 23, 35] He had a council, but its composition was irregular and its powers were no more than advisory. [*153*, p. 24] Custom and traditional law played a large part in his government, but when so disposed he could set aside the most fundamental customs. While all chiefs were more or less sacred, the monarch was held in some sense to be an incarnate god. [*159*, p. 8] Royal blood, being divine, was kept pure by brother-sister marriage, a custom otherwise unknown to the Polynesians. There was no law of succession, but the ruler named his own successor. [*153*, p. 22] The royal dignity was guarded as hardly anywhere else. It was death for a commoner to remain standing when the king's name was mentioned in song, or when his food, water, or clothing was carried past, to walk near the king's enclosure with paint on one's face, to touch any object of his use, to approach him other than prostrate. [*153*, p. 22; *154*, p. 77; *160*, p. 57; *161*, p. 21] The punishment for violating these tabus was to be burned to ashes, strangled, or stoned to death; and many were the victims, although a mild ruler might temper justice and spare the culprit's life. [*160*, p. 57] For efficiency and dispatch, the king took executioners with him when he went on tour. [*161*, p. 21] Glory was also served by a huge suite and crowd of servants, retainers and hangers-on, priests, singers, dancers, runners, fly swatters, spittoon carriers, pipe lighters, cloak holders, storytellers, and sundry other attendants, plus the many who lingered simply to eat without working. [*152*, pp. 128–130; *150*, p. 27] Kamehameha went traveling with a retinue of about a thousand persons. [*150*, p. 28] During the illness of the king, the people were practically immobilized, as no one could walk abroad or cook. [*161*, pp. 21–22] So fully did the king represent all authority that on his death there was an orgy of crime and violence until the new ruler asserted his position. [*153*, p. 23]

There was also a sacred aristocracy sharply set off from the lowly commoners, with many distinctions of rank, appropriate tabus, and ceremonies. The hierarchies were quite elaborate, with six or seven layers below the monarch. [*154*, p. 73] The deepest chasm, however, lay between ruling class and subjects. The former, for example, had names that could not be given to nonnobles. [*152*, p. 142] Like the Incas, members of the ruling class had a court language for use among themselves, and they discarded any word that became known to the vulgar. [*157*, p. 23] They had the better life; the chiefly classes were so much better developed physically than the ordinary people that some foreigners thought they must be of different racial stock. [*156*, p. 134]

The nobility, however, were insecure. Although civil and priestly ranks were hereditary, office- and landholding were not, and the king created or debased nobles at will. [*153*, p. 22] Owning everything, even the fish in the sea, he parceled out lands to great chiefs, whose holdings he could and sometimes did repossess upon the least failure of obedience or for any other reason. [*158*, p. 21; *154*, p. 73] Chiefs in turn assigned to subtenants, and these to lower holders, and so on for several steps. Subtenants were likewise insecure, but they had an advantage denied those holding directly from the king, as they could try to strengthen their position by holding parcels from several higher chiefs. [*157*, p. 24] All were particularly liable to dispossession when a new king mounted the throne and redivided everything. [*150*, p. 29] Property rights were so feeble that there were no laws regarding them; and if a person wished to recover something taken from him, he could hope to do so only by the favor of a person of higher rank than the guilty party. [*160*, pp. 57–58] Commerce was backward, to say the least, and the only important articles of foreign trade (to European ships), pork and sandalwood, were royal monopolies. [*159*, p. 83] It was a sign of the growth of new influences when these monopolies were given up in 1819.

The good living of the aristocrats and of the swarm of parasites around the throne laid a heavy burden on the working population.

There were regular taxes, accounts of which were kept by knotted cords in Inca style [*156*, p. 155]; otherwise, all grades in authority extracted or extorted what they could or needed in produce, compulsory presents, and forced labor. [*153*, pp. 25–26] If anyone of the lower orders improved his plot, it was likely to be snatched away; if a chief smelled a succulent roasting pig, it might be invited to the chief's table; if a commoner made a good house or large fishnet, or if he dressed well, he was inviting trouble. In all, possibly two-thirds of the fruits of the labors of ordinary people were taken by their betters. [*154*, pp. 74–76; *153*, p. 26] Some of what was gathered, especially foodstuffs, the chiefs returned as handouts. [*161*, p. 18] But the burden was doubtless heavy. As noted, the physical development of the commoners was markedly inferior. Difficulties of existence led parents to kill probably more than half of their offspring. [*151*, pp. 31–32] There was a brighter side; insecurity brought generosity, as people freely gave away what was likely to be snatched. [*157*, p. 24]

To this oppression, the people reacted, or failed to react, with remarkable passivity. When the king grew so greedy for revenues from sale of sandalwood that he drove the people to exhaustion and physical weakness, there was no complaint. [*159*, p. 90] On the contrary, it was widely accepted that the king was appointed to help the oppressed and to succor those in trouble. [*160*, p. 53] The missionaries of the beginning of the nineteenth century saw the ordinary folk as so inert that it was hardly worth trying to convert them, but only the chiefs [*158*, p. 49]; and when the latter adopted Christianity, their subjects duly followed. So revered was such a king as Kamehameha that upon his death many mourners mutilated themselves and some sought to commit suicide. [*156*, p. 170]

The apparatus of control was elaborate and multiform. There were many spies, guards, and executioners. But emphasis was on the religious-ideological. The king's enemies were likely to be picked for religious sacrifices, and a reader of signs might be put to death if he made an error. [*154*, p. 77; *152*, p. 130] Political propaganda was made by historians, genealogists, and storytellers, who rehearsed the ancient lore and modified it as needed. [*152*, pp. 130, 134] The semidivine king also gained popular acceptance by occasionally deigning to work with his own hands at gardening and fishing. [*156*, p. 158] There were all manner of required rites for every occasion, and several days each month were given to ceremonies. The religious system had no ethical content or abstract beliefs of importance, but was mostly designed to surround the royal person and the upper classes with awe. [*157*, p. 25] Most of all, and this was a peculiarity of the Hawaiian system, obedience rested on innumerable tabus, violation of which was at once a sin and a crime. Many burdensome prohibitions, as against men and women eating together, or against women eating bananas, pork, coconut, and other foods, were not of direct political significance. However, the rulers promulgated their desires in the form of tabus, under pain of earthly and spiritual punishment, upon any particular place or thing as desired, upholding social barriers and profound respect for superiors. [*153*, p. 44] "Tabu" meant most of all the sacredness of the rulers. They do not seem to have realized how thoroughly the tabu system worked for their benefit, but they honestly believed in its rightness and justice as part of the order of the universe.

The tabus, however, were not embedded in the Hawaiian personality, but were readily unmade as they had been made, by political authority. Circumcision, a widespread and traditional practice, came to an end when the king forbade it. [*154*, p. 11] More remarkable, the weightiest tabus were ended by royal example and decree; cults were tossed aside, and the people were left virtually without a religion. After the death of the strong Kamehameha in 1819, a less autocratic and more indolent personality, Liholiho, came to the throne. Faith in the power of the tabus had been shaken by the increasingly frequent sight of visitors who ignored them without being fulminated. There were also rumors that the tabus had been overthrown in Tahiti without the dire results predicted. [*156*, p. 176] High chiefs began to lose faith, and women of the royal household, upon whom the prohibitions rested with special severity, persuasively urged the king to give more freedom. Liholiho himself wanted more latitude in his dissipations. [*151*, p. 43] After some hesitation, the king went to dine with his women, and they together ate forbidden foods. Others followed, at first with trepidation and then freely, while the high priest resigned his office and joined in making a bonfire of the wooden idols. [*154*, pp. 124–130; *156*, pp. 181–183] Horrified conservatives rebelled, but they were defeated without difficulty in a single battle. This was a victory, not of Christianity, which was adopted later, but of the foreign example.

It would thus seem that the exceptionally constraining and irrational ideology that supported the totality of Hawaiian despotism could not stand up against diverse influences. On the other hand, strong beliefs in spiritual influences need not have such consequences as in Hawaiian despotism. Among the Eskimos, who had practically no political organization, tabus were very numerous. But the consequence of violation was bad luck and sickness for the sinner, not chastisement by authorities. Only quite exceptionally, if it were felt that the transgressions were so serious as to threaten calamity for all, might the community take action, and then only to exclude the transgressor. [495, pp. 70–71]

SIZE: PRIMITIVE EMPIRES

The size of an organization or state works hand in hand with isolation to make for stronger authority. The two can hardly be separated, because as organizations grow they reduce the number of their competitors and themselves turn inward; internal relations become more important relative to external. Yet many bureaucratic-oligarchic tendencies are closely correlated with sheer bigness. The larger the organization, necessarily the greater the distance between inferiors and superiors, the greater the importance of hierarchic relations. Everyone knows the difference between small groups, with intimate contacts and personal involvement, and a large, possibly efficient, but indifferent conglomerate with its impersonal rules and goals. In a small group the leader must fairly well answer the needs or expectations of the members; in a large one, he answers more the needs or possibilities of the organization. Dealing with the organization and manipulating its functions become more important than purposes exterior to the organization. Control of positions, patronage, and communications is the key to power, and it belongs to the hierarchy; hence oligarchy is characteristic of the big organization. Conviviality, personality, and loyalty become prime conditions of success, while administrators rank above thinkers. [530, pp. 41, 21, 23]

Up to a certain point, of course, bigness improves rationality of decision and effectiveness of use of resources by joining human intelligences and energies into larger wholes. It may make possible the application of technology far beyond the abilities of small groups. Yet, as a modern student remarked, "Size by itself introduces a pathological element in organization." [530, p. 4] The impersonality of the apparatus, which lends itself to exploitation and manipulation, tends to treat people like things, and acceptance and loyalty become primary virtues. The organization raises its own values over those of individuals. Becoming less effective as an individual, man becomes more of an instrument and is expected to like it. In sum, the bigger organization is more an institution and less a group of individual people; its effectiveness is less personal and more organizational.

The differences between large and small organizations are somewhat like those between the elephant and the rabbit: the former is less agile and flexible in the measure that it is more ponderous; far from hopping like a rabbit, it cannot lift itself off the ground; it has a much slower metabolism; it spends much more of its energy simply holding itself up; it moves about less and is less nervous. As dimensions change, relations of qualities change; in the large organization multipliable and general action gains importance, while strictly individual action and motivation recede. The organizational or collective ethos particularly comes to the fore. The more workers carrying the beam, the less personal reason for any of them to refrain from ducking to ease his back and the greater need for a synthetic conviction, rational or not, that the organizational purpose be served. Like the great empire, the big organization needs a cultivated morale, an image of purpose, necessity for compliance, and unanimity, which when manufactured may be effective but easily turns into routine and pretense.

It is commonplace that large organizations of all kinds, from charities to corporations, are usually run by a rather small group or a single leader or driving spirit, who may be attentive to needs of others in varying degrees, but who certainly has a hand on the levers of the apparatus and probably controls its formal channels. As the apparatus of political parties grows, they become less purposeful and dynamic and more sluggish in action and thought, less disposed to risk or to innovate as the organization becomes sacred and a purpose in itself instead of a means to supposedly primary goals. [516, pp. 371–373] Big trade unions become almost the antithesis of primitive workingmen's protective associations, with bureaucratic controls, formal recruitment of staff, distance between leaders and led, strong emphasis on the rights of the organization per se, and policies often differing from the wishes of the membership. [H. Wilensky in *474*, pp. 221 ff.] Great corporations take on bureaucratic forms and vices, intrigue not rarely prevailing over technical-economic considerations. Their bureaucrats must study the relations of power and the predilections of the bosses. [M. Dalton in *474*, p. 215] They are much concerned with image building, not only for the sake of sales but for internal harmony, loyalty, and the prestige of leadership. The bigger the corporation, the more attention it is likely to give to indoctrination or propaganda, showing itself great, wise, beneficent, and socially necessary. It is notable that, although there is an optimum size that is frequently exceeded, corporations are often amalgamated but very seldom split except by outside pressure; directors, like the politicians they usually have to be, like to build empires. Legislative bodies are formal and structured roughly in proportion to their size. For example, on the American scene, although the House of Representatives is only a little more than four times larger than the Senate, differences are quite marked: the House has been much more subject to the rule of a czar; in it, small and exclusive committees are far more decisive; individual members have fewer rights and little voice; and the whole body is more amenable to executive leadership than is the Senate.

Size is an unhappily inexact concept in this connection. Even corporations might be differently graded according to such indexes as volume of transactions, number of employees, capital, importance in the market, and the like. The politically effective size of states is hardly measurable. Perhaps its main component might be population, but area is also important, as extensive territories reduce communications among people, isolating them from one another and the outside world. A ruler may be distant and mysterious partly because his subjects are numerous and he is correspondingly elevated; he may be so also to many of his subjects because he dwells far away in a city they can seldom or never visit. There is some relation of effective size to economy: a pastoral people will have far broader contacts and more familiarity with their rulers than the same number fixed on their fields; well-developed commerce likewise tends to integrate a realm and so make it in effect smaller. In this sense, political size has such components as the relation of the inside to the outside, or the extent to which the world of human experience is dominated by a single authority; the ability of rulers to elevate themselves above the mass of men; the ability of men to communicate with their fellows through nonofficial channels, to organize and make themselves felt politically; the degree of intimacy or the feeling that people share a destiny; the feeling of superiority to those without the state.

Particularly important are the effects of technology. Usually, improvements in capabilities increase the range of interaction and so make smaller a state of given physical dimensions. Higher civilization means more specialization and hence trade, more travel, more wealth, at least for some, and leisure for political organization and activity; most of all, it provides better means of learning about the state and the world. A primitive state of a few thousand square miles looks to its subjects more like a universal empire than does a modern nation of nearly continental dimensions.

Much of this volume has dwelt upon relations of size of the state to the controls that it permits and the ways in which it affects life and thought. These considerations may be generalized by a brief review of societies less civilized than the universal empires of history. One such is the Hawaiian kingdom, whose oppressiveness rested not only upon isolation but also upon relative size. A primitive state of 150,000 souls could not be fraternal as could one of 1,000. In smaller islands of Polynesia, chieftainship was less autocratic and religion less tyrannical than in Hawaii [157, p. 34], and the proportion of product taken by nonproducers was less. [161, p. 132] The aristocracy was set off sharply from commoners, but land was held by hereditary and indefeasible right, even by commoners; the position of subchief was hereditary, and the highest chiefs or kings had to heed the advice of the council and the demands of the priesthood. [162, pp. 255, 259] On quite small islands there was a good deal of primitive democracy, as the most powerful body was an equalitarian council of elders; privileges of chiefs were slight, and they and ordinary folk were alike responsible for their actions. [161, p. 105]

In Africa, which remained through the nineteenth century the world's largest preserve of primitive and near-primitive political institutions, strength and oppressiveness of kingship and social stratification seem to have been substantially correlated with size of political unit, varying from small bands not much larger than a big family to states of tens or hundreds of thousands. There was tremendous diversity and there were many complex arrangements; in the intertwining of political, religious, and social institutions, it was often difficult to say where, if anywhere, there resided something like political sovereignty. There were also many "federal" arrangements, whereby a higher chief stood for the unity of more or less self-governing clans or "states," as among the Ashanti of the Gold Coast. But so far as centralized political organizations have been described, there seems to have been a fairly regular progression of rulership with size. As examples one might take the equalitarian bands of Bushmen, the moderate-sized and moderately governed Hottentot tribes, the strongly ruled larger Bantu nations [541, p. 31], and the refined and complex despotisms of Dahomey, the Ganda, and others.

The Bushmen and Bergdamas lived in rather loose independent kinship groups of from ten to about a hundred souls, subsisting by hunting and gathering and independent of, usually antagonistic to, similar groups in the vicinity. [270, p. 9; 272, p. 11] There were no social classes and no distinctions except that of the chief, who became such by no formalities but by general recognition; he was most likely a son of a preceding chief, but did not have to be. There was little contention over the chiefship because it carried little power to hurt or help anyone. [270, pp. 62, 193; 272, p. 183] The chief was practically indistinguishable in appearance and bearing [272, p. 10] and no wealthier than the rest; he commanded no tribute or services and had no insignia. [271, p. 150] He had no legislative or judicial functions; if anything had to be decided, he talked it over with the men. If it was felt that anyone needed correction, the assembled group discussed and judged his conduct. [270, pp. 87–90] The chief had some honors, performed rituals, and was a symbol of unity; but he had no special assistants. Some men were considered possessors of magical powers, but there were no priests. Art was realistic and unconventional. [271, pp. 196, 213] The primitive means of subsistence impeded gathering into larger groups, and warfare did not bring about the subjection of one to another; the defeated would lose territory, perhaps, and might move away. Sometimes a forceful leader would try to claim tribute from neighboring bands and arbitrate over them, but such arrangements were temporary. Only as European influence penetrated did some Bergdama groups amalgamate; then there emerged a stronger chiefship, like that of the Hottentots. [270, pp. 133–134]

The pastoral Hottentots lived in tribes of 500 to 2,500. There was a simple division of class, partly based on ownership of cattle, lacking which the poor became dependents of the rich, partly based on origins, whereby some were citizens and others, mostly aliens, were servants without a share in tribal government. [270, pp. 61, 121] The powers of the chief were far larger than among the Bushmen or Bergdamas, but were by no means autocratic. Although there were sometimes dynastic conflicts, the chieftainship was not extremely coveted and was sometimes renounced. At his accession the chief had to promise to respect the laws and the rights of the people. [271, p. 328] The chief was judge with powers of sentencing to death, but he had no corps to enforce his decision, which might be carried out by the warriors if they approved. [270, pp. 189, 116] Hardly a lawmaker, he was first among equals in his council; crucial decisions, as of peace and war, were made by a general assembly. The chief organized hunts and regulated grazing, but otherwise possessed no extensive control of the economy. [270, pp. 82, 117] Surrounded by no formal etiquette, he lived much like his subjects. He did, however, enjoy some political revenues, such as tribute on game killed and part of such fines as might be levied [271, p. 334]; and he was usually the richest member of the tribe. There were subchiefs over the clans within the tribe, and the chief had no right to intervene in clan affairs. The rulership was also limited by the fact that a sector could secede if displeased. [270, pp. 115, 198, 190]

The Bantus, with a heavier population density based on mixed farming as well as cattle raising, had larger tribes, ranging from 5,000 or so to more than 100,000. Stratification was complicated, with nobles, commoners, serfs, and aliens. [270, p. 56] In a class by himself was the great chief or king, among some tribes held semidivine or so magically potent that he could kill a man by pointing a finger at him. [265, p. 383; 270, p. 107] He was surrounded by much ceremony and adulation and addressed in terms of formal flattery; his personal name was sometimes tabu. He lived somewhat secluded; he would not eat with subjects and occasionally might disappear in order to make an impression of mystery. Those approaching him patted hands continually while murmuring his praises, going down on hands and knees as they drew into the presence. [265, pp. 382–384; 270, pp. 97–98] The king was the most important bond of unity of the tribe; and allegiance to him, not kinship or blood, was the mark of affiliation. Looked up to as father of his people, he was the bearer of general prosperity [265, p. 375], more or less responsible for the general welfare. [270, pp. 29, 68–69] He was extolled in long eulogies recited on public occasions, which were almost all that people would remember of him; and from childhood they were taught loyalty to him. [270, pp. 98–99, 105]

As much of an autocrat as his personality permitted, the Bantu chief was master of his subjects' life and property. As judge he had the power of death, sometimes symbolized by handing him spear, ax, and club at his installation. [270, p. 102] His verdict was carried out by his retainers, and fines went into his pocket. [267, p. 222] He might feel obliged to follow traditional law in his judgments, but he could also coerce extrajudicially. Once, for example, a Zulu king was constrained to decide a case against a favorite on grounds of custom, but he negated this concession by ordering the murder of the successful litigant and his family. [M. Gluckman in 263, p. 33] The kraal was held responsible for the misdeeds of any inmate, and failure to report a crime made one guilty with the criminal. There was no trial for treason, as suspicion sufficed to cause the village of the suspect to be wiped out. [267, pp. 223–224] As legislator, the Bantu chief supplemented or modified traditional law; he would hear the opinions of a council, but the decision was his. [270, p. 141] He controlled the army and made war. He was the center of tribal magic, which assumed great importance [270, pp. 72–73] and facilitated administration; for example, some tribes regarded it as sinful and dangerous for commoners to consume the first fruits, which had ceremoniously to be handed over to the gods and the rulers. [265, pp. 394–395]

The chief's economic powers were wide. He distributed land and regulated agricultural activities. Taxation was irregular according to his needs [267, p. 221]; he exacted a large tribute from crops, cattle, and hunting. It was dangerous to acquire much wealth, as he might kill and confiscate [270, pp. 71, 111]; rich men were sometimes accused of witchcraft, a crime punished by the most gruesome death and confiscation of property. [267, p. 219] The culture did not offer notable luxuries, but the king possessed much more of everything than anyone else, especially scores or hundreds of wives. Those about him were wholly dependent, as they held property on loan from him only and he could strip them of it at will. [270, p. 110]

Effective power, as everywhere, depended on administration, and it was hard for the king to do much that those highly placed around him disapproved of. But he had his subchiefs, lieutenants, and executive staff at his disposal. The tribe was divided into sections for more effective management. Nobles were ordinarily placed over the sections, but commoners were preferred for the king's lieutenants and ministers, as they were held more trustworthy. [270, p. 57] Many spies also helped ensure obedience. [M. Gluckman in 263, p. 42]

The rulership was much coveted and often violently disputed. The heir was usually a son by the great or principal wife. In some tribes the chief did not take a great wife until after inauguration in order that he should be less troubled by the ambitions of a grown heir; however, this often made a regency necessary. [270, p. 172] There was much trouble with revolts and civil wars, usually started by a member of the royal family and hence potential monarch. One remedy was to send near relatives of the king to govern outlying areas; another was to kill them. Brothers were often murdered, usually for real or supposed conspiracy, but sometimes simply as a precaution. Some prudent chiefs of the Zulu, one of the largest Bantu groups, had all their sons killed at birth, or all but a few. One had his wives murdered as soon as each became pregnant. [270, pp. 173–174], such was the anxiety to guard power. On the other hand, if the king was exceptionally bad, unpopular, or dangerous, he was likely to be assassinated by his relatives. That is, the high aristocracy sometimes rose against the person of the sacred ruler, but not against the autocratic powers, which were believed necessary. [270, p. 105] The people did not criticize or revolt. Discontented groups might try to withdraw, but this was a difficult and desperate remedy. [270, p. 154]

Bantu kingship rose to a zenith in the Zulu kingdom built up early in the nineteenth century by Shaka Zulu, a truly imperial figure like Genghis Khan. Before him, Bantu tribes had been fighting limited and indecisive wars mostly for glory; but Shaka, perhaps inspired by infiltrating European influences, determined to drive for hegemony. He made his beaten enemies his booty, taking their wives and cattle and drafting their surviving men into an ever growing army. [267, p. 10] Turning his nation into full-time warriors, he conquered some 100,000 square miles and destroyed the independence of about 300 tribes comprising half a million persons. [265, p. 359] The nation was his tool. Men were called "Warshields of the king," and they, like land, were his property; he received a fine as indemnity in case of murder. His soldiers married when he commanded and whom he chose. [M. Gluckman in 263, pp. 29, 44] Each household owed him a girl. Like a good imperialist, Shaka reshaped institutions, doing away with the old clans as units [270, pp. 101, 28] and assuming personal charge of magic, expelling or killing many of the previously powerful priesthood. [M. Gluckman in 263, p. 31; 269, p. 242] So strong was his grip that when he was slightly wounded by a would-be assassin his regiments fell on one another and massacred a large number in their zeal to punish those not evincing sufficiently passionate grief. [267, p. 223] Famous for his bloodiness, Shaka slaughtered wholesale and on the slightest caprice, devising the cruelest punishments, like impaling, for those who displeased him. So monstrous was his despotism that in mourning for his mother's death he decreed that cultivation should be ended, milk should be spilled on the ground, and all women becoming pregnant should be killed with their husbands. The first orders were kept in force three months, the last a year. [267, p. 16] For his excesses, Shaka was finally cut down by his brothers.

Another first-class despotism was that of Dahomey in West Africa, with a population of about 130,000 farmers and hunters and an area of about 4,000 square miles. Society was stratified: at the bottom were slaves, mostly employed on the king's plantations, who were treated more harshly than usual in Africa; over them were free farmers and a middle class, who were by law denied the use of many items of visible wealth, such as chairs, hammocks, bedspreads, and the like; above was a privileged class of priests and officials who did not work in the ordinary sense. [264, I, 99, 107, 102; P. Mercier in 262, p. 210] The king was high above all, treated with such deference that before him even the ministers prostrated themselves in the dust and threw dirt upon their heads; and the royal scepter, carried by messengers, was received with ceremony as though it were the king himself. [264, II, 33–34] His powers were absolute, of course, within the framework of the general culture.

Owner of all in theory, the king secured his due. As judge, he sometimes confiscated property; anyone who seemed to be gaining independent wealth was in danger of finding himself a penniless slave. [264, I, 78, 99n] There was an elaborate system for checking all farmers and their harvests; livestock, hunting, hives, spices, and so on were all taxed, as were craft production and sales. [264, I, 114, 117–120] Dual accounting was supposed to make cheating difficult, and the king had some thousand tax gatherers, but it is said that only a small part of the take reached the royal coffers. [264, I, 109] Taxation, moreover, was entwined with controls in general. It was attempted to plan agriculture so that proper amounts of each crop were planted. A certain nut tree was prohibited entirely on grounds that profits from it made it harder to get slaves; when it proved difficult to make this ban effective, the tree was permitted in restricted numbers. [264, I, 112] On other occasions the king forbade or limited the growing of attractive crops, like coffee, sugarcane, rice, and tobacco, as though simply to make his power felt.

The main indulgences or displays of the king were in the use of people. He had a harem of some 2,000 girls, and he enjoyed having men do his bidding. He once stationed men at arm's length over the whole 90 miles between the coast and the capital to pass along messages and goods, an extremely wasteful use of manpower. [264, II, 45, 56–57] He also sacrificed slaves lavishly. On solemn occasions, as a royal funeral, hundreds would be slain, and some dozens at yearly festivals in orgies of blood. Any important ceremony, in fact, required a few beheadings; and routinely, every morning, the king had a man and a woman killed to carry glad greetings to his ancestors. The king alone had the right to make human offerings or to authorize them, as for the opening of a new cult house. But this use was much less religious rite than conspicuous consumption. Slaves were expensive, and the right to slice them up was a suitable ornament of royalty. [264, II, 50–55]

The administrative system was nothing if not sophisticated. Administrators were drawn not from the nobility but from the middle classes to secure more wholehearted adherence. No member of the royal family could hold office; the crown prince, who was any son designated by the king, had no part in the government. Ministers were to be always at the king's call; if one did not appear instantly when summoned, it was cause for disciplinary action. [264, II, 39,

31, 43] There were most elaborate controls to ensure faithfulness and accuracy. Each administrative title was conferred on a man outside and a woman inside the palace; the latter was to check the former and guard the royal interest. [P. Mercier in 262, p. 232] Each official report was presented in three different ways and before three sets of witnesses, who had to agree. [264, I, 111] Police secretly followed all suspicious persons, especially travelers. The taxation system doubled as a political control, pebbles corresponding to the people in each place and category being deposited appropriately in the capital. For local administration there were provincial chiefs, village chiefs, headmen of groups of compounds, and sib heads, all named or at least confirmed by the king. [264, II, 28, 76–77, 5, 37] The king might even determine the headship of families by his prerogative of approving all inheritances.

The Dahomese, as practiced autocrats, believed in ruling as much by psychology as by force. The king was depicted as supremely just. Upon enstoolment, he would give the people a quantity of cowry shells in "payment" of the land, which thereby became his by purchase as well as by royal right. [264, I, 80] Similarly, when taxes were being gathered, he would conspicuously pay to himself part of the harvest from his own fields, thus showing his impartiality. [264, I, 115] Various tricks were also played with magic and superstition. For example, to learn how many sheep, goats, or cattle people owned, the officials would spread word that a great plague was coming unless everyone offered to the appropriate deity a shell for each animal he owned. After the people had brought their shells and the king had added an impressive number, the officials would rejoice that the plague had been averted and begin their calculations as to how many animals could be taken from each village. [264, I, 118–119] Cults were manipulated [P. Mercier in 262, p. 214], and the priesthood was kept under close royal control. Not only did it instill fear and docility into the hearts of the multitude in the name of a pyramidal pantheon (corresponding to the political realities) [264, II, 294], but each cult house was expected to keep an accounting of its members and report to the king. Somewhat like Hawaiian tabus under Western influence, the whole ideological system collapsed when the French overcame the native despotism. [260, p. 99]

It is difficult to tell how representative these samples may be of the great complexity of African political forms. But various parallel examples might be cited from other parts of the continent. The Lele of the Congo, hunters and farmers like the Bantu but dwellers in villages of twenty to a hundred huts, practically enjoyed the anarchist's dream of no political authority at all. The nominal chief was merely the oldest man, respected for his age but correspondingly feeble as a leader. [M. Douglas in 262, p. 15] Advanced toward autocracy were the Shilluk of the Upper Nile, a people of about a hundred thousand, but divided into two moieties and enjoying a good deal of local autonomy. The king was in theory absolute and divine, an incarnation of the founding spirit of the nation; but in fact he was more like a high priest, had to be chosen by a consensus of national leaders, and was frequently overthrown. [261, pp. 72–81; G. Lienhardt in 262, pp. 139–153] A clearer example is that of the Ganda, a nation of about a million, the largest in the lake region of East Africa, where despotism was nearly perfect. Absolute master by his command of the standing army, the king was dignified by many titles suggestive of supernatural powers. He traced his lineage through numerous exalted ancestors, for many of whom there were kept up shrines like those of Inca mummies, with a prime minister, royal sister, descendants of wives, and the like in attendance. [268, pp. 43–45] When the king went abroad, he had an escort of executioners as did the Hawaiian monarch; respectfully or prudently, the people would remain indoors. [266, p. 170] To maintain the proper attitudes, the king would destroy houses, sell people into slavery or have them burnt alive or cut to pieces for trivial offenses, such as sneezing in the royal presence, or sometimes for no offense at all but simply to manifest power. [268, p. 45] Although there was a noble class, the king was the master of status. The fiefs he gave out were not hereditary but his to resume, their holders had frequently to visit the capital, and about a thousand scions of upper-class families were kept in the palace. It was a dubious privilege to belong to the royal family, as the king excluded his brothers and his children from administration and not infrequently killed them. [268, p. 48; 266, p. 84] On the other hand, anyone might rise by catching the eye and favor of the ruler. He was, with his vizier, center of the administrative system, appointing governors and maintaining various sets of officials to report on one another. [266, pp. 50–52] All taxes were supposed to be paid into the royal purse, whence sums were returned as needed for local administration. It is noteworthy that this centralized monarchic system was influential over lesser kingdoms of the region; however, these remained less fully autocratic. Thus, in the smaller state of the Soga, with a population of about ten thousand, nobles held substantial hereditary positions, there was no standing army, and the royal princes had considerable rights. [266, pp. 41, 82]

Thus, among many primitive and supposedly simple peoples, the encompassing of relatively large groups in a single state has enabled autocracy to grow to respectable fullness. And despite the crudity of material culture, it has functioned in principle much as it has in vastly larger and more highly civilized empires. The empire of Constantine, the great Chinese dynasties, Russian tsardom of the sixteenth century, and possibly even some imperial states of the twentieth century have shared many things with the Hawaiian kingdom of half-naked fishers, the Zulus, whose palaces were built of latticed sticks covered with thatch, and the primitive cultivators of Dahomey or the Ganda. In all of them a mortal man was upraised and glorified beyond reason as a symbol of unity, with theoretically complete and final powers over everything within his vast domain; a large part of the produce of the land was taken for the pleasure and glory of the autocrat and those who could clamber onto the political apparatus; to maintain control, there were employed much cruelty and an apparatus of terror, as well as psychological devices to give suitable ideas and keep men in a proper frame of mind. Such various despotisms have been kin in their troubles, also: the problem of succession, a pervasive atmosphere of suspicion, intrigues, and rivalries as men reached for the intoxicating cup of power, and the growth of a large class who feasted on the fruits of others' labors. Unchallenged power raises problems that have not much changed.

WAYS OF POWER

Isolation and size are fairly simple and concrete factors promoting imperial ways and hierarchic power, although they must be weighed in terms of other factors, such as means of communication and ranges of interaction. The very large and essentially isolated state seems inevitably autocratic, even if, as in the case of

Rome, institutions and ideas of the constitutional state are only slowly laid aside. But not only does the close unity promote Caesarism; causation also proceeds in the opposite direction: concentration on power and glory, the stressing of force and domination, is an essential factor in the formation of the great empire and the establishment of the autocratic imperial system. And just as isolation or size usually inclines toward ways of the empire, likewise an emphasis on crude power, the reliance on force, gives imperial aspects to fairly small states.

Whatever the importance of general utility and free consent (apart from that engineered by various psychological devices or controls), compulsion and force are the foundation of empire building; the more ruthless the struggle for supremacy, the harder for independent states to maintain themselves, and the best candidates for the prize of world rule are the most ruthless and determined seekers after power. Domination and glory also isolate; superiority of power is felt as moral superiority, which relieves of any necessity to learn from or take seriously into account political inferiors. The possession of power justifies its use and renders it important, and the need for power justifies autocracy, which sanctions itself by success, that is, by power.

Autocracy is not especially productive of military strength. In their maturity the universal empires, founded on conquest, have regularly become quite flabby. They tend, probably contrary to desires and for reasons beyond control, to a pacifistic frame of mind, even while continuing to rely internally on arbitrary force to a large degree. At the same time and probably for related reasons, some of the most efficient fighting states, at least in defense, have been among the freest. The Swiss for centuries were the best soldiers of Europe while their country was a lone beacon of republican liberties; the Dutch were perhaps freest when they were battling successfully against heavy odds for independence; and the Athenians far outclassed the Persians as soldiers. But the Swiss and the Dutch, strong as they were in their times, could not or did not wish to apply this strength to territorial expansion (not considering the Netherlands overseas empire, commercial in origin). The Greeks could beat back the Persians; but it was the Persians, not the Greeks, who made an immense empire. Power-mindedness, a characteristic of the state or social order, indicates little about the quality of the people as raw material for armies, although one may imagine that militaristic values, indoctrination, and drill should produce at least fair soldiers.

Military strength, at least on the defensive, does not require a militaristic regime; on the other hand, states like Prussia or Ch'in prior to the unification of China, which for whatever reason come to stress force and domination, have taken on more than a few attributes of autocratic empires. The Spartans, who were small-scale empire builders ruling a much larger population of serfs and dependents, not only laid strong emphasis on matters of direct military utility, such as sports, physical strength, constancy, and bravery; they also tried largely to isolate their citizens from foreign contact, denigrated commerce and forbade its exercise, made their land a cultural desert, required total conformism for full citizenship [116, p. 237], and, much more than other Greeks, gave their constitution a supernatural basis, submitting it to the Delphic oracle before proclaiming it to the people. [Xenophon in 327, p. 239] The example of Prussia is equally familiar. With its stress on kingly power and hierarchic status, its scorn for commerce and interference in the economy, the court of the successors of Frederick the Great might have been that of a much greater autocracy. The outstanding difference was that, as in Japan, the hereditary nobility retained importance because of its supposed military virtues; even so, the nobility was to a large degree converted from a class in its own right to a rank in service in imperial style. Only the king and a few ministers had any real responsibility, and public spirit was strangled. [235, p. 41] The militaristic ordering of Prussia particularly reduced intellectual capacities. Frederick the Great himself was French by education, and the creators of Prussian organization and thought — Scharnhorst, Stein, Gneisenau, Clausewitz, and Moltke — were all non-Prussians; no less striking, the glorifiers of Prussian power, Hegel and Treitschke, were likewise brains from freer and less ambitious parts of Germany who gave themselves to Prussian ambition. [noted by 240, p. 123]

Similarly, the state of Ch'in, driving for universal empire, drew from other lands its leading organizers and ideologues of power who helped convert it from a feudal conglomerate to a centralized bureaucratic state in imperial style. The guidebook of one of its developers, Lord Shang, gives a stark picture of its imperial ways. State and people were sharply set apart; it was frankly sought to weaken them to make it stronger. [16, p. 82] Merchants and the commercial mentality were held noxious in the extreme, while nobility in a complicated ranking was made dependent only on military merit, and obedience was held the sole virtue [*16*, pp. 15, 85]; there was as much emphasis on internal authority as on external strength; to denounce a culprit was as meritorious as slaying an enemy, and there was "one reward against nine punishments." [*16*, pp. 14, 84] The most obvious shortcoming was the disinclination to gild the realities of power.

A correlation between power-mindedness and aspects of the imperial order is also discernible in organizations directly devoted to the use of compulsion, such as the armed forces and the police. Although police departments, like the governments they serve, are varied, they are apt to be authoritarian and politically conservative. One would have to look far to find police forces exerting pressure for liberalization of the government or intervening on the liberal side of a dispute, but they have frequently resisted dilution of autocracy, either because they are beneficiaries of state power or because it suits their mentality. Both within the service [*455*, p. 114] and in relation to the political authority, the police are usually strongly imbued with principles of loyalty. They may be, of course, valiant defenders of liberty; but it is probably fair to say that the more important the role of police, the less free the community.

A better example is that of the armed forces, which are much larger and more integrated than the police and much more set apart as a self-contained and self-ordering organization. Large armies, at least until the technological revolution of modern times, seem to have displayed numerous parallels with the model or ideal imperial apparatus. They have tended to isolate themselves from a surrounding society regarded as weak and inferior. The generals, like the emperors, have had no great liking for law, international, civilian, even military, preferring personal relations and understanding; the term "sea lawyer" in the navy and its equivalent in the army connote opprobrium for those who would avail themselves of legalities for their personal welfare and to the detriment of needs of the service. Armies have always much stressed glory, prestige, and honor; and honor has meant for the military as for the empire complete loyalty and utter obedience. Like the imperial spirit, the military spirit has been inimical to business and scornful of commercial values. The rewards of miltary leaders have been noncommercial, not large salaries but social and sometimes political status, economic security and many perquisites of membership in the elite, from the use of horses and personal servants to free medical care and solemn funerals. Like empires, armies have a strong hierarchic structure, stress the organization over the individual and character over intelligence, are much given to ceremony and tradition, and are lamentably uninventive; like empires, too, they bask in the awe that men have for power. Generalship, like imperial rulership, is concerned with the effective control of men by compulsion and indoctrination. Like the universal empire, the military have usually been highly conservative and hostile to change; they have rejected the idea of real progress in history, emphasizing the permanent evil, the truculence, pride, and selfishness of human nature. [229, p. 257]

With the justification of the exceptional nature of their profession, armies have segregated themselves with their own laws, social values, morality, and economy, divorced so far as possible from the civilian world and the marketplace. When the boy puts on a uniform he is supposed to think of himself as a changed being stepping into another sphere. Sometimes, as in the German army of the nineteenth century, there was great hauteur and snobbery; to be friendly with civilians was to be unreliable. [222, p. 233] According to Bismarck, no antimilitarist, many officers considered all civilians as "alien enemies." [239, p. 296] The American army, with less pride, lived at the same time very much to itself. It has also tried consciously to keep apart. It is symptomatic that the faculties of the academies, which stand at the heart of the military esprit, have been drawn almost entirely from within the services, even for nonmilitary subjects, the naval academy providing a partial exception. The discipline of the academies also has promoted complacency and feelings of superiority to the civilian universe and values left behind. To help develop the mentality of separateness, cadets are not allowed off the grounds during the first year, even for Christmas [221, p. 144]; and they are permitted to have no money but are issued only a few tokens for purchases on the grounds. [221, p. 22] As a result of such withdrawal, armies have become introverted and concerned with internal matters and the needs of the organization. [239, p. 15] For this reason also, armies may, like completed empires, become rather unaggressive and reluctant to undertake the disturbance of war. They have, in any event, been frequently very successful in building up a corporate sense of honor and pride of status, so that officers of nonmilitary or bourgeois background, far from introducing their values into the establishment, have so far as possible shed their skins and taken on its ways, even to exaggeration, as in the Prussian army. [222, p. 238]

The military has felt itself apart from and above parliamentary and popular politics, viewed as low and disorderly; military contempt for the dealing politician is traditional. The feeling is that decisions should be made not by competitive forces, bargaining and maneuver, but by professionals and those duly authorized. Above all the military approach is anti-individualistic and anti-democratic. So far as the army has a political stance, in settled societies it is almost invariably conservative, as has been notoriously true of the professional sectors of the armies of Germany, France, England, Russia before 1917, and other countries. In Europe it has been widely felt that officers should be aristocrats to ensure loyalty to the established order; and they have seldom been enamored of constitutions but have preferred the mystic authority of a king, even when they might have profited materially by republicanism. Thus the German army had political ideals varying from feudal to absolutist, but never constitutional; the army swore loyalty only to the Supreme War Lord as long as he kept the throne; and the officers, who were subject to discharge for taking a liberal position, regarded themselves as the only sure bulwark of monarchy. [222, pp. 236–237] They looked upon the Reichstag as something like a personal enemy; the Prussian Minister of War, the intelligent Roon, for example, spoke of the "spreading constitutional confusion of ideas." [239, p. 190] After the French Third Republic was established in 1870, the army remained wholly monarchist in sympathies for a generation, and anyone expressing republican ideas was ostracized. [228, p. 51]

As the United States turned more liberal after the Civil War, the army became more conservative and fearful of the effects of democratization. [229, pp. 257, 260] A post-1918 ROTC manual written in the War Department defined "democracy" in these terms: "Authority derives through mass mutiny or any other forms of direct expression. . . . Attitude toward property is communistic – negating property rights. . . . Results in demagogism, agitation, discontent and anarchy." [239, p. 410] Only a very small fraction of American army officers regard themselves as liberals, but most are frankly conservative, and the higher in rank the more so. [*230*, pp. 236–239]

If American officers are strongly conservative, this does not imply that they have been very fond of free business enterprise. On the contrary, they have been more than a little scornful of business mentality and usually quite willing to see a large measure of governmental controls and a high level of taxation. [*230*, p. 246] Military circles tend to look to orderly, that is, monopolistic, relations. Before the First World War, the war ministries of Europe made no effort to stimulate competition in the supplying of munitions but rather favored cartelization. [*239*, p. 367] "Prussian socialism," whereby the productive forces of the nation should be mobilized and directed for maximum strength, is in the military style, which can only scorn the mentality of the tradesman. Profit seeking is dishonorable and unpatriotic. Continental officers of the eighteenth century looked down upon their British counterparts as representatives of shopkeepers, while British officers looked down on their own commercial classes who made British greatness. [*239*, p. 59] Rather few military leaders have come from business circles; the mentality of landed interests fits much better, as in the imperial system. [*230*, pp. 86–87, 95] In the eighteenth and nineteenth centuries, French, British, and German officer corps alike had strong relations with the landed aristocracy to the relative exclusion of merchants and industrialists. In this spirit also, armies have traditionally been rather careless of costs, unimpressed with their economic dependence, and ready to spend whatever might seem necessary to get what they feel is required.

While the military mind has little sympathy for open politics, political struggles go on under cover within the organization. They are inevitable where relations are fundamentally political. Although little comes to public knowledge, partly because of professional solidarity, it can be observed that the higher, if not the lower echelons, show much politicking and timeserving, and engage in keen contests for promotion and prestige. [*239*, p. 266] Bernhardi called the peacetime army the "school of cold-blooded climbing." [*239*, p. 298] Even in the supreme trial of war, personal spite may dominate. Although such behavior is usually camouflaged, many examples might be cited from military history. More than once did a Napoleonic marshal fail to support another for personal reasons, and Ney and Murat almost had a duel over the command while facing the enemy. One Russian general, Rennenkampf, left his colleague, Samsonov, in the lurch in 1914, thereby bringing on the disastrous defeat of Tannenberg. [*239*, pp. 268–269] Sundry accusations have come out of the Second World War, as that the American air force declined to send bombers in support of the army in Normandy lest its independence be shadowed. [*230*, p. 25]

To keep some kind of political order, the military services have resorted, even more than bureaucracies, to rank and promotion by seniority. At least up to the rank of captain or major, all an officer had to do in order to progress properly in any peacetime army was to avoid serious trouble. [*239*, p. 298] For example, in the French army of the nineteenth century, promotion was almost entirely by seniority [*227*, p. 68], and the American army had a flat rule that seniority should guide except in case of disability. [*224*, p. 17] Rank has even been made dependent upon the exact date of appointment. To a large extent, this principle has prevailed also at very high levels, up to positions of such importance as to be decided by the chief of the state or military department. In the United States, for example, even generals and admirals are to a large extent graded by seniority unless the President or his immediate advisers reach down to pass an outstanding man ahead of his seniors.

Advancement by seniority harmonizes perfectly with conservatism, and both of these conform with the fundamental of military organization, strict subordination. Rigid rules from above are its essence; insubordination is its crime, and command must be unadulterated; it is technical mutiny for soldiers to present a joint petition. At the top of the hierarchy, as in a great bureaucracy, relations may be fairly free and fluid; a general can argue with his superior general or even take liberties with orders in a rather unmilitary way as the corporal cannot do with the sergeant or the lieutenant with the captain. [*239*, p. 297] As natural for an organization dedicated to exerting force, the mentality is primarily of compulsion; and there is much more emphasis on punishment than on reward. The command structure is a pyramid of autocracies, the officer who is subjected to the rule of his superiors compensating himself by the government of his subordinates. Above, there is usually a supreme figure; fond of hero worship, armies have often made their commander into a demigod, a symbol of leadership regarded as essential for spirit and unity.

The exaltation of the one or the few means the contrary for the many. One of the most marked characteristics of armies has been the gulf between the officers and the ranks, a gulf deeper than that between classes in civilian society. There is little respect for the personal dignity of inferiors, and individuality is regarded as somewhat subversive. All must dress and should act alike, except for the distinctions conferred by the hierarchy; men should even have identical haircuts. Much of military drill and procedure is designed essentially to humiliate and to make responses automatic, that is, mindless. All should march and think in step. It is the general assumption of the military approach that "men" in the ranks (as distinguished from officers) are naturally bad and must be reshaped, disciplined out of their natures into passive instruments of superior command. It has been fairly well assumed (at least until armies were thrust into the new technological age) that they might be strong and brave, but that they also were more or less dolts of whom no thinking was expected or desired, that they should respond not intelligently but docilely. It was a Roman maxim that the soldiers should fear their officers more than the enemy. [314, I, 10] Frederick the Great said exactly the same thing and tried to bring it about. For such obedience and fear, familiarity is dangerous, and the enlisted man has been treated much like an inferior race or like the populace of a well-developed empire, conspicuously differentiated by dress and style of life, housed apart, with separate recreations and the like. Segregation has extended to the offspring; children of officers and men were formerly strictly separated, even in the military establishment of free America, proud of its classless society. [230, p. 180] As a Polish-Saxon king said in the eighteenth century, "For the officers, honor is reserved; for the common man, obedience and loyalty." [239, p. 72]

In this situation a certain moral crudity creeps in, the amorality of those whose superiority is incontestable, supported by prerogative and force. Military leaders frequently lack compunction in bullying, deceiving, or sometimes killing outsiders. A French writer who had to deal with military communiqués commented, "A military education involves a training in casuistry." [234, p. 53] Twelve years were required to bring justice in the Dreyfus affair, as the French officers were quite willing to ignore truth and justice for their and the army's prestige; the honor they professed loudly consisted not of uprightness and rectitude but of self-interest and refusal to admit an error. Even when all the evidence was in the record and the forgeries had been proved, the army refused to admit the innocence of Dreyfus but freed him for "extenuating circumstances" which did not exist, while there was no effort to punish the guilty. [228, p. 47] Many generals seem to have regarded those under their command not as fellow humans but as things that might be usefully spent, sometimes in the furtherance of the crassest ambitions. A few years ago, an American Air Force general could make in peacetime so unsophisticated a statement of national policy as, "Let's start killing people. People need to respect the United States, and when we start killing people there will be more respect for the United States." [230, p. 273] This is, of course, no reflection of native character; great power inclines to the cynical view of human nature and to an overestimation of the utility and rightness of force.

With authority and caste go ornamentation, symbolism, myth, and belief. The military makes a fetish of marks of status more than any other sector of society, with chevrons, epaulets, stripes, ribbons, braids, pompons, sashes, plumes, medals, and a host of insignia taking the place of the mandarins' buttons and other ornaments of rank; like mandarins, generals are also distinguished by many other status symbols, such as the means of transportation they rate and the appointments of their places of work and residence. Of all professions (with the possible exception of the diplomatic, also much preoccupied with power), the military is the most protocol-ridden, with standard operating procedures and prescribed forms for everything imaginable, especially for the manner of treating superiors. [230, p. 196] There is ceremony from the bugle notes of reveille until taps, from formal induction of recruits to the pageantry of the military funeral; there are flying banners, spirited songs, and martial music; there is the colorful parade ground, true symbol of the military way, the compulsive emotion of countless men all marching to the roll of drums and blare of trumpet in cadenced step, the image of power. At West Point, gestures have extraordinary importance; for example, the handshake of an upperclassman could make the social status of a plebe. [221, p. 27] Etiquette is partly based on jealously guarded tradition, but it is kept not because it is traditional but because it is felt necessary in the military way; the fresh new United States Air Force is at least as etiquette-conscious as the other branches. [*230*, p. 199]

Just as it is much entranced with forms, the military loves the past, seeking legitimation by reference to bygone days and history from the Roman empire onward. The histories of nation and regiment are taught for inspiration, to make men disposed to sacrifice themselves in favor of an organic continuity much greater than the individual. West Point is filled with all manner of carefully cultivated and strictly followed traditions, supported by a myriad of symbols, monuments, and memorials of past greatness. Military science has also been strongly past-oriented; until shaken by the First World War, it was seeking eternal truths of strategy valid since Hannibal. [*239*, p. 29] There has also been an inclination to interpret history to serve the purposes of military prestige, not only in treating the national past as a series of battles but in making the best of these. For example, the Prussian army insisted that all was wise and planned even when there was accident and bumbling, and persecuted anyone so disloyal as to differ. [*239*, p. 26]

Within this framework, captains are inclined to believe that success depends most of all on morale and character; and the best qualifications for advancement are (aside from endurance) team spirit, bearing, and loyalty mixed with the proper amount of individual push or even good-natured brashness. The military rewards a mixture of self-assertiveness with diplomacy, good-fellowship and self-submergence in adherence to the corps and its ways. There is also an emphasis on will, which derives from the importance of coercion. As Foch said and as other French generals believed, before war proved the naïveté of such an approach, "Victory equals will power"; one had only to dash into the fray with maximum faith and impetus. [*239*, p. 350] Consequently, there has always been heavy stress on character training, indoctrination, inculcation of conformity, and obedience as a value. [*223*, p. 80] This is the purpose not only of drills and direct education but also of hazing and many equivalent practices, designed to promote loyalty and submissiveness in new entrants from the anarchic civilian world. This is also a reason for the emphasis usual in military establishments on athletics, especially of group coordination, much favored, for example, at American service academies. [*230*, pp. 129–130] West Point has made much of character formation by compulsion, with many demerits for dereliction but no specific reward for doing one's duty. [*221*, p. 49] This policy falls most heavily on newcomers, who are called "beasts" and treated as such for the purpose of crushing any fragment of individual will. In his first year, the plebe is or was required to speak only when spoken to by a superior, never to walk but to trot, to sit only on a 3-inch edge of his chair, to repeat inane set answers to a host of inane set questions, and to submit to a multitude of other indignities which in another context would be considered ridiculous puerilities [*221*, pp. 5–8, 10 ff.], but which are less inhumane than the physical tortures formerly practiced as hazing. It has also been considered a very fine thing for soldiers to have a religion, preferably of more or less authoritarian cast, to improve their morals and to give them proper attitudes. Church attendance is compulsory at all four American service academies. European army officers have usually been expected to be good members of the established church. After 1870, as France was becoming more secular, the army grew more and more Catholic, virtually requiring profession of faith. [*228*, p. 21] Clemenceau, a strong anticlerical in politics but a believer in national strength, wanted the army to have religious instruction. [*239*, p. 351]

Armies have preferred parade-ground excellence to more realistic practice in preparing for combat. Not only did this viewpoint prevail under Russian or Prussian monarchs who thought of regiments mostly as ornaments and considered precision of movement more important than battle readiness; the army of republican France before the First World War looked much more to making men automatons than effective soldiers. Instead of training for battles, they tried to turn battles into mere bayonet charges to fit the training. [*227*, pp. 112–113] The attitude of the old Russian army is typified by an incident under Paul. An irritated officer shouted that a peasant who had annoyed him should be hanged, and the soldiers proceeded to do so. The tsar praised the officer for the blind obedience of his men. [*395*, p. 40]

Stress on obedience and loyalty at best means some sacrifice of intelligence and initiative. Many writers take for granted the mediocrity of the military mind [*229*, p. 59], and this expression ordinarily connotes crudity and ham-handedness. Debate and suasion can hardly be part of the military way; independent thought is inconvenient or even dangerous, and intelligence or the capacity to compare and criticize marks a man as potentially insubordinate. Philosophers and soldiers do not mix, and unusual brightness has blighted many a military career. Until modern technology forced itself upon the profession, bookishness has been little esteemed. It is typical that the Gothic court of the early Middle Ages objected to education for the prince on the ground that letters were not needed for victory, and such sentiments continued in German military circles into the nineteenth century. An officer seen with a book was long looked upon with suspicion. [223, p. 74] Most Prussian officers were ignorant even by the standards of the day [235, pp. 37–38], quite innocent of education and proud of it until the reforms brought by defeat at the hands of Napoleon. [223, p. 75] Thereafter the Prussian military succeeded better than most in reconciling intelligence with the primacy of obedience, but something of the old attitudes persisted. In 1859, for example, the War Minister tried to introduce educational requirements for entry into the officer corps, but it was violently and successfully objected that lack of schooling should be overlooked if "character" (meaning chiefly background) was suitable. [239, pp. 194–195] In the French army of the nineteenth century, anti-intellectualism was marked; initiative and originality were reprehensible [226, p. 157]; independent judgment smacked of critical spirit and potential disloyalty; to read books, except the rule book, was to be suspect. [227, p. 108] General discussion was abhorred because it risked casting doubt on sacred virtues. [228, p. 31]

The American army has shared the feeling that intellectual brilliance or even military genius is superfluous if not harmful, as exceptional talent would disturb the neatness of the organization. An officer expressed the general sentiment: "Military obedience is invaluable because it never reasons." [229, pp. 257–258] Today the military recognizes the importance of science, yet friction remains between scientists and military administrators of research, for the latter prefer order and loyalty to the spirit of free investigation dear to the scientists. [530, chap. ix] The forces have insisted upon education for their officers, but the content has been restricted. It has been the frank view of the military academy that an open and inquiring mind leads to indecisiveness if not worse. [231, p. 231] The curriculum, without elective or optional courses [221, p. 31], has emphasized memorizing more than thinking, facts and details more than general principles, such as specifics of gunnery rather than the physical bases. Very little attention has been paid to social

sciences and political studies, although there is much stress on social amenities, and cadets are required to learn to dance well.
[*231*, chap. x, p. 219] Debate is undesirable; according to the
rules, radio programs "must be devoid of opinion, editorializing
or other comments," and controversial speakers are seldom permitted. [*231*, p. 243] Asking unnecessary questions is a demerit
offense. [*221*, p. 51] A catechism for plebes began with a question —
"What happens when a plebe thinks?" — and the prescribed answer
is, in effect, that thinking is a dangerous deviation. [*231*, p. 243]
Academic excellence or class standing has been found to bear practically no relation to subsequent attainment of high rank. With
some well-known exceptions, such as General Douglas MacArthur,
it makes almost no difference for a cadet's chances of acquiring
stars if he rates near the top or well below the middle, despite the
fact that a large part of the courses are strictly military and grades
include estimated leadership ability. On the other hand, there is
a high correlation between athletic participation and career success [*230*, p. 134], although it is doubtful that games and sports
have anything to do with generalship. [*225*, p. 81]

Unhappily, doubt and inquiry, the urge to look beyond the
given, are essential for improvement. And if there is no relation
between academy grades and later rise in rank, one must conclude
that the grades bear little relation to intelligence (which would
imply a serious failure in grading or teaching) or, more likely, that
intelligence beyond a certain necessary and acceptable level is
of little use in climbing the military ladder. The effect is, of course,
cumulative; if those of limited brainpower come to positions of
command, they are more likely to distrust those sharper than themselves than to advance them. In any event, it has often appeared
that the military machine has run to a remarkable extent upon
routine — "The army is perhaps not the birthplace of routine but
is its adopted land," as a French writer has put it [*227*, p. 108] —
and it has shone more for imbecility than for brilliance. The maxim
has been to stick to the tried and true, even at enormous cost to
effectiveness. Standing for the fixed order, armies have hardly ever
in the past looked for new weapons; a serious student can assert
flatly that great military inventions have all been made by nonmilitary men, not by professionals. [*239*, p. 370] If a general uses
a modicum of imagination and springs a strategic surprise, as
Epaminondas did against the Spartans at Leuctra, Hannibal at

Cannae, or Schlieffen in his plan for envelopment of the French forces, this is held to be highest genius, although the ingenuity involved is extremely modest compared with that of high-level chess.

Not only have military leaders been uninventive; they have all too often made gross, even childish, errors of judgment. A myriad of these errors have, of course, been neutralized or obscured by equally egregious errors of the opponent; but many have been all too obvious. For example, one recalls the foolishness of British redcoats marching in formation against American Indians hiding behind the trees, because their officers could not imagine that tactics suitable in Europe might need modification for a different enemy in colonial America. Nor were such tactics of the parade battle really suitable in Europe. In the wars of the French Revolution, Prussian and other soldiers were forbidden to protect themselves from enemy fire by lying down; such conduct was not seemly and did not follow the rules. [239, p. 113]

In the first part of the nineteenth century, the French army had to suffer years of torture (and 2,000 suicides) from heat in Algeria before adopting a bearable uniform. [226, p. 153] Even at the beginning of the First World War, many thousands of deaths were needed to teach the French army that red pantaloons were more ornamental than useful. Technological backwardness of the military may be fairly understandable in an age unaccustomed to the idea of progress, but a minister of war of Napoleon III, when the industrial revolution was nearly a century old, denied that "we need new devices to sustain our glory"; and the emperor had to force on his army a breech-loading rifle eleven years after it had been invented and turned down by a military technical commission. [226, p. 165] He also had trouble getting the army to adopt the machine gun, which had been shown to be effective in the American Civil War. When that would-be Caesar in 1867 convened his leading officers for a discussion of the strategic situation, in the lack of ideas he found nothing better than to have a general read aloud passages of Thier's *History of the Consulate and the Empire*. [226, p. 160] About the same time a high French officer said that maps were of no value; it was enough to get hold of a peasant and make him show the way. [227, pp. 109–110] The defeat of 1870 brought a reaction against military anti-intellectualism and an avidity for new weapons, but soon energies were lost in dull routine and regulations, and the posture of marksmen again became more important than hitting the target. [228, pp. 9, 54]

Incompetence of military management was especially evident in the First World War, perhaps because in the long preceding period of peace there was little drive to rethink anything; even the German General Staff, perhaps the most enlightened, was distinctly hostile to technical improvements. [231, p. 35] In 1909 a French military spokesman said, "You talk of heavy artillery. Thank God, we have none." [228, p. 55] French generals trusted all to élan and character; the result was, of course, massive butchery of brave but stupidly commanded men. [239, pp. 221, 351] They cared little for machine guns, having only 2,500 at the beginning of the war against 50,000 in the German army; the French army suffered countless casualties while this deficiency was being corrected. [233, p. 23] As for devices, what they had sufficed. A French general said, brushing off the inventor of a grenade, "We have been preparing for this war for forty-four years. If we needed such a device, we wouldn't have waited for a sapper to make it." [233, p. 38] The story of Winston Churchill's battle to get the tank into production is familiar. British, French, and German officers were all apathetic or hostile to the idea, although it was no startling novelty; armored cars had been in use on a small scale for a decade or more. [239, p. 232] In the same spirit, the American army clung nostalgically to horse cavalry until the eve of the Second World War. [230, p. 25] When tanks were hesitantly introduced, the advantages of surprise were thrown away, and two and a half years were required to get them really into action. [239, p. 231] Other inventions similarly neglected were legion.

Military planning was hardly better. Although trenches had been extensively and successfully used in the Russo-Turkish War, the Boer War, the Russo-Japanese War, and the Balkan War of 1912, the generals entirely failed to prepare for trench warfare. [239, pp. 352–353] The Entente before 1914 gave practically no thought to wartime connections with their presumptive ally, Russia, and the use of the only secure port, Archangel. [239, p. 346] Despite warnings that the Germans contemplated marching through Belgium, the French army resolutely refused to credit this possibility [233, pp. 26–27]; in fact, the general staff made a military study of all parts of France *except* the region adjoining Belgium. [239, p. 344] Headquarters on both sides during the war showed an incredible lack of imagination; their general approach was to strike the enemy not where he was weak but where he was strong, as at Verdun; they did not shrink from the idiocy of a war of attrition between two nearly equal powers. After the halting of their initial planned offensive, the German army had no idea what to do except to grind away. [235, pp. 147–148] The chief of operations refused support for the army in the east, which was making real progress, while the western front was a sorry slugging match, specifically contending that they should hit where the enemy was. [239, p. 274] One of the few imaginative moves, the Gallipoli campaign, pushed by Churchill, failed for lack of support by the regulars. Similarly, military estimates of their own and enemy capacities were egregiously erroneous. In 1914 the heads of the British and French armies were sure that they could beat the Germans alone, not merely without American help, which eventually saved them, but without the Russians as well, not to speak of the Italians. [239, p. 335] After stopping the Germans at the Marne in the initial rush, Allied generals were arguing whether it would take three or four weeks to throw the enemy back across the frontier. [235, p. 147] In 1917 the Germans judged that removal of restrictions on submarine warfare was more important than having the United States enter the war against them. An elementary study of productive capacities, the United States then possessing close to half of the world's heavy industry, should have shown the folly of the gamble. Equally striking was the universal failure of planning beyond the opening of hostilities. None of the belligerents thought of economic mobilization or even increased munitions production. [239, p. 352] None made the slightest preparation for a conflict lasting more than a few weeks or at most a few brief months, although there had been many long wars in European history, and critics freely predicted a drawn-out, grinding conflict. [239, p. 349] The French had no plans to make any guns or explosives at all after the fighting began, having made provision for only two and one-fourth shells per day per cannon. [233, pp. 22, 35–36] Even after the war was well under way and settled down to a contest of attrition, consuming gargantuan quantities of matériel, production was undertaken with extreme reluctance. Only 170 guns had been made in France by March, 1915, and plans began to move only when civilians pushed. [233, p. 36]

It may be necessary for the military to be characterized by devotion to traditional ways and routine, by a stern hierarchy of command, stress on obedience, by punctilio and convention, and correspondingly by uninventiveness. Armies seem to be of this character with remarkable unanimity, despite wide social and political differences among the societies that support them. The reason given is, of course, that they must be strongly organized for their exceptional goal of destruction. To the military, individualism equals anarchy [229, p. 258] and ineffectiveness. Debating societies are useless in battle; there can be no questioning of orders in an emergency, and all should be trained to give necessary obedience by reflex. Strikes could hardly be permitted in any military force. Yet whether the military organization is best for its purpose of national defense and enforcement of the will of the state is very difficult to judge. Despite much written about tactics and battles and a good deal on the relations of military to civilian authorities, very little has been published on the political sociology of the military profession and on its organizational principles; the military establishment screens its inner dynamics. Little or no effort has been made to analyze such matters as the need for saluting, the desirability of segregating officers from their charges as against camaraderie, the possible usefulness of broader discussion, or at least explanation of policies, and so on; still less have armies been disposed to experiment.

One might argue the opposite case; it has been contended that military ways dull by routine, rather deaden than fortify fighting spirit, and instead of heightening potentialities of leadership, reduce them. [230, pp. 151, 153] It is plausible but not absolutely convincing to argue that needs of battle require the mechanization of men. How much more important is it for soldiers to obey blindly, as in "squads left," than to meet new situations intelligently? When men really share a visible danger, the prevalent spirit is more likely to be one of informality and equality. Military punctilio has been largely or entirely superfluous to battle and often a positive hindrance, especially but not only in the decorative armies of the eighteenth century. Where men are really under pressure, as in submarines or combat planes, relations are relatively free and easy. For truly difficult tasks, coordination is best achieved not by pure command but through intelligent cooperation based on understanding and shared purpose, as in an exploratory expedition. Although the military usually abhor critical thought, a large measure of it may well be useful for effective working together. This is virtually admitted in practice; when direly pressed or defeated, armies tend to relax much of their stiffness — the reform of the Prussian army after defeat by Napoleon being the best example — only to revert to traditional authoritarian patterns in peacetime [230, p. 46] when they are free to be themselves. It may also be guessed that the best planner of battle tactics would be a mild intellectual of mathematical bent who would be good for nothing on the parade ground or dueling field, and who would never aspire to a military career.

Much of the military way is called for, however, by the essence of irrational authority. It is necessary to teach men to do effectively what they might find silly or wrong, and as the need for sacrifice is distant and difficult to understand, spirit is reinforced by ideology, drill, religion, and appeals to the past. Obedience to officers is like obedience to God, and it is easier to feel that we are doing right when we are carrying on in the way consecrated by dead heroes. Ceremony in the armed forces, as everywhere, supports conformity. Etiquette and formality are more necessary when visible danger does not furnish a strong common purpose; without habitual respect supported by rigid rules, the command system would probably break down in general slackness and disorder; men in the army, unlike factory workers, can hardly be effectively controlled by threat of discharge. The Greeks could discipline by democracy and persuade instead of commanding the execution of a plan of battle [236, p. 19; 237, p. 57], but they could do so only because of the exceptional cohesion of the polis. The Swiss army of the fifteenth and sixteenth centuries could discipline largely by force of opinion, the common purpose, and pride in the unit; but no modern society is sufficiently well integrated to elect officers and run the army democratically. Hence there is need for the emotional security of fully prescribed behavior and all devices to subordinate and freeze the individual will and make reactions mechanical. Like big empires, big impersonal armies need synthetic unity and purpose.

The military establishment thus shares some of the needs of the imperial order and meets them similarly. But just as the empire is in part the result of opportunity for power, something of the military order undoubtedly answers the urges of the powerful. It is easy for commanders to believe that unchallengeable command is suitable if not indispensable; it certainly is much easier and more gratifying than having to persuade. They are the less fond of free-thinking intelligence and critical attitudes because these mean questioning of themselves and their orders, or at least a need to justify orders—which are much better not called into discussion. Marks of status, fine protocol, and deferential manners of approach may serve to regularize relations; they also are good for the egos of superiors. Whether or not the sharp distinction between officers and men makes obedience easier, it certainly helps the self-esteem of those above the line who make the rules. Masses of men marching in precision drill and responding in beautiful uniformity provide agreeable spectacles for those on the reviewing stand, whether or not robotization makes better soldiers. Hazing and indignities piled on new recruits in many armies, like the brutalities to which Prussian soldiers were subjected, may help shape character and may also represent a bit of sadism. And without its many ceremonies, military life, especially in peacetime, would be much more tedious. Technology, on the other hand, is rather a nuisance for those who are pleased with power over men, as it complicates, makes for impersonality, and raises demands on intelligence. The military order is thus shaped by the type of character it attracts, especially those enjoying direct and unequivocal power over others, by the traits that it rewards with advancement, and by the opportunities it gives leaders to shape the system.

In any organization, those in charge would like to run it to please themselves. The peculiarity of the military establishment is that it represents power. There is little to prevent generals from organizing the army as they please; even in a society like that of the United States, with traditional civilian supremacy, the politicians are very respectful of the military men; in many countries, the latter are effective bosses so far as they choose to be, not only of their own house but of the country. The military establishment, shaping its own institutions, represents a world of its own, dedicated to power and based upon it. Consequently, its virtues and its faults, its principles of organization and its rewards, are kin to those of the universal empire.

THE IMPERIAL ORDER

The universal empire, like the command of military force, is the incarnation of power. It has no obvious relation to race: white men are apparently as capable of kissing the feet of their master as are yellow, brown, or black. It seems to have little or nothing to do with climate, as despotic empires have flourished in the bracing climate of north China, the chill of Muscovy, the monotonously cool Andean highlands, and the sweltering plains of India. It bears no simple relation to geography. Imperial despotism is not peculiarly Asiatic or oriental; it is odd that Asia or the Orient should be associated with any political form, as that huge region has the utmost diversity of cultures, races, and conditions, which have little in common except distance from the West. Africa and Indo-America have shown themselves likewise prone to autocratic rule. The fact that Europe has escaped a strong unification since the Roman empire and has emerged as the land of individualism must be credited partly to luck, as several attempts at European empire have only narrowly failed. One or another would doubtless have succeeded were it not for the natural barriers guarding the independence of states; particularly the English Channel has been decisive for the maintenance of the balance of power. Nor does technology appear to be of basic importance for the character of empire, although rulers naturally use the most effective means they know, and arts of civilization facilitate wide dominion. The more remarkable fact is the general resemblance of despotisms of a Stone Age level to civilized ones.

It has seemed a qualification for the building of empire not to be much given to commerce; agricultural Rome was better equipped than commercial Athens to drive for world supremacy, and empires have looked with more favor on farming than trade. On the other hand, it may be contended that intensity of international intercourse paves the way for unification. But empire building has seemed in small degree to answer an economic need. Merchants have probably never played a leading role in promoting world conquest. Nor does unification have any obvious relation to the great works of which the empire is capable, particularly irrigation projects, as argued by Karl Wittfogel [570], despite possible advantages of strong and extensive government in management of water resources. The first great empires arose where men, using rivers to water dry valleys, built the first great civilizations. But the development of irrigation systems in Sumeria, China, and probably Egypt was the work of small states; and in the first two of these, independent states had a long and creative history before being overtaken by imperial unification. Need for cooperation in waterworks may conceivably create a tradition of forced labor and help prepare psychologically for large-scale self-subordination; it might also teach voluntary cooperation and community spirit. Irrigation in China has mostly been on a small scale, requiring no wide imperial coordination, and was less necessary in antiquity when the population was only a fraction of that of modernity. Nor has the empire been very useful; irrigation works in imperial China seem to have been undertaken mostly on local initiative, while the regime looked on passively, except when military interests were involved. [*18*, p. 43] Waterworks have been local or of secondary importance for the great empires of India, Rome, highland Peru, Persia (except in the province of Babylonia), Turkey, the Mongols, and Russia. On the other hand, the Ifugao of northern Luzon, wholly dependent on irrigation, had no chieftains and none but the most informal government. [*495*, p. 101] In Holland and Flanders the need for keeping up the dikes fostered village cooperation, self-government, and independence. Holland, of all nations most dependent on collective coping with the watery element, was long an island of freedom in absolutist Europe. Habits of self-subordination to community needs are the strength of small states; it is when they are lost that the conquerors can easily make the land their own. To be sure, some empires have earned respect and gratitude by building roads, canals, bridges, and the like; but others, like that of the Moguls, did practically nothing for their taxpayers beyond keeping sufficient order for the elite to enjoy their status. It would not appear that any people has called the aggressor state to rule over them in order that it might construct grand projects, hydraulic or other.

One might contend that the great empire justifies itself by bringing peace. Peoples weary of endless and purposeless strife of nations may well hail whoever can impose a single rule, feeling that it is better that all be ruled, no matter by whom, that they can no longer hurt one another. Probably politically more operative than this diffuse longing is the ability of a rising nation to promise protection to fearful states or groups within states. When a conquering state is gathering formerly independent lands together, there would seem to be almost always a party favorable to its purposes, which rightly or not regards the conqueror as a redeemer of sorts, as the pro-Romans in Greece, the pro-Muscovites in Novgorod, or the pro-French or pro-Empire forces in medieval Italy. But such feelings have served only somewhat to enfeeble resistance; the great empires have been made by strong swords and wills, mostly if not entirely because some thirsted for dominion and managed to impose their yoke on the rest.

There is no more need to postulate that the imperial state exists to serve a useful function for the subject peoples than that slavery corresponds to the interests of the slaves. When a number of men freely join to protect their families and fortunes from marauders and to settle pacifically disputes among themselves, this may be a government, as were the brotherhood-communes of the Middle Ages. When a brigand band goes beyond robbery to keep its victims in permanent subjugation, to deprive them of most of their income, and to enjoy their humiliation, this may also be a government. More gently stated, there are contrasting purposes of government, to help men live better or to maintain the advantages of those on top. No regime can be purely the one or the other: in the best, there are opportunities for leaders to use their status somehow for their own benefit; in the worst, there is likely to be some pretense of promoting the well-being of at least a large sector of the population. But "imperium" meant "command" before it became synonymous with the realm commanded. The great empires seem to be purpose in themselves more than means to social purposes, as Schumpeter stressed [542], and they come close to following

> The simple plan,
> That they should take who have the power
> And they should keep who can. [Quoted by 156, p. 133]

When the master makes the rules, he inevitably makes them to suit himself, subject only to such practical checks and necessities as may restrict his arbitrariness. As Herodotus had a Persian conspirator say, "How is it possible that monarchy should be a well-adjusted thing, when it allows a man to do as he likes without being answerable? Such license is enough to stir strange and unwonted thoughts in the hearts of the worthiest of men. Give a person this power, and straightway his manifold good things puff him up with pride." [Bk. III, 80] Even if the ruler thinks of himself as responsible for his people, he interprets their needs in his own terms. Although the love of shepherd and sheep may be mutual and sincere, and he may like to have them sleek and fat, the sheep nonetheless exist for the benefit of the shepherd. Sometimes it would seem, indeed, that the millions exist for the sake of slavery. Montesquieu felt that the Roman empire, which was probably one of the less oppressive of the genus, destroyed a hundred nations and shed oceans of blood for no better purpose than to elevate to glory a handful of middling to monstrous men. [337, chap. xv] This may be too strongly stated, but the purpose of empire hardly need transcend the frank boast of Tiglath-Pileser, restorer of Assyrian greatness: "I carried away their possessions, I burned their cities with fire. I demanded from their hostages tribute and contributions, I laid on them the heavy yoke of my rule." [462, p. 31] It would be pleasant to think that the great empires arise and subsist because they are beneficial; one might also regard them as punishment for human frailty, just as natural calamities were formerly regarded as retribution for sins of the flesh.

The empire does well to give itself a mission, such as the preservation of peace or the spread of civilization. But its prime function and the one it best accomplishes is the maintenance of the superiority of some over others. It is characterized by hierarchy and its fundament is inequality. The essence of Confucianism, the best imperial ideology, is the subordination of everyone to someone else, the consecration of inequality. [53, p. 7] Human relations may be divided roughly into two kinds, those between equals, based on mutual gain and with initiative from either or both, and those between unequals, in which values are imposed and wherein a superior has most choice while an inferior adapts himself. [541, pp. 2–3] The imperial order means the prevalence of the latter (vertical relations) and the reduction of the former (free or horizontal relations) between persons and groups. The empire and the military organization have this in common, that they are based on command or vertical relations, whether or not aggressive in temper. The large organization, with its greater ordering structure and higher and stronger pyramid of power, also represents the victory of vertical relations, with more gradations, greater distance between ordinary people and deciders, and weaker checks from below. Similarly, isolation from outside influences reduces horizontal relations to the benefit of the vertical by eliminating competition, comparison, external support for dissidence, and the like; in the isolated state men cannot look for help or inspiration to equals abroad, while the rulers are not themselves checked by confrontation with other sovereign powers. Unity serves authority.

Verticality prevails the more strongly because it transmits itself through the social fabric, much as a magnetic alignment: the more dipoles line up in a certain direction, the more force exerted upon others to fall in line. Authority works downward, and the despotism of one means countless petty despotisms. Submission to superior authority authorizes and inclines toward strong rule over inferiors; as one is treated by his superiors, he is likely to treat those subject to his will; obeying the higher law, one demands obedience in its name, enjoying at once the security of self-subordination and the pleasures of commanding. At all levels and in all relations, the cultivation of authoritarian ways and traits of personality promotes both acceptance of rule and the demand that others accept it. Strong ordering of society, moreover, impedes the horizontal relations that might attenuate the vertical, as a general discipline is imposed.

Serfdom is most oppressive when the lords are under strong central rule [*466*, p. 7], no doubt partly because serfs are prevented from changing landlords, partly because obedience is an accepted value of all. The Russian landowner who was at the mercy of his tsar was lord of his serfs, and the peasant felt entitled to beat his wife because of the beatings he received from the master or the overseer. [*394*, p. 34] Within the peasant household, the head was master of all, including grown and married sons unless or until the family split, and had control of all earnings; he ordered work and punished the wayward [*413*, pp. 34–37]; sometimes he claimed, like the seigneur, the *jus primae noctis*. The wife was frequently treated like a domestic animal [*394*, pp. 105–106], and younger brothers were expected to defer to elder. [*413*, p. 35] After the end of serfdom in 1861, the old family began to break up, the authority of the father became less oppressive, and women gained more recognition as humans. [*394*, p. 108] Still, in 1911, a peasant who killed his son was found guilty by a rural court, not of murder, but of failure to inculcate filial obedience. [*413*, p. 38] As St. Augustine perceived, "Every family then being a part of the city . . . the family's peace adheres unto the city's, that is, the orderly command, and obedience in the family has real reference to the orderly rule and subjection in the city." [*City of God*, Bk. 19, chap. xvi] In the Chinese system, as the mandarins were slaves of the emperor, they were lords of their districts, as the head of the family was supreme in the household, mothers-in-law bossed young wives, who were patient scullions while awaiting their day of domestic tyranny, and at the bottom of the scale little girls oppressed by their brothers lorded it over younger sisters. Those accustomed from infancy to total authority above could hardly think of challenging the emperor's right.

No analogy can be more than suggestive of the complex political realities; and it must be recognized that, just as the empire is not pure exploitation, relations are not of pure subordination but are mixed with elements of cooperation and mutuality. Dominance is seldom or never absolute and is not sharply set off from collaboration. The slaveowner serves a managerial function, and astute slaves may profit by his weaknesses. The relation of employee to employer is typically a vertical one, but the degree of subordination varies enormously. The plantation lord may hold his slaves, peons, or serfs as he does his oxen or pigs; a surgeon furnishes his patient indispensable services in his own discretion and at his own price. But many aspects of the imperial order can be interpreted in terms of the verticality of social relations. For example, the superiority of any group over another, by race, nationality, caste, or social class, conduces to something like the imperial mentality, with its formalism, need for mythical or ideological justification, conservatism, and emphasis on traditional authority. Landlordism, whereby tenants or serfs stand below large owners instead of as equal smallholders, is a natural accompaniment of the imperial structure. Poverty and backwardness favor despotism by reducing communication and interaction between equals more than they weaken bonds of rule from above. Military and political victories, exalting the position of the rulers, also strengthen relations of superiority; for this reason, defeat commonly tends to disperse political power while victory favors its concentration and nourishes autocratic tendencies, quite apart from likely incidental expansion of the state. On the other side, independent organizations of the people promote horizontal relations. The autocrat wishes to have his subjects isolated and unorganized, except so far as he can control the organization; individually each is wholly at his mercy, whereas he would be much restrained if they could even assemble in one place and sense the general opinion and their potential strength. Organizations cutting across the vertical order, wherein citizens can act together on their own volition, or autonomous groups capable of standing against the authorities, make society freer. In this logic, the empire has no strong liking for commercial relations, which are typically horizontal, based on free choice of both sides and mutual advantage, the antithesis of the political. Communication in general facilitates horizontal relations; this is the basic reason that technical progress is usually liberalizing and permits more freedom in large states.

Some degree of organization whereby the elect command their fellows is necessary for civilized society; not only are there strong and weak, but there must be leaders and led, some who give directions and others who follow. Regulation can effectively increase freedom, as traffic flows better under control of rules than it could in anarchy. But the dominance of vertical relations, which is equivalent to unfreedom, has grave negative implications. Morality slips away as one deals with inferiors; self-respect, with superiors. Political struggle is harsher and more demoralizing than economic conflict, as the stakes are higher and compromise is harder to achieve. Parasitism may be expected to be roughly proportional to the degree that some hold power over others and that gains are more substantial and easier from taking than from producing. In the marketplace, when there are multiple buyers and sellers, prices are more or less objectively fixed by supply and demand; when a single seller or buyer holds the reins, prices become political, concern shifts from the furnishing of desired commodities to the maintenance of position; relations become haughty or servile, and exploitation becomes more attractive than production. Generally, the prevalence of vertical relations must shift energies and values from the economic to the political, with the consequent impoverishment of many and the enrichment of a few. This very fact contributes to the stability of relations of superiority; unlike relations of equals, they represent entrenched interests and cannot be changed without injury to the holders of power; hence they may be equated with the rigidities of the social order. The first law of power is self-preservation; those on top find change inherently threatening and undesirable, and they are in a position to block it.

The prevalence of vertical relations is also anti-intellectual and

antiprogressive. There is a contrariety between intellectual freedom and authority of any kind; the one is hostile to the other, as
truth and power stand apart. So far as men can achieve their needs
by commanding, they spare themselves the trouble of thinking;
power will dispense with intelligence if it can, and he who can
convince by force will probably do so. Discussion and the need to
persuade tend to realism and objectivity; relations between equals
have to be more or less rational and follow mutually accepted
values. But authority can and does act without rational justification; and so far as it is irrational it may have recourse to magic,
tradition, or other means of playing upon the frailty of the mind;
inquiry and free criticism are bothersome, and the criterion of
truth becomes political. Advantage can be used to maintain advantage, power to fortify power; the better it is able to do so, the
more of an imposition it becomes.

Power is self-sanctifying because the strong esteem it and the
weak respect it; but it is a moral affliction. Men hardly learn from
the exercise of it but are spoiled by it; many a ruler, moderate and
dedicated in early years of authority, has grown capricious, deaf
to good advice, and blind to reality, the victim of his own power.
Only those who must cope with great forces beyond their control,
like Abraham Lincoln, mature and ripen in high office. Along with
truth, humanity and justice depart from the power-ordered world;
arrogance and servility come in. The more one controls his subordinates, the less they encourage his virtues. If there is no need to
take others into account, men easily come to ignore them; if there
is no pressure to be good, men become bad. The sense of unshakable dominion is poisonous to the conscience, as rulers make and
stand above rules. According to Henry IV, Pope Gregory said, "The
spirit of the ruler is elevated in accord with the number of those
subject to him, and he believes that he knows more than all because
he sees that he can do more than all." [543, p. 141] Perhaps it seems
incumbent upon him to act the autocrat, lest mildness be thought
weakness. In the days of Ivan the Terrible, Peresvetov wrote, "If
a tsar rules mildly, his realm declines and his fame decreases."
[411, p. 106] The difficulty of reconciling power and justice is the
outstanding problem of theology: how can God be at once wholly
good and yet omnipotent when evil is around us?

The unbridled potentate forgets the humanity both of himself
and his subjects. As the Mogul Jahangir had it, "It is said that a

king shall deem no one his relation." [*199*, pp. 240–241] According to Sallust, "Absolute princes are always more jealous of the good than of the bad, because another man's virtue, as they take it, is a diminution of their prestige and therefore dangerous." [*Conspiracy of Cataline*, chap. iii] Those who use propaganda or myth to justify themselves pass on to plain lies and destroy the sense of fair truth both in themselves and in those upon whom they press. Success needs no justification. Plato wrote that, for the mighty, justice is "Doing good to your friends and harm to your enemies." [*Republic* in 327, p. 172] As Herodotus put it, "A King, besides, is beyond all others inconsistent with himself. Pay him court in moderation and he is angry because you do not show him more profound respect. . . . he sets aside the laws of the land, puts men to death without trial, and rapes women." [Bk. III, 80] Power dislikes law, as Cleon is said to have urged when the Athenians debated how to treat their rebellious subjects: "If right or wrong you are resolved to rule them, rightly or wrongly they must be punished for your good. Otherwise you must give up your empire, and when virtue is no longer dangerous you may be virtuous as you please." [Thucydides, Bk. III, 40] Men suppose those below them to be worse than themselves; those who are born to serve the autocrat are expected to be poor creatures and in need of the whip. Under the absolute power, punishment is used less to deal with wrong than to vindicate authority, which is in any event superior to right. Caprice is the rule: the despot is likely to reduce millions to beggary while loading with favors and riches a handful who tickle his fancy or play upon his foibles.

The story of the misuse of power, which is the outcome of the possession of too much of it, is an old one; it may cause wonder, pity, or even indignation. But for the countless millions whose lives are broken and made senseless for the evil and vanity of their masters, it is worse than tragedy. The power of men to raise themselves upon the backs of others represents the frustration of humanity and the cheating of the promise of intelligence. Because of the oppression of man by man, progress, which seemingly should be consistent, cumulative, and as though automatic once the preconditions have been achieved, has been exceptional in the chronicles of our species, while stultification if not degradation has been the usual rule. Only when circumstances have in some special fashion favored the division and consequent weakening of political powers have the exploitative and antiprogressive forces yielded to the productive and progressive.

Nothing is more difficult than to curb excess of power. We find psychological or spiritual support in that which is dazzlingly great; giving loyalty to that which stands above, we find surety and purpose. Men stand breathless before the harsh egotist whom they would despise if he had not known how to elevate himself to power, that is, to greatness. Thus an intelligent, unindoctrinated foreigner could be reduced to gibbering ecstasy by a glimpse of Napoleon. That Heine was a poet adds to the lyricism of his description, but does not falsify his feelings:

The trembling leaves bowed toward him as he advanced, the sunbeams quivered, frightened yet curious, through the green leaves. . . . He rode a white steed, which stepped with such calm pride, so confidently, so nobly — had I then been crown prince of Prussia I would have envied that steed. . . . Even the face had that hue which we find in the marble of Greek and Roman busts; the traits were as nobly cut as in the antique, and on the face was written, "Thou shalt have no Gods before me." A smile which warmed and soothed every heart, flitted over the lips — and yet all knew those lips needed but to whistle — *et la Prusse n'existait plus*. . . . It was an eye clear as heaven; it could read the hearts of men, it saw at a glance all the things of this world. . . . The brow was not so clear, the phantoms of future battles were nestling there; there was a quiver which swept over that brow, and those were the creative thoughts, the great seven-mile-boot thoughts, wherewith the spirit of the Emperor strode invisibly over the world — and I believe that every one of those thoughts would have given to a German author full material wherewith to write, all the days of his life. [Quoted by 476, pp. 62–63]

It is less amazing that ordinary Frenchmen gladly gave their lives for the glory of the little Corsican, and that he thought it was their simple duty to do so. For the downtrodden as for the exalted, empire is a holy thing.

It may be that men are spiritually overwhelmed by power and bow happily to the man who treads upon their necks because he is only doing what they, in some recess of their hearts if not with conscious will, long to do. The exercise of power, not in a vague metaphysical sense but in deciding the destinies of other humans, preferably those with whom we are in contact and by whom we measure ourselves, is so sweet that it easily takes precedence over

almost everything. Hardly any strong personality is entirely free
of it. Not everyone would like to be a drill sergeant, but almost all
take delight in somehow swaying others. Power is so general a
means that it must be a general end, like money, but more so, and
it becomes a substitute for other purposes. To be powerful is to be
important, a little godlike. Harmless, bookish scholars, the more
scholarly for their political ineptitude, are often pleased to have
an opportunity to administer money and their professional colleagues, to the neglect of intellectual concerns. That dangers are
many and rewards insecure does not deter from the game of power;
many a man has resolved either to reign or perish, knowing that
his predecessors have perished miserably, even if they managed
briefly to sit atop the slippery pole. Although the vizier was usually
executed after a brief tenure, candidates always came forward.
Nothing is so alluring as to arrive at that blissful state where one's
wish is law; the highest desideratum of the weary and the eager
is to be able to do by merely willing. This is in prospect the pleas-
antest of sensations and the dream of fairy tales.

One hardly imagines that power could be ill or dangerous in his
own hands; this would be a denial of the personality, as the thirst
for power is its affirmation. Those who hold reins over men and
things never think of themselves as corrupted by the vices of
power. To become powerful enchants good men as well as bad,
for it means the ability to achieve for good or evil; in a broad sense
it is the essence of vitality, of life itself, which never rests but
always wishes to accomplish. It is inseparable from prestige and
glory, which is superiority to others if not control over them; it is
akin to the yearning for immortality, whereby a man hopes by
greatness to rise, at least in symbols and remembrance, above the
common fate of oblivion. When one becomes powerful and able
to satisfy material wants and give himself all manner of luxuries,
these wants lose importance; but the desire for power is an addiction that hardly ever leaves those who have tasted the sweet.
Rather, the mania for power turns into a great ideal.

Primitives are probably quite as subject to the vice as are civilized creatures. Indeed, it transcends the limits of the human genus,
as apes, too, have their chiefships, a powerful male usually standing more or less imperiously over females, young, and tolerated
inferior males. [C. Carpenter in 546, p. 41] Dominance is given by
strength and the disposition to fight for it, and each ape in a group

is fearful lest a stronger come along to usurp its social position. [574, p. 237] Although social patterns vary widely [565, p. 1544], rank commonly determines not only possession of females but priority in satisfying other wants; in case of shortage, the dominant will take food or whatever they desire from their inferiors, who generally submit without contest or protest and may fear to serve themselves until the superior goes away. [574, p. 234] Males and females alike adopt a posture of sexual invitation before superiors. Ordinarily responding to aggression by submission, as do humans, the weaker members of the primate community try to secure food and favor by ingratiation [574, p. 238] and smile deferentially at superiors, as courtiers would. [451, p. 91] Chimpanzees have been observed to act as though trained in a palace. On the approach of a dominant male (who in one case seemed to owe his position to the frightful noise he learned to make with an empty gasoline tin) inferiors would pant, bow to the ground, and submissively hold out their hands; he might accept their humble greetings or, if in a sour mood, slap the crouching subject. [505, pp. 813, 825] An ordinary chimpanzee would have to share his prey, willy-nilly, but a chief would yield only what he did not want and then require the others to beg for it. [483, p. 307] Among gorillas, the nearest of apes to *Homo sapiens*, single males dominate groups of some ten to twenty individuals; others below the boss accept their status — males over females, females over juveniles — with little fighting, while various unattached males wander about. The superior individual takes what he wants, usually allows no other mature male in his company, has first if not exclusive access to the females, and always has the right of way; he also governs his small state, deciding or initiating movements and activities like nest building. [540, pp. 115–116, 132, 192; 539, pp. 237–238, 254] It would thus seem that aggressiveness must have been advantageous through eons of evolution, as the self-assertive appropriated most females and in times of shortage ate better than the less masterful. Considering the likelihood that those who most strongly push themselves have had more offspring through hundreds of thousands of generations, it is perhaps remarkable that human truculence is no greater. If we do not suffer the bestial disposition of baboons, which, when the leadership is called into question, will mangle one another in struggling for the possession of a female (often killed in the melee) [574, pp. 252–257], the relative or frequent mildness of our tribe may be ascribed to counteracting advantages of compassion in the raising of children and of mutual help and cooperativeness in enterprises too complex for a single individual, like hunting large animals or making war. There could be no civilization without such virtues.

Government the more readily becomes oppression because power is exercised mostly by those most imbued with the lust for it. The qualities that enable a man to rise above his fellows, and often at their expense, bear no close relation to those that make for good government. A prime qualification for holding the helm and a likely disqualification for steering carefully is self-confidence. For political success, appearances are more important than realities, cunning than intelligence, self-love than generosity. Competition for power tends to drive out virtue, as one can hardly be more self-denying than his rivals without penalizing himself; and the attainment of power rises above the need to be virtuous, or provides a substitute for what would be required as virtues in common people. For kings and emperors the chief, almost the only, law is success.

People sense that might makes right, although they say the contrary, because right has been often made by might. Power is haloed, as those who are powerful make an atmosphere of reverence for institutions, if not for men, in which people comply because they feel they should and must. The ideas and many of the ways of the great empire are as immortal as anything can be on earth because they suit holders of power at all layers of the social order. All manner of authoritarian and traditionalist voices are loud because they tend to maintain the given structure, and they are louder when vested positions are becoming shaky. Ideas that do not suit the holders of power have a doubtful life; even a great religion like Buddhism could be driven out of India and practically out of Chinese life and thought because the elite preferred Hinduism or Confucianism; and the moral profundity of Christianity made limited progress until the Caesars took it up. The dominant ideas in religion, ethics, philosophy, economics, and government are necessarily those patronized by the dominant sectors of society. Holders of power at times support philosophies of no utility to their position; but the less sound and rational their status, the more they feel the need for irrational justification.

What intelligence can do when fully set free is the prime wonder of the universe. What is attainable is perhaps best exemplified by mathematics, wherein there have not usually been substantial material or social rewards, but where inhibitions and preconceptions have been minimal; the steps of careful thinking required to reach the height of mathematical analysis are unrivaled except in closely related fields, such as theoretical physics. In the eighteenth century mathematics was a science of marvelous sophistication while biology was still in its infancy. The latter fairly well burst out from the chains of its implications for society only in the nineteenth century, while social and political thinking, even closer to social values, is still far from attaining similar detachment and intellectual power, although it had excellent beginnings as long ago as Aristotle. It may be guessed — it can hardly be proved — that the prejudices, the fears of thinking really new thoughts, the fixations and inhibitions that have so largely prevented the effective use of human intelligence, have been brought on mostly by the command and status structure of society and the urge of vested interests of one kind or another to preserve an atmosphere favorable to themselves. That is, the mental as well as institutional rigidities of humanity may be laid to the excess of vertical, unequal relations.

If it is desired, then, to apply the chief attribute of humanity to the solution of humanity's considerable problems, it is necessary to find the best ways that people can work together on an adequate scale — which nowadays means a very large scale — without an excess of power in the hands of any, to find the right ground between needs for order and needs for freedom, between the requirements for coordination and for vision and responsibility for persons at different levels, between the necessity of compulsion and the desirability of autonomy. The distortion is usually, one may feel sure, in the direction of too much control. Even in a free and competitive society men find it difficult fully to recognize the desirability of letting people manage for themselves. The spirit of empire building invades even scientific laboratories, as those who graduate from research to administration forget that the most fruitful work is done personally, not by handling others through whom their intelligence operates at a long remove.

The crux of the problem is that power does not check itself but is checked only by offsetting power or by incapacity to govern. Complete and deadening unification has been avoided only by an inability to conquer the whole world or to manage effectively the conquered universe. Limitations of power arise not from sage design, for power does not aim to limit itself, but from happy accidents of geography, economic factors, the decay of instruments of control, and the like, whereby authority reaches its limits or slackens its grip in favor of lesser powers.

Human design and desire have usually operated, not for the checking of power, but toward unity and ipso facto for a greater role for political power. The leadership finds unity a great value and treasures it in the name of the community. The principle of togetherness, the great whole, is inherently stronger than that of disunity: the unionist movement overrides opposition and strengthens itself, while divisive movements work toward weakness, and secessions are themselves subject to fission. Union always promises an immediate gain, and empire raises a vision of utopia justifying power, the possibility of an engineered solution for the woes of mankind. And the empire seems to be following the road of progress, which leads toward unity as spheres of interaction widen.

Always, indeed, we need a higher power to prevent us from abusing our little powers and hurting one another; we need to be ruled. Let someone save us from ourselves. We long to have peace and security, an untroubled life, and an assured and protected future. Yet we cannot have all this with freedom, for freedom means the ability to be disorderly, to make trouble, to do things contrary to the will of others, ultimately the freedom to try to settle differences in our way; order and security mean letting some higher power govern our lives. This we do in the state. Still the states themselves reserve a higher freedom called sovereignty, which signifies insecurity for all. To overcome this there must be world rule, or world empire. And yet, in universal empire likewise there is no sweet security and perfect peace, but only a suffocation instead of turmoil and a different kind of danger.

It is easy to predict that the next stage of history might be world empire. If any state glimpses an opportunity to do so, it cannot fail to claim world hegemony in the name of its own security and the safety of mankind; and it may well be deemed a worthy sacrifice to assume the onerous responsibility of assuring the supposed welfare of all. Some power might even feel impelled to risk destruction for the sake of bringing about millennial peace instead of nuclear dangers. Then history as it has been and progress, insofar as it depends upon free intelligence, would presumably come to an end, to be renewed, if at all, only after a long and tortured degradation.

But if this is the course to which the past seems to point, it can hardly be deemed fate. Civilization began some five thousand years ago and probably cannot endure much longer; it must either come to a finale, breaking down with a crash or setting out on the road to decay, or else it must transcend politics and be transfigured into a higher way. A real and creative reformation of human society can be effected not by any political action but by application of science and technology and the uninhibited drawing of conclusions from their reality.

Perhaps something of this will come. At least, the international contest has visibly changed. Although the habit remains of trying to direct and guide the development of weaker nations, it is probably not productive of power; and the idea of war between leading states seems absurd, the more so as techniques of destruction advance beyond measure. But there are as yet only hints that mankind may be able to leap out of the political morass into a new era of freedom with security. To take this leap would be nearly miraculous, like jumping out of our skins psychologically; but intelligence has worked miracles before.

BIBLIOGRAPHY

(Works cited by number in the text are included; classics cited by conventional subdivisions and biblical sources are not included.)

CHINA

1. Liby Abegg. *The Mind of East Asia.* London: Thames and Hudson, 1952.
2. Etienne Balazs. *Chinese Civilization and Bureaucracy.* New Haven: Yale University Press, 1964.
3. John Barrow. *Travels in China.* London, 1804.
4. E. Blackhouse and J. O. P. Bland. *Annals and Memoirs of the Court of Peking.* Boston: Houghton Mifflin, 1914.
5. Derk Bodde. *China's First Unifier.* Leiden: E. J. Brill, 1938.
6. ———. "Physical Science and Engineering in China" (review), *Science,* CXLIX (Aug. 20, 1965).
7. Demetrius Boulger. *A Short History of China.* London: Gibbings & Co., 1900.
8. Chung-li Chang. *The Chinese Gentry.* Seattle: University of Washington Press, 1955.
9. J. C. Cheng. *Chinese Sources for the Taiping Rebellion, 1850–1864.* Hong Kong: Hong Kong University Press, 1963.
10. Maurice Collis. *The Great Within.* London: Faber & Faber, 1941.
11. H. G. Creel. *Chinese Thought from Confucius to Mao Tse-tung.* New York: Mentor Books, 1953.
12. Raymond Dawson, ed. *The Legacy of China.* Oxford: Clarendon Press, 1964.
13. W. A. C. H. Dobson. "Micius," in *The Far East: China and Japan.* Supplement to the *University of Toronto Quarterly.* Toronto: University of Toronto Press, 1961.
14. Justus Doolittle. *Social Life of the Chinese.* New York: Harper, 1865. 2 vols.
15. Robert K. Douglas. *Society in China.* London: Ward, Lock & Co., 1901.
16. J. J. L. Duyvendak. *The Book of Lord Shang.* Chicago: University of Chicago Press, 1963.
17. Wolfram Eberhard. *A History of China.* London: Routledge & Kegan Paul, 1950.

18. ———. *Conquerors and Rulers: Social Forces in Medieval China.* Leiden: E. J. Brill, 1952.
19. John K. Fairbank, ed. *Chinese Thought and Institutions.* Chicago: University of Chicago Press, 1959.
20. John K. Fairbank. *The United States and China.* 2d ed. New York: Viking Press, 1962.
21. Fan Wen-lan. *Drevniaia istoriia Kitaia.* Moscow: Akademiia Nauk, 1958.
22. Albert Feuerwerker. *China's Early Industrialization.* Cambridge: Harvard University Press, 1958.
23. C. P. Fitzgerald. *China: A Short Cultural History.* London: Cresset Press, 1950.
24. ———. *The Empress Wu.* Melbourne: F. W. Chesire, 1955.
25. Alfred Forke. *Geschichte der alten chinesischen Philosophie.* Hamburg: Cram, de Gruyter & Co., 1964.
26. ———. *Geschichte der mittelalterlichen chinesischen Philosophie.* Hamburg: Cram, de Gruyter & Co., 1964.
27. ———. *Geschichte der neueren chinesischen Philosophie.* Hamburg: Cram, de Gruyter & Co., 1964.
28. L. Carrington Goodrich. *A Short History of the Chinese People.* New York: Harper, 1951.
29. Herbert H. Gowen. *An Outline History of China.* Boston: Sherman, French & Co., 1913. 2 vols.
30. Marcel Granet. *Chinese Civilization.* London: Kegan Paul, 1930.
31. J. J. M. de Groot. *Sectarianism and Religious Persecution in China.* Amsterdam, 1903–1904. 2 vols.
32. Emily Hahn. *China Only Yesterday, 1850–1950.* Garden City, N.Y.: Doubleday, 1963.
33. Clarence H. Hamilton. *Buddhism in India, Ceylon, China and Japan.* Chicago: University of Chicago Press, 1931.
34. James P. Harrison. "Communist Interpretations of the Peasant Wars," *China Quarterly,* no. 24 (Oct.–Dec., 1965).
35. Frederick Hirth. *The Ancient History of China.* New York: Columbia University Press, 1911.
36. Kung-chuan Hsiao. *Rural China, Imperial Control in the Nineteenth Century.* Seattle: University of Washington Press, 1960.
37. M. Huc. *A Journey through the Chinese Empire.* New York: Harper, 1878. 2 vols.
38. Charles O. Hucker. *The Traditional Chinese State in Ming Times.* Tucson: University of Arizona Press, 1961.
39. E. A. Kracke, Jr. *Civil Service in Early Sung China, 960–1067.* Cambridge: Harvard University Press, 1953.
40. Kenneth S. Latourette. *The Chinese: Their History and Culture.* New York: Macmillan, 1934.

41. Owen Lattimore. *Inner Asian Frontiers of China.* New York: American Geographical Society, 1940.
42. Owen and Eleanor Lattimore. *The Making of Modern China.* New York: W. W. Norton, 1944.
43. Louis LeCompte. *Journey through the Empire of China.* London, 1697.
44. Mabel Ping-hua Lee. *The Economic History of China.* New York: Columbia University Press, 1921.
45. Li Chien-nung. *The Political History of China, 1840–1928.* Princeton: D. Van Nostrand Co., 1956.
46. Liang Chi-chao. *History of Chinese Political Thought.* London: Kegan Paul, 1930.
47. James T. C. Liu. *Reform in Sung China.* Cambridge: Harvard University Press, 1959.
48. Lou Kan-jou. "Histoire sociale de l'époque Tcheou." Unpublished dissertation. University of Paris, 1935.
49. Klaus Mehnert. *Peking and Moscow.* New York: G. P. Putnam's Sons, 1963.
50. G. E. Morrison. *An Australian in China.* London, 1895.
51. Mu Fu-sheng. *The Wilting of the Hundred Flowers.* New York: Frederick A. Praeger, 1962.
52. Joseph Needham. *Science and Civilization in China.* Vol. I. Cambridge: The University Press, 1954.
53. M. Frederick Nelson. *Korea and the Old Order in Eastern Asia.* Baton Rouge: Louisiana State University Press, 1946.
54. John L. Nevius. *China and the Chinese.* New York: Harper & Bros., 1869.
55. David S. Nivison and Arthur F. Wright, eds. *Confucianism in Action.* Stanford: Stanford University Press, 1959.
56. Pao Chao Hsieh. "The Government of China (1644–1911)." Unpublished dissertation. Johns Hopkins University, 1925.
57. Edward H. Parker. *The Financial Capacity of China.* Shanghai, 1887.
58. L. S. Perelomov. *Imperiia Tsin'.* Moscow: Akademiia Nauk, 1962.
59. Edwin G. Pulleyblank. *The Background of the Rebellion of An Lu-Shan.* London: Oxford University Press, 1955.
60. Edwin O. Reischauer. *Ennin's Travels in T'ang China.* New York: Ronald Press, 1955.
61. Edwin O. Reischauer and John K. Fairbank. *East Asia: The Great Tradition.* Boston: Houghton Mifflin, 1960.
62. Edward R. Schafer. *The Empire of Min.* Rutland, Vt.: Charles E. Tuttle Co., 1954.
63. Shan Iue. *Ocherki istorii Kitaia.* Moscow: Akademiia Nauk, 1959.
64. Arthur H. Smith. *Chinese Characteristics.* New York: Young People's Missionary Movement, 1907.

65. ———. *Village Life in China*. New York: Young People's Missionary Movement, 1907.
66. Hans O. H. Stange. *Leben, Persönlichkeit und Werk Wang Mangs*. Berlin, 1934.
67. Elbert B. Thomas. *Chinese Political Thought*. New York: Prentice-Hall, 1927.
68. Laurence G. Thompson. *Ta T'ung Shu: The One-World Philosophy of K'ang Yu-wei*. London: Allen & Unwin, 1958.
69. Richard L. Walker. *The Multi-State System of Ancient China*. Hamden, Conn.: Shoe String Press, 1953.
70. Wang Yü-ch'üan. "The Rise of Land Tax and the Fall of Dynasties in Chinese History," *Pacific Affairs*, IX (1936).
71. Burton Watson. *Ssu-ma Ch'ien: Grand Historian of China*. New York: Columbia University Press, 1958.
72. Max Weber. *The Religion of China*. Glencoe, Ill.: Free Press, 1951.
73. W. F. Wertheim. *East-West Parallels*. Chicago: Quadrangle Books, 1964.
74. Léon Wieger. *Textes historiques*. Vol. I. Hien-hien, 1929.
75. C. Martin Wilbur. *Slavery during the Former Han Dynasty*. Field Museum of Natural History, Anthropological Series, vol. 34. 1943.
76. S. Wells Williams. *The Middle Kingdom*. Vol. I. New York: John Wiley, 1859.
77. Arthur F. Wright. *Buddhism in Chinese History*. Stanford: Stanford University Press, 1959.
78. Arthur F. Wright, ed. *The Confucianist Persuasion*. Stanford: Stanford University Press, 1960.
79. Mary Clabaugh Wright. *The Last Stand of Chinese Conservatism*. Stanford: Stanford University Press, 1957.
80. Wu, Kuo-cheng. *Ancient Chinese Political Theories*. Shanghai: Commercial Press, 1932.
81. Lien-sheng Yang. *Studies in Chinese Institutional History*. Cambridge: Harvard University Press, 1963.
82. Martin C. Yang. *A Chinese Village*. New York: Columbia University Press, 1945.
83. Y. C. Yang. *China's Religious Heritage*. Nashville: Abingdon-Cokesbury Press, 1943.
84. Hawkling L. Yen. *A Survey of Constitutional Development of China*. New York: Columbia University Press, 1911.

EGYPT AND ANCIENT NEAR EAST

88. Cyril Aldred. *The Egyptians*. New York: Frederick A. Praeger, 1961.

89. Klaus Baer. *Rank and Title in the Old Kingdom.* Chicago: University of Chicago Press, 1960.

90. James Baikie. *A History of Egypt.* London: A. & C. Black, 1929. 2 vols.

91. Dimitri Baranki. *Phoenicia and the Phoenicians.* Beirut: Khayats, 1961.

92. James H. Breasted. *The Dawn of Conscience.* New York: Charles Scribner's Sons, 1934.

93. ———. *A History of Egypt.* New York: Charles Scribner's Sons, 1905.

94. ———. *A History of Egypt.* 2d ed. London: Hodder & Stoughton, 1950.

95. Wallis Budge. *Egyptian Religion.* New Hyde Park, N.Y.: University Books, 1959.

96. Eugène Cavaignac. *Les Hittites.* Paris: Maisonneuve, 1950.

97. V. Gordon Childe. *Man Makes Himself.* New York: New American Library, 1951.

98. Georges Contenau. *Everyday Life in Babylon and Assyria.* London: Edward Arnold, 1954.

99. Leonard Cottrell. *The Lost Pharaohs.* New York: Grosset & Dunlap, 1963.

100. I. M. D'iakonov. *Obshchestvennyi i gosudarstvennyi stroi drevnego dvurech'ia Shumer.* Moscow: Akademiia Nauk, 1959.

101. V. N. D'iakov and S. I. Kovalev, eds. *Istoriia drevnego mira.* Moscow, 1962.

102. Walter A. Fairservis, Jr., *The Ancient Kingdoms of the Nile.* New York: Thomas Y. Crowell, 1962.

103. Sidney N. Fisher. *The Middle East.* New York: Knopf, 1959.

104. Henri Frankfort. *Ancient Egyptian Religion.* New York: Harper, 1948.

105. ———. *The Birth of Civilization in the Near East.* Bloomington: Indiana University Press, 1954.

106. ———. *Kingship and the Gods.* Chicago: University of Chicago Press, 1948.

107. C. J. Gadd. *The Cities of Babylonia.* Fascicle of *Cambridge Ancient History.* Rev. ed. Vol. I, chap. xiii. Cambridge: The University Press, 1962.

108. ———. *The Dynasty of Agade and the Gutian Invasion.* Fascicle of *Cambridge Ancient History.* Rev. ed. Vol. I, chap. xix. Cambridge: The University Press, 1963.

109. Cyrus H. Gordon. *Before the Bible.* New York: Harper & Row, 1962.

110. O. R. Gurney. *The Hittites.* Harmondsworth, Middlesex: Penguin Books, 1952.

111. H. R. Hall. *The Ancient History of the Near East*. London: Methuen, 1932.
112. Donald Harden. *The Phoenicians*. New York: Frederick A. Praeger, 1962.
113. Jacquetta Hawkes and Sir Leonard Wooley. *Prehistory and the Beginnings of Civilization*. New York: Harper & Row, 1963.
114. William C. Hayes. *Egypt: Internal Affairs from Tuthmosis I to the Death of Amenophis III*. Parts I, II. Fascicles of *Cambridge Ancient History*. Rev. ed. Cambridge: The University Press, 1962.
115. ———. *The Scepter of Egypt*. Cambridge: Harvard University Press, 1953.
116. Richard M. Haywood. *Ancient Greece and the Near East*. New York: David McKay, 1964.
117. Fritz M. Heichelheim. *An Ancient Economic History*. Vol. I. Leiden: A. W. Sizthoff, 1958.
118. Philip K. Hitti. *Lebanon in History*. London: Macmillan, 1957.
119. Bedrich Hrozny. *Ancient History of Western Asia, India and Crete*. Prague, 1951.
120. Hermann Kees. *Ancient Egypt: A Cultural Topography*. Chicago: University of Chicago Press, 1961.
121. Samuel N. Kramer. *From the Tablets of Sumeria*. Indiana Hills, Colo.: Falcon's Wing Press, 1956.
122. ———. *The Sumerians*. Chicago: University of Chicago Press, 1963.
123. W. F. Leemans. *The Old-Babylonian Merchant: His Business and Social Position*. Leiden: E. J. Brill, 1950.
124. Pierre Montet. *Everyday Life in Egypt in the Days of Rameses the Great*. London: Edward Arnold, 1958.
125. Sabatino Moscati. *The Face of the Ancient Orient*. London: Routledge & Kegan Paul, 1960.
126. Margaret A. Murray. *The Splendor That Was Egypt*. New York: Hawthorn Books, 1963.
127. A. T. Olmstead. *History of Assyria*. Chicago: University of Chicago Press, 1960.
128. ———. *Western Asia in the Days of Sargon*. New York: Henry Holt, 1908.
129. A. Leo Oppenheim. *Ancient Mesopotamia*. Chicago: University of Chicago Press, 1964.
130. André Parrot. *Sumer*. London: Thames and Hudson, 1960.
131. Jacques Pirenne. *Histoire de la civilisation de l'Egypte Ancienne*. Vol. I. Paris: Albin Michel, 1961.
132. Ernesto Pontieri, dir. *Storia Universale*. Milan: Francesco Vallardi, 1959.
133. George Rawlinson. *History of Phoenicia*. London: Longmans, Green, 1889.

134. Elizabeth Riefstahl. *Thebes in the Time of Amunhotep III.* Norman: University of Oklahoma Press, 1964.
135. Georges Roux. *Ancient Iraq.* Cleveland: World Publishing Co., 1964.
136. H. W. F. Saggs. *The Greatness That Was Babylon.* New York: Hawthorn Books, 1962.
137. Hartmut Schmökel. *Sumeri, Assiri e Babilonesi.* Rome: Editrice Primato, 1957.
138. Robert Silverberg. *Akhnaten the Rebel Pharaoh.* Philadelphia: Chilton Books, 1964.
139. W. Stevenson Smith. *The Old Kingdom in Egypt.* Fascicle of *Cambridge Ancient History.* Rev. ed. Vol. I, chap. xiv. Cambridge: The University Press, 1962.
140. George Steindorff and Keith C. Steele. *When Egypt Ruled the East.* Chicago: University of Chicago Press, 1957.
141. Jon M. White. *Everyday Life in Ancient Egypt.* New York: G. P. Putnam's Sons, 1963.
142. John A. Wilson. *The Burden of Egypt.* Chicago: University of Chicago Press, 1951.

HAWAII

150. W. D. Alexander. *A Brief History of the Hawaiian People.* New York: American Book Co., 1891.
151. Rufus Anderson. *The Hawaiian Islands.* Boston: Gould & Lincoln, 1864.
152. Martha W. Beckwith, ed. *Kepelino's Traditions of Hawaii.* Honolulu: Bernice P. Bishop Museum, 1932.
153. William F. Blackman. *The Making of Hawaii.* New York: Macmillan, 1899.
154. Sheldon Dibble. *A History of the Sandwich Islands.* Honolulu: Thos. G. Thrum, 1909.
155. H. R. Hays. *The Kingdom of Hawaii.* Greenwich: New York Graphic Society, 1964.
156. Manley Hopkins. *Hawaii.* London, 1862.
157. James J. Jarves. *History of the Hawaiian Islands.* Honolulu: Charles E. Hitchcock, 1847.
158. Gerrit P. Judd IV. *Hawaii: An Informal History.* New York: Collier Books, 1961.
159. Ralph S. Kuykendall. *The Hawaiian Kingdom, 1778–1854.* Honolulu: University of Hawaii, 1938.
160. David Malo. *Hawaiian Antiquities.* Honolulu: Bernice P. Bishop Museum, 1951.

161. Marshall D. Sahlins. *Social Stratification in Polynesia.* Seattle: University of Washington Press, 1958.
162. Robert W. Williamson. *Essays in Polynesian Ethnology.* Cambridge: The University Press, 1939.
163. Robert W. Williamson. *Religion and Social Organization in Central Polynesia.* Cambridge: The University Press, 1937.

INCAS

170. Louis Baudin. *A Socialist Empire: The Incas of Peru.* Trans. Katherine Woods. Princeton: D. Van Nostrand Co., 1961.
171. Wendell C. Bennet and Junius B. Bird, *Andean Cultural History.* New York: Museum of Natural History, 1949.
172. Joseph Bram. *An Analysis of Inca Militarism.* New York: American Ethnological Society, 1941.
173. Burr C. Brundage. *Empire of the Inca.* Norman: University of Oklahoma Press, 1963.
174. G. H. S. Bushnell. *Peru.* New York: Frederick A. Praeger, 1957.
175. Victor W. von Hagen. *Realm of the Incas.* New York: Mentor Books, 1961.
176. Edward Hyams and George Ordash. *The Last of the Incas.* London: Longmans, 1963.
177. Phillip A. Means. *Ancient Civilizations of the Andes.* New York: Charles Scribner's Sons, 1931.
178. Sally Falk Moore. *Power and Property in Inca Peru.* New York: Columbia University Press, 1958.
179. Harold Osborne. *Indians of the Andes.* Cambridge: Harvard University Press, 1952.
180. Julian H. Steward, ed. *Handbook of the South American Indians.* Washington: Government Printing Office, 1946.
181. Garcilaso de la Vega. *The Incas.* New York: Orion Press, 1961.

INDIA

188. A. S. Altekar. *State and Government in Ancient India.* Delhi: Banarsidass, 1958.
189. Narayanchandra Bandyopadhyaya. *Economic Life and Progress in Ancient India.* Vol. I. Calcutta: University of Calcutta, 1945.
190. A. C. Basham. *The Wonder That Was India.* New York: Hawthorn Books, 1963.
191. François Bernier. *Travels in the Mogul Empire.* Trans. Archibald Constable. London: Oxford University Press, 1934.

192. Atindranath Bose. *Social and Rural Economy of Northern India, 600 B.C.–200 A.D.* Calcutta: University of Calcutta, 1945.
193. *Cambridge History of India.* Vol. IV. Ed. Richard Burn. Cambridge: The University Press, 1937.
194. Santosh K. Das. *The Economic History of Ancient India.* Calcutta: Mithra Press, 1925.
195. Michael Edwardes. *A History of India.* London: Thames and Hudson, 1961.
196. Gertrude Emerson. *The Pageant of Indian History.* New York: Longmans, Green, 1948.
197. G. T. Garratt, ed. *The Legacy of India.* Oxford: Clarendon Press, 1938.
198. U. N. Ghoshal. *A History of Indian Political Ideas.* Bombay: Oxford University Press, 1959.
199. Edward S. Holden. *The Mogul Emperors of Hindustan.* New York: Charles Scribner's Sons, 1895.
200. R. P. Kangle. *The Kautilya Arthasastra.* Bombay: University of Bombay, 1963.
201. D. D. Kosambi. *An Introduction to the Study of Indian History.* Bombay: Popular Books, 1956.
202. Stanley Lane-Poole. *Aurangzib.* Oxford: Clarendon Press, 1893.
203. R. C. Majumdar, ed. *The History and Culture of the Indian People.* Vols. I, II. London: Allen & Unwin, 1953.
204. Radha K. Mookerji. *Chandragupta Maurya and His Times.* Delhi: Rajkamal Publications, 1952.
205. W. H. Moreland. *From Akbar to Aurangzeb.* London: Macmillan, 1923.
206. V. S. Naipaul. *An Area of Darkness.* London: André Deutsch, 1964.
207. Jawaharlal Nehru. *The Discovery of India.* New York: John Day, 1946.
208. K. A. Nilakanta Sastri, ed. *A Comprehensive History of India.* Vol. II. Bombay: Orient Longmans, 1957.
209. D. Pant. *The Commercial Policy of the Moguls.* Bombay: D. B. Taraporevala & Sons, 1930.
210. Stuart Pigott. *Prehistoric India.* Harmondsworth, Middlesex: Penguin Books, 1950.
211. Beni Prasad. *The State in Ancient India.* London: Arthur Probsthain, 1928.
212. H. G. Rawlinson. *India: A Short Cultural History.* New York: D. Appleton-Century, 1938.
213. Jadunath Sarkar. *The Mughal Administration.* Putna: Putna University, 1920.
214. Sri Ram Sharma. *Mughal Government and Administration.* Bombay: Hind Kitabs, 1951.

215. Vincent A. Smith. *The Early History of India.* Oxford: Clarendon Press, 1914.
216. Percival Spears. *India.* Ann Arbor: University of Michigan Press, 1961.
217. Romila Thapar. *Asoka and the Decline of the Mauryas.* London: Oxford University Press, 1961.
218. Mortimer Wheeler. *Early India and Pakistan.* London: Thames and Hudson, 1954.
219. Philip Woodruff. *The Founders of Modern India.* New York: St. Martin's Press, 1954.

MILITARY ORGANIZATION

220. Stanislaw Andrzejewski. *Military Organization and Society.* London: Routledge & Kegan Paul, 1954.
221. Kendall Banning. *West Point Today.* New York: Funk & Wagnalls, 1937.
222. Gordon A. Craig. *The Politics of the Prussian Army, 1640–1945.* Oxford: Clarendon Press, 1955.
223. Karl Demeter. *Das deutsche Offizierkorps.* Frankfurt a. M.: Bernard & Graefe, 1962.
224. James B. Fry. *Military Miscellanies.* New York: Brentano's, 1889.
225. J. F. C. Fuller. *Generalship: Its Diseases and Their Cure.* Harrisburg, Pa.: Military Service Publishing Co., 1936.
226. Charles de Gaulle. *La France et son armée.* Paris: Plon, 1938.
227. Raoul Girardet. *La Société militaire dans la France contemporaine.* Paris: Plon, 1953.
228. Paul-Marie de la Gorce. *The French Army.* New York: George Braziller, 1963.
229. Samuel P. Huntington. *The Soldier and the State.* Cambridge: Harvard University Press, 1957.
230. Morris Janowitz. *The Professional Soldier.* New York: Free Press of Glencoe, 1960.
231. John W. Masland and Laurence I. Radway. *Soldiers and Scholars.* Princeton: Princeton University Press, 1957.
232. Joseph Monteilhet. *Les institutions militaires de la France.* Paris: Felix-Alcan, 1932.
233. André Morizet. *De l'incapacité de militaires à faire la guerre.* Paris: Editions Clarté, 1921.
234. Jean de Pierrefeu. *French Headquarters, 1915–1918.* London: Geoffrey Bles, 1924.
235. Herbert Rosinski. *The German Army.* New York: Harcourt, Brace, 1940.

236. Oliver L. Spaulding. *Pen and Sword in Greece and Rome.* Princeton: Princeton University Press, 1937.
237. Oliver L. Spaulding, Hoffman Nickerson, and John W. Wright. *Warfare.* Washington: Infantry Journal Press, 1937.
238. John R. Swomley, Jr. *The Military Establishment.* Boston: Beacon Press, 1964.
239. Alfred Vagts. *Militarism.* New York: Meridian Books, 1959.
240. Esmé Wingfield-Stratton. *They That Take the Sword.* New York: William Morrow, 1931.

PERSIA

245. Arthur Christensen. *L'Iran sous les Sassanides.* 2d. ed. Paris: Annales du Musée Guimet, 1944.
246. William Culican. *The Medes and Persians.* New York: Frederick A. Praeger, 1965.
247. "Persia," in *Encyclopaedia Britannica.* 1964 ed.
248. "Mazdakism," in *Encyclopaedia Britannica.* 1964 ed.
249. Richard N. Frye. *The Heritage of Persia.* London: Weidenfeld & Nicolson, 1962.
250. Clément Huart. *Ancient Persia and Iranian Civilization.* New York: Knopf, 1927.
251. Otakar Klima. *Mazdak.* Prague, 1957.
252. A. T. Olmstead. *History of the Persian Empire.* Chicago: University of Chicago Press, 1948.
253. Percy M. Sykes. *A History of Persia.* Vols. I, II. London: Macmillan, 1951.
254. R. C. Zaehner. *The Dawn and Twilight of Zoroastrianism.* New York: G. P. Putnam's Sons, 1961.

PRIMITIVE AFRICA

260. David E. Apter. *The Politics of Modernization.* Chicago: University of Chicago Press, 1965.
261. E. E. Evans-Pritchard. *Essays in Social Anthropology.* New York: Free Press of Glencoe, 1963.
262. Daryll Forde, ed. *African Worlds.* London: International African Institute, 1954.
263. M. Fortes and E. E. Evans-Pritchard, eds. *African Political Systems.* London: Oxford University Press, 1950.
264. Melville J. Herskovits. *Dahomey.* New York: J. J. Augustin, 1938. 2 vols.

265. Henri A. Junod. *The Life of a South African Tribe*. Vol. I. New Hyde Park, N.Y.: University Books, 1962.
266. Apolo Kagwa. *The Customs of the Baganda*. Ed. M. Mandelbaum. New York: Columbia University Press, 1934.
267. Eileen Jensen Krige. *The Social System of the Zulus*. Pietermaritzburg: Shuter & Shooter, 1962.
268. Audrey I. Richards, ed. *East African Chiefs*. London: Faber & Faber, 1960.
269. E. A. Ritter. *Shaka Zulu*. London: Longmans, Green, 1955.
270. I. Schapera. *Government and Politics in Tribal Societies*. London: Watts, 1965.
271. ———. *The Khoisan Peoples of South Africa*. London: Routledge & Kegan Paul, 1930.
272. Elizabeth M. Thomas. *The Harmless People*. New York: Knopf, 1959.

ROME, GREECE, AND BYZANTIUM

275. Andrew Alföldi. *A Conflict of Ideas in the Late Roman Empire*. Oxford: Clarendon Press, 1952.
276. Cyril Bailey, ed. *The Legacy of Rome*. Oxford: Clarendon Press, 1928.
277. Ernest Barker. *Social and Political Thought in Byzantium*. Oxford: Clarendon Press, 1957.
278. Norman H. Baynes. *Byzantine Studies and Other Essays*. London: Athlone Press, 1955.
279. Norman H. Baynes and H. B. Moss. *Byzantium*. Oxford: Clarendon Press, 1948.
280. Julius Beloch, "Der Verfall der antiken Kultur," *Historische Zeitschrift*, 84 (1900), 1–38.
281. Hermann Bengtson. *Griechische Geschichte*. Munich: C. H. Beck, 1950.
282. E. Beurlier. *Le culte rendu aux empereurs romains*. Paris: Ernest Thorin, 1890.
283. Raymond Bloch. *The Etruscans*. New York: Frederick A. Praeger, 1958.
284. Raymond Bloch and Jean Cousin. *Rome et son destin*. Paris: Armand Colin, 1960.
285. Arthur E. R. Boak. *A History of Rome to 565 A.D.* New York: Macmillan, 1943.
286. C. M. Bowra. *The Greek Experience*. London: Weidenfeld & Nicolson, 1957.

287. James Bryce. *The Holy Roman Empire*. New York: Macmillan, 1905.
288. Jacob Burckhardt. *The Age of Constantine the Great*. New York: Pantheon Books, 1949.
289. J. B. Bury. *History of Greece*. London: Macmillan, 1959.
290. *Cambridge Ancient History*. Vol. XI: *The Imperial Peace*, A.D. 70–192. Cambridge: The University Press, 1936.
291. *Cambridge Ancient History*. Vol. XII: *The Imperial Crisis and Recovery*, A.D. 193–324. Cambridge: The University Press, 1939.
292. *Cambridge Medieval History*. Vol. IV: *The Eastern Roman Empire, 717–1455*. Cambridge: The University Press, 1929.
293. M. Cary. *A History of the Greek World from 323 to 146* B.C. London: Methuen, 1959.
294. ———. *A History of Rome*. London: Macmillan, 1962.
295. M. Cary and T. J. Haarhoff. *Life and Thought in the Greek and Roman World*. London: Methuen, 1940.
296. Shirley J. Case. *The Evolution of Early Christianity*. Chicago: University of Chicago Press, 1960.
297. Martin P. Charlesworth. *The Roman Empire*. London: Oxford University Press, 1951.
298. F. R. Cowell. *The Revolutions of Ancient Rome*. London: Thames and Hudson, 1962.
299. Franz Cumont. *The Oriental Religions in Roman Paganism*. Chicago: Open Court Publishing Co., 1911.
300. William S. Davis. *The Influence of Wealth in Imperial Rome*. New York: Macmillan, 1910.
301. Charles Diehl. *Byzantium: Greatness and Decline*. New Brunswick, N.J.: Rutgers University Press, 1957.
302. Samuel Dill. *Roman Society from Nero to Marcus Aurelius*. London: Macmillan, 1905.
303. ———. *Roman Society in the Last Century of the Western Empire*. London: Macmillan, 1905.
304. L. E. Elliott-Binns. *The Beginnings of Western Christendom*. Greenwich, Conn.: Seabury Press, 1957.
305. "Brigantaggio," in *Enciclopedia Italiana*. Rome, 1949.
306. "Dead Sea Scrolls," in *Encyclopaedia Britannica*. 1964 ed.
307. "Roman Law," in *Encyclopaedia Britannica*. 1964 ed.
308. Gugliemo Ferrero. *The Greatness and Decline of Rome*. Vol. V. New York: G. P. Putnam's Sons, 1909.
309. ———. *The Ruin of Ancient Civilization and the Triumph of Christianity*. New York: G. P. Putnam's Sons, 1921.
310. ———. *The Women of the Caesars*. London: T. Fisher Unwin, 1911.
311. George Finlay. *History of the Byzantine Empire*. London: J. M. Dent & Sons, 1906.

312. Tenney Frank. *An Economic History of Rome*. Baltimore: Johns Hopkins Press, 1927.
313. Ludwig Friedländer. *Roman Life and Manners under the Early Empire*. London: George Routledge & Sons, 1909.
314. Edward Gibbon. *The Decline and Fall of the Roman Empire*. New York: Modern Library, 1932. 2 vols.
315. Gustave Glotz. *Ancient Greece at Work*. New York: Knopf, 1926.
316. ———. *The Greek City and Its Institutions*. London: Kegan Paul, 1929.
317. T. R. Glover. *Democracy in the Ancient World*. Cambridge: The University Press, 1927.
318. Moses Hadas. *Hellenistic Culture*. New York: Columbia University Press, 1959.
319. Mason Hammond. *City-State and World State*. Cambridge: Harvard University Press, 1951.
320. David J. Hill. *A History of Diplomacy in the International Development of Europe*. Vol. I: *The Struggle for Universal Empire*. London: Longmans, Green, 1911.
321. Leon Homo. *Roman Political Institutions*. New York: Knopf, 1929.
322. Walter W. Hyde. *Paganism to Christianity in the Roman Empire*. Philadelphia: University of Pennsylvania Press, 1946.
323. Trevor G. Jalland. *The Church and the Papacy*. London: Society for Promoting Christian Knowledge, 1944.
324. H. F. Jolowicz. *Historical Introduction to the Study of Roman Law*. Cambridge: The University Press, 1961.
325. A. H. M. Jones. *Athenian Democracy*. Oxford: Basil Blackwell, 1957.
326. ———. *The Later Roman Empire*. Norman: University of Oklahoma Press, 1964. 2 vols.
327. Donald Kagan, ed. *Sources in Greek Political Thought*. New York: Free Press, 1965.
328. J. A. O. Larsen. *Representative Government in Greek and Roman History*. Berkeley and Los Angeles: University of California Press, 1955.
329. Kenneth S. Latourette. *A History of the Expansion of Christianity*. Vol. I. New York: Harper & Bros., 1937.
330. Naphtali Lewis and Meyer Reinhold. *Roman Civilization*. New York: Columbia University Press, 1955.
331. Ferdinand Lot. *The End of the Ancient World*. New York: Knopf, 1931.
332. John P. Mahaffy. *The Silver Age of the Greek World*. Chicago: University of Chicago Press, 1906.
333. Harold Mattingly. *The Imperial Civil Service of Rome*. Cambridge: The University Press, 1910.

334. ———. *Roman Imperial Civilization*. London: Edward Arnold, 1957.
335. G. R. S. Mead. *Fragments of a Faith Forgotten*. New Hyde Park, N.Y.: University Books, 1960.
336. William Miller. *Trebizond: The Last Greek Empire*. London: Society for Promoting Christian Knowledge, 1926.
337. Charles L. de Montesquieu. *Consideration on the Causes of the Greatness of the Romans and Their Decline*. New York: Free Press, 1965.
338. Martin P. Nilsson. *Imperial Rome*. New York: Harcourt, Brace, 1926.
339. G. Ostrogorsky. "The Byzantine Emperor and the Hierarchical World Order," *Slavonic and East European Review*, XXXV (Dec., 1956).
340. Erik Peterson. *Der Monotheismus als politisches Problem*. Leipzig: Jakob Hegner, 1935.
341. Coleman Phillipson. *The International Law and Custom of Ancient Greece and Rome*. London: Macmillan, 1911. 2 vols.
342. M. Rostovtzeff. *The Social and Economic History of the Roman Empire*. Oxford: Clarendon Press, 1957.
343. Ernest G. Sihler. *From Augustus to Augustine*. Cambridge: The University Press, 1923.
344. Vladimir G. Simkhovitch. "Rome's Fall Reconsidered," *Political Science Quarterly*, XXXI (June, 1916).
345. Chester G. Starr. *Civilization and the Caesars*. Ithaca: Cornell University Press, 1954.
346. G. H. Stevenson. *Roman Provincial Administration*. Oxford: Basil Blackwell, 1949.
347. Louis M. Sweet. *Roman Emperor Worship*. Boston: Richard G. Badger, 1919.
348. Ronald Syme. *The Roman Revolution*. Oxford: Clarendon Press, 1939.
349. Tacitus. *Complete Works*. New York: Modern Library, 1942.
350. W. W. Tarn. *Hellenistic Civilization*. London: Edward Arnold, 1936.
351. Lily Ross Taylor. *The Divinity of the Roman Emperor*. Middletown, Conn.: American Philological Association, 1931.
352. Jules Toutain. *The Economic Life of the Ancient World*. London: Kegan Paul, Trench, Trubner, 1930.
353. A. A. Vasiliev. *History of the Byzantine Empire*. Madison: University of Wisconsin Press, 1952.
354. Lawrence Waddy. *Pax Romana and World Peace*. New York: W. W. Norton, n.d.
355. Johannes Weiss. *Earliest Christianity*. Vol. I. New York: Harper & Bros., 1959.

356. E. G. Weltin. *The Ancient Popes*. Westminster, Md.: The Newman Press, 1964.
357. W. L. Westermann. "The Economic Basis of the Decline of Ancient Culture," *American Historical Review*, XX (July, 1915).
358. Edward Lucas White. *Why Rome Fell*. New York: Harper & Bros., 1927.

RUSSIA

359. *Absoliutizm v Rossii (XVII–XVIII vv) sbornik statei*. Moscow: Akademiia Nauk, 1964.
360. Gregor Alexinsky. *Modern Russia*. London: T. Fisher Unwin, 1913.
361. A. Babaevskii. In *Vozrozhdenie* (Paris) (July, 1963), p. 39.
362. R. Beerman. "Soviet and Russian Anti-Parasite Laws," *Soviet Studies*, XV (April, 1964).
363. Nikolai A. Berdiaev. *The Russian Idea*. Boston: Beacon Press, 1962.
364. V. N. Bernadskii. *Novgorod i novgorodskaia zemlia v XV veke*. Moscow: Izd. Akademiia Nauk, 1961.
365. Jerome Blum. *Lord and Peasant in Russia*. Princeton: Princeton University Press, 1961.
366. Charles B. Boynton. *The Russian Empire*. Cincinnati, 1856.
367. Michael Cherniavsky. *Tsar and People*. New Haven: Yale University Press, 1961.
368. Gaëtan Combes de Lestrade. *Le Russie économique et sociale*, Paris, 1896.
369. Frederick C. Conybeare. *Russian Dissenters*. Cambridge: Harvard University Press, 1921.
370. William Coxe. *Travels into Poland, Russia, Sweden*. Dublin, 1784. 3 vols.
371. Theodore Dan. *The Origins of Bolshevism*. New York: Harper & Row, 1964.
372. E. J. Dillon. *The Eclipse of Russia*. London: J. M. Dent & Sons, 1918.
373. M. D'jakanov. *Skizzen zur Gesellschafts und Staatsordnung des alten Russlands*. Breslau: Osteuropa Institut, 1931.
374. "Russia," *Encyclopaedia Britannica*. 11th ed.
375. Merle Fainsod. *How Russia Is Ruled*. Cambridge: Harvard University Press, 1963.
376. Louis Fischer. *The Life of Lenin*. New York: Harper & Row, 1964.
377. Michael T. Florinsky. *Russia: A History and an Interpretation*. Vol. I. New York: Macmillan, 1953.

378. Michael T. Florinsky. *The End of the Russian Empire*. New Haven: Yale University Press, 1931.

379. Constantin de Grunwald. *Peter the Great*. London: Douglas Saunders, 1956.

380. August von Haxthausen. *The Russian Empire*. London: Chapman & Hall, 1856. 2 vols.

381. Sigismund von Herberstein. *Notes upon Russia*. New York: Hakluyt Society, 1851.

382. A. Herzen. *Collected Works*. Vol. VII. Moscow, 1956.

383. Barbara Jelavich. *A Century of Russian Foreign Policy, 1814–1914*. New York: J. B. Lippincott, 1964.

384. J. L. H. Keep. "Bandits and the Laws in Muscovy," *Slavonic Review*, XXXV (Dec., 1956).

385. A. F. Kerensky. *The Crucifixion of Liberty*. London: Arthur Barker, 1934.

386. *Khrestomatiia po istorii SSSR XVIII v.* Ed. L. G. Beskrovnyi and B. B. Kafengauz. Moscow, 1963.

387. A. I. Klibanov. *Istoriia religioznogo sektantsva v Rossii*. Moscow, 1965.

388. V. O. Kluchevsky. *A History of Russia*. London: J. M. Dent & Sons, 1912. 5 vols.

389. Samuel Kucherov. *Courts, Lawyers and Trials under the Last Three Tsars*. New York: Frederick A. Praeger, 1953.

390. E. B. Lanin. *Russian Characteristics*. London: Chapman & Hall, 1892.

391. Joseph La Palombara, ed. *Bureaucracy and Political Development*. Princeton: Princeton University Press, 1963.

392. Theodore H. von Laue. *Why Lenin? Why Stalin?* New York: J. B. Lippincott, 1964.

393. Ivo J. Lederer, ed. *Russian Foreign Policy*. New Haven: Yale University Press, 1962.

394. Anatole Leroy-Beaulieu. *The Russian Peasant*. Ed. Henry J. Tobias. Sandoval, N.M.: Coronado Press, 1962.

395. Carlo Lozzi. *Vecchia Russia*. Rome: A. F. Formiginni, 1934.

396. Robert Lyall. *The Character of the Russians*. London, 1823.

397. ———. *Travels in Russia*. . . . London, 1825. 2 vols.

398. James Mavor. *An Economic History of Russia*. Vol. I. London: J. M. Dent & Sons, 1914.

399. Alfred G. Meyer. *The Soviet Political System*. New York: Random House, 1965.

400. Bernard Pares. *Russia and Reform*. London: Archibald & Constable, 1907.

401. I. I. Polosin. *Sotsial'no-politicheskaia istoriia Rossii XVI-nachala XVII v.* Moscow: Akademiia Nauk, 1963.

402. Sergei Pushkarev. *The Emergence of Modern Russia, 1801–1917.* New York: Holt, Rinehart & Winston, 1963.

403. Peter Putnam, ed. *Seven Britons in Imperial Russia.* Princeton: Princeton University Press, 1952.

404. Nicholas V. Riasanovsky. *A History of Russia.* New York: Oxford University Press, 1963.

405. *Russia at the Close of the Sixteenth Century.* Ed. Edward A. Bond. London: Hakluyt Society, 1956.

406. Stepniak (pseud. of Sergei M. Kravchinski). *The Russian Peasantry.* London: Swan Sonnenschein, Lowrey, 1888.

407. B. H. Sumner. *Peter the Great and the Emergence of Russia.* New York: Macmillan, 1951.

408. Stuart R. Tompkins. *Russia through the Ages.* New York: Prentice-Hall, 1940.

409. Donald W. Treadgold, ed. *The Development of the USSR.* Seattle: University of Washington Press, 1964.

410. Henri Troyat. *Daily Life in Russia under the Last Tsar.* London: Allen & Unwin, 1961.

411. Dmitrij Tschižewskii. *Das heilige Russland: russische Geistesgeschichte I.* Hamburg: Rowohlt, 1959.

412. S. V. Utechine. *Russian Political Thought.* New York: Frederick A. Praeger, 1963.

413. Nicholas Vakar. *The Taproot of Soviet Society.* New York: Harper & Bros., 1962.

414. G. Vasilevski. *Krinitsa.* St. Petersburg, 1908.

415. A. T. Vassilyev. *The Ochrana.* Philadelphia: J. B. Lippincott, 1930.

416. George Vernadsky. *The Mongols and Russia.* New Haven: Yale University Press, 1953.

417. ———. *Russia at the Dawn of the Modern Age.* New Haven: Yale University Press, 1959.

418. Luigi Villari. *Russia under the Great Shadow.* London: T. Fisher Unwin, 1905.

419. Donald Mackenzie Wallace. *Russia.* New York: Henry Holt, 1877.

420. Warren B. Walsh, ed. *Readings in Russian History.* Syracuse: Syracuse University Press, 1948.

421. Robert G. Wesson. *Soviet Communes.* New Brunswick, N.J.: Rutgers University Press, 1963.

422. Peter Wiles. "On Physical Immortality," *Survey,* no. 56 (July, 1965).

423. Nevin O. Winter. *The Russian Empire of Today and Yesterday.* London: Simpkin, Marshall, Hamilton, Kent, 1914.

424. James F. C. Wright. *Slava Bohu: The Story of the Dukhobors.* New York: Farrar & Rinehart, 1940.

425. Sergei Zenkovsky. "The Russian Church Schism: Its Background and Repercussions," *Russian Review,* XVI (Oct., 1957).

TURKEY

430. A. D. Alderson. *The Structure of the Ottoman Dynasty.* Oxford: Clarendon Press, 1956.
431. George J. S. Eversley. *The Turkish Empire.* London: T. Fisher Unwin, 1954.
432. Hamilton Gibb and Harold Bowen. *Islamic Society and the West.* Vol. I, Pts. I, II. London: Oxford University Press, 1950.
433. Stanley Lane-Poole. *The Story of Turkey.* New York: G. P. Putnam's Sons, 1890.
434. Emil Lengyel. *Turkey.* New York: Random House, 1941.
435. Albert H. Lyber. *The Government of the Ottoman Empire in the Time of Suleiman the Magnificent.* Cambridge: Harvard University Press, 1963.
436. Roger B. Merriman. *Suleiman the Magnificent.* Cambridge: Harvard University Press, 1944.
437. Herbert J. Muller. *The Loom of History.* New York: Harper & Bros., 1958.
438. Paul Wittek. *The Rise of the Ottoman Empire.* London: Royal Asiatic Society, 1938.
439. Walter L. Wright, Jr. *Ottoman Statecraft.* Princeton: Princeton University Press, 1935.

VARIOUS AND GENERAL

450. Sebastiano Aglianò. *Questa Sicilia.* Verona: Arnoldo Mondadori, 1950.
451. Richard J. Andrew. "The Origins of Facial Expressions," *Scientific American,* 213 (Oct., 1965).
452. Thomas W. Arnold. *The Caliphate.* Oxford: Clarendon Press, 1924.
453. *Babeuf et les problèmes du babouvisme.* Paris, Editions Sociales, 1963.
454. Edward C. Banfield. *The Moral Basis of a Backward Society.* Glencoe, Ill.: Free Press, 1958.
455. Michael Banton. *The Policeman in the Community.* London: Tavistock Publications, 1964.
456. Joseph Baratz. *The Story of Dagania.* Tel Aviv, 1937.
457. Adriaan J. Barnouw. *The Pageant of Netherlands History.* New York: Longmans, Green, 1952.
458. E. T. Bell. *The Development of Mathematics.* New York: McGraw-Hill, 1940.
459. Avraham C. Ben-Yosef. *The Purest Democracy in the World.* New York: Herzl Press, 1963.

460. Marie Louise Berneri. *Journey through Utopia*. London: Routledge & Kegan Paul, 1950.

461. G. L. Brook. *A History of the English Language*. London: André Deutsch, 1958.

462. Charles J. Bullock. *Politics, Finance and Consequences*. Cambridge: Harvard University Press, 1939.

463. John F. Cady. *Southeast Asia: Its Historical Development*. New York: McGraw-Hill, 1964.

464. W. F. Church. *The Greatness of Louis XIV: Myth or Reality*. Boston: D. C. Heath, 1959.

465. Benjamin Constant. *Prophecy from the Past*. Ed. and trans. H. B. Lippmann. New York: Reynal & Hitchcock, 1941.

466. Rushton Coulborn, ed. *Feudalism in History*. Princeton: Princeton University Press, 1956.

467. Francis M. Crawford. *Southern Italy and Sicily and the Rulers of the South*. New York: Macmillan, 1926.

468. A. C. Crombie, ed. *Scientific Change*. New York: Basic Books, 1963.

469. Charles C. Cumberland. *The Mexican Revolution*. Austin: University of Texas Press, 1952.

470. Rupert Emerson. *From Empire to Nation*. Cambridge: Harvard University Press, 1960.

471. "Mafia," *Encyclopaedia Britannica*. 1964 ed.

472. "Satan," *Encyclopaedia Britannica*. 1964 ed.

473. Alfred Espinas. *La philosophie sociale du XVIII siècle et la révolution*. Paris: Felix-Alcan, 1898.

474. Amitai Etzioni, ed. *Complex Organizations*. New York: Holt, Rinehart & Winston, 1962.

475. ———. *Modern Organizations*. Englewood Cliffs, N.J.: Prentice-Hall, 1964.

476. H. A. L. Fisher. *Bonapartism*. Oxford: Clarendon Press, 1908.

477. Lillian E. Fisher. *The Background of the Revolution for Mexican Independence*. Boston: Christopher Publishing House, 1934.

478. George M. Foster. *Traditional Cultures and the Impact of Technological Change*. New York: Harper & Bros., 1962.

479. Leopoldo Franchetti. *La Sicilia nel 1876: Condizioni politiche e amministrative*. Florence: G. Barbera, 1877.

480. F. G. Friedman. "The World of La Miseria," *Partisan Review*, XX (March-April, 1953).

481. Raymond Frost. *The Backward Society*. New York: St. Martin's Press, 1961.

482. Andrew Gemant. *The Nature of the Genius*. Springfield, Ill.: Charles C Thomas, 1961.

483. Jane Goodall. "My Life among Wild Chimpanzees," *National Geographic*, CXXIV (Aug., 1963).

484. Louis Gottschalk, ed. *Generalization in the Writing of History.* Chicago: University of Chicago Press, 1963.
485. Ernest Gruening. *Mexico and Its Heritage.* New York: Century Co., 1928.
486. G. E. von Grunebaum. *Medieval Islam.* Chicago: University of Chicago Press, 1953.
487. Romano Guardini. *Der Heilbringer in Mythos, Offenbarung und Politik.* Stuttgart: Deutsche Verlags-Anstalt, 1945.
488. Edward V. Gulick. *Europe's Classical Balance of Power.* Ithaca: Cornell University Press, 1955.
489. Everett E. Hagen. *On the Theory of Social Change.* Homewood, Ill.: Dorsey Press, 1962.
490. Norman Hampson. *A Social History of the French Revolution.* London: Routledge & Kegan Paul, 1963.
491. Marvin Harris. *Town and Country in Brazil.* New York: Columbia University Press, 1956.
492. Frederick Hertz. *The Development of the German Public Mind.* Vol. I. New York: Macmillan, 1962.
493. Philip K. Hitti. *The History of the Arabs.* New York: St. Martin's Press, 1953.
494. E. J. Hobsbawm. *Primitive Rebels.* New York: Frederick A. Praeger, 1963.
495. E. Adamson Hoebel. *The Law of Primitive Man.* Cambridge: Harvard University Press, 1954.
496. Eric Hoffer. *The True Believer.* New York: Harper & Bros., 1951.
497. Irving L. Horowitz. *The Anarchists.* New York: Dell Publishing Co., 1964.
498. ———. *Revolution in Brazil.* New York: Dutton, 1964.
499. Herman G. James. *Brazil after a Century of Independence.* New York: Macmillan, 1925.
502. Vera Kelsey. *Seven Keys to Brazil.* New York: Funk & Wagnalls, 1941.
503. E. S. de Klerck. *History of the Netherlands East Indies.* Rotterdam: W. L. and J. Brusse, N.V., 1938.
504. Vittorio Lanternari. *The Religions of the Oppressed.* New York: Knopf, 1963.
505. Jane and Hugo van Lawick. "New Discoveries among Africa's Chimpanzees," *National Geographic,* CXXVIII (Dec., 1965).
506. Daniel Lerner. *The Passing of Traditional Society.* Glencoe, Ill.: Free Press, 1958.
507. Carlo Levi. *Christ Stopped at Eboli.* New York: Farrar, Strauss, 1963.
508. Oscar Lewis. *Life in a Mexican Village.* Urbana, Ill.: University of Illinois Press, 1951.

509. Hubertus zu Loewenstein. *The Germans in History*. New York: Columbia University Press, 1945.

510. John Lough. *An Introduction to Seventeenth Century France*. London: Longmans, Green, 1954.

511. Robert H. Lowie. *The Origin of the State*. New York: Harcourt, Brace, 1927.

512. Louis Madelin. *La France de l'Empire*. Paris: Plon, 1926.

513. Joseph Maier and Richard W. Weatherhead. *Politics of Change in Latin America*. New York: Frederick A. Praeger, 1964.

514. Pierre Mendès-France. *A Modern French Republic*. New York: Hill and Wang, 1963.

515. Charles E. Merriam. *Political Power*. Glencoe, Ill.: Free Press, 1950.

516. Robert Michels. *Political Parties*. Glencoe, Ill.: Free Press, 1949.

517. Morelly. *Code de la Nature, ou le véritable esprit de ses loix*. Paris: Paul Guenther, 1755. Repr. 1910.

518. Hans J. Morgenthau. *Politics among Nations*. New York: Knopf, 1960.

519. Fritz Morstein-Marx. *The Administrative State*. Chicago: University of Chicago Press, 1957.

520. S. Mowinckel. *He That Cometh*. New York: Abingdon Press, 1954.

521. V. S. Naipaul. *The Middle Passage*. London: André Deutsch, 1962.

522. Franz Neumann. *The Democratic and Authoritarian State*. Glencoe, Ill.: Free Press, 1957.

523. Harold Nicolson. *Monarchy*. London: Weidenfeld, Nicolson, 1962.

524. John B. Noss. *Man's Religions*. New York: Macmillan, 1949.

525. Ragnar Numelin. *The Beginnings of Diplomacy*. London: Oxford University Press, 1959.

526. Arthur Nussbaum. *A Concise History of the Law of Nations*. New York: Macmillan, 1947.

527. Henry B. Parkes. *A History of Mexico*. Boston: Houghton-Mifflin, 1960.

528. J. Roland Pennock and David G. Smith. *Political Science: An Introduction*. New York: Macmillan, 1964.

529. Henri Pirenne. *Economic and Social History of Medieval Europe*. New York: Harcourt, Brace, 1937.

530. Robert Presthus. *The Organizational Society*. New York: Knopf, 1962.

531. Herbert I. Priestley. *The Mexican Nation: A History*. New York: Macmillan, 1935.

532. Paul Radin. *The World of Primitive Man*. New York: Henry Schuman, 1953.

533. Rudolf Rocker. *Die Entscheidung des Abendlandes*. Hamburg: Friedrich Oetinger, 1949.

534. Ernesto Rossi. *Il malgoverno*. Bari: Laterza, 1955.
535. Hans K. Röthel. *Die Hansestädte*. Munich: Prestel-Verlag, 1955.
536. Alvin Z. Rubinstein and Garold W. Thumm. *The Challenge of Politics*. Englewood Cliffs, N.J.: Prentice-Hall, 1965.
537. Frank M. Russell. *Theories of International Relations*. New York: D. Appleton-Century, 1936.
538. George Sansom. *A History of Japan, 1334-1615*. Stanford: Stanford University Press, 1961.
539. George B. Schaller. *The Mountain Gorilla*. Chicago: University of Chicago Press, 1963.
540. ———. *The Year of the Gorilla*. Chicago: University of Chicago Press, 1964.
541. Richard A. Schermerhorn. *Society and Power*. New York: Random House, 1961.
542. Joseph A. Schumpeter. *Imperialism and Social Classes*. New York: Augustus M. Kelley, 1951.
543. Kenneth M. Setton and Henry R. Winkler, eds. *Great Problems in European Civilization*. New York: Prentice-Hall, 1954.
544. J. C. L. Sismondi. *History of the Italian Republics*. Rev. by William Boultin. London: George Routledge & Sons, 1906.
545. Albert Soboul. *The Partisan Sans-Culottes and the French Revolution, 1793-1794*. Oxford: Clarendon Press, 1964.
546. Charles H. Southwick. *Primate Social Behavior*. Princeton: D. Van Nostrand, 1963.
547. Melford E. Spiro. *Kibbutz: Venture in Utopia*. Cambridge: Harvard University Press, 1956.
548. Bertold Spuler. *The Muslim World*. P. I. Leiden: E. J. Brill, 1960.
549. Boris Stern. *The Kibbutz That Was*. Washington: Public Affairs Press, 1965.
550. Hilgard O. Sternberg. "Brazil: Complex Giant," *Foreign Affairs*, XLIII (Jan., 1965).
551. Eric Strauss. *The Ruling Servants*. New York: Frederick A. Praeger, 1961.
552. Ragnar Svanstrom and Carl F. Palmstierna. *A Stort History of Sweden*. Oxford: Clarendon Press, 1934.
553. John A. Symonds. *The Age of the Despots*. New York: G. P. Putnam's Sons, 1960.
554. Frank Tannenbaum. *Peace by Revolution*. New York: Columbia University Press, 1933.
555. René Taton, ed. *Histoire générales des sciences*. Vol. I. Paris: Presses Universitaires de France, 1957.
556. Alexis de Tocqueville. *The Old Regime and the Revolution*. New York: Harper, 1876.
557. Crawford H. Toy. *Introduction to the History of Religion*. Cambridge: Harvard University Press, 1948.

558. Gordon Tullock. *The Politics of Bureaucracy.* Washington: Public Affairs Press, 1965.

559. George Vernadsky. "Scope and Content of Chingis Khan's Yasa," *Harvard Journal of Asiatic Studies,* III (Dec., 1938).

560. Bernard H. M. Vlekke. *Nusantara: A History of the East Indian Archipelago.* Cambridge: Harvard University Press, 1943.

561. Charles Wagley. *An Introduction to Brazil.* New York: Columbia University Press, 1963.

562. Thomas A. Walker. *A History of the Law of Nations.* Vol. I. Cambridge: The University Press, 1899.

563. Edmund A. Walsh, ed. *The History and Nature of International Relations.* New York: Macmillan, 1922.

564. *Walsingham's Manual: A Practical Guide for Ambitious Politicians.* Ed. George Tullock. Columbia: University of South Carolina Press, 1961.

565. S. L. Washburn *et al.* "Field Studies of Old World Apes and Monkeys," *Science,* CL (Dec. 17, 1965).

566. Max Weber. *Essays in Sociology.* New York: Oxford University Press, 1958.

567. ———. *The Theory of Social and Economic Organization.* New York: Oxford University Press, 1947.

568. Murray Weingarten. *Life in a Kibbutz.* New York: Reconstruction Press, 1955.

569. Lynn White, Jr. *Medieval Technology and Social Change.* Oxford: Clarendon Press, 1962.

570. Karl A. Wittfogel. *Oriental Despotism.* New Haven: Yale University Press, 1957.

571. Ronald Wraith and Edgar Simpkins. *Corruption in Developing Countries.* New York: Norton, 1964.

572. Quincy Wright. *A Study of War.* Chicago: University of Chicago Press, 1941. 2 vols.

573. Práxedes Zancada. *El Obrero en España.* Barcelona. 1902.

574. S. Zuckerman. *The Social Life of Monkeys and Apes.* London: Kegan Paul, Trench, Trubner, 1932.

INDEX